ACCA

STUDY TEXT

PAPER P7

ADVANCED AUDIT AND ASSURANCE (UNITED KINGDOM)

In this new syllabus first edition approved by ACCA

- We **discuss** the **best strategies** for studying for ACCA exams

- We **highlight** the **most important elements** in the syllabus and the **key skills** you will need

- We **signpost** how each chapter links to the syllabus and the study guide

- We **provide** lots of **exam focus points** demonstrating what the examiner will want you to do

- We **emphasise key points** in regular **fast forward summaries**

- We **test your knowledge** of what you've studied in **quick quizzes**

- We **examine your understanding** in our **exam question bank**

- We **reference all the important topics** in our **full index**

BPP's **i-Learn** and **i-Pass** products also support this paper.

FOR EXAMS IN DECEMBER 2007 AND JUNE 2008

First edition June 2007

ISBN 9780 7517 3306 8

British Library Cataloguing-in-Publication Data
A catalogue record for this book
is available from the British Library

Published by

BPP Learning Media Ltd
BPP House, Aldine Place
London W12 8AA

www.bpp.com/learningmedia

Printed in Great Britain by Ashford Colour Press

We are grateful to the Association of Chartered
Certified Accountants for permission to reproduce past
examination questions. The suggested solutions in the
exam answer bank have been prepared by BPP
Learning Media Ltd.

Contents

The BPP Learning Media Effective Study Package

Distance Learning from BPP Professional Education

You can access our exam-focussed interactive e-learning materials over the **Internet**, via BPP Learn Online, hosted by BPP Professional Education.

BPP Learn Online offers **comprehensive tutor support**, **revision guidance** and **exam tips**.

Visit www.bpp.com/acca/learnonline for further details.

Learning to Learn Accountancy

BPP's ground-breaking **Learning to Learn Accountancy** book is designed to be used both at the outset of your ACCA studies and throughout the process of learning accountancy. It challenges you to consider how you study and gives you helpful hints about how to approach the various types of paper which you will encounter. It can help you **focus your studies on the subject and exam**, enabling you to **acquire knowledge**, **practise and revise efficiently and effectively**.

How the BPP ACCA-approved Study Text can help you pass

How the BPP ACCA-approved Study Text can help you pass

Tackling studying

We know that studying for a number of exams can seem daunting, particularly when you have other commitments as well.

- We therefore provide guidance on **what you need to study efficiently and effectively** – to use the limited time you have in the best way possible

- We explain the **purposes** of the **different features** in the BPP Study Text, demonstrating how they help you and improve your chances of passing

Developing exam awareness

We never forget that you're aiming to pass your exams, and our Texts are completely focused on helping you do this.

- In the section **Studying P7** we introduce the key themes of the syllabus, describe the skills you need and summarise how to succeed

- The **Introduction** to each chapter of this Study Text sets the chapter in the context of the syllabus and exam

- We provide specific tips, **Exam focus points**, on what you can expect in the exam and what to do (and not to do!) when answering questions

And our Study Text is **comprehensive**. It covers the syllabus content. No more, no less.

Using the Syllabus and Study Guide

We set out the Syllabus and Study Guide in full.

- Reading the **introduction to the Syllabus** will show you what **capabilities** (skills) you'll have to demonstrate, and how this exam links with other papers.

- The topics listed in the **Syllabus** are the **key topics** in this exam. By quickly looking through the Syllabus, you can see the breadth of the paper. Reading the Syllabus will also highlight topics to look out for when you're reading newspapers or *student accountant* magazine.

- The **Study Guide** provides the **detail**, showing you precisely what you'll be studying. Don't worry if it seems a lot when you look through it; BPP's Study Text will carefully guide you through it all.

- Remember the Study Text shows, at the start of every chapter, which areas of the Syllabus and Study Guide are covered in the chapter.

Testing what you can do

Testing yourself helps you develop the skills you need to pass the exam and also confirms that you can recall what you have learnt.

- We include **Questions** within chapters, and the **Exam Question Bank** provides lots more practice.

- Our **Quick Quizzes** test whether you have enough knowledge of the contents of each chapter.

- Question practice is particularly important if English is not your first written language. ACCA offers an **International Certificate in Financial English** promoting language skills within the international business community.

BPP
LEARNING MEDIA

Example chapter

Topic list

The Topic list gives an overview of the chapter.

Introduction

The Introduction sets the chapter in the context of the whole syllabus.

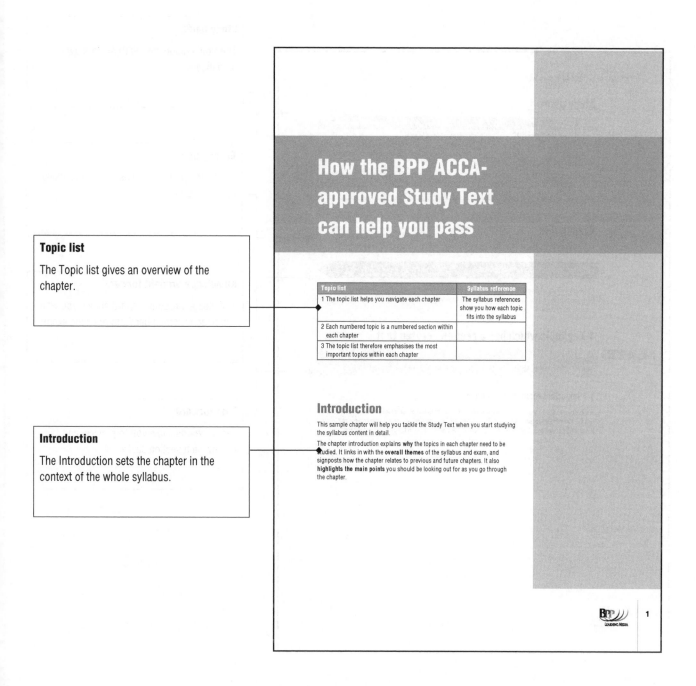

How the BPP ACCA-approved Study Text can help you pass

Topic list	Syllabus reference
1 The topic list helps you navigate each chapter	The syllabus references show you how each topic fits into the syllabus
2 Each numbered topic is a numbered section within each chapter	
3 The topic list therefore emphasises the most important topics within each chapter	

Introduction

This sample chapter will help you tackle the Study Text when you start studying the syllabus content in detail.

The chapter introduction explains **why** the topics in each chapter need to be studied. It links in with the **overall themes** of the syllabus and exam, and signposts how the chapter relates to previous and future chapters. It also **highlights the main points** you should be looking out for as you go through the chapter.

Study guide

	Intellectual level
We list the topics in ACCA's Study guide that are covered in each chapter	The intellectual level indicates the depth in which the topics will be covered

Exam guide

The Exam guide highlights ways in which the main topics covered in each chapter may be examined.

Knowledge brought forward from earlier studies

Knowledge brought forward boxes summarise information and techniques that you are **assumed to know** from your earlier studies. As the exam may test your knowledge of these areas, you should **revise** your previous study material if you are unsure about them.

1 Key topic which has a section devoted to it

FAST FORWARD Fast forwards give you a **summary** of the content of each of the main chapter sections. They are listed together in the roundup at the end of each chapter to allow you to review each chapter quickly.

1.1 Important topic within section

The headings within chapters give you a good idea of the **importance** of the topics covered. The larger the header, the more important the topic is. The headers will help you navigate through the chapter and locate the areas that have been highlighted as important in the front pages or in the chapter introduction.

Study guide

The Study guide links with ACCA's own guidance.

Exam guide

The Exam guide describes the examinability of the chapter.

Knowledge brought forward

Knowledge brought forward shows you what you need to remember from previous exams.

Fast forward

Fast forwards allow you to preview and review each section easily.

Example

Examples show you how theory is put into practice.

Key term

Key terms are the core vocabulary.

Exam focus point

Exam focus points provide specific links to the exam.

Formula to learn

You must remember these formulae in the exam.

Question

Questions provide vital practice of what you've learnt.

Case Study

Case Studies link what you've learnt with the business environment.

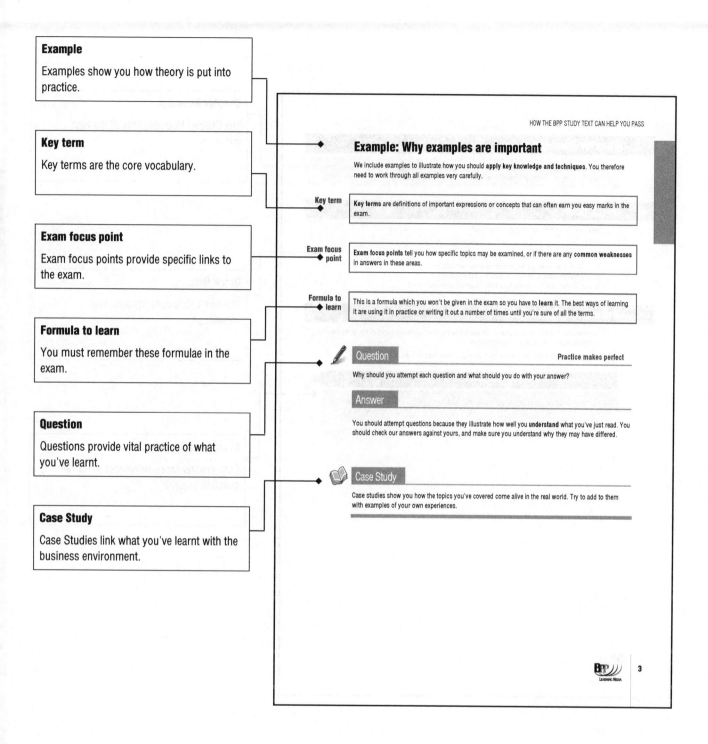

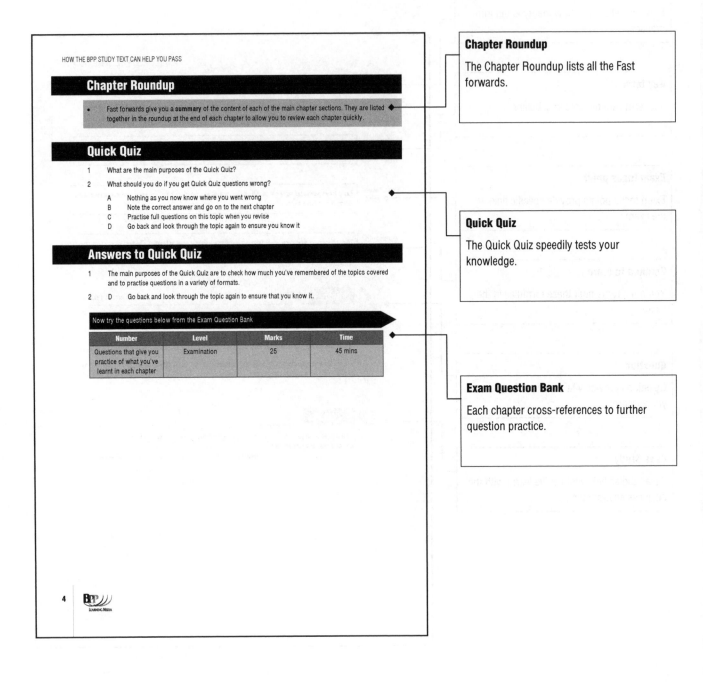

Chapter Roundup

- Fast forwards give you a **summary** of the content of each of the main chapter sections. They are listed together in the roundup at the end of each chapter to allow you to review each chapter quickly.

Quick Quiz

1   What are the main purposes of the Quick Quiz?

2   What should you do if you get Quick Quiz questions wrong?

    A   Nothing as you now know where you went wrong
    B   Note the correct answer and go on to the next chapter
    C   Practise full questions on this topic when you revise
    D   Go back and look through the topic again to ensure you know it

Answers to Quick Quiz

1   The main purposes of the Quick Quiz are to check how much you've remembered of the topics covered and to practise questions in a variety of formats.

2   D   Go back and look through the topic again to ensure that you know it.

Now try the questions below from the Exam Question Bank

Number	Level	Marks	Time
Questions that give you practice of what you've learnt in each chapter	Examination	25	45 mins

Chapter Roundup

The Chapter Roundup lists all the Fast forwards.

Quick Quiz

The Quick Quiz speedily tests your knowledge.

Exam Question Bank

Each chapter cross-references to further question practice.

4

Learning styles

BPP's guide to studying, *Learning to Learn Accountancy*, provides guidance on identifying how you learn and the variety of intelligencies that you have. We shall summarise some of the material in *Learning to Learn Accountancy*, as it will help you understand how to you are likely to approach the Study Text:

If you like	Then you might focus on	How the Study Text helps you
Word games, crosswords, poetry	Going through the detail in the Text	Chapter introductions, Fast forwards and Key terms help you determine the detail that's most significant
Number puzzles, Sudoku, Cluedo	Understanding the Text as a logical sequence of knowledge and ideas	Chapter introductions and headers help you follow the flow of material
Drawing, cartoons, films	Seeing how the ways material is presented show what it means and how important it is	The different features and the emphasis given by headers and emboldening help you see quickly what you have to know
Attending concerts, playing a musical instrument, dancing	Identifying patterns in the Text	The sequence of features within each chapter helps you understand what material is really crucial
Sport, craftwork, hands on experience	Learning practical skills such as preparing a set of accounts	Examples and question practice help you develop the practical skills you need

If you want to learn more about developing some or all of your intelligencies, *Learning to Learn Accountancy* shows you plenty of ways in which you can do so.

Studying efficiently
and effectively

What you need to study efficiently and effectively

Positive attitude

Yes there is a lot to learn. But look at the most recent ACCA pass list. See how many people have passed. They've made it; you can too. Focus on all the **benefits** that passing the exam will bring you.

Exam focus

Keep the exam firmly in your sights throughout your studies.

- Remember there's lots of **helpful guidance** about P7 in this first part of the Study Text.
- Look out for the **exam references** in the Study Text, particularly the types of question you'll be asked.

Organisation

Before you start studying you must organise yourself properly.

- We show you how to **timetable** your study so that you can ensure you have enough time to cover all of the syllabus – and revise it.
- Think carefully about the way you take **notes**. You needn't copy out too much, but if you can summarise key areas, that shows you understand them.
- Choose the notes **format** that's most helpful to you; lists, diagrams, mindmaps.
- Consider the **order** in which you tackle each chapter. If you prefer to get to grips with a theory before seeing how it's applied, you should read the explanations first. If you prefer to see how things work in practice, read the examples and questions first.

Active brain

There are various ways in which you can keep your brain active when studying and hence improve your **understanding** and **recall** of material.

- Keep asking yourself how the topic you're studying fits into the **whole picture** of this exam. If you're not sure, look back at the chapter introductions and Study Text front pages.
- Go carefully through every **example** and try every **question** in the Study Text and in the Exam Question Bank. You will be thinking deeply about the syllabus and increasing your understanding.

Review, review, review

Regularly reviewing the topics you've studied will help fix them in your memory. Your BPP Texts help you review in many ways.

- Important points are emphasised **in bold**.
- **Chapter Roundups** summarise the **Fast forward** key points in each chapter.
- **Quick Quizzes** test your grasp of the essentials.

BPP Passcards present summaries of topics in different visual formats to enhance your chances of remembering them.

Timetabling your studies

As your time is limited, it's vital that you calculate how much time you can allocate to each chapter. Following the approach below will help you do this.

Step 1   Calculate how much time you have

Work out the time you have available per week, given the following.

- The standard you have set yourself

- The time you need to set aside for work on the Practice & Revision Kit, Passcards, i-Learn and i-Pass

- The other exam(s) you are sitting

- Practical matters such as work, travel, exercise, sleep and social life

Hours

Note your time available in box A.   A [   ]

Step 2   Allocate your time

- Take the time you have available per week for this Study Text shown in box A, multiply it by the number of weeks available and insert the result in box B.   B [   ]

- Divide the figure in box B by the number of chapters in this Study Text and insert the result in box C.   C [   ]

Remember that this is only a rough guide. Some of the chapters in this Study Text are longer and more complicated than others, and you will find some subjects easier to understand than others.

Step 3   Implement your plan

Set about studying each chapter in the time shown in box C. You'll find that once you've established a timetable, you're much more likely to study systematically.

Short of time: Skim study technique

You may find you simply do not have the time available to follow all the key study steps for each chapter, however you adapt them for your particular learning style. If this is the case, follow the **Skim study** technique below.

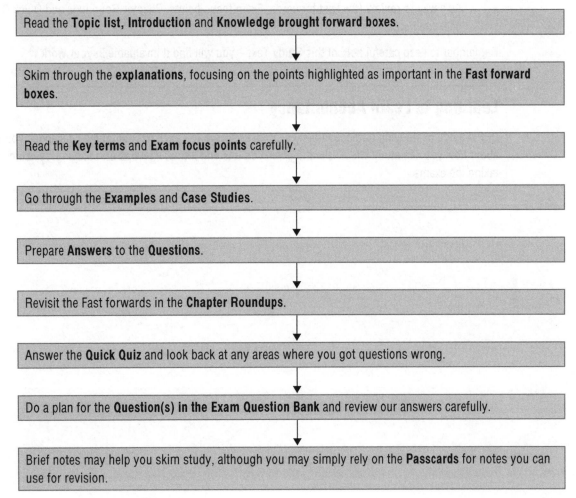

Read the **Topic list, Introduction** and **Knowledge brought forward boxes**.

Skim through the **explanations**, focusing on the points highlighted as important in the **Fast forward boxes**.

Read the **Key terms** and **Exam focus points** carefully.

Go through the **Examples** and **Case Studies**.

Prepare **Answers** to the **Questions**.

Revisit the Fast forwards in the **Chapter Roundups**.

Answer the **Quick Quiz** and look back at any areas where you got questions wrong.

Do a plan for the **Question(s) in the Exam Question Bank** and review our answers carefully.

Brief notes may help you skim study, although you may simply rely on the **Passcards** for notes you can use for revision.

Revision

When you are ready to start revising, you should still refer back to this Study Text.

- As a source of **reference** (you should find the index particularly helpful for this)
- As a way to **review** (the Fast forwards, Exam focus points, Chapter Roundups and Quick Quizzes help you here)

Remember to keep careful hold of this Study Text – you will find it invaluable in your work.

Learning to Learn Accountancy

BPP's guide to studying for accountancy exams, **Learning to Learn Accountancy**, challenges you to think about how you can study effectively and gives you lots and lots of vital tips on studying, revising and taking the exams.

Studying P7

Approaching P7

1   What P7 is about

The purpose of the P7 syllabus is to analyse, evaluate and conclude on the assurance engagement and other audit and assurance issues in the context of best practice and current developments.

The syllabus begins by introducing the legal and regulatory environment, examining the topics of money laundering and the consideration of laws and regulations. It then goes on to consider the ethical and professional issues that accountants need to be aware of in their work, including professional liability.

Practice management is considered in the context of quality control and advertising for work, tendering and professional appointments. This area considers more of the specific ethical and professional issues that were introduced earlier.

The syllabus then moves onto various assurance assignments, focussing on the external audit of a set of financial statements. It also considers other assurance engagements and the different levels of assurance that can be given to users.

The end-product of an assignment is the report to users and this is covered in some depth, examining the external audit report, review reports, environmental and social audit reports, for example.

Current issues and developments are covered throughout the syllabus wherever they are relevant.

2   What's required?

P7 builds on the knowledge and understanding gained from Paper 2.6 *Audit and Internal Review*/F8 *Audit and Assurance*. You will also be expected to be familiar with your financial reporting studies in Paper 2.5/F7 *Financial Reporting* and Paper 3.6 *Advanced Corporate Reporting*/ P2 *Corporate Reporting*.

You must possess good technical knowledge of audit and financial reporting but one of the key skills you will need is the ability to be able to apply your knowledge to the particular facts in the scenario.

You will also need to be able to explain key ideas, techniques and approaches. Your explanations and descriptions need to be clearly focussed on the particular circumstances in the question.

Section A of the paper will consist of two compulsory questions worth in total between 50 and 70 marks. They will be of the case study type of question and probably split into several parts. In this case, another key skill you will require is the ability to stick rigidly to the time allocation for each question, and where it is split into several parts, to stick to the time allocated to each part.

Section B of the paper will consist of three questions, of which you must answer two. These questions will tend to be more focussed towards specific topic areas, such as ethical and professional issues and auditors' reports. Again they could be based on mini scenarios which you will have to comment on and discuss.

3   How to pass

Cover the whole syllabus

Although Section B of the paper contains an optional element, the two questions in Section A are compulsory and could cover a range of topics from across the syllabus. Question spotting at this level is unwise and not recommended.

Question practice

Question practice is a key part of your revision and will allow you to develop your application skills. Use the questions in the question bank at the back of this Study Text and later in the BPP *Practice and Revision Kit* for P7.

Analysis and answering of questions

You need to consider the question requirements carefully so that you answer the actual question that has been set. For example, if the question asks you to 'explain' or 'discuss' or 'comment on', make sure that you do so, rather than just produce a list of bullet points or omit to answering the whole requirement.

When answering questions at this level, you need to ensure that your answers are relevant to the scenario in the question – producing a general answer covering everything you know about a particular topic will not score you many marks and is an inefficient use of your time.

Employ good exam technique

The following points will stand you in good stead when it comes to answering questions in the real exam.

- **Sub-headings** and leaving **spaces between paragraphs** help to demonstrate that your answer is clearly structured and emphasise the points you are making.

- **Short paragraphs** (2-3 sentences) help you keep to the point, but avoid 2-3 word bullet points.

- **Time management** is key in this paper but less likely to be a problem if you do the longest questions (Questions 1 and 2) first.

- **Reading the question carefully** first is important in ensuring that you answer the question set.

4   Brought forward knowledge

The P7 syllabus assumes knowledge brought forward from Paper 1.1 *Preparing Financial Statements*, Paper 2.5/F7 *Financial Reporting* and Paper 3.6 *Advanced Corporate Reporting*/P2 *Corporate Reporting**. It's very important to be comfortable with your financial reporting studies because such aspects are likely to come up in scenario-based questions in both Sections A and B of this paper.

Students who took Paper 3.1 in June 2007 under the old syllabus and are retaking in December 2007 may not have the brought forward knowledge required from Paper 3.6 *Advanced Corporate Reporting**.

* The examiner has stated that she will not test any of the accounting topics that only appear in the Corporate Reporting syllabus in the **first two sittings** as this could be unfair for some students who will sit P7 before P2 under the transitional arrangements.

Advanced Audit and Assurance (UK) (P7)

This syllabus and study guide is designed to help with planning study and to provide detailed information on what could be assessed in any examination session.

THE STRUCTURE OF THE SYLLABUS AND STUDY GUIDE

Relational diagram of paper with other papers

This diagram shows direct and indirect links between this paper and other papers preceding or following it. Some papers are directly underpinned by other papers such as Advanced Performance Management by Performance Management. These links are shown as solid line arrows. Other papers only have indirect relationships with each other such as links existing between the accounting and auditing papers. The links between these are shown as dotted line arrows. This diagram indicates where you are expected to have underpinning knowledge and where it would be useful to review previous learning before undertaking study.

Overall aim of the syllabus

This explains briefly the overall objective of the paper and indicates in the broadest sense the capabilities to be developed within the paper.

Main capabilities

This paper's aim is broken down into several main capabilities which divide the syllabus and study guide into discrete sections.

Relational diagram of the main capabilities

This diagram illustrates the flows and links between the main capabilities (sections) of the syllabus and should be used as an aid to planning teaching and learning in a structured way.

Syllabus rationale

This is a narrative explaining how the syllabus is structured and how the main capabilities are linked. The rationale also explains in further detail what the examination intends to assess and why.

Detailed syllabus

This shows the breakdown of the main capabilities (sections) of the syllabus into subject areas. This is the blueprint for the detailed study guide.

Approach to examining the syllabus

This section briefly explains the structure of the examination and how it is assessed.

Study Guide

This is the main document that students, tuition providers and publishers should use as the basis of their studies, instruction and materials. Examinations will be based on the detail of the study guide which comprehensively identifies what could be assessed in any examination session. The study guide is a precise reflection and breakdown of the syllabus. It is divided into sections based on the main capabilities identified in the syllabus. These sections are divided into subject areas which relate to the sub-capabilities included in the detailed syllabus. Subject areas are broken down into sub-headings which describe the detailed outcomes that could be assessed in examinations. These outcomes are described using verbs indicating what exams may require students to demonstrate, and the broad intellectual level at which these may need to be demonstrated (*see intellectual levels below).

Reading lists

ACCA has two approved publishers: BPP Professional Education and Kaplan Publishing Foulks Lynch. Both these publishers base their study texts on the detailed contents of the study guides as published by ACCA. ACCA takes no editorial responsibility for the detailed content of these study texts although ACCA examiners will annually review their content for general appropriateness and relevance in supporting effective study towards ACCA examinations.
In addition ACCA examiners will recommend other text books where appropriate, which students may read in order to widen their reading beyond the approved study texts. Relevant articles will also be published in *student accountant*.

1

INTELLECTUAL LEVELS

The syllabus is designed to progressively broaden and deepen the knowledge, skills and professional values demonstrated by the student on their way through the qualification.

The specific capabilities within the detailed syllabuses and study guides are assessed at one of three intellectual or cognitive levels:

Level 1: Knowledge and comprehension
Level 2: Application and analysis
Level 3: Synthesis and evaluation

Very broadly, these intellectual levels relate to the three cognitive levels at which the Knowledge module, the Skills module and the Professional level are assessed.

Each subject area in the detailed study guide included in this document is given a 1, 2, or 3 superscript, denoting intellectual level, marked at the end of each relevant line. This gives an indication of the intellectual depth at which an area could be assessed within the examination. However, while level 1 broadly equates with the Knowledge module, level 2 equates to the Skills module and level 3 to the Professional level, some lower level skills can continue to be assessed as the student progresses through each module and level. This reflects that at each stage of study there will be a requirement to broaden, as well as deepen capabilities. It is also possible that occasionally some higher level capabilities may be assessed at lower levels.

LEARNING HOURS

The ACCA qualification does not prescribe or recommend any particular number of learning hours for examinations because study and learning patterns and styles vary greatly between people and organisations. This also recognises the wide diversity of personal, professional and educational circumstances in which ACCA students find themselves.

Each syllabus contains between 23 and 35 main subject area headings depending on the nature of the subject and how these areas have been broken down.

GUIDE TO EXAM STRUCTURE

The structure of examinations varies within and between modules and levels.

The Fundamentals level examinations contain 100% compulsory questions to encourage candidates to study across the breadth of each syllabus.

The Knowledge module is assessed by equivalent two-hour paper based and computer based examinations.

The Skills module examinations are all paper based three-hour papers. The structure of papers varies from ten questions in the *Corporate and Business Law* (F4) paper to four 25 mark questions in *Performance Management* (F5) and *Financial Management* (F9). Individual questions within all Skills module papers will attract between 10 and 30 marks.

The Professional level papers are all three-hour paper based examinations, all containing two sections. Section A is compulsory, but there will be some choice offered in Section B.

For all three hour examination papers, ACCA has introduced 15 minutes reading and planning time.

This additional time is allowed at the beginning of each three-hour examination to allow candidates to read the questions and to begin planning their answers before they start writing in their answer books. This time should be used to ensure that all the information and exam requirements are properly read and understood.

During reading and planning time candidates may only annotate their question paper. They may not write anything in their answer booklets until told to do so by the invigilator.

The Essentials module papers all have a Section A containing a major case study question with all requirements totalling 50 marks relating to this case. Section B gives students a choice of two from three 25 mark questions.

Section A of each of the Options papers contains 50-70 compulsory marks from two questions, each attracting between 25 and 40 marks. Section B will

2

offer a choice of two from three questions totalling 30-50 marks, with each question attracting between 15 and 25 marks

GUIDE TO EXAMINATION ASSESSMENT

ACCA reserves the right to examine anything contained within the study guide at any examination session. This includes knowledge, techniques, principles, theories, and concepts as specified.

For the financial accounting, audit and assurance, law and tax papers, ACCA will publish *examinable documents* every six months to indicate exactly what regulations and legislation could potentially be assessed at the following examination session. Knowledge of new examinable regulations will not be assessed until at least six calendar months after the last day of the month in which documents are issued or legislation is passed. The relevant cut-off date for the June examinations is 30 November of the previous year, and for the December examinations, it is 31 May of the same year.

The study guide offers more detailed guidance on the depth and level at which the examinable documents will be examined. The study guide should therefore be read in conjunction with the examinable documents list.

3

Syllabus

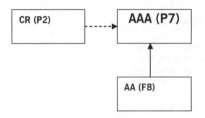

AIM

To analyse, evaluate and conclude on the assurance engagement and other audit and assurance issues in the context of best practice and current developments.

MAIN CAPABILITIES

On successful completion of this paper, candidates should be able to:

A Recognise the legal and regulatory environment and its impact on audit and assurance practice

B Demonstrate the ability to work effectively on an assurance or other service engagement within a professional and ethical framework

C Assess and recommend appropriate quality control policies and procedures in practice management and recognising the auditor's position in relation to the acceptance and retention of professional appointments

D Identify and formulate the work required to meet the objectives of audit and non-audit assignments and the application of the International Standards on Auditing (UK and Ireland)

E Evaluate findings and the results of work performed and drafting suitable reports on assignments

F Understand the current issues and developments relating to the provision of audit-related and assurance services

RELATIONAL DIAGRAM OF MAIN CAPABILITIES

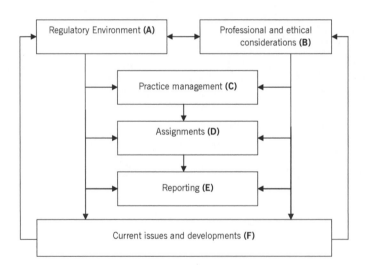

RATIONALE

The Advanced Audit and Assurance syllabus is essentially divided into six areas.

The syllabus starts with the legal and regulatory environment including money laundering, and procedures in practice management, including quality control and the acceptance and retention of professional engagements. This then leads into professional and ethical considerations, including the Code of Ethics and professional liability.

The syllabus then covers various assignments, including an audit of financial statements, audit-related services, and other assurance assignments, as well as the reporting of these assignments.

The final section covers current issues and developments relating to the provision of audit-related and assurance services.

DETAILED SYLLABUS

A   Regulatory Environment

1.   International regulatory frameworks for audit and assurance services

2.   Money laundering

3.   Laws and regulations

B   Professional and Ethical Considerations

1.   Code of Ethics and Conduct

2.   Fraud and error

3.   Professional liability

C   Practice Management

1.   Quality control

2.   Advertising, publicity, obtaining professional work and fees

3.   Tendering

4.   Professional appointments

D   Assignments

1.   The audit of historical financial information including;
     i)   Planning, materiality and assessing the risk of misstatement
     ii) Evidence
     iii) Evaluation and review

2.   Group audits

3.   Audit-related services

4.   Assurance services

5.   Prospective financial information

6.   Forensic audits

7.   Internal audit

8.   Outsourcing

E.   Reporting

1.   Auditor's reports

2.   Reports to management

3.   Other reports

F   Current Issues and Developments

1.   Professional, ethical and corporate governance

2.   Information technology

3.   Transnational audits

4.   Social and environmental auditing

5.   Other current issues

5

APPROACH TO EXAMINING THE SYLLABUS

The examination is a three hour paper constructed in two sections. Questions in both sections will be almost entirely discursive. However, candidates will be expected, for example, to be able to assess materiality and calculate relevant ratios where appropriate.

Section A questions will be based on 'case study' type questions. That is not to say that they will be particularly long, rather that they will provide a setting within a range of topics, issues and requirements can be addressed. Different types of question will be encountered in Section B and will tend to be more focussed on specific topics, for example 'auditor's reports', 'quality control' and topics of ISAs (UK and Ireland) which are not examinable in Paper F8, *Audit and Assurance*. (This does not preclude these topics from appearing in Section A). Current issues will be examined across a number of questions.

Number of marks

Section A: 2 compulsory questions	50-70
Section B: Choice of 2 from 3 questions	30-50
	100

Study Guide

A   REGULATORY ENVIRONMENT

1.   International regulatory frameworks for audit and assurance services

a)   Explain the need for laws, regulations, standards and other guidance relating to audit, assurance and related services.[2]

b)   Outline and explain the legal and professional framework including:[2]
    i)   the national and international standard-setting process
    ii)   the authority of national and international standards
    iii)   public oversight and principles of corporate governance
    iv)   the role of audit committees.

c)   Discuss the effectiveness of the different ways in which the auditing profession and audit markets are regulated.[2]

2.   Money laundering

a)   Define 'money laundering'.[1]

b)   Explain how international efforts seek to combat money laundering.[2]

c)   Explain the scope of criminal offences of money laundering and how professional accountants may be protected from criminal and civil liability.[2]

d)   Explain the need for ethical guidance in this area.[2]

e)   Describe how accountants meet their obligations to help prevent and detect money laundering including record keeping and reporting of suspicion to the National Criminal Intelligence Service (NCIS).[2]

f)   Explain the importance of 'know your customer' (KYC) information.[2]

g)   Recognise potentially suspicious transactions and assess their impact on reporting duties.[2]

h)   Describe, with reasons, the basic elements of an anti-money laundering program.[2]

3.   Laws and regulations

a)   Compare and contrast the respective responsibilities of management and auditors concerning compliance with laws and regulations in an audit of financial statements.[2]

b)   Describe the auditors considerations of compliance with laws and regulations and plan audit procedures when possible non-compliance is discovered.[2]

c)   Discuss how and to whom non-compliance should be reported.[2]

d)   Recognise when withdrawal from an engagement is necessary.[2]

B   PROFESSIONAL AND ETHICAL CONSIDERATIONS

1.   Code of Ethics and Conduct

a)   Explain the Fundamental Principles and the conceptual framework approach.[1]

b)   Identify, evaluate and respond to threats to compliance with the fundamental principles.[3]

c)   Discuss and evaluate the effectiveness of available safeguards.[3]

d)   Recognise and advise on conflicts in the application of fundamental principles.[3]

2.   Fraud and error

a)   Define and clearly distinguish between the terms 'error', 'irregularity', 'fraud' and 'misstatement'.[2]

b)   Compare and contrast the respective responsibilities of management and auditors for fraud and error.[2]

c)   Describe the matters to be considered and procedures to be carried out to investigate actual and/or potential misstatements in a given situation.[2]

7

d) Explain how, why, when and to whom fraud and error should be reported and the circumstances in which an auditor should withdraw from an engagement.[2]

e) Discuss the current and possible future role of auditors in preventing, detecting and reporting error and fraud.[2]

3. Professional liability

a) Recognise circumstances in which professional accountants may have legal liability.[2]

b) Describe the factors to determine whether or not an auditor is negligent in given situations.[2]

c) Explain the other criteria for legal liability to be recognised (including 'due professional care' and 'proximity') and apply them to given situations.[2]

d) Compare and contrast liability to client with liability to third parties.[3]

e) Comment on precedents of case law.[2]

f) Evaluate the practicability and effectiveness of ways in which liability may be restricted, including professional indemnity insurance (PII).[3]

g) Discuss how audit and other opinions may be affected by limiting auditors' liability.[2]

h) Discuss the advantages and disadvantages of claims against auditors being settled out of court.[2]

i) Discuss and appraise the principal causes of audit failure and other factors that contribute to the 'expectation gap' (e.g. responsibilities for fraud and error).[3]

j) Recommend ways in which the expectation gap might be bridged.[2]

C PRACTICE MANAGEMENT

1. Quality control

a) Explain the principles and purpose of quality control of audit and other assurance engagements.[1]

b) Describe the elements of a system of quality control relevant to a given firm.[2]

c) Select and justify quality control procedures that are applicable to a given audit engagement.[3]

d) Assess whether an engagement has been performed in accordance with professional standards and whether reports issued are appropriate in the circumstances.[3]

2. Advertising, publicity, obtaining professional work and fees

a) Explain the need for guidance in these areas.[2]

b) Recognise situations in which specified advertisements are acceptable.[2]

c) Discuss the restrictions on practice descriptions, the use of the ACCA logo and the names of practising firms.[2]

d) Discuss the extent to which reference to fees may be made in promotional material.[2]

e) Outline the determinants of fee-setting and justify the bases on which fees and commissions may and may not be charged for services.[3]

f) Discuss the ethical and other professional problems involved in establishing and negotiating fees for a specified assignment.[3]

3. Tendering

a) Discuss the reasons why entities change their auditors/professional accountants.[2]

b) Recognise and explain the matters to be considered when a firm is invited to submit a proposal or fee quote for an audit or other professional engagement.[2]

c) Identify the information required for a proposal.[2]

d) Prepare the content of an engagement proposal document.[2]

e) Discuss and appraise the criteria that might be used to evaluate tenders received from audit firms in a given situation.[3]

f) Discuss reasons why audit fees may be lowered from the previous year's fees. [2]

g) Explain 'lowballing' and discuss whether or not it impairs independence.[2]

4. Professional appointments

a) Explain the matters to be considered and the procedures that an audit firm/professional accountant should carry out before accepting a specified new client/engagement including:[3]
   i) client acceptance
   ii) engagement acceptance
   iii) agreeing the terms of engagement.

b) Recognise the key issues that underlie the agreement of the scope and terms of an engagement with a client.[2]

c) Outline the procedures for the transfer of books, papers and information following a new appointment.[1]

D ASSIGNMENTS

1. The audit of historical financial information

a) Describe the key features of the following audit methodologies:[1]
   i) risk-based auditing
   ii) 'top down' approach
   iii) systems audit
   iv) balance sheet approach
   v) transaction cycle approach
   vi) directional testing.

b) Justify an appropriate approach to a given assignment and recognise when an approach is unsuitable.[3]

1(i) Planning, materiality and assessing the risk of misstatement

a) Specify the matters that should be considered in planning a given assignment including:[3]
   i) logistics (e.g. staff and client management, multiple locations, deadlines)
   ii) use of IT in administration
   iii) time budgets
   iv) assignment objectives and reports required
   v) client interface (e.g. communication methods)
   vi) preliminary materiality assessment
   vii) key financial statement risks
   viii) an overall audit strategy.

b) Define materiality and demonstrate how it should be applied in financial reporting and auditing.[2]

c) Apply the criteria that determine whether or not a matter is material and discuss the use and limitations of prescriptive rules in making decisions about materiality.[3]

d) Identify and explain business risks in given situations.[2]

e) Describe the factors that influence the assessment of a specified risk (e.g. inherent risk, financial statement risk) for a given assignment.[2]

f) Explain how and why the assessments of risks and materiality affect the nature, timing and extent of auditing procedures in a given situation.[2]

g) Select and apply appropriate risk assessment procedures, including analytical procedures, to obtain an understanding of a given entity and its environment.[3]

h) Assess the risk of misstatement at the financial statement level and assertion level and design audit procedures in response to assessed risks.[3]

i) Recognise and assess the implications of a specified computer system (e.g. network) on an assignment.[2]

9

1(ii) Evidence

a) Evaluate the appropriateness and sufficiency of different sources of audit evidence and the procedures by which evidence may be obtained including:[3]
   i) analytical procedures
   ii) management representations
   iii) the work of others
   iv) audit sampling
   v) external confirmations
   vi) audit automation tools.

b) Specify audit procedures to obtain sufficient audit evidence from identified sources.[2]

c) Apply the criteria for assessing the extent to which reliance can be placed on substantive analytical procedures and recognise situations in which analytical procedures may be used extensively.[3]

d) Apply analytical procedures to financial and non-financial data.[2]

e) Identify and evaluate the audit evidence expected to be available to:[3]
   i) verify specific assets, liabilities, transactions and events; and
   ii) support financial statement assertions and accounting treatments (including fair values).

f) Explain the reasons for preparing and retaining documentation and the importance of reviewing working papers.[1]

g) Explain the specific audit problems and procedures concerning related parties and related party transactions.[2]

h) Recognise circumstances that may indicate the existence of unidentified related parties and select appropriate audit procedures.[2]

i) Demonstrate the use of written management representations as the primary source of audit evidence and as complementary audit evidence.[2]

j) Discuss the implications of contradictory evidence being discovered.[2]

k) Recognise when it is justifiable to place reliance on the work of an expert (e.g. a surveyor employed by the audit client).[2]

l) Assess the appropriateness and sufficiency of the work of internal auditors and the extent to which reliance can be placed on it.[2]

1(iii) Evaluation and review

a) Explain review procedures (including the use of analytical procedures and checklists) and assess their role in detecting material misstatements.[3]

b) Evaluate findings quantitatively and qualitatively, e.g:[3]
   i) the results of audit tests and procedures
   ii) the effect of actual and potential misstatements.

c) Compare and contrast how the auditor's responsibilities for corresponding figures, comparative financial statements, 'other information', subsequent events and going concern are discharged.[3]

d) Apply the further considerations and audit procedures relevant to initial engagements.[2]

e) Discuss the courses of action available to an auditor if a material inconsistency or misstatement of fact exists.[2]

f) Specify audit procedures designed to identify subsequent events that may require adjustment to, or disclosure in, the financial statements of a given entity.[2]

g) List indicators that the going concern basis may be in doubt and recognise mitigating factors.[2]

h) Evaluate the evidence that might be expected to be available and assess the appropriateness of the going concern basis in given situations.[3]

i) Assess the adequacy of disclosures in financial statements relating to going concern and explain the implications for the auditor's report with regard to the going concern basis.[3]

10

j)   Evaluate the matters (e.g. materiality, risk, relevant accounting standards, audit evidence) relating to:[3]
   i)   stocks
   ii)   standard costing systems
   iii)   cash flow statements
   iv)   changes in accounting policy
   v)   long-term contracts
   vi)   taxation
   vii)   segmental reporting
   viii) fixed assets
   ix)   fair value
   x)   leases
   xi)   revenue recognition
   xii)   pension costs
   xiii) government grants
   xiv)   finance costs
   xv)   related parties
   xvi)   earnings per share
   xvii) impairment
   xviii) provisions, contingent liabilities and contingent assets
   xix)   goodwill
   xx)   brands
   xxi)   research and development
   xxii) other intangible assets
   xxiii) capital instruments
   xxiv) financial instruments
   xxv)   investment properties
   xxvi) transition to International Financial Reporting Standards (IFRS)
   xxvii) share-based payment transactions
   xxviii) business combinations
   xxix) discontinued operations
   xxx)   held for sale non-current assets.

2.   **Group audits**

a)   Recognise the specific matters to be considered before accepting appointment as principal auditor to a group in a given situation.[3]

b)   Compare and contrast the organisation, planning, management and administration issues specific to group audits with those of joint audits.[2]

c)   Recognise the specific audit problems and describe audit procedures in a given situation relating to:[3]
   i)   the correct classification of investments

   ii)   differing accounting policies and frameworks
   iii)   fair values on acquisition
   iv)   intangibles
   v)   taxation
   vi)   goodwill on consolidation
   vii)   intra-group balances, transactions and profits
   viii) related parties
   ix)   share options
   x)   post balance sheet events
   xi)   entities in developing countries.

d)   Discuss letters of support ('comfort letters') as audit evidence.[2]

e)   Identify and describe the matters to be considered and the procedures to be performed when a principal auditor uses the work of other auditors in a given situation.[3]

f)   Explain the implications for the auditor's report on the financial statements of an entity where the opinion on a component is qualified or otherwise modified in a given situation.[2]

3.   **Audit-related services**

a)   Describe the nature of audit-related services, the circumstances in which they might be required and the comparative levels of assurance provided by professional accountants.[2]

b)   Distinguish between:[2]
   i)   audit-related services and an audit of historical financial statements
   ii)   an attestation engagement and a direct reporting engagement.

c)   Plan review engagements, for example:[2]
   i)   a review of interim financial information
   ii)   a 'due diligence' assignment (when acquiring a company, business or other assets).

d)   Explain the importance of enquiry and analytical procedures in review engagements and apply these procedures.[2]

e)   Describe and apply the general principles and procedures relating to a compilation engagement (e.g. to prepare financial statements).[2]

f) Explain why agreed-upon procedures and compilation engagements do not (usually) meet the requirements for an assurance engagement.[1]

g) Illustrate the form and content of: [2]
   i)   a report of factual findings
   ii) a compilation report.

4. Assurance services

a) Describe the main categories of assurance services that audit firms can provide and assess the benefits of providing these services to management and external users:[3]
   i)   risk assessments
   ii)   business performance measurement
   iii) systems reliability
   iv)   electronic commerce.

b) Justify a level of assurance (reasonable, high, moderate, limited, negative) for an engagement depending on the subject matter evaluated, the criteria used, the procedures applied and the quality and quantity of evidence obtained.[3]

c) Recognise the ways in which different types of risk (e.g. strategic, operating, information) may be identified and analysed and assess how management should respond to risk.[3]

d) Recommend operational measures and describe how the reliability of performance information systems is assessed (including benchmarking).[2]

e) Describe a value for money audit and recommend measures of economy, efficiency and effectiveness.[2]

f) Explain the demand for reliable and more timely reporting on financial information and the development of continuous auditing.[2]

g) Select procedures for assessing internal control effectiveness.[2]

h) Describe how entities are using core technologies (e.g. EDI, e-mail, Internet, World Wide Web) and explain how e-commerce affects the business risk of a given entity.[2]

5. Prospective financial information

a) Define 'prospective financial information' (PFI) and distinguish between a 'forecast', a 'projection', a 'hypothetical illustration' and a 'target'.[1]

b) Explain the principles of useful PFI.[1]

c) Identify and describe the matters to be considered before accepting a specified engagement to report on PFI.[2]

d) Discuss the level of assurance that the auditor may provide and explain the other factors to be considered in determining the nature, timing and extent of examination procedures.[1]

e) Describe examination procedures to verify forecasts and projections relating to:[2]
   i)   revenue
   ii)   capital expenditure
   iii) revenue expenditure
   iv)   profits
   v)   cash flows
   vi)   working capital.

f) Compare the content of a report on an examination of PFI with reports made in providing auti-related services.[2]

6. Forensic audits

a) Define the terms 'forensic accounting', 'forensic investigation' and 'forensic audit'.[1]

b) Describe the major applications of forensic auditing (e.g. fraud, negligence, insurance claims) and analyse the role of the forensic auditor as an expert witness.[2]

c) Apply the fundamental ethical principles to professional accountants engaged in forensic audit assignments.[2]

d) Select investigative procedures and evaluate evidence appropriate to determining the loss in a given situation.[3]

e) Explain the terms under which experts make reports.[2]

12

7. Internal audit

a) Compare the objectives and principal characteristics of internal audit with other assurance engagements.[2]

b) Compare and contrast operational and compliance audits.[2]

c) Justify a suitable approach (e.g. cyclical compliance) to specified multi-site operations.[3]

d) Discuss outsourcing internal auditing services.[2]

8. Outsourcing

a) Explain the different approaches to 'outsourcing' and compare with 'insourcing'.[2]

b) Discuss and conclude on the advantages and disadvantages of outsourcing finance and accounting functions including:[3]
   i) data (transaction) processing
   ii) pensions
   iii) information technology (IT)
   iv) internal auditing
   v) due diligence work
   vi) taxes.

c) Recognise and evaluate the impact of outsourced functions on the conduct of an audit.[3]

E   REPORTING

1   Auditor's reports

a) Critically appraise the form and content of a standard unmodified auditor's report.[3]

b) Recognise and evaluate the factors to be taken into account when forming an audit opinion in a given situation.[3]

c) Justify audit opinions that are consistent with the results of audit procedures relating to the sufficiency of audit evidence and/or compliance with accounting standards (including the going concern basis). [3]

d) Draft extracts suitable for inclusion in an audit report.[3]

e) Discuss the implications for the auditor's report on financial statements that report compliance with IFRSs.[2]

f) Assess whether or not a proposed audit opinion is appropriate.[3]

g) Discuss 'a true and fair view'.[2]

h) Describe special purpose auditors' reports (e.g. on summary financial statements) and analyse how and why they differ from an auditor's report on historical financial information.[2]

2.   Reports to management

a) Draft suitable content for a report to management, on the basis of given information, including statements of facts, their potential effects and appropriate recommendations for action.[3]

b) Critically assess the quality of a management letter.[3]

c) Advise on the content of reports to those charged with governance in a given situation.[3]

d) Explain the need for timely communication, clearance, feedback and follow up.[2]

e) Discuss the relative effectiveness of communication methods.[2]

3.   Other reports

a) Analyse the form and content of the professional accountant's report for an assurance engagement as compared with an auditor's report.[2]

b) Draft the content of a report on examination of prospective financial information.[2]

c) Discuss the effectiveness of the 'negative assurance' form of reporting and evaluate situations in which it may be appropriate to express a reservation or deny a conclusion.[3]

13

situations in which it may be appropriate to express a reservation or deny a conclusion.[3]

F   CURRENT ISSUES AND DEVELOPMENTS

Discuss the relative merits and the consequences of different standpoints taken in current debates and express opinions supported by reasoned arguments.

1.   Professional, ethical and corporate governance

a)   Discuss the relative advantages of an ethical framework and a rulebook.[2]

b)   Evaluate the adequacy of existing ways in which objectivity may be safeguarded and suggest additional measures to improve independence.[3]

c)   Identify and assess relevant emerging ethical issues and evaluate the safeguards available.[3]

d)   Discuss IFAC developments including: [2]
    i)   the implementation and adoption of International Standards on Auditing (ISAs) (UK and Ireland) by the Auditing Practices Board (APB)
    ii)   significant current assurance issues being dealt with by APB.

e)   Assess the relative advantages and disadvantages of partnership status, limited liability partnerships and incorporation of audit firms.[2]

f)   Discuss current developments in the limitation of auditors' liability and the practical ways in which the risk of litigation and liability can be reduced in a given situation.[3]

g)   Discuss innovations in corporate governance (e.g. enterprise-wide risk management) and their impact on boards of directors, audit committees and internal auditors.[3]

2.   Information technology

a)   Describe recent trends in IT and their current and potential impact on auditors (e.g. the audit implications of 'cyberincidents' and other risks).[2]

b)   Explain how IT may be used to assist auditors and discuss the problems that may be encountered in automating the audit process.[2]

3.   Transnational audits

a)   Define 'transnational audits' and explain the role of the Transnational Audit Committee (TAC) of IFAC.[1]

b)   Discuss how transnational audits may differ from other audits of historical financial information (e.g. in terms of applicable financial reporting and auditing standards, listing requirements and corporate governance requirements).[2]

c)   Discuss the need for international audit firm networks in implementing international auditing standards.[2]

d)   Distinguish, for example, between 'global auditing firms' and second tier firms.[2]

e)   Discuss the impact of globalisation on audit firms and their clients.[2]

f)   Explain the advantages and problems of current trends (e.g. to merge, to divest consultancy services).[2]

4.   Social and environmental auditing

a)   Discuss the increasing importance of policies that govern the relationship of an organization to its employees, society and the environment.[2]

b)   Describe the difficulties in measuring and reporting on economic, environmental and social performance and give examples of performance measures and sustainability indicators.[2]

c)   Explain the auditor's main considerations in respect of social and environmental matters and how they impact on entities and their financial statements (e.g. impairment of assets, provisions and contingent liabilities).[2]

d)   Describe substantive procedures to detect potential misstatements in respect of socio-environmental matters.[2]

14

e) Discuss the form and content of an independent verification statement (e.g. on an environmental management system (EMS) and a report to society).[2]

5. Other current issues

a) Discuss how the potential problems associated with the audit of small enterprises may be overcome.[2]

b) Explain how International Standards on Auditing (UK and Ireland) affect smaller firms.[2]

c) Discuss the dominance of the global firms and their influence and impact on the accounting profession.[2]

d) Discuss the impact of developments in public company oversight on external auditors.[2]

e) Explain current developments in auditing standards including the need for new and revised standards and evaluate their impact on the conduct of audits.[3]

f) Discuss other current legal, ethical, other professional and practical matters that affect accountants, auditors, their employers and the profession.[3]

15

The exam paper

The exam is a three-hour paper consisting of two sections.

Section A consists of two compulsory questions which must be attempted. These questions will be based on case study type scenarios. These will provide detailed information and could include extracts from financial statements and audit working papers, and strategic and operational details for a client business. They will over topics from across the syllabus.

Section B will consist of three questions, of which two must be answered. These questions will tend to be more focused on specific topics, such as audit reports and quality control for example.

The paper will have a global focus; no numerical questions will be set.

		Number of marks
Section A:	2 compulsory questions	50-70
Section B:	Choice of 2 from 3 questions	50-70
		100

Analysis of pilot paper

Section A

1 Business risks comfort letters, group audits
2 Forensic accounting, matters to consider and audit procedures (losses, stock)

Section B

3 Quality control issues
4 Audit reports
5 Ethical and professional issues

The pilot paper is reproduced in full from page 41

Pilot paper

Paper P7

Advanced Audit and Assurance

Time allowed

Reading and planning: 15 minutes
Writing: 3 hours

This paper is divided into two sections:

Section A – This ONE question is compulsory and MUST be attempted

Section B – TWO questions ONLY to be attempted

Do NOT open this paper until instructed by the supervisor.

During reading and planning time only the question paper may be annotated. You must NOT write in your answer booklet until instructed by the supervisor.

This question paper must not be removed from the examination hall.

Warning

The pilot paper cannot cover all of the syllabus nor can it include examples of every type of question that will be included in the actual exam. You may see questions in the exam that you think are more difficult than any you see in the pilot paper.

Question 1

This is typical of the case study type question you can expect to find in Section A. In part (a) note that you need to identify the business risks, as opposed to the audit risks. Your explanation needs to be sufficiently clear and detailed to score well. Part (c) should be fairly straightforward but again you need to explain your answer to score good marks. Use the information in the scenario to help generate ideas for part (b). For each question part, make sure you don't overrun on time.

This question is covered by the material in Chapters 6, 7 and 11 of this Study Text.

Question 2

This question is a scenario-based one on a non-audit assignment. You should be able to score well on part (a) on forensic auditing and its application to fraud investigations. For the remainder of the question, use the information in the scenario to help you. When describing the tests you should perform in parts (c) and (d), make sure they are specific and well explained so that you can achieve maximum marks in these parts of the question.

This question is covered by the material in Chapters 9, 12 and 14 of this Study Text.

Question 3

This 20 mark question on quality control is split into five separate scenarios. Notice the question requirement to comment on the implications – it's not enough just to identify them if you want to score well.

This question is covered by the material in Chapters 4, 9 and 10 of this Study Text.

Question 4

This question is a fairly straightforward one on audit reports. You are presented with four scenarios and need to assess the suitability of the proposed report. Taking each scenario in turn and dealing with it in the allocated time available is the best approach. Where you disagree with the proposed report, you must explain why to score well.

This question is covered by the material in Chapter 17 of this Study Text.

Question 5

This question is on ethical and professional issues. In part (a) you need to discuss the adequacy of existing guidance and comment on it. Part (b) is split into three separate scenarios – use the information in these to help you. The requirement also asks you to state what action the company should take in each case – do not overlook this part of the question.

This question is covered by the material in Chapters 2 and 3 of this Study Text.

Section A – BOTH questions are compulsory and MUST be attempted

1   You are an audit manager in Ribi & Co, a firm of Chartered Certified Accountants. One of your audit clients Beeski Ltd provides satellite broadcasting services in a rapidly growing market.

In November 2005 Beeski purchased Xstatic Ltd, a competitor group of companies. Significant revenue, cost and capital expenditure synergies are expected as the operations of Beeski and Xstatic are being combined into one group of companies.

The following financial and operating information consolidates the results of the enlarged Beeski group:

	Year end 30 September	
	2006 (Estimated)	2005 (Actual)
	£m	£m
Turnover	6,827	4,404
Cost of sales	(3,109)	(1,991)
Distribution costs and administrative expenses	(2,866)	(1,700)
Research and development costs	(25)	(22)
Depreciation and amortisation	(927)	(661)
Interest expense	(266)	(202)
Loss before taxation	(366)	(172)
Customers	14·9m	7·6m
Average revenue per customer (ARPC)	£437	£556

In August 2006 Beeski purchased MTbox Ltd, a large cable communications provider in India, where your firm has no representation. The financial statements of MTbox for the year ending 30 September 2006 will continue to be audited by a local firm of Chartered Certified Accountants. MTbox's activities have not been reflected in the above estimated results of the group. Beeski is committed to introducing its corporate image into India.

In order to sustain growth, significant costs are expected to be incurred as operations are expanded, networks upgraded and new products and services introduced.

Required:

(a)   Identify and describe the principal business risks for the Beeski group.   (9 marks)

(b)   Explain what effect the acquisitions will have on the planning of Ribi & Co's audit of the consolidated financial statements of Beeski Ltd for the year ending 30 September 2006.   (10 marks)

(c)   Explain the role of 'support letters' (also called 'comfort letters') as evidence in the audit of financial statements.   (6 marks)

(d)   Discuss how 'horizontal groups' (ie non-consolidated entities under common control) affect the scope of an audit and the audit work undertaken.   (5 marks)

(30 marks)

2   You have been asked to carry out an investigation by the management of Xzibit Ltd. One of the company's subsidiaries, Efex Engineering Ltd, has been making losses for the past year. Xzibit's management is concerned about the accuracy of Efex Engineering's most recent quarter's management accounts.

The summarised income statements for the last three quarters are as follows:

Quarter to	30 June 2006 £000	31 March 2006 £000	31 December 2005 £000
Turnover	429	334	343
Opening stock	180	163	203
Materials	318	251	200
Direct wages	62	54	74
	560	468	477
Less: Closing stock	(162)	(180)	(163)
Cost of goods sold	398	288	314
Gross profit	31	46	29
Less: Overheads	(63)	(75)	(82)
Net loss	(32)	(29)	(53)
Gross profit (%)	7·2%	13·8%	8·5%
Materials (% of revenue)	78·3%	70·0%	70·0%
Labour (% of revenue)	14·5%	16·2%	21·6%

Xzibit's management board believes that the high material consumption as a percentage of turnover for the quarter to 30 June 2006 is due to one or more of the following factors:
(1) under-counting or under-valuation of closing stock;
(2) excessive consumption or wastage of materials;
(3) material being stolen by employees or other individuals.

Efex Engineering has a small number of large customers and manufactures its products to each customer's specification. The selling price of the product is determined by:
(1) estimating the cost of materials;
(2) estimating the labour cost;
(3) adding a mark-up to cover overheads and provide a normal profit.

The estimated costs are not compared with actual costs. Although it is possible to analyse purchase invoices for materials between customers' orders this analysis has not been done.

A physical stock count is carried out at the end of each quarter. Stock items are entered on stocksheets and valued manually. The company does not maintain perpetual stock records and a full physical count is to be carried out at the financial year end, 30 September 2006.

The direct labour cost included in the stock valuation is small and should be assumed to be constant at the end of each quarter. Historically, the cost of materials consumed has been about 70% of turnover.

The management accounts to 31 March 2006 are to be assumed to be correct.

Required:

(a) **Define 'forensic auditing' and describe its application to fraud investigations.**   (5 marks)

(b) **Identify and describe the matters that you should consider and the procedures you should carry out in order to plan an investigation of Efex Engineering Ltd's losses.**   (10 marks)

(c) (i) **Explain the matters you should consider to determine whether closing stock at 30 June 2006 is undervalued; and**
     (ii) **Describe the tests you should plan to perform to quantify the amount of any undervaluation.**   (8 marks)

(d) (i) **Identify and explain the possible reasons for the apparent high materials consumption in the quarter ended 30 June 2006; and**
     (ii) **Describe the tests you should plan to perform to determine whether materials consumption, as shown in the management accounts, is correct.**   (7 marks)

(30 marks)

Section B – TWO questions ONLY to be attempted

3   You are a manager in Ingot & Co, a firm of Chartered Certified Accountants, with specific responsibility for the quality of audits. Ingot was appointed auditor of Argenta Ltd, a provider of waste management services, in July 2006. You have just visited the audit team at Argenta's head office. The audit team is comprised of an accountant in charge (AIC), an audit senior and two trainees.

Argenta's draft accounts for the year ended 30 June 2006 show turnover of £11·6 million (2005 – £8·1 million) and total assets of £3·6 million (2005 – £2·5 million). During your visit, a review of the audit working papers revealed the following:

(a)   On the audit planning checklist, the audit senior has crossed through the analytical procedures section and written 'not applicable – new client'. The audit planning checklist has not been signed off as having been reviewed.

(4 marks)

(b)   The AIC last visited Argenta's office when the final audit commenced two weeks ago on 1 August. The senior has since completed the audit of tangible fixed assets (including property and service equipment) which amount to £0·6 million as at 30 June 2006 (2005 – £0·6 million). The AIC spends most of his time working from Ingot's office and is currently allocated to three other assignments as well as Argenta's audit.   (4 marks)

(c)   At 30 June 2006 trade debtors amounted to £2·1 million (2005 – £0·9 million). One of the trainees has just finished sending out first requests for direct confirmation of customers' balances as at the balance sheet date.

(4 marks)

(d)   The other trainee has been assigned to the audit of the consumable supplies that comprise stock amounting to £88,000 (2005 – £53,000). The trainee has carried out tests of controls over the perpetual stock records and confirmed the 'roll-back' of a sample of current quantities to book quantities as at the year end.   (3 marks)

(e)   The AIC has noted the following matter for your attention. The financial statements to 30 June 2005 disclosed, as unquantifiable, a contingent liability for pending litigation. However, the AIC has seen a letter confirming that the matter was settled out of court for £0.45 million on 14 September 2005. The auditor's report on the financial statements for the year ended 30 June 2005 was unmodified and signed on 19 September 2005. The AIC believes that Argenta's management is not aware of the error and has not brought it to their attention.   (5 marks)

Required:

Identify and comment on the implications of these findings for Ingot & Co's quality control policies and procedures.

Note: The mark allocation is shown against each of the five issues.

(20 marks)

5

4   You are the manager responsible for four audit clients of Axis & Co, a firm of Chartered Certified Accountants. The year end in each case is 30 June 2006.

You are currently reviewing the audit working paper files and the audit seniors' recommendations for the auditors' reports. Details are as follows:

(a) Mantis Ltd is a subsidiary of Cube Ltd. Serious going concern problems have been noted during this year's audit. Mantis will be unable to trade for the foreseeable future unless it continues to receive financial support from the parent company. Mantis has received a letter of support ('comfort letter') from Cube Ltd.

The audit senior has suggested that, due to the seriousness of the situation, the audit opinion must at least be qualified 'except for'.   (5 marks)

(b) During the year Lorenze Ltd has changed its accounting policy for purchased brands from amortisation over their estimated useful lives to annual impairment review. No disclosure of this change has been given in the financial statements. The carrying amount of brands in the balance sheet as at 30 June 2006 is the same as at 30 June 2005 as management's impairment review shows that it is not impaired.

The audit senior has concluded that a qualification is not required but suggests that attention can be drawn to the change by way of an emphasis of matter paragraph.   (6 marks)

(c) The directors' report of Abrupt Ltd states that investment property rental forms a major part of turnover. However, a note to the financial statements shows that property rental represents only 1·6% of total turnover for the year. The audit senior is satisfied that the turnover figures are correct.

The audit senior has noted that an unqualified opinion should be given as the audit opinion does not extend to the directors' report.   (4 marks)

(d) Audit work on the after-date bank transactions of Jingle Ltd has identified a transfer of cash from Bell Ltd. The audit senior assigned to the audit of Jingle has documented that Jingle's finance director explained that Bell commenced trading on 7 July 2006, after being set up as a wholly-owned foreign subsidiary of Jingle.

The audit senior has noted that although no other evidence has been obtained an unmodified opinion is appropriate because the matter does not impact on the current year's financial statements.   (5 marks)

Required:

For each situation, comment on the suitability or otherwise of the audit senior's proposals for the auditors' reports. Where you disagree, indicate what audit modification (if any) should be given instead.

Note: The mark allocation is shown against each of the four issues.

                                                                                                          (20 marks)

6

5 (a) **Comment on the need for ethical guidance for accountants on money laundering.** (5 marks)

(b) You are senior manager in Dedza & Co, a firm of Chartered Certified Accountants. Recently, you have been assigned specific responsibility for undertaking annual reviews of existing clients. The following situations have arisen in connection with three clients:

(i) Dedza was appointed auditor and tax advisor to Kora Ltd last year and has recently issued an unmodified opinion on the financial statements for the year ended 31 March 2006. To your surprise, HM Revenue & Customs has just launched an investigation into the affairs of Kora on suspicion of underdeclaring income.

(7 marks)

(ii) The chief executive of Xalam Ltd, an exporter of specialist equipment, has asked for advice on the accounting treatment and disclosure of payments being made for security consultancy services. The payments, which aim to ensure that consignments are not impounded in the destination country of a major customer, may be material to the financial statements for the year ending 31 December 2006. Xalam does not treat these payments as tax deductible.

(4 marks)

(iii) Your firm has provided financial advice to the Pholey family for many years and this has sometimes involved your firm in carrying out transactions on their behalf. The eldest son, Esau, is to take up a position as a senior government official to a foreign country next month.

(4 marks)

Required:

Identify and comment on the ethical and other professional issues raised by each of these matters and state what action, if any, Dedza & Co should now take. (15 marks)

Note: The mark allocation is shown against each of the three situations.

(20 marks)

End of Question Paper

Part A
Regulatory environment

International regulatory frameworks for audit and assurance services

Topic list	Syllabus reference
1 International regulatory frameworks for audit and assurance services	A1
2 Audit committees	A2
3 Internal control effectiveness	A3
4 Money laundering	A2
5 Law and regulation	A3

Introduction

This chapter covers a wide range of regulations that affect the work of audit and assurance professionals. You need to be aware of the international nature of the audit and assurance market and the main issues driving the development of regulatory frameworks.

The detailed requirements relating to money laundering are then discussed. You should be prepared to explain the responsibilities of professional accountants in this area and to outline the procedures that audit firms should implement.

The final section looks at the auditor's responsibilities in respect of laws and regulations that apply to an audit client. This is a topic that could be built in to a practical case study question.

Study guide

		Intellectual level
A1	**Regulatory environment**	
	International regulatory frameworks for audit and assurance services	
(a)	Explain the need for laws, regulations, standard and other guidance relating to audit, assurance and related services.	2
(b)	Outline and explain the legal and professional framework including:	2
(i)	The national and international standard-setting process	
(ii)	The authority of national and international standards	
(iii)	Public oversight and principles of corporate governance	
(iv)	The role of audit committees	
(c)	Discuss the effectiveness of the different ways in which the auditing profession and audit markets are regulated.	2
A2	**Money laundering**	
(a)	Define 'money laundering'.	1
(b)	Explain how international efforts seek to combat money laundering.	2
(c)	Explain the scope of criminal offences of money laundering and how professional accountants may be protected from criminal and civil liability.	2
(d)	Explain the need for ethical guidance in this area.	2
(e)	Describe how accountants meet their obligations to help prevent and detect money laundering including record keeping and reporting of suspicion to the National Criminal Intelligence Service (NCIS).	2
(f)	Explain the important of 'know your customer' (KYC) information.	2
(g)	Recognise potentially suspicious transactions and assess their impact on reporting duties.	2
(h)	Describe, with reasons, the basic elements of an anti-money laundering program.	2
A3	**Laws and regulations**	
(a)	Compare and contract the respective responsibilities of management and auditors concerning compliance with laws and regulations in an audit of financial statements.	2
(b)	Describe the auditors considerations of compliance with laws and regulations and plan audit procedures when possible non-compliance is discovered.	2
(c)	Discuss how and to whom non-compliance should be reported.	2
(d)	Recognise when withdrawal from an engagement is necessary.	2

Exam guide

The technical content of this part of the syllabus is mainly drawn from your earlier studies. Questions in this paper are unlikely to ask for straight repetition of this knowledge, but rather to require explanation or discussion of the reasons behind the regulations.

1 International regulatory frameworks for audit and assurance services

FAST FORWARD

Major developments in international regulation of audit and assurance are currently taking place.

1.1 The need for laws, regulations, standards and other guidance

Corporate scandals, such as Encon and Worldcom in the USA, and Parmalat in Italy have brought the audit profession under close scrutiny from investors, businesses, regulators and others.

Businesses have become more complex and global, and firms of accountants have expanded their range of services well beyond traditional assurance and tax advice. This has led to a great deal of re-examination of regulatory and standard-setting structures both nationally and internationally in recent years.

1.2 The legal and professional framework

You have studied the regulatory framework in earlier papers. The following summaries will provide a quick reminder.

1.2.1 Overview of the UK regulatory framework

The EU 8th Directive on company law requires that persons carrying out statutory audits must be approved by the authorities of EU member states. The authority to give this approval in the UK is delegated to Recognised Supervisory Bodies (RSBs). An auditor must be a member of an RSB and be eligible under its own rules. The ACCA is a RSB.

The RSBs are required to have rules to ensure that persons eligible for appointment as a company auditor are either (4(1), Sch 11, CA 1989):

- Individuals holding an appropriate qualification
- Firms controlled by qualified persons

Financial Reporting Council

The FRC

The Financial Reporting Council (FRC) is the UK's independent regulator for corporate reporting and governance.

Its aim is to promote confidence in corporate reporting and governance.

In pursuit of this aim its six objectives are to promote:

1   high quality corporate reporting
2   high quality auditing
3   high quality actuarial practice
4   high standards of corporate governance
5   the integrity, competence and transparency of the accountancy and actuarial professions
6   its effectiveness as a unified independent regulator

The functions it exercises in pursuit of these six objectives can be summarised as follows:

- setting, monitoring and enforcing accounting and auditing standards
- setting actuarial standards
- statutory oversight and regulation of auditors
- operating an independent investigation and discipline scheme for public interest cases
- overseeing the regulatory activities of the professional accountancy and actuarial bodies
- promoting high standards of corporate governance

The structure of the FRC is illustrated below and the elements most relevant to this syllabus have been cross-referenced to the sections where you will find more detailed coverage.

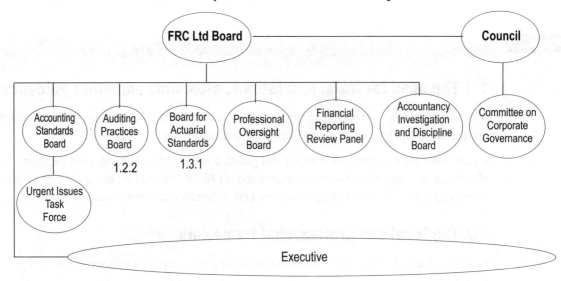

1.2.2 National and international standard setting

Auditing Standards are set by the Auditing Practices Board (APB).

The APB makes three categories of pronouncement:

- Auditing Standards (Quality control, engagement and ethical)
- Practice notes
- Bulletins

The APB has adopted International Standards on Auditing. In many cases, the Standards have been augmented by UK requirements (shown in grey shade in the Standards) so in UK, ISAs are styled International Standards on Auditing (UK and Ireland). Complying with these is a requirement when carrying out statutory audits.

International Standards on Auditing are produced by the International Audit and Assurance Standards Board (IAASB), a technical standing committee of the International Federation of Accountants (IFAC). An explanation of the workings of the IAASB, the authority of the ISAs and so on are laid out in the *Preface to International Standards on Quality Control, Auditing, Assurance and Related Services*.

The *Preface* restates the mission of IFAC as set out in its constitution: 'The development and enhancement of an accountancy profession with harmonised standards able to provide services of consistently high quality in the public interest'.

Within each country, local regulations govern, to a greater or lesser degree, the practices followed in the auditing of financial or other information. Such regulations may be either of a statutory nature, or in the form of statements issued by the regulatory or professional bodies in the countries concerned.

National standards on auditing and related services published in many countries differ in form and content. The IAASB takes account of such documents and differences and, in the light of such knowledge, issues ISAs which are intended for international acceptance.

1.2.3 The authority attached to ISAs

The Preface also lays out the authority attached to ISAs in general.

Authority of International Standards on Auditing

International Standards on Auditing (ISAs) are to be applied in the audit of historical financial information.

The IAASB's Standards contain basic principles and essential procedures (identified in bold type black lettering) together with related guidance in the form of explanatory and other material, including appendices. The basic principles and essential procedures are to be understood and applied in the context of the explanatory and other material that provide guidance for their application. It is therefore necessary to consider the whole text of a standard to understand and apply the basic principles and essential procedures.

In exceptional circumstances, an auditor may judge it necessary to depart from an ISA in order to more effectively achieve the objective of an audit. When such a situation arises, the auditor should be prepared to justify the departure.

Any **limitation** of the applicability of a specific ISA is made clear in the standard, for example, it might contain a passage such as the following:

Application to public sector

'The Public Sector Perspective (PSP) issued by the Public Sector Committee of the International Federation of Accountants is set out at the end of an ISA. Where no PSP is added, the ISA is applicable in all material respects to the public sector'. For example, ISA 320 *Audit materiality* includes a PSP that points out that in assessing materiality. The public sector auditor must, in addition to exercising professional judgement, consider any legislation or regulation which may impact that assessment.

1.2.4 Working procedures of the IAASB

The working procedure of the IAASB is to select subjects for detailed study by a **subcommittee** established for that purpose. The IAASB delegates to the subcommittee the initial responsibility for the preparation and drafting of accounting standards and statements.

As a result of that study, an **exposure draft** is prepared for consideration by the IAASB. If approved, the exposure draft is widely distributed for comment by member bodies of IFAC, and to such international organisations that have an interest in auditing standards as appropriate.

The comments and suggestions received as a result of this exposure are then considered by the IAASB and the exposure draft is **revised** as appropriate. Provided that the revised draft is approved it is issued as a definitive **International Standard on Auditing** or as an **International Auditing Practice Statement** and becomes operative.

1.2.5 Current ISAs (UK and Ireland)

No	Title
200	Objective and general principles governing an audit of financial statements
210	Terms of audit engagements
220	Quality control for audits of historical financial information
230	Audit documentation
240	The auditor's responsibility to consider fraud in an audit of financial statements
250	Consideration of laws and regulations in an audit of financial statements
260	Communication of audit matters with those charged with governance
300	Planning an audit of financial statements
315	Obtaining an understanding of the entity and its environment and assessing the risks of material misstatement
320	Audit materiality
330	The auditor's procedures in response to assessed risks
402	Audit considerations relating to entities using service organisations
500	Audit evidence
501	Audit evidence – additional considerations for specific items
505	External confirmations
510	Initial engagements – opening balances and continuing engagements – opening balances
520	Analytical procedures
530	Audit sampling and other means of testing
540	Audit of accounting estimates
545	Auditing fair value measurements and disclosures
550	Related parties
560	Subsequent events
570	Going concern
580	Management representations
600	Using the work of another auditor
610	Considering the work of internal audit
620	Using the work of an expert
700	The auditor's report on financial statements
710	Comparatives
720	Other information in documents containing audited financial statements and the auditors' statutory reporting responsibility in relation to directors' reports

Notes

1   Students should be aware of the nature and meaning of the audit report and should be able to discuss the contents and wording of the report. Students would not be asked to reproduce the audit report in full in an exam question, but they may be requested to prepare explanatory paragraphs for inclusion in the report particularly in situations leading to a modified report.

2   Students are advised that questions will be based on the principles and good practice set out in the International Standards on Auditing.

Exam focus point

> International standards are quoted throughout this text and you must understand how they are applied in practice. These standards were all listed as being examinable in this syllabus at the time of writing, you should check the list of examinable documents for your exam in *Student Accountant* prior to your sitting.

Point to note

> Throughout the rest of this book, for convenience, ISAs (UK and Ireland) are referred to simply as ISAs. Note that if you need to refer to an ISA in the exam, you should give it its full title, eg ISA (UK and Ireland) 200 *Objective and general principles governing an audit of financial statements*. However, it is unlikely that you will need to refer to an ISA by name in the exam.

1.3 Public oversight

FAST FORWARD

> Public oversight of the audit profession and of standard-setting has been a trend in recent regulatory developments within the UK and internationally.

1.3.1 Public oversight in the UK

In the UK the Professional Oversight Board contributes to investor, market and public confidence in the financial and governance stewardship of listed and other entities by:

- independent oversight of the regulation of the auditing profession by the recognised supervisory and qualifying bodies;

- monitoring the quality of the auditing function in relation to economically significant entities;

- independent oversight of the regulation of the accountancy profession by the professional accountancy bodies;

- independent oversight of the regulation of the actuarial profession by the professional actuarial bodies and promoting high quality actuarial work.

In relation to audit, the Board achieves its aims by:

1   Authorising professional accountancy bodies to act as supervisory bodies and/or to offer a recognised professional qualification. As part of this activity, the Board will assess whether:

- the recognised supervisory and qualifying bodies comply with all the statutory requirements for recognition set out in the Companies Act 1989;

- the recognised supervisory bodies comply with the independent standard setting, monitoring and disciplinary arrangements which the legislation provides for

2   Monitoring the audit quality of economically significant entities through an independent Audit Inspection Unit (AIU). The unit monitors audit quality by reviewing audit processes including audit judgements. It:

- agrees with audit firms amendments to their procedures where appropriate;

- makes recommendations to the recognised supervisory bodies for appropriate regulatory action; and where appropriate refers matters to the AIDB and the FRRP.

1.3.2 Public oversight internationally

In February 2005 the **Public Interest Oversight Board** was launched to exercise oversight for all of IFAC's 'public interest activities' including its standard-setting bodies such as the IAASB. Its work involves

- monitoring the standard-setting boards
- overseeing the nomination process for membership of these boards
- co-operation with national oversight authorities.

1.3.3 Other examples of public oversight

In the USA, the Public Company Accounting Board (PCAOB) is a private sector body created by the Sarbanes-Oxley Act, 2002. Its aim is to oversee the auditors of public companies. Its stated purpose is to 'protect the interests of investors and further the public interest in the preparation of informative, fair and independent audit reports'. Its powers include setting auditing, quality control, ethics, independence and other standards relating to the preparation of audit reports by issuers. It also has the authority to regulate the non-audit services that audit firms can offer – this power was awarded to it as a result of the Enron and Worldcom scandals.

The standards issued by the PCAOB have increasing relevance for UK auditors. Firstly, the PCAOB standards relating to Sarbanes-Oxley compliance, such as AS 2 on internal control, have direct relevance to the auditors of UK companies with joint listings on the US stock exchange. Secondly, the PCAOB standards are likely to influence IAASB thinking as they develop new standards.

1.4 Principles of corporate governance

FAST FORWARD Listed companies are required to conform to the requirements of the Combined Code.

The Combined Code is issued as part of the Stock Exchange guidance and so generally relates to listed companies. However, this does not mean that following the guidance is not good practice for other companies also.

1.4.1

Principles of the Combined Code	
The board	Every company should be headed by an effective board, which is collectively responsible for the success of the company.
	There should be a clear division of responsibilities at the head of the company between the running of the board and the executive responsibility for the running of the company's business. No one individual should have unfettered powers of decision.
	The board should include a balance of executive and non-executive directors (and in particular independent non-executive directors) such that no individual or small group of individuals can dominate the board's decision taking.
	There should be a formal, rigorous and transparent procedure for the appointment of new directors to the board.
	The board should be supplied in a timely manner with information in a form and of a quality appropriate to enable it to discharge its duties. All directors should receive induction on joining the board and should regularly update and refresh their skills and knowledge.
	The board should undertake a formal and rigorous annual evaluation of its own performance and that of its committees and individual directors.

Principles of the Combined Code	
	All directors should be submitted for re-election at regular intervals, subject to continued satisfactory performance. The board should ensure planned and progressive refreshing of the board.
Remuneration	Levels of remuneration should be sufficient to attract, retain and motivate directors of the quality required to run the company successfully, but a company should avoid paying more than is necessary for this purpose. A significant proportion of executive directors' remuneration should be structured so as to link rewards to corporate and individual performance.
	There should be formal and transparent procedures for developing policy on executive remuneration and for fixing the remuneration packages of individual directors. No director should be involved in deciding his or her own remuneration.
Accountability and audit	The board should present a balanced and understandable assessment of the company's position and prospects.
	The board should maintain a sound system of internal control to safeguard shareholders' investment and the company's assets.
	The board should establish formal and transparent arrangements for considering how they should apply the financial reporting and internal control principles and for maintaining an appropriate relationship with the company's auditors.
Relations with institutional shareholders	There should be a dialogue with shareholders based on the mutual understanding of objectives. The board as a whole has responsibility for ensuring that a satisfactory dialogue with shareholders takes place.
	The board should use the AGM to communicate with investors and to encourage their participation.

> Depending on the size of the company, this may involve setting up an internal audit department.

1.4.2 Corporate governance statement

The stock exchange rules require that, as part of the **annual report**, a company must **include** a narrative **statement of how it has applied the principles set out in the Combined Code**. This statement must include an explanation which allows the shareholders to evaluate how the company have applied the principles.

The statement must also provide explanation of whether the company has **complied** with the principles of the Combined Code.

They must also provide a statement showing how they have applied the principles relating to directors' remuneration (not examined in detail here).

The auditors must review the corporate governance statement before it is published. Their duty to review it extends to the following items:

- Directors should explain in their annual report their responsibility for preparing the accounts and there should be statement by the auditors about their reporting responsibilities.

- The board should, at least annually, conduct a review of the group's system of internal controls and should report to shareholders that they have done so. The review should cover all material controls, including financial, operational and compliance controls and risk management systems.

- The board should establish an audit committee of at least three, or in the case of smaller companies two, members, who should all be independent non-executive directors. The board should satisfy itself that at least one member of the audit committee has recent and relevant financial experience.

- The main role and responsibilities of the audit committee should be set out in written terms of reference and should include:

    - To monitor the integrity of the financial statements of a company, and any formal announcements relating to the company's performance, reviewing significant financial reporting judgements contained in them.

    - To review the company's internal financial controls and, unless expressly addressed by a separate board risk committee composed of independent directors or by the board itself, to review the company's internal control and risk management systems.

    - To monitor and review the effectiveness of the company's internal audit function.

    - To make recommendations to the board, for it to put to shareholders for their approval in general meeting, in relation to the appointment, re-appointment and removal of the external auditor and to approve the remuneration and terms of engagement of the external auditor.

    - To review and monitor the external auditor's independence and objectivity and the effectiveness of the audit process, taking into consideration relevant UK professional and regulatory requirements.

    - To develop and implement policy on the engagement of the external auditor to supply non audit services, taking into account relevant ethical guidance regarding the provision of non-audit services by the external audit firm; and to report to the board, identifying any matters in respect of which it considers that action and improvement is needed and making recommendations as to the steps to be taken.

- The terms of reference of the audit committee, including its role and the authority delegated to it by the board, should be made available. A separate section of the annual report should describe the work of the committee in discharging those responsibilities.

- The audit committee should review arrangements by which staff of the company may, in confidence, raise concerns about possible improprieties in matters of financial reporting or other matters. The audit committee's objective should be to ensure that arrangements are in place for the proportionate and independent investigation of such matters and for appropriate follow-up action.

- The audit committee should monitor and review the effectiveness of internal control activities. Where there is no internal audit function, the audit committee should review annually whether there is a need for an internal audit function and make a recommendation to the board, and the reasons for the absence of such a function should be explained in the relevant section of the report.

- The audit committee should have primary responsibility for making a recommendation on the appointment, reappointment or removal of the external auditors. If the board does not accept the audit committee's recommendation, it should include in the annual report, and in any papers recommending appointment or re-appointment, a statement from the audit committee explaining the recommendation and should set out the reasons why the board has taken a different position.

- The annual report should explain to shareholders how, if the auditor provides non audit services, auditor objectivity and independence is safeguarded.

1.4.3 Benefits of a voluntary code

The Combined Code is a **voluntary code**. The Stock Exchange requires that disclosures be made as to whether it has been complied with, but there are **no statutory requirements to comply** with it.

The main benefit in having a voluntary code is that the code can be **applied flexibly**, where management believe that it is relevant. The **disclosure** requirements ensure that **shareholders** are **aware** of the position and they can make any points they want to about compliance with the code at the AGM.

It has been argued that making such a code obligatory would have **punitive effects** on some companies, due to their size or investor make up and that legislation would create a **burden of requirement** which **could be excessive in many cases**.

Critics of the view would argue:

- Disclosure of non-compliance is insufficient as the AGM is still not sufficient protection for shareholders.

- Having a voluntary code allows some companies not to comply freely, to the detriment of their shareholders.

- The requirement to disclose is only a Stock Exchange requirement, and there are many unlisted companies who should be encouraged to apply the codes.

The government has shown concern for this area in the past and it is believed that it **might take action in the future to regulate this area** more heavily.

However, at the moment, having a **voluntary code is a compromise** based on the points made above.

2 Audit committees

FAST FORWARD

Audit committees are made up of non-executive directors and are perceived to increase confidence in financial reports.

2.1 Combined Code provisions

Audit committees were the subject of the Smith Report in 2003. The Smith Report contained a summary of recommendations which have been included in the revised Combined Code.

Combined Code provisions

The board **would establish** an audit committee of **at least three, or in the case of smaller companies, two members**.

The main role and responsibilities should be set out in **written terms of reference** and should include:

(a) To monitor the integrity of the financial statements of the company and any formal announcements relating to the company's financial performance, reviewing significant financial reporting issues and judgements contained in them.

(b) To review the company's internal financial controls and, unless expressly addressed by a separate board risk committee composed of independent directors or by the board itself, the company's control and risk management systems.

(c) To monitor and review the effectiveness of the company's internal audit function.

(d) To make recommendations to the board for it to put to the shareholders for their approval in general meeting in relation to the appointment of the external auditor and to approve the remuneration and terms of engagement of the external auditors.

(e) To monitor and review the external auditor's independence, objectivity and effectiveness, taking into consideration relevant UK professional and regulatory requirements.

(f) To develop and implement policy on the engagement of the external auditor to supply non-audit services, taking into account relevant ethical guidance regarding the provisions of non-audit services by the external audit firm and to report to the board, identifying any matters in respect of which it considers that action or improvement is needed, and making recommendations as to the steps to be taken and to report to the board, identifying any matters in respect of which it considers that action or improvement is needed, and making recommendations as to the steps to be taken.

The audit committee should be provided with **sufficient resources** to undertake its duties.

2.2 Advantages and disadvantages of audit committees

The key advantage to an auditor of having an audit committee is that a committee of independent non-executive directors provides the auditor with an independent point of reference other than the executive directors of the company, in the event of disagreement arising.

Other **advantages** that are claimed to arise from the existence of an audit committee include:

(a)   It will lead to **increased confidence** in the credibility and objectivity of financial reports.

(b)   By specialising in the problems of financial reporting and thus, to some extent, fulfilling the directors' responsibility in this area, it will allow the **executive** directors to **devote their attention to management**.

(c)   In cases where the interests of the company, the executive directors and the employees conflict, the audit committee might provide an **impartial body** for the auditors to consult.

(d)   The internal auditors will be able to report to the audit committee.

Opponents of audit committees argue that:

(a)   There may be **difficulty selecting** sufficient non-executive directors with the necessary competence in auditing matters for the committee to be really effective.

(b)   The establishment of such a **formalised reporting procedure** may **dissuade** the **auditors** from raising matters of judgement and limit them to reporting only on matters of fact.

(c)   **Costs** may be **increased**.

2.3 Role and function of audit committees

In an appendix to the *Cadbury Report*, the Committee expands on the role and function of the audit committee.

'If they operate effectively, audit committees can bring significant benefits. In particular, they have the potential to:

(a)   improve the quality of financial reporting, by reviewing the financial statements on behalf of the Board;

(b)   create a climate of discipline and control which will reduce the opportunity for fraud;

(c)   enable the non-executive directors to contribute an independent judgement and play a positive role;

(d)   help the finance director, by providing a forum in which he can raise issues of concern, and which he can use to get things done which might otherwise be difficult;

(e)   strengthen the position of the external auditor, by providing a channel of communication and forum for issues of concern;

(f)   provide a framework within which the external auditor can assert his independence in the event of a dispute with management;

(g)   strengthen the position of the internal audit function, by providing a greater degree of independence from management;

(h)   increase public confidence in the credibility and objectivity of financial statements.'

Question
Voluntary codes

Explain the benefits of corporate governance codes being voluntary.

Answer

- Code can be applied flexibly, as is best for the company.
- Burden of statutory requirement is not created

Question
Audit committees

Since 1978 all public companies in the United States of America have been required to have an audit committee as a condition of listing on the New York Stock Exchange.

(a)   Explain what you understand by the term audit committee.
(b)   List and briefly describe the duties and responsibilities of audit committees.
(c)   Discuss the advantages and disadvantages of audit committees.

Answer

(a)   An **audit committee** reviews financial information and liases between the auditors and the company. It normally consists of the non-executive directors of the company, though there is no reason why other senior personnel should not also be involved.

(b)   (i)   To monitor the integrity of the financial statements of the company, reviewing significant financial reporting issues and judgements contained in them.

(ii)   To review the company's internal financial control system and, unless expressly addressed by a separate risk committee or by the board itself, risk management systems.

(iii) To monitor and review the effectiveness of the company's internal audit function.

(iv)   To make recommendations to the board in relation to the appointment of he external auditor and to approve the remuneration and terms of engagement of the external auditors.

(v)   To monitor and review the external auditor's independence, objectivity and effectiveness, taking into consideration relevant UK professional and regularly requirements.

(vi)   To develop and implement policy on the engagement of the external auditor to supply non-audit services, taking into account relevant ethical guidance regarding the provisions of non-audit services by the external audit firm.

In addition to these responsibilities, any responsible audit committee is likely to want:

(1)   To **ensure that the review procedures** for interim statements, rights documents and similar information are **adequate;**

(2)   To **review both the management accounts** used internally and the **statutory accounts** issued to shareholders for reasonableness;

(3)   To make **appropriate recommendations for improvements in management control.**

(c)   There are a number of advantages and disadvantages.

Disadvantages

(1)   Since the finding of audit committees are rarely made public, it is **not** always **clear what they do** or how effective they have been in doing it.

(2)   It is possible that the audit committee's **approach** may prove somewhat **pedestrian,** resolving little of consequence but acting as a drag on the drive and entrepreneurial flair of the company's senior executives.

(3)   Unless the requirement for such a body were made compulsory, as in the US, it is likely that those **firms most in need** of an audit committee would nevertheless **choose not to have one**. (Note that the Combined Code now requires listed companies to have an audit committee.)

Advantages

(1)   By its very existence, the audit committee should make the **executive directors more aware of their duties and responsibilities.**

(2)   It could act as a **deterrent to the commission of illegal acts** by the executive directors and may discourage them from behaving in ways which could be prejudicial to the interests of the shareholders

(3)   Where **illegal or prejudicial acts** have been carried out by the executive directors, the **audit committee** provides an **independent body** to which the auditor can turn. In this way, the problem may be resolved without the auditor having to reveal the matter to the shareholders, either in his report or at the AGM.

3 Internal control effectiveness

FAST FORWARD

Internal control is a key part of good corporate governance. Directors are responsible for maintaining a system of control that will safeguard the company's assets.

3.1 Importance of internal control and risk management

Internal controls are essential to management, as they contribute to

- Safeguarding the company's assets
- Helping to prevent and detect fraud
- Therefore, safeguarding the shareholders' investment

Good internal control helps the business to run efficiently. A control system reduces identified risks to the business. It also helps to ensure reliability of reporting, and compliance with laws.

3.2 Directors' responsibilities

The **ultimate responsibility** for a company's system of internal controls lies with the board of directors. It should set procedures of internal control and regularly monitor that the system operates as it should.

Part of setting up an internal control system will involve **assessing the risks** facing the business, so that the **system** can be **designed** to ensure those **risks are avoided**. This is discussed in more detail in Chapter 12.

As you know from your earlier studies in auditing the system of internal control in a company will reflect the **control environment**, which includes the attitude of the directors towards risk, and their awareness of it.

Internal control systems will always have **inherent limitations**, the most important being that a system of internal control cannot eliminate the possibility of human error, or the chance that staff will collude in fraud.

Once the directors have set up a system of internal control, they are responsible for **reviewing** it regularly, to ensure that it **still meets its objectives**.

The board may decide that in order to carry out their review function properly they have to employ an **internal audit function** to undertake this task. The role of internal audit is discussed in more detail in Chapter 16, but this is potentially part of its function.

If the board does not see the need for an internal audit function, the Combined Code suggests that it revisits this decision on an annual basis, so that the **need for internal audit is regularly reviewed**.

The Combined Code recommends that the board of directors **report** on their review of internal controls as part of their annual report. The statement should be based on an annual assessment of internal control which should confirm that the board has considered **all significant aspects** of internal control. In particular the assessment should cover:

(a) The **changes** since the last **assessment** in **risks** faced, and the company's **ability** to **respond** to **changes** in its business environment

(b) The **scope** and **quality** of management's monitoring of risk and internal control, and of the work of internal audit, or consideration of the need for an internal audit function if the company does not have one

(c) The **extent** and **frequency** of reports to the board

(d) **Significant controls**, **failings** and **weaknesses** which have or might have material impacts upon the accounts

(e) The effectiveness of the public reporting processes

3.3 Auditors' responsibilities

The Auditing Practice Board's Bulletin 2006/5 *The Combined Code on Corporate Governance: Requirements of Auditors Under the Listing Rules of the Financial Services Authority* considers what auditors should do in response to a statement on internal controls by directors.

The guidance states that the auditors should concentrate on the review carried out by the board. The objective of the auditors' work is to assess whether the company's summary of the process that the board has adopted in reviewing the effectiveness of the system of internal control is supported by the documentation prepared by the directors and reflects that process.

The auditors should make appropriate enquiries and review the statement made by the board in the accounts and the supporting documentation.

Auditors will have gained some understanding of controls due to their work on the accounts; however what they are required to do by auditing standards is narrower in scope than the review performed by the directors.

Auditors therefore are not expected to assess whether the directors' review covers all risks and controls, and whether the risks are satisfactorily addressed by the internal controls. To avoid misunderstanding on the scope of the auditors' role, the Bulletin recommends that the following wording be used in the audit report.

'We are not required to consider whether the board's statements on internal control cover all risks and controls, or form an opinion on the effectiveness of the company's corporate governance procedures or its risk and control procedures.'

The Bulletin also points out that it is particularly important for auditors to communicate quickly to the directors any material weaknesses they find, because of the requirements for the directors to make a statement on internal control.

The directors are required to consider the material internal control aspects of any significant problems disclosed in the accounts. Auditors work on this is the same as on other aspects of the statement; the auditors are not required to consider whether the internal control processes will remedy the problem.

The auditors may report by exception if problems arise such as:

(a) The **board's summary** of the process of review of internal control effectiveness does **not reflect** the **auditors' understanding** of that process.

(b) The **processes** that **deal with** material internal control aspects of **significant problems** do **not reflect** the **auditors' understanding** of those processes.

(c) The board has **not made** an **appropriate disclosure** if it has **failed** to **conduct** an **annual review**, or the disclosure made is not consistent with the auditors' understanding.

The report should be included in a separate paragraph below the opinion paragraph. The Bulletin gives the following example.

Other matter

We have reviewed the board's description of its process for reviewing the effectiveness of internal control set out on page x of the annual report. In our opinion the boards comments concerning ... do not appropriately reflect our understanding of the process undertaken by the board because...

Critics of recent developments have argued that listed company directors ought to be able to report on the effectiveness of internal controls, and that this is part of the responsibility and accountability expected of listed company directors. The debate is likely to continue over the next few years.

3.4 Assurance services

Accountants may also provide assurance services relating to internal control systems. This is discussed in Chapter 12.

4 Money laundering

FAST FORWARD

Money laundering law is an increasingly important issue for auditors to be aware of.

Key term

'**Money laundering** is the process by which criminals attempt to conceal the true origin and ownership of the proceeds of their criminal activity, allowing them to maintain control over the proceeds and, ultimately, providing a legitimate cover for their sources of income.'   ACCA Code of Ethics and Conduct

Money laundering is a particularly hot topic internationally. Clearly, auditors should consider it when assessing compliance risks at a client.

4.1 International recommendations and UK law

An inter-governmental body, the Financial Action Task Force on Money Laundering (FATF) was established to set standards and develop policies to combat money laundering and terrorist financing. In 1990, FATF issued recommendations for governments on how to combat these offences and these recommendations have now been endorsed by more than 130 countries.

Relevant legislation in the UK includes:

- the Terrorism Act 2000
- the Proceeds of Crime Act 2002
- the Money Laundering Regulations 2003.

The ACCA has issued *Technical Factsheets 94 and 131 on Anti-money laundering (Proceeds of Crime and Terrorism)* as guidance for its members on their responsibilities under this legislation.

4.2 Ethical guidance

ACCA's Code of Ethics and Conduct (covered in detail in chapter 2) contains guidance in respect of money laundering. Its requirements are very similar to those in the Technical Factsheets, but less detailed. The Technical Factsheets give guidance in the context of current UK law, whereas the ethical guidance emphasises the international nature of money laundering and the need for ACCA members to be aware of local legal frameworks and the basic procedures to be applied, irrespective of where in the world their work is taking place.

4.3 Accountants' obligations

The basic requirements are for accountants to keep records of clients' identity and to report suspicions of money laundering to the **Serious Organised Crime Agency (SOCA).**

Elements of a money-laundering program

Procedures	Explanations
• appoint an *MLRO* and implement internal reporting procedures	• The MLRO should have a suitable level of seniority and experience. • Individuals should make internal reports of money laundering to the MLRO. • The MLRO must consider, and document the process, whether to report to SOCA.
• train *individuals* to ensure that they are aware of the relevant legislation, know how to recognise and deal with potential *money laundering*, how to report suspicions to the *MLRO*, and how to identify *clients*	• Individuals should be trained in the firm's obligations under law, and their personal obligations. • They must be made aware of the firm's identification, record-keeping and reporting procedures.

• establish internal procedures appropriate to forestall and prevent *money laundering*, and make relevant *individuals* aware of the procedures	• Procedures should cover
	  – client acceptance
	  – gathering "know your client" (KYC) information such as expected patterns of business to assist in spotting suspicious transactions
	  – controls over client money and transactions through the client account
	  – advice and services to clients that could be of use to a money launderer
	  – internal reporting lines
	  – the role of the MLRO

• verify the identity of new *clients* and maintain evidence of identification	• The firm must be able to establish that new clients are who they claim to be
	• Typically, this will include taking copies of evidence such as
	  – passports
	  – driving licences
	  – utility bills
	• For a company this will include
	  – identities of directors
	  – certificate of incorporation

Procedures	Explanations
• maintain records of *client* identification, and any transactions undertaken for or with the *client*	• Special care needs to be taken when handling clients' money to avoid participation in a transaction involving money laundering.
• *report* suspicions *of money laundering* to SOCA.	• SOCA has designed standard disclosure forms

4.4 Risk-based approach

On any assignment, the accountants should assess the risk of money laundering activities. Clearly, every circumstance is different, but the following diagram illustrates some key risk factors.

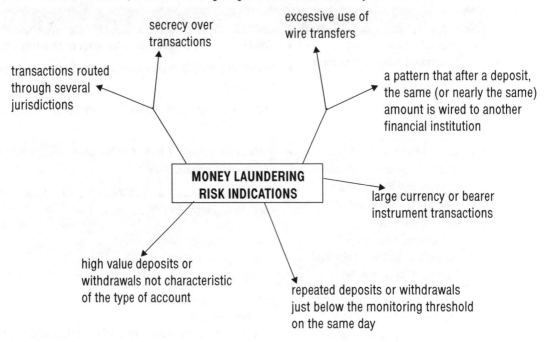

4.5 The scope of criminal offences

The firm requires these procedures to avoid committing any of the wide range of offences under the Regulations.

4.5.1 Money laundering offences are:

- concealing criminal property
- 'arranging' – becoming involved in an arrangement which is known or is suspected of facilitating the acquisition of criminal property
- acquiring using or possessing criminal property.

Defences to these offences include:

- reporting to SOCA or the MLRO before the act took place
- reporting to SOCA or the MLRO after the act took place if there was good reason for the failure to report earlier

4.5.2 Failure to Report Offences under the legislation

Key terms

> **Knowledge**
>
> - actual knowledge
>
> - shutting one's mind to the obvious
>
> - deliberately deterring a person from making disclosures, the content of which one might not care to have
>
> - knowledge of circumstances which would indicate the facts to an honest and reasonable person
>
> - knowledge of circumstances which would put an honest and reasonable person on inquiry and failing to make the reasonable inquiries which such a person would have made.
>
> **Suspicion**
>
> Suspicion is not defined in existing legislation. Case law and other sources indicate that suspicion is more than speculation but it falls short of proof or knowledge. Suspicion is personal and subjective but will generally be built on some objective foundation and so there should be some degree of consistency in how a *business's MLRO* treats possible causes of suspicion.

- Failure by an individual in the regulated sector to inform SOCA or the MLRO as soon as practicable of knowledge or suspicion of money laundering.

- Failure by the MLRO to pass on a report to SOCA as soon as possible.

  The defences here for an individual would include that there was reasonable excuse for not having made a report, or that the person does not know or suspect money laundering and their employer has not provided them with appropriate training.

  The defence for the MLRO is that there is a reasonable excuse for not having made a report. The Court would consider whether relevant guidance, such as the ACCA technical factsheet, had been followed.

4.5.3 Tipping Off and other Offences

- Tipping off is when the MLRO or any individual discloses something that might prejudice any investigations. It is a defence if the person did not know or suspect that it was likely to prejudice the investigation.

- Falsifying, concealing, destroying or disposing of documents relevant to the investigation.

- MLROs also commit an offence if they consent to a transaction which they know or suspect is money laundering, where consent has not been received from SOCA.

5 Law and regulation

Auditors must be aware of law and regulations as part of their planning and must be aware of any statutory duty to report non-compliance by the company.

5.1 Legal requirements relating to the company

The Codes of Best Practice discussed above are all voluntary codes of practice. However, companies are increasingly subject to laws and regulations with which they must comply as well. Some examples are given in the diagram below.

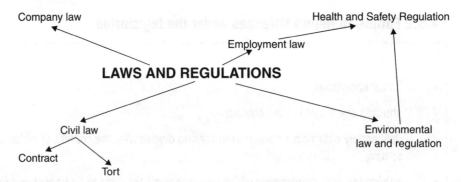

An auditor must be aware of the effect that non-compliance with the laws and regulations would have on the financial statements.

ISA (UK and Ireland) 250 *Consideration of Laws and Regulations in an audit of Financial Statements* provides guidance on the auditor's responsibility to consider laws and regulations in an audit of financial statements.

> **ISA 250.2**
>
> When designing and performing audit procedures and in evaluating and reporting the results thereof, the auditor should recognise that non-compliance by the entity with laws and regulations may materially affect the financial statements.

An audit **cannot** detect non-compliance with **all** laws and regulations.

'Non-compliance' refers to acts of omission or commission by the entity being audited, either intentional or unintentional, which are contrary to the prevailing laws or regulations. Such acts include transactions entered into by the entity, or on its behalf by its management or employees. It does **not** include personal misconduct.

Whether an act constitutes non-compliance is a legal matter that may be beyond the auditor's professional competence, although the auditor may have a fair idea in many cases though his knowledge and training. Ultimately such matters can only be decided by a court of law.

Laws and regulations governing a business entity can vary enormously (financial disclosure rules, health and safety, pollution, employment, etc). The further removed non-compliance is from the events and transactions normally reflected in the financial statements, the less likely the auditor is to become aware of it or recognise non-compliance.

5.2 Responsibility of management for compliance

Management are responsible for ensuring a client's operations are conducted in accordance with laws and regulations.

The following policies and procedures, among others, may assist management in discharging its responsibilities for the prevention and detection of non-compliance.

- **Monitor legal requirements** and ensure that operating procedures are designed to meet these requirements

- **Institute and operate** appropriate systems of **internal control** including internal audit and an audit committee

- **Develop, publicise and follow a code of conduct**

- Ensure **employees** are properly **trained** and **understand the code of conduct**

- **Monitor compliance** with the code of conduct and act appropriately to **discipline** employees who fail to comply with it

- **Engage legal advisors** to assist in monitoring legal requirements
- **Maintain a register** of significant laws with which the entity has to comply within its particular industry and a record of complaints

5.3 The auditor's consideration of compliance

As with fraud and error, the auditor is not, and cannot be held responsible for preventing non-compliance. The fact that an annual audit is carried out may, however, act as a deterrent.

Certain factors will increase the risk of material misstatements due to non-compliance with laws and regulations not being detected by the auditor.

(a) There are many laws and regulations, relating principally to the operating aspects of the entity, that typically do **not have a material effect on** the financial statements.

(b) The effectiveness of audit procedures is affected by the **inherent limitations** of the accounting and internal control systems and by the use of testing.

(c) Much of the **audit evidence** obtained by the auditor is **persuasive** rather than conclusive.

(d) Non-compliance may involve conduct **designed to conceal** it, such as collusion, forgery, deliberate failure to record transactions, senior management override of controls or intentional misrepresentations being made to the auditor.

ISA 250.13

In accordance with ISA 200 *Objective and general principles governing an audit of financial statements*, the auditor should plan and perform the audit with an attitude of professional scepticism recognising that the audit may reveal conditions or events that would lead to questioning whether an entity is complying with laws and regulations.

The auditor would only test for compliance with specific laws and regulations if engaged to do so.

ISA 250.15

In order to plan the audit, the auditor should obtain a general understanding of the legal and regulatory framework applicable to the entity and the industry and how the entity is complying with that framework.

In obtaining this general understanding the auditor should obtain an understanding of the procedures followed by the entity to ensure compliance. He should recognise that some laws and regulations may have a **fundamental effect** on the operations of the entity, ie they may cause the entity to cease operations or call into question the entity's continuance as a going concern. For example, non-compliance with the requirements of the entity's license or other title to perform its operations could have such an impact (for example, for a bank, non-compliance with capital or investment requirements).

The auditor would usually obtain a general understanding of laws and regulations affecting the entity in the following ways.

- **Use the existing knowledge** of the entity's industry and business
- **Enquire of management** concerning the entity's **policies and procedures** regarding compliance with laws and regulations
- **Enquire of management** as to the laws or regulations that may be expected to have a fundamental effect on the operations of the entity
- **Discuss with management** the **policies or procedures** adopted for identifying, evaluating and accounting for **litigation claims and assessments**

ISA 250.18/19

After obtaining the general understanding, the auditor should perform procedures to help identify instances of non-compliance with those laws and regulations where non-compliance should be considered when preparing financial statements, specifically:

(a)   inquiring of management as to whether the entity is in compliance with such laws and regulations;

(b)   inspecting correspondence with the relevant licensing or regulatory authorities.

(c)   Enquiring of those charged with governance as to whether they are on notice of any such possible instances of non-compliance with law or regulations.

In the UK and Ireland, the auditor's procedures should be designed to help identify possible or actual instances of non-compliance with those laws and regulations which provide a legal framework within which the entity conducts its business and which are central to the entity's ability to conduct its business and hence to its financial statements.

Further, the auditor should obtain sufficient appropriate audit evidence about compliance with those laws and regulations generally recognised by the auditor to have an effect on the determination of material amounts and disclosures in financial statements. The auditor should have a sufficient understanding of these laws and regulations in order to consider them when auditing the assertions related to the determination of the amount to be recorded and the disclosures to be made.

These laws and regulations may relate to the form and content of financial statements, accounting for transactions under government contracts, laws determining the circumstances under which a company is prohibited from making a distribution except out of available profits and laws which require auditors expressly to report non compliance, such as not keeping proper records. They should be well established and known to the entity and they should be considered on a recurring basis each year.

Except for such matters, the auditors will not test or perform other procedures on the entity's compliance with laws and regulations since this would be outside the scope of the audit.

ISA 250.22

The auditor should be alert to the fact that procedures applied for the purpose of forming an opinion on the financial statements may bring instances of possible non-compliance with laws and regulations to the auditor's attention. … the auditor should be alert for those instances of possible or actual non compliance with laws and regulations that might incur obligations … to report money laundering offices.

Examples include reading minutes of management meetings and substantive procedures. Representations from management are important.

ISA 250.23

The auditor should obtain written representations that management has disclosed to the auditor all known actual or possible non-compliance with laws and regulations whose effects should be considered when preparing financial statements. Where applicable, the written representations should include the actual or contingent consequences which may arise from the non-compliance.

In the absence of evidence to the contrary, the auditor is entitled to assume the entity is in compliance with these laws and regulations.

The ISA sets out examples of the type of information that might come to the auditor's attention that may indicate non-compliance.

- **Investigation** by a **government department** or payment of fines or penalties

- **Payments** for **unspecified services** or loans to consultants, related parties, employees or government employees

- **Sales commissions** or agents' fees that appear excessive in relation to those normally paid by the entity or in its industry or to the services actually received

- **Purchasing** at **prices significantly above** or **below market price**

- **Unusual payments** in **cash**, purchases in the form of cashiers' cheques payable to bearer or transfers to numbered bank accounts

- Complex corporate structures including offshore companies where ownership cannot be identified

- **Unusual transactions** with companies registered in **tax havens**

- Tax evasion such as the wider declaring of income and overclaiming of expenses

- **Payments for goods or services made other than to the country from which** the goods or services **originated**

- **Payments without proper exchange control documentation**

- **Existence** of an **accounting system** that **fails**, whether by design or by accident, to **provide adequate audit trail** or sufficient evidence

- **Unauthorised transactions** or improperly recorded transactions

- **Media comment**

- Transactions undertaken by the entity that have no apparent purpose or that make no obvious economic sense

- Where those charged with governance of the entity refuse to provide necessary information and explanation to support transactions and other dealings of the company

5.3.1 Procedures when non-compliance is discovered

ISA 250.26

When the auditor becomes aware of information concerning a possible instance of non-compliance, the auditor should obtain an understanding of the nature of the act and the circumstances in which it has occurred, and sufficient other information to evaluate the possible effect on the financial statements.

When evaluating the possible effect on the financial statements, the auditor should consider the following.

- The **potential financial consequences**, such as fines, penalties, damages, threat of expropriation of assets, enforced discontinuation of operations and litigation

- Whether the **potential financial consequences** require **disclosure**

- Whether the potential financial consequences are so serious as to call into question the **true and fair view** (fair presentation) given by the financial statements

ISA 250.28

When the auditor believes there may be non-compliance, the auditor should document the findings and discuss them with management.

Such discussions are subject to the laws concerning 'tipping off' (see Section 5.7). If information provided by management is not satisfactory, the auditor should consult the entity's lawyer and, if necessary, his own lawyer on the application of the laws and regulations to the particular circumstances.

ISA 250.30/31

When adequate information about the suspected non-compliance cannot be obtained the auditor should consider the effect of the lack of audit evidence on the auditor's report.

The auditor should consider the implications of non-compliance in relating to other aspects of the audit particularly the reliability of management representations.

On this last point, as with fraud and error, the auditor must reassess the risk assessment and the validity of management representations.

5.4 Reporting of non-compliance

5.4.1 To management

ISA 250.32/33/34

The auditor should, as soon as practicable, either communicate with the audit committee, the board of directors and senior management, or obtain evidence that they are appropriately informed, regarding non-compliance that comes to the auditor's attention.

If in the auditor's judgement the non-compliance is believed to be intentional and material, the auditor should communicate the finding without delay.

If the auditor suspects that members of senior management, including members of the board of directors, are involved in non-compliance, the auditor should report the matter to the next higher level of authority at the entity, if it exists, such as an audit committee or a supervisory board.

In the UK, the auditor must report if the non-compliance is believed to be intentional **or** material. It does **not** have to be both.

In relation to the last point, where no higher authority exists, or if the auditor believes that the report may not be acted upon or is unsure as to the person to whom to report, the auditor should consider seeking legal advice.

5.4.2 The users of the auditor's report

ISA 250.35/36/37

If the auditor concludes that the non-compliance has a material effect on the financial statements, and has not been properly reflected in the financial statements, the auditor should express a qualified or an adverse opinion.

If the auditor is precluded by the entity from obtaining sufficient appropriate audit evidence to evaluate whether non-compliance that may be material to the financial statements, has, or is likely to have, occurred, the auditor should express a qualified opinion or a disclaimer or opinion on the financial statements on the basis of a limitation on the scope of the audit.

If the auditor is unable to determine whether non-compliance has occurred because of limitations imposed by the circumstances rather than by the entity, the auditor should consider the effect on the auditor's report.

In the UK, if the view given by the financial statements is affected by uncertainty due to suspected or actual non compliance with law and regulations, an explanatory (called **emphasis of matter**) paragraph might be appropriate, subject to the laws relating to tipping off.

5.4.3 To regulatory and enforcement authorities

Confidentiality is an issue again here, but it may be overridden by the law, statute or the courts of law. The auditor should obtain legal advice. If the auditor has a statutory duty to report, he should do so without delay. Alternatively, it may be necessary to make disclosures in the public interest.

5.5 Withdrawal from the engagement

As is the case for fraud or error, withdrawal may be the only option if the entity does not take the remedial action the auditor thinks is necessary, even for non-material matters.

5.6 Practical problems with ISA 250

5.6.1 Distinction between types of law

The most difficult distinction in practice is between:

- Laws which are **central** to the ability of the client to conduct its business
- Other laws and regulations

In practice:

(a) For some business, certain laws and regulations will be central, for other businesses the **same** laws and regulations will not be central.

(b) For some businesses, laws and regulations which were not central last year may be central this year, (for example where the maximum penalty for a first offence is a warning, but subsequent infringements may lead to closure of the business).

5.6.2 Procedures that should be performed

There is a distinction between checking systems of compliance and checking actual compliance. An example would be emissions from a chemical factory; auditors would review the company's systems for keeping these under control, and would also review correspondence with the environmental authority. However, the auditors would not be expected to check the actual emissions.

Chapter Roundup

- Major developments in international regulation of audit and assurance are currently taking place.

- Public oversight of the audit profession and of standard – setting has been a trend in recent regulatory developments within the UK and internationally.

- Listed companies are required to conform to the requirements of the Combined Code.

- Audit committees are made up of non-executive directors and are perceived to increase confidence in financial reports.

- Internal control is a key part of good corporate governance. **Directors** are **responsible** for maintaining a system of control that will safeguard the company's assets.

- Money laundering law is an increasingly important issue for auditors to be aware of.

- Auditors must be aware of law and regulations as part of their planning and must be aware of any statutory duty to report non-compliance by the company.

Quick Quiz

1   List the six functions of the Financial Reporting Council

(1)   ....

(2)   ....

(3)   ....

(4)   ....

(5)   ....

(6)   ....

2   Independent oversight of the audit profession in the UK is the responsibility of the ....
.... Monitoring of the audit quality of economically
significant entities is carried out by the ....

3   Name four potential duties of the audit committee.

(1)   ....

(2)   ....

(3)   ....

(4)   ....

4   Auditors are responsible for a company's system of internal controls

True   ☐

False   ☐

5   List the main elements of an anti-money-laundering program that should be followed by a firm of
professional accountants

(1)   ....

(2)   ....

(3)   ....

(4)   ....

(5)   ....

(6)   ....

6   Name four areas of law which might affect a company.

(1)   ....

(2)   ....

(3)   ....

(4)   ....

7   In the absence of evidence to the contrary, auditors are entitled to assume the entity is in compliance with
laws and regulations relevant to preparing financial statements.

True   ☐

False   ☐

Answers to Quick Quiz

1   (1)   Setting, monitoring and enforcing accounting and auditing standards
    (2)   Setting actuarial standards
    (3)   Statutory oversight and regulation of auditors
    (4)   Operating an independent investigation and discipline scheme for public interest cases
    (5)   Overseeing the regulatory activities of the professional accountancy and actuarial bodies
    (6)   Promoting high standards of corporate governance

2   Professional Oversight Board
    Audit Inspection Unit

3   (1)   Review of financial statements
    (2)   Liaison with external auditors
    (3)   Review of internal audit
    (4)   Review of internal controls

4   False – this is the directors' duty

5   (1)   Appoint a Money Laundering Reporting Officer (MLRO) and set up internal reporting procedures
    (2)   Train individuals about the legal requirements and the firm's procedures
    (3)   Establish appropriate internal procedures
    (4)   Verify the identity of new clients
    (5)   Maintain records of client identification
    (6)   Report suspicions of money laundering to SOCA

6   From:

    (1)   Company law
    (2)   Contract law
    (3)   Tort law
    (4)   Employment law
    (5)   Environmental law

7   True

Now try the question below from the Question Bank

Number	Level	Marks	Time
Q5	Examination	20	36 mins

Part B

Professional and ethical considerations

Code of ethics and conduct

2

Topic list	Syllabus reference
1 Fundamental principles and the conceptual framework approach	B1
2 Specific guidance: Independence	B1
3 APB ethical standards	B1
4 Specific guidance: Confidentiality	B1
5 Specific guidance: Conflicts of interest	B1
6 Conflicts in application of the fundamental principles	B1

Introduction

You have already learnt about ethical rules for auditors. We will examine the issues in more detail and consider some of the complex ethical issues that auditors may face, and the ethical guidance issued by the APB.

We also refer to the ethical guidance of the International Federation of Accountants. This is also identical to ACCA's guidance. Both approach issues of ethics in a conceptual manner.

Some of this chapter is likely to be revision, but that does not mean you should ignore it. Ethics are a key syllabus area. Complex ethical issues are introduced in this chapter. You particularly need to work through the questions given so that you practise **applying** ethical guidelines in given scenarios.

Study guide

		Intellectual level
A1	**REGULATORY ENVIRONMENT**	
	International regulatory frameworks for audit and assurance services	
B	**CODE OF ETHICS AND CONDUCT**	
(a)	Explain the fundamental principles and the conceptual framework approach	1
(b)	Identify, evaluate and respond to threats to compliance with the fundamental principles	3
(c)	Discuss and evaluate the effectiveness of available safeguards	3
(d)	Recognise and advise on conflicts in the application of fundamental principles	3

Exam guide

Professional ethics are of vital importance to the audit and assurance profession so this area is likely to be a regular feature of the exam.

Questions are likely to be practical, giving scenarios where you are required to assess whether the situations are acceptable. Some of these can be answered by reference to specific guidance in the ACCA Code of Ethics and Conduct but others may require you to apply your understanding of the fundamental principles underlying the Code.

You may also have to suggest appropriate safeguards that the audit firm should implement.

1 Fundamental principles and the conceptual framework approach

FAST FORWARD

Accountants require an ethical code because they hold positions of trust, and people rely on them.

1.1 The importance of ethics

IFAC's *Code of Ethics* gives the key reason why accountancy bodies produce ethical guidance: the public interest.

'A distinguishing mark of the accountancy profession is its acceptance of the responsibility to act in the public interest. Therefore, a professional accountant's responsibility is not exclusively to satisfy the needs of an individual client or employer.

The public interest is considered to be the collective well-being of the community of people and institutions the professional accountant serves, including clients, lenders, governments, employers, employees, investors, the business and financial community and others who rely on the work of professional accountants.'

The **key reason** that **accountants need** to have an **ethical code** is that **people rely on them and their expertise.**

Accountants deal with a range of issues on behalf of clients. They often have access to confidential and sensitive information. Auditors claim to give an independent view. It is therefore critical that accountants, and particularly auditors, are, and are seen to be, independent.

As the auditor is required to be, and seen to be, ethical in his dealings with clients, ACCA publishes guidance for its members, the *Code of Ethics and Conduct*. This guidance is given in the form of fundamental principles, guidance and explanatory notes.

IFAC also lays down fundamental principles in its *Code of Ethics*. The fundamental principles of the two associations are extremely similar.

1.2 The fundamental principles

ACCA
• **Integrity.** Members should be **straightforward** and **honest** in all professional and business relationships.
• **Objectivity.** Members **should not allow bias, conflict of interest or undue influence of others** to override professional or business judgements.
• **Professional Competence and Due Care**. Members have a continuing duty to maintain professional knowledge and skill at a level required to ensure that a client or employer receives the advantage of competent professional service based on current developments in practice, legislation and techniques. Members should act diligently and in accordance with applicable technical and professional standards when providing professional services.
• **Confidentiality.** Members should respect the confidentiality of information acquired as a result of professional or business relationships **and should not disclose** any such information to third parties without proper and specific authority **unless there is a legal or professional right or duty to disclose**. Confidential information acquired as a result of professional and business relationships should not be used for the personal advantage of the professional accountant or third parties.
• **Professional Behaviour**. Members should **comply with relevant laws and regulations and should avoid any action that discredits the profession.**

1.3 The conceptual framework

The ethical guidance discussed above is in the form of a conceptual framework. It contains some rules, for example, ACCA prohibits making loans to clients, but in the main it is flexible guidance. It can be seen as being a **framework rather than a set of rules**. There are a number of advantages of a framework over a system of ethical rules. These are outlined in the table below.

Advantages of an ethical framework over a rules based system
A framework of guidance places the onus on the auditor to **actively consider** independence for every given situation, rather than just agreeing a checklist of forbidden items. It also requires him to **demonstrate** that a responsible conclusion has been reached about ethical issues.
The framework **prevents auditors interpreting legalistic requirements narrowly** to get around the ethical requirements. There is an extent to which rules engender deception, whereas principles encourage compliance.
A framework **allows for** the variations that are found in every **individual situation**. Each situation is likely to be different.
A framework can accommodate a **rapidly changing environment**, such as the one that auditors are constantly in.
However, a **framework can contain prohibitions** (as noted above) where these are necessary as safeguards are not feasible.

1.4 Threats to compliance with the fundamental principles

There are five general sources of threat:

- **Self-interest** threat (example, having a financial interest in a client)

- **Self-review** threat (example, auditing financial statements prepared by the firm)

- **Advocacy** threat (example, promoting shares in a listed entity when that entity is a financial statement audit client)

- **Familiarity** threat (example, an audit team member having family at the client)

- **Intimidation** threat (example, threats of replacement due to disagreement)

1.5 Available safeguards

There are three general categories of safeguard:

- Safeguards created by the profession, legislation or regulation
- Safeguards in the work environment
- Safeguards created by the individual

Examples of safeguards created by the **profession**, **legislation** or **regulation**:

- Educational training and experience requirements for entry into the profession

- Continuing professional development requirements

- Corporate governance regulations

- Professional standards

- Professional or regulatory monitoring and disciplinary procedures

- External review by a legally empowered third party of the reports, returns, communication or information produced by a professional accountant.

IFAC issues ethical standards, quality control standards and auditing standards (the APB issues ethical standards and auditing standards) which work together to ensure independence is safeguarded and quality audits are carried out. The regulatory framework was discussed in Chapter 1.

Examples of safeguards in the **work environment**:

- Involving an additional professional accountant to review the work done or otherwise advise as necessary

- Consulting an independent third party, such as a committee of independent directors, a professional regulatory body or another professional accountant

- Appropriate disciplinary processes;

- Timely communication of the employing organisation's policies and procedures, including any changes to them, to all employees and appropriate training and education on such policies and procedures;

- Using different partners and engagement teams with separate reporting lines for the provision of non-assurance services to clients;

- Discussing ethical issues with those in charge of client governance

- Disclosing to those charged with governance the nature of services provided and extent of fees charged

- Involving another firm to perform or reperform part of the engagement

Example of safeguards created by **the individual**:

- Complying with continuing professional development requirements;
- Keeping records of contentious issues and approach to decision-making;
- Maintaining a broader perspective on how similar organisations function through establishing business relationships with other professionals;
- Using an independent mentor;
- Maintaining contact with legal advisors and professional bodies.

The **specific** threats arising within these general areas and the effectiveness of the available safeguards will be considered in section 2.

2 Specific guidance: Independence

FAST FORWARD ⟩⟩ IFAC's and ACCA's guidance is very similar.

2.1 Objective of the guidance

You should be familiar with the concept of independence from your earlier studies. ACCA has recently revised its guidance and it is now very similar to that required by IFAC and the APB.

The IFAC Code discusses independence in the light of the wider term 'assurance engagements' rather than focusing solely on audits.

The guidance states its purpose in a series of steps. It aims to help firms and members:

Step 1   **Identify threats** to independence

Step 2   **Evaluate** whether the threats are insignificant

Step 3   If the threats are not insignificant, **identify and apply safeguards** to eliminate risk, or reduce it to an acceptable level.

It also recognises that there may be occasions **where no safeguard is available**. In such a situation, it is only appropriate to

- **Eliminate the interest** or activities causing the threat
- **Decline the engagement**, or discontinue it

2.1.1 Current issues in ethical guidance

The International Ethics Standards Board for Accountants (IESB) of IFAC recently issued an exposure draft proposing changes to enhance the independence and objectivity of professional accountants carrying out assurance engagements.

Some of the main proposals in this exposure draft are:

- Splitting the guidance into separate sections, one for audit and review engagements, the other for all other assurance assignments. All types of assurance engagements are combined in the existing guidance.
- Clarifying the types of "management functions" that compromise independence.
- Strengthening the rules relating to the provision of IT Systems services

The IESBA is also planning to approve an exposure draft very soon that addresses three specific independence issues: provision of internal audit services, fees and contingent fees.

Exam focus point

You should apply these three steps when approaching questions of independence, and show the examiner that you have done so in your answer. Remember, if there appears to be no safeguard, you must consider the fallback option of not continuing with the professional relationship.

2.2 What is independence?

A provider of assurance services must be, and be seen to be, independent. What is required for this to be the case?

Key term

Independence of mind: The state of mind that permits the provision of an opinion without being affected by influences that compromise professional judgement, allowing an individual to act with integrity, and exercise objectivity and professional scepticism.

Independence in appearance: The avoidance of facts and circumstances that are so significant that a reasonable and informed third party, having knowledge of all relevant information, including safeguards applied, would reasonably conclude a firm's, or a member of the assurance team's, integrity, objectivity or professional scepticism had been compromised.

The degree of independence required is less stringent for a low level assurance engagement to non-audit clients than for audit. This is summarised in the following table:

	Audit	Non-audit, general use	Non-audit, restricted use
Audit client	The assurance team, the firm and the network firm must all be independent of the client.	The assurance team, the firm and the network firm must all be independent of the client.	The assurance team, the firm and the network firm must all be independent of the client.
Non-audit assurance client	N/A	The assurance team and the firm must be independent of the client.	The assurance team and the firm must have no material financial interest in the client.

2.3 When must the assurance provider be independent?

The team and the firm should be independent '**during the period of the engagement**'.

The period of the engagement is from the commencement of work until the signing of the final report being produced. For a **recurring audit**, independence may only cease on **termination of the contract** between the parties.

FAST FORWARD

Both the ACCA rules and the IFAC code give examples of a number of situations where independence might be threatened and suggests safeguards to independence.

2.4 Revision of threats to independence

The area of threats to independence should not be new to you. You should be aware of many of the threats to independence from your earlier studies in auditing. To refresh your memory about independence issues, try the following question.

Question			Revision of audit independence I

From your knowledge brought forward from your previous studies, and any practical experience of auditing you may have, write down as many potential ethical risk areas as you can in the areas below. (Some issues may be relevant in more than one column.)

Personal interests	Review of your own work	Disputes	Intimidation

Answer

Personal interests	Review of your own work	Disputes	Intimidation
Undue dependence on an audit client due to fee levels	Auditor prepares the accounts	Actual litigation with a client	Any threat of litigation by the client
Overdue fees becoming similar to a loan	Auditor participates in management decisions	Threatened litigation with a client	Personal relationships with the client
An actual loan being made to a client	Provision of any other services to the client	Client refuses to pay fees and they become long overdue	Hospitality
Contingency fees being offered			Threat of other services provided to the client being put out to tender
Accepting commissions from clients			Threat of any services being put out to tender
Provision of lucrative other services to clients			
Relationships with persons in associated practices			
Relationships with the client			
Long association with clients			
Beneficial interest in shares or other investments			
Hospitality			

The APB guidance requires that the engagement partner considers threats to independence:

- When considering whether to accept/retain an audit

- When planning the audit

- When forming an opinion on financial statements

- When considering whether to accept or retain an engagement to provide non audit services to an audit client

- When potential threats are reported to him

The APB's remaining ethical standards (2-5) and the ACCA and IFAC codes give extensive lists of examples of threats to independence and applicable safeguards. In the rest of this section, these threats and some relevant factors and potential safeguards will be outlined. Definite rules are shown in bold. You should learn these.

Exam focus point

> It is important that you read through this section and think about the issues raised in each example, rather than just trying to learn rules for each situation. In this exam, it is important that you can apply the spirit of the guidance to a given situation, using the three steps given in section 2.1.

2.5 Self-interest threat

The ACCA Code of Ethics and Conduct highlights a great number of areas in which a self-interest threat might arise.

2.5.1 Financial interests

Key term

A **financial interest** exists where an audit firm has a financial interest in a client's affairs, for example, the audit firm owns shares in the client, or is a trustee of a trust that holds shares in the client.

A financial interest in a client constitutes a substantial self-interest threat. According to both ACCA and IFAC, **the parties listed below are not allowed to own a direct financial interest or an indirect material financial interest in a client**:

- The assurance firm
- A member of the assurance team
- An immediate family member of a member of the assurance team

The following safeguards will therefore be relevant:

- Disposing of the interest
- Removing the individual from the team if required
- Keeping the client's audit committee informed of the situation
- Using an independent partner to review work carried out if necessary

Such matters will involve judgement on the part of the partners making decisions about such matters. For example, what constitutes a material interest? A small percentage stake in a company might be material to its owner. How does the firm judge the closeness of a relationship between staff and their families, in other words, what does immediate mean in this context?

Audit firms should have quality control procedures requiring staff to disclose relevant financial interests for themselves and close family members. They should also foster a culture of voluntary disclosure on an ongoing basis so that any potential problems are identified on a timely basis.

You are the Ethics Partner at Stewart Brice, a firm of Chartered Certified Accountants. The following situations exist.

Teresa is the audit manager assigned to the audit of Recreate, a large quoted company. The audit has been ongoing for one week. Yesterday, Teresa's husband inherited 1,000 shares in Recreate. Teresa's husband wants to hold on to the shares as an investment.

The Stewart Brice pension scheme, which is administered by Friends Benevolent, an unconnected company, owns shares in Tadpole Group, a listed company with a number of subsidiaries. Stewart Brice has recently been invited to tender for the audit of one of the subsidiary companies, Kermit Co.

Stewart Brice has been the auditor of Kripps Bros, a limited liability company, for a number of years. It is a requirement of Kripps Bros' constitution that the auditor owns a token $1 share in the company.

Required

Comment on the ethical and other professional issues raised by the above matters.

Answer

(1)   Teresa is at present a member of the assurance team and a member of her immediate family owns a direct financial interest in the audit client. This is unacceptable.

    In order to mitigate the risk to independence that this poses on the audit, Stewart Brice needs to apply one of two safeguards:

    •   Ensure that the connected person divests the shares
    •   Remove Teresa from the engagement team

    Teresa should be appraised that these are the options and removed from the team while a decision is taken whether to divest the shares. Teresa's husband appears to want to keep the shares, in which case, Teresa should be removed from the team immediately.

    The firm should appraise the audit committee of Recreate of what has happened and the actions they have taken. The partners should consider whether it is necessary to bring in an independent partner to review audit work. However, given that Teresa's involvement is subject to the review of the existing engagement partner and she was not connected with the shares while she was carrying out the work, a second partner review is likely to be unnecessary in this case.

(2)   The audit firm has an indirect interest in the parent company of a company it has been invited to tender for by virtue of its pension scheme having invested in Tadpole Group.

    This is no barrier to the audit firm tendering for the audit of Kermit Co.

    Should the audit firm win the tender and become the auditors of Kermit Co they should consider whether it is necessary to apply safeguards to mitigate against the risk to independence on the audit as a result of the indirect financial interest.

    The factors that the partners will need to consider are the materiality of the interest to either party and the degree of control that the firm actually has over the financial interest.

    In this case, the audit firm has no control over the financial interest. An independent pension scheme administrator is in control of the financial interest. In addition, the interest is unlikely to be substantial and is therefore immaterial to both parties. IFAC states that only if the threat is significant should the interest be divested.

    It is likely that this risk is already sufficiently minimal as to not require safeguards. However, if the audit firm felt that it was necessary to apply safeguards, they could consider the following:

- Notifying the audit committee of the interest
- Requiring Friends Benevolent to dispose of the shares in Tadpole Group

(3) In this case, Stewart Brice has a direct financial interest in the audit client, which is technically forbidden by ACCA rules. However, it is a requirement of any firm auditing the company that the share be owned by the auditors.

The interest is not material. The audit firm should safeguard against the risk by not voting on its own re-election as auditor. The firm should also strongly recommend to the company that it removes this requirement from its constitution as it is at odds with ethical requirements for auditors.

2.5.2 Close business relationships

Examples of when an audit firm and an audit client have an inappropriately close business relationship include:

- Having a material financial interest in a joint venture with the assurance client
- Arrangements to combine one or more services or products of the firm with one or more services or products of the assurance client and to market the package with reference to both parties
- Distribution or marketing arrangements under which the firm acts as distributor or marketer of the assurance client's products or services or vice versa

Again, it will be necessary for the partners to judge the materiality of the interest and therefore its significance. However, **unless the interest is clearly insignificant, an assurance provider should not participate in such a venture with an assurance client**. Appropriate safeguards are therefore to end the assurance provision or to terminate the (other) business relationship.

If an individual member of an assurance team had such an interest, he should be removed from the assurance team.

However, if the firm or a member (and immediate family of the member) of the assurance team has an interest in an entity when the client or its officers also has an interest in that entity, the threat might not be so great.

Generally speaking, **purchasing goods and services from an assurance client on an arm's length basis does not constitute a threat to independence**. If there are a substantial number of such transactions, there may be a threat to independence and safeguards may be necessary.

2.5.3 Employment with assurance client

It is possible that staff might transfer between an assurance firm and a client, or that negotiations or interviews to facilitate such movement might take place. Both situations are a threat to independence:

- An audit staff member might be motivated by a desire to impress a future possible employer (objectivity is therefore affected)
- A former partner turned Finance Director has too much knowledge of the audit firm's systems and procedures

The extent of the threat to independence depends on various factors, such as the role the individual has taken up at the client, the extent of his influence on the audit previously, the length of time that has passed between the individual's connection with the audit and the new role at the client.

Various safeguards might be considered:

- Considering modifying the assurance plan

- Ensuring the audit is assigned to someone of sufficient experience as compared with the individual who has left

- Involving an additional professional accountant not involved with the engagement to review the work done

- Carrying out a quality control review of the engagement

In respect of **audit clients, a partner should not accept a key management position at an audit client until at least two years have elapsed since the conclusion of the audit he was involved with.**

An individual who has moved from the firm to a client should not be entitled to any benefits or payments from the firm unless these are made in accordance with pre-determined arrangements. If money is owed to the individual, it should not be so much as to compromise the independence of the assurance engagement.

A firm should have quality control procedures setting out that an individual involved in serious employment negotiations with an audit client should notify the firm and that this person would then be removed from the engagement.

Exam focus point

> In an exam under the previous syllabus, there was a case where a senior audit team member had had interviews with the client for a senior post, but had not disclosed this fact to the firm.

2.5.4 Partner on client board

A partner or employee of an assurance firm should not serve on the board of an assurance client.

It may be acceptable for a partner or an employee of an assurance firm to perform the role of company secretary for an assurance client, if the role is essentially administrative.

2.5.5 Family and personal relationships

Family or close personal relationships between assurance firm and client staff could seriously threaten independence. Each situation has to be evaluated individually. Factors to consider are:

- The individual's responsibilities on the assurance engagement
- The closeness of the relationship
- The role of the other party at the assurance client

When an immediate family member of a member of the assurance team is a director, an officer or an employee of the assurance client in a position to exert direct and significant influence over the subject matter information of the assurance engagement, the individual should be removed from the assurance team.

The audit firm should also consider whether there is any threat to independence if an employee who is not a member of the assurance team has a close family or personal relationship with a director, an officer or an employee of an assurance client.

A firm should have quality control policies and procedures under which staff should disclose if a close family member employed by the client is promoted within the client.

If a firm inadvertently violates the rules concerning family and personal relationships they should apply additional safeguards, such as undertaking a quality control review of the audit and discussing the matter with the audit committee of the client, if there is one.

2.5.6 Gifts and hospitality

Unless the value of the gift/hospitality is clearly insignificant, a firm or a member of an assurance team should not accept.

Ethical questions involving gifts and hospitality are likely to appear in the exam.

2.5.7 Loans and guarantees

The advice on loans and guarantees falls into two categories:

- The client is a bank or other similar institution
- Other situations

If a lending institution client lends an immaterial amount to an audit firm or member of assurance team on normal commercial terms, there is no threat to independence. If the loan were material it would be necessary to apply safeguards to bring the risk to an acceptable level. A suitable safeguard is likely to be an independent review (by a partner from another office in the firm).

Loans to members of the assurance team from a bank or other lending institution client are likely to be material to the individual, but provided that they are on normal commercial terms, these do not constitute a threat to independence.

An audit firm or individual on the assurance engagement should not enter into any loan or guarantee arrangement with a client that is not a bank or similar institution.

2.5.8 Overdue fees

In a situation where there are overdue fees, the auditor runs the risk of, in effect, making a loan to a client, whereupon the guidance above becomes relevant.

Audit firms should guard against fees building up and being significant by discussing the issues with those charged with governance, and, if necessary, the possibility of resigning if overdue fees are not paid.

2.5.9 Percentage or contingent fees

Contingent fees are fees calculated on a predetermined basis relating to the outcome or result of a transaction or the result of the work performed.

A firm should not enter into any fee arrangement for an assurance engagement under which the amount of the fee is contingent on the result of the assurance work or on items that are the subject matter of the assurance engagement.

It would also usually be inappropriate to accept a contingent fee for non assurance work from an assurance client. Factors to consider in whether a contingent fee is acceptable or not include:

- The range of possible fee outcomes
- The degree of variability in the fee
- The basis on which the fee is to be determined
- Whether the transaction is to be reviewed by an independent third party
- The effect on the transaction on the assurance engagement

In other circumstances it may be appropriate to accept a contingent fee for non assurance work if suitable safeguards are in place. Examples include:

- Making disclosures to the audit committee about the fees
- Review or determination of the fee by an unrelated third party
- Quality control policies and procedures

2.5.10 High percentage of fees

A firm should be alert to the situation arising where when the total fees generated by an assurance client represent a large proportion of a firm's total fees. Factors such as the structure of the firm and the length of time it has been trading will be relevant in determining whether there is a threat to independence. It is also necessary to beware of situations where the fees generated by an assurance client present a large proportion of the revenue of an individual partner.

Safeguards in these situations might include:

- Discussing the issues with the audit committee
- Taking steps to reduce the dependency on the client
- Obtaining external/internal quality control reviews
- Consulting a third party such as ACCA

The public may perceive that a member's objectivity is likely to be in jeopardy where the fees for audit and recurring work paid by one client or group of connected clients exceed 15% of the firm's total fees. Where the entity is listed or public interest, this figure should be 10%.

It will be difficult for new firms establishing themselves to keep outside of these limits and firms in this situation should make use of the safeguards outlined.

2.5.11 Lowballing

When a firm quotes a significantly lower fee level for an assurance service than would have been charged by the predecessor firm, there is a significant self-interest threat. If the firm's tender is successful, the firm must apply safeguards such as:

- Maintaining records such that the firm is able to demonstrate that appropriate staff and time are spent on the engagement

- Complying with all applicable assurance standards, guidelines and quality control procedures

2.5.12 Recruitment

Recruiting senior management for an assurance client, particularly those able to affect the subject matter of an assurance engagement creates a self-interest threat for the assurance firm.

Assurance providers must not make management decisions for the client. Their involvement could be limited to reviewing a shortlist of candidates, providing that the client has drawn up the criteria by which they are to be selected.

2.6 Self-review threat

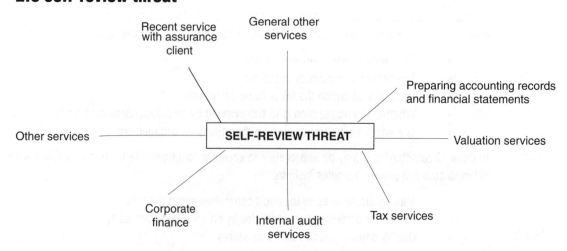

The key area in which there is likely to be a self-review threat is where an assurance firm provides services other than assurance services to an assurance client (providing multiple services). There is a great deal of guidance in the ACCA and IFAC rules about various other services accountancy firms might provide to their clients, and these are dealt with below.

The distinction between listed companies, or public limited companies, and private companies is perceived to be an important issue in the question of providing other services to clients.

Key term

Listed companies are those whose shares have been admitted to a recognised exchange, such as the Stock Exchange, or the AIM.

Public interest companies are those which for some reason (size, nature, product) are in the 'public eye'. Auditors should treat these as if they are listed companies.

Exam focus point

In exam questions, bear in mind the nature of the entity being audited. Is it a small owner-managed business where the auditor is in effect an all-round business adviser and accountant, or is it a listed company where the above rule is relevant?

In the United States rules concerning auditor independence for **listed** companies state that an accountant is not independent if they provide certain non-audit services to an audit client. The relevant services are:

- Bookkeeping
- Financial information systems design and implementation
- Appraisal or valuation services or fairness opinions
- Actuarial services
- Internal audit services
- Management functions
- Human resources
- Broker-dealer services
- Legal services

The rules, found in the Sarbanes-Oxley Act, apply to **any** company listed on the US Stock Exchange so they impact on international auditors.

2.6.1 Recent service with an assurance client

Individuals who have been a director or officer of the client, or an employee in a position to exert direct and significant influence over the subject matter information of the assurance engagement in the period under review or the previous two years should not be assigned to the assurance team.

If an individual had been closely involved with the client prior to the time limits set out above, the assurance firm should consider the threat to independence arising and apply appropriate safeguards, such as:

- Obtaining a quality control review of the individual's work on the assignment
- Discussing the issue with the audit committee

2.6.2 General other services

For assurance clients, accountants are not allowed to:

- **Authorise, execute or consummate a transaction**
- **Determine which recommendation of the company should be implemented**
- **Report in a management capacity to those charged with governance**

Having custody of an assurance client's assets, supervising client employees in the performance of their normal duties, and preparing source documents on behalf of the client also pose significant self-review threats which should be addressed by safeguards. These could be:

- Ensuring non assurance team staff are used for these roles
- Involving an independent professional accountant to advise
- Quality control policies on what staff are and are not allowed to do for clients
- Making appropriate disclosures to those charged with governance
- Resigning from the assurance engagement

2.6.3 Preparing accounting records and financial statements

There is clearly a significant risk of a self-review threat if a firm prepares accounting records and financial statements and then audits them.

On the other hand auditors routinely assist management with the preparation of financial statements and give advice about accounting treatments and journal entries.

Therefore, assurance firms must analyse the risks arising and put safeguards in place to ensure that the risk is at an acceptable level. Safeguards include:

- Using staff members other than assurance team members to carry out work
- Obtaining client approval for work undertaken

The rules are more stringent when the client is listed or public interest. **Firms should not prepare accounts or financial statements for listed or public interest clients**, unless an emergency arises.

For any client, assurance firms are also not allowed to:

- **Determine or change journal entries without client approval**
- **Authorise or approve transactions**
- **Prepare source documents**

2.6.4 Valuation services

Key term

> A **valuation** comprises the making of assumptions with regard to future developments, the application of certain methodologies and techniques, and the combination of both in order to compute a certain value, or range of values, for an asset, a liability or for a business as a whole.

If an audit firm performs a valuation for which will be included in financial statements audited by the firm, a self-review threat arises.

Audit firms should not carry out valuations on matters which will be material to the financial statements. If the valuation is for an immaterial matter, the audit firm should apply safeguards to ensure that the risk is reduced to an acceptable level. Matters to consider when applying safeguards are the extent of the audit client's knowledge of the relevant matters in making the valuation and the degree of judgement involved, how much use is made of established methodologies and the degree of uncertainty in the valuation. Safeguards include:

- Second partner review
- Confirming that the client understands the valuation and the assumptions used
- Ensuring the client acknowledges responsibility for the valuation
- Using separate personnel for the valuation and the audit

2.6.5 Taxation services

The provision of taxation services is generally not seen to impair independence.

2.6.6 Internal audit services

A firm may provide internal audit services to an audit client. However, it should ensure that the client acknowledges its responsibility for establishing, maintaining and monitoring the system of internal controls. It may be appropriate to use safeguards such as ensuring that an employee of the client is designated responsible for internal audit activities and that the client approves all the work that internal audit does.

2.6.7 Corporate finance

Certain aspects of corporate finance will create self-review threats that cannot be reduced to an acceptable level by safeguards. Therefore, **assurance firms are not allowed to promote, deal in or underwrite an assurance client's shares. They are also not allowed to commit an assurance client to the terms of a transaction or consummate a transaction on the client's behalf**.

Other corporate finance services, such as assisting a client in defining corporate strategies, assisting in identifying possible sources of capital and providing structuring advice may be acceptable, providing that safeguards, such as using different teams of staff, and ensuring no management decisions are taken on behalf of the client.

2.6.8 Other services

The audit firm might sell a variety of other services to audit clients, such as:

- IT services
- Temporary staff cover
- Litigation support
- Legal services

The assurance firm should consider whether there are any barriers to independence, such as if the firm were asked to design internal control IT systems, which it would then review as part of its audit, or if the firm were asked to provide an accountant to cover the chief accountant's maternity leave. The firm should consider whether the threat to independence could be reduced by appropriate safeguards.

2.7 Advocacy threat

An advocacy threat arises in certain situations where the assurance firm is in a position of taking the client's part in a dispute or somehow acting as their advocate. The most obvious instances of this would be when a firm offered legal services to a client and, say, defended them in a legal case or provided evidence on their behalf as an expert witness. Advocacy threat might also arise if the firm carried out corporate finance work for the client, for example, if the audit firm was involved in advice on debt reconstruction and negotiated with the bank on the client's behalf.

As with the other threats above, the firm has to appraise the risk and apply safeguards as necessary. Relevant safeguards might be using different departments in the firm to carry out the work and making disclosures to the audit committee. Remember, the ultimate option is always to withdraw from an engagement if the risk to independence is too high.

Question	Advocacy threat

Explain why contingent fees represent an advocacy threat.

Answer

If an accountant is paid fees on a contingency basis, then his will and the client's become too closely aligned. They will both want the same thing to occur (ie the thing the fee is contingent on) and the risk is that the accountant will act in the interests of the client to ensure it happens.

2.8 Familiarity threat

A familiarity threat is where independence is jeopardised by the audit firm and its staff becoming over familiar with the client and its staff. There is a substantial risk of loss of professional scepticism in such circumstances.

We have already discussed some examples of when this risk arises, because very often a familiarity threat arises in conjunction with a self-interest threat.

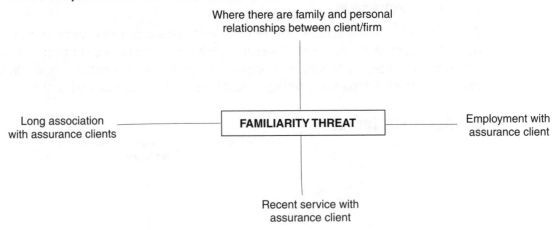

2.8.1 Long association of senior personnel with assurance clients

It can be a significant threat to independence if senior members of staff at an audit firm have a long association with a client. All firms should therefore monitor the relationship between staff and established clients and use safeguards to independence such as rotating senior staff off the assurance team, involving second partners to carry out reviews and obtaining independent (but internal) quality control reviews.

In addition, the Code of Ethics and Conduct sets out specific rules for listed and public interest entities in this situation. These state that **for the audit of listed and other public interest entities:**

- **The engagement partner should be rotated after a pre-defined period, normally no more than five years, and should not return to the engagement until a period of five years has elapsed.**

- **Other key audit partners should be rotated after a pre-defined period, normally no more than seven years, and should not return to the engagement until a period of two years (or five years if returning as engagement partner) has elapsed; and**

- **The individual responsible for the engagement quality control review should be rotated after a pre-defined period, normally no more than seven years, and should not return to the engagement until a period of two years has elapsed**.

When an entity becomes a listed entity, the length of time the staff involved with the audit have been involved should be taken into consideration, but **the engagement partner, other key partners and quality control person should only continue in those position for another two years**.

These rules should be followed, but there may be circumstances in which it is necessary to be flexible, such as when the firm is so small as to make rotation impracticable and when the person involved is particularly important to the audit. However, the firm should apply safeguards in such circumstances.

2.9 Intimidation threat

An intimidation threat arises when members of the assurance team have reason to be intimidated by client staff.

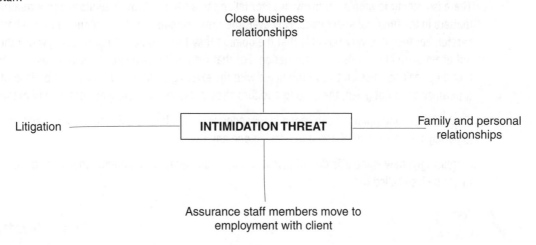

These are also examples of self-interest threats, largely because intimidation may only arise significantly when the assurance firm has something to lose.

2.9.1 Actual and threatened litigation

The most obvious example of an intimidation threat is when the client threatens to sue, or indeed sues, the assurance firm for work that has been done previously. The firm is then faced with the risk of losing the client, bad publicity and the possibility that they will be found to have been negligent, which will lead to further problems. This could lead to the firm being under pressure to produce an unqualified audit report when they have been qualified in the past, for example.

Generally, assurance firms should seek to avoid such situations arising. If they do arise, factors to consider are:

- The materiality of the litigation
- The nature of the assurance engagement
- Whether the litigation relates to a prior assurance engagement

The following safeguards could be considered:

- Disclosing to the audit committee the nature and extent of the litigation
- Removing specific affected individuals from the engagement team
- Involving an additional professional accountant on the team to review work

However, if the litigation is at all serious, it may be necessary to resign from the engagement, as the threat to independence is so great.

2.9.2 Second opinions

Another way that auditors can suffer an intimidation threat is when the audit client is unhappy with a proposed audit opinion, and seeks a **second opinion** from a different firm of auditors.

In such a circumstance, the second audit firm will not be able to give a formal audit opinion on the financial statements – only an appointed auditor can do that. However, the problem is that if a different firm of auditors indicates to someone else's audit client that a different audit opinion might be acceptable, the appointed auditor may feel under pressure to change the audit opinion. In effect, a self-interest threat arises, as the existing auditor may feel that he will lose next year's audit if he does not change this year's opinion.

There is nothing to stop a company director talking to a second firm of auditors about treatments of matters in the financial statements. However, the firm being asked for a second opinion should be very careful, because it is very possible that the opinion they form could be incorrect anyway if the director has not given them all the relevant information. For that reason, firms giving a second opinion should ensure that they seek permission to communicate with the existing auditor and they are appraised of all the facts. If permission is not given, the second auditors should decline to comment on the audit opinion.

Given that second opinions can cause independence issues for the existing auditors, audit firms should generally take great care if asked to provide one anyway.

Increasingly, new standards do not give a choice of accounting treatments, meaning that second opinions might be less called for.

Question

Threats to independence

You are a partner in a firm of chartered certified accountants. The following issues have emerged in relation to three of your clients:

(1) Easter is a major client. It is listed on a major Exchange. The audit team consists of 8 members, of whom Paul is the most junior. Paul has just invested in a personal pension plan that invests in all the listed companies on the Exchange.

(2) You are at the head of a team carrying out due diligence work at Electra, a limited company which your client, Powerful, is considering taking over. Your second in command on the team, Peter, has confided in you that in the course of his work he has met the daughter of the managing director of Electra, and he is keen to invite her on a date.

(3) Your longest standing audit client is Teddies, which you have been involved in for ten years, four as engagement partner. You recently went on an extended cruise with the managing director on his yacht.

Required

Comment on the ethical and other professional issues raised by the above matters. (Note: your answer should outline the threat arising, the significance of the threat, any factors you have taken into account, and, if relevant, any safeguards you could apply to eliminate or mitigate against the threat.)

Answer

(1) In relation to Easter, there is a threat of self-interest arising, as a member of the audit team has an indirect financial interest in the client.

The **relevant factors** are as follows:

- The interest is unlikely to be **material** to the client or Paul, as the investment is recent and Paul's interest is in a pool of general investments made in the Exchange on his behalf

- Paul is the **audit junior** and **does not have a significant role** on the audit in terms of drawing audit conclusions or audit risk areas

The risk that arises to the independence of the audit here is **not significant**. It would be inappropriate to require Paul to divest his interest in the audit client. If I wanted to eliminate all elements of risk in this situation, I could simply change the junior assigned to my team, but such a step is not vital in this situation.

(2) In relation to Powerful, two issues arise. The first is that the firm appears to be providing multiple services to Powerful, which could raise a **self-interest threat**. The second is that the manager assigned to the due diligence assignment wants to engage in a personal relationship with a person connected to the subject of the assignment, which could create a **familiarity or intimidation threat**.

With regard to the issue of multiple services, **insufficient information** is given to draw a conclusion as to the significance of the threat. **Relevant factors** would be matters such as the nature of the services, the fee income and the team members assigned to each. **Safeguards** could include using different staff for the two assignments. The risk is likely to be significant only if one of the services provided is **audit**, which is not indicated in the question.

In relation to the second issue, the **relevant factors** are these:

- The assurance team member has a significant role on the team as second in command
- The other party is closely connected to key staff member at the company being reviewed
- Timing

In this situation, the firm is carrying out a one off review of the company, and **timing is a key issue**. Presently Peter does not have a personal relationship which would significantly threaten the independence of the assignment. In this situation, the **safeguard is to request that Peter does not take any action in that direction until the assignment is completed**. If he refuses, then I may have to consider rotating my staff on this assignment, and removing him from the team.

(3) In relation to Teddies, there is a risk that my long association and personal relationship with the client will result in a **familiarity** threat. This is compounded by my acceptance of significant hospitality on a personal level.

The **relevant factors** are:

- I have been involved with the client for ten years and have a personal relationship with client staff

- The company is not a listed or public interest company

- It is an audit assignment

The risk arising here is **significant**, but as the client is not listed, it is not insurmountable. However, it would be a good idea to implement some safeguards to mitigate against the risk. I could invite a second partner to provide a **hot review** of the audit of Teddies, or even consider requesting that I am **rotated** off the audit of Teddies for a period, so that the engagement partner is another partner in my firm. In addition, I must cease accepting hospitality from the directors of Teddies unless it is clearly insignificant.

2.10 Quality control: Independence

The new quality control standard for firms, ISQC 1 *Quality control for firms that perform audits and reviews of historical financial information, and other assurance and related services engagements*, which we shall look at in detail in Chapter 4, contains a section looking at the firm's procedures with regard to ethics and, in particular, independence.

> **ISQC 1.14**
>
> The firm should establish policies and procedures designed to provide it with reasonable assurance that the firm and its personnel comply with relevant ethical requirements.

The policies and procedures should be in line with the fundamental principles, which should be reinforced by:

- The leadership of the firm
- Education and training
- Monitoring
- A process for dealing with non-compliance

The standard sets out some detailed requirements with regard to independence:

> **ISQC 1.18**
>
> The firm should establish policies and procedures designed to provide it with reasonable assurance that the firm, its personnel and, where applicable, others subject to independence requirements (including experts contracted by the firm and network firm personnel), maintain independence where required by the IFAC Code and national ethical requirements. Such policies and procedures should enable the firm to:
>
> (a) Communicate its independence requirements to its personnel and, where applicable, others subject to them, and
>
> (b) Identify and evaluate circumstances and relationships that create threats to independence, and to take appropriate action to eliminate those threats or reduce them to an acceptable level by applying safeguards, or, if considered appropriate, to withdraw from the engagement.
>
> **ISQC 1.19**
>
> Such policies and procedures should require:
>
> (a) Engagement partners to provide the firm with relevant information about client engagements, including the scope of services, to enable the firm to evaluate the overall impact, if any, on independence requirements.
>
> (b) Personnel to promptly notify the firm of circumstances and relationships that create a threat to independence so that appropriate action can be taken, and

(c)   The accumulation and communication of relevant information to appropriate personnel so that:

    (i)   The firm and its personnel can readily determine whether they satisfy independence requirements

    (ii)   The firm can maintain and update its records relating to independence, and

    (iii)   The firm can take appropriate action regarding identified threats to independence

ISQC 1.20

The firm should establish policies and procedures designed to provide it with reasonable assurance that it is notified of breaches of independence requirements, and to enable it to take appropriate actions to resolve such situations. The policies and procedures should include requirements for:

(a)   All who are subject to independence requirements to promptly notify the firm of independence breaches of which they become aware

(b)   The firm to promptly communicate identified breaches of these policies and procedures to:

    (i)   The engagement partner who, with the firm, needs to address the breach, and

    (ii)   Other relevant personnel in the firm and those subject to the independence requirements who need to take appropriate action, and

(c)   Prompt communication to the firm, if necessary, by the engagement partner and the other individuals referred to in subparagraph (b)(ii) of the actions taken to resolve the matter, so that the firm can determine whether it should take further action.

ISQC 1.23

At least annually, the firm should obtain written confirmation of compliance with its policies and procedures on independence from all firm personnel required to be independent by the IFAC Code and national ethical requirements.

2.10.1 Familiarity threat

Lastly, the ISQC sets out some specific guidance in relation to the threat of over-familiarity with clients.

ISQC 1.25

The firm should establish policies and procedures:

(a)   Setting out criteria for determining the need for safeguards to reduce the familiarity threat to an acceptable level when using the same senior personnel on an assurance engagement over a long period of time, and

(b)   For all audits of financial statements of listed entities, requiring the rotation of the engagement partner after a specified period in compliance with the IFAC Code and national ethical requirements that are more restrictive.

3 APB ethical standards

ES1.36/39

If the audit engagement partner identifies threats to the auditors' objectivity, including any perceived loss of independence, he or she should identify and assess the effectiveness of the available safeguards and apply such safeguards as are sufficient to eliminate the threats or reduce them to an acceptable level. The audit engagement partner should not accept or should not continue an audit engagement if he or she concludes that any threats to the auditors' objectivity and independence cannot be reduced to an acceptable level.

Many of the APB rules are the same as ACCA's, for example, a person involved with an audit should not hold a direct or indirect financial interest in a client. Auditors should not accept, make loans or issue guarantees in favour of audit clients and should not accept loans form them unless the client is a bank or similar institution and the loan is made on similar commercial terms. Here is a summary of the rules.

3.1 ES 2: Financial, business, employment and personal relationships

Financial relationships

General considerations

'The audit firm, any partner in the audit firm, a person in a position to influence the conduct and outcome of the audit or an immediate family member of such a person should not hold:

(a)   any direct financial interest in an audit client or an affiliate of an audit client; or

(b)   any indirect financial interest in an audit client or an affiliate of an audit client, where the investment is material to the audit firm or the individual and to the intermediary; or

(c)   any indirect financial interest in an audit client or an affiliate of an audit client where the person holding it has both:

    (i)   the ability to influence the investment decisions of the intermediary; and
    (ii)   actual knowledge of the existence of the underlying investment.

In the above cases the threats to the auditors' objectivity are such that no safeguards can eliminate them or reduce them to an acceptable level.

Where the financial interest is held by the audit firm, a partner or an immediate family member **the entire interest should be disposed of** (or a sufficient amount of an indirect interest is disposed of so that the remaining interest is no longer material) or **the firm should not accept or should withdraw from the audit**.

Where a financial interest is acquired **unintentionally**, for example through inheritance, the **disposal of the financial interest** is required immediately or as soon as possible. Where disposal does not take place immediately, the audit firm must adopt safeguards. These may include the temporary exclusion of the person in a position to influence the conduct and outcome of the audit.

Where a person in a position to influence the outcome of the audit or a partner in the audit firm becomes aware that a close family member holds a financial interest, it should be reported to the audit engagement partner. If there is any doubt as to the action to be taken the audit engagement partner should resolve the issue through **consultation with the ethics partner**.

Loans and guarantees

Audit firms, persons in a position to influence the conduct and outcome of the audit and immediate family members of such persons should not make a loan to/accept a loan from, or guarantee the borrowings of/have their borrowings guaranteed by, an audit client or its affiliates unless this represents a deposit made with a bank or similar deposit taking institution in the ordinary course of business and on normal business terms.

Business relationships

'Audit firms, persons in a position to influence the conduct and outcome of the audit and immediate family members of such persons should not enter into business relationships with an audit client or its affiliates except where they involve the purchase of goods and services from the audit firm or the audit client in the ordinary course of business and on an arm's length basis and the value involved is not material to either party.'

Where a business relationship has been entered into either the relationship is terminated or the firm does not accept (withdraws) from the engagement/or that person does not retain a position in which they exert such influence on the audit engagement.

Employment relationships

'An audit firm should not admit to the partnership or employ a person to undertake audit work if that person is also employed by the audit client or its affiliates ('dual employment').

A partner or employee of the audit firm should not accept appointment:

 (a)   to the board of directors

 (b)   to any subcommittee of that board

 (c)   to such a position in an entity which holds more than 20% of the voting rights in the audit client, or in which the audit client holds directly or indirectly more than 20% of the voting rights.

Loan staff assignments

'An audit client should not enter into an agreement with an audit client to provide a partner or employee to work for a temporary period as if that individual were an employee unless the audit client:

 (a)   agrees that the individual concerned will not hold a management position
 (b)   acknowledges its responsibility for directing and supervising the work to be performed.'

On completion of the loan staff assignment that individual should not be given any role on the audit involving any function or activity that they performed or supervised during that assignment.

Partners and engagement team members joining an audit client

Partners, senior members of the engagement team and other members of the engagement team should notify the firm of any situation involving their potential employment with an audit client. The individual should be removed from the team and any work performed by them on the most recent audit should be reviewed.

'Where a partner leaves the firm and is appointed as a director (including as a non-executive director) or to a key management position with an audit client, having acted as audit engagement partner at any time in the **two years** prior to his appointment, the firm should resign as auditors. The firm should not accept reappointment as auditors until a two-year period, commencing when the former partner ceased to act for the client, has elapsed or the former partner ceases employment with the former client, whichever is sooner.'

Where the above situation applies to a member of the engagement team the audit firm should consider whether the composition of the audit team is appropriate.

Directors and employees joining an audit firm

Where a director or a former employee joins an audit firm that individual should not be assigned to a position in which he or she is able to influence the conduct and outcome of the audit for a period of two years.

Family members employed by an audit client

As a general governance issue ES 2 states that the audit firm should have policies and procedures that require partners and professional staff to report family relationships involving audit clients.

Where a person in a position to influence the conduct and outcome of the audit, or a partner in the firm becomes aware that an immediate family member is employed by an audit client in a position to exercise influence on the accounting records or financial statements, that individual should cease to have any further role in the audit.

In the case of a close family member the matter should be reported to the audit engagement partner to take appropriate action.

3.2 ES 3: Long association with the audit engagement

3.2.1 General provisions

Where audit engagement partners, key audit partners and staff in senior positions have a long association with the audit safeguards should be applied. **Where they cannot be applied the audit firm should either resign or not stand for reappointment**.

Safeguards include:

- **Rotating the audit partner** and other senior members of the audit team after a pre-determined number of years

- Involving an **additional partner**

- Applying **independent internal quality reviews**

Once an audit partner has held the role for a continuous period of ten years careful consideration should be given to whether objectivity would have the appearance of being impaired.

3.2.2 Additional provisions for listed companies

The firm should establish policies to ensure that:

(a)   no one should act as audit engagement partner or independent partner for a continuous period longer than **five years**

(b)   they should not hold a position of responsibility regarding this audit client again until a further period of five years has elapsed

Where senior staff have been involved on an audit for a continuous period longer than seven years the audit engagement partner should review the safeguards put in place.

In addition, key audit partners (an audit partner other than the engagement partner who is involved at a *group* level) should not act for more than seven years. If the engagement partner becomes a key partner, the total for his combined roles must not exceed seven years.

3.3 ES 4: Fees, remuneration and evaluation policies, litigation, gifts and hospitality

Fees

An audit should not be undertaken on a **contingent fee** basis.

The audit fee should reflect the **time spent** and the **skills and experience** of the personnel performing the audit.

Where fees are **overdue** the auditor needs to consider whether the firm can continue as auditors.

Where it is expected that the fees for both audit and non-audit services receivable from a listed audit client and its subsidiaries will regularly exceed **10% of the annual fee income of the audit firm** (15% for non-listed), the firm should **not act as the auditors** and should either resign or not stand for reappointment.

Where the above fees will regularly exceed **5% of the annual fee income** the audit engagement partner should **disclose** this to the ethics partner and those charged with governance and consider whether safeguards should be applied.

New firms should not undertake any audits of listed companies, where fees would represent 10% or more of the annual fee income of the firm. In addition, for a period not exceeding two years, independent reviews should be performed on those audits of unlisted entities that represent more than 10% of the annual fee income.

Performance criteria and remuneration of staff should not depend on the selling of non-audit services.

Threatened and actual litigation

Where litigation between the audit client and the audit firm is already in progress or is probable, the audit firm should either not continue or should not accept the engagement.

Gifts and hospitality

The audit firm, those in a position to influence the conduct and outcome of the audit and immediate family members should **not accept gifts from the audit client**, unless the value is clearly insignificant.

Hospitality should not be accepted either, unless it is **reasonable** in terms of its frequency, nature and cost.

3.4 ES 5: Non-audit services provided to audit clients

This standard issues general guidance regarding the approach to non-audit services but also goes on to describe how these principles should be applied to specific non-audit services.

General approach

ES 5 does not prohibit the provision of other services. However, it requires the audit engagement partner to:

- Consider whether the objectives of the proposed engagement would be perceived to be inconsistent with the objectives of the audit
- Identify and assess the significance of any related threats to the auditors' objectivity
- Identify and assess the effectiveness of the available safeguards

Where the engagement partner considers it probable that the objectives of the two assignments are inconsistent, the audit firm should either not undertake the non-audit service or not accept/withdraw from the audit engagement.

Safeguards

Where there is a threat to the auditors' objectivity the audit engagement partner should assess whether there are safeguards that could be applied which would eliminate the threat or reduce it to an acceptable level. If safeguards can be applied the non-audit service can be provided. If safeguards cannot be applied, the audit firm should either not undertake the non-audit work, or not accept, or withdraw from, the audit engagement.

3.5 Application of general principles to specific non-audit services

These include the following:

Internal audit services

In general terms this service can be provided assuming that adequate safeguards are in place.

Safeguards include:

- Using different staff for internal and external audit purposes
- Review of the audit of the financial statements performed by a partner who is not involved with the external audit.

However the firm should not undertake the engagement where the auditor will place significant reliance on internal audit as part of the audit of the financial statements or where the audit firm would be taking on a management role.

Information technology services

The audit firm should not undertake an engagement to design, provide or implement information technology systems for an audit client where:

- The system concerned would be important to any significant part of the accounting system or to the production of the financial statements and the auditor would place significant reliance upon them as part of the audit of the financial statements; or
- The audit firm would undertake part of the role of management.

Valuation services

The audit firm should not provide a valuation to a client where the valuation would:

- Involve a significant degree of subjective judgement; and
- Have a material effect on the financial statements.

Actuarial valuation services

The audit firm should not provide actuarial valuation services to an audit client unless they are satisfied the significant judgement will be made by informed management or the valuation has no material effect on the financial statements.

Tax services

In general terms tax services may be provided although the auditor must assess the possible threats to objectivity.

Safeguards would include:

- Use of different staff
- Tax services reviewed by an independent tax partner
- External independent advice on tax work
- Tax computations prepared by the audit team are reviewed by a partner or senior staff member who is not a member of the audit team

The audit firm **should not** provide tax services:

- Where the fee for tax work is calculated on a contingent fee basis and the engagement fees are material to the audit firm
- Where the engagement would involve the audit firm undertaking a management role
- Where it would involve acting as an advocate for the client

Litigation support or legal services

The audit client should not accept such work if relevant matters might have a material impact on financial statements.

Recruitment and remuneration services

The audit firm should not provide a service which would involve the firm taking responsibility for the appointment of any director or employee of the audit client.

For a **listed company** the audit firm should not provide a recruitment service in relation to a key management position.

Corporate finance

This term covers a range of activity but the key threat is that the auditor takes on the role of management. The engagement partner needs to ensure that appropriate safeguards are applied. For example:

- The use of different staff
- Advice is reviewed by an independent corporate finance partner

There are certain circumstances where the corporate finance work should not be undertaken. These include:

- Where the engagement would involve the audit firm taking responsibility for dealing in, underwriting or promoting shares

- Where the partner doubts the appropriateness of an accounting treatment related to the advice provided

- The corporate finance fee is calculated on a contingent basis and is material to the audit firm

Transaction related services

Such services should not be accepted if the audit engagement partner has (or ought to have) doubt about the appropriateness of accounting treatments used, or there are contingent fees and the matter is material or is dependent on significant judgements in financial statements.

Accounting services

These should not be provided to any listed client or where it would involve the auditor taking management decisions.

Glossary of terms used in the Ethical Standards

Close family	A non-dependent parent, child or sibling
Immediate family	A spouse (or equivalent) or dependent
Person in a position to influence the conduct and outcome of the audit	Any person who is directly involved in the audit including the audit partners, audit managers, audit staff, professional personnel from other disciplines involved in the audit and those who provide quality control or direct oversight of the audit. It also includes any person who forms part of the chain of command for the audit within the firm or any person within the firm who may be in a position to exert influence.

There are other practical safeguards individual members and firms can use. Some of these have been suggested in the guidance outlined above. They are discussed in more detail in the rest of this section.

3.6 Ethical standard-provisions available for small entities (ES-PASE)

The APB is aware that a limited number of the requirements in Ethical Standards 1 to 5 are difficult for certain audit firms to comply with, particularly when auditing a small entity and accepts that certain dispensations are appropriate to facilitate the cost effective audit of the financial statements of Small Entities. As a result the ES-Pase was issued.

ES-PASE provides alternative provisions for auditors of Small Entities to apply in respect of the threats arising from economic dependence and where tax or accounting services are provided and allows the option of taking advantage of exemptions from certain of the requirements in APB Ethical Standards 1 to 5 Small Entity audit engagement. Where an audit firm takes advantage of the exemptions within this Standard, it is required to disclose in the audit report the fact that the firm has applied APB Ethical Standard – Provisions Available for Small Entities.

3.7 Current issue: Review of APB Ethical standards

The APB are about to start a review of their Ethical standards in line with the revisions currently being made by IFAC to their ethical code. Some of the key issues likely to be raised during this review are:

- Are the 10% and 15% limits for fee dependence reasonable? It can be argued that there is no evidence to support these thresholds. Should more allowance should be given for the specific circumstances and the implementation of alternative safeguards?

- Should the ES- PASE be withdrawn? The APB's original intention was to have ethical standards that applied to all audits and only issued the ES-PASE in response to lobbying by the professional bodies. The main argument against its retention relates to the fact that the required disclosure of its use in the auditors' report may be seen to devalue the audit opinion.

4 Specific guidance: Confidentiality

FAST FORWARD

> Both IFAC and ACCA recognise a duty of confidence and several exceptions to it.

4.1 Duty of confidence

The ACCA give guidance relating to confidentiality in the *Code of Ethics and Conduct*. A member acquiring information in the course of his professional work should not use, nor appear to use, that information for his personal advantage or for the advantage of a third party. A member must make clear to a client that he may only act for him if the client agrees to disclose in full to the member all information relevant to the engagement.

Where a member agrees to serve a client in a professional capacity both the member and the client should be aware that it is an implied term of that agreement that the member will not disclose the client's affairs to any other person save with the client's consent within the terms of certain recognised exceptions.

4.2 Recognised exceptions to the rule of confidence

ACCA Statement

Obligatory disclosure. If a member knows or suspects his client to have committed an offence of treason he is obliged to disclose all the information at his disposal to a competent authority. Local legislation may also require auditors to disclose other infringements.

Voluntary disclosure. In certain cases voluntary disclosure may be made by the member where:

- Disclosure is reasonably required to protect the member's interests
- Disclosure is required by process of law
- There is a public duty to disclose

IFAC extends this list in its guidance.

IFAC Code of Ethics

- To comply with technical standards and ethical requirements
- To comply with the quality review of a member or professional body
- To respond to an inquiry or investigation by a member body or regulatory body

Also, having decided that confidential information can be disclosed, accountants should consider:

- Whether all relevant facts are known and substantiated
- What type of communication is expected and to whom should it be addressed
- Whether the accountant will incur legal liability as a result of disclosure

---

If an ACCA member is requested to assist the police, the tax authorities or any other authority by providing information about a client's affairs in connection with enquiries being made he should enquire under what **statutory authority** the information is demanded.

Unless he is satisfied that such statutory authority exists he should decline to give any information until he has obtained his client's authority. If the client's authority is not forthcoming and the demand for information is pressed, he should not accede unless advised to by a solicitor.

If an ACCA member knows or suspects that a client has committed a wrongful act he must give careful thought to his own position. He is under no obligation, even in a criminal matter (excluding treason, money-laundering and terrorist offences), to convey his information to a competent authority, but he must ensure that he has not prejudiced himself by, for example, relying on incorrect information.

However, it would be a criminal offence for a member to act positively, without lawful authority or reasonable excuse, in such a manner as to impede with intent the arrest or prosecution of a client whom he knows or believes to have committed an arrestable offence.

4.3 Disclosure in the public interest

FAST FORWARD

ACCA gives further on disclosure 'in the public interest'. Accountants should usually seek legal advice before making disclosures.

The courts have never given a definition of 'the public interest'. This means that again, the issue is left to the judgement of the auditor. It is often therefore appropriate for the member to seek legal advice.

It is only appropriate for information to be disclosed to certain authorities, for example,

- The police
- The Financial Services Authority
- The Department of Trade and Industry

The ACCA guidance states that there are several factors that the member should take into account when deciding whether to make disclosure.

ACCA guidance

- The size of the amounts involved and the extent of likely financial damage
- Whether members of the public are likely to be affected
- The possibility or likelihood of repetition
- The reasons for the client's unwillingness to make disclosures to the authority
- The gravity of the matter
- Relevant legislation, accounting and auditing standards
- Any legal advice obtained

Under ISA 250, if auditors become aware of a suspected or actual instance of non-compliance with law and regulation which gives rise to a statutory right or duty to report, they should report it to the proper authority immediately. They should also seek legal advice.

Exam focus point

> If you are required to make judgements about whether such a disclosure should be made in a given scenario, you should apply a checklist like this to the scenario to ensure you have shown evidence of your consideration of all the relevant factors.

5 Specific guidance: Conflicts of interest

FAST FORWARD

> Auditors should identify potential conflicts of interest as they could result in the ethical codes being breached.

Audit firms should take reasonable steps to identify circumstances that could pose a conflict of interest. This is because a conflict of interest could result in the ethical code being breached (for example, if it results in a self-interest threat arising).

5.1 Conflicts between members' and clients' interests

A conflict between members' and clients' interests might arise if members compete directly with a client, or have a joint venture or similar with a company that is in competition with the client.

The rules state that **members and firms should not accept or continue engagements in which there are, or are likely to be, significant conflicts of interest between members, firms and clients**.

Members should evaluate the threats arising from a conflict of interest, and unless they are clearly insignificant, they should apply safeguards. The test of whether a threat is significant is whether a reasonable and informed third party, having knowledge of all relevant information, including the safeguards applied, would consider the conflict of interest as likely to affect the judgement of members and firms.

5.2 Conflicts between the interests of different clients

Assurance firms are at liberty to have clients who are in competition with each other. However, the firm should ensure that it is not the subject of a dispute between the clients. It must also manage its work so that the interests of one client do not adversely affect the client. **Where acceptance or continuance of an engagement would, even with safeguards, materially prejudice the interests of any client, the appointment should not be accepted or continued**.

Auditors often give their clients business advice unrelated to audit. In such a position, they may well become involved when clients are involved in issues such as:

- Share issues
- Takeovers

Neither situation is inherently wrong for an auditor to be in. With regard to **share issues**, auditor firms should not underwrite an issue of shares to the public of a client they audit. In a **takeover situation**, if the auditors are involved in the audits of both predator and target company, they must take care in a takeover situation. They should not:

- Be the principal advisors to either party
- Issue reports assessing the accounts of either party other than their audit report

If they find they possess material confidential information, they should contact the appropriate body or regulator.

Exam focus point

The issues arising in a takeover were examined in the previous syllabus.

5.2.1 Managing conflicts between clients' interests

When considering whether to accept a client or when there is a change in a client's circumstances, assurance firms should take reasonable steps to ascertain whether there is a conflict of interest or if there is likely to be one in the future. Relationships that ended two or more years earlier are unlikely to create a conflict.

Disclosure is the most important safeguard in connection of conflicts between clients' interests. Safeguards would usually include:

- Notifying the client of the interest/activities that may cause a conflict of interest and obtaining their consent to act in the circumstances, or

- Notifying all known relevant parties that the member is acting for two or more parties in respect of a matter where their respective interests are in conflict, and obtaining their consent so to act, or

- Notifying the client that the member does not act exclusively for any one client in the provision of proposed services, and obtaining their consent so to act

Other safeguards:

- Using separate engagement teams
- Procedures to prevent access of information (such as special passwords)
- Clear guidelines for the respective teams on issues of security and confidentiality
- The use of confidentiality agreements signed by the partners and staff
- Regular review of the safeguards by an independent partner
- Advising one or both of the clients to obtain additional independent advice

6 Conflicts in application of the fundamental principles

The Code of Ethics and Conduct gives some general guidance to members who encounter a conflict in the application of the fundamental principles.

6.1 Matters to consider

The resolution process should include consideration of:

- relevant facts
- ethical issues involved
- fundamental principles related to the matter in question
- established internal procedures
- alternative courses of action

6.1.1 Unresolved conflict

If the matter is unresolved, the member should consult with other appropriate persons within the firm. They may wish to obtain advice from ACCA or legal advisers.

If after exhausting all relevant possibilities, the ethical conflict remains unresolved, members should consider withdrawing from the engagement team, a specific assignment, or to resign altogether from the engagement.

6.2 Example

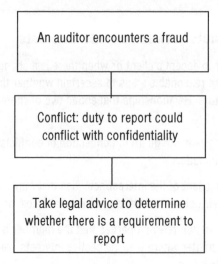

An auditor encounters a fraud

Conflict: duty to report could conflict with confidentiality

Take legal advice to determine whether there is a requirement to report

Chapter Roundup

- Accountants require an ethical code because they hold positions of trust, and people rely on them.

- IFAC's and ACCA's guidance is very similar.

- Both the ACCA rules and the IFAC code give examples of a number of situations where independence might be threatened and suggest safeguards to independence.

- Both IFAC and ACCA recognise a duty of confidence and several exceptions to it.

- ACCA gives further guidance on disclosure 'in the public interest'. Accountants should usually seek legal advice before making disclosures.

- Auditors should identify potential conflicts of interest as they could result in the ethical codes being breached.

Quick Quiz

1 Match the fundamental principle to the characteristic.

   (a)   Integrity

   (b)   Objectivity

      (i)   Members should be straightforward and honest in all professional and business relationships.

      (ii)   Members should not allow bias, conflict or interest or undue influence of others to override professional or business judgements.

2 Name five general threats to independence

   (1)   ....

   (2)   ....

   (3)   ....

   (4)   ....

   (5)   ....

3 Name four relevant safeguards against a financial interest in a client.

   (1)   ....

   (2)   ....

   (3)   ....

   (4)   ....

4 Complete the definition

   .... are fees calculated on a pre-determined basis relating to the outcome or result of a transaction of the result of the work performed.

5 What is a specialist valuation?

Answers to Quick Quiz

1   (a)(i), (b)(ii)

2   (1)   Self-review
     (2)   Self-interest
     (3)   Familiarity
     (4)   Intimidation
     (5)   Advocacy

3   (1)   Disposing of the interest
     (2)   Removing the relevant individual from the assurance team
     (3)   Informing the audit committee of the situation
     (4)   Independent partner review of work undertaken

4   Contingent fees.

5   They include:

     Actuarial valuation, valuation of intellectual property and brands, other intangible assets, property and unquoted investments

Now try the questions below from the Exam Question Bank			
Number	**Level**	**Marks**	**Time**
Q1	Examination	15	27 mins

Professional liability

Topic list	Syllabus reference
1 Legal liability	B3
2 Negligence	B3
3 Restricting liability and professional indemnity insurance	B3
4 Current issues in auditor liability	F1
5 Fraud and error	B2
6 The expectation gap	B3

Introduction

Auditors have responsibilities to several parties. This chapter explores the various **responsibilities** and the **liability that can arise** in respect of them. It also looks at ways of restricting liability, including professional indemnity insurance.

The auditors' responsibility to members and other readers of the accounts in tort and contract can give rise to **liability,** particularly in the event of **negligence.** Case law on this matter is complex and not wholly satisfactory. It results in auditors being liable to some readers and not others. However, **auditors' liability** is a dynamic issue in that it **evolves as cases are brought to court.**

There are some interesting **current developments** for auditors with regard to liability, for example **limited liability partnerships**. This and other current issues pertaining to the topics covered in this chapter are discussed in section 4.

Critically, and contrary to widespread public belief, **auditors do not have a responsibility to detect and prevent fraud.** The responsibilities that auditors do have with regard to fraud and error are outlined in Section 5. Auditors are required to follow the guidance of ISA (UK and Ireland) 240 *The auditor's responsibility to consider fraud in an audit of financial statements.*

Reasons for audit failure and other factors contributing to the 'expectation gap' are covered in section 6.

Study guide

		Intellectual level
B2	**Fraud and error**	
(a)	Define and clearly distinguish between the terms 'error', 'irregularity', 'fraud and 'misstatement'.	2
(b)	Compare and contrast the respective responsibilities of management and auditors for fraud and error.	2
(c)	Describe the matters to be considered and procedures to be carried out to investigate actual and/or potential misstatements in a given situation.	2
(d)	Explain how, why, when and to whom fraud and error should be reported and the circumstances in which an auditor should withdraw from an engagement.	2
(e)	Discuss the current and possible future role of auditors in preventing, detecting and reporting error and fraud.	2
B3	**Professional liability**	
(a)	Recognise circumstances in which professional accountants may have legal liability.	2
(b)	Describe the factors to determine whether or not an auditor is negligent in given situations.	2
(c)	Explain the other criteria for legal liability to be recognised (including 'due professional care' and 'proximity') and apply them to given situations.	2
(d)	Compare and contrast liability to client with liability to third parties.	2
(e)	Comment on precedents of case law.	2
(f)	Evaluate the practicability and effectiveness of ways in which liability may be restricted, including professional indemnity insurance (PII).	2
(g)	Discuss how audit and other opinions may be affected by limiting auditors' liability.	2
(h)	Discuss the advantages and disadvantages of claims against auditors being settled out of court.	2
(i)	Discuss and appraise the principal causes of audit failure and other factors that contribute to the 'expectation gap' (eg responsibilities for fraud and error).	3
(j)	Recommend ways in which the expectation gap might be bridged.	2

Exam guide

Auditors' liability is a key issue facing the profession globally, and ways of restricting liability are being compared and debated. This area can be examined in topical discussion questions, or in practical scenarios considering whether an auditor may be held to have been negligent in specific circumstances.

The extent of auditors' responsibilities in relation to fraud and error is a critical element of the public's perception of the auditor's role. The requirements of ISA 240 in this regard are core knowledge for this paper and may have to be applied in practical scenarios.

1 Legal liability

Professional accountants may have professional liability under statutory law.

Under certain legislation, notably **insolvency** legislation, auditors may be found to be officers of the company and could be charged with criminal offences or found liable for civil offences in connection with the winding up of the company.

Auditors may also be found guilty of the offence of **insider dealing**, which is a criminal offence, as they are privy to inside information.

Auditors could be found guilty of a criminal offence if they knew or suspected a person was laundering money and they failed to report their suspicions to the proper authority.

2 Negligence

Auditors may have professional liability in the tort of negligence.

Negligence is a common law concept. It seeks to provide compensation to a person who has suffered loss due to another person's wrongful neglect. To succeed in an action for negligence, an injured party must prove three things:

(a) A **duty of care** which is enforceable at law existed.

(b) This duty of care was **breached**.

(c) The breach caused the injured party **loss**. In the case of negligence in relation to financial advisers/auditors, this loss must be pecuniary (ie financial) loss.

2.1 Who might bring an action for negligence?

The parties likely to want to bring an action in negligence against the auditors, for example, if they have given the wrong audit opinion through lack of care, are parties such as:

- The company
- Shareholders
- The bank
- Other lenders
- Other interested third parties

A key differences between the various potential claimants is the **nature** of the **duty of care** owed to them.

2.2 The audit client

The auditor owes a duty of care to the audit client automatically under law.

The audit client is the **company**. It is a basic maxim of company law that the company is all the shareholders acting as a body. In other words, the company in this respect, cannot be represented by a single shareholder.

| COMPANY | = | SHAREHOLDERS AS A BODY |

| COMPANY | ≠ | SHAREHOLDER | + | SHAREHOLDER |

The **company** has a **contract** with the audit firm. In the law of many countries, a contract for the supply of a service such as an audit has a duty of reasonable care implied into it by statute.

In other words, whatever the express terms of any written contract between the company and the audit firm, the law always implies a duty of care into it. Therefore, if the company (all the shareholders acting as a body) want to bring a case for negligence, the situation would be as follows.

CLIENT	
Duty of care exists?	AUTOMATIC
Breached?	MUST BE PROVED
Loss arising?	MUST BE PROVED

In order to prove whether a duty of care had been breached, the court has to give further consideration to what the duty of 'reasonable' care means in practice.

2.2.1 The auditors' duty of care

The standard of work of auditors is generally as defined by legislation. A number of judgements made in law cases show how the auditors' duty of care has been gauged at various points in time because legislation often does not state clearly the manner in which the auditors should discharge their duty of care. It is also not likely that this would be clearly spelt out in any contract setting out the terms of an auditors' appointment.

Case Study

Re Kingston Cotton Mill

When Lopes L J considered the degree of skill and care required of an auditor in he declared:

'... it is the duty of an auditor to bring to bear on the work he has to perform that skill, care and caution which a reasonably competent, careful and cautious auditor would use. What is reasonable skill, care and caution, must depend on the particular circumstances of each case.'

Lopes was careful to point out that what constitutes reasonable care depends very much upon the **facts** of a particular case. Another criteria by which the courts will determine the adequacy of the auditors' work is by assessing it in relation to the generally accepted auditing standards of the day.

Case Study

The courts will be very much concerned with accepted advances in auditing techniques, demonstrated by Pennycuick J in *Re Thomas Gerrard & Son Ltd 1967* where he observed:

'... the real ground on which *Re Kingston Cotton Mill* ... is, I think, capable of being distinguished is that the standards of reasonable care and skill are, upon the expert evidence, more exacting today than those which prevailed in 1896.'

Case Study

Lord Denning in the case of *Fomento (Sterling Area) Ltd v Selsdon Fountain Pen Co Ltd 1958* sought to define the auditors' proper approach to their work by saying:

'... they must come to it with an inquiring mind - not suspicious of dishonesty .... - but suspecting that someone may have made a mistake somewhere and that a check must be made to ensure that there has been none.'

The auditors have a responsibility to keep themselves abreast of professional developments. Auditing Standards are likely to be taken into account when the adequacy of the work of auditors is being considered in a court of law or in other contested situations.

When the auditors are exercising judgement they must act both honestly and carefully. Obviously, if auditors are to be 'careful' in forming an opinion, they must give due consideration to all relevant matters. Provided they do this and can be seen to have done so, then their opinion should be above criticism.

However if the opinion reached by the auditors is one that no reasonably competent auditor would have been likely to reach then they would still possibly be held negligent. This is because however carefully the auditors may appear to have approached their work, it clearly could not have been careful enough, if it enabled them to reach a conclusion which would be generally regarded as unacceptable.

If the auditors' suspicions are aroused, they must conduct further investigations until such suspicions are either confirmed or allayed. Over the years, there have been many occasions where the courts have had to consider cases in which it has been held, on the facts of those cases, that the auditors ought to have been put upon enquiry.

2.3 Third parties

FAST FORWARD

The auditor only owes a duty of care to parties other than the audit client if one has been established.

'Third parties' in this context means anyone other than the company (audit client) who wished to make a claim for negligence. It therefore includes any individual shareholders in the company and any potential investors. It also includes, importantly, the bank, who is very often a key financier of the company.

The key difference between third parties and the company is that third parties have no contract with the audit firm. There is therefore no implied duty of care. The situation is therefore as follows.

THIRD PARTIES	
Duty of care exists?	MUST BE PROVED
Breached?	MUST BE PROVED
Loss arising?	MUST BE PROVED

Traditionally the courts have been **averse** to **attributing a duty of care to third parties** to the auditor. We can see this by looking at some past cases that have gone to court.

A **very important case** is *Caparo Industries plc v Dickman and Others 1990*, which is described here.

 Case Study

The **facts as pleaded** were that in 1984 Caparo Industries purchased 100,000 Fidelity shares in the open market. On June 12 1984, the date on which the accounts (audited by Touche Ross) were published, they purchased a further 50,000 shares. Relying on information in the accounts, further shares were acquired. On September 4, Caparo made a bid for the remainder and by October had acquired control of Fidelity. Caparo alleged that the accounts on which they had relied were misleading in that an apparent pre-tax profit of some £1.3 million should in fact have been shown as a loss of over £400,000. The plaintiffs argued that Touche owed a duty of care to investors and potential investors.

The conclusion of the **House of Lords** hearing of the case in February 1990 was that the auditors of a public company's accounts owed **no duty of care** to members of the public at large who relied upon the accounts in deciding to buy shares in the company. And as a purchaser of further shares, while relying upon the auditors' report, a shareholder stood in the same position as any other investing member of the public to whom the auditor owed no duty. The purpose of the audit was simply that of fulfilling the statutory requirements of CA 1985. There was nothing in the statutory duties of company auditors to suggest that they were intended to protect the interests of investors in the market. And in particular, there was no reason why any special relationship should be held to arise simply from the fact that the affairs of the company rendered it susceptible to a takeover bid.

In its report *The Financial Aspects of Corporate Governance*, the Cadbury Committee gave an opinion on the situation as reflected in the *Caparo* ruling. It felt that *Caparo* did not lessen auditors' duty to use skill and care because auditors are **still fully liable in negligence** to the companies they audit and their shareholders collectively. Given the number of different users of accounts, it was impossible for the House of Lords to have broadened the boundaries of the auditors' legal duty of care.

The decision in *Caparo v Dickman* considerably **narrowed the auditors' potential liability to third parties**. The judgement appears to imply that members of various such user groups, which could include creditors, potential investors or others, will not be able to sue the auditors for negligence by virtue of their placing reliance on audited annual accounts.

Case Study

In *James McNaughton Paper Group Ltd v Hicks Anderson & Co 1990*, Lord Justice Neill set out the following position in the light of *Caparo* and earlier cases:

'(a)   In England a restrictive approach was now adopted to any extension of the scope of the duty of care beyond the person directly intended by the maker of the statement to act upon it.

(b)   In deciding whether a duty of care existed in any particular case it was necessary to take all the circumstances into account,

(c)   Notwithstanding (b), it was possible to identify certain matters which were likely to be of importance in most cases in reaching a decision as to whether or not a duty existed.'

A more recent court case produced a **development** in the subject of audit liability. In December 1995, a High Court judge awarded electronic security group ADT £65m plus interest and costs (£40m) in damages for negligence against the former BDO Binder Hamlyn (BBH) partnership.

Case Study

The firm had jointly audited the 1988/89 accounts of Britannia Security Group (BSG), which ADT acquired in 1990 for £105m, but later found to be worth only £40m. Although, under *Caparo*, auditors do not owe a duty of care in general to third parties, the judge found that BBH audit partner Martyn Bishop, who confirmed that the firm stood by BSG's accounts at a meeting with ADT in the run-up to the acquisition, had thereby **taken on a contractual relationship** with ADT. This development has occurred, apparently, because (post-*Caparo*) solicitors and bankers are advising clients intent on acquisitions to get direct assurances from the target's auditors on the truth and fairness of the accounts.

BBH appealed this decision; the liable partners, because of a shortfall in insurance cover, were left facing the prospect of coming up with £34m. An out of court settlement was reached with ADT.

A case in 1997 appeared to take a slightly different line, although this case related to some management accounts on which no written report had been issued.

Case Study

In *Peach Publishing Ltd v Slater & Co 1997* the Court of Appeal ruled that accountants are not automatically liable if they give oral assurances on accounts to the purchaser of a business. The case involved management accounts, which the accountant stated the accounts were right subject to the qualification that they had not been audited. The Court held that the purpose of giving the assurance was not to take on responsibility to the purchaser for the accuracy of the accounts. The purchaser's true objective in this case was to obtain a warranty from the accountant's client, the target. Therefore the accountant was not assuming responsibility to the purchaser but giving his client information on which it could decide whether or not to give the warranty. The Court of Appeal also observed that the purchaser should not have relied on the management accounts without having them checked by its advisers.

Case Study

In a further case the Court of Appeal gave guidance on the effect of a disclaimer which stated that the report had been prepared for the client only and no-one else should rely on it. In *Omega Trust Co Ltd v Wright Son & Pepper 1997* (which related to surveyors but the facts of which can be applied to accountants) the court held that the surveyor was entitled to know who his client was and to whom his duty was held. He was entitled to refuse liability to an unknown lender or any known lender with whom he had not agreed.

All this case law raised some **problems**. In spite of the judgement in *Caparo*, the commercial reality is that creditors and investors (especially institutional ones) do use audited accounts. S 241 CA 1985 requires a company to file accounts with the Registrar. Why is this a statutory requirement? It is surely because the public, including creditors and potential investors, have a need for a credible and independent view of the company's performance and position.

It would be unjust if auditors, who have **secondary responsibility** for financial statements being prepared negligently, bore the full responsibility for losses arising from such negligence just because they are insured. It would also be unjust if the auditors could be sued by all and sundry. While the profession has generally welcomed *Caparo*, two obvious problems are raised by decision.

- Is a restricted view of the usefulness of audited accounts in the profession's long-term interests?

- For private companies there will probably be an increase in the incidence of personal guarantees and warranties given by the directors to banks and suppliers.

Recent developments in the US appear to try and redress the **balance of liability** by highlighting the responsibilities of management with regard to published financial statements. The Sarbanes-Oxley Act requires chief executive officers and finance officers to certify that the accounts of listed companies are not misleading and present the company's financial positional and results fairly. In addition, they are required to confirm that they are responsible for internal controls ad have reported significant control weakness to the auditors/audit committee.

The UK Companies Act requires directors not to make misleading statements to the auditors. However, auditors retain liability to shareholders for negligence and breach of duty, therefore they need to corroborate statements made to them and ensure they are not relying on representations recklessly.

Exam focus point

> A discussion question appeared under the previous syllabus on the impact of recent developments in auditor liability.

2.3.1 Banks and other major lenders

Banks and other major lenders have generally been excluded from the extent of negligent auditors' liability by the decision in Caparo.

Banks often include clauses in loan agreements referring to audited accounts and requesting that they have access to audited accounts on a regular basis or when reviewing the loan facility. In other words, banks may **document a 'relationship'** with the auditors to establish that a duty of care exists.

A recent Scottish case involved a situation similar to this and may suggest that judicial thinking on the matter is developing.

 Case Study

In a *Royal Bank of Scotland v Bannerman Johnstone Maclay and Others 2002* the bank, who provided an overdraft facility to the company being audited, claimed the company had misstated its position due to a fraud and that the auditors were negligent in not discovering the fraud. The auditors claimed that they had no duty of care to the bank. However, the judge determined that the auditors would have known that the bank required audited accounts as part of the overdraft arrangement and could have issued a disclaimer to the bank. The fact that they had not issued a disclaimer was an important factor in deciding that the auditors did owe a duty of care to the bank.

2.3.2 Assurance services

The audit firm might be able and prepared to **offer assurances** to the bank in relation to financial statements, position, internal controls or other matters of interest to a primary lender. If this is the case, and the service is required by the bank, the **auditor should seek to create an engagement with the bank itself**. This will be considered further in Chapter 15.

You should bear in mind that providing assurance services to a lender could result in a **conflict of interest** arising, of course.

2.4 Settlements out of court

Many liability claims are settled out of court. The advantages of doing so are claimed to be a **saving** in **time** and **cost**, and also perhaps a **lower settlement**. An out of court settlement also avoids a high profile court case which **potentially damages** a firm's **reputation**.

Arguments against an out-of-court settlement include the allegations that they often arise through the **unwillingness** of an auditors' **insurance company** to risk a settlement in court. An out of court settlement also **leaves** the **question** of the audit **firm's responsibility unsettled**, but nevertheless the firm's **insurance premiums** may **rise**.

2.5 Disclaimers

FAST FORWARD

> Auditors may attempt to limit liability to clients. This may not always be effective in law.

The cases above suggest that a duty of care to a third party may arise when an accountant does not know that his work will be relied upon by a third party, but only knows that it is work of a kind which is liable in the ordinary course of events to be relied upon by a third party.

Conversely, an accountant may sometimes be informed or be aware, before he carries out certain work, that a third party will rely upon the results. An example is a report upon the business of a client which the accountant has been instructed to prepare for the purpose of being shown to a potential purchaser or potential creditor of that business. In such a case an accountant should assume that he will be held to owe the same duty to the third party as to his client. The Bannermann case suggests this will also be necessary for **audit work**. Since the Bannermann case, many audit firms have included a disclaimer in their audit report.

When ACCA's Council considered the use of disclaimers, their view was:

"Standard disclaimers are not an appropriate or proportionate response to the Bannermann decision. Their incorporation as a standard feature of the audit report could have the effect of devaluing that report."

However there are areas of professional work (for example when acting as an auditor under the Companies Act on behalf of shareholders), where it is not possible for liability to be limited or excluded. There are other areas of professional work (for example when preparing reports on a business for the purpose of being submitted to a potential purchaser) where although such a limitation or exclusion may be included, its effectiveness will depend on the view which a court may subsequently form of its reasonableness.

2.6 Litigation avoidance

The other aspect of how firms are trying to deal with litigation is what they are trying to do to avoid litigation. This strategy has various aspects.

- **Client acceptance procedures** are very important, particularly the screening of new clients and the use of engagement letters. This is covered in more detail in Chapter 5.
- **Performance of audit work**. Firms should make sure that all audits are carried out in accordance with professional standards and best practice.
- **Quality control**. This includes not just controls over individual audits but also stricter 'whole-firm' procedures. This is considered in more detail in Chapter 4.
- **Issue of appropriate disclaimers**. We discussed above the importance of these.

In ACCA's view the best way of restricting liability is for auditors to carry out their audit work in accordance with auditing standards. Where work is properly conducted the auditor should not need to subject it to blanket disclaimers.

Exam focus point

> Read the financial and accountancy press on a regular basis between now and your examination and note any new cases or developments in the question of auditor liability.

 Question

Negligence claims

Although auditors can incur civil liability under various statutes it is far more likely that they will incur liability for negligence under the common law, as the majority of cases against auditors have been in this area. Auditors must be fully aware of the extent of their responsibilities, together with steps they must take to minimise the danger of professional negligence claims.

Required

(a)   Discuss the extent of an auditors' responsibilities to shareholders and others during the course of their normal professional engagement.

(b)   List six steps which auditors should take to minimise the danger of claims against them for negligent work.

Answer

(a)   *Responsibility under statute*

An auditor of a limited company has a responsibility, imposed upon him by statute, to form and express a professional opinion on the financial statements presented by the directors to the shareholders. He must report upon the truth and fairness of such statements and the fact that they comply with the law. In so doing, the auditor owes a duty of care to the company imposed by statute. But such duty also arises under contract and may also arise under the common law (law of tort).

Responsibility under contract

The Companies Act does not state expressly the manner in which the auditor should discharge his duty of care; neither is it likely that this would be clearly spelt out in any contract setting out the terms of an auditor's appointment (eg the engagement letter). Although the articles of a company may extend the auditor's responsibilities beyond those envisaged by the Companies Act, they cannot be used so as to restrict the auditor's statutory duties, neither may they place any restriction upon the auditor's statutory rights which are designed to assist him in the discharge of those duties.

The comments of Lopes L J when considering the degree of skill and care required of an auditor in *Re Kingston Cotton Mill* are still relevant.

> '... It is the duty of an auditor to bring to bear on the work he has to perform the skill, care and caution which a reasonably competent, careful and cautious auditor would use. What is reasonable skill, care and caution must depend on the particular circumstances of each case.'

Clearly, with the advent of auditing standards, a measure of good practice is now available for the courts to take into account when considering the adequacy of the work of the auditor.

Responsibility in tort

The law of tort has established that a person owes a duty of care and skill to 'our neighbours' (common and well-known examples of this neighbour principle can be seen in the law of trespass, slander, libel and so on). In the context of the professional auditor the wider implications, however, concern the extent to which the auditor owes a duty of care and skill to third parties who rely on financial statements upon which he has reported but with whom he has no direct contractual or fiduciary relationship.

Liability to third parties

In *Caparo Industries plc v Dickman & Others 1990*, it was held that the auditors of a public company's accounts owed no duty of care to members of the general public who relied upon the accounts in deciding to buy shares in the company. And as a purchaser of more shares, a shareholder placing reliance on the auditors' report stood in the same position as any other investing member of the public to whom the auditor owed no duty. This decision appeared to radically reverse the tide of cases concerning the auditor's duty of care. The purpose of the audit was simply that of meeting the statutory requirements of the Companies Act 1985. There was nothing in the statutory duties of a company auditor to suggest that they were intended to protect the interests of investors in the market. In particular, there was no reason why any special relationship should be held to arise simply from the fact that the affairs of the company rendered it susceptible to a take-over bid.

A case between BDO Binder Hamlyn and ADT seems to have moved the argument on. In this case it was argued that proximity between a prospective investor and the auditors of a company could be created if the investor asked the auditors whether they stood by their last audit. An appeal is likely in this case as the auditors involved face a large shortfall in insurance proceeds. The recent Scottish Bannerman case suggests that judges may be more likely to impute a duty of care to the auditors if they were aware that the bank made use of audited accounts and did not disclaim liability to them.

(b)   In order to provide a means of protection for the auditor arising from the comments in (a) above, the following steps should be taken.

(i)   Agreements concerning the duties of the auditor should be:

(1)   Clear and precise
(2)   In writing
(3)   Confirmed by a level of engagement, including matters specifically excluded

(ii)   Audit work should be:

(1)   Relevant to the system of internal control, which must be ascertained, evaluated and tested. Controls cannot be entirely ignored: for the auditor to have any confidence in an accounting system there must be present and evident the existence of minimum controls to ensure completeness and accuracy of the records)

(2)   Adequately planned before the audit commences

(3)   Reviewed by a senior member of the firm to ensure qualify control of the audit and to enable a decision to be made on the form of audit report

(iii)   Any queries arising during the audit should be:

(1)   Recorded on the current working papers
(2)   Cleared and filed

(iv)   A management letter should be:

(1)   Submitted to the client or the Board of Directors in writing immediately following an audit

(2)   Seen to be acted upon by the client

(v)   All members of an auditing firm should be familiar with:

(1)   The standards expected throughout the firm

(2)   The standards of the profession as a whole by means of adequate training, which should cover the implementation of the firm's audit manual and the recommendations of the professional accountancy bodies

(vi)   Insurance should be taken out to cover the firm against possible claims.

3 Restricting liability and professional indemnity insurance

ACCA requires that auditors take out professional indemnity insurance.

3.1 Professional indemnity insurance?

Key terms

Professional indemnity insurance is insurance against civil claims made by clients and third parties arising from work undertaken by the firm.

Fidelity guarantee insurance is insurance against liability arising through any acts of fraud or dishonesty by any partner, director or employee in respect of money or goods held in trust by the firm.

It is important that accountants have insurance so that if negligence occurs, the client can be **compensated** for the error by the accountant. The appropriate compensation could be far greater than the resources of the accountancy firm.

Remember that accountants usually trade as **partnerships,** so all the partners are jointly and severally liable to claims made against individual partners.

3.2 ACCA requirements

ACCA requires that firms holding practising certificates and auditing certificates have professional indemnity insurance with a reputable insurance company. If the firm has employees, it must also have fidelity guarantee insurance.

The insurance must cover 'all civil liability incurred in connection with the conduct of the firm's business by the partners, directors or employees'.

The cover must continue to exist for **6 years** after a member ceases to engage in public practice.

3.3 Advantages and disadvantages

The key **advantage** of such insurance is that it provides funds for an innocent party to be compensated in the event of a wrong having been done to them.

An **advantage** to the auditor is that it provides some protection against bankruptcy in the event of successful litigation against the firm. This is particularly important for a partnership, as partners may be sued personally for the negligence of their fellow partners.

A key **disadvantage** is that the existence of insurance against the cost of negligence might encourage auditors to take less care than

- Would otherwise be the case
- Their professional duty requires.

Another problem associated with such insurances are that there are limits of cover (linked with the cost of buying the insurance) and any compensation arising from a claim could be higher than those limits. This could lead to partners being bankrupted despite having insurance. A simple disadvantage associated with the above is the regular cost of the insurance to the partnership.

3.4 Incorporation

The major accountancy firms have been interested in methods of reducing personal liability for partners in the event of negligence for some time. For example, some years ago KPMG (one of the big four accountancy firms) incorporated its UK audit practice. This is allowed under Companies Act 1989.

The new arrangement created 'a firm within a firm'. KPMG Audit plc is a limited company wholly owned by the partnership, KPMG. The reason behind this is to protect the partners from the crushing effects of litigation. The other side of incorporation means that KPMG Audit plc are subject to the statutory disclosure requirements of companies.

An alternative to incorporation as a company is incorporation as a limited liability partnership.

Limited liability partnership can be operated in some countries, for example, some of the states in the USA and the UK.

3.5 Limited liability partnerships (LLPs)

The Limited Liability Partnership Act 2000 enabled UK firms to establish limited liability partnerships as separate legal entities. These combine the flexibility and tax status of a partnership with limited liability for members.

The effect of this is that the partnership, **but not its members**, will be liable to third parties; however the personal assets of **negligent** partners will still be at risk.

Limited liability partnerships could be formed from 6 April 2001. Several prominent professional partnerships have incorporated as LLPs.

Limited liability partnerships are set up by similar procedures to those for incorporating a company. An incorporation document is sent to the Registrar of Companies. The Registrar will issue a certificate of incorporation to confirm that all statutory requirements have been fulfilled.

In a similar way to traditional partnerships, relations between partners will be governed by internal partner agreements, or by future statutory regulations.

Each member of the partnership will still be an agent of the partnership unless he has no authority to act and an outside party is aware of this lack of authority.

3.6 Advantages and disadvantages of different structures

	Advantages	Disadvantages
Partnership	• Less regulation than for companies • Financial statements not on public record	• Joint and several liability • Personal assets at risk
Incorporation	• Limited liability	• Public filing of audited financial statements • Management must comply with Companies Acts
LLP	• Protection at personal assets • Limited liability of members • Similar tax effect to partnership • Flexible management structures	• Public filing of audited financial statements

4 Current issues in auditor liability

FAST FORWARD

> As auditor liability is an important practical issue, there are regularly developments in this area.

Even with PII and other means of restricting liability there has been great concern throughout the audit profession globally at the remaining risks to firms survival in the face of claims which might exceed their insurance cover.

The profession has lobbied for further protection in the form of *proportionate liability* or *capping liability*.

Key term

> *Proportionate liability* would allow claims arising from successful negligence claims to be split between the auditors and the directors of the client company, the split being determined by a judge on the basis of where the fault was seen to lie. This would require the approval of shareholders.
>
> *Capping liability* would set a maximum limit on the amount that the auditor would have to pay out under any claim.

4.1 UK Companies Act 2006

The new Companies Act has introduced a provision for "liability limitation agreements". These would allow the auditor, with authorisation from the members of the company to agree a limit to the auditors liability.

The agreement may specify the limit by any mechanism agreed between the auditor and the company. Examples might be

- a specific sum
- multiples of the audit fee
- proportionate liability

A new agreement must be drawn up and authorised for each financial year.

4.2 Ongoing debate

There have been concerns that the new regulations may distort competition in the audit market. If the biggest firms set caps at very high levels, mid-tier firms could be disadvantaged. The government has left a provision for the Secretary of State to issue specific rules specifying what can and cannot be included in agreements in case competition problems arise.

There are also arguments that capping liability will reduce the value of the audit to investors and may bring pressure on firms to reduce fees.

Overall the profession has reacted positively to the new rules. The reaction has been less positive to the other major effect of the new bill, introducing a criminal offence of 'knowingly or recklessly' including in the auditors report any matter that is misleading, false or deceptive in a material particular.

The government saw this as being a necessary change in order to maintain audit quality.

5 Fraud and error

Misunderstanding of the auditor's responsibilities in respect of fraud is a major component of the 'expectation gap'

5.1 What is fraud?

Key term

Fraud is an intentional act by one or more individuals among management, those charged with governance (management fraud), employees (employee fraud) or third parties involving the use of deception to obtain an unjust or illegal advantage. Fraud may be perpetrated by an individual, or colluded in with people internal or external to the business.

Fraud is a wide legal concept, but the auditor's main concern is with fraud that causes a material misstatement in financial statements. It is distinguished from error, which is when a material misstatement is caused by mistake, for example, in the application of an accounting policy. Specifically, there are two types of fraud causing material misstatement in financial statements:

- Fraudulent financial reporting
- Misappropriation of assets

5.1.1 Fraudulent financial reporting

This may include:

- Manipulation, falsification or alteration of accounting records/supporting documents
- Misrepresentation (or omission) of events or transactions in the financial statements
- Intentional misapplication of accounting principles

Such fraud may be carried out by overriding controls that would otherwise appear to be operating effectively, for example, by recording fictitious journal entries or improperly adjusting assumptions or estimates used in financial reporting.

Aggressive earnings management is a topical issue and, at its most aggressive, may constitute fraudulent financial reporting. Auditors should consider issues such as unsuitable revenue recognition, accruals, liabilities, provisions and reserves accounting and large numbers of immaterial breaches of financial reporting requirements to see whether together, they constitute fraud.

Exam focus point

The assessor for the old syllabus equivalent paper wrote an article on this issue in Student Accountant April 2004 which you should be aware of. It deals with the content of the ISA discussed here when it was an exposure draft.

5.1.2 Misappropriation of assets

This is the theft of the entity's assets (for example, cash, inventory). Employees may be involved in such fraud in small and immaterial amounts, however, it can also be carried out by management for larger items who may then conceal the misappropriation, for example by:

- Embezzling receipts (for example, diverting them to private bank accounts)
- Stealing physical assets or intellectual property (inventory, selling data)
- Causing an entity to pay for goods not received (payments to fictitious vendors)
- Using assets for personal use

5.2 Responsibilities with regard to fraud

Management and those charged with governance in an entity are primarily responsible for preventing and detecting fraud. It is up to them to put a strong emphasis within the company on fraud prevention.

Auditors are responsible for carrying out an audit in accordance with international auditing standards, one of which is ISA (UK and Ireland) 240 *The auditor's responsibility to consider fraud in an audit of financial statements*, the details of which we shall look at now.

5.3 The auditors' approach to the possibility of fraud

5.3.1 General

The key requirement for an auditor is set out early in the ISA.

ISA 240.3

In planning and performing the audit to reduce audit risk to an acceptably low level, the auditor should consider the risks of material misstatements in the financial statements due to fraud.

An overriding requirement of the ISA is that auditors are aware of the possibility of there being misstatements due to fraud.

ISA 240.24

The auditor should maintain an attitude of professional scepticism throughout the audit, recognising the possibility that a material misstatement due to fraud could exist, notwithstanding the auditor's past experience with the entity about the honesty and integrity of management and those charged with governance.

ISA 240.27

Members of the engagement team should discuss the susceptibility of the entity's financial statements to material misstatements due to fraud.

The engagement partner must consider what matters discussed should be passed on to other members of the team not present at the discussion. The discussion itself usually includes:

- An exchange of ideas between the engagement team about how fraud could be perpetrated

- A consideration of circumstances that might be indicative of aggressive earnings management

- A consideration of known factors that might give incentive to management to commit fraud

- A consideration of management's oversight of employees with access to cash/other assets

- A consideration of any unusual/unexplained changes in lifestyle of management/employees

- An emphasis on maintaining professional scepticism throughout the audit

- A consideration of the types of circumstance that might indicate fraud

- A consideration of how unpredictability will be incorporated into the audit

- A consideration of what audit procedures might be carried out to answer any suspicions of fraud

- A consideration of any allegations of fraud that have come to the auditors' attention

- A consideration of the risk of management override of controls

5.3.2 Risk assessment procedures

The auditor would undertake risk assessment procedures as set out in ISA 315 (see Chapter 7) which would include assessing the risk of fraud. These procedures will include:

- Inquiries of management and those charged with governance
- Consideration of when fraud risk factors are present
- Consideration of results of analytical procedures
- Consideration of any other relevant information

In identifying the risks of fraud, the auditor is required by the ISA to carry out some specific procedures.

ISA 240.34

When obtaining an understanding of the entity and its environment, including its internal control, the auditor should make enquiries of management regarding:

(a) Management's assessment of the risk that the financial statements may be materially misstated due to fraud

(b) Management's process for identifying and responding to the risks of fraud in the entity, including any specific risks of fraud that management has identified or account balances, classes of transactions or disclosures for which a risk of fraud is likely to exist

(c) Management's communication, if any, to those charged with governance regarding its processes for identifying and responding to the risks of fraud in the entity, and

(d) Management's communication, if any, to employees regarding its views on business practices and ethical behaviour

ISA 240.38

The auditor should make enquiries of management, internal audit and others within the entity as appropriate, to determine whether they have knowledge of any actual, suspected or alleged fraud affecting the entity.

ISA 240.43

The auditor should obtain an understanding of how those charged with governance exercise oversight of management's processes for identifying and responding to the risks of fraud in the entity and the internal control that management has established to mitigate these risks.

ISA 240.46

The auditor should make inquiries of those charged with governance to determine whether they have knowledge of any actual, suspected or alleged fraud affecting the entity.

ISA 240.48

When obtaining an understanding of the entity and its environment, including its internal control, the auditor should consider whether the information obtained indicates that one or more fraud risk factors are present.

Examples of fraud risk factors

ISA 240 does not attempt to provide a definitive list of risk factors but, in an appendix, identifies and gives examples of two types of fraud that are relevant to auditors:

- fraudulent financial reporting, and
- misstatements arising from misappropriation of assets

For each of these, the risk factors are classified according to three conditions that are generally present when misstatements due to fraud occur:

- incentives/pressures
- opportunities
- attitudes/rationalisations

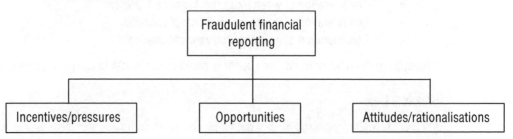

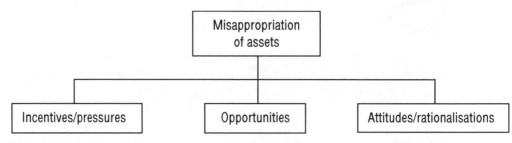

> **ISA 240.57**
>
> When identifying and assessing the risks of material misstatement at the financial statement level, and at the assertion level for classes of transactions, account balances and disclosures, the auditor should identify and assess the risks of material misstatement due to fraud. Those assessed risks that could result in a material misstatement due to fraud are significant risks and accordingly, to the extent not already done so, the auditor should evaluate the design of the entity's related controls, including relevant control activities, and determine whether they have been implemented.

The auditor:

- Identifies fraud risks
- Relates this to what could go wrong at a financial statement level
- Considers the likely magnitude of potential misstatement

Question	Fraud risk

You are an audit manager for Elle and Emm, Certified Accountants. You are carrying out the planning of the audit of Sellfones plc, a high street retailer of mobile phones in the UK, for the year ending 30 September 20X7. The notes from your planning meeting with Pami Desai, the financial director, include the following:

1   One of Sellfones' main competitors ceased trading during the year due to the increasing pressure on margins in the industry and competition from online retailers.

2   A new management structure has been implemented, with 10 new divisional managers appointed during the year. The high street shops have been allocated to these managers, with approximately 20 branch managers reporting to each divisional manager. The divisional managers have been set challenging financial targets for their areas with substantial bonuses offered to incentivise them to meet the targets. The board of directors have also decided to cut the amount that will be paid to shop staff as a Christmas bonus.

3   In response to recommendations in the prior year's Report to Management, a new stock system has been implemented. There were some teething problems in its first months of operation but a report has been submitted to the board by Steven MacLennan, the chief accountant, confirming that the problems have all been resolved and that information produced by the system will be accurate. Pami commented that the chief accountant has had to work very long hours to deal with this new system, often working at weekends and even refusing to take any leave until the system was running properly.

4   The company is planning to raise new capital through a share issue after the year end in order to finance expansion of the business into other countries in Europe. As a result, Pami has requested that the auditor's report is signed off by 15 December 20X7 (6 weeks earlier than in previous years).

5   The latest board summary of results includes:

9 Months to 30 June 20X7 *(unaudited)*		*Year to 30 September 20X6* *(audited)*	
	£m		£m
Turnover	320	Turnover	280
Cost of sales	215	Cost of sales	199
Gross profit	105	Gross profit	81
Operating expenses	(89)	Operating expenses	(70)
Exceptional profit on sale of properties	30		–
Profit before tax	40		11

6   Several shop properties owned by the company were sold under sale and leaseback arrangements.

Required

Identify and explain any fraud risk factors that the audit team should consider when planning the audit of Sellphones plc.

Answer

In this scenario there are a large number of factors that should alert the auditors to the possibility of misstatements arising from fraudulent financial reporting, and others that could indicate a risk of misstatements arising from misappropriation of assets.

1   **Operating conditions within the industry**

The failure of a competitor in a highly competitive business sector highlights the threat to the survival of a business such as Sellphones and this could place the directors under pressure to overstate the performance and position of the company in an attempt to maintain investor confidence, particularly given the intention to raise new share capital.

2   **Management structure and incentives**

It is not clear in the scenario how much involvement the new divisional managers have in the financial reporting process but the auditors would need to examine any reports prepared or reviewed by them very carefully as their personal interest may lead them to overstate results in order to earn their bonuses.

3   **New stock system/chief accountant**

The problems with the implementation of the new stock system suggest that there may have been control weaknesses and errors in the recording of stock figures. Misstatements, whether deliberate or not, may not have been identified. The amount of time spent by the chief accountant on the implementation of the new stock system could be seen as merely unlining the severity of the problems, but the fact that he has not taken any leave should also be considered as suspicious and the auditors should be alert to any indication that he may have been involved in any deliberate misstatement of figures.

4   **Results**

The year on year results look better than might be expected given the business environment. The gross profit margin has increased to 32.8% (20X6 25.3%) and the operating profit margin has increased to 5% (20X6 3.9%). This seems to conflict with what is known about the industry and should increase the auditors' professional scepticism in planning the audit.

5 **Exceptional gain**

The sale and leaseback transaction may involve complex considerations relating to its commercial substance. It may not be appropriate to recognise a gain or the gain may have been miscalculated.

6 **Time pressure on audit**

The auditors should be alert to the possibility that the tight deadline may have been set to reduce the amount of time the auditors have to gather evidence in the post balance sheet period and this may have been done in the hope that certain deliberate misstatements will not be discovered.

7 **Risk of misappropriation of assets**

The nature of the stocks held in the shops increases the risk that staff may steal goods. The risk is perhaps increased by the fact that the attitude of the staff towards their employer is likely to have been damaged by the cut in their Christmas bonus. The problems with the new stock recording system increase the risk that any such discrepancies in stock may not have been identified.

5.3.3 Responding to assessed risks

The auditor must then come up with responses to the assessed risks.

> **ISA 240.61**
>
> The auditor should determine overall responses to address the assessed risks of material misstatement due to fraud at the financial statement level and should design and perform further audit procedures whose nature, timing and extent are responsive to the assessed risks at the assertion level.
>
> **ISA 240.66**
>
> In determining overall responses to address the risks of material misstatement due to fraud at the financial statement level the auditor should:
>
> (a) Consider the assignment and supervision of personnel
>
> (b) Consider the accounting policies used by the entity, and
>
> (c) Incorporate an element of unpredictability in the selection of the nature, timing and extent of audit procedures

The auditor may have to **amend** the **nature, timing or extent** of planned audit procedures to address assessed risks. The auditor should also consider the following:

- Audit procedures responsive to management override of controls
- Journal entries and other adjustments
- Accounting estimates
- Business rationale for significant transactions

> **ISA 240.76**
>
> To respond to the risk of management override of controls, the auditor should design and perform audit procedures to:
>
> (a) Test the appropriateness of journal entries recorded in the general ledger and other adjustments made in the preparation of the financial statements
>
> (b) Review accounting estimates for biases that could result in material misstatements due to fraud, and

> (c) Obtain an understanding of the business rationale of significant transactions that the auditor becomes aware of that are outside of the normal course of business for the entity, or that otherwise appear to be unusual given the auditor's understanding of the entity and its environment.

Examples: specific audit procedures

The auditor might to choose to attend previously unvisited branches to carry out stock or cash checks.

The auditor might perform detailed analytical procedures using disaggregated data, for example, comparing sales and costs of sales by location.

Use an expert to assess management estimates in a subjective area.

5.4 Evaluation of audit evidence

The auditor evaluates the audit evidence obtained to ensure it is consistent and that it achieves its aim of answering the risks of fraud. This will include a consideration of results of analytical procedures and other misstatements found. The auditor must also consider the reliability of management representations.

The auditor must obtain written representation that management accepts its responsibility for the prevention and detection of fraud and has made all relevant disclosures to the auditors.

5.5 Documentation

The auditor must document:

- The significant decisions as a result of the team's discussion of fraud
- The identified and assessed risks of material misstatement due to fraud
- The overall responses to assessed risks
- Results of specific audit tests
- Any communications with management

5.6 Reporting

There are various reporting requirements in ISA 240.

> **ISA 240.93**
>
> If the auditor has identified a fraud or has obtained information that indicates a fraud may exist, the auditor should communicate these matters as soon as practicable to the appropriate level of **management**.
>
> **ISA 240.95**
>
> If the auditor has identified fraud involving:
>
> (a) Management
> (b) Employees who have significant roles in internal control, or
> (c) Others, where the fraud results in a material misstatement in the financial statements
>
> the auditor should communicate these matters to **those charged with governance** as soon as practicable.

The auditor should also make relevant parties within the entity aware of material weaknesses in the design or implementation of controls to prevent and detect fraud which have come to the auditor's attention, and consider whether there are any other relevant matters to bring to the attention of those charged with governance with regard to fraud.

The auditor may have a **statutory duty** to report fraudulent behaviour to **regulators** outside the entity. If no such legal duty arises, the auditor must consider whether to do so would breach their **professional duty of confidence**. In either event, the auditor should take **legal advice**.

5.7 Withdrawal from the engagement

The auditor should consider the need to withdraw from the engagement if the auditor uncovers exceptional circumstances with regard to fraud.

Exam focus point

> Remember your confidentiality checklist from Chapter 2. Refer back to it on page 111. When you are considering whether to make a public interest disclosure, you should always bear it in mind.

Question — Detection of fraud

Required

(a)   Discuss what responsibility auditors have to detect fraud.

(b)   Explain how the auditors might conduct their audit in response to an assessed risk of:

  (i)   Misappropriation
  (ii)   Fraudulent financial reporting

Answer

(a)   The primary responsibility for the prevention and detection of fraud and irregularities rests with management and those charged with governance. This responsibility may be partly discharged by the institution of an adequate system of internal control including, for example, authorisation controls and controls covering segregation of duties.

The auditors should recognise the possibility of material irregularities or frauds which could, unless adequately disclosed, distort the results or state of affairs shown by the financial statements. ISA 240 states that in planning and performing the audit to reduce audit risk to an acceptably low level the auditor should consider the risks of material misstatements in the financial statements due to fraud. Auditors are required to carry out their audit with professional scepticism.

Auditors are required to carry out risk assessment procedures in respect of fraud. This will involve making inquiries of management, considering if any risk factors (such as the existence of pressure for management to meet certain targets) are present and to consider the results of analytical procedures if any method or unexpected relationships have been identified.

If these is an assessed risk of fraud, the auditor must make suitable responses. Overall responses include considering the personnel for the assignment (for example, using more experienced personnel), considering the accounting policies used by the entity (have they changed? Are they reasonable?) and incorporating an element of unpredictability into the audit.

Specific responses to the risk of misstatement at the assertion level due to fraud will vary depending on the circumstances but could include:

*   Changing the nature of audit tests (for example, introducing CAATs if more detail is required about a computerised system)

*   Changing the timing of audit tests (for example, testing throughout an audit period, instead of extending audit conclusions from an interim audit)

*   Changing the extent of audit tests (for example, increasing sample sizes)

(b)   (i)   **Misappropriation**

Employee frauds such as misappropriation are likely to take place when controls are weak. If controls are weak, auditors may not test controls and hence evidence of employee fraud might go undetected. However, if auditors have identified a risk of employee fraud, they might as a response test controls in the relevant area (such as purchases or sales) in order to identify any unexplained patterns in the company's procedures. For example, if a purchase fraud is suspected, auditors might scrutinise authorisation controls to see of a particular member of staff always authorises certain items/for certain people, where the system does not require that.

Many substantive procedures normally performed by the auditors may assist in isolating employee frauds, if they are occurring. For example, tests performed on the receivables ledger may be aimed at revealing overstatement or bad debts, but the design of such tests also assists with cash understatement objectives and may reveal irregularities such as 'teeming and lading'.

(ii) **Fraudulent financial reporting**

If the auditors conclude that there is a high risk of fraudulent financial reporting by management they will concentrate on techniques such as analytical procedures, scrutiny of unusual transactions and all journal entries, review of post balance sheet events (including going concern evaluation), and review of the financial statements and accounting policies for any changes or material distortions.

6 The expectation gap

ISA 240 sets out the current position on the auditor's responsibility to consider fraud, and increased the level of work done by applying the audit risk model. There remains a debate as to whether this is sufficient as the area of fraud is a key part of the expectation gap between what users of auditor's reports believe to be the purposes of the audit compared with the actual nature of the assurance reported to them by auditors.

1   Narrowing the expectation gap

The expectation gap could, theoretically, be narrowed in two ways.

Educating users – the auditor's report as outlined in ISA 700 includes an explanation of the auditor's responsibilities. It is not clear that any further information would help, and it might even have the effect of bringing the value of the audit into question. One suggestion is that auditors could highlight circumstances where they have had to rely on directors' representations.

Extending the auditor's responsibilities – research indicates that extra work by auditors with the inevitable extra costs is likely to make little difference to the detection of fraud because

- most material frauds involve management

- more than half of frauds involve misstated financial reporting but do not include diversion of funds from the company

- management fraud is unlikely to be found in a financial statement audit

- far more is spent on investigating and prosecuting fraud in a company than on its audit

Suggestions for expanding the auditor's role have included:

- requiring auditors to report to boards and audit committees on the adequacy of controls to prevent and detect fraud

- encouraging the use of targeted forensic fraud reviews (see Chapter 14)

- increasing the requirement to report suspected frauds.

Chapter Roundup

- Professional accountants may have professional liability under statutory law.

- Auditors may have professional liability in the tort of negligence.

- The auditor owes a duty of care to the audit client automatically under law.

- The auditor only owes a duty of care to parties other than the audit client if one has been established.

- Auditors may attempt to limit liability to clients. This may not always be effective in law.

- ACCA requires that auditors take out professional indemnity insurance.

- As auditor liability is an important practical issue, there are regularly developments in this area.

- Misunderstanding of the auditor's responsibilities in respect of fraud is a major component of the 'expectation gap'.

Quick Quiz

1   Define fraud

2   Draw a table showing the reporting requirements of ISA 240

3   What three matters must a plaintiff satisfy the court in an action for negligence?

(1)   ....

(2)   ....

(3)   ....

4   Name four aspects of litigation avoidance.

(1)   ....

(2)   ....

(3)   ....

(4)   ....

5   Professional indemnity insurance is insurance against liability arising through any acts of fraud or dishonesty by partners in respect of money held in trust by the firm.

True   ☐

False   ☐

Answers to quick quiz

1   Fraud is the use of deception to obtain unjust or illegal financial advantage and intentional misrepresentation by management, employees or third parties.

2   **REPORTING REQUIREMENTS OF ISA 240**

Management	If the auditors suspect or detect any fraud (even if immaterial) or if a material error is discovered, as soon as they can they should tell management
Those charged with governance	If the auditor has identified fraud involving management, employees with significant roles in internal control, or others, if it results in a material misstatement, they must report it to those charged with governance.
Third parties	Auditors may have a statutory duty to report to a regulator
	Auditors are advised to take legal advice if reporting externally to the company.

3   (1)   A duty of care existed
    (2)   Negligence occurred
    (3)   The client suffered pecuniary loss as a result

4   (1)   Client acceptance procedures
    (2)   Performance of audit work in line with ISAs
    (3)   Quality control
    (4)   Disclaimers

5   False. That is fidelity guarantee insurance.

Now try the question below from the Exam Question Bank

Number	Level	Marks	Time
Q4	Examination	15	27 mins

Part C
Practice management

Quality control

Topic list	Syllabus reference
1 Principles and purpose	C1
2 Quality control at a firm level	C1
3 Quality control on an individual audit	C1

Introduction

The role performed by auditors represents an activity of significant public interest. Quality independent audit is crucial, both to users and to the audit profession. Poor audit quality damages the reputation of the firm and leads to loss of clients and subsequently loss of fees as well as increased litigation and professional insurance costs.

As well as all the specific standards giving guidance on how auditors should perform their work with satisfactory quality these can never cater for every situation. There are two standards dealing with quality at a broader level. These are ISQC1 *Quality Control for firms that Perform Audits and Reviews of Historical Financial Information and other Assurance and Related Services Engagements,* and ISA 220 *Quality Control for Audits of Historical Financial Information.*

Study guide

		Intellectual level
C1	**PRACTICE MANAGEMENT**	
	Quality control	
(a)	Explain the principles and purpose of quality control of audit and other assurance engagements.	1
(b)	Describe the elements of a system of quality control relevant to a given firm.	2
(c)	Select and justify quality control procedures that are applicable to a given audit engagement.	3
(d)	Assess whether an engagement has been performed in accordance with professional standards and whether reports issued are appropriate in the circumstances.	3

Exam guide

Issues relating to quality control can be linked with ethics and liability. You could be asked to suggest quality control procedures that a firm should implement in specific circumstances, or to review a firm's procedures and assess their adequacy.

1 Principles and purpose

Audit quality is not defined in law or through regulations, nor do auditing standards provide a simple definition.

Although each stakeholder in the audit will give a different meaning to audit quality, at its heart it is about delivering an appropriate professional opinion supported by the necessary evidence and objective judgements.

Many principles contribute to audit quality including good leadership, experienced judgement, technical competence, ethical values and appropriate client relationships, proper working practices and effective quality control and monitoring review processes.

The standards on audit quality provide guidance to firms on how to achieve these.

2 Quality control at a firm level

FAST FORWARD

The international standard on quality control (ISQC 1) helps audit firms establish quality standards for their business.

The fact that auditors follow international auditing standards provides a general quality control framework within which audits should be conducted. There are also specific quality control standards.

2.1 Purpose of ISQC 1

ISQC 1.3

The firm should establish a system of quality control designed to provide it with reasonable assurance that the firm and its personnel comply with professional standards and regulatory and legal requirements and that reports issued by the firm or engagement partners are appropriate in the circumstances.

All quality control policies and procedures 'should be **documented** and **communicated** to the firm's personnel'.

We have already considered the sections of this standard relating to ethics in Chapter 2 and those relating to client acceptance will be covered in Chapter 5 of this Study Text. We shall now consider the requirements of the rest of the standard, which fall in the following areas:

- Leadership responsibilities for quality within the firm
- Human resources
- Engagement performance (see also below, the requirements of ISA 220)
- Monitoring

2.2 Leadership responsibilities for quality within the firm

The standard requires that the firm implements policies such that the **internal culture** of the firm is one where **quality** is considered **essential**. Such a culture must be inspired by the leaders of the firm, who must sell this culture in their actions and messages. In other words, the entire business strategy of the audit firm should be driven by the need for quality in its operations.

The firm may appoint an individual or group of individuals to oversee quality in the firm. Such people must have:

- Sufficient and appropriate experience
- The ability to carry out the job
- The necessary authority to carry out the job

2.3 Human resources

The firm's overriding desire for quality will necessitate policies and procedures on ensuring excellence in its staff, to provide the firm with 'reasonable assurance that it has sufficient personnel with the **capabilities**, **competence**, and **commitment to ethical principles** necessary to perform its engagements in accordance with professional standards and regulatory and legal requirements, and to enable the firm or engagement partners to issue reports that are appropriate in the circumstances'.

These will cover the following issues:

- Recruitment
- Capabilities
- Career development
- Compensation

- Performance evaluation
- Competence
- Promotion
- The estimation of personnel needs

The firm is responsible for the ongoing excellence of its staff, though continuing professional development, education, work experience and coaching by more experienced staff.

2.4 Assignment of engagement teams

The assignment of engagement teams is an important matter in ensuring the quality of an individual assignment.

The responsibility for assigning engagement teams is given to the audit engagement partner. The firm should have policies and procedures in place to ensure that:

- Key members of client staff and those charged with governance are aware of the identity of the audit engagement partner
- The engagement partner has appropriate capabilities, competence, authority and time to perform the role
- The engagement partner is aware of his responsibilities as engagement partner

The engagement partner should ensure that he assigns staff of sufficient capabilities, competence and time to individual assignments so that he will be able to issue an appropriate report.

2.5 Engagement performance

The firm should take steps to ensure that engagements are performed correctly, that is, in accordance with standards and guidance. Firms often produce a **manual of standard engagement procedures** to give to all staff so that they know the standards they are working towards. These may be electronic.

Ensuring good engagement performance involves a number of issues:

- Direction
- Supervision
- Review
- Consultation
- Resolution of disputes

Many of these issues will be discussed in the context of an individual audit assignment (see below).

ISQC 1.51

The firm should establish policies and procedures designed to provide it with reasonable assurance that:

(a)   Appropriate consultation takes place on difficult or contentious matters
(b)   Sufficient resources are available to enable appropriate consultation to take place
(c)   The nature and scope of such consultations are documented, and
(d)   Conclusions resulting from consultations are documented and implemented

---

This may involve consulting externally, for example with other firms, or the related professional body (ACCA), particularly when the firm involved is small.

When there are differences of opinion on an engagement team, a report should not be issued until the dispute has been resolved. This may involve the intervention of the quality control reviewer.

Key terms

A **peer review** is a review of an audit file carried out by another partner in the assurance firm.

A **hot review** is a peer review carried out before the audit report is signed.

A **cold review** is a peer review carried out after the audit report is signed.

The firm should have policies and procedures to determine when a quality control reviewer will be necessary for an engagement. This will include all audits of financial statements for listed companies. When required, such a review must be completed before the report is signed.

The firm must also have standards as to what constitutes a suitable quality control review (the nature, timing and extent of such a review, the criteria for eligibility of reviewers and documentation requirements).

Quality control reviews	
Nature, timing and extent	It ordinarily includes discussion with the engagement partner, review of the financial statements/other subject matter information and the report, and consideration of whether the report is appropriate. It will also involve a selective review of working papers relating to significant judgements made.
Eligibility	The reviewer must have sufficient technical expertise and be objective towards the assignment.

Quality control reviews	
Documentation	Documentation showing that the firm's requirements as to a review have been met, that the review was completed before the report was issued and a conclusion that the reviewer is not aware of any unresolved issues.
Listed companies	The review should include: • The engagement team's evaluation of the firm's independence in relation to the specific engagement • Significant risks identified during the engagement and the responses to those risks • Judgements made, particularly with respect to materiality and significant risks • Whether appropriate consultation has taken place on matters involving differences of opinion or other difficult or contentious matters, and the conclusions arising from those consultations • The significance and disposition of corrected and uncorrected misstatements identified during the engagement • The matters to be communicated to management and those charged with governance and, where applicable, other parties such as regulatory bodies • Whether working papers selected for review reflect the work performed in relation to the significant judgements and support the conclusions reached • The appropriateness of the report to be issued

2.6 Monitoring

The standard states that firms must have policies in place to ensure that their quality control procedures are:

- **Relevant**
- **Adequate**
- **Operating effectively**
- **Complied with**

In other words, they must monitor their system of quality control. Monitoring activity should be reported on to the management of the firm on an annual basis.

There are two types of monitoring activity, an ongoing evaluation of the system of quality control and period inspection of a selection of completed engagements. An ongoing evaluation might include such questions as, 'has it kept up to date with regulatory requirements?'

A period inspection cycle would usually fall over a period such as three years, in which time, at least one engagement per engagement partner would be reviewed.

The people monitoring the system are required to evaluate the effect of any **deficiencies** found. These deficiencies might be one-offs. Monitors will be more concerned with **systematic or repetitive deficiencies that require corrective action**. When evidence is gathered that an inappropriate report might have been issued, the audit firm may want to take legal advice.

Corrective action

- Remedial action with an individual
- Communication of findings with the training department
- Changes in the quality control policies and procedures
- If necessary, disciplinary action

3 Quality control on an individual audit

FAST FORWARD

ISA 220 requires firms to implement quality control procedures over individual audit engagements.

The requirements concerning quality control on individual audits are found in ISA (UK and Ireland) 220 *Quality control for audits of historical financial information*. This ISA applies the general principles of the ISQC we looked at in the previous section to an audit.

ISA 220.2

The engagement team should implement quality control procedures that are applicable to the individual audit engagement.

The burden of this falls on the audit engagement partner, who is responsible for the audit and the ultimate conclusion.

3.1 Leadership responsibilities

The engagement partner is required to set an example with regard to the importance of quality.

ISA 220.6

The engagement partner should take responsibility for the overall quality on each audit engagement to which that partner is assigned.

3.2 Ethical requirements

ISA 220.8

The engagement partner should consider whether members of the engagement team have complied with ethical requirements.

This includes the Code of Ethics, with its fundamental principles and all the other detailed requirements. The ISA also contains some detailed guidance about independence in particular.

ISA 220.12

The engagement partner should form a conclusion on compliance with independence requirements that apply to the audit engagement. In doing so, the engagement partner should:

(a)   Obtain relevant information from the firm and, where applicable, network firms, to identify and evaluate circumstances and relationships that create threats to independence

(b)   Evaluate information on identified breaches, if any, of the firm's independence policies and procedures to determine whether they create a threat to independence for the audit engagement

(c)   Take appropriate action to eliminate such threats or reduce them to an acceptable level by applying safeguards. The engagement partner should promptly report to the firm any failure to resolve the matter for appropriate action, and

(d)   Document conclusions on independence and any relevant discussions with the firm that support these conclusions.

3.3 Acceptance/continuance of client relationships and specific audit engagements

The partner is required to ensure that the requirements of the ISQC in respect of accepting and continuing with the audit. If the engagement partner obtains information that would have caused him to decline the audit in the first place he should communicate that information to the firm so that swift action may be taken.

3.4 Assignment of engagement teams

As discussed in the previous section, this is also the responsibility of the audit engagement partner. He must ensure that the team is appropriately qualified and experienced as a unit.

3.5 Engagement performance

There are several factors involved in engagement performance, as previously discussed.

3.5.1 Direction

The partner directs the audit. He is required by other auditing standards to hold a meeting with the audit team to discuss the audit, in particular the risks associated with the audit. This ISA suggests that direction includes 'informing members of the engagement team of:

(a) Their responsibilities (including objectivity of mind and professional scepticism)
(b) The nature of the entity's business
(c) Risk-related issues
(d) Problems that may arise
(e) The detailed approach to the performance of the engagement'

3.5.2 Supervision

The audit is supervised overall by the engagement partner, but more practical supervision is given within the audit team by senior staff to more junior staff, as is also the case with review (see below). It includes:

- Tracking the progress of the audit engagement

- Considering the capabilities and competence of individual members of the team, and whether they have sufficient time and understanding to carry out their work

- Addressing significant issues arising during the audit engagement and modifying the planned approach appropriately

- Identifying matters for consultation or consideration by more experienced engagement team members during the audit engagement

3.5.3 Review

Review includes consideration of whether:

- The work has been performed in accordance with professional standards and regulatory and legal requirements

- Significant matters have been raised for further consideration

- Appropriate consultations have taken place and the resulting conclusions have been documented and implemented

- There is a need to revise the nature, timing and extent of work performed

- The work performed supports the conclusions reached and is appropriately documented
- The evidence obtained is sufficient and appropriate to support the auditor's report, and
- The objectives of the engagement procedures have been achieved

Before the audit report is issued, the engagement partner must be sure that sufficient and appropriate audit evidence has been obtained to support the audit opinion.

3.5.4 Consultation

The partner is also responsible for ensuring that if difficult or contentious matters arise that the team takes appropriate consultation on the matter and that such matters and conclusions are properly recorded.

If differences of opinion arise between the engagement partner and the team, or between the engagement partner and the quality control reviewer, these differences should be resolved according to the firm's policy for such differences of opinion.

3.5.5 Quality control review

The audit engagement partner is responsible for **appointing** a reviewer, if one is required. He is then responsible for discussing significant matters arising with the review and for not issuing the audit report until the quality control review has been completed.

A quality control review should include:

- An evaluation of the **significant judgements** made by the engagement team
- An evaluation of the **conclusions** reached in formulating the auditor's report

A quality control review for a listed entity will include a review of:

- The engagement team's evaluation of the firm's independence towards the audit
- The significant risks identified during the engagement and the responses to those risks (including assessment and response to fraud)
- Judgements made, particularly with respect to materiality and significant risks
- Whether appropriate consultations has taken place on differences of opinion/contentious matters and the conclusions drawn
- Significance and disposition of corrected and uncorrected misstatements identified during the audit
- Matters to be communicated with management/those charged with governance
- Whether the audit documentation selected for review reflects the work performed in relation to significant judgements/supports the conclusions reached
- The appropriateness of the proposed audit report

3.6 Monitoring

The audit engagement partner is required to consider the results of monitoring of the firm's quality control systems and consider whether they have any impact on the specific audit he is conducting.

Question | Quality control issues

You are an audit senior working for the firm Addystone Fish. You are currently carrying out the audit of Wicker Ltd, a manufacturer of waste paper bins. You are unhappy with Wicker's inventory valuation policy and have raised the issue several times with the audit manager. He has dealt with the client for a number of years and does not see what you are making a fuss about. He has refused to meet you on site to discuss these issues.

The former engagement partner to Wicker retired two months ago. As the audit manager had dealt with Wicker for so many years, the other partners have decided to leave the audit of Wicker in his capable hands.

Required

Comment on the situation outlined above.

Answer

Several quality control issues are raised in the above scenario:

Engagement partner

An engagement **partner** is usually appointed to each audit engagement undertaken by the firm, to take responsibility for the engagement on behalf of the firm. Assigning the audit to the experienced audit manager is not sufficient.

The lack of audit engagement partner also means that several of the requirements of ISA 220 about ensuring that arrangements in relation to independence and directing, supervising and reviewing the audit are not in place.

Conflicting views

In this scenario the audit manager and senior have conflicting views about the valuation of inventory. This does not appear to have been handled well, with the manager refusing to discuss the issue with the senior.

ISA 220 requires that the audit engagement partner takes responsibility for settling disputes in accordance with the firm's policy in respect of resolution of disputes required by ISQC 1. In this case, the lack of engagement partner may have contributed to this failure to resolve the disputes. In any event, at best, the failure to resolve the dispute is a breach of the firm's policy under ISQC 1. At worst, it indicates that the firm does not have a suitable policy concerning such disputes as required by ISQC 1.

3.7 Quality control regulations

The regulation of audit is the same for all audit firms regardless of size. However, it is logical to see that it will impact on large and small firms differently.

For example, a large firm may have international quality control procedures. If not, it will certainly have national and regional ones. In order to meet some of the quality control requirements of the APB, small, single-partner firms may need to make extensive use of external experts.

Chapter Roundup

- The international standard on quality control (ISQC 1) helps audit firms establish quality standards for their business.
- ISA 220 requires firms to implement quality control procedures over individual audit engagements.

Quick Quiz

1   The purpose of ISQC 1 is to:

'Establish a system of .... designed to provide it with .... assurance that the firm and its personnel comply with .... standards and .... requirements and that .... issued by the firm or engagement partners are .... in the circumstances.'

2   List five issues relating to good engagement performance that should be addressed in an audit firm's procedures manual

(1)

(2)

(3)

(4)

(5)

3   Who carries out review in an audit of financial statements?

Answers to Quick Quiz

1   Quality control, reasonable, reports, appropriate

2   (1)   Direction
      (2)   Supervision
      (3)   Review
      (4)   Consultation
      (5)   Resolution of dispute

3   Audit work is generally reviewed by the staff member next more senior on the team than the person who
      did the work. The partner must carry out a review to ensure there is sufficient and appropriate evidence to
      support the audit opinion. It might also be necessary under the firm's quality control policies to obtain a
      quality control review by a suitable person outside the audit team. This will be necessary if the audit is of a
      listed entity.

Now try the question below from the Pilot Paper Question Bank

Number	Level	Marks	Time
Q3	Examination	20	36 mins

Obtaining and accepting professional appointments

5

Topic list	Syllabus reference
1 Change in auditors	C3
2 Advertising and fees	C2
3 Tendering	C3
4 Acceptance	C4
5 Agreeing terms	C4
6 Books and documents	C4

Introduction

It is a commercial fact that companies change their auditors. The question that firms of auditors need to understand the answer to is; **why do companies change their auditors?** We shall examine some of the common reasons here.

Related to the fact that entities change their auditors is the fact that **many auditing firms advertise their services**. The ACCA have set out rules for members who advertise their services. We shall examine these rules and the reasons behind them in Section 2.

As we will discover in section 1, the **audit fee** can be a very key item for an entity when it makes decisions about its auditors. Determining the price to offer to potential clients can be a difficult process, but it is just one part of the whole process that is **tendering**. Audits are often put out to tender by companies. We shall examine all the matters firms consider when tendering for an audit in Section 3.

Linked in with the tendering process is the process **of determining whether to accept the audit engagement** if it is offered. ISQC I sets out some basic requirements for all audit firms accepting engagements. This is discussed in Sections 4 and 5.

The general issues surrounding transferring **books and documents** are discussed in Section 6.

Study guide

		Intellectual level
2	**Advertising, publicity, obtaining professional work and fees**	
(a)	Explain the need for guidance in these areas.	2
(b)	Recognise situations in which specified advertisements are acceptable.	2
(c)	Discuss the restrictions on practice descriptions, the use of the ACCA logo and the names of practising firms.	2
(d)	Discuss the extent to which reference to fees may be made in promotional material.	2
(e)	Outline the determinants of fee-setting and justify the bases	2
(f)	Discuss the ethical and other professional problems involved in establishing and negotiating fees for a specified assignment.	2
3	**Tendering**	
(a)	Discuss the reasons why entities change their auditors/professional accountants.	2
(b)	Recognise and explain the matters to be considered when a firm is invited to submit a proposal or fee quote for an audit or other professional engagement.	2
(c)	Identify the information required for a proposal.	2
(d)	Prepare the content of an engagement proposal document.	2
(e)	Discuss and appraise the criteria that might be used to evaluate tenders received from audit firms in a given situation.	2
(f)	Discuss reasons why audit fees may be lowered from the previous year's fees.	2
(g)	Explain 'lowballing' and discuss whether or not it impairs independence.	2
4	**Professional appointments**	
(a)	Explain the matters to be considered and the procedures that an audit firm/ professional accountant should carry out before accepting a specified new client/engagement including:	2
(i)	client acceptance	
(ii)	engagement acceptance	
(iii)	agreeing the terms of engagement	
(b)	Recognise the key issues that underlie the agreement of the scope and terms of an engagement with a client.	2
(c)	Outline the procedures for the transfer of books, papers and information following a new appointment.	1

Exam guide

Ethics is a key topic area and many of the issues in this chapter are ethical. You could be faced with a change in appointment scenario in the exam. The issues surrounding a change in auditors has often been examined in the past with scenarios featuring tendering and audit staffing.

BPP
LEARNING MEDIA

1 Change in auditors

Common reasons behind companies changing the auditor include audit fee, auditor not seeking re-election and size of company.

1.1 Why do companies change their auditors?

It is a fact of life that companies change their auditors sometimes. Not all new clients of a firm are new businesses, some have decided to change from their previous auditors. Obviously, it is often not in the interests of audit firms to lose clients. Therefore a key issue in practice management for auditors is to understand why companies change their auditors, so that, as far as they are able, they can seek to prevent it.

Question

Change of auditors

Before you read the rest of this chapter, spend a minute thinking about the reasons that companies might change their auditors. You might want to shut the Study Text and write them down and then compare them with the reasons that we give in the rest of this section.

Answer

Read through the rest of section 1 and compare your answer to ours.

The following diagram shows some of the more common reasons that companies might change their auditors.

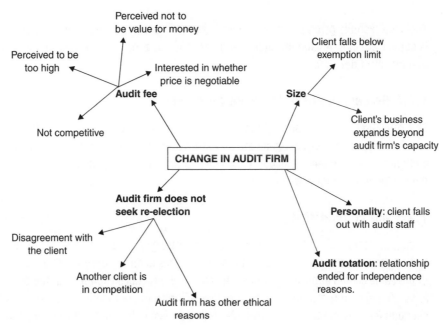

1.2 Audit fee

The audit fee can be a very **sensitive issue**. Audit is required by statute. Many people perceive that it has very little intrinsic value. Therefore, when setting audit fees, auditors must take account of the fact that clients may hold this opinion. Setting fees will be discussed later in the chapter. Here, we shall explore some of the fee related reasons that companies change their auditors.

1.2.1 Perceived to be too high

This is a common reason for auditors being changed. It is strongly linked to people's perception that audit has no intrinsic value. If directors of a company believe that audit is a necessary evil, they will seek to obtain it for as little money as they can.

Much of the 'value', in cost terms, of an audit is carried out away from a client's premises. This is because the most expensive audit staff (managers and partners) often do not carry out their audit work on site. If the client does not understand this, the following sort of situation may arise.

 Case Study

Bob is the owner-manager of Fixings Ltd, a small business which manufactures metal fixings. It has a turnover of £4.5 million and the auditors come in for the second week of October every year. Every year a different senior is in charge and he or she asks similar questions to the ones asked the previous year, because the business rarely changes and the audit is low risk. The partner and manager rarely attend the audit itself because it is not considered cost effective or necessary to do so.

Bob's audit fee was set at £4,500 five years ago when the business was incorporated for tax and inheritance reasons, and has gone up at three percent a year ever since. It now stands at £5,200. During that time, he has paid the same firm £1,200 a year to organise his tax return and deal with the tax authorities on his behalf. He considers this service far more valuable as he has no understanding of tax issues and is exceedingly nervous of a taxation inspection.

Bob cannot understand how the audit fee is four times the size of the tax fee when the auditors attend for a week and do the same work every year. He is also irritated that it continues to steadily rise while the service does not change.

The case example given above is a little exaggerated and generalisations have been made. However, there is some truth in it. An auditor understands the costs that go in to making up the audit fee. It is essential that the client does too.

1.2.2 Perceived not to be value for money

This often goes hand in hand with the audit fee being seen to be too high. In the above example of Bob and Fixings Ltd, this was certainly the case. However, it is possible that a company could be paying their audit firm a fee that they consider reasonable for an audit, they just believe that another firm could give them a better audit for a similar fee.

1.2.3 Not competitive

Again, this issue can be linked with the value for money perception. It is true to say that in some cases, audit firms will offer audit services at low prices. This is on the grounds that they then sell other services to the same clients at profitable prices. It is through practices like this that the problem of lowballing can arise. You should remember the issue of lowballing from your earlier studies. In such conditions, a well-set audit fee may not be competitive even if it is a reasonable fee for the service provided.

1.2.4 Interest in whether price is negotiable

This reason may be linked to all of the above fee-related issues, or it may just arise out of interest on the client's part. It costs the client very little except some time on his part to put his audit out to tender. He might even do this with every intention of keeping the present auditor.

Putting the audit out to tender would give him more insight into how competitive his audit fee is and keep his auditor 'honest', in that he will have to justify his fee and risk it being higher than competitors in the tender.

The by-product might be that he receives a competitive tender which offers him far more than he receives from his current auditor and he changes his auditor anyway. It could also mean that, when forced to justify his position, the current auditor reassesses his service and comes up with a far more competitive deal.

1.3 The auditor does not seek re-election

Another key reason for the auditor changing is that the auditor chooses not to stand for election for another year. You should be familiar with many of the reasons behind this:

- There could be ethical reasons behind the auditor choosing not to stand
- The auditor might have to resign for reasons of competition between clients
- The auditor might disagree with the client over accounting policies
- The auditor might not want to reduce his audit fee

Question	Ethical reasons

Name three ethical reasons why an auditor might not seek re-election or might resign, explaining the nature of the problem and the reasoning behind the resignation.

Answer

As you know from your earlier studies and from studying Chapter 2, there are countless ethical issues that could have arisen. Here are some common ones. Refer to Chapter 2 if you have included one that does not appear here.

(a)   **Fee level**

The audit fee which is necessary to carry out the audit at a profit may have reached a level which is inappropriate according to the ACCA's guidance on fee levels. If the audit fee constituted more than 15% of the total practice income, this would be considered to be an independence problem. This is because the audit opinion might be influenced by a fear of losing the client.

In such a situation, or if the practice had a large client below the limits but whose forecast suggested future growth, it might be necessary for the auditor to end the relationship to ensure that he did not become dependent on the client.

(b)   **Integrity of management**

The auditor might feel that he has reason to doubt the integrity of management. There are many reasons why this could be the case. It could be as a result of a breakdown in relationship, or an unproven suspected fraud.

However, if the auditor does not feel that the client is trustworthy he should not continue his relationship with him.

(c)   **Other services**

The auditor may offer a number of services to the client. He may be offered some lucrative consultancy work by the client which he wants to undertake, but he feels that the independence of the audit will be severely affected by the provision of the consultancy work because of the heavy involvement that means he will have in the client's business.

As the audit fee is substantially lower than the fees associated with the consultancy work and the auditor is trying to develop his business advice department, he may decide to resign from the audit to take on the consultancy.

1.4 Size of the company

This can be a major reason for a change in auditors. There are two key reasons, one of which has been touched on already.

- Client experiences rapid growth to the point where the audit is no longer practicable for the audit firm.

- Client retrenches or restructures in such a way that it no longer needs a statutory audit.

In the first instance, the auditor may no longer be able to provide the audit for several reasons:

- Insufficient resources
- Staff
- Time
- Fee level issue

In the second instance, the client has chosen no longer to take advantage of the audit.

In either situation, there is little that the auditor can do to prevent losing the work.

1.5 Other reasons

These reasons may have been touched on in relation to the other reasons given above. We shall consider them briefly here.

1.5.1 Personality

For many small owner-managed companies, audit is almost a personal service. The relationship between such a client and auditor may be strongly based on personality, and if relationships break down, it may be necessary for the audit relationship to discontinue.

Personality may not be such an issue for bigger entities and audit firms where the audit engagement partner could be transferred if required, while the audit stayed within the firm.

1.5.2 Audit rotation

Rotation of audit staff was discussed in Chapter 2 as a safeguard to audit independence. However, the partners in a firm may sometimes conclude that the firm as a whole has been associated too long with a client and divest the audit.

Exam focus point

From the nature of the issues raised above, it is clear that some of them will affect small firms and not larger ones and some will more pre-dominantly affect larger ones. You should bear that in mind when approaching exam questions, and as usual, apply common sense.

BPP
LEARNING MEDIA

Question   **Control over re-appointment**

(a) Of the reasons for a change in auditors given above, which do you feel that an auditor may have control over and which he can therefore guard against? Ignore the cases when the auditor does not seek re-election or resigns.

(b) What should the auditor do to guard against the issues you have identified in part (a)?

Answer

(a) **Issues auditor may have control over**

There are two key issues identified above that an auditor may have some control over:

(i) **Fees**

- Perception
- Competitiveness

(ii) **Personality**

(b) **Actions to guard against issues arising**

(i) With regard to fees, the auditor can ensure that the audit is conducted in such a way as to foster the perception that the audit is good value for the fee. This can be done by encouraging the attitude of audit staff and ensuring that a professional manner is always maintained. It also requires a constant awareness by staff of the need to add value, and to ensure that the audit provides more of a service than fulfilling a statutory requirement. This can be achieved by offering relevant advice to the client as a by-product of the audit, predominantly through the report to management, but also as an integral part of the culture of the audit.

(ii) Also with regard to fees, the auditor can ensure he is competitive in the first instance, by setting reasonable fees and in the second instance by conducting research into what his competitors charge. As companies have to file accounts and the audit fee must be disclosed, this is readily available information.

(iii) Personality is obviously not an issue that an auditor can legislate against. However, part of an auditor's professionalism is to ensure that if personality problems arise, they are handled sensitively and they arise only due to issues on the side of the client.

If serious conflict arise, firms should have a procedure for rotating audits between audit partners.

2 Advertising and fees   6/04

FAST FORWARD

ACCA's general rule on advertising is 'the medium used should not reflect adversely on the member or the accountancy profession'.

2.1 ACCA guidance

Auditors are in business, and in business it is necessary to advertise. However, accountants are professional people and people rely on their work. It is important therefore that their advertisements do not project an image that is inconsistent with that fact.

ACCA gives guidance about advertising in the Code of Ethics and Conduct. In general, ACCA allows members to advertise their work in any way they see fit. In other words, it is a matter of judgement for the member. This is subject to the following general rule:

> **ACCA STATEMENT**
>
> 'The medium used to advertise **should not reflect adversely** on the member, ACCA or the accountancy profession.'

And the following guidance.

> **ACCA STATEMENT**
>
> Advertisements and promotional material should **not**:
>
> - Discredit the services offered by others whether by claiming superiority for the member's or firm's own services or otherwise
> - Be misleading, either directly or by implication
> - Fall short of the requirements of the British Code of Advertising Practice and the IBA Code of Advertising Standards and Practices, including
>   - Legality
>   - Decency
>   - Clarity
>   - Honesty
>   - Truthfulness

2.2 Fees

FAST FORWARD

It is generally inappropriate to advertise fees.

Three issues arise with regard to fees:

- Referring to fees in promotional material
- Commissions
- Setting and negotiating fees

The last two issues are inter-related and are also closely connected with tendering, which is discussed in the next section.

2.2.1 Advertising fees

The fact that it is difficult to explain the service represented by a single fee in the context of an advertisement and that **confusion might arise as to what a potential client might expect to receive in return for that fee** means that it is **seldom appropriate** to include information about fees in short advertisements.

In longer advertisements, where reference is made to fees in promotional material, the **basis** on which those fees are calculated, hourly and other charging rates etc, **should be clearly stated**.

The key issue to remember with regard to advertising fees is that the **greatest care should be taken to not mislead potential clients**. It is appropriate to advertise free consultations to discuss fee issues. This free consultation will allow fees to be explained, thus avoiding the risk of confusion. It is inappropriate to advertise discounts on existing fees.

2.2.2 Setting and negotiating fees

As this is a key part of the tendering process, this is discussed below in Section 3.

2.2.3 Commissions

Members may accept or pay referral fees if appropriate safeguards exist.

ACCA members may offer commission (and by implication receive commission) for introducing clients. However, they should only do so if there are appropriate safeguards such as making full disclosure.

2.3 Use of the ACCA logo

Members of the ACCA may be either associates or fellows. In which case they are allowed to use the designatory letters ACCA or FCCA behind their name.

A firm may describe itself as a firm of 'Chartered Certified Accountants' where:

- At least half of the partners are ACCA members, and
- Those partners hold at least 51% of voting rights under the partnership agreement

A firm in which all the partners are Chartered Certified Accountants may use the description 'Members of the Association of Chartered Certified Accountants'.

A firm which holds a firm's auditing certificate from ACCA may describe itself as Registered Auditors.

Question
Advertising and fees

Felicity Carr and Frank Harrison both qualified as chartered certified accountants five years ago. They have now decided to set up in practice together. Their new firm holds an auditing certificate from ACCA and they intend to undertake small audits and some tax work. They will charge themselves out at £100 per hour initially. They will operate from Frank's home. They are a little rusty on the rules concerning advertising and obtaining professional work and so have asked you to advise them.

They have decided to call their practice Harrison Carr and to advertise in the local paper. As they are launching themselves, they have decided to take out a full page advertisement one week and then run a series of smaller adverts in the future. They have also decided to advertise in a local business newspaper.

Required

(a) Explain the ACCA guidance on advertising, including advertising fees.

(b) Advise Harrison Carr how they should proceed in relation to:

    (i) How they may describe the firm
    (ii) The adverts in the paper

Answer

(a) **General guidance on advertising**

Generally members may not advertise in a manner that reflects adversely on themselves and their profession. This means that they should consider the quality of the paper they intend to advertise in. The local paper is appropriate. They should also ensure that they do not discredit the services offered by others in their advert.

Advertising fees

The key issue of importance when advertising fees is to ensure that the reference to fees is not misleading. Generally, it is seldom appropriate to mention fees on a small advert.

(b) (ii) **Description of firm**

As both partners are chartered certified accountants it is acceptable to advertise the firm as being a member of the association of chartered certified accountants. They may also describe themselves as registered auditors.

(iii) **The proposed advertisements**

While they are planning a larger advert followed by several smaller ones, it may still not be appropriate to mention fees. This is because while they could refer to charge out rates, it would be impossible in the paper to describe how much each service would cost without estimating the time jobs would take. It is impossible to generalise such matters and the reference to fees could therefore be misleading.

It would be more appropriate to advertise that they will give free consultations to discuss fees. They may include all the details given above, their name, the membership of the ACCA and their registered auditor status.

3 Tendering

When approaching a tender, it is important to consider both fees and practical issues.

3.1 Approach

A firm puts together a tender if

- It has been approached by a prospective client, and
- The partners have decided that they are capable of doing the work for a reasonable fee.

When approached to tender, the auditor has to consider whether he wants to do the work. You should be aware of all the ethical considerations that would go into this decision. The auditor will also have to consider

- Fees
- Practical issues

3.1.1 Fees

Determining whether the job can be done for a reasonable price will involve a substantial number of estimates. The key estimate will be how long the partner thinks it will take to do the work. This will involve meeting with the prospective client to discuss their business and systems and making the estimate from there.

The first stage of setting the fee is therefore to ascertain **what the job will involve**. The job should be broken down into its respective parts, for example, audit and tax, or if it is a complex and/or pure audit, what aspects of the job would be undertaken by what level staff.

The second stage is closely linked with the first, therefore. It involves **ascertaining which staff**, or which level of staff, **will be involved** and in what proportions they will be involved.

Once estimates have been made of how long the work will take and what level of expertise is needed in each area, **the firm's standard charge out rates can be applied** to that information, and a **fee estimated**.

Clearly, it is **commercially vital** that the estimates of time and costs are **reasonable**, or the audit firm will be seeking to undertake the work at a loss. However, it is also ethically important that the fee estimate is reasonable, or the result will be that the client is being misled about the sustainable fee level.

3.1.2 Lowballing

Problems can arise when auditing firms appear to be charging less than this, or at least less than the 'market rate' for the audit. The practice of undercutting, usually at tender for the audit of large companies, has been called **lowballing**. In other cases, the audit fee has been reduced even though the auditors have remained the same. The problem here is that, if the audit is being performed for less than it is actually worth, then the auditors' independence is called into question.

This is always going to be a topical debate, but in terms of negotiating the audit fee the following factors need to be taken into account.

(a)   The audit is perceived to have a fluctuating 'market price' as any other commodity or service. In a recession, prices would be expected to fall as companies aim to cut costs everywhere, and as auditors chase less work (supply falls). Audit firms are also reducing staffing levels and their own overhead costs should be lower.

(b)   Companies can **reduce external audit costs** through various legitimate measures:

- Extending the size and function of internal audit
- Reducing the number of different audit firms used world-wide
- Selling off subsidiary companies leaving a simplified group structure to audit
- The tender process itself simply makes auditors more competitive
- Exchange rate fluctuations in audit fees

(c)   Auditing firms have increased productivity, partly through the use of more sophisticated information technology techniques in auditing.

The ACCA's guidance on quotations states that it is **not improper** to secure work by **quoting a lower fee** so long as the **client has not been misled** about the level of work that the fee represents.

In the event of investigations into allegations of unsatisfactory work, the level of fees would be considered with regard to member's conduct with reference to the ethical guidelines.

3.1.3 Practical issues

The firm will have to consider the practical points arising from the approach. Common considerations include:

- Does the proposed timetable for the work fit with the current work plan?
- Does the firm have suitable personnel available?
- Where will the work be performed and is it accessible/cost effective?
- Are (non-accounting) specialist skills necessary?
- Will staff need further training to do the work?
- If so, what is the cost of that further training?

Certain information will be required to put together a proposal document. This has already been touched on briefly, when discussing the audit fee. It is likely that audit staff would have to have a meeting with the prospective client to discuss the following issues:

- What the client requires from the audit firm, for example:

    - Audit
    - Number of visits (interim and final)
    - Tax work

- What the future plans of the entity are, for example:

    - Is it planning to float its shares on an exchange in the near future?
    - Is growth, or diversification anticipated?

- Whether the entity is seeking its first auditors and needs an explanation of audit

- Whether the entity is seeking to change its auditors
- If the entity is changing its auditors, the reason behind this

3.2 Content of an audit proposal

An audit proposal, or tender, does not have a set format. The prospective client will indicate the format that he wants the tender to take. This may be merely in document form, or could be a presentation by members of the audit firm.

Although each tender will be tailored to the individual circumstances, there are some matters which are likely to be covered in every one. These are set out below.

Matters to be included in audit proposal
• The fee, and how it has been calculated
• An assessment of the needs of the prospective client
• An outline of how the firm intends to meet those needs
• The assumptions made to support that proposal
• The proposed approach to the engagement
• A brief outline of the firm
• An outline of the key staff involved

If the tender is being submitted to an **existing client**, some of those details will be unnecessary. However, if it is a competitive tender, the firm should ensure they submit a comparable tender, even if some of the details are already known to the client. This is because the tender must be **comparable** to competitors and must appear professional.

3.3 Evaluation of a tender

Each company will have its own criteria for what it wants from a firm of auditors. This means that there are no hard and fast rules about how a tender will be evaluated. However, there are some general points to bear in mind when putting together a proposal.

Evaluation factors	
Fee	The fee, as discussed earlier, **can be the most important factor** for people assessing tenders. It is possible that a reader might look at the fee and decide not to continue reading the tender, despite the rest of the content.
Professionalism	Auditors provide a **professional service** and the first impressions a prospective client may have of the firm are the staff involved with the proposal and the tender document itself. It is therefore vital that the professionalism which should mark the audit relationship is clear.
Proposed approach	An audit can cause a disruption to the ordinary course of a business, particularly in the finance department. The client might be seeking the **least disruptive approach**. This might mean they look for an audit with the shortest number of proposed days on site.
Personal service	It is important that the relationship between the auditors and the management of the entity is good and the client perceives that they are getting value for money. It is important to highlight key staff and to **foster relationships** with management from the outset of a relationship, and this means during the tender process.

4 Acceptance

FAST FORWARD

ISQC 1 sets out what a firm must consider and document in relation to accepting or continuing engagement, which is, the integrity of the client, whether the firm is competent to do the work, whether the firm meets the ethical requirements in relation to the work.

4.1 Ethical requirements

There are a number of ethical procedures associated with accepting engagements which you have studied previously.

Knowledge brought forward from earlier studies

From paper F8 Audit and Assurance (or equivalent)

Procedures before accepting nomination

(a) Ensure that there are **no ethical issues** which are a **barrier** to accepting nomination.

(b) Ensure that the auditor is **professionally qualified** to act and that there are no legal or technical barriers.

(c) Ensure that the existing **resources** are **adequate** in terms of staff, expertise and time.

(d) Obtain **references for the directors** if they are not known personally to the audit firm.

(e) **Consult the previous auditors** to ensure that there are not any reasons behind the vacancy which the new auditors ought to know. This is also a courtesy to the previous auditors.

Procedures after accepting nomination

(a) **Ensure** that the **outgoing auditors' removal** or **resignation** has been **properly conducted** in accordance with the law.

   The new auditors should see a valid notice of the outgoing auditors' resignation, or confirm that the outgoing auditors were properly removed.

(b) **Ensure** that the **new auditors' appointment is valid**. The new auditors should obtain a copy of the resolution passed at the general meeting appointing them as the company's auditors.

(c) Set up and **submit a letter of engagement** to the directors of the company (see below).

4.2 Requirements of ISQC 1

We touched on some of the bulk of the requirements of ISQC 1 *Quality control for firms that perform audits and reviews of historical information and other assurance and related services assignments* in Chapter 4. However, it sets out standards and guidance in connection with the acceptance and continuance of client relationships and specific engagements which we shall consider here.

> **ISQC 1.28**
>
> The firm should establish policies and procedures for the acceptance and continuance of client relationships and specific engagements designed to provide it with reasonable assurance that it will only undertake or continue relationships and engagements where it:
>
> (a)   Has considered the integrity of the client and does not have information that would lead it to conclude that the client lacks integrity
>
> (b)   Is competent to perform the engagement and has the capabilities, time and resources to do so, and
>
> (c)   Can comply with ethical requirements.
>
> The firm should obtain such information as it considers necessary in the circumstances before accepting an engagement with a new client, when deciding whether to continue an existing engagement, and when considering acceptance of a new engagement with an existing client. Where issues have been identified, and the firm decides to accept or continue the client relationship or a specific engagement, it should document how the issues were resolved.

The firm should carry out the following steps:

Step 1   Obtain relevant information

Step 2   Identify relevant issues

Step 3   If resolvable issues exist, resolve them and document that resolution

4.2.1 Obtain information

The standard outlines three general sources of information:

- The communications auditors must make with the previous auditors according to the IFAC code
- Other relevant communications, for example with other parties in the firm, bankers or legal counsel
- Searches on relevant databases

In deciding whether to continue an engagement with an existing client, or to accept a new engagement with an existing client, the firm should also consider significant matters that have arisen in the course of the previous/existing relationship, for example, expansion into a business area in which the audit firm has no experience.

4.2.2 Identify issues

The standard gives a list of matters that the auditors might consider in relation to the acceptance decision.

Matters to consider	
Integrity of a client	The identity and business reputation of the client's principal owners, key management, related parties and those charged with governance
	Nature of the client's operations, including its business practices
	Information concerning the attitude of the client's principal owners, key management, those charged with governance towards matters such as aggressive interpretation of accounting standards/internal control environment
	Whether the client is aggressively concerned with maintaining the firm's fees as low as possible
	Indications of an inappropriate limitation in the scope of work
	Indications that the client might be involved in money laundering or other criminal activities
	The reasons for the proposed appointment of the firm and non-reappointment of the previous firm

Matters to consider	
Competence of the firm	Do firm personnel have knowledge of relevant industries/subject matters?
	Do firm personnel have experience with relevant regulatory or reporting requirements, or the ability to gain the necessary skills and knowledge effectively?
	Does the firm have sufficient personnel with the necessary capabilities and competence?
	Are experts available, if needed?
	Are individuals meeting the criteria and eligibility requirements to perform the engagement quality control review available where applicable?
	Is the firm able to complete the engagement within the reporting deadline?

In addition, the firm needs to consider whether acceptance would create any conflicts of interest.

ISQC 1.34

Where the firm obtains information that would have caused it to decline an engagement if that information had been available earlier, policies and procedures on the continuance of the engagement and the client relationship should include consideration of:

(a)   The professional and legal responsibilities that apply to the circumstances, including whether there is a requirement for the firm to report to the person or persons who made the appointment or, in some cases, to regulatory authorities, and

(b)   The possibility of withdrawing from the engagement or from both the engagement and the client relationship

---

Such procedures might include discussions with client management and those charged with governance, and, if required, discussions with the appropriate regulatory authority.

Exam focus point

In a past exam, 10 marks of a case study question were available for outlining matters to consider before accepting a due diligence engagement. It is important, when attempting such a question, to tailor your answer to the question and not just give a list of general points, such as those given above. So, for instance instead of "consider management", identify key personnel and refer to them by name in your answer highlighting any specific concerns you might have about them specifically from information given in the question.

Question

Accepting nomination

You are a partner in Hamlyn, Jones and Co, a firm of Chartered Certified Accountants. You have just successfully tendered for the audit of Lunch Limited, a chain of sandwich shops across West London. The tender opportunity was received cold, that is, the company and its officers are not known to the firm. The company has just been incorporated and has not previously had an audit. You are about ready to accept nomination.

(a)   Explain the procedures should you carry out prior to accepting nomination.

In the course of your acceptance procedures you received a reference from a business contact of yours concerning one of the five directors of Lunch Limited, Mr V Loud. It stated that your business contact had done some personal tax work for Mr Loud ten years previously, when he had found Mr Loud to be difficult to keep in contact with, slow to provide information and he had suspected Mr Loud of being economical with the truth when it came to his tax affairs. As a result of this distrust, he had ceased to carry out work for him.

(b)   Comment on the effect this reference would have accepting nomination.

Answer

(a)   The following procedures should be carried out:

- Ensure that I and my audit team are professionally qualified to act and consider whether there are ethical barriers to my accepting nomination.

- Review the firm's overall work programme to ensure that there are sufficient resources to enable my firm to carry out the audit.

- Obtain references about the directors as they are not known personally by me or anyone else in my firm.

(b)   The auditor must use his professional judgement when considering the responses he gets to references concerning new clients. The guidance cannot legislate for all situations so it does not. In the circumstance given above there is no correct answer therefore, in practice an auditor would have to make a justified decision which he then documented.

Matters to be considered

The reference raises three issues for the auditor considering accepting nomination.

- The issue that the director has been difficult to maintain a relationship with in the past
- The issue that the director was slow to provide information in the past
- The suspicion of a lack of integrity in relation to his tax affairs.

The auditor must **consider** these **in the light of several factors**:

- The length of time that has passed since the events

- What references which refer to the interim time say

- The difference between accepting a role of auditing a company and personal tax work

- The director's role in the company and therefore the audit

- The amount of control exercised by the director

  - Relationships with other directors
  - Influence

At this stage he **should not be considering** how highly he **values** the **opinion** of the referee. That should have been considered before he sent the reference. At this stage he should only be considering the implications of the reference for his current decision.

Auditing a company is different from auditing personal affairs in terms of obtaining information and contacting personnel. In this case, the **key issue** is the question over the **integrity** of the director.

As we do not have information about interim references and details of the business arrangements it is difficult to give a definite answer to this issue. However, Mr Loud is likely to only have **limited control over decisions** of the entity being one of five directors, which might lead to the auditor deciding that the reference was insufficient to prevent him accepting nomination. If Mr Loud were the **finance director**, the auditor would be more inclined not to take the nomination.

Exam focus point	You can see from the answer above that there are no easy answers to ethical questions. You might be asked questions in the exam similar to the one above as part of a scenario highlighting several ethical issues. It is not enough just to state the rules at this level, you must **explain** what the practical issues are and try to **draw conclusions** based on the facts you know. Once qualified, you may face issues like this in your working life and will have to make judgements like this in practice. That is what the exam is trying to imitate.

4.3 Money laundering

As we discussed in Chapter 2, accountants are now required to carry out specific client identification procedures when accepting new clients.

'**Know your client**' (KYC) is an important part of being in a position to comply with the law on money laundering, because as we mentioned in Chapter 2, knowledge of the client is at the bottom of 'suspicion' in the context of making reports about money laundering.

It is important from the outset of a relationship with a new client to obtain KYC information, such as,

- Expected patterns of business
- The business model of the client
- The source of the client's funds

When the client's money is to be handled by the professional, there is a higher than normal risk to the professional, so even more detailed KYC procedures will be required.

4.4 Politically exposed persons (PEPs)

Being involved with PEPs may be particularly risky for firms, particularly in terms of reputation risks if things go wrong.

Key term

> **Politically exposed persons** are individuals who are, or have been, entrusted with prominent public functions in a foreign country (for example, heads of state or senior politicians and officials).

Firms and institutions should have risk management systems set up to determine whether an individual is a PEP when client identification procedures are being carried out. When a person has been identified as a PEP, a member of senior management should approve establishing a business relationship with that person.

The firm should then take reasonable measures to establish the source of that individual's wealth and funds and conduct enhanced ongoing monitoring of the firm's relationship with that individual.

4.5 Client screening

Many audit firms use a client acceptance checklist to assist them in making the decision. and ensuring that such requirements are met. An example of a client acceptance checklist is given in the appendix towards the back of this Study Text.

5 Agreeing terms

FAST FORWARD

Certain issues must be agreed in writing when an audit is accepted.

5.1 Clarifying the agreement

It is important when entering into a contract to provide services to ensure that both parties fully understand what the agreed services are. Misunderstanding could lead to a break down in the relationship, and eventually result in legal action being undertaken.

5.2 Engagement letter

An auditor will outline the basis for the audit agreement in his tender to provide services. However, once he has accepted nomination, it is vital that the basis of his relationship is discussed with the new client and laid out in contractual form. This is the role of the **engagement letter**, which you should be familiar with.

Matters which should be clarified in the audit agreement

- **Responsibilities** of both parties
    - Auditor is responsible for reporting on the financial statements to members
    - Directors have a statutory duty to maintain records and take responsibility for the financial statements
    - Directors are responsible for the detection and prevention of fraud
- **Fees**
    - Level
    - Billing and credit terms
    - Potential increases
- **Timing**
    - Audit timing

An example of an engagement letter is given in the appendix of this text. You should already be familiar with it. ISA (UK and Ireland) 210, *Terms of audit engagements* sets out best practice concerning engagement letters.

In practice, the auditor and the new client will meet to negotiate the terms of the audit agreement, which the auditor will later clarify in the engagement letter. The first audit should not take place until the client has returned the engagement letter with an indication that he agrees to its terms.

 Question **Engagement letter**

ISA 210 lists a series of matters which may be referred to in an engagement letter. What are they?

Answer

The ISA includes the following matters in paragraphs 6 to 8:

- The objective of the audit of financial statements
- Management's responsibility for the financial statements
- The applicable reporting framework
- The scope of the audit, including reference to applicable legislation, regulations, or pronouncements of professional bodies to which the auditor adheres
- The form of any reports or other communication of results of the engagement
- The fact that because of the test nature and other inherent limitations of an audit, together with the inherent limitations of any accounting and internal control system, there is an unavoidable risk that even some material misstatement may remain undiscovered
- Unrestricted access to whatever records, documentation and other information requested in connection with the audit.
- Arrangements regarding the planning of the audit
- Expectations of receiving from management written confirmation concerning representations made in connection with the audit
- Request for the client to confirm the terms of engagement by acknowledging receipt of the engagement letter

- Description of any other letters or reports the auditor expects to issue to the client
- Basis on which fees are computed and any billing arrangements
- Arrangements concerning the involvement of other auditors and experts in some aspects of the audit
- Arrangements concerning the involvement of internal auditors and other client staff
- Arrangements to be made with the predecessor auditor, if any, in the case of an initial audit
- Any restriction of the auditor's liability when such possibility exists
- A reference to any further agreements between the auditor and the client.

Exam focus point

In exam questions you might be asked to discuss matters that an auditor in a particular scenario should discuss with his potential client, in order to come to an agreement about the audit. You should therefore be aware of this list of items, as well as the points made at para 5.3, and be prepared to identify which are relevant in any given circumstance.

6 Books and documents

FAST FORWARD

Audit working papers belong to the auditor.

6.1 Ownership

As you know, **audit working papers are owned by the auditor**. In the event of auditors taking over an audit from another firm, they are **not entitled** to take over all the audit files that that firm has put together on the client.

The ACCA rules state that in order to ensure continuity of a client's affairs, the previous auditors must provide the new auditors will all the **reasonable carry-over information** they request, and they should do this **promptly**. The previous auditor should ensure that he transfers all the books and documents belonging to the client to the new auditors without delay. He is only allowed to keep the books where he is entitled to exercise a **lien**.

6.2 The right of lien

Key term

A **lien** is a creditor's right to retain possession of a debtor's property until the debtor pays what is owed to the creditor.

If the previous auditor is still owed fees by the client, he may have a right to exercise a lien over some of the client's books. General liens over property can rarely be established. However, it may be possible for an auditor to have a particular lien when a debtor owes a debt specifically in respect of that property.

A right of particular lien will only exist where the following conditions are fulfilled.

- The documents must be the property of the client itself (not a closely related third party)
- The documents must have come into the member's possession by proper means
- The work must have been done and a fee note rendered in respect of it
- The fee must relate to the retained documents

6.3 Third party rights to information

As discussed in Chapter 2, the auditor owes a duty of confidentiality to the client. This means that documents containing information about the client should not be given to third parties unless:

- The client agrees to the disclosure before it is made
- Disclosure is required by statute or court order
- Disclosure is otherwise in accordance with the rules of professional conduct

6.4 Client rights to information

Audit working papers are the property of the auditor and as such, the **client has no right of access to them**. The member may allow the client access to the working papers if he so chooses.

However, the position is more complicated when the work undertaken is something other than audit. For example, if the accountant puts together the **financial statements** on behalf of the client, those financial statements will belong to the client.

With tax work, documents created in carrying out **tax compliance work** will belong to the client.

Chapter Roundup

- Common reasons behind companies changing the auditors include audit fee, auditor not seeking re-election and size of company.

- ACCA's general rule on advertising is 'The medium used should not reflect adversely on the member, ACCA or the accountancy profession'.

- It is generally inappropriate to advertise fees.

- Members may accept or pay referral fees if appropriate safeguards exist.

- When approaching a tender, it is important to consider both fees and practical issues.

- ISQC 1 sets out what a firm must consider and document in relation to accepting or continuing engagement, which is the integrity of the client, whether the firm is competent to do the work, whether the firm meets ethical requirements in relation to the work.

- Certain issues must be agreed in writing when an audit is accepted.

- Audit working papers belong to the auditor.

Quick Quiz

1   Name three reasons why an auditor might not seek re-election.

2   Fill in the blanks

Advertising and promotional material should not:

–   ……………………… the service offered …………………………. ………………………….

–   Be …………………………., either directly or by implication

–   Fall short of the requirements of the ……………………………. ………………………….
………………………….. …………………………….. ………………………….

3   Why should accountants not usually advertise fees?

4   List five practical issues that an auditor should consider when approaching a tender.

5   Draw a diagram showing the key stages in a tender, explaining what happens at each stage.

6   List three sources of information about a new client given in ISQC 1

7   According to ISQC 1, when considering whether to accept an engagement with a new or existing client, the auditors must consider whether a ……………………………. …….. ……………………………. arises.

8   List five matters which may be referred to in an engagement letter.

Answers to Quick Quiz

1   (1)   Ethical reasons (eg fees)
       (2)   Another client in competition
       (3)   Disagreement over accounting policy

2   Discredit, by others, misleading, British Code of Advertising Practice

3   The advert is unlikely to be detailed, and facts given about fees could mislead potential clients

4   (1)   Does the timetable fit with current work plan?
       (2)   Are suitable personnel available
       (3)   Where will work be performed? Is it cost effective
       (4)   Are specialist skills needed?
       (5)   Will staff need further training? If so, what is the cost?

5

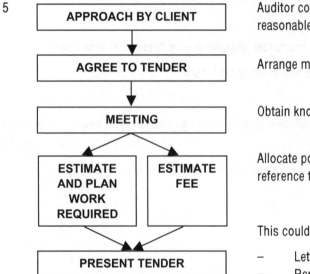

Auditor considers if it is possible to undertake work at a reasonable fee

Arrange meeting to obtain information prior to tender

Obtain knowledge of the business and the service required

Allocate potential staff to work plan and calculate fee by reference to standard charge out rates

This could be in the form of:

−   Letter
−   Report
−   Presentation

6   (1)   Communications with existing/previous auditors
       (2)   Communications with other third parties (eg bankers/legal counsel)
       (3)   Relevant databases

7   Conflict of interest

8   See the answer to question 5 in the body of the chapter

Now try the question below from the Exam Question Bank

Number	Level	Marks	Time
Q3	Examination	20	36 mins

Part D
Assignments

Planning and risk assessment

Topic list	Syllabus reference
1 Revision: overview of audit planning	D1(i)
2 Audit methodologies	D1
3 Materiality	D1(i)
4 Risk	D1(i)
5 Analytical procedures	D1(i)
6 General planning matters	D1(i)

Introduction

The issue of audit planning should not be new to you. You learnt how to plan an audit in your previous auditing studies. Why then is this chapter here? There are two answers:

- To **revise** the details that should be included in an **audit plan** and the general considerations included in planning

- To **consider** some of the **finer points of planning** from the point of view of the engagement partner, specifically to consider the issue of the **risk associated with the assignment** (which is a personal risk to the partner in the event of litigation arising)

Risk is an important factor in the audit. It falls into two categories:

- Specific **assignment risk** (known as audit risk) which you have studied previously

- **Business risk** associated with the client which may form a part of inherent risk and therefore impacts on the audit

Risk is a key issue in an audit, and the most common approach to audits incorporates a recognition of those risks in the approach taken. This and other audit methodologies are compared in section 2.

Study guide

		Intellectual level
D1	**ASSIGNMENTS**	
	The audit of historical financial information	
(a)	Describe the key features of the following audit methodologies:	1
(i)	risk-based auditing	
(ii)	'top down' approach	
(iii)	systems audit	
(iv)	balance sheet approach	
(v)	transaction cycle approach	
(vi)	directional testing.	
(b)	Justify an appropriate approach to a given assignment and recognise when an approach is unsuitable.	3
D2	**Planning, materiality and assessing the risk of misstatement**	
(a)	Specify the matters that should be considered in planning a given assignment including:	3
(i)	logistics (eg staff and client management, multiple locations, deadlines)	
(ii)	use of IT in administration	
(iii)	time budgets	
(iv)	assignment objective and reports required	
(v)	client interface (eg communication methods)	
(vi)	preliminary materiality assessment	
(vii)	key financial statement risks	
(viii)	an overall audit strategy	
(b)	Define materiality and demonstrate how it should be applied in financial reporting and auditing.	2
(c)	Apply the criteria that determine whether or not a matter is material and discuss the use and limitations of prescriptive rules in making decisions about materiality.	2
(d)	Identify and explain business risks in given situations.	2
(e)	Describe the factors that influence the assessment of a specified risk (eg inherent risk, financial statement risk) for a given assignment.	2
(f)	Explain how and why the assessments of risks and materiality affect the nature, timing and extent of auditing procedures in a given situation.	2
(g)	Select and apply appropriate risk assessment procedures, including analytical procedures, to obtain an understanding of a given entity and its environment.	3
(h)	Assess the risk of misstatement at the financial statement level and assertion level and design audit procedures in response to assessed risks.	3
(i)	Recognise and assess the implications of a specified computer system (eg network) on an assignment.	2
F5	**Other current issues**	
(a)	Discuss how the potential problems associated with the audit of small enterprises may be overcome.	2

Exam guide

Exam case study questions are often set in the context of audit planning, identifying risk areas and considering the audit strategy to apply to the audit. This is the case in the pilot paper and questions of this type have appeared very regularly under the previous syllabus.

1 Revision: overview of audit planning

FAST FORWARD > Auditors must plan their work so that it is undertaken in an effective manner.

1.1 ISA 300

ISA (UK and Ireland) 300 *Planning an audit of financial statements* requires auditors to plan the audit to ensure that attention is paid to the correct areas on the audit, and the work is carried out in an effective manner.

The ISA refers to two documents, the **overall audit strategy**, setting out in general terms how the audit is to be carried out, and the **audit plan**, which details specific procedures to be carried out to implement the strategy and complete the audit

1.2 ISA (UK and Ireland) 315 *Understanding the entity and its environment and assessing the risks of material misstatement*

ISA (UK and Ireland) 315 *Obtaining an understanding of the entity and its environment and assessing the risks of material misstatement* states that 'the auditor should obtain an understanding of the entity and its environment, including its internal control, sufficient to identify and assess the risks of material misstatement of the financial statements whether due to fraud or error, and sufficient to design and perform further audit procedures'. It sets out various methods by which the auditors may obtain this understanding:

- Inquiries of management and others within the entity
- Analytical procedures
- Observation and inspection
- Audit team discussion of the susceptibility of the FS to material misstatement
- Prior period knowledge (subject to certain requirements)

The auditors must use a combination of the top three techniques, and must engage in the discussion for every audit. The auditor may use his prior period knowledge, but must carry out procedures to ensure that there have not been changes in the year meaning that it is no longer valid.

The ISA sets out a number of areas of the entity and its environment that the auditor should gain an understanding of. These are summarised here, but more detail is given in a mindmap included in the appendix to this Study Text.

- Nature of the entity
- Industry, regulatory and other external factors
- Objectives, strategies and relating business risks
- Measurement and review of the company's performance
- Internal control

The purpose of obtaining the understanding is to **assess the risks of material misstatement** in the financial statements for the current audit. The ISA says that 'the auditor should identify and assess the risks of material misstatement at the financial statement level, and at the assertion level for classes of transactions, account balances and disclosures'. It requires the auditor to take the following steps:

Step 1   **Identify risks** throughout the process of obtaining an understanding of the entity

Step 2   **Relate the risks** to what can go wrong at the **assertion level**

Step 3   Consider whether the risks are of a **magnitude** that **could result in a material misstatement**

Step 4   Consider the **likelihood** of the risks causing a material misstatement

---

Simple example

The audit team at Ockey Ltd has been carrying out procedures to obtain an understanding of the entity. In the course of making inquiries about the stock system, they have discovered that Ockey Ltd designs and produces tableware to order for a number of high street stores. It also makes a number of standard lines of tableware, which it sells to a number of wholesalers. By the terms of its contracts with the high street stores, it is not entitled to sell uncalled stock designed for them to wholesalers. Ockey Ltd regularly produces 10% more than the high street stores have ordered, in order to ensure that they meet requirements when the stores do their quality control check. Certain stores have more stringent control requirements than others and regularly reject some of the stock.

The knowledge above suggests two risks, one that the company may have obsolescent stock, and another that if their production quality standards are insufficiently high, they could run the risk of losing custom.

We shall look at each of these risks in turn and relate them to the assertion level.

Stock

If certain of the stocks are obsolescent due to the fact that it has been produced in excess of the customer's requirement and there is no other available market for the stock, then there is a risk that stock as a whole in the financial statements will not be carried at the appropriate value. Given that stock is likely to be a material balance in the balance sheet of a manufacturing company, and the value could be up to 10% of the total value, this has the capacity to be a material misstatement.

The factors that will contribute to the likelihood of these risks causing a misstatement are matters such as:

- Whether management regularly review stock levels and scrap items that are obsolescent
- Whether such items are identified and scrapped at the stock count
- Whether such items can be put back into production and changed so that they are saleable

Losing custom

The long term risk of losing custom is a risk that in the future the company will not be able to operate (a going concern risk, which we shall revise in Chapter 9). It could have an impact on the financial statements, if sales were attributed to them that they dispute, sales and debtors could be overstated, that is, not carried at the correct value. However, it appears less likely that this would be a material problem in either area, as the problem is likely to be restricted to a few number of customers, and only a few number of sales to those customers.

Again, review of the company's controls over the recording of sales and the debt collection procedures of the company would indicate how likely these risks to the financial statements are to materialise.

Some risks identified may be **significant risks** (indicated by the following factors), in which case they present **special audit considerations** for the auditors.

- Risk of **fraud**
- Its relationship with **recent developments**
- The degree of **subjectivity** in the financial information
- The fact that it is an **unusual** transaction
- It is a significant transaction with a **related party**
- The **complexity** of the transaction

Routine, non-complex transactions are less likely to give rise to significant risk than unusual transactions or matters of director judgement because the latter are likely to have more management intervention, complex accounting principles or calculations, greater manual intervention or there is a lower opportunity for control procedures to be followed.

When the auditor identifies a significant risk, if he hasn't done so already, he should evaluate the design and implementation of the entity's controls in that area.

Point to note

Internationally, there is currently an ED of ISA 540 which includes additional risk assessments in relation to estimates in line with the new risk assessment procedures in ISA 315.

1.3 ISA (UK and Ireland) 330 *The auditor's procedures in response to assessed risks*

The main requirement of ISA (UK and Ireland) 330 *The auditor's procedures in response to assessed risks* is 'in order to reduce audit risk to an acceptably low level, the auditor should determine overall responses to assessed risks at the financial statement level, and should design and perform further audit procedures to respond to assessed risks at the assertion level'.

Overall responses including emphasising to the audit team the need for professional scepticism, assigning additional/alternative staff to the audit, using experts, providing more supervision on the audit and incorporating more unpredictability into the audit.

The evaluation of the control environment that will have taken place as part of the assessment of the client's internal control systems will help the auditor determine whether they are going to take a **substantive approach** (focusing mainly on substantive procedures) or a **combined approach** (tests of control and substantive procedures).

In accordance with this approach, the auditor should then determine **further audit procedures** designed to answer the assessed risks.

The auditor **must** carry out substantive procedures on material items. In addition, the auditor must carry out the following substantive procedures:

- Agreeing the financial statements to the underlying accounting records
- Examining material journal entries
- Examining other adjustments made in preparing the financial statements

1.4 Documentation requirements

ISAs 315 and 330 contain a number of documentation requirements. The following matters should be documented:

- The discussion among the audit team concerning the susceptibility of the financial statements to material misstatements, including any significant decisions reached

- Key elements of the understanding gained of the entity including the elements of the entity and its control specified in the ISA as mandatory, the sources of the information gained and the risk assessment procedures carried out

- The identified and assessed risks of material misstatement

- Significant risks identified and related controls evaluated

- The overall responses to address the risks of material misstatement

- Nature, extent and timing of further audit procedures linked to the assessed risks at the assertion level

- If the auditors have relied on evidence about the effectiveness of controls from previous audits, conclusions about how this is appropriate

Question	Revision of audit planning

You have been informed by the senior partner of your firm that you are to be in charge of the audit of a new client, Peppermint Chews, for the year ended 31 December 20X4. She tells you that the company is engaged in the manufacture and wholesaling of sweets and confectionery, with turnover of approximately £5,000,000 and a work force of about 150. The company has one manufacturing location, sells mainly to the retail trade but also operates 10 shops of its own. The senior partner asks you to draw up an outline audit plan for the assignment showing when you anticipate visits to the client will be made and what kind of work will be carried out during each visit. The deadline for your audit report is 28 February 20X5.

Required

Draw up an outline plan for the audit of Peppermint Chews for the year ended 31 December 20X4, including:

(a) Approximate timing in the company's year of each stage of the audit of this new client. State why you have selected the approximate timing

(b) The objective of each stage

(c) The kind of work that will be carried out at each stage

Answer	

Initial visit

(a) Timing. As this is a new client, this visit should take place as soon as possible after the terms of engagement have been agreed with and accepted by the directors of Peppermint Chews.

(b) Objective. To build up a background knowledge of the company to assist in the more detailed planning of audit work that will be required at a later stage.

(c) Audit work. We shall need to obtain details of the following:

- The history and development of the company
- The nature of the commercial environment within which the company operates
- The nature of the company's products and manufacturing processes

- The plan of organisation within the company
- The accounting and internal control systems operating within the company
- The accounting and other records of the company and how they are maintained

The above will be obtained using such techniques as interview, observation, reviewing client's systems documentation, and so on.

We shall not at this stage carry out detailed tests of controls on the company's systems, but we should carry out 'walk-through' tests to gain confirmation that the systems outlined to them in theory appear to operate that way in practice.

Interim visit(s)

(a) Timing. As this is the first audit of Peppermint Chews, it may, in view of the extra work involved, be necessary to have more than one interim visit. If we decided that only one such visit would be needed, however, then ideally it should take place reasonably close to the year end, in, say, October 20X4. If it were decided that more than one visit were needed, then perhaps the first interim visit should take place in April/May 20X4.

(b) Objective. The purpose of interim audits is to carry out detailed tests on a client's accounting and internal control systems to determine the reliance that may be placed thereon.

(c) Audit work. Following the initial visit to the client, we should have completed their documentation of the client's systems using narrative notes and flowcharts. We should also have assessed the strengths and weaknesses of the systems and determined the extent to which they wish to place reliance on them.

Given effective controls, we shall select and perform tests designed to establish compliance with the system. We shall therefore carry out an appropriate programme of tests of controls. The conclusion from the results may be either:

(i) That the controls are effective, in which case we shall only need to carry out restricted substantive procedures; or

(ii) That the controls are ineffective in practice, although they had appeared strong on paper, in which case we shall need to carry out more extensive substantive procedures.

After carrying out tests of controls, it is normal practice, as appropriate, to send management a letter identifying any weaknesses and making recommendations for improvements.

Final visit

(a) Timing. This may well be split into a pre-final visit in December 20X4 and a final audit early in 20X5, or it could be a continuous process.

(b) Objective. We should visit the client prior to the year end to assist in the planning of the final audit so as to agree with the client detailed timings such as year end stock count and trade debtors circularisation, preparation of client schedules, finalisation of accounts and so forth.

The object of the final audit is to carry out the necessary substantive procedures, these being concerned with substantiating the figures in the accounting records and, eventually, in the financial statements themselves. The completion of these tests, followed by an overall review of the financial statements, will enable us to decide whether they have obtained 'sufficient appropriate audit evidence to be able to draw reasonable conclusions' so that they are in a position to express an opinion on the company's financial statements, the expression of an opinion in their audit report being the primary objective of the audit.

(c) Audit work. The audit work to be carried out at this final stage would include the following:

- Consideration and discussion with management of known problem areas
- Attendance at stock count
- Verification of assets and liabilities/income and expenditure
- Following up interim audit work

- Carrying out review of post balance sheet events
- Analytical procedures
- Obtaining management representations
- Reviewing financial statements
- Drafting the audit report

2 Audit methodologies

The audit strategy document will describe the audit methodology to be used in gathering evidence. This section describes the main methodologies currently used by auditors.

2.1 Risk-based audit

Risk-based auditing refers to the development of auditing techniques that are responsive to risk factors in an audit. As we set out in section 4, the auditors apply judgement to determine what level of risk pertains to different areas of a client's system and devise appropriate audit tests.

This approach should ensure that the greatest audit effort is directed at the areas in which the financial statements are most likely to be misstated, so that the chance of detecting errors is improved and time is not spent on unnecessary testing of 'safe' areas.

The increased use of risk-based auditing reflects two factors.

(a) The growing complexity of the business environment increases the danger of fraud or misstatement. Factors such as the developing use of computerised systems and the growing internationalisation of business are relevant here.

(b) Pressures are increasingly exerted by audit clients for the auditors to keep fee levels down while an improved level of service is expected.

The risk approach is best illustrated by a small case study.

 Case Study

Audit risk approach

Your audit firm has as its client a small manufacturing company. This company owns the land and buildings in its balance sheet, which it depreciates over 50 years (buildings only) and has always valued at cost.

The other major item in the balance sheet is stock.

Looking at these two balance sheet items from the point of view of the audit firm, the following conclusions can be drawn.

There is only a small chance that the audit engagement partner will draw an inappropriate conclusion about land and buildings.

In a manufacturing company, stock is likely to be far more complex. There may be a significant number of lines to count and value, the quantity will change all the time, stock may grow obsolete. The chance of the audit engagement partner drawing an inappropriate conclusion about stock is higher than the risk in connection with land and buildings.

The auditors will have to do less work to render audit risk acceptable for land and buildings than on stock. The audit risk approach will mean doing less work on land and buildings than stock.

ISA 315 requires that auditors consider the entity's process for assessing its own business risks, and the impact that this might have on the audit in terms of material misstatements. Auditors consider:

- What factors lead to the problems which may cause material misstatements?
- What can the audit contribute to the business pursuing its goals?

This 'business risk' approach was developed because it is sometimes the case that the auditors believe the risk of the financial statements being misstated arises predominantly from the business risks of the company.

2.2 'Top-down' approach

FAST FORWARD

With a 'top-down' approach (also known as the business risk approach) controls testing is aimed at high level controls and substantive testing is reduced.

The table below highlights some of the factors that exist.

Principal risk	Immediate Financial Statement Implications
Economic pressures causing reduced unit sales and eroding margins.	Stock values (SSAP 9) Going concern
Economic pressures resulting in demands for extended credit	Debtors recoverability
Product quality issues related to inadequate control over supply chain and transportation damage.	Stock values – net realisable value and stock returns
Customer dissatisfaction related to inability to meet order requirements.	Going concern
Customer dissatisfaction related to invoicing errors and transportation damage.	Debtors valuation
Unacceptable service response call rate related to poor product quality	Going concern Litigation – provisions and contingencies Stock – net realisable value
Out of date IT systems affecting management's ability to make informed decisions.	Anywhere

Exam focus point

Exam scenarios often contain two requirements linked to business risk – first, to identify business risks in a scenario and second, to link those risks to potential misstatements in the financial statements. Looking at this issue in **practice** is the best way to learn.

Question
Business risk

State what category of business risk each of the risks in the above table falls under.

Answer

1	Financial
2	Financial
3	Operational
4	Operational
5	Operational
6	Operational
7	Operational

The business risk audit approach tries to mirror the risk management steps that have been taken by the directors. In this way, the auditor will **seek to establish that the financial statement objectives have been met**, through an investigation into whether all the other business objectives have been met by the directors.

This approach to the audit has been called a **'top-down' approach**, because it starts at the business and its objectives and works back down to the financial statements, rather than working up from the financial statements which has historically been the approach to audit. The 'top-down approach' has an **effect on the procedures used in the audit**, as follows.

Audit procedure	Effect of 'top-down' approach
Tests of controls	As the auditor pays greater attention to the high level controls used by directors to manage business risks, controls testing will be focused on items such as the control environment and corporate governance than the detailed procedural controls tested under traditional approaches.
Analytical procedures	Analytical procedures are used more heavily in a business risk approach as they are consistent with the auditor's desire to understand the entity's business rather than to prove the figures in the financial statements.
Detailed testing	The combination of the above two factors, particularly the higher use of analytical procedures will result in a lower requirement for detailed testing, although substantive testing will not be eliminated completely.

The other key element of a business risk approach is that as it is focused on the business more fully, rather than the financial statements, there is greater opportunity for the auditor to add value to the client's business and to assist him in managing the risks that the business faces.

2.2.1 Advantages of business risk approach

There are a number of reasons why firms who use the business risk approach prefer it to historic approaches.

- Added value given to clients as the approach focuses on the business as a whole

- Audit attention focused on high level controls and high use of analytical procedures increase audit efficiency and therefore cost

- Does not focus on routine processes, which technological developments have rendered less prone to error than has historically been the case

- Responds to the importance that regulators and the government have placed on corporate governance in recent years

- Lower engagement risk (risk of auditor being sued) through broader understanding of the client's business and practices

2.3 Systems audit

An auditor may predominantly test controls and systems, but substantive testing can **never** be eliminated entirely.

You should be familiar with the systems and controls approach to auditing, from your previous studies. It is always used in conjunction with another approach, because as you are aware, **substantive testing can never be eliminated completely**.

As you studied the concept of controls testing in detail in your previous studies in auditing, we shall only briefly revise it here.

> Management are required to institute a system of controls which is capable of fulfilling their duty of safeguarding the assets of the shareholders.
>
> Auditors assess the system of controls put in place by the directors and ascertain whether they believe it is effective enough for them to be able to rely on it for the purposes of their audit.
>
> If they believe that the system is effective, they carry out tests of controls to ensure that the control system operates as it is supposed to. If they believe that the control system is ineffective, they assess control risk as high and undertake higher levels of substantive testing (see Sections 4 and 5).
>
> The key control objectives and procedures over the main cycles of sales, purchases and wages were studied at length at paper 2.6 (old paper 6). If you do not feel confident in what they are, you should go back to your Study Text in these areas and revise them now.

FAST FORWARD

> An auditor may choose predominantly to carry out substantive tests on the transactions of the business in the relevant period.

2.4 Balance sheet approach

FAST FORWARD

> An auditor may choose predominantly to carry out substantive tests on year end balances.

2.4.1 Balance testing

An alternative to the cycles (or transactions) approach to auditing is to take the balance sheet approach. This is the **most common approach to the substantive part of the audit**, after controls have been tested.

The balance sheet shows a snapshot of the financial position of the business at a point in time. It follows that it if is fairly stated and the previous snapshot was fairly stated then it is reasonable to undertake lower level testing on the transactions which connect the two snapshots, for example, analytical review (examined in Section 6).

Under this approach, therefore, the auditors seek to concentrate efforts on substantiating the closing position in the year, shown in the balance sheet, having determined that the closing position from the previous year (also substantiated) has been correctly transferred to be the opening position in the current year.

You should be aware of the financial statement assertions and the substantive tests in relation to the major items on the balance sheet from your previous studies. Some further tests are detailed in Chapter 11.

2.4.2 Relationship with business risk approach

It is stated above that the substantive element of an audit undertaken under a business risk approach is restricted due to the high use of analytical procedures. However, the element of substantive testing which remains in a business risk approach can be undertaken under the balance sheet approach.

In some cases, particularly **small companies**, the business risks may be strongly connected to the fact that management is concentrated on one person. Another feature of small companies may be that their balance sheet is uncomplicated and contains one or two material items, for example, receivables or inventory.

When this is the case, it is **often more cost-effective to undertake a highly substantive balance sheet audit than to undertake a business risk assessment**, as it is relatively simple to obtain the assurance required about the financial statements from taking that approach.

2.4.3 Limitations of the balance sheet approach

When not undertaken in conjunction with a risk based approach or systems testing, the **level of detailed testing** can be high in a balance sheet approach, rendering it **costly**.

2.5 Transaction cycle approach

Cycles testing is in some ways closely linked to systems testing, because it is based on the same systems. However, while in Section 2.2 we considered the systems of the business in terms of controls testing, here we are looking at them in terms of substantive testing.

When auditors take a cycles approach, they test the transactions which have occurred, resulting in the entries in the profit and loss account (for example, sales transactions, stock purchases, asset purchases, wages payments, other expenses).

They would select a sample of transactions and test that each transaction was complete and processed correctly throughout the cycle. In other words, they substantiate the transactions which appear in the financial statements.

Exam focus point

> The auditors may assess the systems of a company as **ineffective.** In this case, they would carry out extensive substantive procedures. The substantive approach taken in this situation could a be cycles approach. In fact, if systems have been adjudged to be ineffective, the auditor is more likely to take a cycles approach, as it will be essential that the auditor substantiates that the transactions have been recorded properly, despite the poor systems.

The key business cycles are outlined below. Remember that you know what the processes should be in the cycle (you have assessed the system and controls in Section 2.2), under this approach, you are ensuring that individual transactions were processed correctly. Hence, the cycles outlined below should correspond to the controls processes you are already aware of and which we discussed in Section 2.2.

2.5.1 Sales

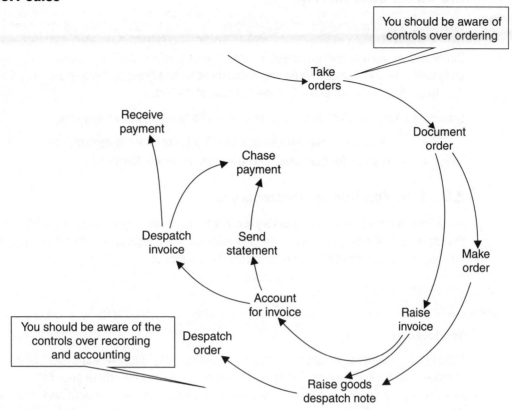

2.5.2 Purchases

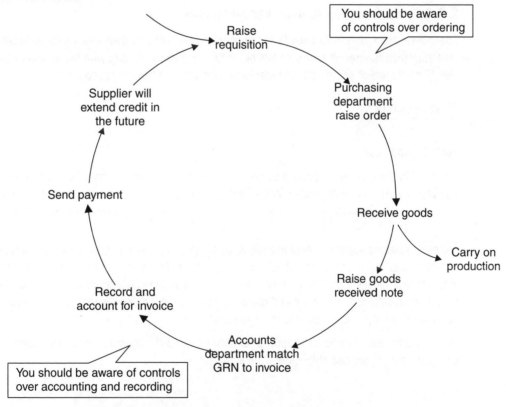

The auditor should be able to find an audit trail for each transaction, for example in the purchases cycle:

- Requisition
- Order
- GRN

- Invoice
- Ledger and daybook entries
- Payment in cashbook/cheque stub

2.6 Directional testing

> Directional testing is a method of discovering errors and omissions in financial statements.

Directional testing has been discussed in detail in your previous auditing studies. It is a method of undertaking detailed substantive testing. Substantive testing seeks to discover errors and omissions, and the discovery of these will depend on the direction of the test.

Broadly speaking, substantive procedures can be said to fall into two categories:

- Tests to discover **errors** (resulting in over- or under-statement)
- Tests to discover **omissions** (resulting in under-statement)

2.6.1 Tests designed to discover errors

These tests will start with the **accounting records** in which the transactions are recorded and check from the entries to supporting documents or other evidence. Such tests should detect any over-statement and also any under-statement through causes other than omission.

 Case Study

Test for errors

If the test is designed to ensure that sales are priced correctly, the test would begin with a sales invoice selected from the sales ledger. Prices would then be checked to the official price list.

2.6.2 Tests designed to discover omissions

These tests must start from **outside the accounting records** and then check back to those records. Understatements through omission will never be revealed by starting with the account itself as there is clearly no chance of selecting items that have been omitted from the account.

 Case Study

Tests for omission

If the test is designed to discover whether all raw material purchases have been properly processed, the test would start, say, with goods received notes, to be checked to the stock records or purchase ledger.

For most systems auditors would include tests designed to discover both errors and omissions. The type of test, and direction of the test, should be recognised before selecting the test sample. If the sample which tested the accuracy and validity of the sales ledger were chosen from a file of sales invoices then it would not substantiate the fact that there were no errors in the sales ledger. The approach known as 'directional testing' applies this testing discipline.

Directional testing is particularly appropriate when testing the financial statement assertions of existence, completeness, rights and obligations, and valuation.

2.6.3 Directional testing and double entry

The concept of directional testing derives from the principle of double-entry bookkeeping, in that for every **debit** there is a **corresponding credit**, (assuming that the double entry is complete and that the accounting records balance). Therefore, any **misstatement** of a **debit entry** will result in either a corresponding **misstatement** of a **credit entry** or a **misstatement** in the opposite direction, of **another debit entry**.

By designing audit tests carefully the auditors are able to use this principle in drawing audit conclusions, not only about the debit or credit entries that they have directly tested, but also about the corresponding credit or debit entries that are necessary to balance the books. Tests are therefore designed in the following way.

Test item	Example
Test debit items (expenditure or assets) for overstatement by selecting debit entries recorded in the nominal ledger and checking value, existence and ownership	If a fixed asset entry in the nominal ledger of £1,000 is selected, it would be overstated if it should have been recorded at anything less than £1,000 or if the company did not own it, or indeed if it did not exist (eg it had been sold or the amount of £1,000 in fact represented a revenue expense).
Test credit items (income or liabilities) for understatement by selecting items from appropriate sources independent of the nominal ledger and ensuring that they result in the correct nominal ledger entry	Select a goods despatched note and check that the resultant sale has been recorded in the nominal ledger sales account. Sales would be understated if the nominal ledger did not reflect the transaction at all (completeness) or reflected it at less than full value (say if goods valued at £1,000 were recorded in the sales account at £900, there would be an understatement of £100).

The matrix set out below demonstrates how directional testing is applied to give assurance on all account areas in the financial statements.

		Primary test also gives comfort on			
Type of account	Purpose of primary test	Assets	Liabilities	Income	Expenses
Assets	Overstatement (O)	U	O	O	U
Liabilities	Understatement (U)	U	O	O	U
Income	Understatement (U)	U	O	O	U
Expense	Overstatement (O)	U	O	O	U

A test for the overstatement of an asset simultaneously gives comfort on understatement of other assets, overstatement of liabilities, overstatement of income and understatement of expenses.

Question

Directional testing

Fill in the blank spaces.

(a)   Based on double-entry bookkeeping, it can be seen from the matrix that assets can only be *understated* by virtue of:

    (i)   Other assets being ....; or

    (ii)   Liabilities being ....; or

    (iii)   Income being ....; or

    (iv)   Expenses being ....

(b)   Similarly, liabilities can only be *overstated* by virtue of:

    (i)   Assets being ....; or

    (ii)   Other liabilities being ....; or

    (iii)   Income being ....; or

    (iv)   Expenses being ....

Answer

(a)	(i)	Overstated	(b)	(i)	Overstated
	(ii)	Understated		(ii)	Understated
	(iii)	Understated		(iii)	Understated
	(iv)	Overstated		(iv)	Overstated

So, by performing the primary tests shown in the matrix, the auditors obtain audit assurance in other audit areas. Successful completion of the primary tests will therefore result in them having tested all account areas both for overstatement and understatement.

The major advantage of the directional audit approach is its cost-effectiveness.

(a)   Assets and expenses are tested for overstatement only, and liabilities and income for understatement only, that is, items are not tested for both overstatement and understatement.

(b)   It audits directly the more likely types of transactional misstatement, ie unrecorded income and improper expense (arising intentionally or unintentionally).

Exam focus point

> Directional testing is particularly useful when there is a high level of detailed testing to be carried out, for example, when the auditors have assessed the company's controls and accounting system as ineffective.

Question

Audit strategy

As audit senior, you have recently attended a meeting with the managing director of Go Shop Ltd (audit client) and the new audit partner assigned to the audit, who has recently joined your firm, Eastlake and Pond. The audit partner is familiarising himself with the client.

Go Shop Ltd is a large limited liability building company set up by John Yeams, who has been managing director since incorporation. It operates in the South of the country, purchasing land outside of major towns and building retail parks, which the company then manages. You are familiar with the client, as you have taken part in the audit for the last three years. The other key member of the board is Kathleen Hadley, who set up the business with John Yeams and is finance director. Kathleen is a qualified accountant, and the accounting systems and procedures at Go Shop have always appeared sound.

You took minutes of the meeting, which are given below.

Minutes of a meeting between Mike Kenton and John Yeams, 30 March 2006

MK introduced himself to JY and asked for a brief history of the business, which was given. Currently, majority of income from property management side, as building market is becoming saturated. With interest rates set to rise, JY is less keen to borrow and build in the current climate.

MK asked JY whether a recent spate of terrorist bomb attacks had had any effect on business. JY commented that there he had been given the impression that retail was down and that customers were staying away from the retail centres – but he felt that some of that could be attributed to rise in interest rates and was likely to be temporary. First months of the year are always poor for retail...

MK asked whether there had been a rise in empty units in the retail centres. JY said there had been a small rise.

MK asked JY about his views in relation to the current bill before Parliament concerning quality standards in the building trade. JY commented that it seemed like a 'load of nonsense' to him, and expressed some dissatisfaction with the current political situation... MK pressed the matter, enquiring as to JY's opinion on the likely effects on his business were more stringent standards to be required in the future. JY is of the firm belief that it would not be passed. MK expressed his fear that the Bill was more than likely to be passed, and would have far-reaching and expensive effects on most builders in the UK. JY repeated some of his previous comments about politicians.

MK enquired as to whether there were any anticipated developments in the business, which he should know about. JY made reference to KH's plans to retire from full time work in the business. MK asked how JY was going to replace her. JY commented that he was hoping to persuade her to stay on as she deals with all the financial side, he'd be lost without her. MK tried to enquire how firm her retirement plans were, but JY was not forthcoming.

After the meeting, Mike Kenton asked you to ring Kathleen and discuss her plans. She confirmed that she does plan to retire. She informed you that she plans to emigrate to Australia, and is not keen to put back her plans. She asked about the possibility of Eastlake and Pond assisting in the recruitment process for her replacement, as she does not feel that John Yeats has the technical ability to recruit someone without her, and has not accepted her plans enough to recruit before her retirement. She said that she has even wondered about the possibility of someone being seconded to the company from Eastlake and Pond to cover her position after she has left and before her replacement is found.

Mike is keen to reappraise the audit strategy taken towards the audit of Go Shop, as he feels the audit could be conducted more efficiently than it has in the past. Historically the audit has been highly substantive.

Required

(a)   Identify and explain the key business risks that exist at Go Shop
(b)   Explain what is meant by the 'business risk approach' to an audit
(c)   Propose and justify a strategy for the audit of Go Shop
(d)   Discuss the ethical implications for the audit of the two suggestions made by Kathleen.

Approaching the answer

As audit senior, you have recently attended a meeting with the managing director of Go Shop (audit client) and the new audit partner assigned to the audit, who has recently joined your firm, Eastlake and Pond. The audit partner is familiarising himself with the client.

Volatile industry

CAKE

Go Shop is a large limited liability building company set up by John Yeams, who has been managing director since incorporation. It operates in the South of the country, purchasing land outside of major towns and building retail parks, which the company then manages. You are familiar with the client, as you have taken part in the audit for the last three years. The other key member of the board is Kathleen Hadley, who set up the business with John Yeams and is finance director. Kathleen is a qualified accountant, and the accounting systems and procedures at Go Shop have always appeared sound.

Good control environment

You took minutes of the meeting, which are given below.

Minutes of a meeting between Mike Kenton and John Yeams, 30 March 2006

MK introduced himself to JY and asked for a brief history of the business, which was given. Currently, majority of income from property management side, as building market is becoming saturated. With interest rates set to rise, JY is less keen to borrow and build in the current climate.

Impact on any borrowing

Going concern

MK asked JY whether a recent spate of terrorist bomb attacks had had any effect on business. JY commented that there he had been given the impression that retail was down and that customers were staying away from the retail centres – but he felt that some of that could be attributed to rise in interest rates and was likely to be temporary. First months of the year are always poor for retail.

Knock on going concern issues?

Pressure on major customers

MK asked whether there had been a rise in empty units in the retail centres. JY said there had been a small rise.

Compliance risk if bill is passed – likely? And going concern?

MK asked JY about his views in relation to the current bill before Parliament concerning quality standards in the building trade. JY commented that it seemed like a 'load of nonsense' to him, and expressed some dissatisfaction with the current political situation… MK pressed the matter, enquiring as to JY's opinion on the likely effects on his business were more stringent standards to be required in the future. JY is of the firm belief that it would not be passed. MK expressed his fear that the Bill was more than likely to be passed, and would have far-reaching and expensive effects on most builders in the UK. JY repeated some of his previous comments about politicians.

MK enquired as to whether there were any anticipated developments in the business, which he should know about. JY made reference to KH's plans to retire from full time work in the business. MK asked how JY was going to replace her. JY commented that he was hoping to persuade her to stay on as she deals with all the financial side, he'd be lost without her. MK tried to enquire how firm her retirement plans were, but JY was not forthcoming.

Operational risk – loss of key staff member, and implications for FS and control environment

---

Independence issues

After the meeting, Mike Kenton asked you to ring Kathleen and discuss her plans. She confirmed that she does plan to retire. She informed you that she plans to emigrate to Australia, and is not keen to put back her plans. She asked about the possibility of Eastlake and Pond assisting in the recruitment process for her replacement, as she does not feel that John Yeats has the technical ability to recruit someone without her, and has not accepted her plans enough to recruit before her retirement. She said that she has even wondered about the possibility of someone being seconded to the company from Eastlake and Pond to cover her position after she has left and before her replacement is found.

Mike is keen to reappraise the audit strategy taken towards the audit of Go Shop, as he feels the audit could be conducted more efficiently than it has in the past. Historically the audit has been highly substantive.

> Link with senior's CAKE – analytical review?? Use of business risk approach. control environment is sound …

Answer plan

(a) **Business risks**

Operational – industry

- Building industry volatile and apparently saturated
- Retail management – retail industry volatile and affected by bomb threats/ interest rates

Operational – personnel

About to lose key management on the financial side and no current plans to replace her. Could severely affect systems in the finance department – could have knock on effects on sales and purchases relationships – suppliers/customers.

Finance

Likely that Go Shop has high borrowings against buildings built and managed – therefore increase in interest rates could be bad – particularly if they have borrowed lots while interest rates were low.

Compliance

Potential statute concerning quality standards:

- Far reaching
- Expensive
- Going concern??

(b) **Business risk approach**

Define BRA – link to ARA, etc…

Indicator of going concern problem?

Debtors' recoverability

Tangible fixed assets impairment

Effect on FS themselves – more prone to error?

Also, impact on control environment?

GC

Interest rates

GC

(c) **Strategy**

BRA – have identified BR

Key risks to FS as identified above – linked strongly…seems reasonable to extend audit risk approach in this way.

Control environment strong – therefore reasonable to do control testing – but question if this will still be the case if KH leaves.

Also, senior has CAKE – therefore analytical procedures will be good. Explanations available for analytical review.

BRA is generally more efficient than highly substantive – due to top down procedures.

(d) **Ethical implications**

Recruitment – mustn't make management decisions.

Secondment – must ensure that there are walls between staff on audit team and seconded staff – may represent too great a loss of objectivity due to familiarity.

Answer

(a) **Key business risks at Go Shop**

Operational – industry

The building industry is generally considered to be a volatile industry and sensitive to changes in economic climate. The managing director has identified that the particular market that the company operates in, retail parks, has become saturated. Go Shop's business is therefore likely to be volatile generally and the market for the services Go Shop provides is saturated. This is an operational risk – what will Go Shop do if it does not do what it has done historically?

The company is not only strongly connected with the building industry, but also the retail industry. This is another industry that is volatile. It has recently been affected by higher interest rates and reduced consumer spending. It has also suffered due to the bomb threats made against retail parks, which have discouraged consumers from shopping.

Operational – personnel

The business is about to lose a key member of personnel on the financial side, and there appear to be no current plans to replace her. This could severely affect systems in the finance department, which could have a knock on effect on crucial supply and customer relations and hence the operations of the wider business.

Finance

It is likely that Go Shop has a **high level of borrowings secured** on the buildings that they have built and now managed. If this is the case, the **increase in interest rates** will adversely affect their business directly in the form of **interest** on these loans. This may be particularly severe if they have over-borrowed when interest rates were low.

Compliance

There is currently legislation before Parliament that is likely to have far-reaching effects on the operations of Go Shop's building arm. The law relates to quality standards in the building industry and is likely to be costly to implement. It is possible that Go Shop will struggle to **afford to implement such standards**. An even more significant concern is that it appears that the director has taken **no steps to mitigate this risk** and has put **no action plans into place** to ensure that the law would be complied with, if passed. This could mean that the company could be liable to legal action and fines.

(b) **Business risk approach**

The business risk approach is an extension of the audit risk approach. When using an audit risk approach, the auditors focus their attention on matters that they feel are the most significantly risky to the financial statements so that they can provide a cost effective audit.

The audit risk approach concentrates on three areas of risk; inherent risk, control risk and detection risk.

In a business risk approach, the auditors determine that the risks that are most likely to adversely affect the financial statements are the business risks of the company, hence they direct their testing to the business risks apparent in the business.

This can be illustrated in the given scenario by looking at the significant links between the business risks identified and the financial statements:

Operational – industry

Volatile industry	Significant issues relating to **going concern** arising, auditors should direct their audit work in this area.
Retail units affected by bomb threats	Potential issues relating to **debtors' recoverability**. Retail units may not be able to pay rent/honour leases if they are not receiving sufficient income from sales.
	The potential fall in income related to the retail units could affect the valuation **of tangible fixed assets** – is there a need for an impairment review?

Operational – personnel

Loss of FD	This could have a significant impact on the **calculation and presentation of the financial statements** if they are now drafted by an inexperienced person.
	There is also a significant impact on the **control environment**, which will affect assessment of control risk.

Finance

Interest rates	The issues relating to high interest will affect the **interest figure** in the profit and loss account. It might also impact on the **going concern** assumption.

Compliance

New law	Depending on the timing of the new legislation and the outcomes discussed above, this could affect **post balance sheet events**, contingencies or **provisions**. It could also potentially affect going concern.

(c) **Audit strategy**

The audit strategy will depend on certain matters such as the date when Kathleen Hadley leaves the business. Assuming that she leaves after the audit, a **business risk approach** would be appropriate.

This is because business risks have already been identified, and, as outlined above, there are **significant links between the business risks and the financial statements.**

The **control environment has historically been strong**, so making use of controls testing would appear to be appropriate. This in particular is highly dependent on the presence of Kathleen Hadley at the audit date.

The **audit senior** has **experience** of the client and significant **knowledge** of the business therefore. It seems appropriate given this, that a high use be made of **analytical procedures**. It also appears that strong explanations will be available for movements on accounts over the period. Again, this is dependent on the presence of Kathleen Hadley.

Lastly, the business risk approach is considered an **efficient approach** as it uses 'top down' procedures, so as strong evidence appears to be available, it is sensible to take the most efficient approach possible, while ensuring that a quality audit is conducted.

(d) **Ethical implications**

(i) *Recruitment*

It is very important that the audit firm do not take management decisions on behalf of the entity. Hence it would be appropriate for them to take a role in the recruitment process, perhaps reviewing CV's and advising as to qualifications and factors to look for. However, they should not get heavily involved in the interviewing process, as this could lead them to, in effect, make management decisions on behalf of the directors.

(ii) *Secondment*

If a staff member of the audit firm is to be seconded to the audit client to work in this significant role, the firm would have to be very clear that there were 'Chinese Walls' in place between that staff member and the audit team. This may in practice be impossible.

However, provided that objectivity can be retained for the audit team and that there is not a problem of familiarity, a secondment might be appropriate.

A problem of familiarity could arise if

- Either, the person seconded had previously worked on the audit and the strategy and approach was not changed,

- Or, the audit team were familiar with the person seconded and had a personal relationship with him that presented a significant risk to objectivity.

3 Materiality

Materiality considerations are important at the planning stage. An item might be material due to its nature, value or impact on readers of the financial statements.

3.1 Revision of materiality

Key term

Materiality is an expression of the relative significance or importance of a particular matter in the context of financial statements as a whole (ISA 320).

Materiality considerations during **audit planning** are extremely important. The assessment of materiality at this stage should be based on the most recent and reliable financial information and will help to determine an effective and efficient audit approach. Materiality assessment will help the auditors to decide:

- **How many** and **what items** to examine
- Whether to use **sampling techniques**
- What **level of error** is likely to lead to a qualified audit opinion

The resulting combination of audit procedures should help to reduce audit risk to an appropriately low level.

MATERIALITY CRITERIA	
An item might be material due to its	
Nature	Given the definition of materiality that an item would affect the readers of the financial statements, some **items** might **by their nature affect readers.** Examples include **transactions related to directors,** such as remuneration or contracts with the company.
Value	Some items will be significant in the financial statements by virtue of their **size,** for example, if the company had bought a piece of land with a value which comprised three-quarters of the asset value of the company, that would be material. That is why materiality is often expressed in terms of **percentages** (of assets, of profits).

| Impact | Some **items may by chance have a significant impact** on financial statements, for example, a proposed journal which is not material in itself could convert a profit into a loss. The difference between a small profit and a small loss could be material to some readers. |

3.2 Rules on materiality

It is clear from the points made about materiality criteria that materiality is judgmental, and something that auditors must be aware of when approaching all their audit work.

However, you will know from your previous studies that generally accepted rules about materiality exist. Examples are:

- Items relating to directors are generally material
- Percentage guidelines are often given for materiality

Exam focus point

In earlier studies, you may have always calculated materiality by taking a weighted average of the calculated percentages of turnover (1-2%), profit before tax (5%) and total assets (2-5%). This is appropriate when calculating preliminary (planning) materiality. In this paper, you will often be calculating materiality in relation to a specific item. You must only use the relevant comparator (for example, total assets if the matter relates to the balance sheet, PBT if the matter impacts upon profit, and both if it relates to the balance sheet and impacts on profit, for example, a provision.)

While materiality **must always be a matter of judgement** for the auditor, it is **helpful to have some rules** to bear in mind. Reasons for this are:

- The rules give the auditor a **framework** within which to base his thoughts on materiality

- The rules provide a **benchmark** against which to assess quality of auditing, for example, in the event of litigation or disciplinary action.

3.3 Problems with materiality

As discussed above, materiality is a matter of judgement for the auditor. Therefore, prescriptive rules will not always be helpful when assessing materiality. A **significant risk** of prescriptive rules is that a **significant matter,** which **falls outside the boundaries of the rules,** could be overlooked, leading to a **material misstatement in the financial statements**.

The percentage guidelines of assets and profits that are commonly used for materiality must be handled with care. The auditor must bear in mind the **focus** of the company being audited.

In some companies, **post tax profit** is the key figure in the financial statements, as the level of dividend is the most important factor in the accounts.

In **owner managed businesses**, if owners are paid salary and are indifferent to dividends, the key profit figure stands higher in the profit and loss account, say at **gross profit** level. Alternatively in this situation, the auditor should consider a figure that does not appear on the profit and loss account: **profit before directors' salaries and benefits**.

Some companies are **driven by assets** rather than the need for profits. In such examples, higher materiality might need to be applied to assets. In some companies, say charities, **costs** are the driving factor, and materiality might be considered in relation to these.

While rules or guidelines are helpful to auditors when assessing materiality, they must always keep in mind the **nature** of the business they are dealing with. Materiality must be **tailored to the business and the anticipated user** of financial statements, or it is not truly materiality. Remember the definition of materiality and consider **all the elements** of it:

"Materiality is a expression of the **relative** significance or importance of a particular matter in the context of the [THESE] financial statements as a whole. A matter is material if it would **reasonably influence a reader**..."

3.4 Current developments

Internationally, there is currently an exposure draft of ISA 320 *Audit materiality* in issue. The key issues in relation to this exposure draft are:

(a) **Definition of materiality**. The ED makes clear that the definition of materiality used by the auditors should be the same as the definition in the applicable reporting framework. (For example, the definition in current ISA 320 is the same as in IAS 1.)

(b) **Users**. The ED says that the auditor should consider users of financial statements as a group for materiality purposes and should not try and consider individual users.

(c) **Percentage benchmarks**. The ED provides more guidance on the use of percentage benchmarks for calculating materiality.

(d) **Reporting.** The ED requires auditors to communicate all discovered misstatements to management, even those that appear trivial.

(e) **Evaluation**. The ED sets out that establishing a materiality level does not mean some matters should be ignored in overall review.

Question   Materiality

You are the manager responsible for the audit of Albreda Co. The draft consolidated financial statements for the year ended 30 September 2006 show turnover of £42.2 million (2005 £41.8 million), profit before taxation of £1.8 million (2005 £2.2 million) and total assets of £30.7 million (2005 £23.4 million). In September 2006, the management board announced plans to cease offering 'home delivery' services from the end of the month. These sales amounted to £0.6 million for the year to 30 September 2006 (2005 £0.8 million). A provision of £0.2 million has been made at 30 September 2006 for the compensation of redundant employees (mainly drivers).

Required

Comment upon the materiality of these two issues.

Answer

Home delivery sales

The appropriate indicator of materiality with regard to the home delivery sales is revenue, as the home delivery sales from part of the total turnover of the company.

£0.6 million is 1.4% of the total turnover for 2006 (see Working 1 below).

An item is generally considered to be material if it is the region of 1% of turnover, so the home delivery services are material.

Provision

The appropriate indicators of materiality with regard to the provision are total assets and profit, as the provision impacts both the balance sheet (it is a liability) and the profit and loss account (it is a charge against profit).

£0.2 million is 0.65% of total assets in 2006 (see Working 2 below). As an item is generally considered to be material if it is the region of 2-5% of total assets, the provision is not material to the balance sheet.

However, £0.2 million is 11% of profit before tax for 2006 (see Working 3 below). An item is considered material to profit before tax if it is in the region of 5%. Therefore, the provision is material to the profit and loss account.

Working 1	Working 2	Workings 3
$\frac{£0.6\text{million}}{£42.2\text{million}} \times 100\% = 1.4\%$	$\frac{£0.2\text{million}}{£30.7\text{million}} \times 100 = 0.65\%$	$\frac{£0.2\text{million}}{£1.8\text{million}} \times 100 = 11\%$

Exam focus point

This question is taken from on old syllabus exam paper. Had you calculated this materiality and commented upon whether these matters were material in the exam, then you could have earned up to two marks out of the twenty available in this question. Given that the question had two further parts which also required analysis of materiality, you could have earned a substantial number of marks for calculating relevant materiality indicators and commenting on them.

In the exam it is not necessary to give such a comment about the relevant indicator of materiality. The bits that would have earned two marks in the exam are shown in grey shade above. When attempting exam questions, when you are given the information to calculate and comment on materiality, do so.

4 Risk

As you know from your earlier studies at 2.6, the auditor must be aware of two types of risk.

- **Audit risk** (sometimes known as assignment or engagement risk)
- **Business risk**

4.1 Audit risk

FAST FORWARD

Auditors must assess the risk of material misstatements arising in financial statements and carry out procedures in response to assessed risks.

Key terms

Audit risk is the risk that auditors may give an inappropriate opinion on the financial statements. Audit risk has two key components; risk of material misstatement in financial statements (**financial statement risk**) and the risk of the auditor not detecting the material misstatements in financial statements (**detection risk**). Financial statement risk breaks down into inherent risk and control risk.

Inherent risk is the susceptibility of an account balance or class of transactions to material misstatement, either individually or when aggregated with misstatements in other balances or classes, irrespective of related internal controls.

Control risk is the risk that a misstatement:

- Could occur in an account balance or class of transactions
- Could be material, either individually or when aggregated with misstatements in other balances or classes, and
- Would not be prevented, or detected and corrected on a timely basis, by the accounting and internal control systems.

Detection risk is the risk that the auditors' substantive procedures do not detect a misstatement that exists in an account balance or class of transactions that could be material, either individually or when aggregated with misstatements in other balances or classes.

Example

In an old syllabus paper, a question gave some details about an oil company, which had abandoned one of its oil rigs. This abandonment was a financial statement risk because the abandonment gave rise to an impairment in the value of the rig, which might not have been reflected in the financial statements. In other words, there was a risk that the financial statements were misstated in respect of this oil rig.

4.1.1 Inherent risk

Inherent risk is the risk that items will be misstated due to characteristics of those items, such as the fact they are estimates or that they are important items in the accounts. The auditors must use their professional judgement and the understanding of the entity they have gained to assess inherent risk. If no such information or knowledge is available then the inherent risk is **high.**

FACTORS AFFECTING CLIENT AS A WHOLE	
Integrity and **attitude to risk** of directors and management	Domination by a single individual can cause problems
Management experience and **knowledge**	Changes in management and quality of financial management
Unusual pressures on management	Examples include tight reporting deadlines, or market or financing expectations
Nature of business	Potential problems include technological obsolescence or over-dependence on single product
Industry factors	Competitive conditions, regulatory requirements, technology developments, changes in customer demand
Information technology	Problems include lack of supporting documentation, concentration of expertise in a few people, potential for unauthorised access

FACTORS AFFECTING INDIVIDUAL ACCOUNT BALANCES OR TRANSACTIONS	
Financial statement **accounts prone to misstatement**	Accounts which require adjustment in previous period or require high degree of estimation
Complex accounts	Accounts which require expert valuations or are subjects of current professional discussion
Assets at risk of being **lost or stolen**	Cash, stock, portable fixed assets (computers)
Quality of **accounting systems**	Strength of individual departments (sales, purchases, cash etc)
High volume transactions	Accounting system may have problems coping
Unusual transactions	Transactions for large amounts, with unusual names, not settled promptly (particularly important if they occur at period-end)
	Transactions that do not go through the system, that relate to specific clients or processed by certain individuals
Staff	Staff changes or areas of low morale

4.1.2 Control risk

Control risk is the risk that client controls fail to detect material misstatements. A **preliminary assessment** of **control risk** at the planning stage of the audit is required to determine the level of controls and substantive testing to be carried out.

4.1.3 Detection risk

Detection risk is the risk that audit procedures will fail to detect material errors. Detection risk relates to the inability of the auditors to examine all evidence. Audit evidence is usually persuasive rather than conclusive so some detection risk is usually present, allowing the auditors to seek 'reasonable confidence'.

The auditors' **inherent and control risk assessments** influence the **nature, timing and extent of substantive procedures** required to reduce detection risk and thereby audit risk.

4.2 Business risk

Business risk is the risk arising to companies through being in operation.

Key terms

> **Business risk** is the risk inherent to the company in its operations. It is risks at all levels of the business. It is split into three categories:
>
> **Financial risks** are the risks arising from the financial activities or financial consequences of an operation, for example, cash flow issues or overtrading.
>
> **Operational risks** are the risks arising with regard to operations, for example, the risk that a major supplier will be lost and the company will be unable to operate.
>
> **Compliance risk** is the risk that arises from non-compliance with the laws and regulations that surround the business. The compliance risk attaching to environmental issues, for example, is discussed in Chapter 16.

In Chapter 14, we will discuss the Turnbull guidelines that highlight the importance of risk management in a business. The above components of business risk are the risks that the company should seek to mitigate and manage.

The **process of risk management** for the business is as follows:

- Identify significant risks which could prevent the business achieving its objectives
- Provide a framework to ensure that the business can meet its objectives
- Review the objectives and framework regularly to ensure that objectives are met

A key part of the process is therefore to **identify the business risks**. There are various tools used to do this that you may have come across before. They are listed below.

- SWOT analysis
- The five forces model
- The PEST analysis
- Porter's value chain

Exam focus point

> The study guide states that you should be able to identify business risks in a question. If you have previously used any of the above techniques, they may be useful to you, but in the exam, it will be better to use common sense as you work through any given question, bearing in mind the three components of business risk given above.

4.2.1 Relationship between business risk and audit risk

On the one hand, business risk and audit risk are completely unrelated:

- Business risk arises in the operations of a business
- Audit risk is focused on the financial statements of the business
- Audit risk exists only in relation to an opinion given by auditors

In other ways, the two are strongly connected. The strong links between them can be seen in the inherent and control aspects of audit risk. In audit risk these are limited to risks pertaining to the financial statements.

Business risk includes all risks facing the business. In other words, inherent audit risk may include business risks.

In response to business risk, the directors institute a system of controls. These will include controls to mitigate against the financial aspect of the business risk. These are the controls that audit control risk incorporates.

Therefore, although audit risk is very financial statements focused, business risk does form part of the inherent risk associated with the financial statements, not least, because if the risks materialise, the going concern basis of the financial statements could be affected.

4.3 Business risks from current trends in IT

4.3.1 The increasing risk of cyber incidents

Increasing connectivity and the openness of computer networks in the global business environment expose businesses to system and network failures and to cyber attack. In a study titled 'The Economic Impact of Cyber Attacks' the US Congressional Research Service reported that recent estimates of the total worldwide losses due to hostile attacks range from US$13 billion (for worms and viruses only) to US$ 226 billion (for all forms of attacks, the study also noted that cyber incidents had the effect of wiping 1% to 5% off the share price of targeted companies.

4.3.2 Audit considerations

Auditors must assess their clients' procedures for identifying and addressing these risks. Some main considerations are:

- Has management established an information and internet security policy?
- How does the entity identify critical information assets and the risk to these assets?
- Does the entity have cyber insurance (many general policies now exclude cyber events)?
- Is there a process for assuring security when linked to third party systems (e.g partners/contractors)?
- What controls are in place to ensure that employees only have access to files and applications that are required for their job?
- Are regular scans carried out to identify malicious activity?
- Are procedures in place to ensure that security is not compromised when the company's systems are accessed from home or on the road?
- What plans are in place for disaster recovery in case of an incident?

These issues will be built into the auditor's assessment of the control environment of the entity and in some cases may influence the auditor's view as to whether there are any uncertainties relating to the going concern status of the entity.

Case Study

Risk in an e-commerce environment

Tripper Ltd is a travel agency operating in three adjacent towns. The directors have recently taken the decision that they should cease their High Street operations and convert into a dot.com. The new operation, Trippers.com, will benefit from enlarged markets and reduced overheads, as they will be able to operate from single, cheaper premises.

Such a business decision has opened Tripper Ltd up to significant new business risks.

Customers

Converting to a dot.com company in this way enforces a loss of 'personal touch' with customers. Trippers staff will no longer meet the customers face to face. In a business such as a travel agency, this could be a significant factor. Customers may have appreciated the service given in branches and may feel that this level of service has been lost if it is now redirected through computers and telephones. Trippers should be aware of the possibility of, and mitigate against, loss of customer due to perceived reduction in service.

Competition

By leaving the local area and entering a wider market, Trippers is opening itself up to much more substantial competition. Whereas previously, Trippers competed with other local travel agents, they will now be competing theoretically with travel agents everywhere that have Internet facilities.

Technology issues

As Trippers has moved into a market that necessitates high technological capabilities, a number of business risks are raised in relation to technological issues:

Viruses

There is a threat of business being severely interrupted by computer viruses, particularly if the staff of Trippers are not very computer literate or the system the company invests in is not up to the standard required.

Viruses could cause interrupted sales and loss of customer goodwill, which could have a significant impact on the going concern status of the company.

Loss of existing custom

Technology could be another reason for loss of existing customers. Their existing customers might not have Internet access or ability to use computers. We do not know what Trippers' demographic was prior to conversion.

However, if conversion means that Trippers lose their existing client base completely and have to rebuild sales, the potential cost in advertising could be excessive.

Cost of system upgrades

Technology is a fast moving area and it will be vital that Trippers' web site is kept up to current standards. The cost of upgrade, both in terms of money and business interruption, could be substantial.

New supply chain factors

Trippers may keep existing links with holiday companies and operators. However, they will have new suppliers, such as Internet service providers to contend with.

Personnel

Due to the conversion, Trippers.com will require technical staff and experts. They may not currently have these staff. If this is the case, they could be at risk of severe business interruption and customer dissatisfaction.

If the directors are not computer literate, they may find that they are relying on staff who are far more expert that they are to ensure that their business runs efficiently.

Legislation

There are a number of issues to consider here. The first is data protection and the necessity to comply with the law when personal details are given over the computer. It is important that the web site is secure.

E-commerce is also likely to be an area where there is fast moving legislation as the law seeks to keep up with developments. Trippers must also keep up with developments in the law.

Lastly, trading over the Internet may create complications as to what domain Trippers are trading in for the purposes of law and tax.

Fraud exposure

The company may find that it is increasingly exposed to fraud in the following ways:

- Credit card fraud relating from transactions not being face to face
- Hacking and fraud relating from the web site not being secure
- Over-reliance on computer expert personnel could lead to those people committing fraud

Trippers' auditors will be regarding the conversion with interest. The conversion will also severely affect audit risk.

Impact on audit risk

Inherent risk

Many of the business risks identified above could have significant impacts on going concern.

Control risk

The new operations will require new systems, many of which may be specialised computer systems.

Detection risk

The conversion may have the following effects:

- Create a 'paper less office' as all transactions are carried out on line – this may make use of CAATs essential

- The auditors may have no experience in e-commerce which may increase detection risk

- There are likely to be significant impacts on analytical review as results under the new operations are unlikely to be very comparable to the old

- There may be a significant need to use the work of experts to obtain sufficient, appropriate audit evidence

4.4 Financial statement risk

4.4.1 Definition

This is the risk that the financial statements are materially misstated. The material misstatement could involve:

- Errors in the amounts recorded in the profit and loss account or balance sheet
- Errors in or omissions from the disclosure notes

4.4.2 Link with business risk

Many, if not all, business risks will produce a financial statement risk.

<table>
<tr><td>**Exam focus point**</td><td>In scenario questions you could be asked to explain either business or financial statement risks. It is important to use the scenario in the correct way and answer the exact question that is being asked.</td></tr>
</table>

Using the information in the previous case study to illustrate the link

Business risk	Financial statement risk
The business may lose sales as a result of computer viruses, which could threaten the company's going concern status.	Uncertainties over going concern may not be fully disclosed.
Breaches of data protection law and other regulations could result in the company suffering financial penalties.	Provisions relating to breaches of regulations may be omitted or understated.
The business may suffer losses from credit card fraud.	Losses arising from frauds may not be recognised in the financial statements.

Exam focus point

In this case study, e-commerce has been used to illustrate the issue of risks. E-commerce is a topical area, and you should be familiar with the issues arising for audit and assurance from e-commerce. However, you need to be able to recognise issues for any business scenario you are given.

Try and learn to let key phrases trigger your thoughts about particular issues such as systems and going concern. Above all, think about the nature of the business in the scenario and the strengths and weaknesses likely to exist at it.

You should attempt the next question, which is a case study question on risks. The answer to this question includes an 'approach' to answering such questions, which you can look at if you struggle to identify risks in the scenario.

Question

Audit risk

Forsythia is a small limited company offering garden landscaping services. It is partly owned by three business associates, Mr Rose, Mr White and Mr Grass, who each hold 10% of the shares. The major shareholder is the parent company, Poppy Ltd. This company owns shares in 20 different companies, which operate in a variety of industries. One of them is a garden centre, and Forsythia regularly trades with it. Poppy Ltd is in turn owned by a parent, White Holdings Ltd.

The management structure at Forsythia is simple. Of the three non-corporate shareholders, only Mr Rose has any involvement in management. He runs the day to day operations of the company (marketing, sales, purchasing etc) although the company employs two landscape gardeners to actually carry out projects. The accounts department employs a purchase clerk and a sales clerk, who deal with all aspects of their function. The sales clerk is Mr Rose's daughter, Justine. Mr Rose authorises and produces the payroll. The company ledgers are kept on Mr Rose's personal computer. Two weeks after the year end, the sales ledger records were severely damaged by a virus. Justine has a single print out of the balances as at year end, which shows the total owed by each customer.

Forsythia owns the equipment which the gardeners use and they pay them a salary and a bonus based on performance. Mr Rose is remunerated entirely on a commission basis relating to sales and, as a shareholder he receives dividends annually, which are substantial.

Forsythia does not carry any stock. When materials are required for a project, they are purchased on behalf of the client and charged directly to them. Most customers pay within the 60 day credit period, or take up the extended credit period which Forsythia offer. However, there are a number of accounts that appear to have been outstanding for a significant period.

Justine and her father do not appear to have a very good working relationship. She does not live at home and her salary is not significant. However, she appears to have recently purchased a sports car, which is not a company car.

The audit partner has recently accepted the audit of Forsythia. You have been assigned the task of planning the first audit.

Required

Identify and explain the audit and engagement risks arising from the above scenario.

Approaching the answer

Try and apply the two points mentioned in the exam focus point above. Look for **key words** and **ask questions** of the information given to you. This is illustrated here:

> **[Debtors likely to be significant]**
>
> Forsythia is a small limited company offering garden landscaping services. It is partly owned by three business associates, Mr Rose, Mr White and Mr Grass, who each hold 10% of the shares. The major
>
> **[Complicated corporate structure – why?]**
>
> shareholder is the parent company, Poppy Ltd. This company owns shares in 20 different companies, which operate in a variety of industries. One of them is a garden centre, and Forsythia regularly trades with it. Poppy Ltd is in turn owned by a parent, White Holdings Ltd. **[Controlling party?]**
>
> **[Key man? Over-reliance?]**
>
> The management structure at Forsythia is simple. Of the three non-corporate shareholders, only Mr Rose has any involvement in management. He runs the day to day operations of the company
>
> **[Is it slightly odd that a landscape gardening business isn't owned by landscape gardeners?]**
>
> (marketing, sales, purchasing etc) although the company employs two landscape gardeners to actually carry out projects. The accounts department employs a purchase clerk and a sales clerk, who deal **[??]** with all aspects of their function. The sales clerk is Mr Rose's daughter, Justine. Mr Rose authorises and produces the payroll. The company ledgers are kept on Mr Rose's personal computer. Two weeks **[Poor controls]** after the yearend, the sales ledger records were severely damaged by a virus. Justine has a
>
> **[No segregation of duties]**
>
> single print out of the balances as at year end, which shows the total owed by each customer.
>
> **[Limitation? And given below, a suspicion of fraud? Teeming and lading?]**
>
> **[Very profit related focused. – management bias?]**
>
> Forsythia owns the equipment which the gardeners use and they pay them a salary and a bonus based on performance. Mr Rose is remunerated entirely on a commission basis relating to sales and, as a shareholder he receives dividends annually, which are substantial.
>
> **[How accounted?]**
>
> Forsythia does not carry any stock. When materials are required for a project, they are purchased on
>
> **[Any laws and regulations relevant?]**
>
> behalf of the client and charged directly to them. Most customers pay within the 60 day credit period, or take up the extended credit period which Forsythia offer. However, there are a number of accounts that
>
> **[Problem with debtors Fraud?]**
>
> appear to have been outstanding for a significant period.

Justine and her father do not appear to have a very good working relationship. She does not live at home and her salary is not significant. However, she appears to have recently purchased a sports car, which is not a company car.

Fraud?

The audit partner has recently accepted the audit of Forsythia. You have been assigned the task of planning the first audit.

Detection risk
Opening balances
Comparatives – audited or not?

Any group planning issues?

Why not all the other group companies? Why do they have different auditors?

Answer plan

Not all the points you notice will necessarily be **relevant** and you may also find that you do not have **time** to mention all the points in your answer. Now you should prioritise your points in a more formal answer plan and then write your answer:

Audit risks

Inherent	*Control*
Related party transactions/group issues	Lack of segregation of duties
Debtors	PC/virus
Fraud – possible indicators, professional scepticism	Suspicion of fraud?
Profit driven management	Key man
Credit extended – accounting/law and regs	*Detection*
	First audit
	Opening bals and comparatives – audited?

Engagement risks

Some questions raised which makes business look odd

- Group (complex/different auditors/who controls?)
- Nature of business – yet landscape gardeners hired

Indicators of potential fraud

Possible indicators of money laundering (complex structure/cash business)

These may be overstated, but auditor must   (a) consider them
                                             (b) be prepared for consequences

Answer

The following matters are relevant to planning Forsythia's audit:

Audit risks – inherent

Related parties and group issues

Forsythia is part of a **complicated group structure**. This raises several issues for the audit:

- There is a risk of related party transactions existing and not being properly disclosed in the financial statements in accordance with FRS 8.

- Similarly, there is a risk that it will be difficult to ascertain the controlling party for disclosure

- There are likely to be some group audit implications. My firm may be required to undertake procedures in line with the principal auditors' requirements if Forsythia is to be consolidated

Debtors

Forsythia is a **service provider**, and it **extends credit** to customers. This is likely to mean that **trade debtors** will be a significant audit balance. However, there is **limited audit evidence** concerning trade debtors due to the effects of a computer virus. There are also indicators of a **possible fraud**.

Fraud?

There are various factors that may indicate a sales ledger fraud has taken/is taking place:

- Lack of segregation of duties
- Extensive credit offered
- The virus only destroyed sales ledger information – too specific?
- Poorly paid sales ledger clerk – with expensive life style
- Sales ledger clerk is daughter of rich shareholder and they do not have a good relationship

None of these **factors** necessarily point to a fraud individually, but **added together raise significant concerns**.

Profit driven management

Mr Rose is motivated for the financial statements to show a profit for two reasons:

- He receives a commission (presumably sales driven, which impacts on profit)
- He receives dividends as shareholder, which will depend on profits

There is a risk that the **financial statements** will be **affected by management bias**.

Credit extended

We should ensure that the credit extended to customers is standard business credit. There are unlikely to be any **complications**, for example, interest, but if there were, we should be aware of any **laws and regulations** which might become relevant, and any **accounting issues** which would be raised.

Audit risk – control

There are three significant control problems at Forsythia.

Segregation of duties

There appears to be a **complete lack of segregation of duties** on the three main ledgers. This may have led to a **fraud** on the sales ledger. The fact that there is no segregation on payroll is also a concern as this is an area where frauds are carried out.

Lack of segregation of duties can also lead to **significant errors** arising and not being detected by the system. This problem means that **control risk** will have to be assessed as **high** and **substantial substantive testing** be undertaken.

Personal Computer

A PC is used for the accounting system. This is likely to have **poor built in controls** and further exacerbate the problems caused by the lack of segregation of duties.

The **security** over PCs is also often poor, as has been the case here, where a **virus** has destroyed evidence about the sales ledger.

Key man

The fact that Mr Rose is dominant in management may also be a control problem, particularly if he were ever to be absent.

Audit risk – detection

The key detection risk is that this is the **first audit**, so we have no CAKE (cumulative audit knowledge and experience) of this client. We have not audited the **opening balances** and **comparatives**. We should have contacted any previous auditors and therefore be aware of whether these have been audited. If there were no previous auditors, these are unaudited. We must ensure that our audit report is clear on this issue.

There is also significant detection risk in relation to **related parties**, as discussed above.

Engagement risk

There are several indicators that Forsythia may be an 'odd' company.

The first indicator is that it is part of a **complex and unexplained group**, and that the group is not audited by the same firm of auditors, although it is unclear how many firms of auditors are involved in the group audit. There may be good reasons for this audit policy, but we should **investigate those reasons**, in case any other reasons appear.

Another indicator is that it seems slightly odd that a small company should exist to provide landscape gardening services, when it appears that the owners are not landscape gardeners, or at least, if they are, they do not work in the business. Again, there may be valid reasons for this, but we should **discover and document them**.

It is particularly important that these issues are cleared up. A complex group structure and a company dealing in cash transactions (Forsythia's potentially are) could indicate the possibility that the owners are trying to **launder money**. There are also indicators of **fraud**. If either of these issues exist, the auditor may have **significant responsibility** to report and co-operate with relevant authorities, and the **professional relationship of client and auditor could be compromised**. Therefore, the audit firm must ensure that it has suitable 'know your client' procedures in place and the appropriate systems for making suspicion reports should a suspicion arise. The partners must ensure that staff have appropriate training so that they are able to comply fully with legal requirements in relation to money laundering.

5 Analytical procedures

FAST FORWARD

Analytical procedures are important at all stages of the audit.

Knowledge brought forward from previous studies

Guidance on analytical procedures is given in ISA (UK and Ireland) 520 *Analytical Procedures*.

Analytical procedures can be used at three stages of the audit:

- Planning
- Substantive procedures
- Overall review

Analytical procedures consist of comparing items, for example, current year financial information with prior year financial information, and analysing predictable relationships, for example, the relationship between debtors and credit sales.

5.1 Use of analytical procedures generally

There are a number of occasions and assignments when an auditor will look to take an analytical procedures approach. One has already been mentioned in this chapter. When auditors use the business risk approach they seek to use a high level of analytical procedures. Other examples include:

- Reviews (Chapter 13)
- Assurance engagements (Chapter 13)
- Prospective financial information (Chapter 15)

5.2 Use of analytical procedures on an audit

Exam focus point

You should note that whether or not auditors choose an analytical procedure approach for an audit, the knowledge you already have of analytical procedures **still applies**. In any audit, analytical procedures are used at the three stages. If the analytical procedures approach is taken, the use of analytical review at the second stage is expanded.

There are a number of factors which the auditors should consider when deciding whether to use analytical procedures as substantive procedures.

Factors to consider	Example
The **plausibility and predictability** of the relationships identified for comparison and evaluation	The strong relationship between certain selling expenses and turnover in businesses where the sales force is paid by commission
The **objectives** of the analytical procedures and the extent to which their results are reliable	
The **detail** to which information can be **analysed**	Analytical procedures may be more effective when applied to financial information or individual sections of an operation such as individual factories or shops
The **availability of information**	Financial: budgets or forecasts Non-financial: eg the number of units produced or sold
The **relevance of the information** available	Whether the budgets are established as results to be expected rather than as tough targets (which may well not be achieved)
The **comparability of the information** available	Comparisons with average performance in an industry may be of little value if a large number of companies differ significantly from the average
The **knowledge gained during previous audits**	The effectiveness of the accounting and internal controls The types of problems giving rise to accounting adjustments in prior periods

Factors which should also be considered when determining the reliance that the auditors should place on the results of substantive analytical procedures are:

Reliability factors	Example
Other audit procedures directed towards the same financial statements assertions	Other procedures auditors undertake in reviewing the collectability of debtors, such as the review of subsequent cash receipts, may confirm or dispel questions arising from the application of analytical procedures to a profit of customers' accounts which lists for how long monies have been owed

Reliability factors	Example
The **accuracy** with which the expected results of analytical procedures can be predicted	Auditors normally expect greater consistency in comparing the relationship of gross profit to sales from one period to another than in comparing expenditure which may or may not be made within a period, such as research or advertising
The **frequency** with which a relationship is observed	A pattern repeated monthly as opposed to annually

Reliance on the results of analytical procedures depends on the auditors' assessment of the **risk** that the procedures may identify relationships (between data) do exist, whereas a material misstatement exists (that is, the relationships, in fact, do not exist). It depends also on the results of investigations that auditors have made if substantive analytical procedures have highlighted significant fluctuations or unexpected relationships (see below).

5.3 Practical techniques

When carrying out analytical procedures, auditors should remember that every industry is different and each company within an industry differs in certain aspects.

Important accounting ratios	Gross profit margins, in total and by product, area and months/quarter (if possible)
	Debtors ratio (average collection period)
	Stock turnover ratio (inventory divided into cost of sales)
	Current ratio (current assets to current liabilities)
	Quick or acid test ratio (liquid assets to current liabilities)
	Gearing ratio (debt capital to equity capital)
	Return on capital employed (profit before tax to total assets less current liabilities)
Related items	Creditors and purchases
	Stock and cost of sales
	Fixed assets and depreciation, repairs and maintenance expense
	Intangible assets and amortisation
	Loans and interest expense
	Investments and investment income
	Debtors and bad debt expense
	Debtors and sales

Ratios mean very little when used in isolation. They should be calculated for **previous periods** and for **comparable companies.** The permanent file should contain a section with summarised accounts and the chosen ratios for prior years.

In addition to looking at the more usual ratios the auditors should consider examining **other ratios** that may be **relevant** to the particular **client's business,** such as revenue per passenger mile for an airline operator client, or fees per partner for a professional office.

Exam focus point

At this level, you are more likely to be required to **justify** why an analytical procedures approach should be taken than to calculate a series of ratios.

However, if you are asked to perform analytical review in the exam, remember that it is vital that you analyse any calculation you have made in your answer. It is very important to make comments and draw conclusions.

Other analytical techniques include:

(a) **Examining related accounts** in conjunction with each other. Often revenue and expense accounts are related to balance sheet accounts and comparisons should be made to ensure relationships are reasonable.

(b) **Trend analysis.** Sophisticated statistical techniques can be used to compare this period with previous periods.

(c) **Reasonableness tests.** These involve calculating **expected value** of an item and comparing it with its actual value, for example, for straight-line depreciation.

(Cost + Additions − Disposals) × Depreciation % = Charge in P & L A/C

5.3.1 Trend analysis

Trend analysis is likely to be very important if an analytical procedure approach is taken. Information technology can be used in trend analysis, to enable auditors to see trends graphically with relative ease and speed.

Methods of trend analysis include:

- 'Scattergraphs'
- Bar graphs
- Pie charts
- Any other visual representations
- Time series analysis
- Statistical regression

Time series analysis involves techniques such as eliminating seasonal fluctuations from sets of figures, so that underlying trends can be analysed. This is illustrated below.

Example

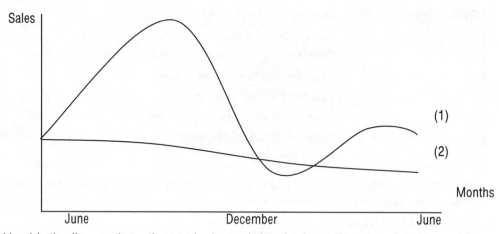

Line 1 in the diagram shows the actual sales made by a business. There is a clear seasonal fluctuation before Christmas. Line 2 shows a level of sales with 'expected seasonal fluctuations' having been stripped out. It shows that sales were lower than expected for December and continued to be low, despite December sales being higher than the other months.

In this analysis the seasonal fluctuations have been estimated. This analysis is useful however, because the estimate is likely to be based on past performance, so that conclusion from this is that there might be a problem:

- Sales are below the levels of previous years
- Sales are below expectation

Exam focus point

Audit approach has been identified as a key topic area. It is an area you should be familiar with from previous auditing studies, and most of the items looked at in this chapter should be revision.

A key point to remember when seeking to identify an appropriate strategy for a particular audit is that the approaches are linked and in some cases it may be best to use two or more together to achieve a good result. For example, directional testing would be used with a balance sheet approach because they are both substantive testing issues.

Remember also to focus on details given in the question to determine what approach is relevant. For example, if the question relates to a business which has a low level of large transactions, a cycles based approach might be relevant. A business with substantial numbers of sales transactions resulting in a balance sheet with substantial receivables in it might benefit from a balance sheet approach. It is likely that a risk approach would be taken in conjunction with these approaches. You should consider whether a business risk approach would be relevant.

6 General planning matters

FAST FORWARD

There are various administrative matters which auditors must also consider as part of their overall audit strategy.

6.1 Logistics

When planning an audit, the audit engagement partner or manager has to consider many practical things. We shall consider a few of them here:

- Staff
- Client management
- Locations of the audit
- Deadlines

6.1.1 Staff

There are several considerations with regard to audit staff, and these are shown in the diagram below.

Exam focus point

Bear in mind that not all will be relevant to all audits, and when answering questions, you should concentrate on the facts given in the question rather than listing all these factors regardless of information given in the question.

 Case Study

Skills in an e-commerce environment

Specialist skills will be required to plan and carry out an audit is where the company engages in e-commerce.

Specialist knowledge is required to carry out various key aspects of the audit:

Inherent risk evaluation	A degree of specialist understanding of the inherent nature of the IT environment will be required to understand the inherent risk arising from the business being involved in e commerce.
Control environment assessment	Similarly, to be able to make intelligent queries about the control environment, and to be able to understand the answers given, a degree of knowledge is required.
Determining procedures	In a heavily IT environment, it is going to be impossible to ascertain what procedures are required, and what the extent and timing of those procedures is going to be, without a specialist knowledge.
Evaluating going concern	An understanding of the technological environment will be required in order to properly assess the impact of that environment on the going concern assumption, the risks that exist and the potential impact of those risks on the business and its ability to continue.

6.1.2 Client management

The management of the client company may have preferences regarding audit staff, for example, a finance director may be keen that there is continuity of audit staff on the assignment, so that last year's semi senior is this year's senior, or that the same staff are used from year to year.

This may not always be possible, but the person planning the audit will try and bear in mind the needs of the client in such matters. Consistency of audit staff may help audit efficiency in terms of knowledge of the business and its staff.

6.1.3 Locations

The person planning the audit will have to give consideration to the location of the audit. There are several issues that could arise.

Factor	Consideration
Location	Distance for audit staff to travel
	Mobility of audit staff
	Location of audit review by manager/engagement partner
Multiple locations	All the above considerations
	Determination of which locations to visit
	Allocation of audit staff to each site
	Liaising with client staff to ensure each site visit is convenient.

6.1.4 Deadlines

It is of vital importance that the audit team know the deadlines involved in the audit. The key dates that the team will need to know are likely to be:

- Date of stock count
- Date the financial statements are due to have been drafted by
- Dates of main audit visit
- Date of manager review
- Date of engagement partner review
- Date of engagement partner's post audit meeting with client management
- Date on which the audit report is due to be signed
- Date of AGM

It is important that the audit team is aware of these dates and that the audit is planned so that the work can be achieved in relation to these dates. It is vitally important, for instance, that the audit is completed by the date on which the audit report is to be signed. It would also be foolish to try and start detailed substantive testing before the financial statements had been drafted.

6.2 Use of IT

The use of IT is increasingly common in auditing. There are several factors which may need to be considered:

- Whether the client has a computerised system
- If so, whether the auditors will make use of CAATs
- Whether the auditor will use computers to complete his working papers
- If so, whether the members of the audit team are equipped with laptops
- What specific audit tasks the engagement partner requires to be done on the computer, for example, analytical review
- Whether the partner wants to be able to contact the audit team electronically on site
- If so, whether the audit team are properly equipped with modems.

6.3 Time budgets

We discussed the importance of time estimation when we discussed setting the fee in Chapter 3. It is important to the engagement partner that the audit is completed in a cost effective manner. Therefore, the time taken to conduct each part of the audit will have been estimated and the fee set accordingly.

These time budgets are an important part of planning then.

- It is important that the time is estimated accurately
- It is important that the audit team is aware of the time budget
- It is important that the audit team record variances from the time budget

The time budget will be based on issues such as:

- Prior year time records
- Risk assessments
- Materiality considerations

In other words, if stock is the most material and risky item on the balance sheet, it will have a large estimate of time attached to it, especially if it took a long time last year. In contrast an item such as long term bank loans could be material, but it is low risk due to the existence of good third party evidence and use can be made of procedures such as analytical review. It may therefore have less time budgeted to it.

6.4 Subsidiary objectives of the assignment

The key purpose of the audit, as you know, is to obtain sufficient, appropriate evidence to express an opinion on the financial statements.

However, there may be subsidiary (non-statutory) objectives of the audit assignment. An example would be the report to management. The audit plan should set out these subsidiary objectives and also set deadlines and any specific requirements for these.

Chapter Roundup

- Auditors must plan their work so that it is undertaken in an effective manner.

- With a business risk ('top-down') approach controls testing is aimed at high level controls and substantive testing is reduced.

- An auditor may predominantly test controls and systems, but substantive testing can never be eliminated entirely.

- An auditor may choose predominantly to carry out substantive tests on the transactions of the business in the relevant period.

- An auditor may choose predominantly to carry out substantive tests on year end balances.

- Directional testing is a method of discovering errors and omissions in financial statements.

- Materiality considerations are important at the planning stage. An item might be material due to its nature, value or impact on readers of the financial statements.

- Auditors must assess the risk of material misstatements arising in financial statements and carry out procedures in response to assessed risks.

- Business risk is the risk arising to companies through being in operation.

- Analytical procedures are important at all stages of the audit.

- There are various administrative matters which auditors must also consider as part of their overall audit strategy.

Quick Quiz

1   What are the five components of an audit strategy document?

   (1) ....

   (2) ....

   (3) ....

   (4) ....

   (5) ....

2   What are the effects of a 'top down' audit approach on:

   (a)   Tests of controls
   (b)   Analytical procedures
   (c)   Detailed testing

3   Name 4 key control objectives for sales.

   (1) ....
   (2) ....
   (3) ....
   (4) ....

4   When undertaking a cycles approach to auditing, the auditor is ensuring that transactions are processed through the cycle.

   True   ☐

   False ☐

5   A balance sheet approach should never be combined with a business risk approach.

   True   ☐

   False ☐

6   Complete the matrix.

Type of account	Purpose of primary test	Primary test also gives comfort on			
		Assets	Liabilities	Income	Expenses
Assets		U	O	O	U
Liabilities		U	O	O	U
Income		U	O	O	U
Expense		U	O	O	U

7   Complete the definition:

   .... is an expression of the

   .... or .... of a particular matter in the context of financial statements.

8   Identify whether the following matters, which represent potential business risks to the company are financial, operational or compliance risks.

Item	Potential business risk
Going concern	
Physical disasters	
Breakdown of accounting systems	
Loss of key personnel	
Credit risk	
Breach of legislation	
Sales tax problems	
Currency risk	
Poor brand management	
Environmental issues	

9   Name four considerations relating to audit staff an audit plan should cover.

(1)   ………………………………….

(2)   ………………………………….

(3)   ………………………………….

(4)   ………………………………….

Answers to Quick Quiz

1   (1)   Understanding the entity and its environment
     (2)   Risk and materiality
     (3)   Nature, timing and extent of procedures
     (4)   Co-ordination, direction, supervision and review
     (5)   Other matters

2   (a)   Tests of control focused on high level controls
     (b)   Analytical procedures used more extensively
     (c)   Detailed testing consequently reduced

3   Any of:

     Ordering and granting of credit

     •   **Goods** and **services** are **only supplied** to **customers** with **good credit ratings**
     •   **Customers** are encouraged to **pay promptly**
     •   **Orders** are **recorded correctly**
     •   **Orders** are **fulfilled**

     Despatch and invoicing

     •   All **despatches** of goods are **recorded**
     •   All **goods and services** sold are **correctly invoiced**
     •   All **invoices** raised **relate to goods and services** that have been **supplied** by the business
     •   **Credit notes** are only given for **valid reasons**

     Recording, accounting and credit control

     •   All sales that have been **invoiced** are **recorded** in the general and sales ledgers
     •   All **credit notes** that have been **issued** are **recorded** in the general and sales ledgers
     •   All **entries** in the sales ledger are **made** to the **correct** sales ledger **accounts**
     •   **Cut-off** is applied correctly to the sales ledger
     •   Potentially **doubtful debts** are **identified**

4   True

5   False

6

Type of account	Purpose of primary test	Primary test also gives comfort on			
		Assets	Liabilities	Income	Expenses
Assets	Overstatement (O)	U	O	O	U
Liabilities	Understatement (U)	U	O	O	U
Income	Understatement (U)	U	O	O	U
Expense	Overstatement (O)	U	O	O	U

7   Materiality, relative significance, importance

8

Item	Potential business risk
Going concern	Financial
Physical disasters	Operational
Breakdown of accounting systems	Financial
Loss of key personnel	Operational
Credit risk	Financial
Breach of legislation	Compliance
Sales tax problems	Compliance
Currency risk	Financial
Poor brand management	Operational
Environmental issues	Compliance

9 From:

(1) Correct level of qualification
(2) Availability
(3) Correct level of experience
(4) Relationship with client staff
(5) Special skills
(6) Travel logistics
(7) Relationship with client staff

Now try the question below from the Exam Question Bank			
Number	**Level**	**Marks**	**Time**
Q21	Examination	25	45 mins

7

Evidence

Topic list	Syllabus reference
1 Audit evidence	D1(ii)
2 Related parties	D1(ii)
3 Management representations	D1(ii)
4 Reliance on the work of an expert	D1(ii)
5 Reliance on the work of internal audit	D1(ii)
6 Revision: documentation	D1(ii)

Introduction

Audit evidence is a vital part of any audit. The **basic issues** relating to **evidence** are that:

- **Auditors must obtain evidence** to support FS assertions. This evidence must be **sufficient and appropriate.**

- Audit evidence must be **documented** sufficiently.

Documentation is revised in Section 6 of this chapter.

Related parties are a difficult area to obtain audit evidence on. The auditor must bear in mind, who evidence is from and how extensive it is. Obtaining evidence about related party transactions is considered in Section 2.

Often the auditors will have to rely on **management representations** about related parties and other issues. Management representations are **subjective evidence**, and the auditor must proceed with caution when dealing with them. This is discussed in Section 3.

Sometimes, the **evidence** the auditor requires is **beyond the expertise of the auditor,** and he will need to **rely on the work of an expert.** The relevant procedures that the auditor must undertake are outlined in Section 4.

Similar considerations arise if the external auditor intends to rely on the work of internal audit.

Study guide

		Intellectual level
D1(ii)	**Evidence**	
(a)	Evaluate the appropriateness and sufficiency of different sources of audit evidence and the procedures by which evidence may be obtained including:	3
(i)	analytical procedures	
(ii)	management representations	
(iii)	the work of others	
(iv)	audit sampling	
(v)	external confirmations	
(vi)	audit automation tools	
(b)	Specify audit procedures to obtain sufficient audit evidence from identified sources.	2
(c)	Apply the criteria for assessing the extent to which reliance can be placed on substantive analytical procedures and recognise situations in which analytical procedures may be used extensively.	3
(d)	Apply analytical procedures to financial and non-financial data.	2
(e)	Identify and evaluate the audit evidence expected to be available to:	3
(i)	verify specific assets, liabilities, transactions and events; and	
(ii)	support financial statement assertions and accounting treatments (including fair values)	
(f)	Explain the reasons for preparing and retaining documentation and the importance of reviewing working papers.	1
(g)	Explain the specific audit problems and procedures concerning related parties and related party transactions.	2
(h)	Recognise circumstances that may indicate the existence of unidentified related parties and select appropriate audit procedures.	2
(i)	Demonstrate the use of written management representations as the primary source of audit evidence and as complementary audit evidence.	2
(j)	Discuss the implications of contradictory evidence being discovered.	2
(k)	Recognise when it is justifiable to place reliance on the work of an expert (eg a surveyor employed by the audit client).	2
(l)	Assess the appropriateness and sufficiency of the work of internal auditors and the extent to which reliance can be placed on it.	2

Exam guide

Specific audit issues examined in this paper are likely to be at a higher level than in your previous auditing exams. Therefore, the more complex evidence issues of related parties, representations and using the work of others are important. You should consider how they link with specific accounting issues in Chapters 9 and 10.

1 Audit evidence

FAST FORWARD

Auditors need to obtain sufficient, appropriate audit evidence.

1.1 Obtaining evidence

You should be aware of the key points audit evidence from your previous auditing studies. We shall revise them briefly here. Substantive procedures are designed to obtain evidence about the financial statement assertions.

Key term

> **Financial statement assertions** are the representations of the directors that are embodied in the financial statements. By approving the financial statements, the directors are making representations about the information therein. These representations or assertions may be described in general terms in a number of ways.

ISA (UK and Ireland) 500 *Audit evidence* states that 'the auditor should use assertions for **classes of transactions**, **account balances**, and **presentation and disclosures** in sufficient detail to form the basis for the assessment of risks of material misstatement and the design and performance of further audit procedures'. It gives examples of assertions in these areas.

Assertions used by the auditor	
Assertions about **classes of transactions** and events for the period under audit	**Occurrence**: transactions and events that have been recorded have occurred and pertain to the entity.
	Completeness: all transactions and events that should have been recorded have been recorded.
	Accuracy: amounts and other data relating to recorded transactions and events have been recorded appropriately.
	Cutoff: transactions and events have been recorded in the correct accounting period (see measurement, above).
	Classification: transactions and events have been recorded in the proper accounts.
Assertions about **account balances** at the period end	**Existence**: assets, liabilities and equity interests exist.
	Rights and obligations: the entity holds or controls the rights to assets, and liabilities are the obligations of the entity.
	Completeness: all assets, liabilities and equity interests that should have been recorded have been recorded.
	Valuation and allocation: assets, liabilities, and equity interests are included in the financial statements at appropriate amounts and any resulting valuation or allocation adjustments are appropriately recorded.
Assertions about **presentation and disclosure**	**Occurrence and rights and obligations**: disclosed events, transactions and other matters have occurred and pertain to the entity.
	Completeness: all disclosures that should have been included in the financial statements have been included.
	Classification and understandability: financial information is appropriately presented and described, and disclosures are clearly expressed.
	Accuracy and valuation: financial and other information are disclosed fairly and at appropriate amounts.

You may find the following mnemonic useful when remembering the financial statement assertions: ACCA COVER

A ccuracy

C ompleteness

C ut-off

A llocation

C lassification (understandability)

O ccurrence

V aluation

E xistence

R ights and obligations

(Each letter of ACCA COVER is the first letter of each of the assertions listed above.)

Auditors obtain evidence by one or more of the following procedures.

PROCEDURES	
Inspection of assets	Inspection of assets that are recorded in the accounting records confirms **existence**, gives evidence of **valuation**, but does not confirm **rights and obligations**
	Confirmation that assets seen are recorded in accounting records gives evidence of **completeness**
Inspection of documentation	Confirmation to documentation of items recorded in accounting records confirms that an asset **exists** or a transaction **occurred**. Confirmation that items recorded in supporting documentation are recorded in accounting records tests **completeness**
	Cut-off can be verified by inspecting reverse population, that is, checking transactions recorded **after** the balance sheet date to supporting documentation to confirm that they occurred after the balance sheet date
	Inspection also provides evidence of **valuation/ measurement**, **rights and obligations** and the nature of items **(presentation and disclosure)**. It can also be used to **compare** documents (and hence test **consistency** of audit evidence) and confirm **authorisation**
Observation	Involves watching a procedure being performed (for example, post opening)
	Of limited use, as only confirms procedure took place when auditor watching
Enquiries	Seeking information from **client staff** or **external sources**
	Strength of evidence depends on knowledge and integrity of source of information
Confirmation	Seeking confirmation from another source of details in client's accounting records for example, confirmation from bank of bank balances
Computations	Checking arithmetic of client's records, for example, adding up ledger account
Audit automation tools	See section on CAATs (1.3 below)
Analytical procedures	See Chapter 6 and 1.4 below

1.2 Sufficient and appropriate audit evidence

'Sufficiency' and 'appropriateness' are interrelated and apply to both tests of controls and substantive procedures.

- **Sufficiency** is the measure of the **quantity** of audit evidence.
- **Appropriateness** is the measure of the **quality** or **reliability** of the audit evidence.

Auditors are essentially looking for enough reliable audit evidence. Audit **evidence usually indicates what is probable** rather than what is definite (is usually persuasive rather than conclusive) so different sources are examined by the auditors. However, auditors can only give **reasonable assurance** that the financial statements are free from misstatement, so **not all sources of evidence will be examined**.

When assessing the sufficiency and appropriateness of audit evidence, auditors must consider whether the evidence is consistent. Where **contradictory evidence** is discovered, for example, where one piece of evidence suggests that a specific liability has been settled prior to the year end whilst another piece of evidence throws doubt on this, the auditors must perform any other procedures necessary to resolve the inconsistency.

ISA (UK and Ireland) 530 *Audit sampling and other means of testing* is based on the premise that auditors do not normally examine all the information available to them; it would be impractical to do so and using audit sampling will produce valid conclusions.

Key terms

> **Audit sampling** involves the application of audit procedures to less than 100% of the items within an account balance or class of transactions such that all sampling units have a chance of selection. This will enable the auditor to obtain and evaluate audit evidence about some characteristic of the items selected in order to form or assist in forming a conclusion concerning the population.
>
> **Statistical sampling** is any approach to sampling that involves random selection of a sample, and use of probability theory to evaluate sample results, including measurement of sampling risk.
>
> **Population** is the entire set of data from which a sample is selected and about which an auditor wishes to draw conclusions.
>
> **Sampling units** are the individual items constituting a population.
>
> **Stratification** is the process of dividing a population into sub-populations, each of which is a group of sampling units, which have similar characteristics (often monetary value).
>
> **Error** means either control deviations, when performing tests of control, or misstatements, when performing substantive procedures
>
> **Expected error** is the error that the auditor expects to be present in the population.
>
> **Tolerable error** is the maximum error in the population that the auditor would be willing to accept.
>
> **Anomalous error** means an error that arises from an isolated event that has not recurred other than on specifically identifiable occasions and is therefore not representative of errors in the population.
>
> **Sampling risk** arises from the possibility that the auditor's conclusion, based on a sample of a certain size, may be different from the conclusion that would be reached if the entire population were subjected to the same audit procedure.
>
> **Non-sampling risk** arises from factors that cause the auditor to reach an erroneous conclusion for any reason not related to the size of the sample. For example, most audit evidence is persuasive rather than conclusive, the auditor might use inappropriate procedures, or the auditor might misinterpret evidence and fail to recognise an error.

Some testing procedures do **not** involve sampling, such as:

- Testing 100% of items in a population (this should be obvious)

- Testing all items with a certain characteristic (for example, over a certain value) as selection is not representative

The ISA distinguishes between **statistically based sampling**, which involves the use of random selection techniques from which mathematically constructed conclusions about the population can be drawn, and **non-statistical methods**, from which auditors draw a judgmental opinion about the population. However the principles of the ISA apply to both methods. You should be aware of the major methods of statistical and non-statistical sampling.

The auditors' judgement as to what is sufficient appropriate audit evidence is influenced by a number of factors.

- **Risk assessment**
- The **nature** of the **accounting and internal control systems**
- The **materiality** of the item being examined
- The **experience gained during previous audits**
- The auditors' **knowledge of the business** and **industry**
- The **results of audit procedures**
- The **source** and **reliability of information** available

If they are unable to obtain sufficient appropriate audit evidence, the auditors should **consider the implications for their report.**

Question   Audit evidence

'The auditor should obtain sufficient and appropriate audit evidence to be able to draw reasonable conclusion on which to base the audit opinion.'   (ISA 500.2)

Discuss the extent to which each of the following sources of audit evidence is sufficient and appropriate.

(a)   Oral representation by management in respect of the completeness of sales where the majority of transactions are conducted on a cash basis

(b)   Flowcharts of the accounting and control system prepared by a company's internal audit department

(c)   Year-end supplier's statements

(d)   Physical inspection of a fixed asset by an auditor, and

(e)   Comparison of profit and loss account items for the current period with corresponding information for earlier periods.

Answer

Appropriate – Relevance

The relevance of audit evidence should be considered in relation to the overall audit objective of forming an opinion and reporting on the financial statements. The evidence should allow the auditor to conclude on the following:

Balance sheet items (Existence, rights and obligations, completeness, valuation and allocation)

Profit and loss account items (Occurrence, completeness, accuracy, cut-off and classification)

(a)   The representations by management in respect of the completeness of sales is relevant to the first of the objectives when gathering evidence on profit and loss account items. Depending on the system operated by the client and the controls over cash sales there may be no other evidence as to the completeness of sales.

(b)   The flowcharts prepared by the internal audit department will not be directly relevant to the auditor's opinion on individual figures in the financial statements, but rather when the auditor is following the requirement in ISA 315 to ascertain the enterprise's system of recording and processing transactions. The auditor will wish to assess the adequacy of the system as a basis for the preparation of financial statements so the flowcharts will be relevant only if they are sufficiently detailed to allow the auditor to carry out this assessment. The auditor would also wish to make an initial assessment of internal controls at this stage so the flowcharts will be more relevant of control procedures are specifically identified.

(c)   Year-end suppliers' statements provide evidence relevant to the auditor's conclusions on:

- The completeness of creditors, as omissions from the purchase ledger listing would be identified by comparing statements received to that listing

- The existence of creditors recorded in the purchase ledger

- The fact that the liabilities are properly those of the enterprise (for example, the statements are not addressed to, say, the managing director in his own name)

- The valuation of creditors at the year end with respect to cut-off of invoices and credit notes, and discounts or allowances.

(d)   The physical inspection of a fixed asset is clearly relevant to the auditor's opinion as to the existence of the asset, and to some extent the completeness of recording of assets, that is, the auditor can check that all the assets inspected have been recorded. In certain circumstances evidence relevant to valuation might be obtained, for example, where a client has written down a building due to permanent diminution in value and the auditor sees it standing unused and derelict.

(e)   The comparison of profit and loss account items with prior periods will provide evidence as to:

(i)   Completeness of recording, as omissions can be identified and investigated

(ii)   Valuation, in cases where the auditor has appropriate information on which to base expectations, for example, if the number of workers has doubled during the year and a set percentage wage increase had been effected in the year

(iii)   Disclosure, as the comparison should highlight any inconsistencies of classification and treatment from year to year.

Appropriate – Reliable

Reliability of audit evidence depends on the particular circumstances but the guideline offers three general presumptions

- Documentary evidence is more reliable than oral evidence

- Evidence obtained from independent sources outside the enterprise is more reliable than that secured solely from within the enterprise

- Evidence originated by the auditor by such means as analysis and physical inspection is more reliable than evidence obtained by others.

(a)   The oral representations by management would be regarded as relatively unreliable using the criteria in the guideline, as they are oral and internal. In the absence of any external or auditor-generated evidence, the auditor should ensure that these representations are included in the letter of representation so that there is at least some documentary evidence to support any conclusions.

(b)   The assessment of how reliable the flowcharts are would depend on the auditor's overall assessment of the internal audit department. The factor to be considered would include its degree of independence, the scope of its work, whether due professional care had been exercised, the technical competence and level of resource available to the internal audit department. This assessment should be documented by the external auditor of he is to make use of the flowcharts in his audit planning and design of tests.

(c)   Suppliers' statements would generally be seen as reliable evidence, being documentary and form sources external to the enterprise. If the auditor had doubts as to the reliability of this evidence, it could be improved by the auditor originating similar evidence by means of a creditor's circularisation rather than relying on suppliers' statements received by the client.

(d)   Physical inspection of a fixed asset is a clear example of auditor-originated evidence, so would usually be considered more reliable than that generate by others.

(e)   Analysis such as this comparison of profit and loss items with the prior periods would again be terms auditor-generated evidence, and would be considered more reliable than evidence generated by others. Ultimately the reliability of such audit evidence depends on the reliability of the underlying data, this should be checked by compliance or substantive testing.

Sufficiency

The auditor needs to obtain sufficient relevant and reliable evidence to form a reasonable basis for his opinion on the financial statements. His judgements will be influenced by factors such as:

- His knowledge of the business and its environment
- The risk of misstatement
- The persuasiveness of the evidence

(a)   To decide if the representations were sufficient with regard to concluding on the completeness of sales the auditor would consider:

- The nature of the business and the inherent risk of unrecorded cash sales

- The materiality of the item; in this case it would appear that cash sales are material

- Any possible management bias

- The persuasiveness of the evidence in the light of other related audit work, for example, testing of cash receipts.

If the auditor believes there is still a risk of material understatement of sales in the light of the above, he should seek further evidence.

(b)   Client-prepared flowcharts are **not** sufficient as a basis for the auditor's evaluation of the system. To confirm that the system does operate in the manner described, the auditor should perform 'walk through' checks, tracing a small number of transactions through the system. There is, however, no need for the auditor to prepare his own flowcharts if he is satisfied that those produced by internal audit are accurate.

(c)   The auditor's decision as to whether the suppliers' statements were sufficient evidence would depend on his assessment of materiality and the risk of misstatement. Its persuasiveness would be assessed in conjunction with the results of other audit work, for example, substantive testing of purchases, returns, and cash payments, and compliance testing of the purchases system.

(d)   Inspection of a non current asset would be sufficient evidence as to the existence of the asset (provided it was carried out at or close to the balance sheet date). Before concluding on the fixed asset figure in the accounts, the auditor would have to consider the results of his work on other aspects as the ownership and valuation of the asset.

(e)   In addition to the general considerations such as risk and materiality, the results of a 'comparison' alone would not give very persuasive evidence. It would have to be followed by a detailed investigation of variances (or lack of variances where they were expected). The results should be compared to the auditor's expectations based on his knowledge of the business, and explanations given by management should be verified. The persuasiveness of the evidence should be considered in the light on other relevant testing, for example, compliance testing of payments systems, or substantive testing of expense invoices.

1.3 Computer assisted audit techniques (CAATs)

1.3.1 Audit software

Audit software performs the sort of checks on data that auditors might otherwise have to perform by hand. Examples of uses of audit software are:

- Interrogation software, which accesses the client's data files
- Comparison programs, which compare versions of a program
- Interactive software for interrogation of on-line systems
- Resident code software to review transactions as they are processed

Although audit interrogation software may be used during many tests of controls and substantive procedures, its use is particularly appropriate during substantive testing of transactions and especially balances. By using audit software, the auditors may **scrutinise large volumes of data** and concentrate skilled manual resources on the investigation of results, rather than on the extraction of information and **selection** of **samples**.

Major considerations when deciding whether to use file interrogation software are as follows.

(a) As a minimum auditors will require a **basic understanding** of data processing and the enterprise's computer application, together with a detailed knowledge of the audit software and the computer files to be used.

(b) Depending on the complexity of the application, the auditors may need to have a sound appreciation of **systems analysis**, operating systems and, where program code is used, experience of the programming language to be utilised.

(c) Auditors will need to consider how easy it is to **transfer** the **client's data** onto the auditors' PC.

(d) The client may **lack full knowledge** of the **computer system**, and hence may not be able to explain fully all the information it produces.

1.3.2 Test data

An obvious way of seeing whether a system is **processing** data in the way that it should be is to input some valid test data and see what happens. The expected results can be calculated in advance and then compared with the results that actually arise. Test data can also be used to check the controls that prevent processing of **invalid data** by entering data with say a non-existent customer code or worth an unreasonable amount, or transactions which may if processed breach limits such as customer credit limits.

A significant problem with test data is that any resulting corruption of the data files has to be corrected. This is difficult with modern real-time systems, which often have built in (and highly desirable) controls to ensure that data entered **cannot** easily be removed without leaving a mark.

Other problems with **test data** are that it only tests the operation of the system at a **single point of time**, and auditors are only testing controls in the programs being run and controls which they know about. The problems involved mean that test data is being used less as a CAAT.

1.3.3 Embedded audit facilities and current issues

The results of using test data would, in any case, be completely distorted if the programs used to process it were not the ones **normally** used for processing. For example a fraudulent member of the IT department might substitute a version of the program that gave the correct results, purely for the duration of the test, and then replace it with a version that siphoned off the company's funds into his own bank account.

To allow a **continuous** review of the data recorded and the manner in which it is treated by the system, it may be possible to use CAATs referred to as 'embedded audit facilities'. An embedded facility consists of audit modules that are incorporated into the computer element of the enterprise's accounting system. Two frequently encountered examples are Integrated Test Facility (ITF) and Systems Control and Review File

(SCARF). Such systems allow auditors to give frequent and fast audit reports on a wide variety of subject matters, key performance indicators and critical success factors. The use of IT to produce such reports means additional risk to auditors. They need to ensure that the reports are replaced properly (ie that no one relies on yesterday's report today) and are protected from interference (hacking). It also widens the amount of expertise needed from auditors, as they will need IT skills as well as expertise in a number of different areas being reported on.

1.4 Substantive analytical procedures

1.4.1 Role of analytical procedures

Chapter 6 covered the use of analytical procedures at the planning stage of the audit, in assessing risk. Analytical procedures are also widely used as a substantive procedure and can be much more cost-effective than carrying out high volumes of tests of details.

1.4.2 Examples

Simple comparisons

A simple year on year comparison could provide very persuasive evidence that an expense such as rent is correctly stated, providing that the auditor has sufficient knowledge of the business, for example knowing that the same premises have been leased year on year and that there has been no rent review.

Comparisons with estimates prepared by the auditors

A common example of this is where a business may have a large number of items of plant and machinery that are depreciated at different rates. The auditor could perform a quick calculation:

$$\boxed{\text{Closing balance of plant and machinery (cost)}} \times \boxed{\text{Average depreciation rate}}$$

If this estimate was similar to the actual depreciation charge, it would go some way to allowing the auditor to conclude that the charge was materially correct.

Relationship between financial and non-financial information

In making an estimate of employee costs, probably for one specific department, such as manufacturing, the auditor might use information about the number of employees in the department, as well as rates of pay increases. The estimate might be

$$\boxed{\text{Prior year wages expense}} \times \boxed{\frac{\text{Average no. of employees current year}}{\text{Average no. of employees prior year}} \times \% \text{ pay increase}}$$

If the actual expense does not make sense when compared to the estimate, explanations would need to be sought and corroborated. For example, management might explain that for several months of the year the factory ran double shifts, so a higher proportion of hours worked were paid at higher overtime rates.

Further examination of production records for those months would be required.

If no explanation is available, then more detailed substantive testing will be required directed towards possible misstatements such as mispostings or frauds such as payments to dummy employees.

1.4.3 Suitability of using analytical procedures

ISA 520 *Analytical procedures* notes that auditors should not rely on analytical procedures alone in respect of material balances but should combine them with tests of detail . Tests of detail are also required in areas where significant risks have been identified at the planning stage.

2 Related parties

Related party transactions can be a difficult area to gain audit evidence about as evidence may be limited to representations by management.

2.1 Importance of related parties

Central to a number of government investigations in various countries have been companies trading with organisations or individuals **other than at arm's length**. Such transactions were made possible by a degree of control or influence exercised by directors over both parties to the transactions. ISA (UK and Ireland) 550 *Related parties* covers this area.

Key terms

Related party: parties are considered to be related if one party has the ability to control the other party or exercise significant influence over the other party in making financial and operating decisions.

Related party transactions are a transfer of resources or obligations between related parties, regardless of whether a price is charged.

ISA 550.2

The auditor should perform audit procedures designed to obtain sufficient appropriate audit evidence regarding the identification and disclosure by management of related parties and the effect of related party transactions that are material to the financial statements.

The auditors' knowledge of the client must be sufficient to identify related party transactions for the following reasons.

(a) The **financial reporting framework** may require **disclosure** in the **financial statements** of certain related party relationships and transactions, such as those required by IAS 24 or FRS 8.

(b) The existence of related parties or related party transactions may **affect the financial statements**. For example tax liability and expense may be affected by the tax laws in various jurisdictions which require special consideration when related parties exist.

(c) The **source of audit evidence** affects the auditors' assessment of its reliability. A greater degree of reliance may be placed on audit evidence that is obtained from or created by unrelated third parties.

(d) A related party transaction may be motivated by **considerations other than ordinary business considerations**, for example, profit sharing or even fraud.

2.2 Inherent difficulties of detection

It may not be self-evident to management whether a party is related. Furthermore, many accounting systems are not designed to either distinguish or summarise related party transactions, so management will have to carry out additional analysis of accounting information.

An audit cannot be expected to detect all material related party transactions. The risk that undisclosed related party transactions will not be detected by the auditors is especially high when:

- **Related party transactions** have **taken place without charge.**

- **Related party transactions** are **not self-evident** to the auditors.

- Transactions are with a party that the auditors could **not reasonably** be expected to **know** is a **related party.**

- **Active steps** have been taken by **management** to **conceal** either the full terms of a transaction, or that a transaction is, in substance, with a related party.

- The **corporate structure** is **complex.**

ISA 550.3

Where there is any indication that such circumstances exist, the auditor should perform modified, extended or additional procedures as are appropriate in the circumstances.

ISA 550.6-3

When planning the audit the auditor should assess the risk that material undisclosed related party transactions, or undisclosed outstanding balances between an entity and its related parties may exist.

2.3 Responsibilities of management

Management is responsible for the identification of related party transactions. Such transactions should be properly approved as they are frequently not at arm's length. Management is also responsible for the **disclosure** of related party transactions.

ISA 550.7-10

The auditor should review information provided by those charged with governance and management identifying the names of all known related parties and should perform the following audit procedures in respect of the completeness of this information:

(a)   Review prior year working papers for names of known related parties;

(b)   Review the entity's procedures for identification of related parties;

(c)   Inquire as to the affiliation of those charged with governance and officers with other entities;

(d)   Review shareholder records to determine the names of principal shareholders or, if appropriate, obtain a listing of principal shareholders from the share register;

(e)   Review minutes of the meetings of shareholders and those charged with governance and other relevant statutory records such as the register of directors' interests;

(f)   Inquire of other auditors currently involved in the audit, or predecessor auditors, as to their knowledge of additional related parties;

(g)   Review the entity's income tax returns and other information supplied to regulatory agencies;

(h)   Review invoices and correspondence from lawyers for indications of the existence of related parties or related party transactions; and

(i)   Inquire of the names of all pension and other trusts established for the benefit of employees and the names of their management.

If, in the auditor's judgement, there is a lower risk of significant related parties remaining undetected, these procedures may be modified as appropriate.

The auditor should review information provided by directors and management identifying related party transactions and should be alert for other material related party transactions.

When obtaining an understanding of the accounting and internal control systems and making a preliminary assessment of control risk, the auditor should consider the adequacy of control procedures over the authorisation and recording of related party transactions.

2.4 Audit procedures

The following are examples of audit procedures.

- **Enquire of management** and the directors as to whether transactions have taken place with related parties that are required to be disclosed by the disclosure requirements that are applicable to the entity

- **Review prior year working papers** for names of known related parties

- **Review minutes** of meetings of shareholders and directors and other relevant statutory records such as the register of directors' interests

- **Review accounting records** for large or unusual transactions or balances, in particular transactions recognised at or near the end of the financial period

- **Review confirmations of loans receivable** and payable and confirmations from banks. Such a review may indicate the relationship, if any, of guarantors to the entity

- **Review investment transactions**, for example purchase or sale of an interest in a joint venture or other entity

- **Enquire** as to the **names** of all pension and other trusts established for the benefit of employees and the names of their management and trustees

- **Enquire** as to the **affiliation** of directors and officers with other entities

- **Review the register of interests in shares** to determine the names of principal shareholders

- **Enquire of other auditors** currently involved in the audit, or predecessor auditors, as to their knowledge of additional related parties

- **Review the entity's tax returns**, returns made under statute and other information supplied to regulatory agencies for evidence of the existence of related parties

- **Review invoices and correspondence** from lawyers for indications of the existence of related parties or related party transactions

In addition during the audit, the auditor should be alert for transactions which may indicate the existence of unidentified related parties. Examples include:

- Transactions which have **abnormal terms of trade**, such as unusual prices, interest rates, guarantees and repayment terms

- Transactions which appear to **lack a logical business reason** for their occurrence

- Transactions in which **substance differs from form**

- Transactions **processed or approved in a non-routine manner** or by personnel who do not ordinarily deal with such transactions

- **Unusual transactions** which are entered into shortly before or after the end of the financial period

- **High volume** or **significant transactions** with certain customers or suppliers as compared with others.

- **Unrecorded transactions** such as the receipt or provision of management services at no charge

2.4.1 Examining identified related party transactions and disclosures

ISA 550.13

In examining the identified related party transactions, the auditor should obtain sufficient appropriate audit evidence as to whether these transactions have been properly recorded and disclosed.

The following procedures are suggested when the audit evidence about a related party transaction is limited.

- **Discuss** the **purpose** of **the transaction** with management or the directors
- **Confirm** the **terms** and **amount** of the **transaction** with the related party
- **Inspect evidence** in the possession of the related party
- **Corroborate** with the **related party** the **explanation** of the purpose of the transaction and, if necessary, confirm that the transaction is *bona-fide*
- **Confirm** or **discuss** information with persons associated with the transactions

2.5 Disclosure relating to control of the entity

ISA 550.8

Where the applicable financial reporting framework requires disclosure of related party relationships, the auditor should be satisfied that the disclosure is adequate.

2.6 Directors' representations

ISA 550.15

The auditors should obtain written representations from management concerning the completeness of information provided regarding the related parties and the adequacy of related party disclosures in the financial statements.

2.7 Audit conclusions and reporting

ISA 550.16

If the auditor is unable to obtain sufficient appropriate audit evidence concerning related parties and transactions with such parties or concludes that their disclosure in the financial statements is not adequate, the auditor should modify the audit report appropriately.

Problems with applying ISA 550	
Identification of controlling party	Auditors may find it very difficult to identify the controlling party if the entity is part of a multi-national group. If the controlling party is a trust, auditors may have problems determining who if anyone controls the trust.
	Alternatively the directors may state that they do not know the identity of the controlling party or that there is no controlling party. These statements may be difficult to disprove.
Materiality	This problem has two aspects:
	(a) Auditors may not be able to determine **whether transactions** are **material** to related parties who are individuals (directors, key management and their families).
	(b) Auditors may have particular problems **applying** the **definition** of **materiality** (an item is material if it affects the decisions of the users of the accounts). As materiality depends on circumstances as well as amounts, auditors have to decide whether the fact that certain transactions are on normal commercial terms influences whether they are disclosed.

2.8 Transactions with directors and management

Auditors may find it difficult to obtain sufficient assurance that they have identified all disclosable transactions because of:

    (a)   The **low value of certain transactions**, making them difficult to detect when using normal audit procedures

    (b)   Any **requirements** for **disclosure of transactions** between the company and the connected persons of a director, given that it may not always be easy for the auditors to identify such connected persons

    (c)   The fact that there may be little or no **documentary evidence** of **transactions** requiring disclosure

The complexity of the relevant legislation may give rise to difficulties of interpretation. For example, advances of expenses or remuneration on account may constitute a disclosable loan if the monies are outstanding for a long time.

2.8.1 Company procedures

Auditors should enquire as to the company's procedures for ensuring that all disclosable transactions are properly identified and recorded. Such procedures are likely to include the following.

- **Advise** all **directors** and **officers** that they have a **responsibility** to disclose transactions in which they have an interest, either directly or through connected persons (Such disclosure should take place at a meeting of the directors)
- **Record** all **transactions** notified in the minutes of directors' meetings
- **Maintain** a **register** in which details of all transactions requiring disclosure are recorded
- **Establish** some **method** of:
  - **Identifying proposed transactions** which will require the approval of the members in general meeting
  - **Ensuring** that the **company does not enter** into any **illegal transaction**

- **Monitor the system** by checking on a regular basis (as a minimum, once a year) that each director is in agreement with the company's record of his disclosable transactions and is satisfied that such records are both complete and accurate
- **Obtain** from **each director** at the end of each financial year a **formal statement** indicating the disclosures necessary for the purposes of the statutory accounts

With smaller organisations, auditors may well find that there may be no formalised procedures or that they are inadequate. Auditors should **advise each director** of his statutory responsibilities, and make a **written request** for **confirmation** of any disclosable transaction in which he has an interest.

2.8.2 Audit procedures

Further audit procedures to be adopted should include the following.

- **Inspect** the **board minutes** and other records of transactions with directors and connected persons to consider their adequacy and whether or not they appear to have been kept up to date

- **Examine** any **agreements** and **contracts** involving **directors and connected persons**, including tracing the details of such transactions to any source documentation available

- **Consider** whether **transactions** disclosed are on **commercial** terms

- **Assess** the **recoverability** of amounts due from directors or connected persons

- **Review** the **legality** of the disclosable transactions recorded by the company. Where auditors are of the opinion that a transaction is illegal, they should:

    - Immediately advise the directors of their view

    - Give careful consideration as to whether any reference to the matter will be required in the audit report

- **Advise** the **client** to **seek legal advice** in those cases where there are doubts as to the legality and/or disclosable nature of a transaction

- **Consider** the **possibility** that the **company's details** of **disclosable transactions** may be incomplete as regards those directors (and connected persons) who have not been in office throughout the year

- **Review subsequent events** in order to consider whether they might have any impact on the matters requiring disclosure

Finally, auditors should consider obtaining **written representations** from each director giving confirmation of any disclosable transaction which relates to himself and any persons connected with him.

2.9 Exposure draft

There is currently an exposure draft of ISA 550 in issue. It seeks to ensure that auditors obtain sufficient appropriate audit evidence about the accounting for, and disclosure of, related party relationships and transactions in the financial statements, by obtaining an understanding of the entity's related party relationships and transactions, by identifying and assessing the associated risks of material misstatement and by responding to those risks.

2.9.1 Minimum risk assessment procedures

- The auditor shall inquire of management at the beginning of the audit regarding the identity of the entity's related parties and the nature of its related party relationships and transactions

- The auditor shall obtain an understanding of how the entity is controlled or significantly influenced and how it controls or significantly influences the related parties

- The auditor shall perform the following risk assessment procedures:

  - Inquire of management and others within the entity about the existence of transactions that are both significant and non routine

  - Where a party appears to actively exert dominant influence over the entity, perform procedures intended to identify the parties to which the dominant party is related, and understand the nature of the business relationships that these parties may have established with the entity, and

  - Review appropriate records or documents that are both significant and non-routine, and for other information that may indicate the existence of previously unidentified or undisclosed related party relationships or transactions. Appropriate records or documents shall include bank and legal confirmations obtained by the auditor and minutes of meetings of shareholders and those charged with governance and other relevant statutory records.

- If the auditor identifies transactions that are both significant and non-routine, the auditor shall consider whether the transactions or their circumstances indicate the possible involvement of previously unidentified or undisclosed related parties.

- Related parties should feature in the discussion carried out by the audit team required by ISA 315

- The audit partner should communicate all known related parties to the audit team as part of the planning process

- The auditor shall obtain an understanding of the business rationale of the entity's related party relationships and transactions to assess whether they give rise to risks of material misstatements in the financial statements. In addition, for those significant and non-routine related party transactions the auditor shall determine whether they have been appropriately authorised and approved

- The auditor shall obtain an understanding of the following in the context of related parties:

  - Internal controls including control environment

  - How those charged with governance oversee related party transactions

  - Controls over related parties in which management has a significant interest

2.9.2 Responsive further procedures

The ED then goes on to outline substantive procedures in response to the risk assessment procedures. As required by ISA 330, assessed risks must be addressed by responsive procedures. In particular, if management assert that related party transactions have occurred at arm's length, the auditor must substantiate that assertion, and if it cannot be substantiated, the auditors should request that management remove the assertion, and consider the implications for their report if management refuse.

If the auditor discovers related parties/transactions previously undisclosed by management, then he should take the following actions:

- Tell the audit team so as to assess the impact of the knowledge on other work done

- Ask management to identify transactions with that related party

- Investigate why the entity's controls failed to recognise it was a related party

- If it appears that the related party was deliberately covered up, communicate this information to those charged with governance and consider the implications for the rest of the audit

2.9.3 Management representations

The auditor should obtain written representations that management and those charged with governance have disclosed related parties and transactions completely and accurately, that the disclosures in the financial statements are accurate and that the accounting for them is appropriate, given their business rationale.

2.9.4 Evaluation

The auditor should evaluate whether related parties and transactions have been accounted for and disclosed appropriated in accordance with the reporting framework and whether the effects of related parties and transactions could make the financial statements misleading.

2.9.5 Communications

The auditor should communicate with those charged with governance:

- The nature, extent, business rationale and disclosure of significant related party relationships and transactions, including those involving actual or perceived conflicts of interest, and

- Significant issues identified during the audit regarding the entity's related party relationships and transactions

2.9.6 Documentation

The auditor shall document the identity of the entity's related parties and the nature of the relationships and the procedures performed to understand the nature of business relationships where a party appears to actively exert dominant influence over the entity.

Question	Related party transactions

You are the senior in charge of the audit of AB Milton Co for the year ended 31 May 20X1. Details of AB Milton Co and certain other companies are given below.

AB Milton Co

A building company formed by Alexander Milton and his brother, Brian.

AB Milton Co has issued share capital of 500 ordinary $1 shares, owned as shown below.

Alexander Milton	210	42%	Founder and director
Brian Milton	110	22%	Founder and director
Catherine Milton (Brian's wife)	100	20%	Company secretary
Diane Hardy	20	4%	
Edward Murray	60	12%	Director

Edward Murray is a local business man and a close friend of both Alexander and Brian Milton. He gave the brothers advice when they set up the company and remains involved through his position on the board of directors. His own company, Murray Design Co, supplies AB Milton Co with stationery and publicity materials.

Diane Hardy is Alexander Milton's ex-wife. She was given her shares as part of the divorce settlement and has no active involvement in the management of the company. Alexander's girlfriend, Fiona Dyson, is the company's solicitor. She is responsible for drawing up and reviewing all key building and other contracts, and frequently attends board meetings so that she can explain the terms of a particular contract to the directors. Her personal involvement with Alexander started in May 20X1 and, since that time, she has spent increasing amounts of time at the company's premises.

Cuts and Curls Co

A poodle parlour, of which 50% of the issued shares are owned by Diane Hardy and 50% by Gillian Milton, who is Alexander and Diane's daughter.

Cuts and Curls operated from premised owned by AB Milton Co for which is pays rent at the normal market rate.

Campbell Milton Roofing Co

A roofing company owned 60% by AB Milton Co and 40% by Ian Campbell, the managing director.

Campbell Milton Roofing Ltd carries out regular work for AB Milton Co and also does roofing work for local customers. Alexander Milton is a director of Campbell Milton Roofing Co and Catherine Milton is the company secretary. All legal work is performed by Fiona Dyson.

(a)   Based on the information given above, identify the potential related party transactions you expect to encounter during the audit of AB Milton Co and summarise, giving your reasons, what disclosure, if any, will be required in the full statutory accounts.

(b)   Prepare notes for a training session for junior staff on how to identify related party transactions. Your notes should include:

(i)   A list of possible features which could lead you to investigate a particular transaction to determine whether it is in fact a related party transaction, and

(ii)   A summary of the general audit procedures you would perform to ensure that all material related party transactions have been identified.

Answer

(a)

Person/entity	Related party	Why	Transaction
Alex Milton	✓	Director	
Brian Milton	✓	Director	No transactions mentioned
Brian's wife	✓	Wife of director	
Edward Murray	✓	Director	Purchases of stationery
Murray Designs	✓	Sub of Director	
Diane Hardy	✗	No longer close family & ≥ 20%	
Fiona Dyson	✓	Presumed close family & shadow director	Contracts drawn
Cuts & Curls	?	(see below)	Rental agreement
Campbell Milton Roofing	✓	Sub of AB Milton	Work done for AB (see below)
Ian Campbell	✓ / ✗	Could be considered key management of group	

Cuts & Curls is not clear cut. For it to be a related party Gillian Milton would need to be in a position to control Cuts & Curls and then due to her relationship with Alex Milton her company would come under the related party umbrella. Gillian only holds 50% and therefore holds joint control with her mother.

Disclosure

One a related party has been identified disclosure is required of any material transaction. Materiality is in most cases determined by considering both parties perspective. For instance, the contracts drawn by Fiona Dyson may be material to her even if not for AB Milton.

Transactions with subsidiaries, that is, Campbell Milton Roofing:

Disclosure is not required of transactions which are cancelled on consolidation. However, if group accounts are not prepared due to a small/medium group exemption material transactions between the two companies would need to be disclosed.

Disclosure should include:

- Names of the transacting related parties

- A description of the relationship

- A description of the transaction and the amounts included

- The amounts due to or form the related party at the end of the year

- Any other element of the transaction necessary for an understanding of the financial statements

(b) Notes for staff training sessions:

(i) A logical place to start the audit of related party transactions would be to identify all possible related parties. This would always include

- Directors and shadow directors
- Group companies

- Pension funds of the company
- Associates

It is likely that the other related parties would include:

- Key management (perhaps identified by which staff have key man cover)
- Shareholder owning > 20% of the shares
- Close relatives associates of any of the above

A related party transaction need to be reported if it is a material either to the reporting entity on to the other party to the transaction.

Related party transactions do not necessarily have to be detrimental to the reporting entity, but those which are will be easier to find. Features which may indicate this may include:

- Unusually generous trade or settlement discounts

- Unusually generous payment terms

- Recorded in the nominal ledger code of any person previously identified as a related party (for example, director)

- Unusual size of transaction for customers (for example, if ABL were paying a suspiciously high legal bill for a building company)

(ii)   Audit steps to find related party transactions may include:

- Identification of excessively generous credit terms by reference to aged trade accounts receivable analysis

- Identification of excessive discounts by reference to similar reports

- Scrutiny of cash book/cheque stubs for payments made to directors or officers of the company (probably more realistic for smaller entities)

- Review of Board minutes for evidence of approval of related party transactions (directors are under a fiduciary duty to not make secret profits)

- Written representations from directors to give exhaustive list of all actual/potential related parties (that is, allow us to make the materiality assessment, not them)

- Review of accounting rewards for large transactions, especially near the year end and with non-established customers/suppliers

- Identification of any persons holding > 20% of the shares in the entity by reference of the shareholders' register

3 Management representations

Management representations may be the only suitable evidence available when knowledge of the facts is confined to management and the matter is principally one of judgement or opinion.

3.1 Representations

The auditors receive many representations during the audit, both unsolicited and in response to specific questions. Some of these representations may be critical to obtaining sufficient appropriate audit evidence. Representations may also be required for general matters, eg full availability of accounting records. ISA (UK and Ireland) 580 *Management representations* covers this area.

> **ISA 580.2**
>
> The auditor should obtain appropriate representations from management. Written confirmation of appropriate representations from management, as required by paragraph 4 below, should be obtained before the audit report is issued.

Key term

> **Management** comprises officers and those who also perform senior managerial functions.

3.2 Acknowledgement by management of their responsibility for the financial statements

> **ISA 580.3**
>
> The auditor should obtain evidence that management acknowledges its responsibility for the fair presentation of the financial statements in accordance with the applicable financial reporting framework and has approved the financial statements. … In the UK and Ireland, the auditor should obtain evidence that those charged with governance acknowledge their collective responsibility for the preparation of the financial statements and have approved the financial statements.

This is normally done when the auditors receive a signed copy of the financial statements which incorporate a relevant statement of management responsibilities. Alternatively, the auditors may obtain such evidence from:

- **Relevant minutes of meetings** of the board of directors or similar body, or by attending such a meeting

- A **written representation** from management

> **ISA 580.5(a)**
>
> The audit should obtain written representations from management that:
>
> (a)   It acknowledges its responsibility for the design and implementation of internal control to prevent and detect error; and
>
> (b)   It believes the effects of those uncorrected financial statement misstatements aggregated by the auditor are immaterial, both individually and in the aggregate, to the financial statements taken as a whole. A summary of such items should be included in or attached to the written representation.

3.3 Representations by management as audit evidence

FAST FORWARD

> Management representations can never be a substitute for evidence the auditors expected to be available.
>
> Oral representations should be confirmed in writing.
>
> Auditors should seek other evidence to corroborate statements made by management.

In addition to representations relating to responsibility for the financial statements, the auditors may wish to rely on management representations as audit evidence.

> **ISA 580.4**
>
> The auditor should obtain written representations from management on matters material to the financial statements when other sufficient appropriate audit evidence cannot be reasonably expected to exist.

Written confirmation of oral representations avoids confusion and disagreement. Such matters should be discussed with those responsible for giving the written confirmation, to ensure that they understand what they are confirming. Written confirmations are normally required of appropriately senior management. Only matters which are material to the financial statements should be included.

When the auditors receive such representations they should:

- Seek **corroborative audit evidence** from sources inside or outside the entity

- **Evaluate** whether the **representations** made by management appear reasonable and are consistent with other audit evidence obtained, including other representations

- **Consider whether the individuals** making the representations can be expected to be **well-informed** on the particular matters

The ISA then makes a very important point.

'Representations by management cannot be a substitute for other audit evidence that the auditor could reasonably expect to be available ... if the auditor is unable to obtain sufficient appropriate audit evidence regarding a matter which has, or may have, a material effect on the financial statements and such audit evidence is expected to be available, this will constitute a limitation in the scope of the audit, even if a representation from management has been received on the matter.'

There are instances where management representations may be the only audit evidence available.

- **Knowledge of the facts is confined to management**, for example, the facts are a matter of management intention.

- The **matter is principally one of judgement or opinion**, for example, the trading position of a particular customer.

There may be occasions when the representations received do not agree with other audit evidence obtained.

ISA 580.9

If a representation by management is contradicted by other audit evidence, the auditor should investigate the circumstances and, when necessary, consider whether it casts doubt on the reliability of other representations made by management.

Investigations of such situations will normally begin with further enquires of management; the representations may have been misunderstood or, alternatively, the other evidence misinterpreted. If explanations are insufficient or unforthcoming, then further audit procedures may be required.

3.4 Documentation of representations by management

The auditors should include in audit working papers evidence of management's representations in the form of a summary of oral discussions with management or written representations from management.

A written representation is better audit evidence than an oral representation and can take the form of:

- A **representation letter** from management

- A **letter from the auditors** outlining the auditors' understanding of management's representations, duly acknowledged and confirmed by management

- **Relevant minutes** of meetings of the board of directors or similar body or a signed copy of the financial statements (note)

Note. A signed copy of the financial statements for a company may be sufficient evidence of the directors' acknowledgement of their collective responsibility for the preparation of the financial statements where it incorporates a statement to that effect. A signed copy of the financial statements, however, is not, by itself, sufficient appropriate evidence to confirm other representations given to the auditor as it does not, ordinarily, clearly identify and explain the specific separate representations.

3.4.1 Basic elements of a management representation letter

A management representation letter should:

- Be **addressed** to the **auditors**
- **Contain specified information**
- Be **appropriately dated** and **signed** by those with specific relevant knowledge

The letter will usually be **dated** on the **day the financial statements are approved**, but if there is any significant delay between the representation letter and the date of the auditors' report, then the auditors should consider the need to obtain further representations.

A management representation letter is usually signed by the members of management who have **primary responsibility** for the entity and its financial aspects (that is, the senior executive officer and the senior financial officer) based on the best of their knowledge and belief.

3.4.2 Example of a management representation letter

An example of a management representation letter is provided in an appendix to the ISA. It is not a standard letter, and representations will vary from one period to the next.

Exam focus point

The most important points to remember about a letter of representation are:

- The circumstances in which it can be used
- The auditors' response if the client fails to agree to it.

You should also be able to draft appropriate representations if asked.

(Entity letterhead)

(To Auditors) (Date)

This representation letter is provided in connection with your audit of the financial statements of ABC Company for the year ended December 31, 20X1 for the purpose of expressing an opinion as to whether the financial statement gives a true and fair view of (or 'present fairly, in all material respects') the financial position of ABC Company as of December 31, 20X1 and of the results of its operations and its cash flows for the year then ended in accordance with (indicate applicable financial reporting framework).

We acknowledge as directors our responsibilities under the Companies Act 1985 for preparing financial statements which give a true and fair view and for making accurate representations to you. All the accounting records have been made available to you for the purpose of your audit and all the transactions undertaken by the company have been properly reflected and recorded in the accounting records. All other records and related information, including minutes of all management and shareholders' meetings, have been made available to you.

We also acknowledge our responsibility for the design and implementation of internal control to prevent and detect fraud.

We confirm, to the best of our knowledge and belief, the following representations:

[Include here representations relevant to the entity. Such representations may include the following.]

- There have been no irregularities involving management or employees who have a significant role in the accounting and internal control systems or that could have a material effect on the financial statements, and we have disclosed to you our assessment of the risk that the financial statements might be materially misstated as a result of fraud.

- We confirm the completeness of the information provided regarding the identification of related parties and that the disclosure concerning related parties transactions is sufficient.
- The financial statements are free of material misstatement, including omissions.

- The company has complied with all aspects of contractual agreements that could have a material effect on the financial statements in the event of non-compliance. There has been no non-compliance with requirements of regulatory authorities that could have a material effect on the financial statements in the event of non-compliance.

- The following have been properly recorded and when appropriate, adequately disclosed in the financial statements.

  (a) The identity of, and balances and transactions with, related parties.
  (b) Losses arising from sale and purchase commitments.
  (c) Agreements and options to buy back assets previously sold
  (d) Assets pledged as collateral

- We have no plans or intentions that may materially alter the carrying value or classification of assets and liabilities reflected in the financial statements.

- We have no plans to abandon lines of product or other plans or intentions that will result in any excess or obsolete stock, and no stock is stated at an amount in excess of net realisable value.

- The company has satisfactory title to all assets and there are no liens or encumbrances on the company's assets, except for those that are disclosed in Note X to the financial statements.

- We have recorded or disclosed, as appropriate, all liabilities, both actual and contingent, and have disclosed in Note X to the financial statements all guarantees that we have given to third parties.

- Other than … described in Note X to the financial statements, there have been no events subsequent to period end which require adjustment of or disclosure in the financial statement or notes thereto.

- The … claim by XYZ company has been settled for the total sum of XXX which has been properly accrued in the financial statements. No other claims in connection with litigation have been or are expected to be received.

- There are no formal or informal compensating balance arrangements with any of our cash and investment accounts. Except as disclosed in Note X to the financial statement, we have no other line of credit arrangements.

- We have properly recorded or disclosed in the financial statements the capital stock repurchase options and agreements, and capital stock reserved for options, warrants, conversions and other requirements.

....

(Senior Executive Officer)

....

(Senior Financial Officer)

3.5 Actions if management refuses to provide representations

ISA 580.15

If management refuses to provide written representation that the auditor considers necessary, this constitutes a limitation of scope for their report and the auditor should express a qualified opinion or a disclaimer of opinion.

In these circumstances, the auditors should consider whether it is appropriate to rely on other representations made by management during the audit.

Question   Management representations

You are an audit manager reviewing the completed audit file of Leaf Oil Co.

(a)   There have been no events subsequent to the period end requiring adjustment in the financial statements.

(b)   The company has revalued 2 properties in the year. The directors believe that the property market is going to boom next year, so have decided to revalue the other 2 properties then.

(c)   The directors confirm that the company owns 75% of the newly formed company, Subsidiary Co, at the year end.

(d)   The directors confirmed that the 500 gallons of oil in Warehouse B belong to Flower Oil Co.

Required

Comment on whether you would expect to see these matters referred to in the management representation letter.

Answer

(a)   I would expect to see this referred to in a management letter. ISA 580 gives this as an example of a matter to be included in the management letter, as management should inform auditors of relevant subsequent events.

(b)   This should not appear on a management representation letter, even though management opinion is involved. This indicates an incorrect accounting treatment which the auditors should be in disagreement with the directors over.

(c)   This should not appear on a management representation letter as there should be sufficient alternative evidence for this matter. The auditor should be able to obtain registered information about Subsidiary Co from the companies' registrar.

(d)   This should not appear on a management representation letter. The auditors should be able to obtain evidence from Flower Oil Co that the inventory belongs to them.

4 Reliance on the work of an expert

FAST FORWARD   Sometimes auditors may need to use the work of an expert to obtain sufficient, appropriate audit evidence.

4.1 Experts

Professional audit staff are highly trained and educated, but their experience and training is limited to accountancy and audit matters. In **certain situations** it will therefore be necessary to employ someone else with **different expert knowledge** to gain sufficient, appropriate audit evidence.

Key term

> An **expert** is a person or firm possessing special skill, knowledge and experience in a particular field other than accounting and auditing.

Auditors have **sole responsibility** for their opinion, but may use the work of an expert. An expert may be engaged by:

- A client to provide **specialist advice** on a particular matter which affects the financial statements
- The auditors in order to obtain **sufficient audit evidence** regarding certain financial statement assertions

ISA (UK and Ireland) 620 *Using the work of an expert* covers this area.

4.2 Determining the need to use the work of an expert

ISA 620.2

When using the work performed by an expert, auditors should obtain sufficient appropriate audit evidence that such work is adequate for the purposes of an audit.

The following list of examples is given by the ISA of the audit evidence which might be obtained from the opinion, valuation etc of an expert.

- **Valuations of certain types of assets**, for example land and buildings, plant and machinery
- **Determination of quantities or physical condition of assets**
- **Determination of amounts** using specialised techniques, for example pensions accounting
- **The measurement of work completed** and **work in progress** on contracts
- **Legal opinions**

When considering whether to use the work of an expert, the auditors should review:

- The **importance** of the matter being considered in the context of the accounts
- The **risk of misstatement** based on the nature and complexity of the matter
- The **quantity** and **quality** of other available **relevant audit evidence**

Exam focus point

Engaging an expert is a costly business and the client and auditors will only want to if there is a real need to do so, in other words, in circumstances where other relevant and reliable audit evidence is not available. When recommending audit procedures in the exam, only recommend using an expert if it is relevant test. It is not a substitute for alternative tests.

Once it is decided that an expert is required, the approach should be discussed with the management of the entity. Where the management is unwilling or unable to engage an expert, the auditors should consider engaging an expert themselves **unless sufficient alternative audit evidence can be obtained.**

4.3 Competence and objectivity of the expert

ISA 620.8/9

When planning to use the work of an expert the auditors should assess the professional competence [including, in the UK, professional qualifications, experience and resources] of the expert. The auditor should evaluate the objectivity of the expert.

This will involve considering:

- The expert's **professional certification**, or licensing by, or membership of, an appropriate professional body
- The expert's **experience and reputation** in the field in which the auditors are seeking audit evidence

The risk that an expert's **objectivity is impaired** increases when the expert is:

- **Employed** by the entity
- **Related** in some other manner to the entity, for example, by being financially dependent upon, or having an investment in, the entity

If the auditors have **reservations** about the competence or objectivity of the expert they may need to carry out **other procedures** to obtain **evidence from another expert.**

4.4 The expert's scope of work

> **ISA 620.11**
>
> The auditors should obtain sufficient appropriate audit evidence that the expert's scope of work is adequate for the purposes of the audit.

Written instructions usually cover the expert's terms of reference and such instructions may cover such matters as follows.

- The **objectives** and **scope** of the expert's work
- A **general outline** as to the specific matters the expert's report is to cover
- The **intended use** of the expert's work
- The **extent** of the **expert's access** to appropriate records and files
- Clarification of the expert's relationship with the entity, if any
- Confidentiality of the entity's information
- Information regarding the **assumptions and methods intended** to be used by the expert and their consistency with those used in prior periods

4.5 Assessing the work of the expert

> **ISA 620.12**
>
> The auditors should assess the appropriateness of the expert's work as audit evidence regarding the financial statement assertions being considered.

Auditors should assess whether the substance of the expert's findings is properly reflected in the financial statements or supports the financial statement assertions. It will also require consideration of:

- The **source data used**
- The **assumptions and methods used**
- **When** the expert carried out the work
- The reasons for any **changes in assumptions and methods**
- The **results** of the expert's work in the light of the auditors' overall knowledge of the business and the results of other audit procedures

The auditors do **not** have the expertise to judge the assumptions and methods used; these are the responsibility of the expert. However, the auditors should seek to obtain an understanding of these assumptions, to consider their reasonableness based on other audit evidence, knowledge of the business and so on.

ISA 620.15

If the results of the expert's work do not provide sufficient appropriate audit evidence, or if the results are not consistent with other audit evidence, the auditor should resolve the matter.

This may involve discussion with both the client and the expert. Additional procedures (including use of another expert) may be necessary.

4.6 Reference to an expert in the audit report

ISA 620.16

When issuing an unmodified audit report, the auditor should not refer to the work of the expert

Such a reference may be misunderstood and interpreted as a qualification of the audit opinion or a division of responsibility, neither of which is appropriate.

If the auditors issue a modified audit report, then they may refer to the work of the expert. In such cases, auditors should obtain permission in advance from the expert. If such permission is not given, then the auditors may have to seek legal advice.

Question

Using an expert

The following situations are both extracted from an exam on the previous syllabus.

(a)   'The useful life of each platform is assessed annually on factors such as weather conditions and the period over which it is estimated that oil will be extracted.' You are auditing the useful lives of the platforms.

(b)   'Piles of copper and brass, that can be distinguished with a simple acid test, have been mixed up.' You are attending the inventory count.

Required

Explain whether it is necessary to use the work of an expert in these situations. Where relevant, you should describe alternative procedures.

Answer

(a)   **Platforms**

It is not necessary to use an expert to audit the useful lives of the platforms as there are many other available services of evidence. Relevant procedures include:

- Obtaining weather reports to see whether managements determination of useful lives is consistent with them.

- Comparing budgeted oil against actual oil extracted (if the budget was optimistic, so might the useful life be).

- Review published industry comparators (such as Shell and BP). If the useful lives of their platforms as published in financial statements is significantly different, discuss with management why that might be.

- Consider whether management's determination of useful lives in the past has been proved accurate.

(b)   It is not necessary to use an expert, as the question states that a 'simple' test is available. The auditors should confirm that the company will be making use of this test during the inventory count to separate the inventory. The auditor should reperform the test on a sample of "brass" and "copper" as counted to ensure it has been separated correctly.

Exam focus point

The exam question will often give a clear indicator of whether an expert is required or not. For instance in (a) above, information was given on what the useful lives were based on – which the auditor should be able to interpret himself. In (b), the words "**simple** acid test" imply an expert is not required.

5 Reliance on the work of internal audit

The principles of relying on work done by anyone other then the audit firm are always the same. The role of internal audit is studied in depth in the earlier paper.

Knowledge brought forward from earlier studies

Reliance on the work of internal auditors by external auditors

The external auditors may make use of the work of internal audit. The guidance over when this appropriate is given to them in ISA (UK and Ireland) 610 *Considering the work of internal audit.*

The ISA states that the external auditors must give consideration first to the scope and organisation of the internal audit department and then evaluate the specific audit work they are interested in.

The following factors must be considered.

- Proficiency and training of the people who have undertaken the work
- Level of supervision, review and documentation of the work of assistants
- Sufficiency and appropriateness of evidence to draw conclusions
- Appropriateness of conclusions drawn
- Consistency of any reports prepared with the work performed
- Whether the work necessitates amendment to the external audit programme

6 Revision: documentation

FAST FORWARD

All evidence obtained should be documented.

6.1 Document what?

All audit work must be documented: the working papers are the **tangible evidence of all work done in support of the audit opinion.** ISA 230 *Documentation* was revised in September 2005.

In the case of area where the evidence is difficult to obtain, such as related parties, and may arise through discussions with management, it is vital that notes are made of conversations and that, as discussed in section 3, representations on material matters are confirmed in writing.

In your previous studies, you have learnt the practical issues surrounding how audit papers should be completed. There is a key general rule concerning what to include on a working paper to remember, which is:

'What would be necessary to provide an experienced auditor, with no previous connection with the audit, with an understanding of the nature, timing, and extent of the audit procedures performed to comply with the ISAs and applicable legal and regulatory requirements and the results of the audit procedures and the audit evidence obtained, and significant matters arising during the audit and the conclusions reached thereon.'

The key reason for having audit papers therefore is that they provide evidence of work done. They may be required in the event of litigation arising over the audit work and opinion given.

The revised ISA sets out certain requirements about what should be recorded, such as the identifying characteristics of the specific items being tested.

It also sets out things an auditor should record in relation to significant matters, such as discussions undertaken with directors and how the auditor addressed information that appeared to be inconsistent with his conclusions in relation to significant matters.

If an auditor felt it necessary to depart from customary audit work required by audit standards, he should document why, and how the different test achieved audit objectives.

The ISA also contains details about how the audit file should be put together and actions in the event of audit work being added after the date of the audit report (for example, if subsequent events results in additional work being carried out).

We shall briefly revise here the review of working papers. **Review** of working papers is important, as it allows a more senior auditor to **evaluate the evidence obtained** during the course of the audit for sufficiency and reliability, so that more evidence can be obtained to support the audit opinion, if required.

6.2 Review of audit working papers

FAST FORWARD

Working papers should be reviewed by a more senior audit staff member before an audit conclusion is drawn.

Work performed by each assistant should be reviewed by personnel of appropriate experience to consider whether:

- The work has been **performed** in **accordance with the audit programme.**

- The work performed and the results obtained have been **adequately documented.**

- Any **significant matters** have been **resolved** or are reflected in audit conclusions.

- The **objectives** of the audit procedures have been **achieved.**

- The **conclusions** expressed are **consistent** with the results of the work performed and support the audit opinion.

The following should be reviewed on a timely basis.

- The **overall audit strategy** and the **audit plan**

- The **assessments of inherent and control risks**

- The **results** of **control** and **substantive procedures** and the conclusions drawn therefrom including the results of consultations

- The **financial statements,** proposed audit adjustments and the proposed auditors' report

In some cases, particular in large complex audits, personnel not involved in the audit may be asked to review some or all of the audit work, the auditors' report etc. This is sometimes called a **peer review** or **hot review.**

Question   **Working papers**

Viewco is a manufacturer of TVs and video recorders. It carries out a full physical stock count at its central warehouse every year on 31 December, its financial year end. Finished goods are normally of the order of £3 million, with components and work in progress normally approximately £1 million.

You are the audit senior responsible for the audit of Viewco for the year ending 31 December 20X1. Together with a junior member of staff, you will be attending Viewco physical stock count.

(a)   Explain why it is necessary for an auditor to prepare working papers.

(b)   State, giving reasons, what information the working papers relating to this stock count attendance should contain.

Answer

(a)   Working papers are necessary for the following reasons:

- So that the reporting partner can be satisfied that work delegated has been properly performed.

- To provide, for future reference, detail of problems encountered, evidence of work performed and conclusions drawn therefrom in arriving at the audit opinion.

- Their preparation encourages a methodical approach.

- To facilitate review.

- To provide evidence that Auditing Standards have been followed.

(b)   *Information*   *Reasons*

1. Administration

Client name	• Enables an organised file to be produced.
Year end	
Title	
Date prepared	• Enables papers to be traced if lost
Initials of preparer	• Any questions can be addressed top the appropriate person
	• Seniority of preparer is indicated
Initials of senior to indicate review of junior's work	• Evidence that guideline on planning, controlling and recording is being followed
	• Evidence of adherence to auditing standards

2. Planning

(i) Summary of different models of TV and Video held and the approximate value of each.	• Enables auditor to familiarise himself with different types of stock line
Summary of different types of raw material held and method of counting small components.	
Summary of different stages of WIP identified by client.	

(ii) Time and place of count.	• Audit team will not miss the count
(iii) Personnel involved.	• Auditor aware who to address questions/ problems to.
(iv) Copy of client's inventory count instructions and an assessment of them.	• Enables an initial assessment of the likely reliability of Viewco's count. • Assists in determining the amount of work audit team need to do. • Enables compliance work to be carried out, that is, checking Viewco staff follow the instructions.
(v) Plan of warehouse	• To ensure all areas covered at count • Clear where to find different models/components • Location of any 3rd party/moving stock clear.
(vi) Details of any known old or slow moving lines	• Special attention can be given to these at count for example, include in test counts
(vii) Scope of tests counts to be performed that is, number/value of items to be counted and method of selection. For Viewco probably more counting of higher value finished goods	• Ensures appropriate amount of work done based on initial assessment. • Clear plan for audit team.
3. Objectives of attendance that is, to ensure that the quality of stock to be reflected in the financial statements is materially accurate.	• Reporting partner can confirm if appropriate/ adequate work done.
4. Details of work done	• Provides evidence for future reference and documents adherence to auditing standards. • Enables reporting partner to review the adequacy of the work and establish whether it meets the stated objective.
A. Details of controls testing work performed – observing Viewco's counters and ensuring they are following the instructions and conducting the count effectively, for example,	• Enable reassessment of likely reliability of Viewco's count. • Enables assessment of chances of items being double counted or omitted.
(i) Note of whether the area was systematically tided.	
(ii) Note of whether or how counted goods are marked.	
(iii) Note of how Viewco record and segregate any goods still moving on count day.	

    (iv) Note of adequacy of supervision and general impression of counters.

- Enables assessment of overall of count and hence likely accuracy.

    (v) Note whether counters are in teams of two and whether any check counts are performed.

- Evidence of independent checks may enhance reliability.

B. Details of substantive work performed

    (i) Details of items of raw materials or finished goods test counted:

- From physical stock to client's count sheet.

  - Evidence to support the accuracy and completeness of Viewco's count sheets

- From Viewco's count sheets to physical stock.

  - Evidence to support the existence of stock recorded by Viewco.

      For both of the above note stock code, description, number of units and quality. Use a symbol to indicate agreement with Viewco's records.

    (ii) Details of review for any old/ obsolete stock for example, dusty/damaged boxes. Note code, description, number of units and problem.

- Details can be followed up at final audit and the net realisable investigated.

    (iii) Details of review of WIP

- Assessment of volume of part complete items of each stage.

  - Evidence in support of accuracy of quantity of WIP

- Assessment of appropriateness of degree of completion assigned to each stage by Viewco (could describe items at various stages).

  - Details can be followed through at final audit to final stock sheets.
  - Basis for discussion of any description.

    (iv) Copies of:

- Last few despatch notes
- Last few goods received notes
- Last few material requisitions
- Last few receipts to finished goods.

  - Enables follow up at final audit to ensure cut-off is correct that is, goods despatched are reflected as sales, goods received as purchases and items in WIP are not also in raw materials and finished goods.

    (v) Copies of client's stock count sheets (where number makes this practical).

- Enables follow up at final audit to ensure that Viewco's final sheets are intact and no alterations have occurred.

5. Summary of Results

In particular:

(i)   Details of any problems encountered.

(ii) Details of any test count discrepancies and notes of investigation into their causes.

(iii) Details of any representations by the management of Viewco.

- Senior/manager can assess any consequences for audit risk and strategy and decide any further work needed.

- Provides full documentation of issues that could require a judgmental decision and could ultimately be the basis for a qualified opinion.

6. Conclusion

- Indicates whether or not the initial objective has been met and whether there are any implications for the audit opinion.

Chapter Roundup

- Auditors need to obtain sufficient, appropriate audit evidence.

- Related party transactions can be a difficult area to gain audit evidence about as evidence may be limited to representations by management.

- Management representations may be the only suitable evidence available when knowledge of facts is confined to management and the matter is principally one of judgement or opinion.

- Sometimes auditors may need to use the work of an expert to obtain sufficient appropriate audit evidence.

- All evidence obtained should be documented.

- Working papers should be reviewed by a more senior audit staff member before an audit conclusion is drawn.

Quick quiz

1   Give five examples of financial statement assertions.

    (1)   ....

    (2)   ....

    (3)   ....

    (4)   ....

    (5)   ....

2   Which of the following is not a procedure designed to obtain evidence?

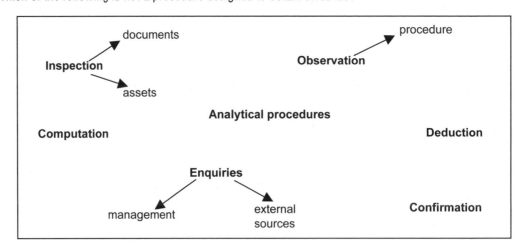

3   Give five instances where the risk of undisclosed related party transactions going undiscovered by the auditors is high.

    (1)   ....

    (2)   ....

    (3)   ....

    (4)   ....

    (5)   ....

4   Management representations might take the form of a letter from the auditors acknowledged and signed by the director.

True   ☐

False   ☐

5   Complete the definition

An .... is a person or firm possessing ...., knowledge and experience in a particular field other than ....

6   Give three examples of audit evidence which can be obtained from an expert.

(1)   ....

(2)   ....

(3)   ....

7   What is a hot review?

Answers to quick quiz

1   (1)   Existence
    (2)   Rights and obligations
    (3)   Occurrence
    (4)   Completeness
    (5)   Valuation
    (6)   Cut-off
    (7)   Classification
    (8)   Accuracy
    (9)   Allocation

2   Deduction

3   (1)   There has been no charge
    (2)   Related parties are not evident to auditors
    (3)   Auditors could not reasonably know party was related
    (4)   Steps have been taken to conceal relationship
    (5)   Corporate structure is complex

4   True

5   Expert, special skill, accountancy

6   (1)   Valuations of assets
    (2)   Determination of quantities of assets
    (3)   Legal opinions

7   A hot review is when a member of staff who has not been involved in the audit is asked to review all the working papers before the audit report is signed.

Now try the question below from the Exam Question Bank

Number	Level	Marks	Time
Q9	Examination	20	36 mins

Evaluation and review (i)

Topic list	Syllabus reference
1 Revision: review procedures and evaluation of findings	D1(iii)
2 Revision: opening balances	D1(iii)
3 Revision: comparatives	D1(iii)
4 Revision: other information	D1(iii)
5 Revision: subsequent events	D1(iii)
6 Revision: going concern	D1(iii)

Introduction

Towards the end of an audit, a series of review and evaluations are carried out. You should be familiar with them from your previous auditing studies.

Section 1 outlines the **overall review** which is undertaken on the financial statements as a whole and the review of errors and potential errors.

In Sections 2 and 3, the issue of **opening balances and comparatives** is discussed. In the event of a recurring audit, both these items are audited by review. In special circumstances, notably the first audit, different considerations and procedures must be followed.

The auditor must review **other information** to establish whether it contradicts the audit report. The detailed procedures and requirements are discussed in section 4.

The auditor conducts reviews of the **going concern** presumption and the period between the balance sheet and the signing of the audit report **(subsequent events)**. There is guidance given on both these areas in ISAs, and they are dealt with in sections 6 and 5 respectively.

Study guide

		Intellectual level
1(iii)	**Evaluation and review**	
(a)	Explain review procedures (including the use of analytical procedures and checklists) and assess their role in detecting material misstatements.	3
(b)	Evaluate findings quantitatively and qualitatively eg	3
(i)	the results of audit tests and procedures	
(ii)	the effect of actual and potential misstatements.	
(c)	Compare and contrast how the auditor's responsibilities for corresponding figures, comparative financial statements. 'other information', subsequent events and going concern are discharged.	3
(d)	Apply the further considerations and audit procedures relevant to initial engagements.	2
(e)	Discuss the courses of action available to an auditor if a material inconsistency or misstatement of fact exits.	2
(f)	Specify audit procedures designed to identify subsequent events that may require adjustment or, or disclosure in, the financial statements of a given entity.	2
(g)	List indicators that the going concern basis may be in doubt and recognise mitigating factors.	2
(h)	Evaluate the evidence that might be expected to be available and assess the appropriateness of the going concern basis in given situations.	3
(i)	Assess the adequacy of disclosures in financial statements relating to going concern and explain the implications for the auditor's report with regard to the going concern basis.	3

Exam guide

Going concern is a particularly important audit review which could be relevant in risks or evidence questions. Bear in mind the links with planning, knowledge of the business and analytical procedures.

1 Revision: review procedures and evaluation of findings

FAST FORWARD

The auditors must perform and document an overall review of the financial statements before they can reach an opinion.

Once the bulk of the substantive procedures have been carried out, the auditors will have a draft set of financial statements which should be supported by appropriate and sufficient audit evidence. As the beginning of the end of the audit process, it is usual for the auditors to undertake an **overall review** of the financial statements. This review of the financial statements, in conjunction with the conclusions drawn from the other audit evidence obtained, gives the auditors a reasonable basis for their opinion on the financial statements. It should be carried out by a senior member of the audit team, with appropriate skills and experience.

1.1 Compliance with accounting regulations

The auditors should consider whether:

(a) The information presented in the financial statements is in accordance with local/national statutory requirements.

(b) The accounting policies employed are in accordance with accounting standards, properly disclosed, consistently applied and appropriate to the entity.

When examining the **accounting policies**, auditors should consider:

- Policies **commonly adopted in particular industries**

- Policies for which there is **substantial authoritative support**

- Whether any **departures from applicable accounting standards** are necessary for the financial statements to give a true and fair view

- Whether the **financial statements reflect the substance** of the underlying transactions and not merely their form

When compliance with local/national statutory requirements and accounting standards is considered, the auditors may find it useful to use a **checklist**.

1.2 Review for consistency and reasonableness

The auditors should consider whether the financial statements are consistent with their knowledge of the entity's business and with the results of other audit procedures, and the manner of disclosure is fair. The principal considerations are as follows.

(a) Whether the financial statements adequately reflect the **information** and **explanations** previously obtained and conclusions previously reached during the course of the audit

(b) Whether it reveals any **new factors** which may affect the presentation of, or disclosure in, the financial statements

(c) Whether analytical procedures applied when completing the audit, such as comparing the information in the financial statements with other pertinent data, **produce results** which assist in arriving at the overall conclusion as to whether the financial statements as a whole are consistent with their knowledge of the entity's business (see Chapter 7)

(d) Whether the **presentation** adopted in the financial statements may have been unduly influenced by the **directors' desire** to present matters in a favourable or unfavourable light

(e) The potential impact on the financial statements of the **aggregate of uncorrected misstatements** (including those arising from bias in making accounting estimates) identified during the course of the audit and the preceding period's audit, if any

1.3 Analytical procedures

In Chapter 6 we discussed how analytical review procedures are used as part of the overall review procedures at the end of an audit. Remember the areas that the analytical review at the final stage must cover.

- Important accounting ratios
- Related items
- Changes in products; customers
- Price and mix changes
- Wages changes
- Variances
- Trends in production and sales
- Changes in material and labour content of production

- Other profit and loss account expenditure
- Variations caused by industry or economy factors

As at other stages, significant fluctuations and unexpected relationships must be investigated and documented.

1.4 Summarising errors

During the course of the audit, errors will be discovered which may be material or immaterial to the financial statements. It is very likely that the client will adjust the financial statements to take account of material and immaterial errors during the course of the audit. At the end of the audit, however, some errors may still be outstanding and the auditors will summarise these **unadjusted errors**.

The summary of errors will not only list errors from the current year, but also those in the previous year(s). This will allow errors to be highlighted which are reversals of errors in the previous year, such as in the valuation of closing/opening stock. Cumulative errors may also be shown, which have increased from year to year. It is normal to show both the balance sheet and the profit and loss effect, as in the example given here.

SCHEDULE OF UNADJUSTED ERRORS

		20X2				20X1			
		P & L account		Balance sheet		P & L account		Balance sheet	
		Dr	Cr	Dr	Cr	Dr	Cr	Dr	Cr
		£	£	£	£	£	£	£	£
(a)	ABC Ltd debt unprovided	10,470			10,470	4,523			4,523
(b)	Opening/ closing stock under-valued*	21,540			21,540		21,540	21,540	
(c)	Closing stock undervalued		34,105	34,105					
(d)	Opening unaccrued expenses								
	Telephone*		453	453		453			453
	Electricity*		905	905		905			905
(e)	Closing unaccrued expenses								
	Telephone	427			427				
	Electricity	1,128			1,128				
(f)	Obsolete stock write off	2,528			2,528	3,211			3,211
Total		36,093	35,463	35,463	36,093	9,092	21,540	21,540	9,092
	*Cancelling items	21,540			21,540				
			453	453					
			905	905					
		14,553	34,105	34,105	14,553				

1.4.1 Evaluating the effect of misstatements

As part of their completion procedures, auditors should consider whether the cumulative effect of unadjusted errors is material.

ISA 320.12

In evaluating whether the financial statements are prepared in all material respects, in accordance with an applicable financial reporting framework, the auditor should assess whether the aggregate of uncorrected misstatements that have been identified during the audit is material.

The aggregate of uncorrected misstatements comprises:

(a) **Specific misstatements** identified by the auditors, including the net effect of uncorrected misstatements identified during the audit of the previous period if they affect the current period's financial statements

(b) Their **best estimate** of **other misstatements** which cannot be quantified specifically (ie projected errors)

If the auditors consider that the aggregate of misstatements may be material, they must consider reducing audit risk by extending audit procedures or requesting management to adjust the financial statements (which management may wish to do anyway).

ISA 320.15

If management refuses to adjust the financial statements and the results of extended audit procedures do not enable the auditor to conclude that the aggregate of uncorrected misstatements is not material, the auditor should consider the appropriate modification to the auditor's report.

If the aggregate of the uncorrected misstatements that the auditors have identified approaches the materiality level, the auditors should consider whether it is likely that undetected misstatements, when taken with aggregated uncorrected misstatements, could exceed the materiality level. Thus, as aggregate uncorrected misstatements approach the materiality level the auditors should consider reducing the risk by

- **Performing additional audit procedures or**
- By **requesting management** to adjust the financial statements for identified misstatements

The schedule will be used by the audit manager and partner to decide whether the client should be requested to make adjustments to the financial statements to correct the errors.

1.5 Completion checklists

Audit firms frequently use checklists which must be signed off to ensure that all final procedures have been carried out, all material amounts are supported by sufficient appropriate evidence, etc.

2 Revision: opening balances

FAST FORWARD Specific procedures must be applied to opening balances.

2.1 Audit procedures

Key term

Opening balances are those account balances which exist at the beginning of the period. Opening balances are based upon the closing balances of the prior period and reflect the effects of:

- Transactions of prior periods
- Accounting policies applied to the prior period

ISA (UK and Ireland) 510 *Initial Engagements – Opening Balances and continuing engagements – opening balances* provides guidance on opening balances.

- When the financial statements of an entity are audited for the first time
- When the financial statements for the prior period were audited by another auditor

> **ISA 510.2**
>
> For initial audit engagements, the auditor should obtain sufficient appropriate audit evidence that:
>
> (a)   the opening balances do not contain misstatements that materially affect the current period's financial statements;
>
> (b)   the prior period's closing balances have been correctly brought forward to the current period or, when appropriate, have been restated; and
>
> (c)   appropriate accounting policies are consistently applied or changes in accounting policies have been properly accounted for and adequately disclosed.

In addition, the auditor should carry out the above on continuing engagements. Appropriate and sufficient audit evidence is required on opening balances and this depends on matters such as the following.

- The **accounting policies** followed by the entity
- Whether the **prior period's financial statements were audited** and, if so, whether the auditors' report was modified
- The **nature of the accounts** and the risk of their misstatement in the current period's financial statements
- The **materiality** of the opening balances relative to the current period's financial statements

The auditor must consider whether **opening balances reflect the application of appropriate accounting policies** and that those policies are **consistently applied** in the current period's financial statements. When there are any changes in the accounting policies or application thereof, the auditor should consider whether they are appropriate and properly accounted for and adequately disclosed.

2.1.1 Prior period balances audited

When the prior period's financial statements were audited by another auditor, the current auditor may be able to obtain sufficient appropriate audit evidence regarding opening balances by **reviewing** the predecessor auditor's **working papers**. In these circumstances, the current auditor would also consider the professional competence and independence of the predecessor auditor. If the prior period's audit report was **modified**, the auditor would pay particular attention in the current period to the matter which resulted in the modification.

Before communicating with the predecessor auditor, the current auditor must consider the relevant parts of IFAC's *Code of Ethics for Professional Accountants*.

Where the prior period balances were audited by the current auditor, and an unqualified opinion was given, procedures relating to opening balances must ensure balances have been appropriately brought forward and accounting policies have been consistently applied. If a qualified opinion was given, the auditors must ensure that the matter has been resolved and dealt with in the current financial statements.

2.1.2 Prior period balances not audited

When the prior period's financial statements were not audited or when the auditor is not able to be satisfied by using the procedures described above, the auditor must perform other procedures such as those discussed below.

For **current assets and liabilities** some audit evidence can usually be obtained as part of the current period's audit procedures. For example, the **collection** (payment) of opening **debtors** (creditors) during the current period will provide some audit evidence of their existence, rights and obligations, completeness and valuation at the beginning of the period.

In the case of **stock**, however, it is more difficult for the auditor to be satisfied as to stock on hand at the beginning of the period. Therefore, additional procedures will usually be necessary such as:

- **Observing a current physical stock count** and reconciling it back to the opening stock quantities

- **Testing the valuation** of the opening stock items

- **Testing gross profit** and cut-off

A combination of these procedures may provide sufficient appropriate audit evidence.

For **non-current assets and liabilities**, the audit will ordinarily examine the records underlying the opening balances. In certain cases, the auditor may be able to obtain confirmation of opening balances with third parties, for example, for long-term debt and investments. In other cases, the auditor may need to carry out additional audit procedures.

2.2 Audit conclusion and reporting

ISA 510.11

If, after performing procedures including those set out above, the auditor is unable to obtain sufficient appropriate evidence concerning opening balances, the auditor's report should include:

(a)   a qualified opinion;

(b)   a disclaimer of opinion; or

(c)   in those jurisdictions where it is permitted, an opinion which is qualified or disclaimed regarding the results of operations and unqualified regarding financial position.

If the opening balances contain misstatements which could materially affect the current period's financial statements, the auditor should inform management, and any predecessor auditor.

ISA 510.12

If the effect of the misstatement is not properly accounted for and adequately disclosed, the auditor should express a qualified opinion or an adverse opinion, as appropriate.

The report will also be modified if **accounting policies** are **not consistently applied**.

ISA 510.13

If the current period's accounting policies have not been consistently applied in relation to the opening balances and if the change has not been properly accounted for and adequately disclosed, the auditor should express a qualified opinion or an adverse opinion as appropriate.

If the prior period auditor's report was modified, the auditor should **consider the effect on the current period's financial statements**. For example, if there was a scope limitation, such as one due to the inability to determine opening stock in the prior period, the auditor may not need to qualify or disclaim the current period's audit opinion. The ISA finishes:

ISA 510.14

However, if a modification regarding the prior period's financial statements remains relevant and material to the current period's financial statements, the auditor should modify the current auditor's report accordingly.

Exam focus point

In an old syllabus paper, a case study question had one part looking at how a new auditor would deal with opening balances.

3 Revision: comparatives

FAST FORWARD

The auditor's responsibilities for comparatives vary depending on whether they are corresponding figures or comparative financial statements.

3.1 What type of comparatives are they?

ISA 710 *Comparatives* establishes standards and provides guidance on the auditors' responsibilities regarding comparatives.

> **ISA 710.2/2-1**
>
> The auditor should determine whether the comparatives comply in all material respects with the financial reporting framework applicable to the financial statements being audited … [and] should obtain sufficient appropriate audit evidence that amounts derived from the preceding period's financial statements are free from material misstatements and are appropriately incorporated into the financial statements for the current period.

Comparatives are presented differently under different countries' financial reporting frameworks. Generally comparatives can be defined as **corresponding amounts** and **other disclosures** for the preceding financial reporting period(s), presented for comparative purposes. Because of these variations in countries' approach to comparatives, the ISA refers to the following frameworks and methods of presentation.

Key terms

Corresponding figures are amounts and other disclosures for the preceding period included as part of the current period financial statements, which are intended to be read in relation to the amounts and other disclosures relating to the current period (referred to as 'current period figures'). These corresponding figures are not presented as complete financial statements capable of standing alone, but are an integral part of the current period financial statements intended to be read only in relationship to the current period figures. This is the usual approach in the UK.

Comparative financial statements are amounts and other disclosures of the preceding period included for comparison with the financial statements of the current period, but do not form part of the current period financial statements.

Comparatives are presented in compliance with the relevant financial reporting framework. The essential audit reporting differences are that:

- For **corresponding figures**, the auditors' report only refers to the financial statements of the current period.

- For **comparative financial statements**, the auditors' report refers to each period that financial statements are presented.

ISA 710 provides guidance on the auditors' responsibilities for comparatives and for reporting on them under the two frameworks in separate sections.

3.2 Corresponding figures

3.2.1 The auditors' responsibilities

> **ISA 710.6**
>
> The auditor should obtain sufficient appropriate audit evidence that the corresponding figures meet the requirements of the applicable financial reporting framework.

Audit procedures performed on the corresponding figures are usually limited to checking that the corresponding figures have been correctly reported and are appropriately classified. Auditors must assess whether:

- **Accounting policies** used for the corresponding figures are **consistent** with those of the current period or whether appropriate adjustments and/or disclosures have been made.

- **Corresponding figures agree** with the **amounts** and other disclosures presented in the prior period or whether appropriate adjustments and/or disclosures have been made.

> **ISA 710.6-1**
>
> In the UK and Ireland, the auditors should obtain sufficient appropriate audit evidence that:
>
> (a)   The accounting policies used for the corresponding amounts are consistent with those of the current period and appropriate adjustments and disclosures have been made where this is not the case.
>
> (b)   The corresponding amounts agree with the amounts and disclosures presented in the preceding period and are free from errors in the context of the financial statements of the current period, and
>
> (c)   Where corresponding amounts have been adjusted as required by relevant legislation and accounting standards, appropriate disclosures have been made.

When the financial statements of the prior period:

- Have been audited by other auditors
- Were not audited

the incoming auditors assess whether the corresponding figures meet the conditions specified above and also follow the guidance in ISA 510.

If the auditors become aware of a possible material misstatement in the corresponding figures when performing the current period audit, then they must perform any necessary additional procedures.

3.2.2 Reporting

> **ISA 710.10**
>
> When the comparatives are presented as corresponding figures, the auditor should issue an audit report in which the comparatives are not specifically identified because the auditor's opinion is on the current period financial statements as a whole, including the corresponding figures.

The auditor's report will only make any specific reference to corresponding figures in the circumstances described below. We will look at specific examples of the wording of auditors' reports in such circumstances below.

Firstly, there is the problem of what happens when the auditor's report for the previous period was modified.

ISA 710.12

When the auditor's report on the prior period, as previously issued, included a qualified opinion, disclaimer of opinion, or adverse opinion and the matter which gave rise to the modification is:

(a)   unresolved, and results in a modification of the auditor's report regarding the current period figures, the auditor's report should also be modified regarding the corresponding figures; or

(b)   unresolved, but does not result in a modification of the auditor's report regarding the current period figures, the auditor's report should be modified regarding the corresponding figures

If a modified report was issued, but the matter which gave rise to it is resolved and properly dealt with in the financial statements, the current report will not usually refer to the previous modification. If the matter is material to the **current period**, however, the auditors may include an **emphasis of matter paragraph** to deal with it.

In performing the audit of the current period financial statements, the auditors, in certain unusual circumstances, may become aware of a material misstatement that affects the prior period financial statements on which an unmodified report has been previously issued.

ISA 710.15

In such circumstances, the auditor should consider the guidance in ISA 560 *Subsequent events* and:

(a)   if the prior period financial statements have been revised and reissued with a new auditor's report, the auditor should be satisfied that the corresponding figures agree with the revised financial statements; or

(b)   if the prior period financial statements have not been revised and reissued, and the corresponding figures have not been properly restated and/or appropriate disclosures have not been made, the auditor should issue a modified report on the current period financial statement modified with respect to the corresponding figures included therein.

In these circumstances, if the prior period financial statements have not been revised and an auditor's report has not been reissued, but the corresponding figures have been properly restated and/or appropriate disclosures have been made in the current period financial statements, the auditors may include an **emphasis of matter paragraph** describing the circumstances and referencing to the appropriate disclosures. In this regard, the auditors also consider the guidance in ISA 560 *Subsequent events*.

3.2.3 Incoming auditors: additional requirements

When the prior period financial statements were audited by other auditors, in some countries the incoming auditors can refer to the predecessor auditors' report on the corresponding figures in the incoming auditor's report for the current period.

ISA 710.17

When the auditor decides to refer to another auditor, the incoming auditor's report should indicate:

(a)   that the financial statements of the prior period were audited by another auditor;

(b)   the type of report issued by the predecessor auditor and, if the report was modified, the reasons therefore; and

(c)   the date of that report.

In the UK, the existing auditor does not make reference to another auditor in his report.

The situation is slightly different if the prior period financial statements were **not audited**.

ISA 710.18

When the prior period financial statements are not audited, the incoming auditor should state in the auditor's report that the corresponding figures are unaudited.

The inclusion of such a statement does not, however, relieve the auditors of the requirement to perform appropriate procedures regarding opening balances of the current period. Clear disclosure in the financial statements that the corresponding figures are unaudited is encouraged. If there is insufficient evidence about corresponding figures or inadequate disclosures, the auditor should consider the implications for his report.

ISA 710.19

In situations where the incoming auditor identifies that the corresponding figures are materially misstated, the auditor should request management to revise the corresponding figures or if management refuses to do so, appropriately modify the report.

3.3 Comparative financial statements

3.3.1 The auditors' responsibilities

ISA 710.20

The auditor should obtain sufficient appropriate audit evidence that the comparative financial statements meet the requirements of the applicable financial reporting framework.

This is effectively involves the auditors following the same procedures on the prior period statements as noted above.

3.3.2 Reporting

ISA 710.24

When the comparatives are presented as comparative financial statements, the auditor should issue a report in which the comparatives are specifically identified because the auditor's opinion is expressed individually on the financial statements of each period presented.

The auditors may therefore express a **modified opinion** or include an **emphasis of matter** paragraph with respect to one or more financial statements for one or more period, whilst issuing a different report on the other financial statements.

The auditors may become aware of circumstances or events that materially affect the financial statements of a prior period during the course of the audit for the current period.

ISA 710.25

When reporting on the prior period financial statements in connection with the current year's audit, if the opinion on such prior period financial statements is different from the opinion previously expressed, the auditor should disclose the substantive reasons for the different opinion in an emphasis of matter paragraph.

3.3.3 Incoming auditors: additional requirements

Again, there are procedures where the prior period financial statements are audited by other auditors.

ISA 710.26

When the financial statement of the prior period were audited by another auditor:

(a)   the predecessor auditor may reissue the audit report on the prior period with the incoming auditor only reporting on the current period; or

(b)   the incoming auditor's report should state that the prior period was audited by another auditor and the incoming auditor's report should indicate:

    (i)   that the financial statements of the prior period were audited by another auditor;

    (ii)   the type of report issued by the predecessor auditor and if the report was modified, the reasons therefor; and

    (iii)   the date of that report.

In performing the audit on the current period financial statements, the incoming auditors may become aware of a material misstatement that affects the prior period financial statements on which the predecessor auditors had previously reported without modification.

ISA 710.28

In these circumstances, the incoming auditor should discuss the matter with management and, after having obtained management's authorisation, contact the predecessor auditor and propose that the prior period financial statements be restated. if the predecessor agrees to reissue the audit report on the restated financial statements of the prior period, the auditor should follow the guidance in [Paragraph 3.24].

The predecessor auditors may not agree with the proposed restatement or they may refuse to reissue the audit report for the prior period financial statements. In such cases, the introductory paragraph of the auditor's report may indicate that the predecessor auditors reported on the financial statements of the prior period before restatement.

In addition, if the incoming auditors are engaged to audit and they perform sufficient procedures to be satisfied as to the appropriateness of the restatement adjustment, they may also include the following paragraph in the report.

'We also audited the adjustment described in Note X that were applied to restate the 20X1 financial statements. In our opinion, such adjustments are appropriate and have been properly applied.'

The other circumstance is that the prior period financial statement may not have been audited.

ISA 710.30

When the prior period financial statements are not audited, the incoming auditor should state in the auditor's report that the comparative financial statements are unaudited.

Again, the inclusion of such a statement does not relieve the auditors of the requirement to carry out appropriate procedures regarding opening balances of the current period. Clear disclosure in the financial statements that the comparative financial statements are unaudited is encouraged.

ISA 710.31

In situations where the incoming auditor identifies that the prior year unaudited figures are materially misstated, the auditor should request management to revise the prior year's figures or if management refuses to do so, appropriately modify the report.

Question
Opening balances and comparatives

Auditing standards have been issued on opening balances for initial engagements and comparatives, and one of the matters considered is where one firm of auditors takes over from another firm. You have recently been appointed auditor of Lowdham Castings, a limited company which has been trading for about thirty years, and are carrying out the audit for the year ended 30 September 20X6. The company's turnover is about £500,000 and its normal profit before tax is about £30,000. Comparatives are shown as corresponding figures only.

Required

Explain your responsibilities in relation to the comparatives included in the accounts for the year ended 30 September 20X6. You should also outline the information you would require from the retiring auditors.

Answer

Consideration of the financial statements of the preceding period is necessary in the audit of the current period's financial statements in relation to three main aspects.

(a) Opening position: obtaining satisfaction that those amounts which have a direct effect on the current period's results or closing position have been properly brought forward.

(b) Accounting policies: determining whether the accounting policies adopted for the current period are consistent with those of the previous period.

(c) Comparatives: determining that the comparatives are properly shown in the current period's financial statements.

The auditors' main concern will therefore be to satisfy themselves that there were no material misstatements in the previous year's financial statements which may have a bearing upon their work in the current year.

The new auditors do not have to 're-audit' the previous year's financial statements, but they will have to pay more attention to them than would normally be the case where they had themselves been the auditors in the earlier period. A useful source of audit evidence will clearly be the previous auditors, and, with the client's permission, they should be contacted to see if they are prepared to co-operate. Certainly, any known areas of weakness should be discussed with the previous auditors and it is also possible that they might be prepared to provide copies of their working papers (although there is no legal or ethical provision which requires the previous auditors to co-operate in this way).

4 Revision: other information

FAST FORWARD

Auditors should always seek to resolve inconsistencies or misstatements of fact between financial statements and other published information.

4.1 What other information?

ISA (UK and Ireland) 720 *Other Information in Documents Containing Audited Financial Statements* establishes standards and provides guidance on the auditors' consideration of other information, on which the auditors have **no obligation to report,** in documents containing audited financial statements.

> **ISA 720.2/2-1**
>
> The auditor should read the other information to identify material inconsistencies with the audited financial statements. If, as a result of reading the other information, the auditor becomes aware of any apparent misstatements therein, or identifies any material inconsistencies with the audited financial statements, the auditor should seek to resolve them.

Key terms

> **Other information** is financial and non-financial information *other than* the audited financial statements and the auditors' report, which an entity may include in its annual report, either by custom or statute.
>
> A **material inconsistency** exists when other information contradicts information contained in the audited financial statements. A material inconsistency may raise doubt about the audit conclusions drawn from audit evidence previously obtained and, possibly, about the basis for the auditors' opinion on the financial statements.

Examples of other information are:

- A report by management or the board of directors on operations
- Financial summaries or highlights
- Employment data
- Planned capital expenditures
- Financial ratios
- Name of officers and directors
- Selected quarterly data

Auditors have no responsibility to report that other information is properly stated because an audit is only an expression of opinion on the truth and fairness of the financial statements. However, they may be **engaged separately**, or **required by statute**, to report on elements of other information. In any case, the auditors should give consideration to other information as inconsistencies with the audited financial statements may undermine their report.

Some countries require the auditors to apply specific procedures to certain other information, for example, required supplementary data and interim financial information. If such other information is omitted or contains deficiencies, the auditors may be required to refer to the matter in their report.

When there is an obligation to report specifically on other information, the auditors' responsibilities are determined by the **nature of the engagement** and by **local legislation** and professional standards. When such responsibilities involve the review of other information, the auditors will need to follow the guidance on **review engagements** in the appropriate ISAs.

You should note that in the UK, auditors are required to state in the audit report whether the directors' report is consistent with the financial statements. This has recently changed. Previously auditors were only required to report this by exception (ie if it did not agree).

4.2 Access to other information

Timely access to other information will be required. The auditors therefore must make arrangements with the client to obtain such information prior to the date of their report. In circumstances where all the other information may not be available prior to that date, the auditors should follow the guidance below.

BPP
LEARNING MEDIA

4.3 Material inconsistencies

> **ISA 720.11/12/13**
>
> If, on reading the other information, the auditor identifies a material inconsistency, the auditor should determine whether the audited financial statements or the other information needs to be amended. If the auditor identifies a material inconsistency the auditor should seek to resolve the matter through discussion with those charged with governance.
>
> If an amendment is necessary in the audited financial statements and the entity refuses to make the amendment, the auditor should express a qualified or adverse opinion.
>
> If an amendment is necessary in the other information and the entity refuses to make the amendment, the auditor should consider including in the auditor's report an emphasis of matter paragraph describing the material inconsistency or taking other actions.

The actions taken by the auditors will depend on the individual circumstances and the auditors may consider taking legal advice. In the UK and Ireland, the auditor has a statutory duty to consider whether the information in the directors' report is consistent with the financial statements with which it is issued.

4.4 Material misstatements of fact

A 'material misstatement of fact' in other information exists when such information, not related to matters appearing in the financial statement, is incorrectly stated and presented.

> **ISA 720.16**
>
> If the auditor becomes aware that the other information appears to include a material misstatement of fact, the auditor should discuss the matter with the entity's management. The auditor should consider whether the other information needs to be amended.

When discussing the matter with the entity's management, the auditors may not be able to evaluate the validity of the other information and management's responses to the auditors' enquiries, and would need to consider whether valid differences of judgement or opinion exist.

> **ISA 720.17/18**
>
> When the auditor still considers that there is an apparent misstatement of fact, the auditor should request management to consult with a qualified third party, such as the entity's legal counsel and should consider the advice received.
>
> If the auditor concludes that there is a material misstatement of fact in the other information which management refuses to correct, the auditor should consider taking further appropriate action.

Such an action could include such steps as notifying those ultimately responsible for the overall direction of the entity and obtaining legal advice. In the UK, if those charged with governance refuse to change the other information the auditors should include an explanatory (emphasis of matter) paragraph in the report.

5 Revision: subsequent events

Auditors should consider the effect of subsequent events (after the balance sheet date) on the accounts.

5.1 Events after the balance sheet date

'Subsequent events' include:

- Events occurring between the period end and the date of the auditor's report
- Facts discovered after the date of the auditor's report

ISA 560 *Subsequent Events* begins by stating that:

ISA 560.2

The auditor should consider the effect of subsequent events on the financial statements and on the auditor's report.

FRS 21 *Events after the balance sheet date* deals with the treatment in financial statement of events, both favourable and unfavourable, occurring after the period end. It identifies two types of event:

- Those that provide further evidence of conditions that existed at the period end
- Those that are indicative of conditions that arose subsequent to the period end

5.2 Events occurring up to the date of the auditor's report

ISA 560.4

The auditor should perform procedures designed to obtain sufficient appropriate audit evidence that all events up to the date of the auditor's report that may require adjustment of, or disclosure in, the financial statements have been identified.

These procedures should be applied to any matters examined during the audit which may be susceptible to change after the year end. They are in addition to tests on specific transactions after the period end, eg cut-off tests.

The ISA lists procedures to identify subsequent events which may require adjustment or disclosure. They should be performed as near as possible to the date of the auditors' report.

PROCEDURES TESTING SUBSEQUENT EVENTS	
Enquiries of management	Status of items involving **subjective judgement**/ accounted for using preliminary data
	New **commitments**, borrowings or guarantees
	Sales or destruction of **assets**
	Issues of **shares/debentures** or changes in business structure
	Developments involving **risk areas, provisions** and **contingencies**
	Unusual accounting adjustments
	Major events (eg going concern problems) affecting appropriateness of accounting policies for estimates
Other procedures	**Consider procedures** of management for identifying subsequent events
	Read minutes of general board/committee meetings
	Review latest accounting records and financial information

Reviews and updates of these procedures may be required, depending on the length of the time between the procedures and the signing of the auditors' report and the susceptibility of the items to change over time.

> **ISA 560.7**
>
> When the auditor becomes aware of events which materially affect the financial statements, the auditor should consider whether such events are properly accounted for and adequately disclosed in the financial statements.

5.3 Facts discovered after the date of the auditor's report but before the financial statements are issued

The financial statements are the management's responsibility. They should therefore inform the auditors of any material subsequent events between the date of the auditors' report and the date the financial statements are issued. The auditors do **not** have any obligation to perform procedures, or make enquires regarding the financial statements **after the** date of their report.

> **ISA 560.9**
>
> When, after the date of the auditor's report but before the financial statements are issued, the auditor becomes aware of a fact which may materially affect the financial statements, the auditor should consider whether the financial statements need amendment, should discuss the matter with the management and should take action appropriate in the circumstances.

When the financial statements are amended, the auditors should **extend the procedures** discussed above to the **date of their new report**, carry out any other appropriate procedures and issue a new audit report dated the day it is signed.

The situation may arise where the statements are not amended but the auditors feel that they should be.

> **ISA 560.11**
>
> When management does not amend the financial statements in circumstances where the auditor believes they need to be amended and the auditor's report has not been released to the entity, the auditor should express a qualified opinion or an adverse opinion.

If the auditors' report has already been issued to the entity then the auditors should notify those who are ultimately responsible for the entity (the management or possibly a holding company in a group), not to issue the financial statements or auditors' reports to third parties. If they have already been so issued, the auditors must take steps to prevent the reliance on the auditors' report. The action taken will depend on the auditors' legal rights and obligations and the advice of the auditors' lawyer.

5.4 Facts discovered after the financial statements have been issued

Auditors have no obligations to perform procedures or make enquiries regarding the financial statements after they have been issued. In the UK, this includes the period up until the financial statements are laid before members at the AGM.

ISA 560.14

When, after the financial statements have been issued, the auditor becomes aware of a fact which existed at the date of the auditor's report and which, if known at that date, may have caused the auditor to modify the auditor's report, the auditor should consider whether the financial statements need revision, should discuss the matter with management, and should take the action as appropriate in the circumstances.

The ISA gives the appropriate procedures which the auditors should undertake when management revises the financial statements.

(a)   **Carry out the audit procedures** necessary in the circumstances

(b)   **Review the steps taken by management** to ensure that anyone in receipt of the previously issued financial statements together with the auditors' report thereon is informed of the situation

(c)   **Issue a new report** on the revised financial statements

ISA 560.16

The new auditor's report should include an emphasis of a matter paragraph referring to a note to the financial statements that more extensively discusses the reason for the revision of the previously issued financial statements and to the earlier report issued by the auditor.

In our opinion, the revised financial statements give a true and fair view (or 'present fairly, in all material respects'), as at the date the original financial statements were approved, of the financial position of the company as of December 31, 20X1, and of the results of its operations and its cash flows for the year then ended in accordance with [relevant national legislation].

In our opinion the original financial statements for the year to December 31, 20X1, failed to comply with [relevant national standards or legislation].

Date   AUDITOR
Address

Where local regulations allow the auditor to restrict the audit procedures on the financial statements to the effects of the subsequent event which caused the revision, the new auditor's report should contain a statement to that effect.

Where the management does **not** revise the financial statements but the auditors feel they should be revised, or if the management does not intend to take steps to ensure anyone in receipt of the previously issued financial statements is informed of the situation, then the auditors should consider steps to take, on a timely basis, to prevent reliance on their report. The actions taken will depend on the auditors' legal rights and obligations (for example, to contact the shareholders directly) and legal advice received. In the UK, the auditor has a legal right to make statements at the AGM.

Exam focus point

Subsequent events have previously appeared in an audit reports question with 5 easy marks for outlining the auditors' responsibilities for subsequent events and then practical application in part (b).

Question

You are auditing the financial statements of Hope Engineering, a limited company, for the year ending 31 March 20X8. The partner in charge of the audit instructs you to carry out a review of the company's activities since the financial year end. Mr Smith, the managing director of Hope Engineering, overhears the conversation with the partner and is surprised that you are examining accounting information which relates to the next accounting period.

Mr Smith had been appointed on 1 March 20X8 as a result of which the contract of the previous managing director, Mr Jones, was terminated. Compensation of £500,000 had been paid to Mr Jones on 2 March 20X8.

As a result of your investigations you find that the company is going to bring an action against Mr Jones for the recovery of the compensation paid to him, as it had come to light that two months prior to his dismissal, he had contractually agreed to join the board of directors of a rival company. The company's lawyer had informed Hope Engineering that Mr Jones' actions constituted a breach of his contract with them, and that an action could be brought against the former managing director for the recovery of the money paid to him.

Required

(a) Explain the nature and purpose of a review of the period after the balance sheet date.

(b) Describe the audit procedures which would be carried out in order to identify any material subsequent events.

(c) Discuss the audit implications of the company's decision to sue Mr Jones for the recovery of the compensation paid to him.

Answer

(a)   The auditors' active responsibility extends to the date on which they sign their audit report. As this date is inevitably after the year end, it follows that in order to discharge their responsibilities, the auditors must extend their audit work to cover the post balance sheet period.

         The objective of the audit of the post balance sheet period is to ascertain whether management has dealt correctly with any events, both favourable and unfavourable, which occurred after the year end and which need to be reflected in the financial statements, if those statements are to show a true and fair view.

         The general rule is that, in the preparation of year end financial statements, no account should be taken of subsequent events unless to do so is required by statute or to give effect to retrospective legislation, or to take into account an event which provides information about a condition existing at the balance sheet date, for example realisable values of stock, or indicates that the going concern concept is no longer applicable. Additionally, certain events may have such a material effect on the company's financial condition, for example a merger, that disclosure is essential to give a true and fair view.

(b)   (i)   Ask management if there have been any material subsequent events.

       (ii)   Identify and evaluate procedures implemented by management to ensure that all events after the balance sheet date have been identified, considered and properly evaluated as to their effect on the financial statements.

       (iii)   Review relevant accounting records to identify subsequent cash received in relation to accounts receivable, to check items uncleared at the year end on the bank reconciliation, to check NRV of inventories from sales invoices.

       (iv)   Review budgets, profit forecasts, cash flow projections and management accounts for the new period to assess the company's trading position.

(v)   Consider known 'risk' areas and contingencies, whether inherent in the nature of the business or revealed by previous audit experience, or by lawyers' letters.

(vi) Read minutes of shareholders' and management meetings, and correspondence and memoranda relating to items included in the minutes to identify any matters arising.

(vii) Consider relevant information which has come to the auditors' attention from sources outside the enterprise, including public knowledge of competitors, suppliers and customers.

(viii) Obtain written representations concerning subsequent events from management.

(c)   The compensation paid to Mr Smith would be disclosed as part of directors' remuneration for the year ended 31 March 20X8. However, the question then arises as to whether or not the financial statements need to take any account of the possible recovery of the compensation payment.

The auditors should first ascertain from the board minutes that the directors intend to proceed with the lawsuit and should then attempt to assess the outcome by consulting the directors and the company's legal advisors. Only if it seems probable that the compensation will be recovered should a contingent gain be disclosed in the notes to the accounts, along with a summary of the facts of the case. A prudent estimate of legal costs should be deducted.

It could be argued that Mr Smith's breach of contract existed at the balance sheet date and that the compensation should therefore be treated as a current asset, net of recovery costs. However, this would not be prudent, given the uncertainties over the court case.

6 Revision: going concern

FAST FORWARD

> Auditors should consider whether the going concern basis is appropriate, and whether disclosure of any going concern problems is sufficient.

6.1 The going concern assumption

Key term

Under the '**going concern assumption**' an entity is ordinarily viewed as continuing in business for the foreseeable future with neither the intention nor the necessity of liquidation, ceasing trading or seeking protection from creditors pursuant to laws or regulations. Accordingly assets and liabilities are recorded on the basis that the entity will be able to realise its assets and discharge its liabilities in the normal course of business'.

ISA (UK and Ireland) 570 *Going concern* states that when preparing accounts, management should make an explicit **assessment** of the entity's ability to continue as a going concern. Most accounting frameworks require management to do so.

When management are making the assessment, the following factors should be considered.

- The **degree of uncertainty** about the events or conditions being assessed increases significantly the further into the future the assessment is made.

- Judgements are made on the basis of the **information available** at the time.

- Judgements are affected by the **size** and **complexity** of the entity, the **nature** and **condition** of the business and the **degree** to which it is **affected** by **external factors**.

ISA 570.2

When planning and performing audit procedures and in evaluating the results thereof, the auditor should consider the appropriateness of management's use of the going concern assumption in the preparation of the financial statements. The auditor should consider any relevant disclosures in financial statements.

The following list gives examples of possible indicators of going concern problems.

(a) **Financial indications**

- Net liabilities or net current liability position

- Necessary borrowing facilities have not been agreed

- Fixed-term borrowings approaching maturity without realistic prospects of renewal or repayment, or excessive reliance on short-term borrowings

- Major debt repayment falling due where refinancing is necessary to the entity's continued existence

- Major restructuring of debt

- Indications of withdrawal of financial support by creditors

- Negative operating cash flows indicated by historical or prospective financial statements

- Adverse key financial ratios

- Substantial operating losses or significant deterioration in the value of assets used to generate cash flows

- Major losses or cashflow problems which have arisen since the balance sheet date

- Arrears or discontinuance of dividends

- Inability to pay creditors on due dates

- Inability to comply with terms of loan agreements

- Reduction in normal terms of trade credit by suppliers

- Change from credit to cash-on-delivery transactions with suppliers

- Inability to obtain financing for essential new product development or other essential investments

- Substantial sales of fixed assets not intended to be replaced

(b) **Operating indications**

- Loss of key management without replacement

- Loss of key staff without replacement

- Loss of a major market, franchises, license, or principal supplier

- Labour difficulties or shortages of important supplies

- Fundamental changes in the market or technology to which the entity is unable to adapt adequately

- Excessive dependence on a few product lines where the market is depressed

- Technical developments which render a key product obsolete

(c) **Other indications**

- Non-compliance with capital or other statutory requirements
- Pending legal proceedings against the entity that may, if successful, result in judgements that could not be met
- Changes in legislation or government policy
- Issues which involve a range of possible outcomes so wide that an unfavourable result could affect the appropriateness of the going concern basis

Exam focus point

A question on going concern might ask you to identify signs that a particular client may not be a going concern.

The significance of such indications can often be **mitigated** by other factors.

(a) The effect of an entity being unable to make its normal debt repayments may be counterbalanced by management's plans to maintain **adequate cash flows** by alternative means, such as by disposal of assets, rescheduling of loan repayments, or obtaining additional capital.

(b) The loss of a principal supplier may be mitigated by the availability of a suitable alternative source of supply.

6.2 Auditors' responsibilities

Auditors are responsible for considering:

- The appropriateness of the going concern assumption
- The existence of **material uncertainties** about the going concern assumption that need to be disclosed in the accounts
- Whether there are adequate disclosures regarding the going concern basis in financial statements

ISA 570.11/12

In obtaining an understanding of the entity, the auditor should consider whether there are events or conditions and related business risks which may cast significant doubt on the entity's ability to continue as a going concern.

The auditor should remain alert for evidence of events or conditions and related business risks which may cast doubt on the entity's ability to continue as a going concern throughout the audit. If such events or conditions are identified, the auditor should, in addition to performing the procedures in Paragraph 26, consider whether they affect the auditor's assessments of the components of audit risk

Management may already have made a preliminary assessment of going concern. If so, the auditors would review potential problems management had identified, and management's plans to resolve them. Alternatively auditors may identify problems as a result of discussions with management.

ISA 570.17

The auditor should evaluate management's assessment of the entity's ability to continue as a going concern. The auditor should assess the adequacy of the means by which those charged with governance have satisfied themselves that:

(a) It is appropriate for them to adopt the going concern basis in preparing the financial statements; and

(b)   The financial statements include such disclosures, if any, relating to going concern as are necessary for them to give a true and fair view.

For this purpose:

(i)   The auditor should make enquiries of those charged with governance and examine appropriate available financial information; and

(ii)   Having regard to the future period to which those charged with governance have paid particular attention in assessing going concern, the auditor should plan and perform procedures specifically designed to identify any material matters which could indicate concern about the entity's ability to continue as a going concern.

The auditors should consider:

- The **process** management used
- The **assumptions** on which management's assessment is based
- Management's **plans** for future action

If management's assessment covers a period of **less than twelve months** from the balance sheet date, the auditor should ask management to extend its assessment period to twelve months from the balance sheet date. In the UK, if the directors have not considered a year from the date of approval of the financial statements and not disclosed that fact the auditor should disclose it in the audit report.

The auditor may need to consider:

- Whether the period considered by management is reasonable
- The company's system for timely identification of future risks
- Quality of budget information
- Appropriateness of key assumptions in budgets
- Sensitivity of budgets
- Obligations owed by the company
- Existence and adequacy of borrowing facilities

The auditor will examine the **borrowing facilities** available to the company. They will confirm the existence and terms of bank facilities and make an assessment of the bankers' intentions towards the company.

Management should not need to make a detailed assessment, and auditors carry out detailed procedures, if the entity has a **history of profitable operations** and **ready access** to **financial resources.**

ISA 570.22

The auditor should inquire of management as to its knowledge of events or conditions and related business risks beyond the period of assessment used by management that may cast significant doubt on the entity's ability to continue as a going concern.

Because the time period is some way into the future, the indications of potential going concern problems would have to be significant. Auditors do not have to carry out specific procedures to identify potential problems which may occur after the period covered by management's assessment. However they should be alert during the course of the audit for any **indications** of future problems.

6.2.1 Additional audit procedures

ISA 570.26

When events or conditions have been identified which may cast significant doubt on the entity's ability to continue as a going concern, the auditor should:

(a)   review management's plans for future actions based on its going concern assessment;

(b)   gather sufficient appropriate audit evidence to confirm or dispel whether or not a material uncertainty exists through carrying out procedures considered necessary, including considering the effects of any plans of management and other mitigating factors; and

(c)   seek written representations from management regarding its plans for future action.

The auditor should consider the need to obtain written confirmations of representations from those charged with governance regarding:

(a)   The assessment of those charged with governance that the company is a going concern

(b)   Any relevant disclosures in the financial statements

When questions arise on the appropriateness of the going concern assumption, some of the normal audit procedures carried out by the auditors may take on an **additional significance**. Auditors may also have to carry out **additional procedures** or to update information obtained earlier. The ISA lists various procedures which the auditors should carry out in this context.

- **Analyse and discuss cash flow**, profit and other relevant forecasts with management

- **Analyse and discuss** the entity's latest available **interim financial statements**

- **Review the terms of debentures and loan agreements** and determine whether they have been breached

- **Read minutes** of the meetings of shareholders, the board of directors and important committees for reference to financing difficulties

- **Enquire** of the entity's lawyer regarding **litigation and claims**

- **Confirm the existence, legality and enforceability** of arrangements to provide or maintain financial support with related and third parties

- **Assess** the **financial ability** of such parties to **provide additional funds**

- **Consider the entity's position** concerning unfulfilled customer orders

- **Review events after the period end** for items affecting the entity's ability to continue as a going concern

The auditors should discuss with management its **plans** for **future action**, for example plans to liquidate assets, borrow money or restructure debt, reduce or delay expenditure or increase capital, and assess whether these are feasible and are likely to improve the situation.

When analysis of cash flow is a significant factor, auditors should consider:

- The **reliability** of the **system** for generating the information
- Whether there is **adequate support** for the assumptions underlying the forecast
- How **recent forecasts** have **differed** from **actual results**

ISA 570.30

Based on the audit evidence obtained, the auditor should determine if, in the auditors' judgement, a material uncertainty exists related to events or conditions that alone or in aggregate, may cast significant doubt on the entity's ability to continue as a going concern. The auditor should document the extent of the auditor's concern (if any) about the entity's ability to continue as a going concern.

An uncertainty will be material if it has so great a potential impact as to require clear disclosure of its nature and implications in the accounts. The accounts should:

- **Adequately describe** the **principal events or conditions** that give rise to the uncertainty about continuance as a going concern, and management's plans to deal with the situation
- **State clearly** that a **material uncertainty exists** and therefore the entity may be unable to realise its assets and discharge its liabilities in the normal course of business

ISA 570.33

If adequate disclosure is made in the financial statements, the auditor should express an unqualified opinion but modify the auditor's report by adding an emphasis of a matter paragraph that highlights the existence of a material uncertainty relating to an event or condition that may cast significant doubt on the entity's ability to continue as a going concern and draws attention to the note in the financial statements that discloses the matters.

6.3 Auditor's report

The auditor's report is considered in detail in Chapter 17. The ISA gives an example of an emphasis of matter paragraph in such circumstances.

'Without qualifying our opinion we draw attention to Note X in the financial statements. The company incurred a net loss of ZZZ during the year ended December 31, 20X1 and, as of that date, the company's current liabilities exceeded its total assets by ZZZ. These conditions, along with other matters as set forth in Note X, indicate the existence of a material uncertainty which may cast significant doubt about the company's ability to continue as a going concern.'

The auditors may express a disclaimer of opinion if for example there are multiple material uncertainties.

ISA 510.34

If adequate disclosure is not made in the financial statements, the auditor should express a qualified or adverse opinion, as appropriate. The report should include explicit reference to the fact that there is a material uncertainty which may cast significant doubt about the company's ability to continue as a going concern.

6.3.1 Adverse opinion

ISA 570.35

If in the auditors' judgement, the entity will not be able to continue as a going concern, the auditor should express an adverse opinion if the financial statements have been prepared on a going concern basis.

This applies whatever the level of disclosure in the accounts. If a basis other than the going concern basis is used, and the auditors consider it appropriate, they can issue an unqualified opinion with an emphasis of matter paragraph.

6.3.2 Limitation of scope

> **ISA 570.37**
>
> If management is unwilling to make or extend its assessment when requested to do so by the auditor, the auditor should consider the need to modify the auditor's report as a result of the limitation on the scope of the auditor's work.

The auditors may be able to obtain sufficient alternative evidence even if management's assessment is inadequate.

6.4 Significant delay

When there is a significant delay in approving the accounts, auditors should consider whether this is due to doubts about the going concern status of the business. The delay may prompt the auditors to perform additional procedures on going concern.

Question	Going concern

You are planning to audit of Truckers whose principal activities are road transport and warehousing services, and the repair of commercial vehicles. You have been provided with the draft accounts for the year ended 31 October 20X5

	Draft 20X5 £'000	Actual 20X4 £'000
Summary profit and loss account		
Turnover	10,971	11,560
Cost of sales	(10,203)	(10,474)
Gross profit	768	1,086
Administrative expenses	(782)	(779)
Interest payable and similar charges	(235)	(185)
Net (loss) profit	(249)	122
Summary balance sheet		
Fixed assets	5,178	4,670
Current assets		
Stock (parts and consumables)	95	61
Debtors	2,975	2,369
	3,070	2,430
Current liabilities		
Bank loan	250	-
Overdraft	1,245	913
Trade creditors	1,513	1,245
Lease obligations	207	–
Other creditors	203	149
	3,481	2,307
Long term liabilities		
Bank loan	750	1,000
Lease obligations	473	–
	1,223	1,000
Net assets	3,544	3,793

You have been informed by the managing director that the fall in turnover is due to:

(1)   The loss, in July, of a long-standing customer to a competitor, and

(2)   A decline in trade in the repair of commercial vehicles.

Due to the reduction in the repairs business, the company has decided to close the workshop and sell the equipment and spares stock. No entries resulting from this decision are reflected in the draft accounts.

During the year, the company replaced a number of vehicles funding them by a combination of leasing and an increased overdraft facility. The facility is to be reviewed in January 20X6 after the audited accounts are available.

The draft accounts show a loss for 20X5 but the forecasts indicate a return to profitability in 20X6 as the managing director is optimistic about generating additional turnover from new contracts.

(a)   State the circumstances particular to Truckers which may indicate that the company is not a going concern. Explain why these circumstances given cause for concern.

(b)   Describe the audit work to be performed in respect of going concern at Truckers.

Answer

(a)

Circumstances	Why cause for concern?
Fall in gross profit % achieved	Whilst the fall in absolute turnover has been explained the fall in gross profit margin is more serious.
	This will continue to be a problem as expenses seem constant and interest costs are growing.
	This will make a future return to profitability difficult.
Losses £249,000	Such levels of losses by comparison to 20X4 profits will make negotiations with bank difficult.
	Especially with the loss of a major customer
Increased debtors balance and increased ageing 20X5 96.7 days 20X4 74.8 days	Worsening debt collection is bad news when the company is making losses and has a deteriorating liquidity position.
	The increase in average debt collection period may be due to a bad debt on the account of the major customer lost in the year.
	A bad debt write-off would cause much increased losses.
Worsening liquidity ratio 20X4 1.03 20X5 0.85	This is a significant fall which will worsen further if a bad debt provision is required
	The company has loan and lease commitments which possibly may not be met.
Increasing reliance on short term finance	This does not secure the future.
	With the company going through so much change this may cause difficulties for the bank overdraft facility negotiations
Gearing will have increased	This leads to an interest commitment which is a drain on future profits.
	This may also cause a problem in negotiating new finance arrangements.
Loss of major customers to competitor	Risk of unprovided bad debts in the accounts
	Other customers could follow suit worsening the company's future prospects.

Circumstances	Why cause for concern?
Loss of commercial customers	Commercial customers normally provide regular income which is important for a company with repayment commitments.
Draft Accounts – final adjustments are outstanding	The company's net asset position could be worsened considerably if fixed assets are written down to recoverable amount, repairs stock written down to net realisable value.
	As mentioned before further bad debt provisions may be necessary.
	The closure may necessitate redundancy provisions.
	All of these factors could increase losses considerably.
Overdraft facility to be reviewed 3 months after the year end	This time period is probably not long enough to see a real improvement in the company's fortunes.
	As auditors we will be reporting when faced with fundamental uncertainty.
	Trying to anticipate the banks likely reaction to the financial statements will be high risk.
Future return to profits anticipated at a time when competitors are achieving success	The concern should be whether this is over optimistic. If so too much reliance being placed upon management representation would be high risk strategy.
	Summary – If the company is not a going concern the accounts would be truer and fairer if prepared in a break-up basis. Material adjustments may then be required to the accounts.

(b)
- Analyse post balance sheet sale proceeds for fixed assets, stock, cash received from customers.

- Review the debt ageing and cash recovery lists. Ask directors if outstanding amounts from lost customer are recoverable.

- Discuss the optimistic view of likely future contracts with the MD. Orders in the post balance sheet period should be reviewed to see if they substantiate his opinion.

- Obtain his opinion about future contracts in a written representation letter.

- Review bank/loan records to assess the extent to which the company has met its loan and lease commitments in the post balance sheet period.

- Review sales orders/sales ledger for evidence of additional lost custom in post balance sheet period.

- Obtain cashflow and profit forecasts:

  - Discuss assumptions with the directors.

  - Perform sensitivity analysis flexing the key assumptions ie interest rates, date of payment of creditors and receipts from customers.

  - Check all commitments have been cleared in accordance with legal agreements.

  - Agree budgets to any actual results achieved in the post balance sheet period.

  - Assess reasonableness of assumptions in the light of the success of the achievement of the company's budgets set for 20X5. Discuss with the directors any targets not achieved.

- Reperform calculations
- Ensure future budgeted profits are expected to meet likely interest charges.

- Review bank records to ensure that the company is operating within its overdraft facility in the post balance sheet period. Review bank certificate for terms and conditions of the facility. Review bank correspondence for any suggestion the bank is concerned about its current position.

- Ask management whether the new vehicle fleet is attracting new contracts as anticipated. Scrutinise any new contracts obtained and check improved gross profit margins will be achieved.

- Obtain management representation as to the likelihood of the company operating for twelve months from the date of approval of the financial statements.

Chapter Roundup

- The auditors must perform and document an **overall review** of the financial statements before they can reach an opinion.
- As part of their completion procedures, auditors should consider whether the cumulative effect of unadjusted errors is material.
- Specific procedures must be applied to **opening balances**.
- The auditors' responsibilities for **comparatives** vary depending on whether they are corresponding figures or comparative financial statements.
- Auditors should always seek to resolve inconsistencies or misstatements of fact between financial statements and other published information.
- Auditors should consider the effect of **subsequent events** (after the balance sheet date) on the accounts.
- Auditors should consider whether the going concern basis is **appropriate,** and whether **disclosure** of going concern problems is **sufficient**.

Quick Quiz

1   Name eight items that analytical review at the final stage must cover.

(1) ....   (5) ....

(2) ....   (6) ....

(3) ....   (7) ....

(4) ....   (8) ....

2   The auditor will maintain a schedule of unadjusted errors. This will include:

- Specific misstatements identified by the auditors
- Best estimate of other misstatements

True ☐

False ☐

3   Where prior period financial statements were unaudited, the auditor should make no reference to the comparatives in his report.

True   ☐

False   ☐

4   Which of the items on the following list are not part of the 'other information' within the scope of ISA 720?

- Directors' report
- Financial ratios
- Cashflow statement
- Employment data
- Auditors' report
- Financial summaries

5   Name 2 elements of 'subsequent events'.

1.   ....

2.   ....

6   List five enquiries which may be made of management in testing subsequent events.

1.   ....

2.   ....

3.   ....

4.   ....

5.   ....

7   Complete the definition

The .... assumption: The enterprise will continue in business for the .... with neither the intention nor the necessity of liquidation.

8   The 'foreseeable future' is always a period of 12 months

True   ☐

False   ☐

Answers to Quick Quiz

1. • Important accounting ratios
   • Related items
   • Changes in products; customers
   • Price and mix changes
   • Wages changes
   • Variances
   • Trends in production and sales
   • Changes in material and labour content of production
   • Other profit and loss account expenditure
   • Variations caused by industry or economy factors

2. True

3. False

4. Cashflow statement and auditors' report

5. (1) Events occurring between the period end and the date of the auditors' report
   (2) Facts discovered after the date of the auditors report

6. From:

   (1) Status of items involving subjective judgement
   (2) Any new commitments
   (3) Sales of assets
   (4) Issues of shares or debentures
   (5) Developments in risk areas
   (6) Unusual accounting adjustments
   (7) Other major events

7. Going concern, foreseeable future

8. False

Now try the question below from the Exam Question Bank

Number	Level	Marks	Time
Q10	Examination	20	36 mins
Q11	Examination	25	45 mins

Evaluation and review (ii) matters relating to specific accounting issues

Topic list	Syllabus reference
1 Fair value	D1(iii)
2 Stock and long term contracts	D1(iii)
3 Tangible fixed assets	D1(iii)
4 Intangible fixed assets	D1(iii)
5 Financial instruments	D1(iii)
6 Investment properties	D1(iii)

Introduction

You must be able to consider four key matters in relation to items appearing in financial statements: risk, materiality, relevant accounting standards and audit evidence. In this chapter, we shall focus on the last two of these, as the first two will depend more on the scenario presented in any given question.

You have previously studied the audit of a basic set of financial statements. At this level, the issues you are presented with will be more complex, but remember that key basic points apply. Bear in mind the relevant **assertions** for the financial statement item.

You need a strong knowledge of all the accounting standards you learnt up to P2 Corporate Reporting to apply in this paper. BPP suggests you keep your previous Study Texts as a reference point when working through this chapter and accounting issues question.

Note. The examiner has stated that in the first two sittings of this paper she will not examine accounting standards that are only examinable in Paper P2. This is being done to ensure that students sitting P7 before P2 under the transitional arrangements are not disadvantaged. All of the topics in this chapter, including financial instruments (at F7/old syllabus 2.5 level) can be examined from this sitting.

Study guide

D	ASSIGNMENTS	Intellectual level
1(iii)	**Evaluation and review**	
(j)	Evaluate the matters (eg materiality, risk, relevant accounting standards, audit evidence)	3
(i)	(i) stock	
(ii)	(ii) standard costing systems	
(iii)	fixed assets	
(iv)	long term contracts	
(v)	fair value	
(iv)	leases	
(viii)	borrowing costs	
(viii)	held for sale fixed assets	
(ix)	impairment	
(x)	goodwill	
(xi)	brand valuations	
(xii)	research and development	
(xiii)	other intangible assets	
	(This list is not exhaustive, in particular, the audit of transactions, balances and other events examined in the earlier paper and is now assumed knowledge) this chapter focuses on assets; further accounting issues are dealt with in the following chapter.	

Exam guide

At this level it is assumed that you can audit all of the items listed above and all items audited at the earlier level.

1 Fair value

 Key assertions relating to assets are existence, completeness, valuation and rights and obligations.

Key term

Fair value is the amount for which an asset or liability could be exchanged between knowledgeable, willing parties in an arm's length transaction.

Fair value accounting is increasingly important and affects the audit of valuation for both assets and liabilities. Many standards now allow valuation at fair value.

For auditors, the determination of fair value will generally be more difficult than determining historical cost. It will be more difficult to establish whether fair value is reasonable for complex assets and liabilities than for more straightforward assets or liabilities which have a market and therefore a market value.

Generally speaking, the trend towards fair value accounting will increase audit work required, not only because determining fair values is more difficult, but because fair values fluctuate in a way that historical costs do not, and will need vouching each audit period.

Exam focus point

In a past paper, there were 6 marks in a current issues question for discussing the impact that fair value accounting was having on auditing.

Fair value is the subject of an auditing standard, ISA 545 *Auditing fair value measurements and disclosures*, which we shall look at now. The standard requires auditors to obtain sufficient appropriate audit evidence that fair value measurements and disclosures are in accordance with the entity's applicable financial reporting framework. This means that the auditor must have a sound knowledge of the accounting requirements relevant to the entity and when fair value is allowed.

2 Stock and long-term contracts

FAST FORWARD

When standard costing is used, the auditors must assess whether the valuation is reasonable.

SSAP 9

Stock should be measured at the lower of cost and net realisable value. Costs include costs of purchase, conversion and others incurred in bringing stock to present location and condition.

2.1 Standard costing

You studied the audit of stock in detail in your studies for 2.6, *Audit and Internal Review*. You should be able to design procedures to verify the existence and valuation of stock. If you are in any doubt in this area, go back to your Paper 2.6 material and revise.

An additional thing to consider in the audit of stock is what **evidence** to obtain about **cost**, when there is a **standard costing system** in operation. Remember that SSAP 9 allows standard costs to be used where prices are fluctuating.

Where standard costing is being used the auditor will have **two objectives**:

- Ensure that standard costing is an **appropriate basis** for valuing stock
- Ensure that the **calculation** of the standard cost is **reasonable**

In evaluating whether standard costs are an appropriate basis, the auditor must

- **Establish whether prices have fluctuated**. This can be done by reviewing purchase invoices, consulting a price index and enquiry of management.

- **Consider if the use of standard costing is the best accounting policy to use**. This should be discussed with the directors.

- If the accounting policy has changed from the previous year, he must **consider the comparability of the accounts.**

- There should also be **disclosure** about any changes of accounting policy in the accounts, which he should ensure is sufficient.

In ensuring that the calculation of the standard cost is reasonable, the auditor must

- Obtain a copy of the calculation of standard cost

- Check the additions and calculations

- Consider whether the calculation is reasonable (for example, based on averages of costs over the year)

- Verify elements of the calculation to appropriate documentation, for example,

  - Purchase prices to invoices
  - Wages and salaries to personnel records
  - Overheads to expenses in the financial statements where possible

- Alternatively, the standard cost may be verifiable by analytical review with comparison to total expense figures in the profit and loss account, for example,

  - Wages should be based on the total wage cost divided by the production total for the year.

Exam focus point

The examiner has set questions on unusual stock items, such as goats and cheese. When tackling such questions, remember the simple assertions you are trying to verify, but tailor how you are going to get the evidence to the unusual asset. So, in June 2005, when asked to audit the carrying value of a goat born on the farm and reared to sell, it would not have been appropriate to say 'verify to purchase invoice'. Instead, reference to their fair (market) value would have been appropriate. So for instance, reviewing recent **sales invoices** for comparable goats. You must think logically about the specific issues raised in an exam question and write relevant answers. You can attempt this question in your Practice and Revision Kit.

2.2 Long term contracts

Before addressing the issue of audit evidence with regard to long term contracts, it is valuable to revise the accounting requirements of SSAP 9.

SSAP 9 Stocks and long term contracts

Turnover and profit recognised must reflect the proportion of work carried out at the accounting date. (This can be calculated on a sales or cost basis)

Where the outcome of a project cannot be foreseen with any reasonable certainty, profit should not be taken up. An expected loss should be provided for in full.

The balance sheet entries could therefore be:

- Stocks (costs to date, less costs recognised)
- Debtors (turnover recognised less payments on account)
- Creditors (payments on account)
- Provisions (for any foreseeable losses)

The auditor will have to audit the calculation of attributable profit or loss and assess if it is reasonable. He will then have to verify all the movements on the balance sheet accounts to that calculation.

The auditor should undertake the following procedures:

- Obtain a copy of the calculation and check the additions and calculations

- Assess whether the basis of calculation is comparable with prior years (FRS 18)

- He should then verify the figures in the calculation:

    - Turnover to certification of work completed to date
    - Total contract price to original contract
    - Cost of work completed to invoices also payroll/clock cards/wage rates
    - Payments on account to remittance advices

- He should discuss with management if there is any chance of a loss arising on the contract

3 Tangible fixed assets

FAST FORWARD

Auditors should ensure that both tangible and intangible assets have been subjected to an annual impairment review.

You covered all the key aspects relating to tangible fixed assets in your earlier studies. If you are in any doubt in this area, go back to your previous material and revise. The issue of fair value discussed in Section 1.1 is likely to impact in an audit of fixed assets.

3.1 Valuation of fixed assets

Fixed assets will be carried at cost or valuation (if an item has been revalued). Cost is straightforward to audit, it can be verified to original purchase documentation. Valuation may be straightforward to audit – it can be verified to the valuation certificate. The carrying value of fixed assets is therefore depreciated cost, or depreciated valuation.

Once a company has revalued assets, it is required to continue revaluing them regularly, at least every five years, so that the valuation is not materially different from the fair value at balance sheet date. The auditors should therefore check that valuation is comparable to market value. They would do this by comparing the existing valuation to current market values (for example, in an estate agent's window).

Assets are depreciated, so their carrying value will not be original cost or valuation. Depreciation can be verified by reperforming the depreciation calculations. Often a 'proof-in-total' check will be sufficient, where auditors calculate the relevant depreciation percentage on the whole class of assets to see if it is comparable to the depreciation charged for that class of assets in the year.

The depreciation rate is determined by reference to the useful life of the asset. This is determined by management based on expectations of how long the asset is expected to be in use in the business. The auditors will audit this by scrutinising those expectations and verifying them where possible – for example, to the minutes of the meeting where management decided to buy the asset, to capital replacement budgets, to past practice in the business.

Exam focus point

In an old syllabus paper, the examiner asked candidates for principal audit procedures to gain evidence about the useful lives of oil platforms. A significant amount of information about what management based their expectations on was given in the question and the examiner expected candidates to use that information. For example, management considered weather conditions that the rigs were subject to. Therefore, to audit the useful life, auditors should obtain weather reports to see if they corroborated the useful life. A platform severely affected by wind and storms will have a shorter useful life than one in calmer conditions.

3.2 Impairment of fixed assets

An asset is impaired when its carrying amount (depreciated cost or depreciated valuation) exceeds its recoverable amount. You should be familiar with the following key terms from your accounting studies.

Key term

> The **recoverable amount** of an asset or cash-generating unit is the higher of its fair value less costs to sell and its value in use.
>
> A **cash-generating unit** is the smallest identifiable group of assets that generates cash inflows that are largely independent of the cash inflows from other assets or groups of assets.
>
> **Value in use** is the present value of the future cash flows expected to be derived from an asset or cash-generating unit.

Management are required to determine if there is any indication that the assets are impaired.

The auditors will consider whether there are any indicators of impairment when carrying out risk assessment procedures. They will use the same impairment criteria laid out in FRS 11 as management do. If the auditors believe that impairment is indicated, they should request that management show them the impairment review that has been carried out. If no impairment review has been carried out, then the auditors should discuss the need for one with management, and if necessary, qualify their report on grounds of disagreement (not conforming with FRS 11) if management refuse to carry out an impairment review.

If an impairment review has been carried out, then the auditors should audit that impairment review. Management will have estimated whether the recoverable amount of the asset/cash generating unit is lower than the carrying amount.

For auditors, the key issue is that recoverable amount requires estimation. As estimation is subjective, this makes it a risky area for auditors.

Management have to determine if recoverable amount is higher than carrying amount. It may not have been necessary for them to estimate both fair value and value in use, because if one is higher than carrying amount, then the asset is not impaired. If it is not possible to make a reliable estimate of net realisable value, then it is necessary to calculate value in use.

Net realisable value is only calculable if there is a active market for the goods, and would therefore be audited in the same way as fair value which was set out in paragraph 1.1.2. Costs to sell such as taxes can be recalculated by applying the appropriate tax rate to the fair value itself. Delivery costs can be verified by comparing costs to published rates by delivery companies, for example, on the internet.

If management have calculated the value in use of an asset or cash-generating unit, then the auditors will have to audit that calculation. The following procedures will be relevant.

> **Value in use**
> - Obtain management's calculation of value in use
> - Reperform calculation to ensure that it is mathematically correct
> - Compare the cash flow projects to recent budgets and projections approved by the board to ensure that they are realistic
> - Calculate/obtain from analysts the long term average growth rate for the products and ensure that the growth rates assumed in the calculation of value in use do not exceed it.
> - Refer to competitors' published information to compare how much similar assets are valued at by companies trading in similar conditions
> - Compare to previous calculations of value in use to ensure that all relevant costs of maintaining the asset have been included
> - Ensure that the cost/income from disposal of the asset at the end of its life has been included

- Review calculation to ensure cash flows from financing activities and income tax have been excluded
- Compare discount rate used to published market rates to ensure that it correctly reflects the return expected by the market

If the asset is impaired and has been written down to recoverable amount, the auditors should review the financial statements to ensure that the write down has been carried out correctly and that the FRS 11 disclosures have been made correctly.

4 Intangible fixed assets

Accounting guidance for intangibles is given in FRSs 10 and 11 and SSAP 13. The types of asset we are likely to encounter under this heading include patents, licences, trade marks, development costs and goodwill.

FRS 10

Positive purchased goodwill should be capitalised and classified as an asset on the balance sheet. Internally generated goodwill should not be capitalised.

An intangible purchased separately from the business should be capitalised at cost. If purchased as part of a business, an intangible should only be capitalised separately if its value can be measured reliably or it becomes part of the price attributed to goodwill.

Internally generated intangibles may be capitalised if they have a readily ascertainable market value. Brands are specifically excluded from this description.

Goodwill and intangibles with a limited useful life should be amortised. Assets may also require impairment reviews under FRS 11.

The auditor should carry out the following procedures

Completeness

- **Prepare analysis** of movements on cost and amortisation accounts

Rights and obligations

- **Obtain confirmation** of all **patents** and **trademarks** held by a patent agent
- **Verify payment** of **annual renewal fees**

Valuation

- **Review specialist valuations** of intangible assets, considering:
  - Qualifications of valuer
  - Scope of work
  - Assumptions and methods used
- **Confirm carried down balances** represent **continuing value**, which are proper charges to future operations

Additions (rights and obligations, valuation and completeness)

- **Inspect purchase agreements, assignments** and **supporting documentation** for intangible assets acquired in period
- **Confirm purchases** have been **authorised**
- **Verify amounts capitalised** of patents developed by the company with supporting costing records

Amortisation
- **Review amortisation**

    – Check computation
    – Confirm that rates used are reasonable

Income from intangibles

- **Review sales returns** and **statistics** to verify the reasonableness of income derived from patents, trademarks, licences etc

- **Examine audited accounts** of third party sales covered by a patent, licence or trademark owned by the company

4.1 Goodwill

Key tests are as follows.

- **Agree consideration** to a **sales agreement**

- **Confirm valuation** of assets acquired is reasonable

- **Check purchased goodwill** is **calculated correctly** (it should reflect the difference between the fair value of the consideration given and the aggregate of the fair values of the separable net assets acquired)

- **Check goodwill** does **not include non-purchased goodwill**

- **Review amortisation**

    – Test calculation
    – Assess whether amortisation rates are reasonable

- **Ensure valuation of goodwill is reasonable** by reviewing prior year's accounts and discussion with the directors

- If useful life is judged to be indefinite, ensure impairment review has been carried out

- Review impairment review for reasonableness

4.2 Development costs

Companies Act 1985
- Development costs can be included in the balance sheet only in special circumstances.
- Development costs capitalised must be amortised.
- Accounts must disclose reasons for capitalisation and period over which the expenditure is to be written off.

SSAP 13

Definitions

Pure (or basic) research

Experimental or theoretical work undertaken primarily to acquire new scientific or technical knowledge for its own sake rather than directed towards any specific aim or application.

Applied research

Original or critical investigation undertaken in order to gain new scientific or technical knowledge and directed towards a specific practical aim or objective.

Development

'Development' is defined as:

'the use of scientific or technical knowledge in order to produce new or substantially improved materials, devices, products or services, to install new processes or systems prior to the commencement of commercial production or commercial applications, or to improving substantially those already produced or installed.'

Expenditure on pure and applied research (other than on fixed assets) is required to be written off in the year of expenditure.

The special circumstances which must be satisfied to justify deferral of development expenditure are:

- There is a clearly defined project.

- The related expenditure is separately identifiable.

- The outcome of such a project has been assessed with reasonable certainty as to:

  - Its technical feasibility

  - Its ultimate commercial viability considered in the light of factors such as likely market conditions (including competing products), public opinion, consumer and environmental legislation

  - The aggregate of the deferred development costs, any further development costs, and related production, selling and administration costs is reasonably expected to be exceeded by related future sales or other revenues

- Adequate resources exist, or are reasonably expected to be available, to enable the project to be completed and to provide any consequential increases in working capital.

The key audit tests largely reflect the criteria laid down in SSAP 13.

- **Check accounting records** to confirm:

  - **Project** is **clearly defined** (separate cost centre or nominal ledger codes)
  - **Related expenditure** can be **separately identified**, and certified to invoices, timesheets

- **Confirm feasibility and viability**.

  - Examine market research reports, feasibility studies, budgets and forecasts
  - Consult client's technical experts.

- **Review budgeted revenues** and **costs** by examining results to date, production forecasts, advance orders and discussion with directors.

- **Review calculations** of **future cash flows** to ensure resources exist to complete the project.

- **Review previously deferred expenditure** to ensure SSAP 13 criteria are still justified.

- **Check amortisation:**

  - Commences with production
  - Charged on a systematic basis

The good news for the auditors in this audit area is that many companies adopt a prudent approach and write off research and development expenditure in the year it is incurred. The auditors' concern in these circumstances is whether the profit and loss account charge for research and development is complete, accurate and valid.

4.3 Brands

The key accounting issue with regard to brands is whether the asset is **internally generated** or not. Remember, FRS 10 forbids the capitalisation of internally generated assets.

If a brand has been purchased separately (that is, not as part of goodwill) then auditors should test the value of the brand according to the sales documentation.

5 Financial instruments

 When auditing investments, the auditors will have to consider both income and the asset.

Key term

An equity instrument of another entity, in other words, a share in another entity is a **financial asset**.

The accounting requirements for financial assets are found in FRS 25 and FRS 26. You should be familiar with the examinable parts of these standards from your financial reporting and corporate reporting studies.

5.1 Valuation of investments

Financial assets are recognised initially at their fair value.

The rules for subsequent measurement are:

Financial assets held to maturity	Amortised cost
Loans and receivables	
Financial assets held for trading	Fair value (changes recognised in profit or loss)
Available for sale financial assets	Fair value (changes recognised in reserves)

The cost of shares can be verified by checking the purchase documentation. The fair value of listed shares will generally be the market price, which can be verified by referring to the stock exchange listings or the quotations published in the financial press.

The classification of the financial instruments should be verified by enquiry of management, as to their intention to sell in the short-term, or hold to maturity. This should be corroborated by a review of events after the balance sheet date and of forecasts and projections.

5.2 Existence of investments

Again, for listed shares, the auditor can check the company exists by reviewing the stock exchange listings. Unlisted companies can be verified by simple enquiries at Companies House.

5.3 Rights and obligations relating to investments

If a company owns shares in another company it should own a share certificate outlining those shares which the auditor can look at. It might be that the company keeps its share certificates in a bank or at a brokers, in which case the auditor confirm with these parties that the share certificate exists (with the client's permission).

5.4 Investment income

We shall look at income in more detail in Chapter 10.

6 Investment properties

A key factor to consider when auditing investment properties is whether one **exists** according to the **criteria** of SSAP 19.

Key term

'.... An **investment property** is an interest in land and/or buildings:

(a)   In respect of which **construction** work and **development** have been **completed**

(b)   Which is held for its **investment potential**, any **rental income** being **negotiated** at **arm's length**.

'....The following are **exceptions** from the definition:

(a)   A property which is **owned** and **occupied** by a company for its **own purposes** is not an investment property.

(b)   A property **let to** and **occupied** by **another group company** is not an investment property for the purposes of its own accounts or the group accounts.'

Substantive tests

- Verify **rental agreements**, ensuring that occupier is not a connected company and that the rent has been negotiated at arm's length.

- If the building has recently been built, check **architect's certificates** to ensure that construction work has been completed

The second important assertion in relation to investment properties is **valuation**. SSAP 19 requires that investment properties be revalued annually at open market value. The auditor should be able to verify this by reference to the valuer's certificate.

Although in most cases the SSAP does not require a qualified valuer, in some cases this will be the case. The auditor should check whether the valuation has been carried out by an appropriate person.

The last key issue with regard to investment properties is **disclosure**. The auditor should review the disclosures made in the financial statements in relation to investment properties to ensure that they have been made appropriately, in accordance with SSAP 19. This includes the disclosures required in relation to the fact that SSAP 19 treatment is a departure from the Companies Act requirement to depreciate buildings made in order to give a true and fair view.

Question	Fixed assets

You are reviewing the file on the audit of Apollo plc, which is nearing completion. Apollo produces two products; the X and the W. Apollo plc purchased two new pieces of plant in the year. Plant is valued at cost. The X103 was bought to replace the X102, which was scrapped at the start of the year. The W103 was bought to replace the W102. The W102 will no longer be used in producing the W, but will be used to test new products, particularly the V, which Apollo is hoping to be able to market and sell in the next two years.

Required

Describe matters you would consider and the audit evidence you would expect to see on file in respect of the valuation of these pieces of plant.

Answer

Matters to consider

The main matter to consider here is the valuation of the W102. Now it will no longer be used in production, it may be impaired. The asset should be valued in the financial statements at the lower of carrying amount or recoverable amount. Recoverable amount will be net realisable value, as the W102 no longer has a value in use because it will not generate cash inflows until the V is marketed. Whether the W102 has a market (fair) value will depend on how specialised a machine it is. The fact that can be transferred to use on a different product to the W suggests that it is not highly specialised and that there may be a second hand market from which a valuation can be taken.

Evidence that should be contained on the audit file

- Indication that the value of the X103 and W103 has been agreed to purchase invoices
- Recalculation of profit/loss on scrapping of X102
- Note of physical inspection to ensure that X102 is no longer on premises
- Minutes of directors' meeting approving the scrapping of the X102 and change in use of the W102 reviewed
- Copy of management's impairment review with regard to the W102
- Fair value of W102 verified by reference to price lists of suppliers of such second hand machines
- Note of observation of operation of machines to ensure W102 no longer used in production

Chapter Roundup

- Key assertions relating to assets are existence, completeness, valuation and rights and obligations.

- When standard costing is used, the auditor must assess whether the valuation is reasonable.

- Auditors should ensure that both tangible and intangible assets have been subjected to an annual impairment review.

- When auditing financial instruments the auditors will have to consider both income and the asset.

Quick Quiz

1   Match the accounting item with the relevant accounting standard(s)

(a)	Long term contracts	(i)	FRS 10
(b)	Intangible fixed assets	(ii)	FRS 11
(c)	Tangible fixed assets	(iii)	FRS 15
		(iv)	SSAP 9

2   Complete the definition.

…………………………….. ……………………………. .is a contract specifically negotiated for the construction of an …………………………. or a …………….. …………………………… that are closely inter-related or interdependent in terms of their design, technology and function or their ultimate purpose or use.

3   Brands may never be capitalised.

True   ☐

False   ☐

Answers to Quick Quiz

1   (a) (iv)
    (b) (i) (ii)
    (c) (ii) (iii)

2   Long term contract, asset, combination of assets.

3   False. Internally generated brands may not be capitalised. Purchased brands with a separately identifiable value may be capitalised.

Now try the questions below from the Exam Question Bank

Number	Level	Marks	Time
Q12	Examination	20	36 mins

BPP
LEARNING MEDIA

Evaluation and review (iii)
Matters relating to further accounting issues

10

Topic list	Syllabus reference
1 Income	D1
2 Liabilities	D1
3 Expenses	D1
4 Disclosures	D1

Introduction

This chapter deals with further accounting issues that could appear in questions where you are required to consider materiality, risk, relevant accounting standards and audit evidence. As in Chapter 9, the content relates to the final two aspects on that list of matters.

Note. The examiner has stated that in the first two sittings of this paper she will not examine accounting standards that are only examinable in Paper P2. This is being done to ensure that students sitting P7 before P2 under the transitional arrangements are not disadvantaged. In the context of Chapter 10, this means that the topics of pensions, and share-based payment will not feature in the first two sittings.

Study guide

		Intellectual level
D1	**Evaluation and review**	
(j)	Evaluate the matters (eg materiality, risk, relevant accounting standards, audit evidence) relating to:	3
(i)	cash flow statements	
(ii)	changes in accounting policy	
(iii)	taxation	
(iv)	segmental reporting	
(v)	leases	
(iv)	revenue recognition	
(vii)	pension costs	
(viii)	government grants	
(ix)	finance costs	
(x)	related parties*	
(xi)	earnings per share	
(xii)	provisions, contingent liabilities and contingent assets	
(xiii)	transition to International Financial Reporting Standards (IFRS)	
(xiv)	share based payment transactions	
(xv)	business combinations*	
(xvi)	discontinued operations	

* Issues relevant to related parties were covered in Chapter 8 and those relevant to business combinations will be covered in Chapter 11.

Exam guide

Scenario questions are likely to appear requiring you to apply your corporate reporting knowledge, to assess whether errors may have been made, determine materiality and identify appropriate evidence. These can feature any of the accounting topics you have studied in your ACCA exams.

1 Income

FAST FORWARD   Revenue recognition is an extremely important issue and completeness is the key assertion to be audited.

1.1 Revenue recognition

We mentioned an important example of revenue recognition earlier, and that was as part of long term contracts. When assessing what income to recognise from a long term contract, the person accounting for it should bear in mind the provisions of FRS 5.

As you are aware, FRS 5 deals with the substance of transactions and thus revenue recognition falls within its specification. Revenue recognition is an issue that is pervasive to financial statements, so is something that the auditor should be aware of when conducting his audit rather than to seek to audit it of itself.

Turnover, or revenue, is commonly audited by analytical review. This is because revenue should be predicable and there are good bases on which to base analytical review, such as:

- Plenty of information, for example, last year's accounts, budget, monthly analyses (companies tend to keep a lot of information about sales)

- Logical relationships with items such as stock and debtors

Unless complex transactions arise where revenue is not as clear cut as a product being supplied and invoiced for, revenue recognition is generally not an issue. However, in some companies, for example, those that deal primarily in long term contracts, revenue recognition can be a **material** issue. Examples of industries where this might be true:

- Building industry
- Engineering industry

In such industries, auditing revenue recognition will be part of auditing construction contracts. The auditor should

---

- Consider whether the basis for recognition is reasonable
- Agree turnover recognised to relevant documents (for example, work certificates or contracts)

 ## Case Study

Revenue recognition in an e-commerce environment

Companies that engage in e-commerce may have particular revenue recognition issues.

The entity may act as a **principal** or as an **agent**. They must determine whether to disclose their gross sales, or merely their commission. For example, Lastminute.com discloses a figure 'TTV', which does not represent statutory turnover, but represents the price at which goods and services has been sold across the group's platforms. Turnover itself is largely made up of commission on selling those goods and services.

The company may engage in **reciprocal arrangements** with other companies whereby they both advertise on each other's website. Whether such an arrangement results in 'revenue' must be considered. It must then be accounted for appropriately.

The company may deal in unusual **discounts** or voucher systems to encourage customers to buy. These must also be reflected.

Lastly, the company must determine a policy for **cut off**. This may be complex if the company acts as an agent. When is the sale made? When the customer clicks 'accept', when the company emails acknowledgement, when the sale is made known to the principal, when the goods are despatched, when the customer receives the goods, when the customer has taken advantage of the services…? The company must determine a reasonable policy for when the sale has been made.

 ## Question   Revenue recognition and other matters

The senior partner of JLPN, a firm of auditors, has issued an 'Audit Risk Alert' letter to all partners dealing with key areas of concern which should be given due consideration by his firm when auditing public companies. The letter outlines certain trends in audit reporting that, if not scrutinised by the auditors, could lead to a loss of reliability and transparency in the financial statements. The following three key concerns were outlined in the letter.

(a) Audit committees play a very important role together with the financial director and auditor in achieving high quality financial control and auditing. Recently the efforts of certain audit committees have been questioned in the press.

(b) The Stock Exchange had reported cases of inappropriate revenue recognition practises including:

  (i) Accelerating revenue prior to the delivery of the product to the customer's site, or prior to the completion of the terms of the sales arrangement

  (ii) Recognition of revenue when customers have unilateral cancellation or termination provisions, other than the normal customary product return provisions

(c) It has been reported that the management of companies had intentionally violated UK Generally Accepted Accounting Practice by immaterial amounts. The reason for this has been the sensitivity of reported earnings per share in a market place where missing the market's expectation of earnings per share by a small amount could have significant consequences.

Required

(a) Explain the importance of the role of an 'Audit Risk Alert' letter to a firm of auditors.

(b) Discuss the way in which the auditor should deal with each of the key concerns outlined in the letter in order to ensure that audit risk is kept to an acceptable level.

Answer

(a) The **'risk alert letter'** is a memorandum used by the reporting partner to notify fellow partners of concerns emerging from dealings with clients, regulatory authorities or stock exchanges. It ensures that:

- Key audit risk areas are reviewed
- Significant trends and irregularities are identified
- Quality is maintained
- Litigation risk is reduced
- Investor confidence is maintained as it reduces manipulation

(b) (i) **Audit Committees** are held to secure good a quality of **internal control** and financial reporting in plc's. If the auditor has doubts about the effectiveness of an audit committee then he should **review its structure, independence and membership** to ensure it meets its objectives. Any shortcomings should be reported to the board and/or the members.

  (ii) **Revenue acceleration** is a **creative accounting device**. Revenue should **not be recognised until earned and realised** (realisable), so the practices described are not acceptable. Only if the risks of ownership have fully transferred to the buyer and the seller has not retained any specific performance obligation should revenue be recognised earlier.

  Extended audit tests concerning revenue recognition and 'cut off' tests may be appropriate if the auditor suspects anomalies.

  (iii) Where **intentional GAAP violations** have occurred, **materiality judgement** may be affected. The auditor must ensure the audit team is aware that violations of GAAP **can affect EPS** for certain clients, and that staff are sufficiently experienced and trained in order to detect such violations. It may be that the errors are individually immaterial, but the **aggregate effect** must be considered. Furthermore, the practice of intentional misstatements may indicate that the **management** of the company **lacks integrity** and the auditor should consider whether the client should be retained.

1.2 Government grants and assistance

Government grants and assistance are accounted for under SSAP 4. They may be either revenue or capital grants.

Revenue grants offer no difficulties to account for or to audit. To audit them, the auditor should:

- Obtain documentation relating to the grant and ensure that it should be classified as revenue

- The value may be agreed to the same documentation (for example, a letter outlining the details of the grant, or a copy of an application form sent by the client)

- The receipt of the grant can be agreed to bank statements

Capital grants can be more difficult to account for. This can raise auditing issues as well.

SSAP 4

Capital grants are cash grants to cover a proportion of the costs of certain items of capital expenditure (for example buildings, plant and machinery).

Grants relating to fixed assets should be credited to revenue over the expected useful life of the assets and this can be done in one of two ways:

(a) **By reducing the acquisition cost of the fixed asset** by the amount of the grant, and providing depreciation on the reduced amount.

(b) By **treating** the amount of the grant **as a deferred credit and transferring a portion of it to revenue** annually.

Audit procedures:

- Consider whether the basis of accounting is comparable to the previous year

- Discuss the basis of accounting with the directors to ensure that the method used is the best method

- Ensure that any changes in accounting method are disclosed

- If method (a) above is used, no further audit work is necessary

- If method (b) is used, the transfer to revenue should be audited, if material. The methods used to audit this would be as for depreciation

Exam focus point

In an old syllabus exam, one of the risks to be identified in the case study was a government grant of a licence to explore for oil. The company had accounted for this at an **estimated** fair value. This was potentially a particularly subjective evaluation, as it was possible that the asset was unique, which made determining a fair value very difficult.

2 Liabilities

The relevant financial statement assertions for liabilities are completeness, rights and obligations and existence. Liabilities must be tested for understatement.

2.1 Leases

The classification of a lease can have a material effect on the financial statements.

First we shall look at the audit of **leases**. The relevant accounting standard for leases is SSAP 21, but the provisions of FRS 5 are also relevant. This is because leases are accounted for according to their **substance** rather than their legal form.

> **SSAP 21**
>
> A finance lease is one where substantially all the risks and rewards of ownership are transferred to the lessee. SSAP 21 provides that such a lease should be recognised on the balance sheet, as is the associated asset.
>
> An operating lease is any lease which is not a finance lease. These are accounted for as the payments are due (in other words, the commitment to future liability is not recognised).

You can see that the **classification** of the lease is **likely to have a material effect on the financial statements**. If the lease is a finance lease, the balance sheet will show substantial assets and liabilities. The net effect will be minimal, but the face of the balance sheet will be materially different from what it would be if it was an operating lease.

It is important that the auditor ensures that the **classification** (which would fall under the assertion existence) is correct. Other important assertions are valuation, and rights and obligations.

The following audit procedures are relevant.

Classification and rights and obligations

- Obtain a copy of the lease agreement

- Review the lease agreement to ensure that the lease has been correctly classified according to SSAP 21

Valuation (finance leases)

- Obtain a copy of the client's workings in relation to finance leases
- Check the additions and calculations of the workings
- Ensure that the interest has been accounted for in accordance with SSAP 21
- Recalculate the interest
- Agree the opening position
- Agree any new assets to lease agreements
- Verify lease payments in the year to the bank statements

Valuation (operating leases)

- Agree payments to the bank statements (if material)

Disclosure

- The auditor should ensure the finance leases have been properly disclosed in the financial statements

---

2.2 Deferred taxation

FAST FORWARD

The auditor needs to audit the movement on the deferred tax provision.

Deferred tax is accounted for under FRS 19.

FRS 19

Full provision must be made for deferred tax assets and liabilities arising from timing differences between the recognition of gains and losses in the financial statements and their recognition in a tax computation, such as:

- Accelerated capital allowances

- Elimination of unrealised intragroup profits on consolidation

- Unrelieved tax losses

- Other sources of short-term timing differences

The FRS permits but does not require entities to adopt a policy of discounting deferred tax assets and liabilities.

The FRS includes other requirements regarding the measurement and presentation of deferred tax to be:

- Measured using tax rates that have been enacted or substantively enacted

- Presented separately on the face of the balance sheet if the amounts are so material that, in the absence of such disclosure, readers may misinterpret the accounts.

Deferred tax is the **tax attributable to timing differences**. Where a company 'saves tax' in the current period by having accelerated capital allowances, a **provision for the tax charge** is **made in the balance sheet**.

The provision is made is because over the course of the asset's life, the tax allowances will reduce until the depreciation charged in the accounts is higher than the allowances. This will result in taxable profit being higher than reported profit and the company will be 'suffering higher tax' in this period.

As part of the **planning process**, if the client receives tax services from the firm, the auditor should consult the tax department as to the company's future tax plans, to ascertain whether they expect a deferred tax liability to arise. This will assist any analytical review they carry out on the deferred tax provision.

Remember that **manipulating the deferred tax figure will not affect the actual tax position**. However, a **deferred tax charge** (the other part of the double entry for the balance sheet provision) **is charged on the profit and loss account before dividends**, even if it is not actually paid to HM Revenue and Customs.

The following procedures will be relevant:

- Obtain an copy of the deferred tax workings and the corporation tax computation

- Check the arithmetical **accuracy** of the deferred tax working

- Agree the **figures used** to calculate timing differences to those on the **tax computation** and the **financial statements**

- Consider the assumptions made in the light of your knowledge of the business and any other evidence gathered during the course of the audit to ensure reasonableness

- Agree the opening position on the deferred tax account to the prior year financial statements

- Review the basis of the provision to ensure:
  - It is line with accounting practice under FRS 19
  - It is suitably comparable to practice in previous years, and
  - Any changes in accounting policy have been disclosed

2.3 Provisions and contingencies

FAST FORWARD

A provision is accounted for as a liability, contingencies are disclosed, so auditors must ensure they have been classified correctly according to FRS 12.

Provisions are accounted for under FRS 12.

FRS 12

A **provision** is a liability that is of uncertain timing or amount, to be settled by the transfer of economic benefits.

A **contingent liability** is either

(a)   A possible obligation arising from past events whose existence will be confirmed only by the occurrence of one or more uncertain future events not wholly within the entity's control; or

(b)   A present obligation that arises from past events but is not recognised because it is not probable that a transfer of economic benefits will be required to settle the obligation or because the amount of the obligation cannot be measured with sufficient reliability.

A **contingent asset** is a possible asset arising from past events whose existence will be confirmed only by the occurrence of one or more uncertain future events not wholly within the entity's control.

FRS 12 states that a provision should be **recognised** as a liability in the financial statements when:

- An entity has a **present obligation** (legal or constructive) as a result of a past event
- It is probable that a **transfer of economic benefits** will be required to settle the obligation
- A **reliable estimate** can be made of the obligation

The audit tests that should be carried out on provisions and contingent assets and liabilities are as follows.

- **Obtain details** of all **provisions** which have been included in the **accounts** and all **contingencies** that have been disclosed

- **Obtain** a **detailed analysis** of all **provisions** showing opening balances, movements and closing balances

- **Determine** for each material provision **whether** the **company** has a **present obligation** as a result of past events by:

  - **Review** of **correspondence** relating to the item

  - **Discussion** with the **directors,** have they created a valid expectation in other parties that they will discharge the obligation?

- **Determine** for each material provision **whether** it is **probable** that a **transfer of economic benefits** will be required to settle the obligation by:

  - **Checking** whether any **payments** have been **made** in the post balance sheet period in respect of the item

  - **Review of correspondence** with solicitors, banks, customers, insurance company and suppliers both pre and post year end

- Sending a **letter** to the **solicitor** to obtain their views (where relevant)

- **Discussing** the **position** of similar **past provisions** with the directors. Were these provisions eventually settled

- **Considering** the **likelihood** of **reimbursement**

- **Recalculate** all **provisions** made

- **Compare** the **amount provided** with any post year end payments and with any amount paid in the past for similar items

- In the event that it is not possible to estimate the amount of the **provision**, check that this **contingent liability** is **disclosed** in the accounts

- **Consider** the **nature** of the **client's business**. Would you expect to see any other provisions, for example, warranties?

- **Consider** whether disclosures of **provisions, contingent liabilities and contingent assets** are correct and sufficient

2.3.1 Obtaining audit evidence of contingencies

Part of ISA 501 *Audit evidence - additional considerations for specific items* covers contingencies relating to litigation and legal claims, which will represent the major part of audit work on contingencies. Litigation and claims involving the entity may have a material effect on the financial statements, and so will require adjustment to/disclosure in those financial statements.

ISA 501.32

The auditor should carry out procedures in order to become aware of any litigation and claims involving the entity which may have a material effect on the financial statements.

Such procedures would include the following.

- **Make appropriate inquiries of management** including obtaining representations
- **Review board minutes** and correspondence with the entity's lawyers
- **Examine legal expense** account
- **Use any information** obtained regarding the entity's business including information obtained from discussions with any in-house legal department

ISA 501.33

When litigation or claims have been identified or when the auditor believes they may exist, the auditor should seek direct communication with the entity's lawyers.

This will help to obtain sufficient appropriate audit evidence as to whether potential material litigation and claims are known and management's estimates of the financial implications, including costs, are reliable.

The ISA discusses the form the letter to the entity's lawyer should take.

ISA 501.34

The letter, which should be prepared by management and sent by the auditor, should request the lawyer to communicate directly with the auditor.

If it is thought unlikely that the lawyer will respond to a general enquiry, the letter should specify the following.

(a)   A list of **litigation and claims**

(b)   **Management's assessment** of the outcome of the litigation or claim and its estimate of the financial implications, including costs involved

(c)   A request that the **lawyer confirm the reasonableness** of management's assessments and provide the auditor with further information if the list is considered by the lawyer to be incomplete or incorrect

The auditors must consider these matters up to the date of their report and so a further, updating letter may be necessary.

A meeting between the auditors and the lawyer may be required, for example where a complex matter arises, or where there is a disagreement between management and the lawyer. Such meetings should take place only with the permission of management, and preferably with a management representative present.

ISA 501.37

If management refuses to give the auditor permission to communicate with the entity's lawyers, this would be a scope limitation and should ordinarily lead to a qualified opinion or a disclaimer of opinion.

If the lawyer refuses to respond as required and the auditor can find no alternative sufficient evidence, a limitation of scope may lead to a qualified opinion or a disclaimer of opinion.

 Question   **Provisions**

In February 20X7 the directors of Newthorpe Engineering plc suspended the managing director. At a disciplinary hearing held by the company on 17 March 20X7 the managing director was dismissed for gross misconduct, and it was decided the managing director's salary should stop from that date and no redundancy or compensation payments should be made.

The managing director has claimed unfair dismissal and is taking legal action against the company to obtain compensation for loss of his employment. The managing director says he has a service contract with the company which would entitle him to two years' salary at the date of dismissal.

The financial statements for the year ended 30 April 20X7 record the resignation of the director. However, they do not mention his dismissal and no provision for any damages has been included in the financial statements.

Required

(a)   State how contingent liabilities should be disclosed in financial statements according to FRS 12 *Provisions, Contingent Liabilities and Contingent Assets.*

(b)   Describe the audit work you will carry out to determine whether the company will have to pay damages to the director for unfair dismissal, and the amount of damages and costs which should be included in the financial statements.

Note. Assume the amounts you are auditing are material.

Answer

(a) FRS 12 states that a provision should be recognised in the accounts if:

- An entity has a **present obligation** (legal or constructive) as a result of a past event
- A **transfer** of **economic benefits** will **probably** be **required** to settle the obligation
- A **reliable estimate** can be **made** of the amount of the obligation.

Under FRS 12 contingent liabilities should not be recognised. They should however be disclosed unless the prospect of settlement is remote. The entity should disclose:

- The **nature** of the liability
- An estimate of its **financial effect**
- The **uncertainties** relating to any possible payments
- The likelihood of any **re-imbursement**

(b) The following tests should be carried out to determine whether the company will have to pay damages and the amount to be included in the financial statements.

(i) **Review** the director's **service contract** and **ascertain** the **maximum amount** to which he would be entitled and the **provisions** in the service contract that would **prevent** him making a **claim**, in particular those relating to grounds for justifiable dismissal.

(ii) **Review** the results of the **disciplinary hearing. Consider** whether the company has acted in accordance with **employment legislation** and its **internal rules,** the **evidence** presented by the **company** and the defence made by the **director.**

(iii) **Review correspondence** relating to the case and **determine** whether the **company** has **acknowledged** any **liability** to the director that would mean that an amount for compensation should be accrued in accordance with FRS 12.

(iv) **Review correspondence** with the company's **solicitors** and **obtain legal advice**, either from the company's solicitors or another firm, about the likelihood of the claim succeeding.

(v) **Review** correspondence and contact the company's solicitors about the likely **costs** of the case.

(vi) **Consider** the **likelihood** of **costs** and **compensation** being **re-imbursed** by **reviewing** the company's **insurance arrangements** and contacting the insurance company.

(vii) **Consider** the **amounts** that should be **accrued** and the **disclosures** that should be made in the accounts. Legal costs should be accrued, but compensation payments should only be accrued if the company has admitted liability or legal advice indicates that the company's chances of success are very poor. However the claim should be disclosed unless legal advice indicates that the director's chance of success appears to be remote.

3 Expenses

Key issues relating to borrowing costs are the measurement rules in FRS 26, and whether any may be capitalised.

3.1 Borrowing costs

FRS 26 gives guidance on how to account for financial instruments which includes debt, so it also gives guidance on how to account for borrowing costs.

> **FRS 26**
>
> The **finance cost** of debt is the difference between the total payments required to be made and the initial carrying value of the debt (that is the interest cost or the dividends plus any premium payable on redemption or other payments). **The carrying amount of debt should be increased by the finance cost** in respect of the reporting period **and reduced by payments made in respect of the debt** in that period.

Payments made in the period will consist of interest and may include an element of capital repayment. Generally, there is unlikely to be a material difference between the way that the lender allocates the finance cost and the way that the entity should allocate it under FRS 26.

If there is no **material** difference, borrowing costs are simple to audit. The **cost of borrowing is interest**, which is disclosed in the profit and loss account.

Interest can often be audited by **analytical review**, as it has a predicable relationship with loans (for example, bank loans or debentures).

Alternatively it can be **verified to payment records** (bank statements) **and loan agreement** documents.

However, if borrowing costs are so substantial that there is likely to be a material difference between the methods, the auditor should carry out the following procedures:

- Obtain the client workings in relation to borrowing costs
- Review them to ensure the method of allocation is in accordance with FRS 26
- Agree relevant figures to accounting information or the financial statements
- Agree figures in respect of interest payments made to statements from lender and/or bank statements

3.2 Pension costs

The matters to consider here will depend on whether the company operates a defined contribution or a defined benefit scheme.

If it is a defined contribution scheme there are no special matters beyond those for any other expense recognised on an accruals basis.

Defined benefit schemes, as you will be aware from your corporate reporting studies, are much more complex and have a potentially material impact on the balance sheet and performance statements.

FRS 17 *Retirement Benefits* provides the rules for accounting for these schemes.

3.2.1 FRS 17 in outline

The balance sheet will include the net surplus or deficit on the scheme, measured as:

Scheme assets at fair value	X
Scheme liabilities (actuarial basis)	(X)
Surplus/(deficit)	X/(X)

These are recalculated each year, and the released gains and losses treated as follows:

Component	Definition	Performance statement
(a) Current service cost	• Increase in the present value of the scheme liabilities expected to arise from employee service in the current period	
(b) interest cost	• Unwinding of one year's discount based on the opening liability	
(c) Expected return on assets	• Estimated return on assets based on long-term expectations at start of period	Profit and loss account
(d) Past service costs	• Increase in PV of scheme liabilities related to service in prior periods arising in current periods as a result of introduction of, or improvement to, retirement benefits	
(e) Gains and losses on settlements and curtailments	• Settlements and curtailments *not* covered by actuarial assumptions. eg (settlements).	
(f) Actuarial gains and losses	• Arising from new valuation or update to valuation. • On assets, differences between expected and actual return. • On liabilities, differences between actuarial assumptions and actual experience during the period, or changes in actuarial assumptions.	Statement of total recognised gains and losses

3.2.2 Audit evidence

Scheme assets (including quoted and unquoted securities, debt instruments, properties)	• ask directors to reconcile the scheme assets valuation at the scheme year end date with the assets valuation at the reporting entity's date being used for FRS 17 purposes; • obtain direct confirmation of the scheme assets from the investment custodian; and • consider requiring scheme auditors to perform procedures

Scheme liabilities	• auditors must follow the principles of ISA 520 *Using the work of an expert* to assess whether it is appropriate to rely on the actuary's work
	
	• specific matters would include
	  – the source data used:
	  – the assumptions and methods used; and
	  – the results of actuaries' work in the light of auditors' knowledge of the business and results of other audit procedures

	Actuarial source data is likely to include: • scheme member data (for example, classes of member and contribution details); and • scheme asset information (for example, values and income and expenditure items).
Actuarial assumptions (for example, mortality rates, termination rates, retirement age and changes in salary and benefit levels)	Auditors will not have the same expertise as actuaries and are unlikely to be able to challenge the appropriateness and reasonableness of the assumptions. Auditors can, however, through discussion with directors and actuaries: • obtain a general understating of the assumptions and review the process used to develop them; • compare the assumptions with those which directors have used in prior years; and • consider whether, based on their knowledge of the reporting entity and the scheme, and on the results of other audit procedures, the assumptions appear to be reasonable and compatible with those used elsewhere in the preparation of the entity's financial statements. • obtain written representations from directors confirming that the assumptions are consistent with their knowledge of the business
Items charged to operating profit (current service cost, past service cost, gains and losses on settlements and curtailments)	• discuss with directors and actuaries the factors affecting current service cost (for example, a scheme closed to new entrants may see an increase year on year as a percentage of pay with the average age of the workforce increasing).
Items charged/credited to finance costs/income (expected return on scheme assets, interest on scheme liabilities)	• consider whether the interest costs reflect an average of the liabilities at the beginning of the year and movement during the year. • ensure that the discount rate reflects the appropriate high quality corporate bond rate at the start of the year and is the same as the rate at which the scheme liabilities were measured at the end of the previous year. • compare the expected return with market indices when dealing with quoted fixed interest and index-linked securities;
Items recognised in the STRGL (actuarial gains and losses)	• discuss with directors and actuaries the underlying reasons for actuarial gains and losses (for example, employee turnover rates or unexpected changes in salaries/medical costs).

Where the results of actuaries' work is inconsistent with the directors' and actuaries. Additional procedures, such as requesting directors to obtain evidence from another actuary, may assist in resolving the inconsistency.

3.3 Share-based payment

FRS 20 *Share-based payment* sets out rules for the measurement of expenses relating to share based payment schemes. These arise most commonly in relation to payments for employee services.

3.3.1 FRS 20 Recap

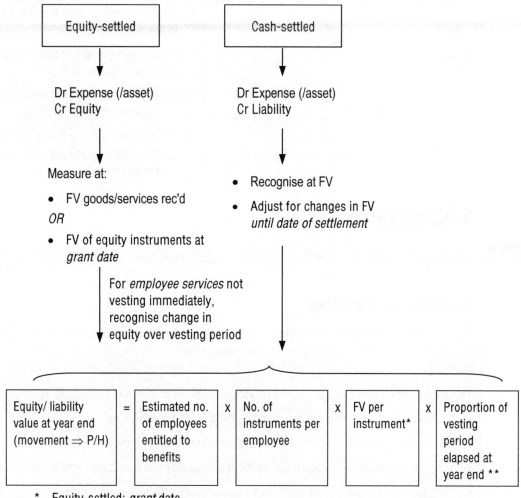

* Equity-settled: *grant* date
Cash-settled: *balance sheet* date

** If length of vesting period relates to performance conditions, it may be revised unless it is a market condition.

3.3.2 Audit evidence

The auditor will require evidence in respect of all the components of the estimated amounts, as well as reperforming the calculation of the expense for the current year.

Issue	Evidence
Number of employees in scheme/number of instruments per employee/length of vesting period.	• Revenue scheme details set out in a contractual documentation
Number of employees estimated to benefit	• Enquire of directors • Compare to staffing numbers per forecasts and prediction
Fair value of instruments	• For equity – settled schemes check that fair value is estimated at **grant date**. • For cash-settled schemes check that the fair value is recalculated at the **balance sheet date**.

Issue	Evidence
	• Check that model used to estimate fair value is in line with FRS 20.

General	• Obtain representations from management confirming their view that
	  – the assumptions used in measuring the expense are reasonable, and
	  – there are no share-based payment schemes in existence that have not been disclosed to the auditors.

4 Disclosures

FAST FORWARD

The auditor must also ensure disclosures in the financial statements are fairly stated.

4.1 Segment reporting

The disclosure of segmental information is governed by the Companies Act 1985 and by SSAP 25.

> **SSAP 25**
>
> **This extends the Companies Act requirements** on analysis of turnover and profits as follows:
>
> • The result as well as turnover must be disclosed for all segments.
>
> • 'Result' for these purposes is profit or loss before tax, minority interests and extraordinary items.
>
> • Each segment's net assets should be disclosed (so that return on capital employed can be calculated).
>
> • Segmental turnover must be analysed between sales to customers outside the group and inter-segment sales/transfers (where material).
>
> Like the CA 1985, SSAP 25 requires analysis by two types of segment, class of business and geographical market.

The following procedures are relevant:

> • Obtain a client schedule of turnover workings
> • Discuss with management the basis for the segmentation
> • Verify a sample of items to backing documentation (invoices) to ensure disclosure is correct

4.2 Earnings per share

Accounting for Earnings per share is governed by FRS 22. It requires that companies of a certain size disclose their earnings per share for the year. This is the profit in pence attributable to each share. FRS 22 describes the various possible complications to calculating earnings per share, but auditing it is straightforward.

The size of the figure is unlikely to be material in itself, but it is key investor figure. As it will be of **interest to all the investors** who read it, it is **material by its nature**.

When considering earnings per share, the auditor must consider **two issues**:

• Whether it been disclosed on a comparable basis to the prior year, and have any changes in accounting policy been disclosed in accordance with FRS 18, and

• Whether it has been calculated correctly.

The audit procedures are as follows:

- Obtain a copy of the client's workings for earnings per share. (If a simple calculation has been used, this can be checked by re-doing the fraction on the face of the profit and loss account.)

- Compare the calculation with the prior year calculation to ensure that the basis is comparable

- Recalculate to ensure that it is correct.

4.3 Discontinued operations

Discontinued operations are accounted for under FRS 3. The FRS requires that discontinued operations are disclosed separately on the face of the balance sheet. This may well be material for the following reasons:

- Potentially material through **size**

- May be **inherently material** if the change in operations is a sign of management policy or a major change in focus of operations

Essentially, the fact that some operations have been discontinued is of interest to shareholders, which is why the FRS 3 disclosures came about. The auditor must be aware of the implications of FRS 3 for the financial statements at all stages of the audit:

(a) At the **planning stage**, if the auditor is aware of an operation being discontinued in the year or in the following period.

(b) While he is doing his **substantive testing**, he must be aware if evidence points to the fact that operations have been discontinued

(c) The issue of discontinued operations is important at the **review stage** of the audit in terms of:

- **Subsequent events** (disclosure requirements of FRS 3 extend beyond the balance sheet date)

- **Going concern** (the discontinued operations may cast doubt on the ability of the company to continue in the foreseeable future)

- Review of financial statements (the auditor needs to be satisfied that the correct **disclosures** have been made)

To audit whether the disclosures have been made correctly, the auditor should undertake the following procedures:

- Discuss the disclosure with management, to ensure that FRS 3 has been correctly applied.
- Review board minutes and any relevant correspondence to ascertain details of the operation being discontinued.
- Obtain a copy of the client's workings to disclose the discontinued operations.
- Review the workings to ensure that the figures are reasonable and agree to the financial statements.
- Trace a sample of items disclosed as discontinuing items to backing documentation (invoices) to ensure that they do related to discontinued operations.

4.4 Cash flow statements

Cash flows are accounted for under the provisions of FRS 1. The cash flow statement is essentially a reconciliation exercise between items on the profit and loss account (operating profit) and the balance sheet (cash).

As such, the cash flow statement is often audited **by the auditor reproducing it from the audited figures in the other financial statements**. This can be done quickly and easily in the modern era by use of computer programmes.

However, if the auditor wished to audit it another way, he could check and recalculate each reconciliation with the financial statements. This would involve checking each line of the statement by working through the client's workings and agreeing items to the accounting records and backing documentation (for example, tax paid to the bank statements) and the other financial statements.

| Question | Cash flow statements |

Why is the cash flow statement relevant to the auditors?

| Answer | |

Report on the cash flow statement

The cash flow statement is specified in the audit report, as a statement the auditors are reporting on. Financial reports are obliged to include a cash flow statement under FRS 1 in order to show a true and fair view. The auditors must therefore assess the truth and fairness of the cash flow statement as required by FRS 1.

Analytical review

The information in the cash flow statement will be used by the auditors as part of their analytical review of the accounts, for example, by adding further information on liquidity. This will be particularly helpful when comparing the statement to previous periods.

Going concern

The cash flow statement may indicate going concern problems due to liquidity failings, overtrading and overgearing. However, the statement is an historical document, prepared well after the year end, and is therefore unlikely to be the first indicator of such difficulties.

Audit evidence

The auditors will obtain very little direct audit evidence from the cash flow statement. It has been prepared by the company (not the auditors or an independent third party) from records which are under scrutiny by the auditors in any case. Thus the auditors will already have most of this information, although in different format.

However, the cash flow statement should provide additional evidence for figures in the accounts, for example, the purchase or sale of tangible fixed assets. Consistency of evidence will be important and complementary evidence is always welcome.

| Question | Accounting issues and audit evidence |

You work for Pitmans, a firm of chartered certified accountants. Tinga Ltd is a long-standing client of your firm, but this is the first year that Pitmans has carried out the audit. The firm also provides a number of other services to Tinga, including a range of tax planning services and business advisory services.

Recently, the firm undertook a review of some forecast financial statements, which Tinga was required to present to the bank.

You have been asked to plan the forthcoming audit of the financial statements for the period ending 31 March 2007. You have been given the following draft balance sheet.

	2007		2006	
	£'000	£'000	£'000	£'000
Assets				
Fixed assets				
Tangible fixed assets		10,101		12,378
Investments		10,000		2,000
Current assets				
Stock	196		191	
Debtors	1012		678	
Bank	–		149	
Prepayments	4		5	
		1,212		1,023
		21,313		15,401
Liabilities and shareholders funds				
Current liabilities				
Trade creditors	938		900	
Bank overdraft	1,168		–	
Bank loan	3,999		–	
		6,150		900
Long term liabilities				
Bank loan		12,325		17,002
Deferred tax		5,000		5,000
Shareholders funds				
Share capital		100		100
Share premium		1,000		1,000
Revaluation reserve		2,000		–
Profit and loss account		(5,262)		(8,601)
		21,313		15,401

Required

Comment on any points arising for your planning of the audit for the year end 31 March 2007. Your comments should include issues relating to risk and materiality, accounting issues and audit evidence issues and any limitations of the review you have undertaken to date. You should also highlight any further information that you intend to seek.

Approaching the answer

You work for Pitmans, a firm of chartered certified accountants. Tinga Ltd is a long-standing client of your firm, but this is the first year that Pitmans has carried out the audit. The firm also provides a number of other services to Tinga, including a range of tax planning services and business advisory services. Recently, the firm undertook a review of some forecast financial statements, which Tinga was required to present to the bank.

You have been asked to plan the forthcoming audit of the financial statements for the period ending 31 March 2007. You have been given the following draft balance sheet.

	2007		2006	
	£'000	£'000	£'000	£'000
Assets				
Fixed assets				
Tangible fixed assets		10,101		12,378
Investments		10,000		2,000
Current assets				
Stock	196		191	
Debtors	1012		678	
Bank	–		149	
Prepayments	4		5	
		1,212		1,023
		21,313		15,401
Liabilities and shareholders funds				
Current liabilities				
Trade creditors	938		900	
Bank overdraft	1,168		–	
Bank loan	3,999		–	
		6,150		900
Long term liabilities				
Bank loan		12,325		17,002
Deferred tax		5,000		5,000
Shareholders funds				
Share capital		100		100
Share premium		1,000		1,000
Revaluation reserve		2,000		–
Profit and loss account		(5,262)		(8,601)
		21,313		15,401

Required

Comment on any points arising for your planning of the audit for the year end 31 March 2007. Your comments should include issues relating to risk and materiality, accounting issues and audit evidence issues and any limitations of the review you have undertaken to date. You should also highlight any further information that you intend to seek.

Answer

Matters arising from preliminary review

Going concern

The balance sheets show a worsening cash position over the year. There are some classic indicators of going concern problems.

- Substantial liabilities
- Excess of current liabilities over current assets
- Bank overdraft
- Substantial increase in debtors
- Bank requiring future profit forecasts, which have been verified by our firm

A profit has been made in the year, but it does not appear that sales are readily being converted into cash.

Sources of audit evidence

- Profit forecasts
- Correspondence with bank
- Any business plans in existence (consult with business advisory department)

Further information required

- We need to confirm for the audit file why the bank required profit forecasts
- We need to review for audit purposes the results of our work on those forecasts
- For the purposes of our audit we must satisfy ourselves that Tinga is a going concern

Three items on the accounts stand out as being particularly interesting at a planning stage. These are:

- Deferred tax
- Increase in investments
- Revaluation in the year

Deferred tax

We will need to confirm what the deferred tax relates to, particularly as the fixed assets in the balance sheet do not seem particularly high. The deferred tax balance does not appear to have moved, despite the movements on fixed assets. We will have to check that deferred tax has been accounted for correctly in accordance with FRS 19.

Increase in investments

Investments are usually a straightforward area to audit with good audit evidence existing in terms of share certificates and valuation certificates.

However, as investments have increased, we must ensure that they have been accounted for correctly. We must also ensure that the increase does not represent a holding in another company that would require the results being consolidated into group results.

Revaluation

There appears to have been a revaluation in the year, although fixed assets have in fact decreased. We must discover what the revaluation reserve relates to, and ensure that it has been accounted for correctly.

Materiality

All the accounting issues discussed above are potentially material to the balance sheet. Fixed assets is the key balance which does not show a liability. As the balance sheet shows high liabilities, any as yet unrecorded impairment in either tangible fixed assets or investments could make the position of the company significantly worse. Conversely, if the liability shown in deferred tax was overstated, this would have the reverse effect.

Limitations of current review

The current review has only taken account of the balance sheet position, so is an incomplete picture. At present, we can only guess at factors on the profit and loss account which have had implications for the balance sheet.

As this is a first year audit, and the audit department is not familiar with this client, we have little knowledge of the business to apply to this review.

It is important as part of the planning process that the audit partner and/or manager enter into discussions with the various departments which have dealings with Tinga to increase their knowledge of the business and to obtain audit evidence on issues such as going concern.

However, it is also important for the audit team to bear in mind that, as auditors, they must maintain their independence towards the audit. There is a danger to the audit firm of loss of objectivity in respect of this audit due to the other services offered to the client, which must not be forgotten.

4.5 Changes in accounting policy

As you have learned in your corporate reporting studies, if a company changes an accounting policy as defined in FRS 18 *Accounting Policies* it is treated as a prior period adjustment.

FRS 3 *Reporting Financial Performance* governs the treatment of prior period adjustments.

4.5.1 Recaps

FRS 18

Accounting policies are defined as comprising an entity's choices of

- recognition
- measurement basis*, and
- presentation

* A choice of *measurement basis* is a policy choice, a choice of *estimation technique* is not.

FRS 3

When a prior period adjustment is made:

- comparatives should be restated using the new policy, and
- the cumulative effect of applying the new policy adjusted through opening reserves

4.6 Transition to International Financial Reporting Standards (IFRS)

Additional considerations arise for the auditor in respect of entities adopting IFRS for the first time.

4.6.1 Recap IFRS 1 First-time adoption of IFRS

An entity prepares an *opening IFRS balance sheet* at the date of transition to IFRS as a starting point for IFRS accounting:

Generally, this will be the beginning of the earliest comparative period shown (ie full retrospective application).

The opening balance sheet itself need not be presented.

The accounting policies used in the opening IFRS balance sheet and throughout all periods presented should be those effective *at the reporting date*. The entity does not apply different versions of IFRS effective at earlier dates.

Preparation of an opening IFRS balance sheet typically involves adjusting the amounts reported at the same date under previous GAAP.

All adjustments are recognised directly in retained earnings (or, if appropriate, another category of equity) not in the income statement.

ILLUSTRATION

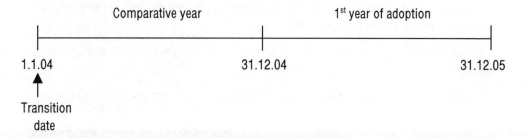

Exemptions from applying IFRS in the opening IFRS balance sheet

(a) In general the standard requires full retrospective application of IFRS

(b) Specific exemptions to full retrospective applications

    (i) Property, plant and equipment and investment properties
        –   Fair value at transition date may be used.

    (ii) Business combinations
        –   Goodwill on acquisitions pre transition date as per UK GAAP

    (iii) Employee benefits

        –   At transition date recognise pension assets, liabilities, gains and losses in accordance with FRS 17 rather than any international equivalent.

    (iv) Cumulative translation differences

        –   At the transition date recognise the cumulative exchange differences relating to the translation of foreign net investments as calculated under UK GAAP rather than any international equivalent.

    (v) Financial instruments

        –   Transitional arrangements apply to existing hedges under the IAS 39 model
        –   Adjustments required at the transition date to reflect existing hedges under the requirements of the IAS.

(c) Disclosures

    (i) Year end 31 December 2005 – normal IFRS disclosures

    (ii) Year end 31 December 2004 (comparatives)

        –   normal IFRS disclosures
        –   reconciliation of profit and equity from UK GAAP to IFRS
        –   changes to cash flow statement

    (iii) 1 January 2004 (start of comparative year)

        –   effect on equity of adjustments from UK GAAP to IFRS
        –   effect on Property, Plant and Equipment of any deemed cost adjustments
        –   impairment disclosures

Chapter Roundup

- Revenue recognition is an extremely important issue and completeness is a key assertion to be audited.

- The relevant financial statement assertions for liabilities are completeness, rights and obligations and existence. Liabilities must be tested for understatement.

- The classification of a lease can have a material effect on the financial statements.

- The auditor needs to audit the movement on the deferred tax provision.

- A provision is accounted for as a liability, contingencies are disclosed, so auditors must ensure they have been classified correctly according to FRS 12.

- Key issues relating to borrowing costs are the measurement rules in FRS26, and whether any may be capitalised.

- The auditor must also ensure disclosures in the financial statements are fairly stated.

Quick Quiz

1   Complete the definition

A .... lease is one that transfers substantially all the .... and .... incident to ownership of an asset.

2   Sort the following valuation tests into those relevant for finance leases and those relevant to operating leases.

- Obtain client's workings
- Ensure interest calculated in accordance with SSAP 21
- Agree the opening position
- Agree new assets to lease agreements
- Verify payments to bank statements

3   Name three types of contingency often disclosed by companies.

(1)   ....

(2)   ....

(3)   ....

4   The auditor may request information directly from the client's solicitors.

True   ☐

False   ☐

5   Link the disclosure issue with the accounting guidance

(a)	Segmental information	(i)	FRS 5
(b)	EPS	(ii)	SSAP 25
(c)	Discontinued operations	(iii)	FRS 3
(d)	Revenue recognition	(iv)	FRS 22

6   Why is EPS disclosure likely to be material?

BPP
LEARNING MEDIA

7   Which of the following is not a reason why revenue is often audited by analytical review?

    (1)   Availability of good, comparable evidence

    (2)   Profit and loss account is not as important as balance sheet

    (3)   It is quicker than detailed substantive testing

    (4)   Turnover has logical relationships with other items in the financial statements

8   Which of the following audit procedures relate to capitalised grants and which to grants put straight to income?

- Obtain relating documentation and ensure classification is correct.

- Agree value receipt of grant to:
    - Documentation (above)
    - Bank statements

- Consider reasonableness of transfers to revenue

- Ensure capitalisation method is comparable

9   Auditors do not report on the cash flow statement (only the balance sheet and profit and loss as recorded in the opinion section of the report).

True   ☐

False ☐

Answers to Quick Quiz

1   Finance, risks, rewards

2
- Obtain client's workings   F
- Ensure interest calculated in accordance with SSAP 21   F
- Agree the opening position   F
- Agree new assets to lease agreements   F
- Verify payments to bank statements   F and O

3   From:

(1)   Guarantees
(2)   Discounted bills of exchange
(3)   Uncalled liabilities on shares
(4)   Lawsuits/claims pending
(5)   Options to purchase assets

4   True. However the letter should be written by management and sent by the auditor.

5   (a)(ii), (b)(iv), (c)(iii), (d)(i).

6   It is of interest to the key readers of accounts – the shareholders.

7   (2) The profit and loss account **is just as important.** However, (3) **is true,** because it is cost effective to use analytical review as a substantive procedure where good evidence is available.

8
- Obtain relating documentation and ensure classification is correct.   C/I

- Agree value receipt of grant to: C/I

  –   documentation (above)
  –   bank statements

- Consider reasonableness of transfers to revenue   C

- Ensure capitalisation method is comparable   C

9   False

Now try the questions below from the Exam Question Bank

Number	Level	Marks	Time
Q13	Examination	20	36 mins
Q14	Examination	20	36 mins
Q16*	Examination	20	36 mins

*Note: Parts (1) and (2) would not be examined in December 2007 or June 2008.

Group audits and transnational audits

11

Topic list	Syllabus reference
1 Appointment as principal auditors	D2
2 Principal auditors and other auditors	D2
3 The consolidation: problems and procedures	D2
4 Joint audits	D2
5 Auditing firms	F3
6 Current developments	F3

Introduction

This is a new auditing topic for you, one which is concerned with practical difficulties of communication between auditors and the problems of geography.

In auditing group accounts, as in so many other areas, the auditors require detailed accounting knowledge in order to fulfil their responsibilities.

Group audits fall into two categories:

(1)   Where the same firm of auditors audits the whole group

(2)   Where one firm of auditors has responsibility for the opinion on the consolidated accounts and a different firm audits part of the group.

Even where the audit of each individual company in the group is carried out by the same firm, there may be administrative complications where some audits are carried out by different branches, perhaps overseas, with different practices and procedures.

Study guide

		Intellectual level
D2	**Group audits**	
(a)	Recognise the specific matters to be considered before accepting appointment as principal auditor to a group in a given situation.	3
(b)	Compare and contrast the organisation, planning, management and administration issues specific to group audits with those of joint audits.	
(c)	Recognise the specific audit problems and describe procedures in a given situation relating to:	3
(i)	the correct classification of investments	
(ii)	differing accounting policies and frameworks	
(iii)	fair values on acquisition	
(iv)	intangibles	
(v)	taxation	
(vi)	goodwill on consolidation	
(vii)	intra-group balances, transactions and profits	
(viii)	related parties	
(ix)	share options	
(x)	post balance sheet events	
(xi)	entities in developing countries	
(d)	Discuss letters of support ('comfort letters') as audit evidence.	2
(e)	Identify and describe the matters to be considered and the procedures to be performed when a principal auditor uses the work of other auditors in a given situation.	3
(f)	Explain the implications for he auditor's report on the financial statements of an entity where the opinion on a component is qualified or otherwise modified in a given situation.	2
F3	**Transnational audits**	
(a)	Define 'transnational audits' and explain the role of the Transnational Audit Committee (TAC) of IFAC.	1
(b)	Discuss how transnational audits may differ from other auditors of historical financial information (eg in terms of applicable financial reporting and auditing standards, listing requirements and corporate governance requirements).	2
(c)	Discuss the need for international audit firm networks in implementing international auditing standards.	2
(d)	Distinguish, for example, between 'global auditing firms' and second tier firms.	2
(e)	Discuss the impact of globalisation on audit firms and their clients.	2
(f)	Explain the advantages and problems of current trends (eg to merge, to divest consultancy services).	2

Exam guide

Group audits are likely to be tested in case study questions. These are likely to include issues relating to acceptance of appointment and working with other auditors as well as matters relating to accounting for the consolidation.

1 Appointment as principal auditors

FAST FORWARD

Principal auditors have a duty to report on the truth and fairness of group accounts.

1.1 Responsibility of principal auditors

Key terms

Principal auditors are the auditors with responsibility for reporting on the financial statements of an entity when those financial statements include financial information of one or more components audited by other auditors.

Other auditors are auditors, other than the principal auditors, with responsibility for reporting on the financial information of a component which is included in the financial statements audited by the principal auditors. Other auditors include affiliated firms, whether using the same name or not, and correspondent firms, as well as unrelated auditors.

Component is a division, branch, subsidiary, joint venture, associated undertaking or other entity whose financial information is included in financial statements audited by the principal auditors.

The duty of the principal auditors is to report on the group accounts, which includes balances and transactions of all the components of the group.

In most jurisdictions, the principal auditors have **sole responsibility** for this opinion even where the group financial statements include amounts derived from accounts which have not been audited by them. As a result, they cannot discharge their responsibility to report on the group financial statements by an unquestioning acceptance of component companies' financial statements, whether audited or not.

1.2 Rights of principal auditors

FAST FORWARD

Principal auditors have the right to require from auditors of subsidiaries the information and explanations they require, and to require the principal company to obtain the necessary information and explanations from subsidiaries.

The principal auditors have all the statutory rights and powers in respect of their audit of the holding company that we identified in the context of the audit of non-group companies in earlier chapters (for example right of access at all times to the holding company's books, accounts and vouchers).

The principal auditors also have the following rights:

(a) The **right to require from the other auditors** such **information and explanations** as they may reasonably require

(b) The right to **require the parent company** to take all reasonable steps to **obtain reasonable information** and explanations from the subsidiary and this will include foreign subsidiaries

Even where their responsibilities in this regard are not set down by statute, the other auditors should appreciate that the component company's financial statements will ultimately form a part of the group financial statements. In principle, the other auditors should therefore be prepared to **co-operate** with the **principal auditors.**

2 Principal auditors and other auditors

FAST FORWARD

Principal auditors should consider whether their involvement in the group audit is sufficient for them to act as principal auditors.

2.1 ISA 600

The principal auditors must decide how to take account of the work carried out by the other auditors. This is dealt with by ISA (UK and Ireland) 600 *Using the work of another auditor.*

Purpose of ISA 600

The purpose is to establish standards and provide guidance when an auditor, reporting on the financial statements of an entity, uses the work of another auditor.

ISA 600.2

When the principal auditor uses the work of another auditor, the principal auditor should determine how the work of the other auditor will affect the audit.

2.2 Acceptance as principal auditors

ISA 600.6

The auditor should consider whether the auditor's own participation is sufficient to be able to act as the principal auditor.

The principal auditors should not be so far removed from large parts of the group audit that they are unable to form an opinion. The ISA suggests that, in this context, the principal auditors should consider the following.

    (a)   The **materiality** of the portion of the financial statements which they do not audit

    (b)   The **degree** of his **knowledge** regarding the business of the components

    (c)   The **risk** of **material misstatements** in the financial statements of the components audited by other auditors

    (d)   The **performance** of **additional procedures** as set out in the ISA regarding the components audited by the other auditor resulting in the principal auditor having significant participation in such an audit, and

    (e)   The nature of the principal auditor's relationship with the firm acting as other auditor

Exam focus point

In addition to these points, the prospective principal auditor should also consider the general points relating to acceptance of appointment discussed in Chapter 2.

2.3 Principal auditors' procedures

ISA 600.7

When planning to use the work of another auditor, the principal auditor should consider the professional competence of the other auditor in the context of the specific assignment. ... [this] should include consideration of the professional qualifications, experience and resources of the other auditor in the context of the specific assignment.

Principal auditors will check:

- The other auditors belong to **a professional body.**

- The **reputation** of any firm to which the other auditors are affiliated. A review of previous audit work by the other auditors may have a bearing.

ISA 600.8

The principal auditor should perform procedures to obtain sufficient appropriate audit evidence that the work of the other auditor is adequate for the principal auditor's purposes, in the context of the specific assignment.

ISA 600 states that the principal auditors should advise the other auditors of:

(a) The **independence requirements** of both the entity and component. The principal auditors should obtain written representations on compliance.

(b) The use to be made of the other **auditors' work** and report. The principal auditors should make sufficient arrangements for the co-ordination of efforts at the planning stages of the audit. The principal auditors should inform the other auditors about the following matters.

- **Areas** requiring **special consideration** (key risks, control environment)
- Procedures for the **identification** of **discloseable inter-company transactions**
- Procedures for notifying principal auditors of **unusual circumstances**
- The **timetable** for completion of the audit

(c) The **accounting, auditing and reporting requirements which are relevant.**

The principal auditors should obtain **written representations** from the other auditors.

The nature, timing and extent of the principal auditors' procedures will depend on the individual circumstances of the engagement, and their assessment of the other auditors' competence.

Procedures that the principal auditors may use include the following.

- **Discussions** with the other auditors about audit procedures
- **Review** of a **written summary** of those procedures (perhaps using a questionnaire)
- **Review** of the other auditors' **working papers**

These procedures may be considered unnecessary if evidence has already been obtained of quality control over the other auditors' work, for example, through inter-firm reviews within affiliated firms.

ISA 600.12

The principal auditor should consider the significant findings of the other auditor.

This consideration may involve:

- **Discussions** with the other auditors and with the management of the component
- **Review** of copies of **reports to directors** or **management** issued by the other auditors
- **Supplementary tests**, performed by the principal auditors or by the other auditors

2.4 Co-operation between auditors

ISA 600.15

The other auditor, knowing the context in which the principal auditor will use the other auditor's work, should co-operate with the principal auditor.

2.4.1 Information supplied by other auditors

Where the component is a subsidiary the other auditors may have a **statutory** duty to co-operate as mentioned in Section 1 above.

If there is no such statutory obligation, but the principal auditors state their intention to use the other auditors' work, then the other auditors may need to obtain permission from the component to communicate with the principal auditors on the auditing matters.

Where this permission is refused, the other auditors should inform the principal auditors of the refusal, so that the principal auditors can agree with the directors of the entity they audit what action to take.

The other auditors should draw to the attention of the principal auditors any matters they discover in their audit which they feel is likely to be relevant to the principal auditors' work.

If the other auditors are unable to perform any aspect of their work as requested, they should inform the principal auditors.

2.4.2 Information supplied by principal auditors

Similarly the principal auditors should advise of any matters that may have an important bearing on the other auditor's work. This is subject however to legal and professional requirements such as confidentiality rules.

2.5 Reporting considerations

> **ISA 600.16**
>
> When the principal auditor concludes that the work of the other auditor cannot be used and the principal auditor has not been able to perform sufficient additional procedures regarding the financial information of the component audited by the other auditor, the principal auditor should express a qualified opinion or disclaimer of opinion because there is a limitation in the scope of the audit.

If the other auditors issue a modified report, the principal auditors should consider whether the nature and significance of the qualification means that the principal auditors' report also needs to be modified.

2.5.1 Division of responsibility

ISA 600 states that the above procedures are always desirable. Nevertheless in some countries the principal auditors can base their opinion solely on the other auditors' audit report.

> **ISA 600.18**
>
> When the principal auditor does so, the principal auditor's report should state this fact clearly and should indicate the magnitude of the portion of the financial statements audited by the other auditor.

In these circumstances the procedures of the principal auditors will be confined to considering the competence of the other auditors, and communicating with the other auditors at the planning stage. In the UK, the principal auditor has **sole responsibility**.

2.6 Other aspects of the audit requiring consideration in a group context

2.6.1 Support letters

It is sometimes the case that a subsidiary, when considered in isolation, does not appear to be a going concern. In the context of group accounts, the parent and the subsidiary are seen to be a complete entity, so if the group as a whole is a going concern, that is sufficient.

When auditing the incorporation of the single company into the group accounts however, the audit will need assurance that the subsidiary is a going concern.

In such a case, the auditor may request a 'support letter' from the director of the parent company. This letter states that the intention of the parent is to continue to support the subsidiary, which makes it a going concern. A support letter is sufficient, appropriate audit evidence on this issue.

2.6.2 Developing countries

Consolidating a subsidiary from a developing country may be a problem, as the basis of preparation of the subsidiary's accounts may be so different to GAAP that the principal auditor will not be able to conclude that the accounts show a true and fair view.

This is only a problem if the accounts, or the differences caused by the basis of preparation are **material to the group.**

The problem can be averted by asking the directors to restate the accounts under GAAP. The principal auditors might require that this restatement process is audited to ensure it is accurate.

Increased internationalisation of accounting practice is **reducing the risk** of this problem arising.

2.6.3 Control environment and systems

Assessment of the control environment and systems will include assessment of the overall group control environment. Factors to consider include:

- Organisational structure of the group
- Level of involvement of the parent company in components
- Degree of autonomy of management of components
- Supervision of components' management by parent company
- Information systems, and information received centrally on a regular basis

2.6.4 Management representations

ISA 580 *Management representations* makes the following comments about obtaining representations in a group situation.

(a)   When the auditors have responsibility for reporting on group financial statements, where appropriate they should obtain **written confirmation** of representations relating to specific matters regarding both the group financial statements and the financial statements of the parent undertaking.

(b)   How they obtain these representations depends on the group's methods of delegation of management control and authority.

Question
Other auditors

You are the main auditor of Mouldings Holdings, a listed company, which has subsidiaries in the UK and overseas, many of which are audited by other firms. All subsidiaries are involved in the manufacture or distribution of plastic goods and have accounting periods coterminous with that of the holding company.

Required

(i)   State why you would wish to review the work of the auditors of the subsidiaries not audited by you
(ii)   Describe the principal audit procedures you would carry out in performing such a review.

Answer

(a) Reasons for reviewing the work of other auditors

The main consideration which concerns the audit of all group accounts is that the holding company's auditors (the 'principal' auditors) are responsible to the members of that company for the audit opinion on the whole of the group accounts.

It may be stated (in the notes to the financial statements) that the financial statements of certain subsidiaries have been audited by other firms, but this does not absolve the principal auditors from any of their responsibilities.

The auditors of a holding company have to report to its members on the truth and fairness of the view given by the financial statements of the company and its subsidiaries dealt with in the group accounts. The principal auditors should have powers to obtain such information and explanations as they reasonably require from the subsidiary companies and their auditors, or from the parent company in the case of overseas subsidiaries, in order that they can discharge their responsibilities as holding company auditors.

The auditing standard ISA 600 *Using the work of another auditor* clarifies how the principal auditors can carry out a review of the audits of subsidiaries in order to satisfy themselves that, with the inclusion of figures not audited by themselves, the group accounts give a true and fair view.

The scope, standard and independence of the work carried out by the auditors of subsidiary companies (the 'other' auditors) are the most important matters which need to be examined by the principal auditors before relying on financial statements not audited by them. The principal auditors need to be satisfied that all material areas of the financial statements of subsidiaries have been audited satisfactorily and in a manner compatible with that of the principal auditors themselves.

(b) Work to be carried out by principal auditors in reviewing the other auditors' work

(i) Send a questionnaire to all other auditors requesting detailed information on their work, including:

(1) An explanation of their general approach (in order to make an assessment of the standards of their work)

(2) Details of the accounting policies of major subsidiaries (to ensure that these are compatible within the group)

(3) The other auditors' opinion of the subsidiaries' overall level of internal control, and the reliability of their accounting records

(4) Any limitations placed on the scope of the auditors' work

(5) Any qualifications, and the reasons for them, made or likely to be made to their audit reports

(ii) Carry out a detailed review of the other auditors' working papers on each subsidiary whose results materially affect the view given by the group financial statements. This review will enable the principal auditors to ascertain whether (*inter alia*):

(1) An up to date permanent file exists with details of the nature of the subsidiary's business, its staff organisation, its accounting records, previous year's financial statements and copies of important legal documents.

(2) The systems examination has been properly completed, documented and reported on to management after discussion.

(3) Tests of controls and substantive procedures have been properly and appropriately carried out, and audit programmes properly completed and signed.

(4)   All other working papers are comprehensive and explicit.

(5)   The overall review of the financial statements has been adequately carried out, and adequate use of analytical procedures has been undertaken throughout the audit.

(6)   The financial statements agree in all respects with the accounting records and comply with all relevant legal requirements and accounting standards.

(7)   Minutes of board and general meetings have been scrutinised and important matters noted.

(8)   The audit work has been carried out in accordance with approved auditing standards.

(9)   The financial statements agree in all respects with the accounting records and comply with all relevant legal and professional requirements.

(10)   The audit work has been properly reviewed within the firm of auditors and any laid-down quality control procedures adhered to.

(11)   Any points requiring discussion with the holding company's management have been noted and brought to the principal auditors' attention (including any matters which might warrant a qualification in the audit report on the subsidiary company's financial statements).

(12)   Adequate audit evidence has been obtained to form a basis for the audit opinion on both the subsidiaries' financial statements and those of the group

If the principal auditors are not satisfied as a result of the above review, they should arrange for further audit work to be carried out either by the other auditors on their behalf, or jointly with them. The other auditors are fully responsible for their own work; any additional tests are those required for the purpose of the audit of the group financial statements.

3 The consolidation: problems and procedures

FAST FORWARD

Consolidation procedures include checking consolidation adjustments have been correctly made, checking treatment of additions and disposals has been correct and arithmetical checks.

3.1 Audit procedures

After receiving and reviewing all the subsidiaries' (and associates') accounts, the principal auditors will be in a position to audit the consolidated accounts. An important part of the work on the consolidation will be checking the consolidation adjustments. Consolidation adjustments generally fall into two categories:

- **Permanent consolidation adjustments**
- **Consolidation adjustments** for the **current year**

The audit steps involved in the consolidation process may be summarised as follows.

Step 1 Compare the audited accounts of each subsidiary/associate to the consolidation schedules to ensure figures have been transposed correctly.

Step 2 Review the adjustments made on consolidation to ensure they are appropriate and comparable with the previous year. This will involve:

- **Recording** the **dates** and **costs** of **acquisitions** of subsidiaries and the assets acquired
- **Calculating goodwill** and **pre-acquisition reserves** arising on consolidation
- **Preparing** an overall **reconciliation** of movements on reserves and minority interests

Step 3 For business combinations determine:

- Whether combination has been **appropriately** treated as an acquisition
- The **appropriateness** of the **date** used as the date of combination
- The **treatment** of the **results** of **investments** acquired during the year
- If acquisition accounting has been used, that the **fair value** or acquired **assets** and **liabilities** is reasonable (to ascertainable market value by use of an expert)
- **Goodwill** has been **calculated correctly** and if amortised, period of amortisation is reasonable

Step 4 For disposals:

- Agree the **date** used as the date for disposal to sales documentation.
- Review management accounts to ascertain whether the **results** of the **investment** have been **included** up to the date of disposal, and whether figures used are reasonable.

Step 5 **Consider** whether **previous treatment** of **existing subsidiaries** or **associates** is still **correct** (consider level of influence, degree of support)

Step 6 Verify the **arithmetical accuracy** of the consolidation workings by recalculating them

Step 7 **Review** the **consolidated accounts** for **compliance** with the legislation, accounting standards and other relevant regulations. Care will need to be taken where:

- Group companies do not have coterminous accounting periods.
- Subsidiaries are not consolidated.
- Accounting policies of group members differ because foreign subsidiaries operate under different rules, especially those located in developing countries
- Elimination of intra-group balances, transactions and profits

Other important areas include:

- Treatment of associates
- Treatment of goodwill and intangible assets
- Foreign currency translation
- Taxation and deferred tax
- Treatment of loss-making subsidiaries
- Treatment of restrictions on distribution of profits of a subsidiary
- Share options

Step 8 **Review** the **consolidated accounts** to confirm that they give a true and fair view in the circumstances (including subsequent event reviews from all subsidiaries updated to date of audit report on consolidated account)

The audit of related party transactions was considered in Chapter 9. Remember that when auditing a consolidation, the relevant related parties are those related to the **consolidated group.** Transactions with consolidated subsidiaries need **not** be disclosed, as they are incorporated in the financial statements

The principal auditors are often requested to carry out the consolidation work even where the accounts of the subsidiaries have been prepared by the client. In these circumstances the auditors are of course acting as accountants **and** auditors and care must be taken to ensure that the **audit** function is carried out and evidenced.

Question   Inter-company balances/profits

Your firm is the auditor of Beeston Industries, a limited company, which has a number of subsidiaries in your country (and no overseas subsidiaries), some of which are audited by other firms of professional accountants. You have been asked to consider the work which should be carried out to ensure that inter-company transactions and balances are correctly treated in the group accounts.

Required

(a) Describe the audit work you would perform to check that inter-company balances agree, and to state why inter-company balances should agree, and the consequences of them not agreeing.

(b) Describe the audit work you would perform to verify that inter-company profit in inventory has been correctly accounted for in the group accounts.

Answer

(a) Inter-company balances should agree because, in the preparation of consolidated accounts, it is necessary to cancel them out. If they do not cancel out then the group accounts will be displaying an item which has no value outside of the group and profits may be correspondingly under or over-stated. The audit work required to check that inter-company balances agree would be as follows.

    (i) Obtain and review a copy of the holding company's instructions to all group members relating to the procedures for reconciliation and agreement of year end inter-company balances. Particular attention should be paid to the treatment of 'in transit' items to ensure that there is a proper cut-off.

    (ii) Obtain a schedule of inter-company balances from all group companies and check the details therein to the summary prepared by the holding company. The details on these schedules should also be independently confirmed in writing by the other auditors involved.

    (iii) Nil balances should also be confirmed by both the group companies concerned and their respective auditors.

    (iv) The details on the schedules in (iii) above should also be agreed to the details in the financial statements of the individual group companies which are submitted to the holding company for consolidation purposes.

(b) Where one company in a group supplies goods to another company at cost plus a percentage, and such goods remain in stock at the year end, then the group stock will contain an element of unrealised profit. In the preparation of the group accounts, best accounting practice requires that a provision should be made for this unrealised profit.

In order to verify that inter-company profit in stock has been correctly accounted for in the group accounts, the audit work required would be as follows.

    (i) Confirm the group's procedures for identification of such stock and their notification to the parent company who will be responsible for making the required provision.

    (ii) Obtain and review schedules of inter-group stock from group companies and confirm that the same categories of stock have been included as in previous years.

(iii) Select a sample of invoices for goods purchased from group companies and check to see that as necessary these have been included in year end inter-group stock and obtain confirmation from other auditors that they have satisfactorily completed a similar exercise.

(iv) Check the calculation of the provision for unrealised profit and confirm that this has been arrived at on a consistent basis with that used in earlier years, after making due allowance for any known changes in the profit margins operated by various group companies.

(v) Check the schedules of inter-group stock against the various stock sheets and consider whether the level of inter-group stock appears to be reasonable in comparison with previous years, ensuring that satisfactory explanations are obtained for any material differences.

4 Joint audits

FAST FORWARD

In joint audits, more than one auditor is responsible for the audit opinion and it is made jointly.

The relationship between principal and other auditors discussed in the previous sections is **not** the same as that between the auditors involved in a joint audit.

Key term

A **joint audit** is one 'where two or more auditors are responsible for an audit engagement and jointly produce an audit report to the client'.

4.1 Reasons for joint audits

Two or more firms of accountants could act as joint auditors for a number of reasons.

(a) **Takeover**. The holding company may insist that their auditors act jointly with those of the new subsidiary.

(b) **Locational problems**. A company operating from widely dispersed locations may find it convenient to have joint auditors.

(c) **Political problems**. Overseas subsidiaries may need to employ local auditors to satisfy the laws of the country in which they operate. It is sometimes found that these local auditors act jointly with those of the holding company.

(d) Companies preferring to use **local accountants**, while at the same time enjoying the wider range of services provided by a large national firm.

4.2 Accepting a joint audit

There are several practical points that must be borne in mind before accepting a joint audit. In particular it will be necessary to assess the **experience** and **standards** of the other firm by looking at the audit techniques used, by scrutinising their working papers and establishing whether they have had experience in similar jobs.

Where there are joint auditors, the audit engagement should be explained in similar terms by each set of auditors. The auditors should agree whether joint or separate letters should be sent to the client. Separate letters would normally need to be sent where other services are provided.

Once a joint position has been accepted the **programme** to be adopted and the **split** of the **detailed work** will have to be discussed.

4.3 Problems with joint audits

One of the major criticisms of joint audits is that they may be expensive. This is probably true, but if the two firms have organised the work between them properly the difference should be minimal. Furthermore, an increase in the fees may be justified by improved services not least because the two firms of accountants are likely to work as efficiently as possible from a sense of professional pride.

Both firms must sign the audit report and both are responsible for the whole audit whether or not they carried out a particular area of the audit programme. It follows that both firms will be **jointly liable** in the event of litigation.

5 Auditing firms

The audit sector is varied, but it has three key elements: Big four, medium firms, small firms.

5.1 Types of firm

The accountancy sector is divided into three generally accepted 'tiers':

(a)   'Big Four' firms – the top four firms by fee incomes.

(b)   Medium sized firms – which is defined more fluidly than the Big Four. One description is firms with more than sixteen partners. This would include about the next fifty firms by fee income.

(c)   Small firms – the remainder

However, a key recent characteristic of the sector has been the tendency of firms to **merge.** So while the above situation is the current picture, it is not the picture of five years ago, and it may well not be the picture of tomorrow.

5.1.1 Big Four

The Big Four audit firms are so called because there is a significant gap in fee income between these firms and the remainder. After this gap, fee income levels fall in a more even curve.

The Big Four so became in 2002 when Andersens merged with Deloitte and Touche. The Big Five became the Big Five in 1998, when two of what had been the Big Six, Coopers and Lybrand and Price Waterhouse, merged. This created a firm at the head of the Big Five which has reported fee income in 1999 of 3.5 times the lowest placed Big Five firm.

5.1.2 Medium sized

As discussed above, there is no one definition of 'medium sized'. The definition given above gives a group of firms with a range in reported income from approximately £160 million to £6 million.

An alternative classification of 'medium-sized' is the next '20 or so' after the bigger firms, but this gives a similar range of fees.

The medium tier is split into two sections, 7 or 8 of the firms with a fee income of £50 million and 'the rest'. Of the 7 or 8, three firms have income of around £100 million.

There is currently a trend for the upper end of the medium sized firms to merge in an attempt to reach up towards the large firms, or at least secure supremacy in the medium tier firms. Examples of this are Grant Thornton and Baker Tilly.

5.1.3 Small firms

By far the largest number of audit and accountancy firms fall into the last sector; the 'small firms'. The local firm with one or two partners is the most common type of accountancy firm.

5.2 Current trends

5.2.1 Globalisation

Globalisation is an issue which affects the larger of the medium-sized firms and the Big Five. There are two approaches to globalisation:

(a) **Affiliation.** This method allows an international brand name to develop and is commonly used by big five firms which have international coverage by a firm using the same name.

(b) **Co-operation.** Medium sized firms often attach themselves to an international co-operative of firms operating under a title which can be incorporated into the firm's name (for example, **BDO** Stoy Hayward) so that a UK firm has an international network of 'sister firms'.

The key benefit of internationalisation is that many clients are companies which are international, so the audit firm can meet their needs around the world. However, as has been the case with Andersens, collapse of the firm in the part of the world can have substantial 'knock-on' effects elsewhere.

5.2.2 Mergers

One key current trend already discussed is merging. This is currently an issue in the medium firm tier as the firms seek to establish dominance over the tier and reach up towards the Big Four.

It is also an issue in the light of the audit exemption limit rising. Many smaller firms face loss of fees through their clients no longer requiring their services. Merging can result in a larger firm with the resources to conduct larger audits.

There are some **disadvantages of mergers,** particularly to clients. A key disadvantage is that it results in **reduced choice** of audit firm for clients.

Another disadvantage, which is specifically relevant to larger firms, is that merger can often result in the new combined firm holding the audits of two highly competitive companies, which often results in one of the audits being lost. These two disadvantages combined represents a particular problem for large, listed companies, whose audits are usually provided by the larger firms.

5.2.3 Divesting services

Another trend is related to the other services audit firms provide. A recent trend of the larger firms has been to divest key other services, such as consultancy.

Other services are a problem for audit firms in relation to their independence ethics. A trend towards divesting was driven by the amendment of the US Securities Exchange Commission's amendment to their rules on auditor independence in 2000.

Exam focus point	Keep an eye on what audit firms are doing or have done in the twelve months prior to your exam.

5.3 Transnational audits

5.3.1 The Forum of Firms

In response to the trend towards globalisation an international grouping, the Forum of Firms (FoF) was founded by the following networks: BDO, Deloitte Touche Tohmatsu, Ernst & Young, Grant Thomton, KPMG and Pricewaterhouse Coopers.

Membership is open to firms and networks that have transnational audit appointments or are interested in accepting such appointments.

These firms have a voluntary agreement to meet certain requirements that are set out in their constitution. These relate mainly to:

- promoting the use of high quality audit practices worldwide, including the use of ISAs
- maintaining quality control standards in accordance with International Standards on Quality Control issued by the IAASB, and conducting globally coordinated internal quality assurance reviews.

5.3.2 The Transnational Auditors Committee

The IAASB has set up the **Transnational Auditors Committee** (TAC) to provide guidance to the members of the FoF.

The TAC has issued the following definition of transnational audit.

Definition	Transnational audit means an audit of financial statements which are or may be relied upon outside the audited entity's home jurisdiction for purposes of significant lending, investment or regulatory decisions; this will include audits of all financial statements of companies with listed equity or debt and other public interest entities which attract particular public attention because of their size, products or services provided.
Guidance	**Other public interest entities** shall include those entities in either the public or the private sectors which **have significant transactions across national borders**, whether or not having either listed equity or debt. These would include, for example, large charitable organisations or trusts, major monopolies or duopolies, providers of financial or other borrowing facilities to commercial or private customers, deposit-taking organisations and those holding funds belonging to third parties in connection with investment or savings activities.
	Significant transactions across national borders – shall include transactions such that there is a reasonable expectation that the financial statements of the entity may be relied upon by a user outside the entity's home jurisdiction for purposes of significant lending, investment or regulatory decisions. Significant in this context does not include use of financial statements to establish normal trade terms with vendors or to open accounts with financial institutions (ie accounts for purposes of collecting customer receipts or making vendor payments). For the avoidance of doubt, an office required solely for the purpose of legal formation and continuing legal existence in a particular jurisdiction does not constitute a significant transaction across national borders.
	In principle, the definition of transnational audit should be applied to the consolidated entity as a whole including the individual entities comprising the consolidated entity.

Examples to illustrate the definition.

Example	Explanation
Private company in US raising debt finance in Canada	This would qualify as a transnational audit as it is reasonable to expect that the financial statements of the company would be used across national borders in obtaining the debt financing
Private Savings and Loans operating entirely in the US (ie only US depositors and US investments)	Although it could be considered a public interest entity, this would not qualify as a transnational audit assuming it can be demonstrated that there are no transnational users.
	In applying the definition of transnational audit, there should be a rebuttable presumption that all banks and financial institutions are included, unless it can be clearly demonstrated that there is no transnational element from the perspective of a financial statement user and that there are no operations across national borders. Potential transnational users would include investors, lenders, governments, customers, regulators, etc.

International charity taking donations through various national branches and making grants around the world	This entity can clearly be considered a pubic interest entity and operating across borders. Further, the international structure would create a reasonable expectation that the financial statements could be used across national borders by donors in other countries if not by others for purposes of significant lending, investment or regulatory decisions.
Private Internet betting company registered in BVI, which operates from Costa Rica and takes wagers by credit card on a worldwide basis via internet	Assuming there is no restriction on gamblers then it would be public interest and operate across borders and therefore classified as a transnational audit.

5.3.3 Features of transnational audits

In the globalised business and financial environment, many audits are clearly transnational, and this produces a number of specific problems which can limit the reliability of the audited financial statements:

- Regulation and oversight of auditors differs from country to country
- Differences in auditing standards from country to country
- Variability in audit quality in different countries

5.3.4 Role of the international audit firm networks

The 'Big 4' and other international networks of firms can be seen as being ahead of governments and institutions in terms of their global influence. They are in a position to establish consistent practices worldwide in areas such as:

- Training and education
- Audit procedures
- Quality control procedures

These firms may as a result be in a better position than national regulators to ensure consistent implementation of high quality auditing standards.

Membership of the Forum of Firms imposes commitments and responsibilities, namely:

- To perform transnational audits in accordance with ISAs
- To comply with the IFAC Code of Ethics
- Be subject to a programme of quality assurance

5.4 Current debate: dominance of the global accounting firms

5.4.1 Competition and choice

The preceding paragraphs have emphasised the strengths of the global accounting firms.

Questions have been raised recently as to whether the concentration in the audit market, with the big four firms supplying audit services to most large companies, creates any risks.

The study 'Competition and choice in the UK audit market' commissioned by the Financial Reporting Council (FRC) and the Department of Trade and Industry (DTI) identifies these potential problems:

- if one or more firms are ineligible due to independence rules, a company may have no effective choice of auditor in the short term.

- if one of the Big Four left the market a few large companies would be unable to find an auditor

- restricted choice may represent a risk to high quality and competitive prices.

5.4.2 Barriers to entry

The situation is unlikely to change in the short term as there are significant barriers to entry to the market for audits of large companies. It may not be economical for other firms to break into this market given the need to demonstrate:

- A credible reputation with large companies, their investors and other stakeholders.

- Appropriate resources and expertise in place to carry out large company audits, including relevant sector-specific skills

- An effective capability to secure timely and reliable audit opinions on overseas subsidiaries for audits of companies with significant international operations.

6 Current developments

FAST FORWARD The International Audit and Assurance Standards Board is currently updating its guidance on groups.

6.1 Revision of ISA 600

IAASB is in the middle of a project to update its guidance on groups which has been running for a number of years. The most recent exposure draft of ISA 600 was issued in March 2006.

Exam focus point

Unsurprisingly therefore, the issue of groups has been focused on in the current issues section of the exam. In December 2004, the original version of this exposure draft was examined, in December 2005 there were six marks for discussing how developments in relation to non–consolidated entities under common control had affected auditing. The new exposure draft will not be examined unless there is an article on *Student Accountant* concerning it. Please note that the examiners article 'Revised group auditing standards' in October 2004 relates to the old ED.

The ISA conforms to the requirements of other ISAs, for example, ISAs 220, 315 and 330, in respect of the procedures required to accept the group audit, obtaining knowledge about the group and assessing risk. The group auditor should gain an understanding of the group as a whole, and assess risks for the group as a whole and for individually significant components. The group auditor has to ensure other auditors are professionally qualified, meet quality control and ethical requirements and will allow the group auditor access to working papers or components.

6.1.1 Objective of the exposure draft

The stated objective of the ISA is to enable auditors to determine whether they can accept an engagement as group auditor and obtain sufficient appropriate evidence to reduce the audit risk for the group financial statements to an acceptably low level. This will be achieved by:

- Determining what work should be carried out on the consolidation process
- Determining what work should be carried out on the components
- Establishing appropriate communication with other auditors
- Evaluating audit evidence about the consolidation process and the components

6.2 Key issues

6.2.1 Significant components

The ED distinguishes between significant components and other components which are not individually significant to the group financial statements.

Key term

A **significant component** is a component identified by the group auditor that due to the nature of, or circumstances specific to, that component or the individual financial significance of the component to the group, has been identified as likely to include significant risks of material misstatement of the group financial statements.

The group auditor should be involved in the assessment of risk in relation to significant components.

If a component is financially significant to the group financial statements then the group auditor will require the other auditors to carry out a full audit of that component, based on the materiality level the other auditors have calculated for that component, or, if it is lower, a materiality level set by the group auditors.

If a component is otherwise significant due to its nature or circumstances, the group auditors will require one of the following:

- A full audit (based on materiality calculated as described above)
- An audit of specified account balances relating to identified significant risks
- Specified audit procedures relating to identified significant risks

The group auditor will perform, or require the other auditors to perform, audit procedures designed to identify subsequent events that may require adjustment to or disclosure in the financial statements of significant components.

If audit work on significant components does not give the group auditor sufficient appropriate audit evidence about the group financial statements, the group auditor would request one of the three procedures outlined above (a full audit, an audit of specified account balances or specified audit procedures) or a review of other individually insignificant components of group financial statements.

Components not subject to these requirements will be subject to analytical review at a group level.

6.2.2 Consolidation

The group auditor will evaluate the appropriateness, completeness and accuracy of the adjustments and reclassifications involved in the consolidation process.

The group auditors will consider whether there are any fraud risk factors or indicators of management bias in connection with the consolidation.

Chapter Roundup

- Principal auditors have a duty to report on the truth and fairness of group accounts.

- Principal auditors have the right to require from auditors of subsidiaries the **information** and **explanations** they require, and to require the principal company to obtain the necessary **information** and **explanations** from subsidiaries.

- Principal auditors should consider whether their **involvement** in the group audit is **sufficient** for them to act as principal auditors.

- Consolidation procedures include:
  - Checking **consolidation adjustments** have been correctly made
  - Checking **treatment of additions and disposals** has been correct
  - **Arithmetical** checks

- In joint audits, more than one auditor is responsible for the audit opinion and it is made jointly.

- The audit sector is varied, but it has three key elements: Big four, medium firms, small firms.

- The International Audit and Assurance Standards Board is currently updating its guidance on groups.

Quick Quiz

1   Match the auditors with the correct definition.

    (a)   Principal auditors   (b)   Other auditors

    (i)   The auditors with responsibility for reporting on the financial statements of an entity when those financial statements include financial information of one or more components by others.

    (ii)   Auditors with responsibility for reporting on the financial information of a component which is included in the financial statements audited by another firm. This includes affiliated firms, whether using the same name or not, and correspondent firms, as well as unrelated auditors.

2   List three rights of principal auditors

3   Complete the matters which the principal auditors must consider in relation to a group audit.

- The .... of the portion of the financial statements which they do not audit.

- The .... regarding the business of the component.

- The .... of their .... with the other auditors.

- Their ability, where necessary, to.............................. ....
  ....

- The risk of .... in the financial statements not audited by them.

4   Name two factors the principal auditors should take into account when planning the nature, timing and extent of their procedures.

5   What is a support letter?

6   List the eight steps involved in auditing a consolidation.

7   If two firms undertake a joint audit, they shall be jointly liable in the event of litigation.

    True   ☐

    False   ☐

8   Name four difficulties which might arise from the audit of a foreign subsidiary.

Answers to Quick Quiz

1   (a)(i), (b)(ii)

2   (1)   Statutory rights and duties in relation to audit of holding company

    (2)   Right to require information and explanations of auditors of a UK incorporated company included in the consolidation

    (3)   Right to require the parent company to take all reasonable steps to obtain information and explanations from the subsidiary.

3   Materiality, degree of their knowledge, nature, relationship, perform additional procedures, material misstatements.

4   From: (1)   Assessment of other auditors
          (2)   Risks
          (3)   Materiality of components
          (4)   Relationships with the client

5   A letter to the auditors from the parent company of a subsidiary which individually does not appear to be a going concern, stating that it intends to continue to support the subsidiary, rendering it a going concern.

6

STEP ONE	Check the transposition from individual audited accounts to the consolidation workings.
STEP TWO	Check consolidation adjustments are correct and comparable with prior years
STEP THREE	Check for, and audit, business combinations
STEP FOUR	Check for, and audit, disposals
STEP FIVE	Consider whether previous treatment of subsidiaries and associates is still correct
STEP SIX	Verify the arithmetical accuracy of the workings
STEP SEVEN	Review the consolidated accounts for compliance with law and standards
STEP EIGHT	Review the consolidated accounts to ensure they give a true and fair view

7   True

8   From:

    (1)   Language difficulties
    (2)   Cultural difficulties
    (3)   Differences in auditing/accounting conventions
    (4)   Specific problems such as high inflation or civil unrest
    (5)   Requirement to obtain a permit to work

Now try the question below from the Exam Question Bank

Number	Level	Marks	Time
Q19	Examination	15	27 mins

Audit-related services and other assurance services

12

Topic list	Syllabus reference
1 Audit related services	D3
2 Assurance engagements	D4
3 Risk assessments	D4
4 Performance measurement	D4
5 Systems reliability	D4
6 Electronic commerce	D4

Introduction

Audit related services are sometimes called **non-audit services**. They are a collection of services, some of which are assurance services and some of which are not. The services outlined in Sections 1 to 3 are:

Reviews: assurance service (ISAE 2400)
Agreed upon procedures: not an assurance service (ISRS 4400)
Compilations: not an assurance service (ISRS 4410)

You must grasp the important distinction between **assurance engagements** (including audit) and **non-assurance engagements**, which will be discussed further in Section 4.

Lastly in this chapter we begin to **explore areas where there may be a need for assurance services.** As you work through the information in Sections 5 to 8 and the rest of Part C, you should consider issues such as:

- Why a need for assurance services might arise in this context
- What sort of criteria the subject matter might be evaluated by
- The level of assurance that can be given about the subject matter
- The qualification/skills required by the accountant to provide assurance

Study guide

		Intellectual level
D3	**Audit-related services**	
(a)	Describe the nature of audit-related services, the circumstances in which they might be required and the comparative levels of assurance provided by professional accountants.	2
(b)	Distinguish between:	2
(i)	audit-related services and an audit of historical financial statements	
(ii)	an attestation engagement and a direct reporting engagement	
(c)	Plan review engagements, for example:	2
(i)	a review of interim financial information	
(ii)	a 'due diligence' assignment (when acquiring a company, business or other assets).	
(d)	Explain the importance of enquiry and analytical procedures in review engagements and apply these procedures.	2
(e)	Describe and apply the general principles and procedures relating to a compilation engagement (eg to prepare financial statements)	2
(f)	Explain why agreed-upon procedures and compilation engagements do not (usually) meet the requirements for an assurance engagement.	2
(g)	Illustrate the form and content of:	2
(i)	A report of factual findings	
(ii)	A compilation report	
4	**Assurance services**	
(a)	Describe the main categories of assurance services that audit firms can provide and assess the benefits of providing these services to management and external users.	3
(i)	risk assessments	
(ii)	business performance measurement	
(iii)	systems reliability	
(iv)	electronic commerce	
(b)	Justify a level of assurance (reasonable, high, moderate, limited, negative) for an engagement depending on the subject matter evaluated, the criteria used, the procedures applied and the quality and quantity of evidence obtained.	3
(c)	Recognise the ways in which different types of risk (eg strategic, operating, information) may be identified and analysed and assess how management should respond to risk.	3
(d)	Recommend operational measures and describe how the reliability of performance information systems is assessed (including benchmarking).	2
(e)	Describe a value for money audit and recommend measures of economy, efficiency and effectiveness.	2
(f)	Explain the demand for reliable and more timely reporting on financial information and the development of continuous auditing.	2
(g)	Select procedures for assessing internal control effectiveness.	2
(h)	Describe how entities are using core technologies (eg EDI, e-mail, Internet, World Wide Web) and explain how e-commerce affects the business risk of a given entity.	2

Exam guide

Assurance and audit-related services are extremely important areas for auditors in practice. Areas such as e-commerce are also particularly topical. Most of these topics have featured in practical questions in the past and are likely to continue to do so.

1 Audit related services

Audit related services may be assurance services (reviews) or not (agreed-upon procedures and compilations).

1.1 Reviews

Review engagements. The objective of a review engagement is to enable an auditor to state whether, on the basis of procedures which do not provide all the evidence that would be required in an audit, anything has come to the auditor's attention that causes the auditor to believe that the financial statements are not prepared, in all material respects, in accordance with an identified financial reporting framework.

Remember the two types of assurance assignments discussed in Chapter 1? These can be applied to reviews, which are an assurance service:

- An **attestation** engagement where the accountant declares that a given premise is either correct or not

- A **direct reporting** engagement, where the accountant reports on issues that have come to his attention during the course of his review

Example: attestation engagement

Auditors may sometimes be asked to **review interim financial information**. In such an engagement, the auditor is being asked to attest assertions made, such as:

- The accounting policies used are consistent with those used in the prior year financial statements.
- No material modifications to the interim financial information as it has been presented are required.

Example: direct reporting engagement

An example of a direct reporting engagement is a **'due diligence'** engagement.

Due diligence reviews are a specific type of review engagement. A typical due diligence engagement is where an advisor (often an audit firm) is engaged by one company planning to take over another to perform an assessment of the material risks associated with the transaction (including validating the assumptions underlying the purchase), to ensure that the acquirer has all the necessary facts. This is important when determining purchase price. Similarly, due diligence can also be requested by sellers.

It may include some or all of the following aspects:

- Financial due diligence (a review of the financial position and obligations of a target to identify such matters as covenants and contingent obligations)

- Operational and IT due diligence (extent of operational and IT risks, including quality of systems, associated with a target business)

- People due diligence (key staff positions under the new structure, contract termination costs and cost of integration)

- Regulatory due diligence (review of the target's level of compliance with relevant regulation)
- Environmental due diligence (environmental, health and safety and social issues in a target)

In a review engagement, the auditor will rely more heavily on procedures such as **enquiry and analytical review** than on more detailed substantive testing. The reasons for this are as follows:

- He is seeking a **lower level of assurance than for an audit**, so these forms of evidence seeking are sufficient due to risk being lower
- Such techniques provide **indicators** to direct work to risk areas and from which to draw conclusions, and they are **quick** and, therefore, **cost-effective**

What the enquiries are about and what matters are the subject of analytical procedure will depend on the specific situation.

Exam focus point

In the previous syllabus, a case study question was set in the context of a due diligence review. A key feature of this question was that it was important to tailor your answer to the facts given in the question. Although it was necessary to know what a due diligence review was, many marks were available for comprehending the key issues in the scenario and applying them in your answer.

International standard on review engagements (ISRE) 2400 *Engagements to review financial statements* contains guidance on review engagements.

ISRE 2400.7

For the purpose of expressing negative assurance in the review report, the auditor should obtain sufficient appropriate evidence primarily through inquiry and analytical procedures to be able to draw conclusions.

ISRE 2400.8

The procedures required to conduct a review of financial statements should be determined by the auditors having regard to the requirements of this ISRE, relevant professional bodies, legislation, regulation and, where appropriate, the terms of the review engagement and reporting requirements.

Many of the requirements of the ISRE are similar to the requirements of an audit because a review is extremely similar to an audit.

- Planning
  - Obtain knowledge of the business
  - Same materiality requirements
  - Using the work of others

- Evidence
  - Document all important matters
  - Apply judgement in determining nature, timing and extent of procedures
  - Enquire about subsequent events
  - Extend procedures if material misstatements are suspected

1.1.1 Reporting

The nature of reporting on reviews was outlined in paper 2.6 so you should be familiar with it. However, we shall revise it here.

An external review is an **exercise similar to an audit**, which is designed to give a **reduced degree of assurance** concerning the proper preparation of a set of financial statements.

As you know from your earlier studies **negative assurance** is given on review assignments.

ISRE 2400.23/24

The review report should contain a clear written expression of **negative assurance.** The auditor should review and assess the conclusion drawn from the evidence obtained as the basis for the expression of negative assurance.

Based on the work performed, the auditor should assess whether any information obtained during the review indicates that the financial statements do not give a true and fair view (or 'are not presented fairly, in all material respects,') in accordance with the identified financial reporting framework.

Key term

Negative assurance is assurance of something in the absence of any evidence arising to the contrary. In effect, this means the auditor is saying, 'I believe that this is reasonable because I have no reason to believe otherwise.'

When no matters have come to the attention of the auditor, he should give a **clear expression of negative assurance** in his report. An example of an unqualified review report is given in the appendix to the ISRE, and it is reproduced here.

Form of Unqualified Review Report

REVIEW REPORT TO...

We have reviewed the accompanying balance sheet of ABC Company at December 31, 20XX, and the related statements of income and cash flows for the year then ended. These financial statements are the responsibility of the Company's management. Our responsibility is to issue a report on these financial statements based on our review.

We conducted our review in accordance with the International Standard on Review Engagements 2400 (or refer to relevant national standards or practices) applicable to review engagements. This Standard requires that we plan and perform the review to obtain moderate assurance as to whether the financial statements are free of material misstatement. A review is limited primarily to inquiries of company personnel and analytical procedures applied to financial data and thus provides less assurance than an audit. We have not performed an audit and, accordingly, we do not express an audit opinion.

Based on our review, nothing has come to our attention that causes us to believe that the accompanying financial statements do not give a true and fair view (or 'are not presented fairly, in all material respects,') in accordance with International Accounting Standards.

Date   *AUDITOR*
Address

If matters have come to the attention of the auditor, he should **describe those matters**. The matters may have the following effects.

Impact	Effect on report
Material	Express a **qualified** opinion of negative assurance
Pervasive	Express an **adverse** opinion that the financial statements do not give a true and fair view

The auditor may feel there has been a limitation in the scope of the work he intended to carry out for the review. If so, he should **describe the limitation.** The limitation may have the following effects.

Impact	Effect on report
Material to one area	Express a **qualified** opinion of negative assurance due to amendments which might required if the limitation did not exist
Pervasive	Do not provide any assurance

1.2 Review of interim financial information performed by the independent auditor of the entity

This subject is covered by ISRE 2410 *Review of interim financial information performed by the independent auditor of the entity.*

1.2.1 General principles

The auditor should comply with ethical principles relevant to the audit when carrying out an interim review. He should apply quality control procedures applicable to the individual engagement. In addition, he should plan and perform the engagement with an attitude of professional scepticism. The auditor should agree the terms of the engagement with the client (these will not be the same terms as for the audit, as the review will result in a lower level of assurance than the annual audit).

1.2.2 Procedures

The procedures outlined below follow the same pattern as an audit, but, because this is a review not an audit, which gives a lower level of assurance, they are not as detailed as audit procedures.

The auditor should possess sufficient understanding of the entity and its environment to understand the types of misstatement that might arise in interim financial information and to plan the relevant procedures (mainly enquiry and analytical) to enable him to ensure that the financial information is prepared in accordance with the applicable financial reporting framework. This will usually include:

- Reading last year's audit and previous review files
- Considering any significant risks that were identified in the prior year audit
- Reading the most recent and comparable interim financial information
- Considering materiality
- Considering the nature of any corrected or uncorrected misstatements in last year's financial statements
- Considering significant financial accounting and reporting matters of ongoing importance
- Considering the results of any interim audit work for this year's audit
- Considering the work of internal audit
- Asking management what their assessment is of the risk that the interim financial statements might be affected by fraud
- Asking management whether there have been any significant changes in business activity, and if so, what effect they have had
- Asking management about any significant changes in internal controls and the potential effect on preparing the interim financial information
- Asking how the interim financial information has been prepared and the reliability of the underlying accounting records

A recently appointed auditor should obtain an understanding of the entity and its environment as it relates to both the interim review and final audit.

The key elements of the review will be:

- Enquiries of accounting and finance staff
- Analytical procedures

Ordinarily procedures would include:

- Reading the minutes of meetings of shareholders, those charged with governance and other appropriate committees
- Considering the effect of matters giving rise to a modification of the audit or review report, accounting adjustments or unadjusted misstatements from previous audits
- If relevant, communicating with other auditors auditing different components of the business
- Analytical procedures designed to identify relationships and unusual items that may reflect a material misstatement
- Reading the interim financial information and considering whether anything has come to the auditors' attention indicating that it is not prepared in accordance with the applicable financial reporting framework
- Agree the interim financial information to the underlying accounting records

Auditors should make enquiries of members of management responsible for financial and accounting matters about:

- Whether the interim financial information has been prepared and presented in accordance with the applicable financial reporting framework
- Whether there have been changes in accounting policies
- Whether new transactions have required changes in accounting principle
- Whether there are any known uncorrected misstatements
- Whether there have been unusual or complex situations, such as disposal of a business segment
- Significant assumptions relevant to fair values
- Whether related party transactions have been accounted and disclosed correctly
- Significant changes in commitments and contractual obligations
- Significant changes in contingent liabilities including litigation or claims
- Compliance with debt covenants
- Matters about which questions have arisen in the course of applying the review procedures
- Significant transactions occurring in the last days of the interim period or the first days of the next
- Knowledge or suspicion of any fraud
- Knowledge of any allegations of fraud
- Knowledge of any actual or possible non compliance with laws and regulations that could have a material effect on the interim financial information
- Whether all events up to the date of the review report that might result in adjustment in the interim financial information have been identified
- Whether management has changed its assessment of the entity being a going concern

The auditor should evaluate discovered misstatements individually and in aggregate to see if they are material.

The auditor should obtain written representations from management that it acknowledges its responsibility for the design and implementation of internal control, that the interim financial information is prepared and presented in accordance with the applicable financial reporting framework and that the effect of uncorrected misstatements are immaterial (a summary of these should be attached to the representations). Also that all significant facts relating to frauds or non compliance with law and regulations has been disclosed to the auditor and that all significant subsequent events have been disclosed to the auditor.

The auditor should read the other information accompanying the interim financial information to ensure that it is not inconsistent with it.

If the auditors believe a matter should be adjusted in the financial information, they should inform management as soon as possible. If management do not respond within a reasonable time, then the auditors should inform those charged with governance. If they do not respond, then the auditor should consider whether to modify the report or to withdraw from the engagement and the final audit if necessary. If the auditors uncover fraud or non compliance with laws and regulations. They should communicate that promptly with the appropriate level of management. The auditors should communicate matters of interest arising to those charged with governance.

1.2.3 Reporting

The ISRE gives the following example standard report.

Report on Review of Interim Financial Information

(Appropriate addressee)

Introduction

We have reviewed the accompanying balance sheet of ABC Entity as of March 31, 20X1 and the related statements of income, changes in equity and cash flows for the three–month period then ended, and a summary of significant accounting policies and other explanatory notes. Management is responsible for the preparation and fair presentation of this interim financial information in accordance with (indicate applicable financial reporting framework). Our responsibility is to express a conclusion on this interim financial information based on our review.

Scope of Review

We conducted our review in accordance with International Standard on Review Engagements 2410, 'Review of Interim financial Information performed by Independent Auditor of the Entity'. A review of interim financial information consists of making inquiries, primarily of persons responsible for financial and accounting matters, and applying analytical and other review procedures. A review is substantially less in scope than an audit conducted in accordance with International Standards on Auditing and consequently does not enable us to obtain assurance that we would become aware of all significant matters that might be identified in an audit. Accordingly, we do not express an audit opinion.

Conclusion

Based on our review, nothing has come to our attention that causes us to believe that the accompanying interim financial information does not give a true and fair view of *(or 'does not present fairly, in all material respects,')* the financial position of the entity as at March 31, 20X1, and of its financial performance and its cash flows for the three–month period then ended in accordance with (applicable financial reporting framework, including a reference to the jurisdiction or country of origin of the financial reporting. Framework when the financial reporting framework used is not International Financial Reporting Standards).

AUDITOR

Date

Address

It also gives examples of modified reports:

Previous paragraphs as per standard report.

Basis for Qualified Conclusion

Based on information provided to us by management, ABC Entity has excluded from property and long–term debt certain lease obligations that we believe should be capitalised to conform with (indicate applicable financial reporting framework). This information indicates that if these lease obligations were capitalised at March 31, 20X1, property would be increased by $ _____, long–term debt by $ _____, and net income and earnings per share would be increased (decreased) by $ _____, $ _____, $ _____, and $ _____, respectively for the three–month period then ended.

Qualified Conclusion

Based on our review, with the exception of the matter described in the preceding paragraph, nothing has come to our attention that caused us to believe that the accompanying interim financial information does not give a true and fair view of *(or 'does not present fairly, in all material respects,')* the financial position of the entity as at March 31, 20X1, and of its financial performance and its cash flows for the three–month period then ended in accordance with (indicate applicable financial reporting framework, including the reference to the jurisdiction or country of origin of the financial reporting framework when the financial reporting framework used is not International Financial Reporting Standards).

AUDITOR

Date

Address

Introduction paragraph – as per standard report

Scope paragraph

Except as explained in the following paragraph .... – as per standard report.

Basis for Qualified Conclusion

As a result of a fire in a branch office on (date) that destroyed its accounts receivable records, we were unable to complete our review of accounts receivable totalling $ _____ included in the interim financial information. The entity is in the process of reconstructing these records and is uncertain as to whether these records will support the amount shown above the related allowance for uncollectible accounts. Had we been able to complete our review of accounts receivable, matters might have come to our attention indicating that adjustments might be necessary to the interim financial information.

Qualified Conclusion

Except for the adjustments to the interim financial information that we might have become aware of had it not been for the situation described above, based on our review, nothing has come to our attention that causes us to believe that the accompanying interim financial information does not give a true and fair view of *(or 'does not present fairly, in all material respects,')* the financial position of the entity as at March 31, 20X1, and of its financial performance and its cash flows for the three–month period then ended in accordance with (indicate applicable financial reporting framework, including a reference to the jurisdiction or country of origin of the financial reporting framework when the financial reporting framework used is not International Financial Reporting Standards).

AUDITOR

Date

Address

1.3 Agreed-upon procedures

Key term

Agreed-upon procedures assignment. In an engagement to perform agreed-upon procedures, an auditor is engaged to carry out those procedures of an audit nature to which the auditor and the entity and any appropriate third parties have agreed and to report on factual findings. The recipients of the report must form their own conclusions form the report by the auditor. The report is restricted to those parties that have agreed to the procedures to be performed since others, unaware of the reasons for the procedures may misinterpret the results.

Agreed upon procedures assignments are discussed in International Standard on Related Services (ISRS) 4400 *Engagements to perform agreed upon procedures regarding financial information*.

1.3.1 Accepting appointment

ISRS 4400.9

The auditor should ensure with representatives of the entity, and ordinarily, other specified parties who will receive copies of the report of factual findings, that there is a clear understanding regarding the agreed procedures and the conditions of the engagement.

1.3.2 Carrying out procedures

The auditors should plan the assignment. They should carry out the agreed upon procedures, documenting their process and findings.

1.3.3 Reporting

ISRS 4400.18

The report of factual findings should contain:

(a)   title;

(b)   addressee (ordinarily the client who engaged the auditor to perform the agreed-upon procedures)

(c)   identification of specific financial or non-financial information to which the agreed-upon procedures have been applied;

(d)   a statement that the procedures performed were those agreed upon with the recipient;

(e)   a statement that the engagement was performed in accordance with the International Standard on Auditing applicable to agreed-upon procedure engagements, or with relevant national standards or practices;

(f)   when relevant a statement that the auditor is not independent of the entity;

(g)   identification if the purpose for which the agreed-upon procedures were performed;

(h)   a listing of the specific procedures performed;

(i)   a description of the auditor's factual findings including sufficient details of errors and exceptions found;

(j)   statement that the procedures performed do not constitute either an audit or a review, and, as such, no assurance is expressed;

(k)   a statement that had the auditor performed additional procedures, an audit or a review, other matters might have come to light that would have been reported;

(l)   a statement that the report is restricted to those parties that have agreed to the procedures to be performed;

(m)   a statement (when applicable) that the report relates only to the elements, accounts, items or financial and non-financial information specified and that it does not extend to the entity's financial statements taken as a whole;

(n)   date of the report;

(o)   auditor's address;

(p)   auditor's signature.

1.4 Compilations

Key term

> **Compilation engagement.** In a compilation engagement, the accountant is engaged to use accounting expertise as opposed to auditing expertise to collect, classify and summarise financial information.

A compilation engagement is one where the accountant is engaged to compile information. Examples include:

- Preparing financial statements
- Preparing tax returns

The information to be compiled does not have to be financial information.

The international guidance on compilation engagements is found in ISRS 4410 *Engagements to compile financial statements*. The most relevant piece of guidance that it contains for us is the guidance on reporting, which is reproduced below.

1.4.1 General principles of a compilation engagement

ISRS 4410 identifies two principles:

(i)   The accountant should comply with IFAC's Code of Ethics, the relevant ethical principles being

- integrity
- objectivity
- professional competence and due care
- confidentiality
- professional behaviour, and
- technical standards

(independence is not a requirement for a compilation engagement)

(ii)   In all circumstances when an accountant's name is associated with financial information compiled by the accountant, the accountant should issue a report.

1.4.2 Procedures

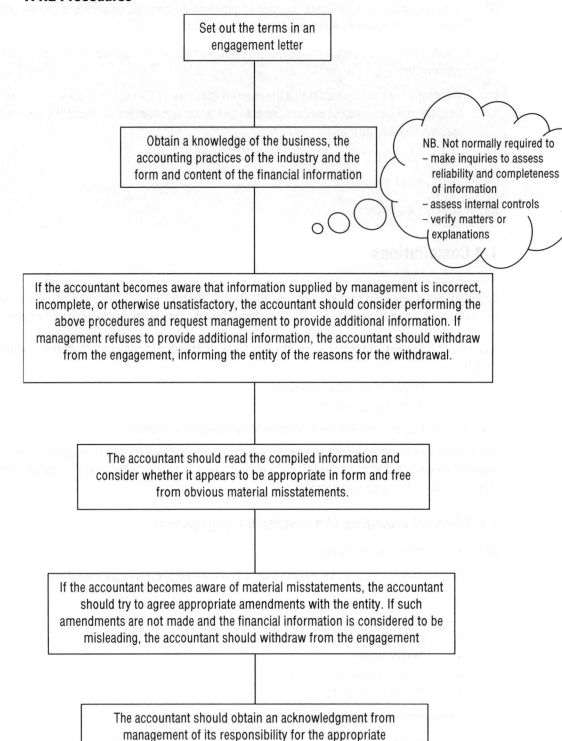

Set out the terms in an engagement letter

Obtain a knowledge of the business, the accounting practices of the industry and the form and content of the financial information

NB. Not normally required to
– make inquiries to assess reliability and completeness of information
– assess internal controls
– verify matters or explanations

If the accountant becomes aware that information supplied by management is incorrect, incomplete, or otherwise unsatisfactory, the accountant should consider performing the above procedures and request management to provide additional information. If management refuses to provide additional information, the accountant should withdraw from the engagement, informing the entity of the reasons for the withdrawal.

The accountant should read the compiled information and consider whether it appears to be appropriate in form and free from obvious material misstatements.

If the accountant becomes aware of material misstatements, the accountant should try to agree appropriate amendments with the entity. If such amendments are not made and the financial information is considered to be misleading, the accountant should withdraw from the engagement

The accountant should obtain an acknowledgment from management of its responsibility for the appropriate presentation of the financial information and of its approval of the financial information

1.4.3 Reporting

The information compiled by the accountant should contain a reference to the fact that it has not been audited.

ISRS 4410.18

Reports on compilation engagements should contain the following:

(a)   title

(b)   addressee

(c)   a statement that the engagement was performed in accordance with the ISA applicable to compilation engagements, or with national standards and practices;

(d)   when relevant, a statement that the accountant is not independent of the entity;

(e)   identification if the financials information noting that it is based on information provided by management

(f)   a statement that neither an audit nor a review has been carried out and that accordingly no assurance is expressed on the financial information;

(g)   a statement that neither an audit nor a review has been carried out and that accordingly no assurance is expressed on the financial information;

(h)   a paragraph, when considered necessary, drawing attention to the disclosure of material departures from the identified financial reporting framework;

(i)   date of the report;

(j)   accountant's address;

(k)   accountant's signature.

2 Assurance engagements

FAST FORWARD

Assurance services improve the quality of decision-making for users of information.

2.1 Elements of an assurance engagement

A definition of an assurance engagement was given in Chapter 1. It is helpful to revise this here.

Key term

An **assurance engagement** is one where a professional accountant evaluates or measures a subject matter that is the responsibility of another party against suitable criteria, and expresses an opinion which provides the intended user with a level of assurance about the subject matter.

In Chapter 1, we set out the basic elements of an assurance engagement. Here, we shall focus on assurance engagements on subjects other than historical financial information (which we have already looked at in the form of audits and reviews) as we look at the guidance in International Standard on Assurance Engagements (ISAE) 3000 *Assurance engagements other than audits or reviews of historical financial information.*

2.2 Assurance given

FAST FORWARD

Assurance engagements may give reasonable assurance or limited assurance.

The ISAE refers to two types of engagement: 'reasonable assurance engagement' and 'limited assurance engagement'. These levels of assurance were also discussed in Chapter 1. Remember that absolute assurance can never be given on an assurance engagement due to the inherent limitations of such engagements.

2.3 Accepting and continuing appointment

 Assurance engagements should only be accepted if the firm meets the requirements of the Code of Ethics and ISQC 1.

The standard requires that practitioners ensure they comply with regard to the Code of Ethics and the Quality Control Standard (ISQC 1) with regard to the assignment. In addition, the standard specifies the following.

> **ISAE 3000.8/9**
>
> The practitioner should accept (or continue where applicable) an assurance engagement only if, on the basis of a preliminary knowledge of the engagement circumstances, nothing comes to the attention of the practitioner to indicate that the requirements of the Code or of the ISAEs will not be satisfied.
>
> The practitioner should accept (or continue where applicable) an assurance engagement only if the practitioner is satisfied that those persons who are to perform the engagement collectively possess the necessary professional competencies.

The engagement must also genuinely be an assurance engagement, that is, it must have the characteristics of an assurance engagement (a three party relationship between the practitioner, the intended user of the information and the party responsible for the information). The responsible party may be an intended user so long as he is not the sole intended user of the information.

> **ISAE 3000.7**
>
> The practitioner should accept (or continue where applicable) an assurance engagement only if the subject matter is the responsibility of a party other than the intended users or the practitioner.

Commonly, the practitioner would ask the responsible party to acknowledge their responsibility for the information in written form.

2.3.1 Agreeing terms

> **ISAE 3000.10**
>
> The practitioner should agree on the terms of the engagement with the engaging party.

For the avoidance of confusion, this should normally be done in writing.

Sometimes, the nature of an assignment being carried out by a practitioner might change, and the responsible party might request that the practitioner provide less or no assurance on an engagement.

> **ISAE 3000.11**
>
> A practitioner should consider the appropriateness of a request, made before the completion of an assurance engagement to a limited assurance engagement or from a reasonable assurance engagement to a limited assurance engagement, and should not agree to a change without reasonable justification.

2.4 Planning and performing the engagement

> **ISAE 3000.12**
>
> The practitioner should plan the engagement so that it will be performed effectively.

This involves developing:

- An overall strategy
- A detailed engagement plan

Matters to be considered

- The terms of the engagement
- The characteristics of the subject matter and identified criteria
- The engagement process and possible sources of evidence
- Understanding of the entity and its environment (risks of material misstatement)
- Identification of intended users and their needs
- Materiality
- Components of assurance engagement risk
- Personnel/expertise requirements (including the potential use of experts)

As with audits, the practitioner should maintain an attitude of professional scepticism.

> **ISAE 3000.15**
>
> The practitioner should obtain an understanding of the subject matter and other engagement circumstances, sufficient to identify and assess the risks of subject matter information being materially misstatement, and sufficient to design and perform further evidence gathering procedures.

Obtaining such an understanding of the entity assists the practitioner when he is exercising professional judgement throughout the engagement.

2.4.1 Appropriateness of the subject matter and criteria

You will remember from Chapter 1 that the subject matter of an assurance engagement must be appropriate to have assurance given on it. The Framework outlines the characteristics of such appropriateness, which include it being identifiable, capable of consistent evaluation and measurement and capable of being subject to procedures and evidence gathering.

> **ISAE 3000.18**
>
> The practitioner should assess the appropriateness of the subject matter.

Equally, the criteria must be appropriate. The Framework also lists characteristics of suitable criteria, including relevance, reliability, completeness, neutrality and understandability. For example, if an assurance subject matter was design of internal controls, internationally recognised criteria such as the COSO framework would be appropriate.

> **ISAE 3000.19**
>
> The practitioner should assess the suitability of the criteria to evaluate or measure the subject matter.

2.4.2 Materiality and engagement risk

> **ISAE 3000.22/24**
>
> The practitioner should consider materiality and assurance engagement risk when planning and performing an assurance engagement.
>
> The practitioner should reduce assurance engagement risk to an acceptably low level in the circumstances of the engagement.

The circumstances of the engagement here refers to the level of assurance that is anticipated, that is, reasonable assurance or limited assurance.

2.4.3 Using the work of an expert

> **ISAE 3000.26/30/32**
>
> When the work of an expert is used in the collection and evaluation of evidence, the practitioner and the expert should, on a combined basis, possess adequate skill and knowledge regarding the subject matter and the criteria for the practitioner to determine that sufficient appropriate evidence has been obtained.
>
> The practitioner should be involved in the engagement and understand the work for which an expert is used, to an extent that is sufficient to enable the practitioner to accept responsibility for the conclusion on the subject matter information.
>
> The practitioner should obtain sufficient appropriate evidence that the expert's work is adequate for the purposes of the assurance engagement.

The practitioner is not expected to have the same degree of skill or expertise as the expert, or there would be no point in using him. However, he is supposed to ensure that the expert is suitably qualified to do the required work, and that he (the practitioner) understands what work is being done, so that the practitioner can give an opinion on the assurance engagement.

2.4.4 Evidence

> **ISAE 3000.33**
>
> The practitioner should obtain sufficient appropriate evidence on which to base the conclusion.

You should be aware of the meaning of sufficiency and appropriateness from your knowledge of auditing. Assurance engagements will involve the use of selective testing methods.

Obtaining sufficient appropriate evidence is likely to include obtaining written management representations from the responsible party where appropriate, particularly where knowledge of facts is confined to the responsible party or it is a matter of judgement of the responsible party.

2.4.5 Subsequent events

> **ISAE 3000.41**
>
> The practitioner should consider the effect on the subject matter information and on the assurance report of events up to the date of the assurance report.

2.5 Reporting

The ISAE makes the following observations about reporting:

ISAE 3000.45/46

The practitioner should conclude whether sufficient appropriate evidence has been obtained to support the conclusion expressed in the assurance report.

The assurance report should be in writing and should contain a clear expression of the practitioner's conclusion about the subject matter information.

In a reasonable assurance engagement, a practitioner should be able to give a 'positive' expression of his conclusion. This does not mean that a report in a reasonable assurance engagement should not be modified, it means the practitioner should be able to draw a conclusion on the basis of the evidence gained.

This is in contrast to a negative opinion, given in a limited assurance engagement, where an auditor gives an opinion as no evidence has been received to the contrary.

2.6 References for a client

Sometimes an auditor will be asked for a reference concerning a client, particularly in relation to his ability to **service a loan**. Where **no additional work is required** to provide a reference, the following matters should be considered:

- Inherent uncertainty of future income and expenditure
- The difficulty of reporting on present solvency (given that the audit is a historic exercise. Such information might be available if a **separate engagement** was made)
- The possibility of a **duty of care** arising
- That clarification might be required (there has been no engagement and no fees, and that liability might have to be expressly disclaimed)

However, the accountants might be able to provide certain information without difficulty:

- The length of time they have acted for the client
- The results declared to the taxation authorities over past years
- A statement of a level of negative assurance given past performance

Where it is necessary to create a separate engagement in order to provide the relevant information, the auditor should consider the guidance in ISAE 3000, discussed above.

In the following sections we shall start to consider some examples of areas where the accountant can provide assurance services.

3 Risk assessments

FAST FORWARD Risk assessment is important to investors and managers and therefore is an important area for assurance services.

We discussed business risk in Chapter 7. It had three elements; financial, operational and compliance. There are a number of specific risks within these elements, some of which are shown the diagram below.

3.1 Need for assurance

Why is there a need for assurance in relation to risk assessment? For what reason would people want an independent opinion that gives them assurance? What criteria should this assurance be in relation to?

The key answer to the first question is that **the risk that the company enters into has a direct impact on the risk of the investment** that anyone purchasing shares in a company or loaning money to a company is making.

Interested stakeholders, **particularly investors**, need assurance that the risk taken by the company, in effect with their investment, is acceptable to them and that the returns that they receive are in accordance with that level of risk.

It is this need for assurance about the risks the company enters into that has led to the **importance of the issue of corporate governance and internal control effectiveness** that we looked at in Chapter 6 and will continue to look at in Chapter 14 in the context of internal audit.

Other stakeholders will also be interested in the effectiveness of risk management in a company. Examples are other creditors and employees. This is because the **ultimate risk is that a business might fail**.

3.2 Possible assurance criteria

The criteria by which risk assessment is evaluated will depend on the specific needs of the company and the user. However, some possibilities are:

- The requirements of the Turnbull guidelines
- Management's policy on risk management

There are no universally recognised criteria suitable for evaluating the **effectiveness** of an entity's risk evaluation. Assurance is likely to be limited to whether evaluation is carried out, rather than the quality of the evaluation.

3.3 Responsibility for risk assessment

There are three sets of people who can be involved in risk assessment in a company:

- Directors/management
- Internal audit
- External audit

We shall discuss the role of internal audit in Chapter 14. The responsibility of the directors has previously been discussed in Chapter 6, and the role of the auditors in risk assessment has been discussed in Chapters 7 and 8.

It is vital that you distinguish between the risk assessment carried out by the auditors and the directors. The directors are responsible for assessing and then managing the risks arising to the business, that is, the business risks.

As part of their audit, the auditors assess audit risk. Audit risk is the risk that the auditors make an inappropriate opinion on financial statements. The auditors may consider business risk as part of their audit risk assessment. However, the **auditors are not responsible for risk management of their clients**.

3.4 Assessing risk

Methods of identifying risk were outlined in Chapter 7. You should be familiar with methods such as SWOT or PEST analysis. In practice, risk identification is likely to be done in all the various departments of a business.

These risks could include, for example:

- Contractual risks (important customers not agreeing to given contractual terms)
- Operational risks (scarce raw materials, risks arising through storage and use)
- Physical risks (for example, health and safety compliance)
- Product distribution (logistics, networks, outlets)
- Regulation (different jurisdictions, internet trading)
- Reputation (brands and staff profile)

The directors of a company need to determine guidelines for assessing risk. Risk might be assessed in terms of

- Significance
- Likelihood
- Capacity to be managed

Mathematical methods could be used to assess risk, for instance using probability factors. Risks can be analysed using a grid such as the example given:

Low likelihood	Low likelihood
High likelihood Low impact	High likelihood High impact

3.5 Responses to risk

There are several responses that management take to risk:

- **Accept** risk (particularly if it is low likelihood, low impact)
- **Reduce** risk (by setting up a system of internal control to prevent the risk arising)
- **Avoid** risk (by not entering that market or not accepting certain contracts)
- **Transfer** risk (by taking out insurance)

If management choose to accept risk, they must set **risk thresholds**, that is, determine levels of risk where they will stop accepting risk and choose one of the other strategies. These thresholds are important because if directors or management are reckless with regard to risk they may be breaching their fiduciary duties.

3.6 Assurance

As stated above, assurance services may be provided. Those relating to **control systems** will be discussed in section 5. External accountants may be able to provide assurance that **management policy** is being adhered to, that **insurance** is sufficient or that a management policy exists.

4 Performance measurement

FAST FORWARD

Performance measurement is another important issue for companies where assurance can be given.

4.1 Revision

Before we consider the benefits of performance measurement we should revise it itself. This is a topic studied in earlier papers.

Performance measurement

Earlier in this Study Text, we discussed how recently measures have been taken to improve the accountability of management to shareholders.

Performance measurement includes a series of measures within the company designed to ensure that people who work in the company are **accountable** to management for their performance.

Here are some benefits of performance measurement.

- Clarifies the objectives of the organisation
- Develops agreed measures of activity
- Gives greater understanding of processes
- Facilitates comparison of performance in different organisations
- Facilitates the setting of targets for the organisation and its managers
- Promotes the accountability of the organisation to its stakeholders

---

The above points refer to the **benefits of performance measurement in itself**. The last bullet point above hints at the benefits of giving assurance on performance measurement.

4.2 Traditional performance measures

4.2.1 Financial

You should be aware of the key financial ratios used to measure performance from your previous studies.

The traditional financial ratios give indicators about:

- Profitability
- Liquidity
- Gearing
- Investment

Whilst these measures are relevant to shareholders, they are measures which investors would expect companies to calculate as a matter of course, and also to calculate them correctly. Therefore, there should not be any need for assurance services in these areas.

However, financial performance could be assessed in further detail in performance measures generally kept for internal use.

- Detail behind figures in financial statements, for example:
  - Sales by product
  - Sales by region
  - Sales by division
- Timeliness of information, whether information is received quickly enough to make good investment decisions.
- Comparisons between the performance of the company and its competitors, or its budgets, or its historic performance.

4.2.2 Operational

Clearly, indicators of operational performance will vary with each business. Measures could include:

- Sales per salesperson
- Number of new products launched each year

The issue performance is measured on will be the key drivers of operation for that particular business.

4.3 Value for money audits

Value for money audits were introduced in your previous auditing studies, as an example of a service that could be undertaken by internal audit. We shall revise them briefly here.

Although much has been written about value for money (VFM), there is no great mystique about the concept. The term is common in everyday speech and so is the idea.

To drive the point home, think of a bottle of Fairy Liquid. If we believe the advertising, Fairy is good 'value for money' because it washes half as many plates again as any other washing up liquid. Bottle for bottle it may be more expensive, but plate for plate it is cheaper. Not only this but Fairy gets plates 'squeaky' clean. To summarise, Fairy gives us VFM because it exhibits the following characteristics.

- **Economy** (more clean plates per pound)
- **Efficiency** (more clean plates per squirt)
- **Effectiveness** (plates as clean as they should be)

The **assessment** of economy, efficiency and effectiveness should be a part of the normal process of any organisation, public or private. Management should carry out **performance reviews** as a regular feature of their control responsibilities.

In a VFM audit, the objectives of a particular programme or activity need to be specified and understood in order for a proper assessment of whether value for money has been achieved to be made.

(a) In a **profit seeking organisation**, objectives can be expressed financially in terms of target profit or return. The organisation, and profit centres within it, can be judged to have operated **effectively** if they have **achieved a target profit** within a given period.

(b) In **non-profit seeking organisations**, effectiveness cannot be measured this way, because the organisation has non-financial objectives. The **effectiveness** of performance in such organisations could be measured in terms of whether **targeted non-financial objectives have been achieved**, but as we have seen there are several problems involved in trying to do this.

Public sector organisations are now under considerable **pressure** to prove that they operate economically, efficiently and effectively, and are encouraged from many sources to draw up **action plans** to achieve value for money as part of the continuing process of good management.

Value for money is important **whatever level of expenditure** is being considered. Negatively it may be seen as an approach to spreading costs in public expenditure fairly across services but positively it is necessary to ensure that the desired impact is achieved with the minimum use of resources.

4.3.1 Revision of value for money terminology

Economy is concerned with the cost of inputs, and it is achieved by **obtaining those inputs at the lowest acceptable cost**. Economy **does not mean straightforward cost-cutting,** because resources must be acquired which are of a suitable **quality** to provide the service to the desired standard. Cost-cutting should not sacrifice quality to the extent that service standards fall to an unacceptable level. Economising by buying poor quality materials, labour or equipment is a 'false economy'.

Efficiency means the following.

(a)   **Maximising output for a given input**, for example maximising the number of transactions handled per employee or per £1 spent.

(b)   **Achieving the minimum input for a given output**. For example, the Department of Social Security is required to pay Unemployment Benefit to millions of people. Efficiency will be achieved by making these payments with the minimum labour and computer time.

Effectiveness means ensuring that the **outputs** of a service or programme have the **desired impacts**; in other words, finding out whether they **succeed in achieving objectives**, and if so, to what extent.

Economy, efficiency and effectiveness can be studied and measured with reference to the following.

(a)   **Inputs**

- Money
- Resources – the labour, materials, time and so on consumed, and their cost

For example, a VFM audit into state secondary education would look at the efficiency and economy of the use of resources for education (the use of schoolteachers, school buildings, equipment, cash) and whether the resources are being used for their purpose: what is the pupil/teacher ratio and are trained teachers being fully used to teach the subjects they have been trained for?

(b)   **Outputs**, in other words the **results of an activity**, measurable as the services actually produced, and the quality of the services.

In the case of a VFM audit of secondary education, outputs would be measured as the number of pupils taught and the number of subjects taught per pupil; how many examination papers are taken and what is the pass rate; what proportion of students go on to further education at a university or college.

(c)   **Impacts**, which are the **effect that the outputs** of an activity or programme have in terms of **achieving policy objectives**.

Policy objectives might be to provide a minimum level of education to all children up to the age of 16, and to make education relevant for the children's future jobs and careers. This might be measured by the ratio of jobs vacant to unemployed school leavers. A VFM audit could assess to what extent this objective is being achieved.

As another example from education, suppose that there is a programme to build a new school in an area. The **inputs** would be the **costs of building** the school, and the resources used up; the **outputs** would be the **school building** itself; and the **impacts** would be the **effect that the new school has on education in the area** it serves.

BPP LEARNING MEDIA

4.4 Need for assurance

It is important to understand why assurance might be required in relation to this kind of information. Why does this information matter to people? Who are these people to whom it matters?

Purpose of assurance: performance measurement	
Financial ratios	The key stakeholders who are likely to be interested in this type of information are **shareholders**. They are interested in the return that they get from their investment. The sort of **criteria** which they are interested in are therefore likely to be: • Industry averages • Percentages of historic performance
Operational ratios	Shareholders may also be interested in operational ratios. However a party who is more likely to be interested in such information is a **customer**, who demands a quality service. In terms of **criteria**, the customer is going to interested in comparisons with competitors, so **industry averages** are likely to feature again
Value for money	In a profit-targeted company, shareholders might be interested in value for money. However, they are more likely to be interested in the financial indicators above. In a **non profit-targeted** company, value for money can be extremely important. Interested parties might be **trustees** and **donors**. In this case, **criteria** would be **objectives set** within the system.

Question

Value for money audit

(a) Outline the basic principles of value for money auditing.
(b) Give examples of the factors which may be quantified in a VFM investigation.

Answer

(a) VFM audit is also known as performance auditing and effectiveness auditing. Traditionally this focused on the elimination of waste and extravagance but today the role is much wider. VFM auditing is concerned with *economy, efficiency* and *effectiveness*.

Economy is taken to mean the achievement of a given result with the least expenditure of money, manpower or other resources. *Efficiency* extends the idea to that of converting resources into a desired product or service in the most advantageous ratio. *Effectiveness* brings into account the goals and objectives which the activity under audit is intended to meet.

The auditor must assess the effectiveness of activities without questioning the policy decisions made and the objectives they serve. He may give advice on improved management or more effective services but must leave policy decisions to elected councillors, members of Parliament or appointed board members.

The VFM auditors may make use of various 'performance indicators' and comparisons to help him to assess whether the organisation matches up to criteria of economy, efficiency and effectiveness. Do proper arrangements (eg appropriate departmental management information systems) exist for securing economy, efficiency and effectiveness? Are these arrangements operating satisfactorily in practice?

(b) The following are examples of the factors which may be quantified in a VFM investigation.

(i) *Productivity*. Measures of work performed per unit of staff time can be compared at different times. Skilled or professional work is more difficult to measure by this criteria than routine and repetitive tasks. For example, it will be relatively easy to measure the productivity of an invoice processing clerk in terms of the number of invoices processed per hour, but it would be more difficult to apply productivity measures to casework carried out by a social worker.

(ii) *Costs*. Unit costs may be compared over time, or between organisations, or in comparison to budget. Care must be taken in making inter-authority comparisons to ensure that like is being compared with like.

(iii) *Service volume*. An example might be the number of hospital beds provided or the number of operations of a particular type carried out.

(iv) *Public demand*. Waiting lists will provide an indication of potential demand, and trends over time will show whether the organisation is meeting those demands.

(v) *Utilisation of services provided*. Percentages of services may be monitored: a typical example in a hospital, say, is that of bed occupancy rates.

Exam focus point

> Questions on performance indicators in the exam could focus on social and environmental factors, see Chapter 16.

5 Systems reliability

FAST FORWARD

> Reliability of systems of internal control is important for financial statements and general business operation.

5.1 Reliable information

As has been pointed out in Chapter 1, the requirement for assurance services is driven by a requirement for reliable information.

This **information about business is often produced by the systems of a business**. Hence it is a pre-requisite of quality business information that a business has quality systems.

This is not a new concept. A fundamental stage of the traditional **audit** is the **assessment of financial systems** to ensure that they are capable of producing financial statements. The concept can be extended beyond financial statements to all the systems of the business from which information can be derived.

It therefore follows that **anyone interested in information from the business** (that is, any stakeholder) will have an **implied interest in assurance on business systems** and that therefore this is an area which businesses are keen to engage accountants.

Of course, anyone who transacts with a business (customers and suppliers) is also relying on the systems working efficiently enough to complete the transaction so that they get their required product/paid on time.

Business systems fall into two categories; **manual and computerised**. In modern times, computerised systems are increasingly important. This is obviously true in the case of companies that trade electronically, but is also generally true in most companies, as most companies have some computerised systems.

Assurance services in both areas will be considered below.

5.2 Internal control systems

In July 2001, the APB in the UK issued a Briefing Paper on the issue of providing assurance in the effectiveness of internal control. This was issued in the light of previous consultation documents by the APB and publications by IFAC about assurance services.

The briefing paper outlines the **APB's thinking in relation to assurance engagements**. **Internal controls** are an area of particular importance in the UK, having been given prominence by the investigations in to **corporate governance** in the 1990s, notably the **Turnbull report**, which concentrated on the risks facing companies, and the need for directors to manage that risk.

5.2.1 Providing assurance on internal control

The APB draw a clear distinction between two areas of assurance:

- Assurance on the **design** of internal control systems
- Assurance on the **operation** of the internal control system, in accordance with the design

These are two very distinct issues, and the two assignments should be approached very differently.

5.2.2 Process of internal control

The APB recognise the following process in relation to internal controls:

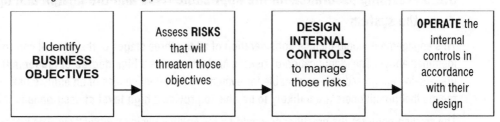

The diagram above also illustrates the points of the process where assurance services can be given:

- Risk identification (see section 2)
- Design of system
- Operation of system

In order to carry out an engagement in relation to the internal controls, the practitioners will require sufficient **knowledge of the business** that they can **identify and understand** the events, transactions and practices which will impact on the system of internal control.

5.2.3 Providing assurance on the operation of the system

The practitioner should establish whether the engagement relates to a period of time or a point of time. The practitioner will only be able to provide a **high level of assurance** on this point if the entity has a detailed description of the design of their system of internal control.

The **report** arising from such an assignment need not be extensive, but is likely to be narrative. This is because practitioners are likely to include such issues as:

- Isolated control failures
- Observation about the abilities of staff involved in operating the system of control
- Potential weaknesses observed which were not contemplated within the design

5.2.4 Providing assurance on the design and operation of the system

In such an engagement practitioners will consider two issues:

- The design of the system in addressing a set of identified risks
- The operation of the system (discussed above)

Such an engagement will involve significant **discussions with management** at the outset, to establish matters such as:

- The desired balance between prevention and detection controls
- The balance between costs and benefits
- The importance of specific control objectives

The outcome of these discussions will necessarily be included in the assurance **report**, to provide a context for their conclusions. The following things will also be included in the report:

- The applicable risks
- Any framework for design used by either the directors or the practitioners
- A description of the design of the system of internal control.

The **level of assurance** given by the practitioners will **depend on several factors**, including the nature of the entity, the knowledge of the business the practitioner possesses and the scope of the engagement. It is likely that the report in this instance would be quite long.

5.2.5 Providing assurance on the applicable risks and the design and operation of the system

This engagement would include consideration of all the three stages of the internal controls process identified above. The identification of risks is likely to involve a **high degree of judgement** as there are no universally recognised criteria suitable for evaluating the effectiveness of an entity's risk evaluation. This means that practitioners are **unlikely to be** able to provide a **high level of assurance** in this area.

The starting point for the practitioner would be the entity's business objectives. The key considerations will include:

- The completeness of the applicable identified risks
- The probability of a risk crystallising
- The materiality of the likely impact of the risk
- The time period over which crystallisation is anticipated

In their **report**, the practitioners would have to outline the business objectives of the entity, a description of the risk identification process and the applicable risks.

5.2.6 Inherent limitations

Internal control systems have inherent limitations, a key one of which is the chance of staff colluding in fraud to override the system. **Any assurance report on internal controls** systems should **include a mention of these inherent limitations**, in order to prevent an unnecessary expectations gap.

5.2.7 Reports

The nature of the individual reports has been touched on above. The discussion paper also includes an example report. However, as the APB make the key point that it is difficult to issue a standard report for assurance services, which are largely dependent on the scope and nature of the individual assignment, this has not been reproduced here.

5.3 Computer systems

A huge number of businesses now use computer systems to run their businesses, and financial information is processed on a computer system.

This means that a number of the controls which the directors are required to put into place to safeguard the assets of the shareholders are incorporated into computer systems.

You learnt about building controls into a computer system in your earlier studies.

It is possible to build controls into computerised processing. A balance must be struck between the degree of control and the requirement for a user friendly system.

Controls can be classified into:

- Security controls
- Integrity controls
- Contingency controls

Integrity controls can be subdivided into two areas:

- Data integrity is preserved when data is the same as it is in source documents and has not been accidentally or intentionally altered, destroyed or disclosed.
- Systems integrity refers to system operation conforming to the design specification despite attempts (deliberate or accidental) to make it behave incorrectly.

When auditors undertake their assessment and testing of controls for the purposes of the statutory audit, they focus on the general and application controls of the system, which relate to security and policies for data input.

In other words, when undertaking the work for the statutory audit, the auditor is interested in the data integrity, as it is the data which is incorporated into the financial statements.

However, it is also important to stakeholders in the company that the system used, which will often impact on operation as well as financial information operates reliably and that risks are mitigated against.

The **two key risks** are:

- The system being put at risk by a virus or some other fault or breakdown which spreads across the system

- The system being invaded by an unauthorised user who could then

    - Affect the smooth operation of the system
    - Obtain commercial sensitive information

The client is likely to have contingency plans in the event of the system being affected by the risks outlined above. However, it is also important to know that the original system is as reliable as could be expected, and whether it is the best system that the company could be using, at the given cost.

The company might seek such assurances from its service provider. However, the service provider has a vested interest in the company believing that its system is reliable and the best available, because he is paid to supply it.

This means that the directors might seek an assurance service from its auditors or another firm of accountants, to undertake work to ascertain if the assertions of the service provider are correct.

If a firm of accountants were to consider taking on such an assurance engagement, they should ensure that they had sufficient skill to undertake the procedures required to ascertain if the assurances were correct. They would have to ensure that they had an IT specialist on the team.

Internal control effectiveness is generally assessed by means of undertaking a systems audit.

5.3.1 Systems audit

You have studied systems audits extensively in your previous auditing studies. As part of any audit, auditors assess the quality and effectiveness of the accounting system. Increasingly, this necessarily includes a consideration of computer systems.

Auditors could accept an assurance engagement to undertake this task outside of the audit and to report specifically on findings. The following are the key areas they are likely to concentrate on to establish how reliable the systems are:

- Management policy
- Segregation of duties
- Security

You should be aware that these are important control considerations in a computer environment. The details that the reporting accountant will consider are outlined below.

Management policy

- Does management have a written statement of policy with regard to computer systems?
- Is it compatible with management policy in other areas?
- Is it adhered to?
- Is it sufficient and effective?
- Is it updated when the systems are updated?
- Does it relate to the current system?

Segregation of duties

- Is there adequate segregation of duties with regard to data input?
- Are there adequate system controls (eg passwords) to enforce segregation of duties?

Security

- Is there a security policy in place:

  - Physical security (locked doors/windows)
  - Access security (passwords
  - Data security (virus shields)

- Is it adhered to?

- Is it sufficient and effective?

5.4 Reporting

It is vital that **management** receive information on the effectiveness of their controls systems and systems reliability generally. This is because, as stated earlier, the operations of the company are likely to rely heavily if not completely on computer systems, and if problems arise, operations could be severely affected.

Problems could arise in terms of:

- No production being possible
- No invoicing being possible
- Invoicing being duplicated or omitted

Other stakeholders, such as customers and suppliers, will also be interested in the reliability of the company's systems, as they will not want to deal with a company who makes mistakes and cannot operate properly.

It is because of the vital importance of this area to business that management may also want to obtain assurance concerning the information it receives on systems reliability.

5.5 Continuous auditing

5.5.1 The demand for information

The traditional model of statutory audit is based on the assumption that the audit report adds credibility to the financial statements. Two significant limitations to the usefulness of this audited information are:

- It is produced only once a year at a specific point in time, and

- There is a long delay between the end of the accounting period and the release of audited information.

In the context of external audit there is an increasing demand for more current disclosure of financial information, and an external audit opinion would add to the credibility of that information.

In the context of internal audit, management's decision-making could be greatly enhanced by real-time internal audit on the functioning of controls and transactions.

5.5.2 Continuous auditing: a definition

There is no universally agreed definition of continuous auditing. Many articles quote a definition from a joint research report by the Canadian Institute of Chartered Accountants (CICA) and the American Institute of Certified Public Accountants (AICPA)

> "A methodology that enables independent auditors to provide written assurance on a subject matter using a series of auditors' reports issued simultaneously with, or a short period of time after, the occurrence of events underlying the subject matter."

Although much research has been done on continuous auditing, its actual use is not yet widespread. From the external audit perspective it is not clear that the benefits would outweigh the costs. Clearly the cost of issuing an audit report on a full set of financial statements each week, month or quarter would be prohibitive. On the other hand, there could be benefits from audit reports covering only specific types of data, such as perhaps, monthly sales information.

5.5.3 Developments

Continuous auditing relies heavily on information technology, and rapid advances in technology make its use more feasible.

> Example
>
> A continuing audit procedure might be designed to identify sales falling outside certain specified parameters. This might trigger an e-mail to the auditor and potentially some other action, such as sending a confirmation request to the customer.

These procedures could be used by both internal and external auditors

5.5.4 Advantages and disadvantages

Advantages

- Overcomes the delays of the traditional audit model
- Can easily allow 100% testing in respect of controls
- Allows management to address control weaknesses more promptly

Disadvantages

- May require significant investment in technology
- Training costs
- Management may be reluctant to allow external auditors the necessary amount of access to their systems.

6 Electronic commerce

E-commerce is a fast-growing area of business.

6.1 Engaging in e-commerce

Key terms

The Internet is a global network connecting millions of computers.

The World Wide Web (WWW) is a system of Internet servers that support specially formatted documents. A group of documents accessed from the same base web site is known as a website.

Electronic data interchange (EDI) is a form of computer to computer data transfer. Information can be transferred in electronic form, avoiding the need for the information to be re-inputted somewhere else.

Electronic mail (e-mail) is a system of communicating with other connected computers or via the internet in written form.

Electronic commerce (e-commerce) means conducting business electronically via a communications link.

The items described above are all now commonly used in business. You are probably familiar with most, if not all of them.

All the items discussed above are (or can be) used in e-commerce. As this is an exceedingly fast growing area of business, it is a very important area for everyone, including accountants, today. You should be familiar with the idea of e-commerce from your previous studies.

A business can engage in 'e-commerce' to a great or small degree. The greater the involvement, the more the risk associated with the involvement. The extent of involvement is explored in the following table.

INVOLVEMENT	RISK
Information provision: A website can be used as a marketing device, to provide information to potential customers, and to enable them to request further information through an email link.	LOW
Transactions with existing customers. Existing customers can be given the opportunity to track current contracts or initiate others over the website.	
Access to new customers. A website can be used as a place where new customers may initiate transactions with the company.	
New business model. A website can be used to diversify into specific web-based products, for example, items that are 'downloadable'	HIGH

There are a variety of **business risks** specific to a company involved in e-commerce, which will exist to a greater or lesser degree depending on the extent of involvement. These have been touched on in Chapter 8 in relation to how they affect financial statements.

- Risk of **non-compliance** with law, issues of where the domain is for legal purposes
- **Contractual issues** arising: are legally binding agreements formed over the Internet?
- Risk of **technological failure** (crashes) resulting in **business interruption**

- Difficulties in determining **accounting policies** (particularly relating to revenue)
- Impact of technology on **going concern assumption**, extent of risk of business failure
- **Security** risks

Many of these issues have implications for the **statutory audit**, and these have been referred to, where relevant, elsewhere in this Study Text. For the purposes of **assurance services**, two key, inter-related issues arise. These are internal controls and systems.

6.2 Internal controls

The question of internal controls and systems reliability was covered in section 5. Obviously a company engaging in e-commerce, reliability of computer systems is going to be an important area, and once which most stakeholders will be interested in.

In particular, controls over **transaction integrity** will be of great importance, as the system will capture transactions and automatically process them. It is also important that the transaction is **processed completely** through the accounting system. The website may not be integrated completely with the underlying accounting system.

Hence the assurance services over the **design and operation of systems** (particularly computerised in this instance) will be of great importance.

6.3 Security

The issue of security in e-commerce is extremely important. It is **important for the business**, as there is a more substantial risk of a **fraud** being perpetrated against the company if transactions are carried out through the website rather than in person. It is important for the **customer**, particularly a **private consumer**, who is **inputting sensitive personal data**.

6.3.1 Lack of trust

A key problem with e-commerce is one of **trust**. In most cultures, consumers grant their trust to business parties that have a close **physical presence**: buildings, facilities and people to talk to. On the Internet these familiar elements are simply not there. The seller's reputation, the size of his business, and the level of customisation in product and service also engender trust.

Internet merchants need to elicit consumer trust when the level of **perceived risk** in a transaction is high. However, research has found that once consumers have built up trust in an Internet merchant such concerns are reduced.

Internet merchants need to address issues such as fear of **invasion of privacy** and abuse of customer information (about their **credit cards**, for example) because they stop people even considering the Internet as a shopping medium.

The parties involved in e-commerce need to have confidence that any communication sent gets to its target destination **unchanged**, and **without being read by anyone else.**

6.4 Web assurance

It has been a feature of electronic commerce that people seem to be happy to browse on line, but less happy to make purchases, due to a lack of knowledge about the company they were dealing with. This led to concerns about

- Processing of the transaction
- Use of the personal information that must be given to complete the sale
- Poor business practices by the company (late delivery/errors in order etc)

Web assurance seeks to remove this barrier by providing assurance to the users of the service. An example of an assurance service developed in relation to e-commerce is WebTrust.

An assurance assignment under WebTrust would involve looking at the assertions of the company relating to the concerns above, and seeking evidence as to whether what they say about their service is true, and whether their systems comply with pre-determined criteria.

The outcome of the exercise is that if the accountant has assurance that the systems comply and the representations made about the service is fair, the Website can be WebTrust accredited.

Exam focus point

In April 2002 the previous examiner wrote an article in the *Student Accountant*, "e-com, 'e-saw, 'e-audit'. This outlines the issues discussed in international guidance relating to e-commerce and the **audit**. It is not designed to give guidance on assurance engagements relating to a business's Internet activities. However, the issue relating to **controls** are relevant in the context of providing assurance on systems.

You should ensure that you read this article and bear in mind that in the exam, a case study or other question could set auditing in an e-commerce situation. You should also think through the issues arising in relation to controls and systems and their implications for assurance services.

Question
Performance review

S plc, a listed company, operates 740 supermarket stores selling food and other household supplies.

There is considerable competition between supermarkets, especially when too many supermarkets attempt to operate in an area in relation to the potential number of customers, or when a local or national price war develops from one operator attempting to gain market share.

Control and performance evaluation within S plc are primarily exercised by:

- Review of league tables of profitability
- Review of key ratios and indicators.

Budgets are used, but are relatively less important as predictable change year-on-year is relatively small. Sales growth for comparable stores that are unaffected by changes in the local competitive situation, is at best 3% excluding inflation. Cost control permits only limited local managerial discretion.

In view of the acute competition the directors have identified a need to review the systems and criteria used for control and performance evaluation, and the possibility of improving these systems.

As part of the review, you have been asked to analyse the data shown for stores A, B and C, which are broadly similar stores in the southern region, using your analysis to illustrate your view on possible system improvements.

Summary data for S plc for the year to 31 December 20X8 are given below.

Required

(a)   Comment on the performance of stores A, B and C, using the available information.

(b)   Explain, with reasons, which key ratios you would recommend be used for operational control and performance valuation of existing stores.

SUMMARY DATA FOR S PLC FOR YEAR TO 31 DECEMBER 20X8

	Store A	Store B	Store C	Group (Total of 740 stores)
Floor area (square metres)	1,200	1,000	1,100	630,000
Number of employees	72	70	67	35,700
	£'000	£'000	£'000	£'000
Revenue	7,680	7,200	7,370	3,849,000
Gross profit	1,698	1,744	1,738	862,000
Labour	917	907	886	434,000
Other costs	731	647	692	328,000
Total costs	1,648	1,554	1,578	762,000
Net profit	50	190	160	100,000
Note. Gross profit is calculated after wastage				
Gross profit pre wastage	24.4%	25.6%	25.5%	24.2%
Wastage	2.3%	1.4%	1.9%	1.8%
Gross profit	22.1%	24.2%	23.6%	22.4%

SIMPLIFIED CAPITAL EMPLOYED IN S PLC SUPERMARKETS AT 31 DECEMBER 20X8

	Store A	Store B	Store C	Group
	£'000	£'000	£'000	£'000
Stock	324	329	343	170,000
less: Creditors	(1,241)	(1,164)	(1,191)	(622,000)
Fixed assets	720	940	1,122	548,000
Net assets	(197)	105	274	96,000

There are no significant debtors.

Year to 31 December 20X7

	Store A	Store B	Store C	Group
	£'000s	£'000s	£'000s	£'000s
Sales	8,320	6,963	7,038	3,739,000
Gross profit	1,947	1,693	1,655	841,000
Net profit	317	232	152	114,000

Answer

(a) Set out below is a commentary on the performance of stores A, B and C. Key ratios are shown in appendix A.

Store A

Store A seems to be **suffering** more than stores B and C from the highly competitive environment in which the group operates, with **revenue down** 7.7% from the previous year and profits having fallen dramatically from £317,000 to £50,000.

Compared with an above average net profit margin of 3.8% in 20X7, the **current year's profit margin** of 0.7% is particularly **disappointing**. A significant contributor to this is the **cost of wastage** – at 2.3% of sales this is almost 28% higher than the average for the group. Combined with an **above average cost base** in terms of both labour and other costs, store A has succeeded in achieving only disappointing levels of profitability.

Although **revenue per square metre** for all three stores is significantly higher than the group average, store A's figure of £6,400 is surprisingly low given that all three stores are in the same region.

There were some **positive aspects** to store A's performance. **Stock turnover**, at 18.46 times, was comfortably above the group average of 17.57 and **fixed asset turnover** (10.67 times) was well above the group average of 7.02.

Given that all three stores are in the same region and given that store A has the greatest floor space and the lowest level of fixed assets (£720,000 compared to £1,122,000 in store C, which is 100 square metres smaller), it is likely that the store **A is operating with older fixtures and fittings**. This may be worth investigating: a refit of the store may halt the decline in sales and newer, more efficient refrigeration and racking systems may improve performance in wastage and other costs such as power.

The low non-current asset base is a major contributory factor to store A having **net liabilities** of £197,000. Although this is hardly a problem given the group's net assets of £96,000,000, the store's management may wish to reflect on the fact that their **suppliers** wait an average of only 75.72 days for payment compared with the 77.87 days which store B's suppliers wait.

Store B

Store B has managed a 3.4% **increase in year-on-year sales**, which is creditable given that sales growth is 'at best 3%, excluding inflation'. This excellent sales growth has led to **higher than average gross profit margins both before and after waste**.

The **net profit margin**, at 2.6%, matches the average earned by the group. This is disappointing given the higher than average gross margin. The main **factor holding back the net profit margin is labour related**. Although **revenue per square metre** is the **highest** of the three stores, **revenue per employee**, at £102,857, is almost 5% **lower** than the average for the group. As well as this apparent inefficiency, **labour costs** (at 12.6% of turnover) are well above the group average of 11.3% and it would be sensible for management to carry out an investigation into this level of labour costs.

The store's **working capital management** figures are in line with group average figures. **Additional inventory days appear to be financed by additional creditor days**, while the fixed asset revenue at 7.66 times is 9% higher than the figure for the average store.

Were management to exercise some control over labour costs and efficiency levels, store B's excellent revenue per square metre and strong gross margins would generate a much more creditable return.

Store C

Like store B, store C has **managed to reverse the group's declining profit** and post an increase in **net profits for the year**. Profits are up from £152,000 to £160,000, an increase of 5.3% and there has been an excellent **increase in revenue** of 4.7%.

Revenue per square metre is comfortably above the group average and **staff efficiency is good**, the 67 employees generating an average of £110,000 each compared to a group average of £107,815.

Like both other stores in the region, **staff costs** (at 12%) are above the group average of 11.3%. Store C also needs to **improve controls over other costs**, as at 9.4% of sales these are substantially in excess of the group average of 8.5% and this is a major contributing factor to the store's disappointing profit margin of 2.2%.

The net assets of store C are much higher than those of the other two stores and the group average. Consequently the stock days and fixed asset turnover figures are particularly poor.

(b)   **Key ratios**

For operational control and performance evaluation purposes of existing stores, the following key ratios could be used.

- **Gross profit margin (before wastage)**. Given both the narrow margins within which S plc operates and what is likely to be limited opportunity for cost control in other areas, this is a key determinant of success. It provides a measure of the effectiveness of the purchasing function and the ability of the store management to pass onto customers increases in purchase prices.

- **Wastage.** This is one of the major areas over which store managers should have direct control and which has a direct and substantial impact on S plc's tight profit margins.

- **Sales growth**. Given the highly competitive nature of the supermarket business and the speed of new store openings, this is a key measure of S plc's on-going competitive success.

- **Revenue per square metre.** This is another key determinant of success for the retail trade and measures the effectiveness of the way in which space is utilised within the store. It is worth noting that store B has both the highest profit margin and revenue per square metre.

- **Revenue per employee**. Hourly pay rates can be set as a matter of group policy and so it is the efficiency of labour which managers can and must control.

- **Net profit margin**. Whilst there is little discretion for cost control on the part of managers, this measure of a store's overall profitability should be included as part of performance evaluation to ensure that managers do still pay some attention to the control of costs

- **Stock in days.** This measure must be carefully monitored as it indicates how well a store is balancing customer needs with effective warehousing.

- **Growth in revenue and net profit.** This measure assesses store management's ability to meet customer needs.

- **Price of key products compared to competitors**. The prices of staple products (milk, bread, butter and so on) should be compared to those of S plc's rivals to ensure that local and national price wars have been responded to sufficiently and adequately.

- **Supplier deliveries on time as a proportion of total deliveries.** Stores must maintain low levels of stock but stockouts must be avoided to ensure high levels of customer satisfaction.

- **Actual customers as a proportion of total customers.** A measure of market share enjoyed by a store is a vital indicator of the effectiveness of a store's policies.

Operational control will be most helped by **a range of financial and non-financial indicators**, possibly based on the **balanced scorecard approach** and hence covering its four perspectives. Those ratios which can be **controlled by store management** are of particular relevance.

The key ratios below (in appendix A) could be **compared over time within each store and with the group average**, as well as **benchmarking** them against best practices in other stores.

Particular attention should be paid to the medium- to long-term movement in sales growth and net profit margin, other ratios being useful indicators of areas of operations that could affect the long-term profitability of a store.

Appendix A

	Store A		Store B		Store C		Group
	20X8	20X7	20X8	20X7	2098	20X7	20X8
Gross profit % (before waste)	24.4%		25.6%		25.5%		24.2%
Gross profit % (after waste)	22.1%	23.4%	24.2%	24.3%	23.6%	23.5%	22.4%
Net profit %	0.7%	3.8%	2.6%	3.3%	2.2%	2.2%	2.6%
Revenue increase/(decrease)	(7.7%)		3.4%		4.7%		2.9%
Net profit increase/(decrease)	(84.2%)		(18.1%)		5.3%		(12.3%)
Revenue per sq metre	£6,400		£7,200		£6,700		£6,110
Revenue per employee	£106,667		£102,857		£110,000		£107,815
Labour costs as % of sales	11.9%		12.6%		12.0%		11.3%
Other costs as % of sales	9.5%		9.0%		9.4%		8.5%
Stock turnover	18.46		16.58		16.42		17.57
Fixed asset turnover	10.67		7.66		6.57		7.02
Creditor days	75.72		77.87		77.19		76.01
Stock days	19.77		22.00		22.23		20.77

Chapter Roundup

- Audit related services may be assurance services (reviews) or not (agreed upon procedures and compilations).

- Assurance services improve the quality of decision making for users of information.

- Assurance engagements may give reasonable assurance or limited assurance.

- Assurance engagements should only be accepted if the firm meet the requirements of the Code of Ethics and ISQC 1 with regard to the assignment.

- Risk assessment is important to investors and managers and therefore is an important area for assurance services.

- Performance measurement is another important issue for companies where assurance can be given.

- Reliability of systems of internal control is important for financial statements and general business operation.

- E-commerce is a fast-growing area of business.

Quick Quiz

1   Name the three types of engagement which comprise audit-related services.

        (1)   ....

        (2)   ....

        (3)   ....

2   Link the review assignment with its description.

        (a)   Attestation engagement

        (b)   Direct reporting engagement

                (i)   The accountant is required to confirm whether:

                        •   Accounting policies are consistent with those in prior year financial statements
                        •   Any material modifications to the presented information are required.

                (ii)   The accountant is required to conduct a review and report on issues arising.

3   In an assurance engagement, the responsible party can also be an intended user.

        A   Never
        B   If there is more than one intended user
        C   If there are more than ten intended users
        D   In exceptional circumstances

4   When carrying out an assurance engagement the practitioner must assess the appropriateness of the subject matter and the criteria.

        True   ☐

        False   ☐

5   The assurance report should be in writing.

        True   ☐

        False   ☐

6   What three concerns does WebTrust seek to allay?

        (1)   ....

        (2)   ....

        (3)   ....

Answers to Quick Quiz

1   Review assignments, agreed-upon procedures assignments and compilation assignments.

2   (a)(i)
     (b)(ii)

3   B

4   True

5   True

6   (1)   The processing of the transaction
     (2)   The security of personal data entered onto the website
     (3)   The past practices of the business

Number	Level	Marks	Time
Q20	Examination	20	36 mins

Now try the question below from the Exam Question Bank

13

Prospective financial information

Topic list	Syllabus reference
1 Reporting on prospective financial information	D5
2 Accepting an engagement	D5
3 Procedures	D5
4 Expressing an opinion	D5

Introduction

Reporting on prospective financial information is covered by ISAE 3400 *The examination of prospective financial information*.

Forecasts are of significant interest to users. Some would say that PFI is of more interest to users of accounts than historic information (HFI), which of course, auditors do report on in the statutory audit.

This is an area in which the **auditors can therefore provide an alternative service to audit, in the form of a review or assurance engagement.** This chapter therefore looks at the considerations that the auditor should consider when taking on such an engagement. The basis for this chapter has been laid in Chapter 12, but in this chapter, we consider issues specific to PFI.

Study guide

		Intellectual level
D5	**Prospective financial information**	
(a)	Define 'prospective financial information' (PFI) and distinguish between a 'forecast', a 'projection', a 'hypothetical illustration' and a 'target'.	1
(b)	Explain the principles of useful PFI.	1
(c)	Identify and describe the matters to be considered before accepting a specified engagement to report to PFI.	2
(d)	Discuss the level of assurance that the auditor may provide and explain the other factors to be considered in determining the nature, timing and extent of examination procedures.	1
(e)	Describe examination procedures to verify forecasts and projections relating to:	2
(i)	revenue	
(ii)	capital expenditure	
(iii)	revenue expenditure	
(iv)	profits	
(v)	cash flows	
(vi)	working capital	
(f)	Compare the content of a report on an examination of PFI with reports made in providing auti-related services.	2

Exam guide

The difficulties of reporting on PFI could be examined. Case studies can easily be set in the context of a PFI assignment.

1 Reporting on prospective financial information

FAST FORWARD

Prospective financial information is difficult to give assurance about because it is highly subjective.

Key term

Prospective financial information is information based on assumptions about events that may occur in the future and possible actions by an entity.

From the definition given above, you can see that prospective financial information is highly subjective. This makes it a difficult area to examine and report on. Guidance on reporting on PFI is given in ISAE 3400 *The examination of prospective financial information.*

The key issues that projections relate to are:

- Capital expenditure
- Profits
- Cashflows

These are the key areas which we will focus on in the procedures part of this chapter.

1.1 Principles of prospective financial information

Increasingly, company directors are producing prospective financial information (PFI), either voluntarily or because it is required by regulators, for example, in the case of a public offering of shares.

Markets and investors need PFI that is understandable, relevant, reliable and comparable. Some specific issues arise in applying these principles to PFI.

Understandable	Disclosure is required of **sources of uncertainty**, **assumptions** made, **determining factors** that will affect whether the assumptions will be borne out, and **alternative outcomes**.
Relevant	No PFI-specific issues arise other than the need for the information to be relevant to the **decision-making** of investors or other users of the information
Reliable	The reliability of PFI **cannot be confirmed** by evidence of past transactions or events. Its reliability depends on it being supported by analysis of the entity's business, strategies and plans.
Comparable	The PFI should be **capable of comparison** with eventual outcomes in the form of historical financial information. The **accounting policies** used in its preparation should also be disclosed.

1.2 Types of prospective financial information

Prospective financial information can be of two types (or a combination of both):

A forecast: Prospective financial information based on assumptions as to future events which management expects to take place and the actions management expects to take (best-estimate assumptions).

A projection: Prospective financial information based on hypothetical assumptions about future events and management actions, or a mixture of best-estimate and hypothetical assumptions.

There are two other terms commonly associated with prospective financial information:

A Hypothetical Illustration: Prospective financial information based on assumptions about uncertain future events and management actions which have not yet been decided on.

A Target: Prospective financial information based on assumptions about the future performance of the entity.

2 Accepting an engagement

FAST FORWARD

The auditor should agree the terms of the engagement with the directors, and should withdraw from the engagement if the assumptions made to put together the PFI are unrealistic.

2.1 General engagement

The ISAE gives the following guidance about accepting an engagement to examine PFI.

> **ISAE 3400.11**
>
> The auditor should not accept, or should withdraw from, an engagement when the assumptions are clearly unrealistic or when the auditor believes that the prospective financial information will be inappropriate for its intended use.

> **ISAE 3000.12**
>
> The auditor and the client should agree on the terms of the engagement.

The ISA also lists the following **factors** which the auditor should consider:

- The **intended use** of the information

- Whether the information will be for general or limited **distribution**

- The **nature of the assumptions**, that is, whether they are best estimate or hypothetical assumptions

- The **elements** to be **included** in the information

- The **period covered** by the information

It also states that the auditor should have sufficient knowledge of the business to be able to evaluate the significant assumptions made.

A firm must also consider practical matters, such as the time available to them, their experience of the staff member compiling the information, any limitations on their work, the degree of secrecy required beyond the normal duty of confidentiality.

3 Procedures

FAST FORWARD

Procedures could include:

- Analytical review (against similar historic projects)
- Verification of projected expenditure to quotes or estimates

3.1 General matters

In carrying out their review, the general matters to which attention should be directed are:

- The nature and background of the company's business
- The accounting policies normally followed by the company
- The assumptions on which the forecast is based
- The procedures followed by the company in preparing the forecast.

3.1.1 The nature and background of the company's business

The accountants will review the company's character and recent history, with reference to such matters as the nature of its activities and its main products, markets, customers, suppliers, divisions, locations, and trend of results.

3.1.2 The accounting policies normally followed by the company

The accountant will wish to establish the accounting principles normally followed by the company and ensure that they have been consistently applied in the preparation of forecasts.

3.1.3 The procedure followed by the company in preparing the forecast

In carrying out their review of the accounting bases and calculations for forecasts, and the procedures followed by the company for preparing them, the main points which the reporting accountants will wish to consider include the following:

(a) Whether the forecast under review is based on forecasts regularly prepared for the purpose of management or whether it has been separately and specially prepared for the immediate purpose.

(b) Where forecasts are regularly prepared for management purposes, the degree of accuracy and reliability previously achieved, and the frequency and thoroughness with which estimates are revised.

(c) Whether the forecast under review represents the management's best estimate of results which they reasonably believe can and will be achieved as distinct from targets which the management have set as desirable.

(d) The extent to which forecast results for expired periods are supported by reliable interim accounts.

(e) The details of the procedures followed to generate the forecast and the extent to which it is built up from detailed forecasts of activity and cash flow.

(f) The extent to which profits are derived from activities having a proved and consistent trend and those of a more irregular, volatile or unproved nature.

(g) How the forecast takes account of any material extraordinary items and prior year adjustments, their nature, and how they are presented.

(h) Whether adequate provision is made for foreseeable losses and contingencies and how the forecast takes account of factors which may cause it to be subject to a high degree of risk, or which may invalidate the assumptions.

(i) Whether working capital appears adequate for requirements; (normally this would require the availability of properly prepared cash-flow forecasts) and where short-term or long-term finance is to be relied on, whether the necessary arrangements have been made and confirmed.

(j) The arithmetical accuracy of the forecast and the supporting information and whether forecast balance sheets and sources and applications of funds statements have been prepared as these help to highlight arithmetical inaccuracies and inconsistent assumptions.

ISAE 3400.17

When determining the nature, timing and extent of examination procedures, the auditor's considerations should include:

(a) the likelihood of material misstatement;

(b) the knowledge obtained during any previous engagement;

(c) management's competence regarding the preparation of prospective financial information;

(d) the extent to which the prospective financial information is affected by the management's judgement; and

(e) the adequacy and the reliability of the underlying data

The ISAE goes on to say that the auditor should **seek appropriate evidence** on those areas which are **particularly sensitive to variation** and have a **material effect** in the information.

3.2 Specific matters

The following list of procedures are procedures which may also be relevant when assessing prospective financial information. The auditor should undertake the review procedures discussed above in addition to these.

Profit forecasts

- Verify projected **income** figures to suitable evidence. This may involve:

    - Comparison of the basis of projected income to similar existing projects in the firm

    - Review of current market prices for that product or service, that is, what competitors in the market charge successfully

- Verify projected **expenditure** figures to suitable evidence. There is likely to be more evidence available about expenditure in the form of:

    - Quotations or estimates provided to the firm
    - Current bills for things such as services which can be used to reliably estimate
    - Market rate prices, for example, for advertising
    - Interest rate assumptions can be compared to the bank's current rates
    - Costs such as depreciation should correspond with relevant capital expenditure projections

Capital expenditure

The auditor should check the capital expenditure for **reasonableness**. For example, if the projection relates to buying land and developing it, it should include a sum for land.

- Projected costs should be **verified to estimates and quotations** where possible

- The projections can be reviewed for **reasonableness**, including a comparison prevailing **market rates** where such information is available (such as for property)

Cash forecasts

- The auditors should review cash forecasts to ensure the **timings involved** are **reasonable** (for example, it is not reasonable to say the building will be bought on day 1, as property transactions usually take longer than that).

- The auditor should check the cash forecast for **consistency with the any profit forecasts** (income/expenditure should be the same, just at different times)

- If there is no comparable profit forecast, the income and expenditure items should be verified as they would have been on a profit forecast.

Exam focus point

When faced with a PFI question in the exam it is important to tailor your answer to the facts given in the question. For example, don't say 'verify projected building costs to builders' quote' if the question states no quote has been obtained.

4 Expressing an opinion

FAST FORWARD

It is impossible to give the same level of assurance about PFI as it is on historical financial information but negative assurance may be given.

4.1 Level of assurance

It is clear that as prospective financial information is subjective information, it is **impossible** for an auditor **to give the same level of assurance** regarding it, as he would on **historic financial information**.

The ISAE suggests that the auditor express an opinion including

- A statement of **negative assurance** that as to whether the **assumptions** provide a reasonable basis for the prospective financial information

- An opinion as to whether the prospective financial information is **properly prepared** on the basis of the assumptions and the relevant reporting framework

- Appropriate **caveats as to the achievability** of the forecasts.

Key term

> **Negative assurance** is assurance of something in the absence of any evidence arising to the contrary. In effect, this means the auditor is saying, 'I believe that this is reasonable because I have no reason to believe otherwise.'

4.2 Report under ISAE 3400

ISAE 3400.27

The report by an auditor on an examination of prospective financial information should contain the following:

(a)   title;

(b)   addressee;

(c)   identification of the prospective financial information;

(d)   a reference to the ISAE or relevant national standards or practices applicable to the examination of prospective financial information;

(e)   a statement that management is responsible for the prospective financial information including the assumptions on which it is based;

(f)   when applicable, a reference to the purpose and/or restricted distribution of the prospective financial information;

(g)   a statement of negative assurance as to whether the assumptions provide a reasonable basis for the prospective financial information.

(h)   an opinion as to whether the prospective financial information is properly prepared on the basis of the assumptions and is presented in accordance with the relevant financial reporting framework;

(i)   appropriate caveats concerning the achievability of the results indicated by the prospective financial information;

(j)   date of the report which should be the date procedures have been completed;

(k)   auditor's address

(l)   signature

ISAE 3400.31

When the auditor believes that the presentation and disclosure of the prospective financial information is not adequate, the auditor should express a qualified or adverse opinion in the report on the prospective financial information, or withdraw from the engagement as appropriate.

ISAE 3400.32

When the auditor believes that one or more significant assumptions do not provide a reasonable basis for the prospective financial information prepared on the basis of best-estimate assumptions or that one or more significant assumptions do not provide a reasonable basis for the prospective financial information given the hypothetical assumptions, the auditor should either express an adverse opinion in the report on the prospective financial information or withdraw from the engagement.

Question

A new client of your practice, Peter Lawrence, has recently been made redundant. He is considering setting up a residential home for old people as he is aware that there is an increasing need for this service with an ageing population (more people are living to an older age). He has seen a large house, which he plans to convert into an old people's home. Each resident will have a bedroom, there will be a communal sitting-room and all meals will be provided in a dining-room. No long-term nursing care will be provided, as people requiring this service will either be in hospital or in another type of accommodation for old people.

The large house is in a poor state of repair, and will require considerable structural alterations (building work), and repairs to make it suitable for an old people's home. The following will also be required:

- New furnishings (carpets, beds, wardrobes and so on for the resident's rooms; carpets and furniture for the sitting-room and dining-room)

- Decoration of the whole house (painting the woodwork and covering the walls with wallpaper)

- Equipment (for the kitchen and for helping disabled residents)

Mr Lawrence and his wife propose to work full-time in the business, which he expects to be available for residents six months after the purchase of the house. Mr Lawrence has already obtained some estimates of the conversion costs, and information on the income and expected running costs of the home.

Mr Lawrence has received about £30,000 from his redundancy. He expects to receive about £30,000 from the sale of his house (after repaying his mortgage). The owners of the house he proposes to buy are asking £50,000 for it, and Mr Lawrence expects to spend £50,000 on conversion on the house (building work, furnishing, decorations and equipment).

Mr Lawrence has prepared a draft capital expenditure forecast, a profit forecast and a cash flow forecast which he has asked you to check before he submits them to the bank, in order to obtain finance for the old people's home.

Required

Describe the procedures you would carry out on:

(a)   The capital expenditure forecast
(b)   The profit forecast
(c)   The cash flow forecast

Answer

All three of the forecasts to be reviewed should be prepared on a monthly basis and the following work would be required in order to consider their reasonableness.

(a)   **Capital expenditure forecast**

(i)   Read estate agent's details and solicitors' correspondence and compare to the capital expenditure forecast to ensure that all expenditure (including sale price, surveyors' fees, legal costs, taxes on purchase) is included.

(ii)   Confirm the estimated cost of new furnishings by agreeing them to supplier price lists or quotations.

(iii)   Verify any discounts assumed in the forecast are correct by asking the suppliers if they will apply to this transaction.

(iv)   Confirm projected building and decoration costs to the relevant suppliers' quotation.

(v)   Confirm the projected cost of specialist equipment (and relevant bulk discounts) to suppliers' price lists or websites.

(vi)   In the light of my experience of other such ventures, consider whether the forecast includes all relevant costs.

(b)   **Profit forecast**

As a first step it will be necessary to recognise that the residential home will not be able to generate any income until the bulk of the capital expenditure has been incurred in order to make the home 'habitable'. However, whilst no income can be anticipated the business will have started to incur expenditure in the form of loan interest, rates and insurance.

The only income from the new building will be rent receivable from residents. The rentals which Mr Lawrence is proposing to charge should be assessed for reasonableness in the light of rental charged to similar homes in the same area. In projecting income it would be necessary to anticipate that it is likely to take some time before the home could anticipate full occupancy and also it would perhaps be prudent to allow for some periods where vacancies arise because of the 'loss' of some of the established residents.

The expenditure of the business is likely to include the following.

(i)   **Wages and salaries.** Although Mr and Mrs Lawrence intend to work full-time in the business, they will undoubtedly need to employ additional staff to care for residents, cook, clean and tend to the gardens. The numbers of staff and the rates of pay should be compared to similar local businesses of which the firm has knowledge.

(ii)   **Rates and water rates.** The estimate of the likely cost of these confirmed by asking the local council and/or the estate agents dealing with the sale of property.

(iii) **Food.** The estimate of the expenditure for food should be based in the projected levels of staff and residents, with some provision for wastage.

(iv)   **Heat and light.** The estimates for heat, light and cooking facilities should be compared to similar clients' actual bills.

(v)   **Insurance.** This cost should be verified to quotes from the insurance broker.

(vi)   **Advertising.** The costs of newspaper and brochure advertising costs should be checked against quotes obtained by Mr Lawrence.

(vii) **Repairs and renewals.** Adequate provision should be made for replacement of linen, crockery and such like and maintenance of the property.

(viii) **Depreciation.** The depreciation charge should be recalculated with reference to the capital costs involved being charged to the capital expenditure forecast.

(ix)   **Loan interest and bank charges.** These should be checked against the bank's current rates and the amount of the principal agreed to the cash forecast.

(c)   **Cash flow forecast**

(i)   Check that the timing of the capital expenditure agrees to the cash flow forecast by comparing the two.

(ii)   Compare the cash flow forecast to the details within the profit forecast to ensure they tie up, for example:

•   Income from residents would normally be receivable weekly/monthly in advance

•   The majority of expenditure for wages etc would be payable in the month in which it is incurred

- Payments to the major utilities (gas, electricity, telephone) will normally be payable quarterly, as will the bank charges

- Rates and taxes are normally paid half-yearly

- Insurance premiums will normally be paid annually in advance.

(iii) Redo the additions on the cash forecast and check that figures that appear on other forecasts are carried over correctly.

Question	More prospective financial information

Gunthorpe Plumbing Supplies ('Gunthorpe') is a wholly owned subsidiary of Lucknow Builders Merchants ('Lucknow') and has been trading at a loss for a number of years. The recent bleak economic climate has led the directors of Lucknow to decide to put Gunthorpe into liquidation and make all the employees redundant, including its three directors.

The three directors of Gunthorpe have decided to form a new company, Gunthorpe Plumbing Supplies (2001) ('Gunthorpe (2001)'), and use their redundancy pay and personal savings to purchase all the shares in the company.

The board of directors of Lucknow have agreed to sell the following assets and liabilities of Gunthorpe to the new company.

(a) All the fixed assets except for one warehouse (see below)
(b) Trading stock, and
(c) Trade debtors and creditors

The price for the fixed assets has been agreed and the value of the trading stock, debtors and creditors, will be confirmed at the date of transfer by an independent valuer.

The directors of Gunthorpe (2001) propose to obtain additional finance in the form of a long term loan from a merchant bank and working capital will be financed by a bank overdraft from their existing bankers.

The directors have asked you to assist them in preparing a profit forecast and cash flow forecast for submission to the two banks. They have provided you with copies of the detailed accounts of Gunthorpe for the past five years, and they point out the following changes which, in their opinion, will enable the new company to trade at a profit.

(a) The substantial management charge imposed by Lucknow will disappear. However, additional costs will have to be incurred for services which were provided by the parent company, such as maintaining the accounting records and servicing the company's vehicles

(b) Initially fewer staff will be employed

(c) Only one of the company's two premises is being taken over – the premises which are not being taken over will be sold by Lucknow on the open market.

The directors have provided you with the following brief details of Gunthorpe's trade. It currently has a turnover of about £1 million and is a wholesaler of plumbing equipment (copper pipes, pipe connections, water taps etc) which are sold mainly on credit to plumbers and builders. Trade discount is given to larger customers. There are some cash sales to smaller customers, but these represent no more than 10% of total sales.

Required

Describe the work you would perform to:

(a) Verify that the value of items included in the profit forecast are reasonable
(b) Verify that the value of items included in the cash flow forecast are reasonable.

Answer

(a) **Verification of items in profit forecast**

The main items appearing in the profit forecast and the required work in relation to them would be as follows:

(i) The budgeted sales income should be considered against that which has actually been achieved in recent years. If the new management are forecasting any increase in the level of sales, the justification for this must be carefully reviewed. Tests should be made to ensure that all expenditure directly related to income is properly accounted for. Confirmation should be sought that the projected income takes proper account of the trade discounts that it is assumed will have to be granted.

(ii) The major term of expenditure is likely to be the purchase of goods for resale. Enquiry should be made as to whether suppliers will continue to grant the new company the same level of trade discounts as the old company and also whether the volume of purchases is such that a similar mark-up will be attained. Management explanations should be sought for any material differences in the anticipated gross profit rate, such explanations being fully investigated as to their plausibility.

(iii) The wages and salaries payable by the new company should be checked by asking management how many people they intend to employ and at what rates. The reasonableness of the projected charge for wages and salaries should be assessed by comparison with the figure for wages and salaries most recently paid by the old company.

(iv) All other major items of expenditure included in the profit forecast (ie selling expenses, finance expenses and administration expenses) should be considered by comparison with the figures of the old company in previous years, ensuring that a reasonable allowance is made for the effects of inflation.

(v) The charges for items previously covered by the management charge should be checked for their completeness and reasonableness.

(vi) An overall review of the projected profits should be undertaken to ensure that it appears to be a realistic forecast and not merely an idealistic target figure.

(b) **Verification of items in the cash flow forecast**

As well as generally checking to ensure that the cash flow forecast appears to be consistent with the profit forecast, specific checks should be made as follows.

(i) The timing of payments due to the parent company.

(ii) The period of credit granted to customers by the old company as it is unlikely that the new company will be in a position to insist on prompter payment by customers.

(iii) The period of credit taken from suppliers should be dealt with in a similar way, although enquiry should be made as to whether creditors are prepared to trade with the new company on the same terms as the old.

(iv) The timing of payment for overhead expenditure should be checked to see that it is reasonable and consistent with established practice.

(v) Although in the early months one would not expect there to be any major purchase or sale of non current assets, the position here should be confirmed by discussion with management of their prolonged plans.

Chapter roundup

- Prospective financial information is difficult to give assurance about because it is highly subjective.

- The auditor should agree the terms of the engagement with the directors, and should withdraw from the engagement if the assumptions made to put together the PFI are unrealistic.

- Procedures could include:

    - Analytical review (against similar historic projects)
    - Verification of projected expenditure to quotes or estimates

- It is impossible to give the same level of assurance about PFI as it is on HFI but **negative assurance** may be given.

Quick quiz

1   Complete the definition

A .... means PFI prepared on the basis of .... as to .... events which management expects to take place and .... management expects to take as of .... the .... is ....

2   Complete the matters an auditor should consider when undertaking a PFI engagement.

- The intended .... of the information
- Whether the information will be general or limited ....
- The nature of the ....
- The .... to be included in the information
- The .... to be covered by the information

3   Identify whether the following procedures are relevant to profit forecasts, capital expenditure forecasts or cash forecasts.

- Ensure the timings are reasonable
- Projected costs should be verified to estimates and quotations
- Analytical review on income (based on comparable projects)
- Review for reasonableness
- Review for consistency with profit forecast.

4   Complete the definition.

.... is assurance of something in the .... of any evidence arising to the ....

5   Reporting accountants are responsible for the PFI they are giving an opinion on.

True   ☐

False   ☐

Answers to quick quiz

1   Forecast, assumptions, future, actions, date, information, prepared.

2   Use, distribution, assumptions, elements, period.

3   • Ensure the timings are reasonable   C
     • Projected costs should be verified to estimates and quotations   P/CapEx
     • Analytical review on income (based on comparable projects)   P
     • Review for reasonableness   P/CapEx/C
     • Review for consistency with profit forecast.   CapEx/C

4   Negative assurance, absence, contrary

5   False

Now try the question below from the Exam Question Bank

Number	Level	Marks	Time
Q22	Examination	20	36 mins

Forensic audits

Topic list	Syllabus reference
1 Definitions	D6
2 Major applications of forensic auditing	D6
3 Ethical principles	D6
4 Procedures and evidence	D6

Introduction

In the current globalised business world there is an increasing demand for forensic services. Audit and assurance professionals are well-placed to provide these.

This chapter introduces forensic accounting and auditing and discusses its applications in practice. It also considers the ethical issues applicable to forensic accountants.

The chapter concludes with a look at investigative procedures and evidence.

Study guide

		Intellectual level
D6	**Forensic audits**	
(a)	Define the terms 'forensic accounting', 'forensic investigation' and 'forensic audit'.	1
(b)	Describe the major applications of forensic auditing eg fraud, negligence, insurance claims) and analyse the role of the forensic auditor as an expert witness.	2
(c)	Apply the fundamental ethical principles to professional accountants engaged in forensic audit assignment.	2
(d)	Select investigative procedures and evaluate evidence appropriate to determining the loss in a given situation.	3
(e)	Explain the terms under which experts make reports.	2

Exam guide

As is illustrated in the pilot paper, this topic can be examined in a very practical way. It is important to have an understanding of the framework but case study questions will involve the application of very similar procedures to those used in traditional audit of financial statements. Some specific knowledge was required of basic definitions, but otherwise the application of audit-style procedures.

1 Definitions

Forensic auditing:	The process of gathering, analysing and reporting on data, in a pre-defined context, for the purpose of finding facts and/or evidence in the context of financial/legal disputes and/or irregularities and giving preventative advice in this area.
Forensic investigation:	Carried out for civil or criminal cases. These can involve fraud, asset tracing for money laundering.
Forensic accounting	Undertaking a financial investigation in response to a particular event, where the findings of the investigation may be used as evidence in court or to otherwise help resolve disputes.

1.1 More general definitions

The range of assignments in this area is vast so to give specific definitions for each is not always practicable. In a recent publication by the Institute of Chartered Accountants of Canada *Standard Practices for Investigative and Forensic Accounting Engagement* (November 2006) following definition is established.

Investigative and forensic accounting engagements are those that:

(a) require the application of professional accounting skills, investigative skills, and an investigative mindset; and

(b) involve disputes or anticipated disputes, or where there are risks concerns or allegations of fraud or other illegal or unethical conduct.

Forensic audit and accounting is a rapidly-growing area. the major accountancy firms all offer forensic service, as do a number of specialist companies. The demand for these services arises partly from the increased expectation of corporate governance codes for:

- company directors to take seriously their responsibilities for the prevention and detection of fraud, and also from

- Governments concerned abut risks arising from criminal funding of terrorist groups.

This section outlines a number of the main application of forensic auditing.

2 Major applications of forensic auditing

Forensic auditing can be applied to a number of situations, including fraud and negligence investigations.

2.1 Fraud

Forensic accountants can be engaged to investigate fraud. This could involve:

- Quantifying losses from theft of cash or goods
- Identifying payments or receipts of bribes
- Identifying intentional misstatements in financial information, such as overstatement of revenue and earnings and understatement of costs and expenses
- Investigating intentional misrepresentations made to auditors

Forensic accountants may also be engaged to act in an advisory capacity to assist directors in developing more effective controls to reduce the risks from fraud.

2.2 Negligence

When an auditor or accountant is being sued for negligence, either or both parties to the case may employ forensic accountants to investigate the work done to provide evidence as to whether it did in fact meet the standards required. They may also be involved in establishing the amount of loss suffered by the plaintiff.

2.3 Insurance claims

Insurance companies often employ forensic accountants to report on the validity of the amounts of losses being claimed, as a means of resolving the disputes between the company and the claimant.

This could involve computing losses following an insured event such as a fire, flood or robbery. If a criminal action arises over an allegation that an insured event was deliberately contrived to defraud the insurance company, the forensic accountant may be called upon as an expert witness (see Section 2.6).

 Case Study

The following example illustrates that investigating fraud is sometimes a matter of applying common sense.

A forensic accountant was asked by an insurance company to quantify the value of loss to a firm following a robbery of gold bars. From the security tapes it was known that the two men, of average height and build, only made one visit to the safe. The accountant compared the amount claimed with a calculation of the weight of gold bars the two men could have physically carried and found that the claim was vastly inflated!

2.4 Other disputes

Forensic accountants can be involved in the investigation of many other types of dispute such as:

- Shareholder disputes
- Partnership disputes
- Contract disputes
- Business sales and purchase disputes
- Matrimonial disputes, including:
    - Valuing the family business
    - Gathering financial evidence
    - Identifying 'hidden' assets
    - Advising in settlement negotiations

2.5 Terrorist financing

In Chapter 1 we saw the legal requirements imposed on professional accountants in this area. In addition, governments are increasingly turning to forensic accountants as part of their counter-terrorism strategy.

The following quote is taken from a speech made by Gordon Brown, the Chancellor of the Exchequer, in October 2006:

'…forensic accounting of transaction trails across continents has been vital in identifying threats, uncovering accomplices, piecing together company structures, and ultimately providing evidence for prosecution. Most recently, forensic accounting techniques have tracked an alleged terrorist bomb maker, using multiple identities, multiple bank accounts and third parties and third countries to purchase bomb making equipment and tracked him to and uncovered an overseas bomb factory.

2.6 The forensic accountant as an expert witness

The preceding sections have identified a number of circumstances where the forensic accountant may be involved as an expert witness in civil or criminal cases. For civil cases in England and Wales the duties of expert witnesses are set out in the **Civil Procedure Rules (CPR)**.

2.6.1 Duties of experts

Experts always owe a duty to exercise reasonable skill and care to those instructing them, and to comply with any relevant professional code of ethics. However when they are instructed to give or prepare evidence for the purpose of civil proceedings in England and Wales they have an overriding duty to help the court on matters within their expertise. This duty overrides any obligation to the person instructing or paying them. Experts must not serve the exclusive interest of those who retain them.

Experts should be aware of the overriding objective that courts deal with cases justly. This includes dealing with cases proportionately, expeditiously and fairly. Experts are under an obligation to assist the court so as to enable them to deal with cases in accordance with the overriding objective. However the overriding objective does not impose on experts any duty to act as mediators between the parties or require them to trespass on the role of the court in deciding facts.

Experts should provide opinions which are independent, regardless of the pressures of litigation. In this context, a useful test of 'independence' is that the expert would express the same opinion if given the same instructions by an opposing party. Experts should not take it upon themselves to promote the point of view of the party instructing them or engage in the role of advocates.

Experts should confine their opinions to matters which are material to the disputes between the parties and provide opinions only in relation to matters which lie within their expertise. Experts should indicate without delay where particular questions or issues fall outside their expertise.

Experts should take into account all material facts before them at the time that they give their opinion. Their reports should set out those facts and any literature or any other material on which they have relied in forming their opinions. They should indicate if an opinion is provisional or qualified, or where they consider that further information is required or if, for any other reason, they are not satisfied that an opinion an be expressed finally and without qualification.

Experts should inform those instructing them without delay of any change in their opinions on any material matter and the reason for it.

Experts should be aware that any failure by them to comply with the Civil Procedure Rules or court orders or any excessive delay for which they are responsible may result in the parties who instructed them being penalised in costs and even, in extreme cases, being debarred from placing the experts' evidence before the court.

2.6.2 Expert witness reports

The Expert Witness Institute has produced a model form of expert's report to help expert witnesses, of whatever profession, to meet their legal duties. The main contents are outlined below:

1.	Index/list of contents	Optional, but desirable
2.	Brief curriculum vitae	Including expert's name, qualifications (eg ACCA) and relevant experience
3.	Summary of conclusions	Brief list of main facts from the evidence and the conclusions/opinions arrived at
4.	Instructions	Must give the substance of all instructions received by the expert, whether written or oral
5.	Issues	The issues to be addressed and the questions to be answered must be clearly set out
6.	Documentation	Full list of all documents and material on which the report is based
7.	Chronology	This must deal only with **factual** evidence, not any matter of opinion
8.	Technical background	Where technical aspects of the issues are outwith the general knowledge or experience of those who will have to deal with the report an explanation of the technical issues in this section may be necessary. For example, in a case involving fraudulent accounting, the requirements of specific accounting standards may have to be explained
9.	Opinion	This should be presented clearly and unambiguously. The reasons for the opinions given should be explicit
10.	References	A numbered list of all items of technical literature relied on. For example in a negligence case this may comprise a list of relevant accounting standards and auditing standards
11.	Declaration	The expert must sign a declaration confirming his understanding of his legal duties, and including the following 'Statement of Truth'.
		I confirm that insofar as the facts stated in my report are within my own knowledge I have made clear which they are and I believe them to be true, and the opinions I have expressed represent my true and complete professional opinion.

3 Ethical principles

FAST FORWARD

The fundamental principles of the *Code of Ethics and Conduct* apply to ACCA members in all professional assignments.

3.1 Example

The following table contains a recap of the fundamental principles. Take a few minutes to think and note down any special relevance you see in them in relation to forensic assignments.

Question	Ethical principles
Integrity	
Objectivity	
Professional competence and due care	
Confidentiality	
Professional behaviour	

Answer

Integrity	Forensic accountants are often, by definition, working in an environment and dealing with individuals who are dishonest and lack integrity. If there is any risk that their own integrity may be compromised they should decline or withdraw from the assignment.
Objectivity	The previous section on the role of the expert witness emphasised the need for independence and objectivity. Any perceived threats to objectivity will undermine the credibility of the accountant's opinion.
Professional competence and due care	Forensic assignments may require very specialised skills, for example, where evidence gathering requires very specific IT skills. A firm should consider very carefully whether they have adequate skills and resources before accepting the assignment.
Confidentiality	Forensic accountants will often be working for one party to a dispute, and have access to very sensitive information. Subject, of course, to legal rules of disclosure in court cases, it is clearly essential to maintain the strictest confidentiality.
Professional behaviour	Fraud cases and other situations such as takeover disputes can be very much in the public eye. Any lapse in the professionalism of, say, an expert witness could do serious damage to the reputation of the profession as a whole.

4 Procedures and evidence

Many of the techniques used in a forensic investigation will be similar to those used in the audit of financial statements but the different objectives and risks of the assignment require some differences in approach.

(a)	Materiality	–	In many investigations there will be no materiality threshold
(b)	Timing	–	Clearly less predictable than audit
		–	Timing of procedures needs to be unpredictable
(c)	Documentation	–	Needs to be reviewed more critically than on an audit
		–	Example 2 shows what an experienced fraud investigator might identify in a fraudulent invoice
(d)	Interviews	–	It may be appropriate to interview a suspected fraudster in the hope of obtaining an admission but this entails some problems:

- Challenging and requires a high skill level

- Legal issues including the risk of being sued for defamation

(e)	Computer-aided techniques	–	Data mining is a key part of many investigation processes. It allows the accountant to access and analyse thousands or millions of transactions that have passed through an accounting system, and identify, say, unusual trends far more quickly than by traditional documentary analysis.
		–	100% of an entity's transactions can be checked for characteristics such as date, time, £ amount, approval, payee etc.
		–	If possible, data should be gathered prior to the initial field visit to reduce the risk of the data being compromised.

4.1 Example 2

Porridge Associates

Invoice

Suite 214
The Castle
Lancaster
LA1 1YL

INVOICE NO: 000796
DATE: February 5, 2007

Registered VAT Number 394/8126/07

To: **Attn: Peter Kenworthy**
Silverfin Enterprises Limited
Century House
Brook Street
London NW3 9HE

Our Reference:

For the period: 1.3.07 to 31/3/07

CONSULTANT	DESCRIPTION		AMOUNT
JFB	Fees in relation to testing of electronic payment systems		
	Total fees:		£8,000.00
	Expenses	£500.00	£500.00
		SUBTOTAL	£8,500.00
		VAT	1,487.50
		TOTAL DUE	£9,987.50

If you have any questions concerning this invoice, call: **0378 279 1789**
or write to **Porridge Associates, UK Head office, 127 Elm Avenue, Nottingham, Notts N12 7PY**

THANK YOU FOR YOUR BUSINESS!

Remittance Advice

Invoice Number: **LIA 000796**

To: Porridge Associates
Bank of Wealth (Jersey) Ltd
St Helier
Jersey

Enclosed please find our cheque for

Account number   87620549
Sort Code   16-58-79

£9,987.50

in settlement of your account

Registered in Jersey: company Registration No. 02470290

'Porridge Associates'

There are fifteen potential 'Red Flags of Fraud' which, taken together, should prevent an invoice such as Porridge's from being paid. However, for the most part these indicators are not correctly recognised for what they really are. As a result fraudulent invoices get paid all the time.

1.   The Castle is in fact 'HM Prison, The Castle, Lancaster'. Fraud investigations routinely check to see whether invoices are generated from prisons. A second indicator in this address is the use of a 'Suite', which suggests temporary accommodation or the use of a business centre.

2.   This is a mobile telephone number. This again suggests a temporary operation or one which does not have a permanent address.

3.   A low invoice number suggests that the company may have begun trading only recently. A comparison against other invoices from the same company may reveal sequential invoice numbering which can indicate that an organisation is the only organisation being invoiced. This may indicate that the organisation is being specifically targeted for fraudulent purposes.

4.   The date of the invoice pre-dates that of the service provided. This may be part of the contract but it is worth checking for clarification.

5.   The VAT number contains a check digit. In this case the number is valid but it does not belong to Porridge Associates. The VAT number, therefore, has been stolen to make this invoice appear legitimate.

6.   All round value payments should be treated with caution. They should be reviewed in detail as they may be staged payments or commissions. They could also be completely false.

7.   Round value expense items may indicate a percentage charge and should be checked carefully.

8.   The address is that of a residential property and appears out of place for a company's UK Headquarters Building. Invoices which contain 'The Close', 'The Crescent', 'The Avenue' or other such locations may all indicate a home address. The more eagle-eyed will notice that the post code N12 is North London and not Nottingham. Fraudsters make mistakes and with care, these can be identified.

9.   Off-shore banking facilities may indicate that the supplier is trying to minimise its tax liability but, it may also be the first leg of transferring fraudulently obtained funds beyond UK legal jurisdiction. The sort code in this case refers to a bank in Gibraltar and not Jersey and this kind of manipulation may suggest a sophisticated money laundering operation.

10.   Company registration numbers follow specific formats and this number is not valid for Jersey.

11.   The absence of a Purchase Order number may indicate a bogus invoice of the type used by certain infamous telex directories. Bogus invoices are routinely sent out by mailshot to hundreds of companies. The fraudsters work on the basis that many low value invoices get paid without being checked.

12.   Vague descriptions of products, service and a lack of backup for expenses should always prompt further enquiries.

13.   There are also different address details which should be looked into further.

14.   Tear off section at bottom is only place that shows bank account details.

and as a general point

15.   Any invoices which contain correction fluid or the use of sticky labels to change an address should be investigated further.

Chapter roundup

- Forensic auditing can be applied to a number of situations, including fraud and negligence investigations.

- The fundamental principles of the *Code of Ethics and Conduct* and apply to ACCA members in all professional assignments.

- Many of the techniques used in a forensic investigation will be similar to those used in the audit of financial statements but the different objectives and risks of the assignment require some differences in approach.

Quick quiz

1   Define the terms forensic auditing, forensic investigation and forensic accounting.

2   State three applications of the use of forensic auditing.

3   State five items that should ideally be included in an expert's report.

Answers to quick quiz

1   Forensic auditing is the process of gathering, analysing and reporting on data in a pre-defined context, for the purpose of finding facts and/or evidence in the context of financial/legal disputes and/or irregularities and giving preventative advice in this area.

Forensic investigations are carried out for civil or criminal cases, which can involve fraud or money laundering.

Forensic accounting is undertaking a financial investigation in response to a particular event, where the findings of the investigation may be used as evidence in court or to other help resolve disputes.

2   Fraud
Negligence
Insurance claims
Terrorist financing

3   Any five of:

Index/list of contents	Chronology
Brief curriculum vitae	Technical background
Summary of conclusions	Opinion
Instructions	References
Issues	Declaration
Documentation	

Now try the question below from the Pilot paper

Number	Level	Marks	Time
Q2 Pilot paper	Examination	30	45 mins

Social and environmental auditing

Topic list	Syllabus reference
1 Importance for the company	F4
2 Measuring social and environmental performance	F4
3 Implications for the statutory audit	F4
4 Implications for assurance services	F4

Introduction

In this chapter we investigate the impact of social and environmental issues on the auditor. This takes two distinct forms:

- Impact on the **statutory audit**
- Impact on the provision of **assurance services** by the auditor.

Increasing importance is placed on social and environmental issues in business. Recent years have seen a substantial weight of environmental legislation passed which puts a **significant burden of compliance** on companies. The danger of non-compliance (fines, bad publicity, impact on going concern) is an aspect of the **environmental risk** which companies face.

Study guide

		Intellectual level
F4	**Social and environmental auditing**	
(a)	Discuss the increasing importance of policies that govern the relationship of an organisation to its employees, society and the environment	2
(b)	Describe the difficulties in measuring and reporting on economic, environmental and social performance and give examples of performance measures and sustainability indicators.	2
(c)	Explain the auditor's main considerations in respect of social and environmental matters and how they impact on entities and their financial statements (eg impairment of assets, provisions and contingent liabilities).	2
(d)	Describe substantive procedures to detect potential misstatements in respect of socio-environmental matters.	2

Exam guide

This topic could be the subject of a current issues discussion question. Measuring social and environmental performance can also be examined as part of a case study question.

1 Importance for the company

FAST FORWARD 〉〉 A company's stakeholders include employees, society and the environment.

1.1 Stakeholders

To recap, there are various **stakeholders** in a company. Traditionally auditors are concerned with one set, the shareholders, to whom they report on the financial statements. The diagram below shows various other stakeholders that a company might have.

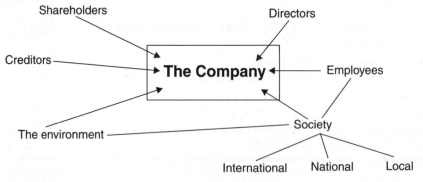

In this chapter we are concerned with the needs of three of the above categories; employees, the environment and society, and the knock on impact this has on the shareholders, directors and the company itself.

The diagram links the first three because in this context they are inextricably linked.

The environment   The environment is directly impacted by many of our corporate activities today. This may be

PRIMARY ⟶ The impact of processes

SECONDARY ⟶ The impact of products

The primary impact is regulated by environmental legislation, which has been prolific in recent years. The secondary impact is governed partly by legislation and partly by consumer opinion.

Society   Society, from the point of view of the company, is made up of consumers or potential consumers. As recognised above, consumers increasingly have opinions about 'green', environmentally friendly products and will direct their purchasing accordingly

Society will also, through lobby groups, often speak out on behalf of the environment as it cannot speak out itself.

Employees   Employees have a relationship with the company in their own right, in terms of their livelihood and also their personal safety when they are at work.

However, from the company's perspective, they are also a small portion of society at large, as they may purchase the products of the company or influence others to do so.

In some ways it is easier to see why the company is important to these stakeholders than why they are important to the company

Environment   The company can cause harm to natural resources in various ways, including:

- Exhausting natural resources such as coal and gas
- Emitting harmful toxins which destroy the atmosphere

Society   Is concerned with the harm to the natural resources as they and their children have to live on the planet and may suffer direct or indirect effects of pollution or waste.

Employees   Have all the concerns that society do and, more immediately, depend on the company for livelihood and safety when at work.

For a company however, there is one simple need. Companies desire above all else to keep making their product and to keep making sales.

Employees are needed to keep making the product, as are natural resources, and consumers' (that is, society's) goodwill is required to keep selling it.

Obviously, loss of employees and consumers is going to make it impossible for companies to stay in business. Therefore it is important for companies to have policies in order to appease these stakeholders and to communicate the policies to them.

Companies are also constrained by prolific legislation regulating their behaviour towards the environment. Many countries have produced environmental legislation in recent years.

1.2 Implications for management

FAST FORWARD

Social and environmental issues might present a risk to the company, and, by implication, the shareholders' investment, which directors are required to mitigate as part of their corporate governance.

The increasing importance of good corporate governance has been discussed in Chapter 1.

The Turnbull guidance states that management are responsible for internal controls which must comprise a sound system to mitigate against risks to the business. For many companies, environmental and social issues might be a significant risk.

The overriding business risk is the risk that the business might fail. Some of the risks arising from social and environmental issues have been discussed above.

Question

Risks

(a)   Describe the key environmental and social risks that a business might face.

(b)   Explain why they might result in the failure of the business.

Answer

(a)   The mindmap below shows the risks that the business faces.

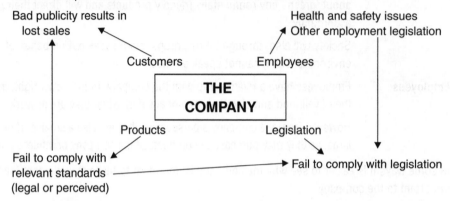

(b)   Any of these issues could be at a level serious enough to cause significant business interruption or even business failure, for the reasons given below.

    (i)   **Bad publicity**. This could lead to customers choosing other products, boycotts and loss of market share significant enough to prevent the business from continuing in operation.

    (ii)   **Legislation**. The company could be discovered not to be complying (through whistleblowing by employees or auditors, or investigation by a regulatory body). This could have the following effects:

- **Fines/compensation**. These could be significant enough to prevent the continuance of the business.

- **Disqualification of directors**. If the staff involved are key members of the organisation, this could threaten the ability of the company to continue.

- **Bad publicity**. See points made above.

1.3 Management controls

The specific controls that management will put into place in line with their duties under the corporate governance codes will vary according to the needs of the business.

They are likely to involve specific measures designed to ensure that environmental legislation is complied with, for example they may relate to protective clothing, disposal of waste etc. The human resources department is likely to design policies to ensure that employment legislation is complied with.

The directors may also seek to incorporate social and environmental values into the corporate culture of the company, so that all employees are aware of the risks arising in these areas, and are focused on avoiding them. This can be achieved by implementing a corporate code, or by setting targets of social and environmental performance.

One such target might be to obtain the British Standards Institute's ISO 14001, relating to Environmental Management Systems. This will involve having an assessment by the BSI, and may involve updating management systems to comply with the standard (ISO 14001).

ISO 14001 is often a formal condition for entry into supply chains and certain markets. It does not require the company to produce an environmental report however. The European equivalent, the Eco-Management and Audit Scheme (EMAS), does.

2 Measuring social and environmental performance

FAST FORWARD

Measuring social and environmental performance can be a difficult area. Auditors can provide assurance services in this area, giving opinions as to whether directors' assertions about performance are fair.

2.1 Targets and indicators

As discussed in Chapter 5, a key part of risk management is monitoring and evaluating results.

Social and environmental performance is not such an easy thing to measure as financial performance. It is less easy to produce ratios and there is unlikely to be an obvious profit appearing from social and environmental activities.

One way to measure social performance is to set targets and sustainability indicators and then appraise whether the targets have been met and the indicators exist.

These targets will vary from business to business, depending on what the issues are. To illustrate the point, a case study based on the Shell report 2000 is given below.

Case Study

Shell

Shell is a large multi-national group of companies that deal in oil, gas and chemicals. There are various issues which make social and environmental issues important to this company:

- They deal in the earth's natural resources
- Their business is heavily environmentally legislated
- They employ a significant number of people
- Some employees work in risky environments
- They operate in areas of the world where Human Rights issues are not given sufficient priority

Targets

In response to the social and environmental issues raised above, Shell have set targets of social and environmental performance which they evaluate and report on to shareholders on an annual basis.

The following are examples of targets which the company has set:

Environmental

- Reduce emissions of carbon dioxide from refinery activity
- Continue to develop cleaner fuels
- Reduce emissions of nitrogen oxides from burning fuel in operations
- Reduce spills of crude oil, oil and chemicals

Social

- Zero employee fatalities in work-related incidents

- Not exploit children in any country where child labour exists, by

    – Employing children under the legal age of employment
    – Dealing with other companies who employ children illegally

- Pursue equal opportunities for men and women in all countries that this is legally possible

Sustainability principles

The company has also set general sustainability principles which all staff should apply in daily business:

- Respect and safeguard people
- Engage and work with stakeholders
- Minimise impact on the environment
- Use resources efficiently
- Maximise profitability
- Maximise benefits to the community

Reporting

The company reports on all these issues to its shareholders, and where-ever possible, the facts included within this report are verified by independent verifiers.

The case study shows a number of targets and sustainability indicators. Some can be measured in mathematical terms, for example:

- Emissions
- Spills
- Elimination of work-related fatalities
- Employment of children

However, some of the targets are not specific enough to be able to measure in that way. For example, it is more difficult to identify whether the company is in relation to achieving a target of developing cleaner fuels until the cleaner fuel appears. Such a development target cannot have a prescribed timescale.

Equally, it is difficult to measure the effect of the general principles which the company has included within the culture of the company.

2.2 Social audits

The process of checking whether a company has achieved set targets may fall within a social audit that a company carries out.

Social audits involve:

- Establishing whether the firm has a rationale for engaging in socially responsible activity

- Identifying that all current environment programmes are congruent with the mission of the company

- Assessing of objectives and priorities related to these programmes

- Evaluating company involvement in such programmes past, present and future

Whether or not a social audit is used depends on the degree to which social responsibility is part of the **corporate philosophy**. A cultural awareness must be achieved within an organisation in order to implement environmental policy, which requires Board and staff support.

In the USA, social audits on environmental issues have increased since the Exxon Valdez catastrophe in which millions of gallons of crude oil were released into Alaskan waters.

The Valdez principles were drafted by the Coalition for Environmentally Responsible Economics to focus attention on environmental concerns and corporate responsibility.

- Eliminate pollutants and hazardous waste
- Conserve non-renewable resources
- Market environmentally safe products and services
- Prepare for accidents and restore damaged environments
- Provide protection for employees who report environmental hazards
- Appoint an environmentalist to their board of directors, name an executive for environmental affairs, and develop an environmental audit of their global operations, which is to be made publicly available

2.3 Environmental audits

Environmental audits seek to assess how well the organisation performs in safeguarding the environment in which it operates, and whether the company complies with its environmental policies.

An environmental audit might be undertaken as part of obtaining or maintaining the BSI's ISO 14001 standard.

The auditor will carry out the following steps:

- Obtain a copy of the company's environmental policy
- Assess whether the policy is likely to achieve objectives:
  - Meet legal requirements
  - Meet British Standards
  - Satisfy key customers/suppliers' criteria
- Test implementation and adherence to the policy by:
  - Discussion
  - Observation
  - 'Walk-though tests' where possible

Exam focus point

A small part of a case study question in December 2003 looked at social and environmental performance indicators in the context of a chain of gyms. In December 2005, a small part of a case study question focused on such indicators in the context of an oil company. These are both relevant to this new syllabus. You can attempt both these questions in your Practice and Revision Kit.

3 Implications for the statutory audit

FAST FORWARD

Social and environmental issues can affect the statutory audit at the planning stage (risk), while undertaking substantive procedures (impairment/provisions) and during audit reviews (going concern).

3.1 Why important?

We now turn from the importance of social and environmental issues to the company and look at why they are important to the auditor in the context of the statutory audit.

The key reason that the issues are important to the statutory audit is that they are important to the company and therefore **can potentially impact on the financial statements**.

In the introduction, the impact of the issues on an audit was divided into three specific areas, which were:

- Planning the audit
- Undertaking substantive procedures
- Audit reviews

Another important point to note is the duties of the auditor arising under ISA (UK and Ireland) 250 *Consideration of law and regulations in an audit of financial statements*. We shall also consider this below.

3.2 Planning the audit

Social and environmental issues impact in two ways:

- Knowledge of the business (ISA 315)
- Inherent risk assessment (ISAs 315 and 330)

You should be aware of the principles involved in these two issues, so there is no need to go into a lot of further detail at this stage.

As part of his knowledge of the business, the auditor should have an awareness of any environmental regulations the business is subject to, and any key social issues arising in the course of the business.

The auditor may be able to obtain knowledge of this aspect of the business by reading the firms procedures or reviewing any quality control documentation they have relating to standards. The auditor may be able to review the results of any environmental audits undertaken by the company.

This will then form part of his assessment of inherent risk.

Exam focus point

Remember that a question does not have to be specifically on social and environmental issues for them to be relevant. Be aware of any implications they might have in a standard question on planning or risks.

3.3 Substantive procedures

Social and environmental issues, although particularly environmental issues, may impact on the financial statements in a number of ways. Some examples are given in the box below.

Examples of the impact of social and environmental matters on financial statements

- Provisions (for example, for site restoration, fines/compensation payments)
- Contingent liabilities (for example, in relation to pending legal action)
- Asset values (issues may impact on impairment or purchased goodwill/products)
- Capital/revenue expenditure (costs of clean up or meeting legal standards)
- Development costs (new products)
- Going concern issues (considered below under reviews)

Exam focus point

When approaching an question about auditing specific items in financial statements, or issuing an audit opinion in regard to them, you should bear in consider whether there is an environmental/social issue which will impact on valuation or disclosure. Use your common sense, however, do not make up such issues where no obvious indicators are given in the question.

The auditor will have to bear in mind the effects of social or environmental issues on the financial statements when designing audit procedures. We will now look at some potential audit procedures that would be relevant in three of the key areas above.

3.3.1 Substantive procedures: asset valuation

The key risk that arises with regard to valuation is that assets might be **impaired**. FRS 11 requires an impairment review to be undertaken with regard to non current assets if certain indicators of impairment exist. We have discussed the audit of impairments in Chapter 11, but shall consider the points specific to environmental and social issues here.

Knowledge brought forward from *Financial Reporting*

FRS 11 gives a list of indicators that an impairment review is required. The indicators relevant here are:

(a)   There is a **current period operating loss** or **net cash outflow** from operating activities, combined with **either** of:

    (i)   **Past** operating losses or net cash outflows from operating activities

    (ii)   An expectation of **continuing** operating losses or net cash outflows from operating activities.

(d)   There is a **significant adverse change** in of the following.

    (ii)   The statutory or other regulatory environment in which the business operates.

The indicator in (a) could be caused by environmental and social issue risks as discussed in the answer to question 1. The indicator in (d) is more specifically relevant to social and environmental issues. It is possible that a significant adverse change could have taken place in the regulatory environment.

The auditor should be aware of the regulatory environment of the client as part of its knowledge of the business (as discussed above), but the following **general procedures** could be undertaken as part of the non current asset testing to **establish whether an impairment review is required**.

- Review the board minutes for indications that the environmental regulatory environment has changed.

- Review relevant trade magazines or newspapers to assess whether any significant adverse change has taken place.

- Discuss the issue with management, particularly those nominated to have responsibility for environmental issues, if such a position exists.

If a significant adverse change has taken place, the directors may or may not have conducted an impairment review. If the directors have not, the auditors should discuss the matter with them. If the directors refuse to conduct an impairment review, the auditors should consider the result of that on their audit report.

If an impairment review has been undertaken, and the valuation of the asset has been adjusted accordingly, the auditor should **audit the impairment review**. This was discussed in Chapter 11.

3.3.2 Substantive procedures: provisions

Guidance on accounting for provisions is given in FRS 12. The audit of provisions has been discussed previously in Chapter 11. We shall consider the points specific to environmental and social issues here.

FRS 12 defines a **provision as a liability of uncertain timing or amount**. A liability is an obligation of an enterprise to transfer economic benefits as a result of past transactions or events. A provision should be recognised when:

- An entity has a **present obligation** (legal or constructive) as a result of a past event
- It is probable that a **transfer of economic benefits** will be required to settle the obligation
- A **reliable estimate** can be made of the obligation

The FRS provides some helpful examples of environmental issues that result in provisions being required, for example one appendix deals with contaminated land and another deals with the issue of implementing new legislation requiring smoke filters. If a company has an environment policy such that the parties would expect the company to clean up contamination, or if the company has broken current environmental legislation then a provision for environmental damage must be made.

The auditor needs to be aware of any circumstances that might give rise to a provision being required, and then apply the recognition criteria to it.

The **general substantive procedures** for **establishing if a provision is required** are the **same as** they were for identifying whether an **impairment review** was required.

If the directors have included provisions in the accounts relating to environmental issues, the **audit procedures** will be the same as were discussed in Chapter 11. Specifically, the auditor may be able to **review correspondence** from any regulatory watchdog, or obtain a copy of the **relevant legislation** to review its requirements.

3.3.3 Substantive procedures: contingent liabilities

Accounting for contingent liabilities is also governed by FRS 12.

FRS 12 defines a contingent liability as either

(a)   A possible obligation that arises from past events whose existence will be confirmed only by the occurrences or non-occurrence of one or more uncertain future events not wholly within the entity's control, or

(b)   A present obligation that arises from past events but is not recognised because it is not probable that a transfer of economic benefits will be required to settle the obligation or because the amount of the obligation cannot be measured with sufficient reliability.

Social and environmental issues may also impact here. In fact, a contingent liability is likely to arise through items being identified in a provision review, when the items highlighted do not meet the recognition criteria for a provision.

This was discussed in Chapter 11. Given their relationship with provisions, the **general audit procedures to establish if contingent liabilities exist** are the **same as** the ones for **provisions**, given above.

If the directors have made **disclosures relating to contingent liabilities** in respect of environmental and social issues, the **procedures** to test them are set out **in chapter 11**. **Specific evidence** would be on similar lines to as for provisions in respect of social and environmental issues: **correspondence with a regulator or relevant legislation**.

3.4 Audit reviews

As discussed in Section 2, environmental and social issues can impact on the ability of the company to continue as a going concern.

The auditor will need to aware of such issues when undertaking his going concern review. The procedures involved in going concern reviews were discussed in Chapter 10.

3.5 Auditor responsibility in the event of non-compliance with law and regulations

FAST FORWARD

The auditor must bear in mind his responsibilities under ISA 250 *Consideration of law and regulations in an audit of financial statements.*

The auditors' responsibility with regard to law and regulations is set out in ISA (UK and Ireland) 250 *Consideration of law and regulations in the audit of financial statements.* This was discussed in Chapter 5, so you should refer back to this to remind yourself of the actions the auditor should take in the event of his discovering non-compliance.

Environmental obligations would be core in some businesses (for example, our oil and chemical company given in the case study above), in others they would not. ISA 250 talks of laws that are 'central' to the entity's ability to carry on business.

Clearly, in the case of a company who stands to lose his operating license to carry on business in the event of non-compliance, environmental legislation is central to the business.

In the case of social legislation, this will be a matter of judgement for the auditor. It might involve matters of employment legislation, health and safety regulation, human rights law and such matters which may not seem core to the objects of the company, but permeate the business due to the need of employees.

The auditor is not expected to be a specialist in environmental law. However, as part of his professional duty, he must ensure that he has enough knowledge to undertake the assignment, or that he engages the use of an expert if necessary.

4 Implications for assurance services

FAST FORWARD

Many different assurance services could be offered within the broad context of social and environmental issues.

4.1 Types of service

Auditors can provide a variety of services in respect of environmental and social issues. Most of these services are familiar to us, so there is no need to speak again about them in length. Remember that most of the services we have discussed could be applied in a environmental and social context:

- Internal audit services (reviewing controls)
- Review of internal controls and procedures
- Management letter concerning controls as a by-product of statutory audit
- Assurance services (see below)

As discussed in the introduction, **management increasingly report to members on social and environmental issues**, and there is a growing public perception that this is an important area.

This means that it is an issue that can give rise to **assurance services**.

Remember!

> The **definition** of an **assurance engagement:**
>
> An **assurance engagement** is one where a practitioner expresses a conclusion designed to enhance the degree of confidence of the intended users other than the responsible party about the outcome of the evaluation or measurement of a subject matter against criteria.

Assurance engagements give rise to assurance reports, which we outlined in Chapter 13. We shall consider the issue of specific verification reports in relation to social and environmental issues here.

If the directors issue an environmental and social report, it may contain figures and statements that are verifiable. Using the example of Shell (above), the directors could make the following assertions:

- Carbon dioxide emissions were x million tonnes in 2001, which represents a 2% decrease from 2000.

- We have implemented a strategy aimed at ensuring that in 5 years time, no one we deal with will have an involvement in child labour.

These assertions can be reviewed and assurance given about them. For instance, in the first case, the level of emission could be traced to records of emission from the refineries, and the percentage calculation could be checked.

In the second instance, the accountants could obtain details of the strategy and ascertain how fully it has been implemented by making enquiries of the staff who should be implementing the strategy. They could also appraise the strategy and give an opinion of the chances of it achieving the objective within the given time frame.

4.2 Contents of an assurance report on environmental issues

There is no guidance in issue as to the contents of such a report. The box below shows some items that should be included as a minimum.

> - Note of the objectives of the review
> - Opinions
> - Basis on which those opinions have been reached
> - Work performed
> - Limitations to the work performed
> - Limitations to the opinion given

 Question

Social and environmental audit

Your audit client, Naturascope Ltd, is a health food and homeopathic remedies retailer, with a strong marketing emphasis on the 'natural' elements of the products and the fact that they do not contain artificial preservatives.

The directors have decided that it would benefit the company's public image to produce a social and environmental report as part of their annual report. There are three key assertions which they wish to make as part of this report:

- Goods/ingredients of products for sale in Naturascope have not been tested on animals
- None of Naturascope's overseas suppliers use child labour (regardless of local laws)
- All Naturascope's packaging uses recycled materials

The directors have asked the audit engagement partner whether the firm would be able to produce a verification report in relation to the social and environmental report.

Required

(a)   Identify and explain the matters should the audit engagement partner consider in relation to whether the firm can accept the engagement to report on the social and environmental report.

(b)   Comment on the matters to consider and the evidence to seek in relation to the three assertions.

Answer

(a)   **Acceptance considerations**

There are four key things that the audit engagement partner should consider:

(i)   **Impact of the new engagement on the audit**

The audit engagement partner needs to ensure that the **objectivity of the audit is not adversely affected** by accepting any other engagements from an audit client. This is of primary importance.

Factors that he will consider include the impact that any fees from the engagement will have on total fees from the client and what staff will be involved in carrying out the new engagement (ie, will they be audit staff, or could be engagement be carried out by a different department).

In favour of the engagement, he would consider that such an engagement should increase his knowledge of the business and its suppliers and systems, and might enhance the audit firm's understanding of the inherent audit risk attaching to the business.

(ii)   **Competence of the audit firm to carry out the assignment**

The audit engagement partner needs to consider whether the firm has the **necessary competence** to carry out the engagement in a quality manner, so as to minimise the risk of being sued for negligence.

This will depend on the nature of the engagement and assurance required (see below) and on whether the auditor felt it would be cost effective to use the work of an expert, if required.

(iii)   **Potential liability of the firm for the report**

As the engagement is not an audit engagement, the partner should consider to whom he would be **accepting liability** in relation to this engagement, and whether the risk that that entails is worth it, in relation to the potential fees and other benefits of doing the work (such as keeping an audit client happy, and not exposing an audit client to the work of an alternative audit firm).

Unless otherwise stated, liability is unlikely to be restricted to the shareholders for an engagement such as this, indeed, it is likely to extend to all the users of the annual report. This could include:

- The bank
- Future investors making ethical investing decisions
- Customers and future customers making ethical buying decisions

The partner should also consider whether it might be possible to limit the liability for the engagement, and **disclaim liability** to certain parties.

(iv)   **Nature of the engagement/criteria/assurance being given**

Before the partner accepted any such engagement on behalf of the firm, he should **clarify** with the directors the **exact nature** of the engagement, the degree of assurance required and the criteria by which the directors expect the firm to assess the assertions.

As the engagement is not an audit engagement, the audit rules of 'truth and fairness', and 'materiality' do not necessarily apply. The partner should determine whether the directors want the firm to verify that the assertions are '**absolutely correct**' or 'correct in x% of cases' and also, what **quality of evidence** would be sufficient to support the conclusions drawn – for example, confirmations from suppliers, or legal statements, or whether the auditors would have to visit suppliers and make personal verifications.

This engagement might be less complex for the audit firm if they could conduct it as an 'agreed-upon procedures' engagement, rather than an assurance engagement.

(b) **Assertions**

(ii) **Animal testing**

The assertion is **complex** because it does not merely state that products sold have not been tested on animals, but that ingredients in the products have not been tested on animals.

This may mean a **series of links** have to be checked, because Naturascope's supplier who is the manufacturer of one of their products may not have tested that product on animals, but may source ingredients from several other suppliers, who may, in turn source ingredients from several other suppliers, etc.

The audit firm may also find that it is a **subjective issue**, and that the assertion 'not tested on animals' is not as clear cut as one would like to suppose. For example, dictionary defines animal as either 'any living organism characterised by voluntary movement…' or 'any mammal, especially man'. This could suggest that the directors could make the assertion if they didn't test products on mammals, and it might still to an extent be 'true', or that products could be tested on 'animals' that, due to prior testing, were paralysed. However, neither of these practices are likely to be thought ethical by animal lovers who are trying to invest or buy ethically.

Potential sources of evidence include: assertions from suppliers, site visits at suppliers' premises, a review of any licenses or other legal documents in relation to testing held by suppliers.

(ii) **Child labour**

This assertion is less complex than the previous assertion because it is restricted to Naturascope's direct overseas suppliers.

However, it contains complexities of its own, particularly the definition of 'child labour', for example in terms of whether labour means 'any work' or 'a certain type of work' or even, 'work over a set period of time', and what the definition of a child is, when other countries do not have the same legal systems and practical requirements of schooling, marriage, voting etc.

There may also be a practical difficulty of verifying how old employees actually are in certain countries, where birth records may not be maintained.

Possible sources of evidence include: assertions by the supplier and inspection by auditors.

(iii) **Recycled materials**

This may be the simplest assertion to verify, given that it is the least specific. All the packaging must have an element of recycled materials. This might mean that the assertion is restricted to one or a few suppliers. The definition of packaging may be wide, for example, if all goods are boxed and then shrink-wrapped, it is possible that those two elements together are termed 'packaging' and so, only the cardboard element need contain recycled materials.

The sources of evidence are the same as previously – assertions from suppliers, inspections by the auditors or review of suppliers' suppliers to see what their methods and intentions are.

Chapter roundup

- A company's stakeholders include employees, society and the environment.

- Social and environmental issues might present a risk to the company, and by implication, the shareholders' investment, which the directors are required to mitigate as part of their corporate governance.

- Measuring social and environmental performance can be a difficult area. Auditors can provide assurance services in this area – giving opinions as to whether directors' assertions about performance are fair.

- Social and environmental issues can affect the statutory audit
  - At the planning stage (risk)
  - While undertaking substantive procedures (impairment/provisions)
  - During audit reviews (going concern)

- The auditor must bear in mind his responsibilities under ISA 250, *Consideration of law and regulations in an audit of financial statements*.

- Many different assurance services could be offered within the broad context of social and environmental issues.

Quick quiz

1   Draw a mindmap showing the major stakeholders in a company.

2   Management have a duty to monitor risks arising from social and environmental issues as part of their corporate governance.

   True   ☐

   False   ☐

3   Name three areas of a statutory audit where social and environmental issues are relevant.

   (1)   ....

   (2)   ....

   (3)   ....

4   Give an example of why social and environmental issues might impact on all of the following financial statement areas:

   - Provisions
   - Contingent liabilities
   - Asset values
   - Capital/revenue expenditure
   - Development costs
   - Going concern

5   List six items which should be covered on an assurance report relating to environmental issues

   (1)   ....   (4)   ....

   (2)   ....   (5)   ....

   (3)   ....   (6)   ....

Answers to quick quiz

1

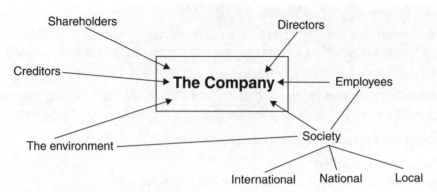

2   True – as we discussed in Chapter 6

3   (1)   Planning (risks)
    (2)   Substantive testing (accounting issues arising)
    (3)   Reviews (going concern)

4   • Provisions   (site restoration or fines/compensation payments)
    • Contingent liabilities   (pending legal action)
    • Asset values   (impairment due to new environmental legislation)
    • Capital/revenue expenditure   (cost of clean up or meeting legal standards)
    • Development costs   (new, environmentally-friendly products)
    • Going concern   (operational existence threatened by new/proposed environmental laws)

5   (1)   Objectives   (4)   Work performed
    (2)   Opinions   (5)   Limitations on work
    (3)   Basis of opinions   (6)   Limitations on opinion

Now try the question below from the Exam Question Bank

Number	Level	Marks	Time
Q24	Examination	15	27 mins

16

Internal audit and outsourcing

Topic list	Syllabus reference
1 Revision: internal audit	D8
2 Other internal audit issues	D8
3 Outsourcing	D8
4 Outsourcing specific functions	D8
5 Impact of outsourcing on an audit	D8

Introduction

In this chapter we **revise internal audit** which you studied in some detail in your earlier auditing studies. Internal auditors provide services to the management of a company. In section two, we **compare the services** that internal auditors provide, **to the assurance and audit-related services we introduced in the previous chapter.** We also introduce a **practical issue,** the internal auditors' approach to **multi-site operations.**

In the second half of the chapter, we look at outsourcing. **Outsourcing is a key issue in business today.** However, the key issues for management are **cost and control.**

The two issues are linked simply because the **question of outsourcing has become a key issue in internal audit.** Businesses are being encouraged to invest in internal audit, because of the benefits that the internal audit department can provide to corporate governance.

However, setting up an internal audit department can be costly and difficult Outsourcing can overcome these problems.

Study guide

		Intellectual level
D7	**Internal audit**	
(a)	Compare the objectives and principal characteristics of internal audit with other assurance engagements.	2
(b)	Compare and contrast operational and compliance audits.	2
(c)	Justify a suitable approach (eg cyclical compliance) to specified multi-site operations.	3
(d)	Discuss outsourcing internal auditing services.	2
8	**Outsourcing**	
(a)	Explain the different approaches to 'outsourcing' and compare with 'insourcing'.	2
(b)	Discuss and conclude on the advantages and disadvantages of outsourcing finance and accounting functions including: (i) data (transaction) processing (ii) pensions (iii) information technology (IT) (iv) internal auditing (v) due diligence work (vi) taxes	3
(c)	Recognise and evaluate the impact of outsourced functions on the conduct of an audit.	3

Exam guide

Outsourcing and internal audit could be examined together or separately. Either or both could feature in a planning scenario question.

1 Revision: internal audit

Internal audit has a key role in corporate governance, providing objective assurance on control and risk management.

1.1 Revision

The internal audit function was considered in detail in the earlier audit and assurance paper. Work through the following question to ensure that you remember the basic principles of internal auditing.

Question   Revision: internal audit

(a) Describe the principal differences between internal and external auditors, considering the following factors.

    (i)   Eligibility
    (ii)   Security of appointment
    (iii)   Main objectives and limitations on the scope of their work

(b) Explain how external auditors would evaluate specific work carried out by internal auditors.

Answer

(a) **Eligibility**

Under the Companies Act 1985, a person is ineligible to act as external auditor if he is an officer or employee of the company, a partner or employee of such a person or a partnership in which such a person is a partner. An internal auditor is an employee of the company.

The Companies Act also requires external auditors to belong to a recognised supervisory body, and this means they must hold an appropriate qualification, follow technical standards and maintain competence.

By contrast anyone can act as an internal auditor even if they do not have a formal accounting qualification. It is up to the company's management who they appoint.

Security

Under the Companies Act, the external auditors are appointed to hold office until the conclusion of the next general meeting. They can be dismissed by an ordinary resolution of shareholders with special notice in general meeting, and have the right to make representations.

External auditors cannot be dismissed by individual directors or by a vote of the board. The only influence directors can have on the removal of external auditors is through their votes as shareholders. The rules on security of tenure are there because of the need for external auditors to protect the interests of shareholders by reporting on directors' stewardship of the business.

By contrast, as internal auditors are employees of the company, they can be dismissed by the directors or lower level of management, subject only to their normal employment rights.

Objectives and limitations on the scope of the audit work

The primary objective of external auditors is laid down by statute, to report on whether the company's accounts show a true and fair view of the state of the company's affairs at the period-end, and of its profit or loss for the period. External auditors are also required to report if certain other criteria have not been met, for example the company fails to keep proper accounting records or fails to make proper disclosure of transactions with directors.

Internal auditors' objectives are whatever the company's management decide they should be. Some of the objectives may be similar to those of external audit, for example to confirm the quality of accounting systems. Other objectives might be in areas which have little or no significance to the external auditor, for example recommending improvements in economy, efficiency and effectiveness.

Statutory rules mean that management cannot limit the scope of external auditors' work. External auditors have the right of access to all a company's books and records, and can demand all the information and explanations they deem necessary. As the objectives of internal audit's work are decided by management, management can also decide to place limitations on the scope of that work.

(b) External auditors should consider whether:

- The work is performed by persons having adequate technical training and proficiency as internal auditors

- The work of assistants is properly supervised, reviewed and documented

- Sufficient appropriate audit evidence is obtained to afford a reasonable basis for the conclusions reached

- The conclusions reached are appropriate in the circumstances

- Any reports prepared by internal audit are consistent with the results of the work performed

- Any exceptions or unusual matters disclosed by internal audit are properly resolved

- Amendments to the external audit programme are required as a result of matters identified by internal audit work

- There is a need to test the work of internal audit to confirm its adequacy.

Hopefully you could answer that question. If you struggled, you might want to refer back to your notes from your previous auditing studies, but here is a summary of the key revision points on internal audit in this syllabus.

Role of internal audit in corporate governance

Internal audit are placed perfectly to assist management in the assessment of risks and internal controls required by the Hampel and Turnbull reports. The Turnbull report in particular highlights the role internal audit can have in providing objective assurance and advice on risk and control.

The Turnbull report sets out some key guidelines for the Board.

TURNBULL GUIDELINES

- Have a **defined process** for the **review** of effectiveness of **internal control.**
- Review **regular** reports on **internal control.**
- Consider **key risks** and how they have been **managed.**
- Check the **adequacy** of **action taken** to remedy weaknesses and incidents.
- Consider the **adequacy** of **monitoring.**
- Conduct an **annual assessment** of risks and the effectiveness of internal control.
- Make a **statement** on this process in the **annual report.**

The traditional definition of internal audit given at the start of the section shows how internal audit can help the directors achieve these objectives; the traditional purpose of internal audit was to review controls.

The third of the Turnbull guidelines refers to risk. All companies face risks arising from their operational activities. Risks arise in different areas.

- Risk the company will go bankrupt
- Risks arising from regulations and law
- Risks arising from publicity

Turnbull requires that risk be managed. This gives rise to another role for the internal audit function, **risk management.**

Risk awareness and management should be the role of everyone in the organisation. The extended role of internal audit with regard to risk is the monitoring of integrated risk management within a company, and the reporting of results to the Board to enable them to report to shareholders.

Internal auditor relationships

Internal auditors have relationships with the following people:

- **Management**: by whom they are employed and may report to
- **Audit committee**: to whom they report
- **External auditors**: who may make use of their work

Reliance on the work of internal auditors by external auditors

The external auditors may make use of the work of internal audit. The guidance over when this appropriate is given to them in ISA (UK and Ireland) 610 *Considering the work of internal audit.*

The ISA states that the external auditors must give consideration first to the scope and organisation of the internal audit department and then evaluate the specific audit work they are interested in.

The following factors must be considered.

- Proficiency and training of the people who have undertaken the work
- Level of supervision, review and documentation of the work of assistants
- Sufficiency and appropriateness of evidence to draw conclusions
- Appropriateness of conclusions drawn
- Consistency of any reports prepared with the work performed
- Whether the work necessitates amendment to the external audit programme

---

1.2 Internal auditors and risk management

The issue of the Turnbull guidance and internal audit's role in relation to risk management was touched on briefly in the box. In response to the Turnbull guidance, directors need to ensure three steps are taken in their business.

- Identify risks
- Control risks
- Monitor risks

It is not internal audit's primary role to manage risk in a company. The process of risk assessment in a company was outlined in Chapter 13. It is the responsibility of the directors, usually delegated to individual managers in various departments.

The risks identified and assessed, and a policy is taken in respect of each of them. To recap, this policy is usually one of four:

- Accept risk (if it is low impact and likelihood)
- Reduce risk (by setting up a system of internal control)
- Avoid risk (by not entering market, accepting contract etc)
- Transfer risk (by taking out insurance)

With their skills in business systems, internal auditors are ideally placed to **monitor** this process and add value to it. They can:

- Give advice on the best design of systems and monitor their operation
- Be involved in a process that continually improves internal control systems
- Provide assurance on systems set up on each department

The involvement of internal audit as a monitoring unit will help to ensure that the process of risk identification and management in a business is a **continual process** rather than a one-off exercise.

2 Other internal audit issues

FAST FORWARD

Internal audit may take on various types of audit.

2.1 Internal audit and assurance engagements

> **REMEMBER**
>
> The definition of an **assurance engagement** is:
>
> An assignment in which a practitioner expresses a conclusion designed to enhance the degree of confidence of the intended users other than the responsible party about the outcome of the evaluation or measurement of a subject matter against criteria.
>
> **Internal audit** can be described as follows:
>
> An independent appraisal function established within an organisation to examine and evaluate its activities.

It is clear from the above definitions that internal audit is in many ways an **assurance function**. Internal auditors, like accountants undertaking an assurance engagement, will evaluate and measure the performance of certain aspects of the company against pre-ordained criteria.

However, in some ways, internal audit can also be compared to an **agreed-upon procedures assignment**, which, as you know from the chapter on audit related services, is not an assurance engagement. This is because the work the internal audit function perform may be pre-ordained by management.

2.2 Operational and compliance audits

Key terms

> **Operational audits** are audits of the operational processes of the organisation and check not only compliance with controls but also the effectiveness of controls as part of the risk management process.
>
> **Compliance audits** are audit checks intended to determine whether the actions of employees are in accordance with company policy or laws and regulations.

Compliance audits are the traditional realm of internal auditors. They involve having a knowledge of the company policy and carrying out tests to ensure that company policy is being followed in practice.

As such, compliance audits tend to fall into the category of internal audit providing assurance services, as discussed above. This is because management are employing them to give them assurance that certain criteria have been met.

However, the work is not assurance in the strict sense of ISAE 3000, because internal audit are not really checking 'assertions' of the employees of the company. They are checking that procedures have been complied with.

Operational audits are different to compliance audits in that the scope is more extensive. As part of an operational audit, the internal audit department might undertake a compliance audit, but the scope **also includes an assessment of the effectiveness** of the procedures that are being audited.

As such, an operational audit is more like an agreed-upon procedures engagement. While an element of assurance is given (particularly with regard to the compliance elements of the assignment), the audit is designed with the intention of the internal auditor drawing his own conclusions about the systems from the work he has done.

2.3 Multi-site operations

Some organisations have several outlets which all operate the same systems. A good example of this would be a retail chain, which would have a number of shops where systems relating to inventory and cash, for example, would be the same.

The objective of audits of multi-site operations is the same as the objective of single site operations. However, as results might vary across the different location, the internal auditor has to take a different approach. Some possible approached to multi-site operations audits are set out below.

(a) **Compliance based audit approach**

With a compliance based audit approach, a master audit programme is drawn up which is used to check the compliance of the branches with the set procedures, after which the results from the branches are compared. There are two possible ways of undertaking the compliance based approach:

- **Cyclical**. This approach is based on visiting all of the sites within a given timeframe.

- **Risk based approach**. This alternative determines which branches are to be visited based on the risk attached to them.

(b) **Process based audit approach**

With a process based audit approach, the audit is planned so that specific key processes are audited. In a retail operation, for example, this could involve the important process of cash handling being audited. This approach can also be undertaken in two ways:

- **Cyclical**. Aims to audit all processes in a business within a set timeframe.

- **Risk-based**. The processes to be audited are determined with reference to the risk attached to them.

2.3.1 Practical considerations

The practical issues to consider in relation to multi-site operations are:

- Which sites to visit
- How often to visit various sites
- Whether to conduct routine or surprise visits and what mix of these types of visit.

Remember that the considerations behind which sites to visit will **not** be the same as for external auditors. Internal auditors may consider issues (among others) such as:

- Size of operation
- History of systems compliance
- Quality/experience of staff on site
- Past results of testing
- Management interest in particular sites

Question   **Audit risk**

You are the Chief Internal Auditor of Adam Ltd, which owns and operates three large departmental stores in Wandon, Thuringham and Tonchester. Each store has more than 22 departments.

You are at present preparing your audit plan and you are considering carrying out detailed audit tests on a rotational basis. You consider that all departments within the stores should be covered over a period of five years but that more frequent attention should be given to those where the 'audit risk' demands it.

Required

Describe the factors which you would consider in order to evaluate the audit risk attaching to each department.

Answer

Risk may be evaluated by considering:

(a)   The probability of an event and

(b)   The potential size of the event.

In the case of an audit the event concerned is undetected material error or fraud.

In evaluating risk in the context of the audit of a company owning and operating three large department stores the factors to be considered are as follows.

(a)   Factors influencing probability

(i)   Strengths and weaknesses in the system of internal control, overall and for each individual store and department in respect of all types of internal control. It would be appropriate to consider such controls under the following headings.

(1)   Organisation of staff

(2)   Segregation of staff

(3)   Physical controls

(4)   Authorisation and approval

(5)   Arithmetic and accounting

(6)   Personnel

(7)   Supervision

(8)   Management

(ii)   Experience derived from previous audits and the conclusion of previous audit reports.

(iii)   Whether the prices of goods sold are fixed by head office or variable by local store or departmental managers.

(iv)   Extent of local purchasing for each store or department.

(v)   The nature of the stock (for example high unit value, attractiveness).

(vi)   Effectiveness of cash-handling systems.

(b)   Factors influencing size

(i)   Relative size of department in terms of:

(1)   Revenue

(2)   Number of transactions

(3)   Average value of stock

(ii)   Internal statistics of losses through shoplifting and staff theft.

(c)   Other general factors

(i)   Comparison among stores and among like departments in the three stores, using ratio analysis.

(ii)   Risk of deterioration or obsolescence of stocks.

(iii)   Rate of turnover of store staff.

Exam focus point   You could have a case study question set in the context of an internal audit.

3 Outsourcing

FAST FORWARD

Outsourcing is the contracting out of certain functions. A business can outsource a small part of the function, or the entire function, or practically all its functions.

3.1 Why outsource?

Key terms

Outsourcing is the process of purchasing key functions from an outside supplier. In other words, it is **contracting-out** certain functions, for example, internal audit or information technology.

Insourcing is when an organisation decides to retain a centralised department for the key function, but brings experts in from an external market on a short term basis to account for 'peak' and 'trough' periods.

There are three general reasons for outsourcing:

- Financial efficiency
- Change management
- Strategy

3.1.1 Financial efficiency

It is often argued that outsourcing **reduces cost**. This **may not necessarily be the case**, but businesses often find that it is worth investigating. If outsourcing is never considered, it is often the case that the cost of maintaining the function in-house is never calculated, and therefore not considered either.

This fact links into the next point about financial efficiency. Outsourcing a function can lead to **greater cost control** over that function. This is as a result of the function now being subject to a contractual fee rather than a previously not completely identified, cost of maintaining the function in-house. This aspect of outsourcing might substantially **improve budgeting and cost control**.

Outsourcing may considerably **reduce the number of employees** for whom the business is responsible. The logistics of shedding staff may make outsourcing a difficult legal and human issue, but the **cost savings** in this area (salary, tax, pension, for example) could be substantial.

Outsourcing can have a fundamental effect on the **shape of an entity's financial statements**, particularly if a function with a high capital investment (for example, information technology) is being outsourced. In some cases, it might be possible to sell the company's assets to the service provider, producing a cash injection, or reduced initial fees.

3.1.2 Change management

Outsourcing can be a way of managing change in a company. For example, if the company decides to change its software, outsourcing the software provision might mean that all **staff training** on the new system is incorporated into the service.

Outsourcing a function such as finance might facilitate the smooth running of a **merger** of two firms who have different accounting systems. This may also be true when a business is **restructured**.

3.1.3 Strategy

Outsourcing can also be part of a strategy to **refocus on the core competencies** of a business, or a thrust to **improve technical services**. It can be a way of **entering a market in the most low risk way**. For example, a previously low-tech business wanting to engage in e-commerce could outsource its website development and maintenance.

3.2 Outsource what?

Generally, if a company chooses to outsource, it will outsource functions which are not perceived to be key competencies. The different approaches which can be taken to outsourcing depend on the extent to which a company contracts out non-core functions. This can be seen by way of an example.

 Case Study

The Toy Company

The Toy Company is a small company, owned and run by Edward T. Bear. It was left to him by his father, T. Bear, who was a skilled toy maker. The business began as a one man operation in the garage and is now has 250 employees and technical computerised processes and is run from its own factory complex.

Edward joined the company on leaving school. He worked alongside his father for ten years. Last year his father died and left the shares in the company to Edward and his sister Victoria. Victoria has never had any role in the company, and is keen to continue that.

The company employed an accountant twenty years previously, and he is still an employee of the firm. In the intervening years, the accounts department has grown to now incorporate five other employees, with one having specific payroll duties. The accounts department has a computer system which is separate from the computer system used in operations.

In operations, there are several divisions: design, manufacture, packaging, sales and marketing.

The company also employs a part time human resources manager who deals with staff matters and recruitment. The office cleaner is the longest serving member of staff. She has worked for Mr Bear since he set up in his first work shop forty years ago.

In the example of the Toy Company, there are several areas where management could consider outsourcing. We will consider the advantages and disadvantages of this below. Here we are only looking to see where the potential lies.

The core competency of the company is the manufacture of toys. This means that there are several functions which do not fall within this competency:

- Accounting
- Human Resources
- Cleaning

Of the above areas, cleaning would be the least risky to outsource because the cleaning does not directly impact on the operation of the business. Cleaning is a common outsourced function in the private sector.

However, we are more interested in the accounting function, being accountants. The accounts department is not part of the core competency, so potentially, it could be outsourced. Within this decision, there are several others. The company could outsource:

- Pension functions
- Tax related functions
- The entire payroll function
- Invoicing
- Credit control
- The entire accounting function

When considering **the extent to which the company wants to adopt outsourcing**, it will must consider the risk involved and the control which management want to maintain over the function. There is less risk involved in outsourcing a part of the payroll function (for example, pensions) than in outsourcing the whole finance function.

Similar subdivisions can be seen when considering the outsourcing of other functions:

Human Resources
Welfare
Health and safety
Recruitment
The entire department

Information Technology
Maintenance
Project management
Network management
The entire IT function

Just to extend the point about outsourcing to its furthest extremes, it is possible to consider outsourcing more of the business than has been discussed above.

In the first instance, Edward could critically appraise the core competency of his business (the manufacture of toys) and subdivide it further. He might decide that the production processes are the core competency and that functions such as design and sales and marketing should be outsourced.

In an extreme case, it is possible to create a **virtual organisation**. For example, Edward could decide that he has no particular personal interest in toy manufacture, but that he does wish to retain the business. In which case, he could outsource all the different functions of the business, but maintain control of the contracts and therefore ultimately the business.

An example of an industry where this could be the case is the airline industry, where it is possible to contract out the aircraft and their maintenance and the crew to fly them.

3.3 Advantages and disadvantages of outsourcing

We will look in detail at the advantages and disadvantages of outsourcing some specific functions in the following sections. For now, however, we shall consider some general advantages and disadvantages of outsourcing that apply to them all.

Advantages of outsourcing
Cost. A key advantage of outsourcing is that it is often cheaper to contract a service out than it is to conduct it in house. It may also significantly improve cost control.
Specialist service. Outsourcing results in specialist being used to provide the service when that would not have been the case if the function was performed in house.
Indemnity. The service organisation may provide indemnity in the event of problems arising. If problems arise in house, there is no such comfort zone.
Cash flow. Obtaining the service through a contract may assist with cash flow, as the contract will represent a flat fee, whereas the cost of providing the service in house might have led to fluctuating costs (for example, if temporary staff are required in a busy period).

Disadvantages of outsourcing
The single biggest disadvantage of outsourcing, is the extent to which the company loses **control** over the function itself, although not over cost control
The **initial cost** of outsourcing may be **substantial,** if an aspect of the decision is to close a current department of the business. The question of **potential redundancies** may dissuade companies from considering outsourcing.

Disadvantages of outsourcing
The contract has to be **managed** to ensure that the service being provided is appropriate and in accordance with the contract. This may take a disproportionate amount of **time**.
The contract might limit the **liability** of the contractor, leading to problems if the contract is not performed well. This might even result in **court action** being required.
Should these disadvantages be realised, the **cost** of outsourcing could outweigh the benefit, even though in theory outsourcing should reduce cost.

4 Outsourcing specific functions

Internal audit is not a core competency and may be outsourced fairly easily.

4.1 Internal audit

Internal audit is rarely a core competency of a company. However, it is a valuable service to management. The corporate codes of recent years that we discussed in Chapter 5 have emphasised the importance of internal audit in assessing controls and monitoring risks.

There are **problems associated with setting up an internal audit department**, however. These are:

- Cost of recruiting staff.

- Difficulty of recruiting staff of sufficient skill and qualification for the company's preference or need.

- The fact that management are not accounting specialist and therefore might struggle to direct the new department in their duties.

- The time frame between setting up the department and seeing the results of having the department.

- The fact that the work required may not be enough to justify engaging full time staff

- The fact that a variety of skills and seniority levels are required, but only one member of full time staff can be justified.

4.1.1 Advantages

The advantage of outsourcing internal audit is that outsourcing can overcome all these problems:

- Staff need not be recruited, as the **service provider has good quality staff**.

- The service provider has **specialist skill** and can assess what management require them to do. As they are external to the operation, this will not cause operational problems.

- Outsourcing can provide an **immediate** internal audit department.

- The service contract can be for the **appropriate time scale** (a two week project, a month, etc)

- Because the **time scale is flexible**, a **team of staff** can be provided if required.

- The service provider could also provide less than at team, but, for example, could provide one member of staff on a full-time basis for a short period, as a **secondment**.

A key advantage of outsourcing internal audit is that **outsourcing can be used on a short term basis**, to:

- Provide immediate services
- Lay the basis of a permanent function, by setting policies and functions
- Prepare the directors for the implications of having an internal audit function
- Assist the directors in recruiting the permanent function.

Outsourced internal audit services are provided by many audit firms, particularly the big five. This can range from a team of staff for a short term project, or a single staff member on a long term project.

4.1.2 Disadvantages

However, the fact that internal audit services are typically provided by external auditors can raise problems as well:

- The company might wish to **use the same firm** for internal and external audit services, but this may lead to **complications for the external auditors**.

- The **cost** of sourcing the internal audit function might be high enough to make the directors choose not to have an internal audit function at all.

4.2 Outsourcing finance and accounting functions

Various functions will be considered in the table below. Remember, however, the key advantages and disadvantages set out in Section 3, they are all likely to be true of the functions discussed more specifically below.

FUNCTION	
Data processing	
Disadvantages	There may be logistical difficulties in outsourcing data processing, due to the high level of paper involved (invoices, goods received notes etc). This information will have to be given to the service organisation.
	A secondary, and more important, effect is that the company might not always have control of their key accounting documentation and records. It is a legal requirement that the directors maintain this information. While they may delegate the practicalities, they are still responsible for maintaining the records.
Pensions	
Advantages	Pensions are a specialist area and there is merit in getting a specialist to operate the company's pension provision.
Disadvantages	Pensions are closely related to the payroll and the company will need to share sensitive information with the pension provider, which may make the situation complicated
Information technology	
Advantages	A key advantage of outsourcing all, or elements of, the IT function is that this will enable the company to keep pace with **rapid technological advances**.
	It also allows the company to take advantage of the work of specialist in a field that many people still find difficult but which they use regularly to carry out their business.
	Outsourcing can provide a useful **safety net** of a technical helpline or indemnity in the event of computer disaster.
	It is also possible that through outsourcing, the company will be able to obtain **added-value,** such as new ways of doing business identified (for example, e-commerce)

FUNCTION	
Due diligence	
Advantages	A key advantage in relation to outsourcing due diligence is the high level of **expertise** that can be brought in. The company can expect **quality** from its service contractor, and can seek **legal compensation** from them in the event of negligence.
Taxes	
Advantages	In relation to taxes, the key advantage is also the buying in of **expertise**.
Disadvantages	The disadvantage of outsourcing tax work is that while the work can be outsourced, the **responsibility** cannot. The tax authorities will deal with the responsible person, not the agent, so the loss of control is particularly risky in this case

5 Impact of outsourcing on an audit

FAST FORWARD
> When a company uses a service organisation, there are special considerations for the auditors.

Exam focus point
> There are both **ethical** and **practical audit implications** of outsourcing on an audit – either could be examined.

5.1 Use of service organisations

The impact of outsourcing on an external audit is considered in ISA (UK and Ireland) 402 *Audit Considerations relating to entities using service organisations*.

Key term
> A **service organisation** is an **organisation** that provides services to another **organisation**.

As we have discussed above, some companies choose to outsource activities necessary to the running of their business to service **organisation**s. Examples of such activities that may be outsourced are:

- Information processing
- Maintenance of accounting records
- Facilities management
- Asset management (for example, investments)
- Initiation or execution of transactions on behalf of the other entity

Some outsourced activities may be directly relevant to the audit. The most obvious example above is the maintenance of accounting records, but most of them actually could impact on the audit.

Auditors need to obtain sufficient, appropriate audit evidence to express an opinion on financial statements. they therefore need to consider an approach towards the parts of the audit affected by the service organisation.

5.2 Considerations of the client auditor

A service organisation may establish and execute policies and procedures that affect a client organisation's accounting and internal control systems. These policies and procedures are physically and operationally separate from the client organisation.

(a)   When the services provided by the service organisation are **limited to recording** and **processing client transactions** and the client retains authorisation and maintenance of accountability, the client may be able to implement effective policies and procedures within its organisation.

(b)   When the service organisation **executes** the client's **transactions** and **maintains accountability**, the client may deem it necessary to rely on policies and procedures at the service organisation.

The ISA states, 'the auditor should determine the significance of service organisation activities to the client and the **relevance** to the audit'.

The ISA lists the following activities as relevant activities. (This is not an exclusive list.)

- Maintenance of accounting records
- Other finance functions
- Management of assets
- Undertaking or making arrangements for transactions as agent of the user entity.

The ISA requires the auditor to understand the terms of the agreement between the service organisation and the user entity. **'User entity and auditors should obtain and document an understanding of:**

(a)   **The contractual terms which apply to relevant activities undertaken by service organisations and**

(b)   **The way that the user entity monitors those activities so as to ensure that it meets its fiduciary and other legal responsibilities.'**

The ISA requires the auditor to consider:

- Whether the terms contain an adequate specification of the information to be provided to the user entity and responsibilities for initiating transactions relating to the activity undertaken by the service organisation.

- The way that accounting records relating to relevant activities are maintained.

- Whether the user entity has right to access to accounting records prepared by the service organisation concerning the activities undertaken, and relevant underlying information held by it, and the conditions in which such access may be sought.

- Whether the terms take proper account of any applicable requirements of regulatory bodies concerning the form of records to be maintained, or access to them.

- The nature of relevant performance standards.

- The way in which the use entity monitors performance of relevant activities and the extent to which its monitoring process relies on controls operated by the service organisation.

- Whether the service organisation has agreed to indemnify the user entity in the event of a performance failure.

- Whether the contractual terms permit the user entity auditors access to source of audit evidence including accounting records of the user entity and the information necessary for the conduct of the audit.

In obtaining an understanding of the entity, the auditor will also consider:

- The **nature of the services** provided by the service organisation

- The **terms of contract** and **relationship** between the client and the service organisation

- The extent to which the client's **accounting and internal control systems interact** with the systems at the service organisation

- The entity's **internal controls** relevant to the service organisation activities.

- The **service organisation's capability** and **financial strength**, including the possible effect of the failure of the service organisation on the client

- Information about the **service organisation** such as that reflected in user and technical manuals

- Information available on **general controls** and **computer systems** controls relevant to the client's applications

If this leads the auditor to decide that the control risk assessment will not be affected by controls at the service organisation, further consideration of this ISA is unnecessary. However, if he concludes that risk is affected, further audit procedures should be carried out.

The client auditor should also consider the existence of **third-party reports** from service organisation auditors, internal auditors, or regulatory agencies as a means of providing information about the accounting and internal control systems of the service organisation and about its operation and effectiveness.

The ISA states that 'if the client auditor concludes that the activities of the service organisation are significant to the entity and relevant to the audit, the auditor should obtain a sufficient understanding of the entity and its environment, including its internal control, to identify and assess the risks of material misstatement and design further audit procedures in response to the assessed risk.'

If information is insufficient, the client auditor should consider asking the service organisation to have its auditor perform such procedures as to supply the necessary information, or the need to visit the service organisation to obtain the information. A client auditor wishing to visit a service organisation may advise the client to request the service organisation to give the client auditor access to the necessary information.

5.2.1 Obtaining audit evidence

The ISA states that **'based on their understanding of the aspects of the user entity's accounting system and control environment relating to relevant activities, user entity auditors should:**

(a) **Assess whether sufficient appropriate audit evidenced concerning the relevant financial statement assessment is available from records held at the user entity; and if not**

(b) **Determine effective procedures to obtain evidence necessary for the audit, either by direct access to records kept by service organisations or through information obtained from the service organisations or their auditors'.**

It also outlines a series of audit procedures

- Inspecting records and documents held by the user entity

- Establishing the effectiveness of controls

- Obtaining representations to confirm balance and transactions from the service organisation

- Performing analytical review on

    - The records maintained by the user entity, or
    - The returns received from the service organisation

- Inspecting records and documents held by the service organisation

- Requesting specified procedures re performed by

    - The service organisation
    - The user entity's internal audit department

- Reviewing information from the service organisation or its auditors concerning the design and operation of its control systems.

5.3 Service organisation auditor's reports

The ISA says 'when using a service organisation auditor's report, the client auditor should consider the nature of and content of that report. If the client auditor uses the report of a service organisation auditor, the auditor should consider making inquiries concerning that auditor's professional competence in the context of the specific assignment undertaken by the service organisation auditor'.

The report of the service organisation auditor will ordinarily be one of two types.

(a) **Report on suitability of design**. This is the basic report.

(b) **Report on suitability of design and operating effectiveness**. This will contain the same as a report on design, **plus** an opinion by the service organisation auditor that the accounting and internal control systems are operating effectively based on the results from the tests of control.

While reports on design may be useful to a client auditor in gaining the required understanding of the accounting and internal control systems, an auditor would not use such reports as a basis for reducing the assessment of control risk.

By contrast a report on operating effectiveness may provide such a basis since tests of control have been performed. If this type of report is maybe to be used as evidence to support a lower control risk assessment, a client auditor would have to consider whether the controls tested by the service organisation auditor are relevant to the client's transactions (significant assertions in the client's financial statements) and whether the service organisation auditor's tests of control and the results are adequate.

The auditor of a service organisation may be engaged to perform **substantive procedures** that are of use to a client auditor. Such engagements may involve the performance of procedure of procedures agreed upon by the client and its auditor and by the service organisation and its auditor.

5.4 Impact on internal audit

External auditors will be affected when outsourced functions impact on the financial statements. Internal audit will be interested in outsourced functions which affect the business (that is, any outsourced function).

Internal audit will be interested in the contractual arrangements made with the service organisation. They may want to pay a visit to the organisation and undertake a review of its systems to ensure that they are sufficient for the business's needs.

| Question | Outsourcing |

(a) Explain the meaning of the word 'outsourcing' and distinguish it from 'insourcing'.

(b) Discuss the risks and benefits of outsourcing the payroll function of a small business, employing a management accountant and an accounts clerk.

(c) You are planning the audit of a company that has just outsourced its credit control function. Describe the planning issues that arise as a result of this action.

| Answer |

(a) **Outsourcing** is the practice of purchasing a specific function from an outside service provider. In other words, it is the practice of contracting-out functions of the business to an expert.

Insourcing, by contrast, is the practice of maintaining a specialist function in house, but buying in external expertise on a short-term basis to balance peaks and troughs in demand for that expertise.

(b) Payroll is a complicated accounting area, particularly due to the issues of taxation arising. It is also susceptible to fraud in the absence of strong controls.

In a small company, such as the one described, there is **little scope for segregation of duties** in relation to payroll. It is likely that payroll would be managed by the accountant, as it the clerk is likely to have a full time job in relation to sales and purchases, and the accountant has greater expertise. However, it is possible that an accountant in such a position, even in a small business, might **not have time to manage payroll** in addition to other accounting duties. In order for there to be **adequate authorisation** and segregation in relation to payroll, **another senior figure should be involved** in authorising the payroll.

In this situation, it might be **cost effective to outsource** the payroll function to an **expert**. This might also **reduce the control problems** inherent in the small department. However, there are some disadvantages related to outsourcing the function. The key issue is one of **confidentiality**, as payroll records contain sensitive data about personnel (for example, their bank details). **Personnel might object** to this information being given to an outside provider. The company would also have to **institute controls over the transfer of data** (such as weekly hours worked) to the service provider.

(c) The auditors should determine whether the outsourced function is **relevant to the audit**. In the case of the credit control function, this is clearly **relevant to receivables** reported in the balance sheet and to **sales and bad debts**.

The auditor must ensure that he **understands the terms of the contract** between the client and the service provider. As part of planning the audit, therefore, he **must obtain a copy** of the contract and **become familiar with its terms**.

The auditor must **ascertain whether he will have access to the records** that he will require as part of his audit evidence. As part of planning he must **make arrangements to enable this access**.

As part of the risk assessment at the planning stage, the auditor must consider whether the outsourcing arrangements affect the risk of material misstatement in the financial statements. In doing so he will consider factors such as the contract (referred to above), the reputation of the service provider and the effectiveness of past controls when the function was maintained in house and present controls over the outsourcing arrangements.

Chapter roundup

- Internal audit has a key role in corporate governance, providing objective assurance on control and risk management.

- Internal audit may take on various types of audit.

- Outsourcing is the contracting out of certain functions. A business can outsource a small part of the function, or the entire function, or practically all its functions!

- Internal audit is not a core competency and may be outsourced fairly easily.

- When a company uses a service organisation, there are special considerations for the auditors.

Quick quiz

1   List six factors which the external auditors should consider in relation to the work of internal audit.

    (1)   ....

    (2)   ....

    (3)   ....

    (4)   ....

    (5)   ....

    (6)   ....

2   Complete the definitions

    .... audits are audits of the ....
    .... of the organisation and check not only compliance with controls but also the
    .... of controls as part of the risk management process.

    .... audits are audit checks intended to determine whether the actions of
    employees are in .... with company .... or
    .... and ....

3   Outsourcing is another term that means staff recruitment

    True   ☐

    False   ☐

4   Name five elements of the accounts function which could be outsourced.

    (1)   ....

    (2)   ....

    (3)   ....

    (4)   ....

    (5)   ....

5   Complete the table, putting the advantages made under the right headings and naming the specific function, if relevant.

General advantages	Function-specific advantages

- Cost
- Keeping pace with technological advance
- Liability/indemnity
- Cashflow
- Specialist service
- Indemnity
- Flexibility (particularly with regard to time scale)

6   The auditor may refer to the responsibility of the service organisation when giving his opinion in financial statements.

True   ☐

False   ☐

Answers to quick quiz

1   (1)   Proficiency and training of staff
     (2)   Level of supervision, documentation and review of the work
     (3)   Sufficiency and appropriateness of evidence
     (4)   Appropriateness of conclusion
     (5)   Consistency of reports with work performed
     (6)   Whether work necessitates amendment to original audit plan

2   Operational, operational processes, effectiveness

     Compliance, accordance, policy, law, regulations

3   False. It is contracting-out functions

4   (1)   Pension
     (2)   Tax
     (3)   Payroll
     (4)   Invoicing
     (5)   Credit control

5

General advantages	Function-specific advantages
• Cost	• Technological advance (IT)
• Liability/indemnity	• Liability/indemnity (IT/due diligence)
• Cashflow	• Immediacy (IA)
• Specialist service	• Flexibility/time scale (IA)
• Flexibility	

6   False

     –   Responsibility for accounting records still lies with directors
     –   Responsibility for auditing them still lies with auditors

Now try the question below from the Exam Question Bank

Number	Level	Marks	Time
Q25	Examination	20	36 mins

Part E
Reporting

Reports

17

Topic list	Syllabus reference
1 Critically appraising the form and content of a standard unmodified auditor's report	E1
2 Forming and critically appraising an open audit	E1
3 Reporting electronically	E1
4 Special purpose audit reports	E1
5 Reporting to those charged with governance	E2

Introduction

As a student at this stage of your studies, you will be familiar with the external audit opinion. If this is not the case, before you read any of this Chapter, you must go back to your previous Study Text and revise the basic features of the report, the various qualifications that can be made, the concept of a true and fair view and the statutory requirements in relation to the audit opinion.

At this level, students are expected not only to know what the audit opinion is and how it is presented. They are required to draw audit opinions and also assess the appropriateness of an audit opinion formed by another person.

In this Chapter we shall also consider the form of the audit report, the criticism that it receives and whether it enables an auditor to express properly a true and fair view.

We shall also look at the occasions when a special audit report is required and we shall also look at the auditors' requirements in relation to reporting to those charged with governance. We have already looked at the issue of reporting on assignments other than audit assignments in Chapter 12 of this Study Text.

Study guide

		Intellectual level
E	**REPORTING**	
1	**Auditor's report**	
(a)	Critically appraise the form and content of a standard unmodified auditor's report.	3
(b)	Recognise and evaluate the factors to be taken into account when forming an audit opinion in a given situation.	3
(c)	Justify audit opinions that are consistent with the results of audit procedures relating to the sufficiency of audit evidence and/or compliance with accounting standards (including the going concern basis).	3
(d)	Draft extracts suitable for inclusion in an audit report.	3
(e)	Discuss the implications for the auditor's report on financial statements that report compliance with IFRSs.	2
(f)	Assess whether or not a proposed audit opinion is appropriate.	3
(g)	Discuss 'a true and fair view'.	2
(h)	Describe special purpose auditors' reports (eg on summary financial statements) and analyse how and why they differ from an auditor's report on historical financial information.	2
2	**Reports to management**	
(a)	Draft suitable content for a report to management, on the basis of given information, including statements of facts, their potential effects and appropriate recommendations for action.	3
(b)	Critically assess the quality of a management letter.	3
(c)	Advise on the content of reports to those charged with governance in a given situation.	3
(d)	Explain the need for timely communication, clearance, feedback and follow up.	2
(e)	Discuss the relative effectiveness of communication methods.	2

Exam guide

Audit reporting questions at this level tend to be challenging, but 'do-able', particularly if you have practised similar questions and have established a step-by-step approach to questions on forming an audit opinion.

1 Critically appraising the form and content of a standard unmodified auditor's report

A standard report is used to promote understandability because the audit report is widely available to both accustomed users and users who are not accustomed to audit and audit language.

1.1 The act of communication

In essence, the auditors' job is straightforward. They carry out tests and enquiries and evaluate evidence received with the purpose of drawing an audit opinion. They then **communicate** that opinion, in the form of an audit report, as we have been discussing. This can cause problems.

The communication problem is caused by a number of different problems that can be identified under three headings, although some of the problems are broadly linked between categories. The three problematic areas are:

- Understandability
- Responsibility
- Availability

1.2 Understandability

Although the essence of the auditors' role is simple, in practice it is surrounded by auditing standards and guidance as it is a **technical** art. It also involves **relevant language**, or 'jargon' that non-auditors may not understand.

This can be seen in a definition of what audit is. 'An audit is an exercise designed to show whether financial statements are free from material misstatement and give a true and fair view.' The highlighted words reveal the problem.

Communicating the audit opinion in a way that people can understand it is a challenge.

1.3 Responsibility

Connected with the problem of what the audit is and what the audit opinion means is a problem of what the auditors are **responsible** for. As far as the **law** is concerned, auditors have a restricted number of duties. **Professional standards** and other bodies, such as the Financial Services Authority, put other duties on auditors.

Users of financial statements, and the public, may not have a very clear perception of what the auditors are responsible for and what the audit opinion relates to, or what context it is in.

The issue of **auditors' liability** ties in here. Audit reports are addressed to shareholders, to whom auditors have their primary and legal responsibility. However, audited accounts are used by significantly more people than that. Should this fact be addressed in the audit report? This issue is also considered in Chapter 4.

1.4 Availability

The availability of audit reports has been increased by the trend to publish financial statements on companies' websites. Auditors should consider the risks of this.

The fact that a significant number of people use audited accounts has just been mentioned. Audit reports are publicly available, as they are often held on **public record**. This fact alone may add to any perception that exists that auditors address their report to more than just shareholders.

The problem of availability is exacerbated by the fact that many companies publish their **financial statements** on their **website**. This means that millions of people around the world have access to the audit report.

This issue may add significant misunderstandings.

- **Language** barriers may cause additional understandability problems
- It may not be clear **which financial information** an audit report refers to
- The audit report may be subject to **malicious tampering** by hackers or personnel

If an audit report is published electronically, auditors lose control of the **physical positioning** of the report, that is, what it is published with. This might significantly impact on understandability and also perceived responsibility. We will look at reporting electronically in Section 3.

1.5 The standard report

The audit report which you are familiar with is the standard UK audit report. This standard report was specifically developed to counter problems of lack of understandability which were inherent in the communication process. This audit report has recently been updated.

INDEPENDENT AUDITOR'S REPORT TO THE SHAREHOLDERS OF XYZ LIMITED

We have audited the financial statements of (name of entity) for the year ended ... which comprise [state the primary financial statements such as the profit and loss account, the balance sheet, the cash flow statement, the statement of total recognised gains and losses] and the related notes. These financial statements have been prepared under the accounting policies set out therein.

Respective responsibilities of directors and auditors

The directors' responsibilities for preparing the annual report and the financial statements in accordance with applicable law and United Kingdom Accounting Standards (UK Generally Accepted Accounting Practice) are set out in the Statement of Directors' Responsibilities.

Our responsibility is to audit the financial statements in accordance with relevant legal and regulatory requirements and International Standards on Auditing (UK and Ireland).

We report to you our opinion as to whether the financial statements give a true and fair view and are properly prepared in accordance with the Companies Act 1985. We report to you whether in our opinion the information given in the directors' report is consistent with the financial statements [The information given in the directors' report includes that specific information presented in the Operating and Financial Review that is cross referred from the Business Section of the directors' report.]

In addition we report to you if, in our opinion, the company has not kept proper accounting records, if we have not received all the information and explanations we require for our audit, or if information specified by law regarding directors' remuneration and other transactions is not disclosed.

We read other information contained in the annual report, and consider whether it is consistent with the audited financial statements. This other information comprises only [the directors' report, the chairman's statement and the operating and financial review]. We consider the implications for our report if we become aware of any apparent misstatements or material inconsistencies with the financial statements. Our responsibilities do not extend to any other information.

Basis of audit opinion

We conducted our audit in accordance with International Standards on Auditing (UK and Ireland) issued by the Auditing Practices Board. An audit includes examination, on a test basis, of evidence relevant to the amounts and disclosures in the financial statements. It also includes an assessment of the significant estimates and judgments made by the directors in the preparation of the financial statements, and of whether the accounting policies are appropriate to the company's circumstances, consistently applied and adequately disclosed.

We planned and performed our audit so as to obtain all the information and explanations which we considered necessary in order to provide us with sufficient evidence to give reasonable assurance that the financial statements are free from material misstatement, whether caused by fraud or other irregularity or error. In forming our opinion we also evaluated the overall adequacy of the presentation of information in the financial statements.

Opinion

In our opinion the financial statements:

- give a true and fair view, in accordance with United Kingdom Generally Accepted Accounting Practice, of the state of the company's affairs as at ... and of its profit [loss] for the year then ended; and

- have been properly prepared in accordance with the Companies Act 1985.

- the information given in the directors' report is consistent with the financial statements.

Registered auditors   *Address*
Date

The audit report has certain elements designed to eliminate common misconceptions:

- It is clearly addressed to shareholders
- Introductory paragraphs outlining what the report refers to
- Paragraphs outlining the responsibilities of directors and auditors
- An explanation of the basis on which the auditors have come to their conclusion
- An expression of opinion

However, some parties still argue that the audit report is a difficult document to understand. It still includes technical terms which require further explanation. It refers to certain items 'by exception' which users might not understand.

It is sometimes argued that the existence of standard report adds complexity to the situation and that users would be better served by having audit reports tailored to each specific client.

1.5.1 Advantages of a standard report

The key advantages of having a standard report is that it is **easier for users to understand** an audit report that has **elements in common** with all other audit reports. It also means that audit reports can be more easily compared.

When a standard report is used, there is less chance of isolated misunderstanding caused by the way one firm of auditors chooses to express itself or in relation to the explanation of a particular issue.

2 Forming and critically appraising an open audit

FAST FORWARD

Auditors express an opinion on financial statements based on the work they have done, the evidence obtained and conclusions drawn in relation to that evidence.

2.1 Forming an audit opinion

When the auditors have gathered all the evidence required, the audit engagement partner will form the audit opinion as to truth and fairness of the financial statements as a whole.

You should already be aware of the various audit opinions that can be given. Examples of the various standard reports in each case are given in the appendix to this Study Text.

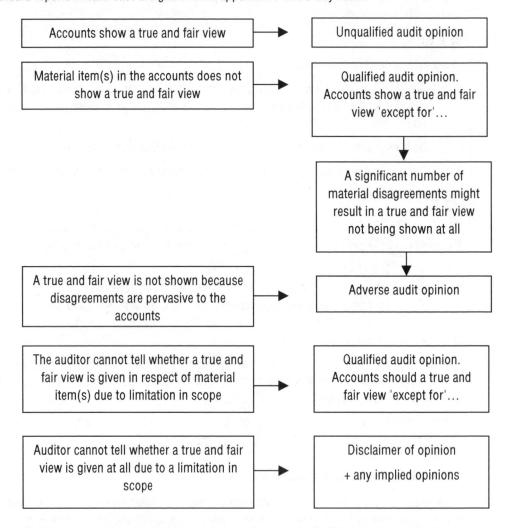

When forming their opinion, there are some key matters that the auditor must consider. These can be illustrated in the form of three questions:

Question 1 Have all the procedures necessary to meet auditing standards and to obtain all the information and explanations necessary for the audit have been carried out?

Question 2 Have the financial statements been prepared in accordance with the applicable accounting requirements?

Question 3 Do the financial statements give a true and fair view?

True: Information is factual and conforms with reality, not false. In addition the information conforms with required standards and law. The accounts have been correctly extracted from the books and records.

Fair: Information is free from discrimination and bias and in compliance with expected standards and rules. The accounts should reflect the commercial substance of the company's underlying transactions.

The process of forming an audit opinion can be summarised in a step format, as follows:

Step 1   Read through all the information given in the question carefully.

Step 2   Analyse the requirement.

Step 3   Read through the information given in the question again in the light of the requirement, making notes of any key factors.

Step 4   Ascertain whether all the evidence reasonably expected to be available has been obtained and evaluated.

Step 5   If not, identify whether the effect of not gaining evidence is such that the financial statements could as a whole be misleading (disclaimer of opinion) or in material part could be misleading ('except for' opinion).

Step 6   Ascertain whether the financial statements have been prepared in accordance with generally accepted accounting principles (GAAP).

Step 7   If not, determine whether departure was required to give a true and fair view and if so, whether it has been properly disclosed.

Step 8   Decide whether any unnecessary departure is material to the financial statements ('except for' opinion) or is pervasive to them (adverse opinion).

Step 9   Conclude whether the financial statements as a whole give a true and fair view.

Even if the answers to steps 4 and 6 are yes, you must still carry out step 9 and make an overall assessment of the truth and fairness of the financial statements in order to conclude that an unqualified opinion is appropriate.

2.2 Emphasis of matter paragraph

Sometimes an auditor may wish to issue an unqualified audit report containing an **emphasis of matter** (explanatory) **paragraph** to highlight a particular matter.

An example of this is when the financial statements are affected by a **fundamental uncertainty**, for example, over the going concern status of the company.

If the financial statements contain sufficient **disclosure** about the matter, the auditor will not need to qualify his opinion, but may wish to **draw attention** to the matter and the disclosures in his report.

An example of an audit report with an emphasis of matter (explanatory) paragraph is given in the appendix.

It is vital for your exam performance that you can analyse a set of facts given to you and draw audit conclusions from them. This is a basic skill at this level. Work through the following question to practice this skill.

Question

You are an audit senior. You are nearing the end of the audit of Nesta Ltd for the year ended 30 June 2006. Nesta Ltd owns a small chain of high-street clothing stores and also has a manufacturing division where it makes it own label brand 'Little Miss'. Own label clothing represents 50% of the inventory and sales of Nesta Co. The financial statements show a profit before tax of £7 million (2005: £3 million) and a balance sheet total of £23 million (2005: £15 million). The following points have arisen on the audit:

(1)   Nesta Ltd owns a number of its retail premises, which it revalues annually. This year several of its shops did rise sharply in value due to inflated property prices in their locality. Nesta also capitalises refits of its shops. Two shops were refitted in the year. The total increase in assets due to refits and revaluations is £10 million. Nesta does not revalue its factory premises, which are held in the Balance Sheet at £175,000.

(2)   Nesta values its stock at the lower of cost or net realisable value. Cost is determined by deducting a suitable estimated profit margin from selling price. Stock in the Balance Sheet at 30 June 2006 was £1,265,000.

(3)   Nesta Ltd has a refunds policy which states that a customer who is not satisfied with their purchase may return their goods within 28 days of purchase and obtain an exchange or a cash refund. Experience has shown that exchanges and refunds are common, as Nesta Ltd's shops do not provide fitting rooms, space being at a premium. Nesta does not make any provision in the financial statements for refunds.

Required

Comment on the matters you will consider in relation to the implications of the above points on the audit report of Nesta Ltd.

Answer

(1)   **Fixed assets**

There are two issues here. The first is whether Nesta's policy of revaluations is correct and the second is whether Nesta should capitalise re-fit costs.

The most important thing to consider is materiality as only material items will affect the audit opinion. The revaluations and refit total is material to the balance sheet. It is possible that any revaluation of the factory premises would also be material.

(i)   **Revaluation policy**

Per FRS 15, fixed assets may be held at cost or valuation. Where a company applies a revaluation policy, FRS 15 requires that all the assets in the relevant class of assets be revalued on a regular basis (at least every 5 years). Nesta revalues annually, so meets the latter requirement.

Nesta revalues property, so the question arises as to whether it should also revalue the factory. This might have a material effect on the balance sheet. However, FRS 15 allows that within the division of assets which are buildings, there could be further subdivisions for the purposes of revaluation. In this case, the classes 'retail premises' and 'manufacturing premises' would appear to be reasonable.

(ii)   **Refits**

Assets should be held at cost or valuation as discussed above. However, in some cases, FRS 15 allows the cost of refits to be added to the original cost of the asset. A retail shop will be subject to refitting and this refitting may enhance its value. However, it is possible in a shop that such refitting might be better classified as expenditure on fixtures and fittings. Nesta's policy should be consistent and comparable, so if they have followed a policy of capitalising refits into the cost of the shop in the past, this seems reasonable.

Conclusion

The issues relating to fixed assets were material and could have affected the auditors' report. However, having considered the issues, it appears that there are no disagreements between the auditors and the directors on these issues. As there appears to have been no limitation on the scope of the auditors' work in relation to fixed assets, the audit opinion would be unqualified in relation to these issues.

(2) **Stock**

SSAP 9 requires that stock be valued at the lower of cost or net realisable value. SSAP 9 defines cost as the expenditure which has been incurred in the normal course of business in bringing the product or service to its present location and condition.

The SSAP outlines a number of methods at arriving at an approximation of cost in the absence of a satisfactory costing system. One such method is the use of a selling price less an estimated profit margin. This is a costing method commonly used in retail enterprises. However, the SSAP states that this is reasonable only if it can be shown that the method gives a reasonable approximation of cost.

Given that 50% of Nesta's stock is manufactured in house, it appears to be unlikely that they cannot ascertain the cost of the stock in a better way than the selling price method. The chain of shops is small, and there should be sufficient controls over stock transfer to enable the company to establish the cost of stock using a FIFO system.

While the auditors might suggest to the directors that they look into the costing systems and make improvements in future years, it is unlikely that they would qualify the audit report in the current year over this matter, assuming that the directors have shown that the accounting policy gives a reasonable approximation of cost.

This is because if a reasonable approximation of cost is given, the difference is not going to be material to the financial statements. Also, if Nesta has had the policy for a long period, the policy is at least consistent with itself, as advised by FRS 18. If the auditors had made recommendations that the system was reviewed in future years and the directors refused to make any amendments to the system in future, the auditors might want to consider taking further action in future years.

Conclusion

If there are no other audit matters arising in relation to stock, the audit report will be unqualified in this respect.

(3) **Provisions**

Nesta offers refunds and exchanges to unhappy customers and experience shows that this offer is commonly taken up. If a sale is refunded, it is as if the sale never took place. It is therefore not prudent for Nesta to recognise profits on such sales. If items are exchanged, the profit element would still exist, so only the stock element would be potentially misstated.

As the refund period is 28 days, the issue is isolated to sales made in the last month of the year. In the absence of specific figures, this approximates to 1/12 of annual turnover and profit, and is therefore potentially material. Using these approximations, this would mean that if more than a quarter of Junes sales were refunded, this could be material to turnover, and potentially to profit.

Given that the accounts are unlikely to be finalised before the end of July, the refunds figure for June should be available to both the directors and to the auditors. They should both be able to assess whether the potential provision required is material to the financial statements, and how much the provision should be, if one is required.

Conclusion

The audit report would only be qualified in respect of this matter if the auditors felt that a material provision was required and the directors refused to include one in the financial statements. In which case, the auditors would issue an 'except for' opinion, on the grounds of disagreement.

Overall conclusion

It appears likely that the auditors will issue an unqualified report for the year ended 30 June 2006.

2.3 Critically appraising an audit opinion

Critiquing an audit opinion is an extension of forming an audit opinion. It is necessary to form an audit opinion yourself in order to ascertain whether someone else's conclusions on the same facts is fair and reasonable.

2.3.1 When will it be necessary to critically appraise an audit opinion?

The obvious answer to this is 'in exam questions'. However, the exams will be based in real-life scenarios and it is important for you to consider the genuine contexts in which audit opinions will be appraised. Consider the following situations:

- Engagement partner reviewing the audit work and conclusions drawn
- Auditor asked for second opinion about an audit opinion
- Second partner required to review an audit file

Stop!

> If you don't know what a second opinion is, go back to Chapter 2. If you don't know why a second partner might be reviewing an audit file, go back to Chapter 4.

Probably the most common example is the engagement partner conducting his file review before drawing his opinion, which he will then give on the audit report that he takes responsibility for. His audit team have carried out the work, and in doing so have drawn audit conclusions about each aspect of the audit work. He must appraise these conclusions and determine whether they are correct or not.

Where a second partner review has been required, for instance, if the client is listed or public interest, one of the things the second partner is required to do is to review the audit opinion suggested and see whether it is reasonable.

The issue of second opinions, as you know, is a tricky one. It is rarely advisable for an auditor to give a second opinion on an audit opinion because he is likely not to be in possession of the full facts.

2.3.2 How should an auditor critically appraise an audit opinion?

An auditor should form his own opinion on the basis of the facts and then evaluate the original audit opinion in the light of his own opinion. As this is a matter of judgement, it is possible that two different, yet reasonable conclusions could be drawn. For instance, auditors might disagree on whether a matter was material or not. If this was the case, further judgements and risk assessments would have to be made.

In exam questions, then, you should bear in mind the step process required to form an audit opinion in the first place. If you work through each step, you may be able to see that the person who formed the original opinion has missed out steps or failed to notice something important.

In the final analysis, this is a skill that you must practise to be able to do well. Try the following question.

Question
Critically appraising an audit opinion

You are an audit partner. Your firm carries out the audit of Branch plc, a listed company. Because the company is listed, you have been asked to perform a second partner review of the audit file for the year ended 30 June 2007 before the audit opinion is finalised. Reported profit before tax is £1.65 million and the balance sheet total is £7.6 million.

You have read the following notes from the audit file:

Earnings per share

As required by FRS 22 *Earning per share*, the company has disclosed both basic and diluted earnings per share. The diluted earnings per share has been incorrectly calculated because the share options held by a director were not included in the calculations. Disclosed diluted earnings per share are 22.9p. Had the share options held by the director been included, this figure would have been 22.4p. This difference is immaterial.

Financial performance statement

The directors have currently not amended certain financial performance ratios in this statement to reflect the changes made to the financial statements as a result of the auditors' work. The difference between the reported ratios and the correct ratios is minimal.

Opinion

We recommend that an unqualified audit report be issued.'

You have noted that there is no evidence on the audit file that the corporate governance statement to be issued as part of the annual report has been reviewed by the audit team. You are aware that the company does not have an audit committee.

You are also aware that the director exercised his share options last week.

Required

Comment on the suitability of the proposed audit opinion and other matters arising in the light of your review. Your comments should include an indication of what form the audit report should take.

Answer

Earnings per share

The problem in the EPS calculation relates to share options held by a director. As they are held by a director, it is unlikely that they are immaterial, as matters relating to directors are generally considered to be material by their nature. The fact that EPS is a key shareholder ratio which is therefore likely to be material in nature to the shareholders should also be considered.

As the incorrect EPS calculation is therefore material to the financial statements, the audit report should be modified in this respect, unless the directors agree to amend the EPS figure. This would be an 'except for' modification, on the grounds of disagreement.

Share options

The share options have not been included in the EPS calculations. The auditors must ensure that the share options have been correctly disclosed in information relating to the director both in the financial statements and the other information, and that these disclosures are consistent with each other. If proper disclosures have not been made, the auditor will have to modify the audit report due to lack of disclosure in this area.

Exercise of share options

The fact that the director has exercised his share options after the year end does not require disclosure in the financial statements. However, it is likely that he has exercised them as part of a new share issue by the company and if so, the share issue would be a non-adjusting post balance sheet event that would require disclosure in the financial statements. We should check if this is the case and, if so, whether it has been disclosed. Non-disclosure would be further grounds for modification.

Financial performance statement

The financial performance statement forms part of the other information that the auditor is required to review under ISA 720. The ISA states that the auditors should seek to rectify any apparent misstatements in this information. The ratio figures are misstated, and the auditor should encourage the directors to correct them, regardless of the negligible difference.

The ISA refers to material items. The ratios will be of interest to shareholders, being investor information and this fact may make them material by their nature. However, as the difference is negligible in terms of value, on balance, the difference is probably not sufficiently material for the auditors to make any modifications or explanations in their audit report.

Corporate governance statement

For the company to meet Stock Exchange requirements, the auditors must review the corporate governance statement. For our own purposes, we should document that we have done so. As having an audit committee is a requirement of the Combined Code and the company does not have one, the corporate governance statement should explain why the company does not have comply with the Code in this respect.

We would not modify our audit report over the corporate governance statement, although we might like to include a reference to it in an emphasis of matter paragraph, if we do not feel the disclosure is sufficient in respect of the non-compliance with the requirement to have an audit committee.

This emphasis of matter paragraph would be contained within the opinion section, after the opinion on the truth and fairness of the financial statements has been given. The opinion would not be modified in this respect.

Overall conclusion

None of the matters discussed above, either singly or seen together are pervasive to the financial statements. The audit report should be modified on the material matter of the incorrect EPS calculation. We should ensure that all the other disclosures are in order and also review the corporate governance statement. If the corporate governance statement does not adequately address the issue of the company not having an audit committee, we will need to include an emphasis of matter paragraph in the opinion section of our report. Our opinion will not be modified in this respect.

Exam focus point

This question required you to evaluate an audit opinion, but did not actually contain a section from an audit report for you to comment on. A question in the exam might. You should try question 'Delphinius' in the Practice and Revision Kit on this area.

3 Reporting electronically

When financial information is available electronically, auditors must ensure that their report is not misrepresented.

3.1 Consent

The problems associated with audit reports being published on websites have been discussed in Section 2. The Auditing Practices Board has issued a bulletin to help the auditor respond properly to a request to publish the audit report electronically.

The Bulletin proposes that the directors should **obtain the consent** of the auditors to publish the audit report on a website. The matter should **ideally be referred to** in the **letter of engagement** between the parties.

The auditors may **reserve the right to decline** the report being so published, if they do not like the presentation of the report and the associated financial statements that the directors propose.

Guidance has been published by another body which advises directors to highlight statutory information given on the website.

3.2 Appropriate wording

The auditors should ensure that their report is worded so that it is appropriate for inclusion on a website. This will include reference to specific financial statements rather than the use of page numbers, for example.

3.3 Controls

Where the auditors' report is to be published electronically, the auditors should carry out a series of checks:

- They should **review the process** for deriving the electronic information from the hard copy financial statements

- They should **check** that the electronic copy is **identical** to the hard copy

- They should **check** that the **presentation** has **not** been **distorted** (ie, that certain items have not been given greater emphasis in the new presentation)

As the directors are responsible for controls in their business, they are responsible for ensuring that the report is not tampered with once it is on the website.

Exam focus point

You should read the accountancy press to follow any developments in this area.

4 Special purpose audit reports

FAST FORWARD

Auditors may issue special reports on summary financial statements, revised accounts and distributions following an audit qualification.

4.1 Summary financial statements

S 251(1) of the Companies Act 1985 provides that a listed public company may issue only summary financial statements to its members instead of the full annual accounts and directors' report. Such statements must comply with Regulations laid down by the Secretary of State.

The summary financial statements must be accompanied by a statement from the company's auditors which states that:

(a) The **summary financial statements** are **consistent** with the **annual accounts** and the **directors' report.**

(b) The **summary financial statements comply** with s 251 Companies Act 1985 and the regulations made under that section (Companies (Summary Financial Statement) Regulations 1995 (SI 1995 2092).

Guidance for auditors is provided by the APB Bulletin 1999/6 *The Auditors' Statement on the Summary Financial Statement.* The terms of the engagement and the extent of the auditors' examination should be agreed in an engagement letter. The fact that auditors are reporting on **consistency** and **compliance** with **s 251**, and **not** on **truth** and **fairness**, will influence the work that they do.

Inconsistencies which auditors will seek include:

(a) **Information** which has been **inaccurately extracted** from the statutory accounts and the directors' report

(b) The **use of headings** in the summary financial statements which are **incompatible** with those used in the full accounts

(c) **Information** which has been **summarised** in a manner which is **inconsistent** with the statutory accounts and the directors' report

(d) **Omission** of **information** which is not required by the regulations but which is necessary to ensure consistency with the statutory accounts and the directors' report (for example information relating to an exceptional item)

If an inconsistency is found auditors should discuss with the directors how to eliminate the inconsistency, for example by including additional information. If the **inconsistency** is **not eliminated,** the auditors should **modify** their **statement.**

When checking for compliance with s 251, auditors should check whether the summary financial statement includes **information** that has **not** been **properly derived** from the full accounts and directors' report. Auditors will also consider whether a **qualified audit report** on the full accounts has been **accurately reproduced** in the summary statements, and any relevant extra information to enable the user to understand the qualification has been given.

The auditors should **read** prior to issue any **other information** which is contained in a document which also contains the summary financial statement. If there is an inconsistency between that other information and the summary financial statement, the auditors should take similar steps to those prescribed in SAS 160 for an inconsistency between the full accounts and other information.

An example unmodified auditors' statement on the summary financial statements is re-produced below.

4.1.1 Example unmodified statement on the summary financial statement

---

Auditors' statement to the shareholders of XYZ plc

We have examined the summary financial statements set out on pages ... .

Respective responsibilities of directors and auditors

The directors are responsible for preparing the [summarised annual report]. Our responsibility is to report to you our opinion on the consistency of the summary financial statement within the [summarised annual report] with the full annual accounts and directors' report, and its compliance with the relevant requirements of s 251 of the Companies Act 1985 and the regulations made thereunder. We also read the other information contained in the [summarised annual report] and consider the implications for our report if we become aware of any apparent misstatements or material inconsistencies with the summary financial statement.

Basis of opinion

We conducted our work in accordance with Bulletin 1999/6 'The auditors' statement on the summary financial statement' issued by the Auditing Practices Board.
Opinion

In our opinion the summary financial statement above/overleaf is consistent with the full annual accounts and directors' report of XYZ plc for the year ended 20..... and complies with the applicable requirements of s 251 of the Companies Act 1985, and the regulations made thereunder.

Registered auditors   *Address*
Date

4.2 Revised accounts

In May 1991 the APC published an exposure draft of an auditing guideline *Auditors' report on revised annual accounts and directors' reports*, which has not yet been replaced by APB guidance. The main provisions are discussed below.

The reason for the publication of a draft guideline is that CA 1989 introduced provisions dealing with the revision of annual accounts and directors' reports which have been found, after their laying or delivering, to be defective.

The revision may be voluntary or by court order, due to non-compliance with the Act. Voluntary revision of the accounts or the report under s 245 is not obligatory.

The revision of the accounts or directors' report may be undertaken by:

- **Revision by replacement**, replacing the original with a new version
- **Revision by supplementary note**

In both these cases, accounts or reports are to be prepared 'as if .... prepared and then approved by the directors as at the date of the original annual accounts', which means that the extent of any revision is limited to that resulting from the facts which were known or discoverable at the original date of approval.

The directors must include a statement in a prominent place in the revised accounts which gives full details of the revision.

The Regulations also state that the duties of the auditors set out in s 237 apply in respect of the report on revised accounts.

The guideline suggests factors to be taken into account when determining the extent of audit work to be performed in relation to the revised accounts.

- Whether the nature of the matter suggest that errors in the accounts may be **pervasive**

- Whether the facts discovered since the approval of the accounts **affect past assumptions** in areas of judgement

- The extent of any consequential **changes** to the form of accounts, which arise from the matter, for example, group accounts may be required for the first time

- The **steps taken by the directors** to investigate and correct the defect

The guideline also lists specific procedures which should be undertaken.

- **Review** the **original audit plans** in the light of the analysis of the matter leading to revision

- **Consider** the extent to which **additional audit evidence** is required

- **Reassess** the **various matters of judgement** involved in the preparation of the original accounts

- **Obtain evidence** that **relates to the adjustments made** to the original accounts

- **Carry out a review** of the **period after the date** on which the original accounts were approved

- **Perform a review** of the **revised accounts**, such as is sufficient, in conjunction with the conclusions drawn from the other audit evidence obtained, to give the auditors a reasonable basis for their opinion on the accounts

- **Consider** any **legal and regulatory consequences** of the revision

---

4.2.1 Examples of the auditors' report on revised accounts

(a)   When revision is effected by replacement

Auditors' report to the members of XYZ Limited

We have audited the revised financial statements on pages ... to ... which have been prepared under the accounting policies set out on pages ... and ... . The revised financial statements replace the original financial statements approved by the directors on ... .

Respective responsibilities of directors and auditors

As described on page ... the directors are responsible for the preparation of financial statements. [*Note*]

It is our responsibility to form an independent opinion, based on our audit, on these revised financial statements and to report our opinion to you. We are also required to report whether in our opinion the original financial statements failed to comply with the requirements of the Companies Act 1985 in the respects identified by the directors.

Bases of opinion

We conducted our audit in accordance with Auditing Standards issued by the Auditing Practices Board. An audit includes examination, on a test basis, of evidence relevant to the amounts and disclosures in the financial statements. It also includes an assessment of the significant estimates and judgements made by the directors in the preparation of the financial statements, and of whether the accounting policies are appropriate to the company's circumstances, consistently applied and adequately disclosed. The audit of revised financial statements includes the performance of additional procedures to assess whether the revisions made by the directors are appropriate and have been properly made.

We planned and performed our audit so as to obtain all the information and explanations which we considered necessary in order to provide us with sufficient evidence to give reasonable assurance that the revised financial statements are free from material mis-statement, whether caused by fraud or other irregularity or error. In forming our opinion, we also evaluated the overall adequacy of the presentation of information in the revised financial statements.

Opinions

In our opinion the revised financial statements give a true and fair view, seen as at the date the original financial statements were approved, of the state of the company's affairs as at ... and of its profit (loss) for the year then ended and have been properly prepared in accordance with the provisions of the Companies Act 1985 as they have effect under the Companies (Revision of Defective Accounts and Report) Regulations 1990.

In our opinion the original financial statements for the year ended ... failed to comply with the requirements of the Companies Act 1985 in the respects identified by the directors in the statement contained in note x to these financial statements.

Registered auditors   *Address*
Date

Note. If the directors' responsibilities with respect to revised financial statements are not set out in a separate statement, the auditors will include a description in their report.

(b)   When the revision is effected by issue of a supplementary note

Auditors' report to the members of XYZ Limited

We have audited the revised financial statements of XYZ Limited for the year ended ... The revised financial statements replace the original financial statements approved by the directors on ... and consist of the attached supplementary note together with the original financial statements which were circulated to members on ... .

Respective responsibilities of directors and auditors

As described on page ... the directors are responsible for the preparation of financial statements.

It is our responsibility to form an independent opinion, based on our audit, on these revised financial statements and to report our opinion to you. We are also required to report whether in our opinion the original financial statements failed to comply with the requirements of the Companies Act 1985 in the respects identified by the directors.

Bases of opinion

We conducted our audit in accordance with Auditing Standards issued by the Auditing Practices Board. An audit includes examination, on a test basis, of evidence relevant to the amounts and disclosures in the financial statements. It also includes an assessment of the significant estimates and judgements made by the directors in the preparation of the financial statements, and of whether the accounting policies are appropriate to the company's circumstances, consistently applied and adequately disclosed. The audit of revised financial statements includes the performance of additional procedures to assess whether the revisions made by the directors are appropriate and have been properly made.

We planned and performed our audit so as to obtain all the information and explanations which we considered necessary in order to provide us with sufficient evidence to give reasonable assurance that the revised financial statements are free from material mis-statement, whether caused by fraud or other irregularity or error. In forming our opinion, we also evaluated the overall adequacy of the presentation of information in the revised financial statements.

475

Opinions

In our opinion the revised financial statements give a true and fair view, seen as at the date the original financial statements were approved, of the state of the company's affairs as at ... and of its profit (loss) for the year then ended and have been properly prepared in accordance with the provisions of the Companies Act 1985 as they have effect under the Companies (Revision of Defective Accounts and Report) Regulations 1990.

In our opinion the original financial statements for the year ended ... failed to comply with the requirements of the Companies Act 1985 in the respects identified by the directors in the supplementary note.

Registered auditors   *Address*
Date

4.3 Distributions following an audit qualification

Under the Companies Act 1985, companies whose accounts have been qualified may only make a distribution (pay a dividend) only under certain circumstances.

The question whether a company has profits from which to pay a dividend is determined by reference to its **'relevant accounts'** which are generally the latest audited annual accounts: s 270. Relevant accounts must be properly prepared in accordance with the requirements of the Companies Acts.

If the auditors have qualified their report on the accounts they must also state in writing whether, in their opinion, the subject matter of their qualification (if it relates to statutory accounting requirements) is material in determining whether the dividend may be paid: s 271 CA 1985.

A copy of this statement must be laid before the company in general meeting. An example is given here.

Auditors' statement to the members of ABC Limited in accordance with Section 271(4) of the Companies Act 1985

We have audited the financial statements of ABC Limited for the year ended (date) in accordance with Auditing Standards issued by the Auditing Practices Board and have expressed a qualified opinion thereon.

Basis of opinion

We have carried out such procedures as we considered necessary to evaluate the effect of the qualified opinion in the context of determining profits available for distribution.

Opinion

In our opinion the subject of that qualification is not material for the purpose of determining, by reference to those financial statements, whether the distribution (interim dividend for the year ended ...) of £ ... proposed by the company is permitted under section 263 of the Companies Act 1985.

Registered auditor

This statement (and the work of the auditors which precedes it) is very important, because a dividend paid **ultra vires** (that is, beyond the powers of the company) can be recovered by the company or the liquidator. This may leave the auditors open to a claim of negligence.

In order to issue a s 271(4) statement, the auditors must reassure themselves that the proposed distribution will be made out of profits available for that purpose (ie distributable profits). These will be **accumulated, realised profits**, so far as not previously utilised by distribution or capitalism, **less accumulated, realised losses**, so far as not previously written off.

S 264(3) defines **undistributable** profits as:

- The share premium account
- The capital redemption reserve
- Any excess of accumulated unrealised profits (not capitalised) over accumulated unrealised losses (not written off)
- Any other reserve which the company is prohibited from distributing by statute, memorandum or articles

5 Reporting to those charged with governance

FAST FORWARD

Auditors must report relevant audit matters to those charged with governance and will also sometimes produce a report to management detailing control weaknesses observed during the audit.

5.1 Report to those charged with governance

ISA (UK and Ireland) 260 *Communication of audit matters with those charged with governance,* gives guidance in this area.

ey term

Governance is the term used to describe the role of persons entrusted with the supervision, control and direction of the entity. Those charged with governance ordinarily are accountable for ensuring that the entity achieves its objectives, financial reporting and reporting to interested parties. Those charged with governance include management only when it performs such functions.

ISA 260.2

The auditor should communicate audit matters of governance interest arising from the audit of financial statements with those charged with governance of an entity.

The scope of the ISA is limited to matters that come to the auditors' attention as a result of the audit; the auditors are not required to design procedures to identify matters of governance interest.

ISA 260.5

The auditor should determine the relevant persons who are charged with governance and with whom audit matters of governance interest are communicated.

The auditors may communicate with the whole board, the supervisory board or the audit committee depending on the governance structure of the organisation. To avoid misunderstandings, the engagement letter should explain that auditors will only **communicate matters** that come to their attention as a **result** of the **performance** of the audit. It should state that the auditors are **not required** to **design procedures** for the purpose of identifying matters of governance interest.

The letter may also:

- **Describe** the **form** which any **communications** on governance matters will take
- **Identify** the **relevant persons** with whom such communications will be made
- **Identify** any **specific matters** of **governance** interest which it has agreed are to be communicated

ISA. 260.11

The auditor should consider matters of governance interest that arise from the audit of the financial statements and communicate them with those charged with governance.

Matters would include:

- Relationships that may bear on the firm's independence and the integrity and objectives of the audit engagement partner and audit staff
- The **general approach** or overall scope of the audit, including limitations or additional requirements
- Selection of, or changes in, **significant accounting policies**
- The potential effect on the financial statements of any **significant risks** and **exposures**, for example pending litigation, that are required to be disclosed in the accounts
- Significant **audit adjustments**
- **Material uncertainties** affecting the organisation's ability to continue as a going concern
- **Significant disagreements** with management
- **Expected modifications** to the audit report
- Other **significant matters** such as material weaknesses in internal control, questions regarding management integrity, and fraud involving management
- Other **matters** mentioned in **terms** of **engagement**

The UK version of the ISA stipulates the following.

ISA 260.11-7

The auditor should communicate to those charged with governance an outline of the nature and scope, including, where relevant, any limitations thereon, of the work the auditor proposes to undertake and the form of the reports the auditor expects to make.

ISA 260.11-12

The auditor should communicate the following findings form the audit to those charged with governance:

(a) The auditor's views about the qualitative aspects of the entity's accounting practices and financial reporting

(b) The final draft of the representation letter, that the auditor is requesting management and those charged with governance to sign. The communication should specifically refer to any matters where management is reluctant to make the representations requested by the auditor

(c) Uncorrected misstatements

(d) Expected modifications to the auditor's report

(e) Material weaknesses in internal control identified during the audit

(f) Matters specifically required by other ISAs (UK and Ireland) to be communicated to those charged with governance, and

(g) Any other audit matters of governance interest

ISA 260.11-19

The auditor should seek to obtain a written representation from those charged with governance that explains their reasons for not correcting misstatements brought to their attention by the auditor.

ISA 260.13

The auditor should consider audit matters of governance interest on a timely basis. ... [and] should plan with those charged with governance the form and timing of communication to them.

5.1.1 Communication methods

Matters may be communicated orally or in writing, but they should be recorded in the audit working papers, however discussed. Auditors should make clear that the audit is not designed to identify all relevant matters connected with governance.

The extent, form the frequency of reports wil be affected by:

- the size and nature of the client
- the attitude of those charged with governance and
- the importance of the issues to be raised.

For example, reports of relatively minor matters to a small client may be best handled orally via a meeting or telephone conversation.

5.1.2 Timing of communication

Reports should be made promptly to allow those charged with governance to take appropriate action.

5.1.3 Current developments

ISA 260 is currently being revised. The ED extends the list of matters to be communicated, particularly matters relating to auditor independence (previously listed entities only).

Keep an eye out for any articles on this topic in *Student Accountant*.

5.2 Reporting to management

Auditors may also issue a report on control weaknesses to management. These reports were a key element in your earlier studies in auditing.

FAST FORWARD

> The primary purpose of the report to management is to inform management of weaknesses in the system of internal controls but the letter can also be used for other purposes.

5.2.1

Recap of key qualities of a report to management

- It should not **include language** that **conflicts** with the **opinion** expressed in the audit report.

- It should state that the **accounting and internal control** system were **considered only** to the **extent necessary** to **determine** the **auditing procedures** to report on the financial statements and not to determine the adequacy of internal control for management purposes or to provide assurances on the accounting and internal control systems.

- It will state that it **discusses only weaknesses** in internal control which have **come to the auditors' attention** as a result of the **audit** and that other weaknesses in internal control may exist.

- It should also include a statement that the **communication is provided for use only** by **management** (or another specific named party).

- The auditors will usually ascertain the actions taken, including the reasons for those suggestions rejected

- The auditors may encourage management to respond to the auditors' comments in which case any response can be included in the report

5.2.2 Form of reports

The form of the report will depend on the type of organisation concerned. It may be appropriate to divide the report into sections, which cover significant and general points for senior management first, and then proceed to more specific, divisional points in subsequent sections. The report covering findings from the audit may typically be formed of a covering letter (see **Example**) and a schedule of points raised.

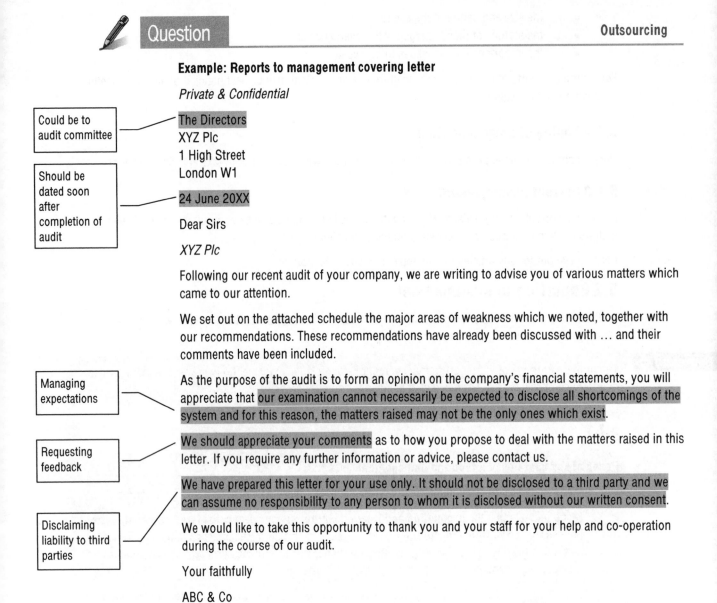

Question

Outsourcing

Example: Reports to management covering letter

Private & Confidential

Could be to audit committee

The Directors
XYZ Plc
1 High Street
London W1

Should be dated soon after completion of audit

24 June 20XX

Dear Sirs

XYZ Plc

Following our recent audit of your company, we are writing to advise you of various matters which came to our attention.

We set out on the attached schedule the major areas of weakness which we noted, together with our recommendations. These recommendations have already been discussed with … and their comments have been included.

Managing expectations

As the purpose of the audit is to form an opinion on the company's financial statements, you will appreciate that our examination cannot necessarily be expected to disclose all shortcomings of the system and for this reason, the matters raised may not be the only ones which exist.

Requesting feedback

We should appreciate your comments as to how you propose to deal with the matters raised in this letter. If you require any further information or advice, please contact us.

Disclaiming liability to third parties

We have prepared this letter for your use only. It should not be disclosed to a third party and we can assume no responsibility to any person to whom it is disclosed without our written consent.

We would like to take this opportunity to thank you and your staff for your help and co-operation during the course of our audit.

Your faithfully

ABC & Co

5.2.3 Specific recommendations

The detailed recommendations included in the appendix would be structured as per the following example.

Sufficient detail
to enable
directors to
follow up

Explain
potential effect
on client
business

Workable
recommendations,
discussed with
management in
advance

Preparation of payroll and maintenance of personnel records

Weakness

Under your present system, just two members of staff are entirely and equally responsible for the maintenance of personnel records and preparation of the payroll. Furthermore, the only independent check of any nature on the payroll is that the chief accountant confirms that the amount of the wages cheque presented to him for signature agrees with the total of the net wages column in the payroll. This latter check does not involve any consideration of the reasonableness of the amount of the total net wages cheque or the monies being shown as due to individual employees.

Implications

It is a serious weakness of your present system, that so much responsibility is vested in the hands of just two people. This situation is made worse by the fact that there is no clearly defined division of duties as between the two of them. In our opinion, it would be far too easy for fraud to take place in this area (eg by inserting the names of 'dummy workmen' into the personnel records and hence on to the payroll) and/or for clerical errors to go undetected.

Recommendations

(i)   Some person other than the two wages clerks be made responsible for maintaining the personnel records and for periodically (but on a surprise basis) checking them against the details on the payroll.

(ii)   The two wages clerks be allocated specific duties in relation to the preparation of the payroll, with each clerk independently reviewing the work of the other.

(iii)   When the payroll is presented in support of the cheque for signature to the chief accountant, that he should be responsible for assessing the reasonableness of the overall charge for wages that week.

Chapter roundup

- A standard format is used to promote understandability because the audit report is widely available to both accustomed users and users who are not accustomed to audit and audit language.

- The availability of audit reports has been increased by the trend to publish financial statements on companies' websites. Auditors should consider the risks of this.

- Auditors express an opinion on financial statements based on the work they have done, the evidence obtained and conclusions drawn in relation to that evidence.

- When financial information is available electronically, auditors must ensure that their report is not misrepresented.

- Auditors may issue special reports on

    - Summary financial statements
    - Revised accounts
    - Distributions following an audit qualification

- Auditors must report relevant audit matters to those charged with governance and will also sometimes produce a report to management detailing control weaknesses observed during the audit.

- The primary purpose of the report to management is to inform management of weaknesses in the system of internal controls but the letter can also be used for other purposes.

Quick quiz

1   Name the opinions auditors may give.

    (1)   ....

    (2)   ....

    (3)   ....

2   Complete the definitions

    (a)   ....: Information is free from .... and
           .... and in compliance with the expected standards and rules.

    (b)   .... is an expression of the relative .... or importance
           of a particular matter in the .... as a whole.

    (c)   ....: Information is .... and conforms with
           ...., not .... Information conforms with required
           standards and law.

3   List the main contents of the ISA 700, standard, unqualified report.

4   Name 5 matters which might be covered in a letter to those charged with governance.

    (1)   ....

    (2)   ....

    (3)   ....

    (4)   ....

    (5)   ....

Answers to quick quiz

1   (1)   Unqualified
     (2)   Modified due to disagreement
     (3)   Modified due to limitation in scope

2   (a)   Fair, discrimination, bias
     (b)   Materiality, significance, financial statements
     (c)   True, factual, reality, false

3   Title, addressee, introductory paragraph, responsibilities of directors/auditors, opinion paragraph, other matters, date, signature, address

4   • The **general approach** or overall scope of the audit, including limitations or additional requirements

     • Selection of, or changes in, **significant accounting policies**

     • The potential effect on the financial statements of any **significant risks** and **exposures**, for example pending litigation, that are required to be disclosed in the accounts

     • Significant **audit adjustments**

     • **Material uncertainties** affecting the organisation's ability to continue as a going concern

     • **Significant disagreements** with management

     • **Expected modifications** to the audit report

     • Other **significant matters** such as material weaknesses in internal control, questions regarding management integrity, and fraud involving management

     • Other **matters** mentioned in **terms** of **engagement**

Now try the question below from the Exam Question Bank

Number	Level	Marks	Time
Q27	Examination	15	27 mins

Part F

Current issues and developments

Current issues

Topic list	Syllabus reference
1 Summary of current issues	Various
2 Update	F5

Introduction

At this level in your studies you are expected to be familiar with current developments affecting the audit and assurance profession. Currently, many of these relate to international regulation.

You must read *Student Accountant* and the wider professional press to keep up to date with these.

Study guide

		Intellectual level
F	**Current issues and developments**	
	Discuss the relative merits and the consequences of different standpoints taken in current debates and express opinions supported by reasoned arguments.	
1	**Professional, ethical and corporate governance**	
(a)	Discuss the relative advantages of an ethical framework and a rulebook.	2
(b)	Evaluate the adequacy of existing ways in which objectivity may be safeguarded and suggest additional measures to improve independence.	3
(c)	Identify and assess relevant emerging ethical issues and evaluate the safeguards available.	3
(d)	Discuss IFAC developments including:	2
(i)	the implementation and adoption of International Standards on Auditing (ISAs) (UK and Ireland) by the Auditing Practices Board (APB)	
(ii)	significant current assurance issues being dealt with by APB.	
(e)	Assess the relative advantages and disadvantages of partnership status, limited liability partnerships and incorporation of audit firms.	2
(f)	Discuss current developments in the limitation of auditors' liability and the practical ways in which the risk of litigation and liability can be reduced in a given situation.	3
(g)	Discuss innovations in corporate governance (eg enterprise-wide risk management) and their impact on boards of directors, audit committees and internal auditors.	3
2	**Information technology**	
(a)	Describe recent trends in IT and their current and potential impact on auditors (eg the audit implications of 'cyberincidents' and other risks).	2
(b)	Explain how IT may be used to assist auditors and discuss the problems that may be encountered in automating the audit process.	2
3	**Transnational audits**	
(a)	Define 'transnational audits' and explain the role of the Transnational Audit Committee (TAC) of IFAC.	1
(b)	Discuss how transnational audits may differ from other audits of historical financial information (eg in terms of applicable financial reporting and auditing standards, listing requirements and corporate governance requirements).	2
(c)	Discuss the need for international audit firm networks in implementing international auditing standards.	2
(d)	Distinguish, for example, between 'global auditing firms' and second tier firms.	2
(e)	Discuss the impact of globalisation on audit firms and their clients.	2
(f)	Explain the advantages and problems of current trends (eg to merge, to divest consultancy services).	2

		Intellectual level
4	**Social and environmental auditing**	
(a)	Discuss the increasing importance of policies that govern the relationship of an organization to its employees, society and the environment.	2
(b)	Describe the difficulties in measuring and reporting on economic, environmental and social performance and give examples of performance measures and sustainability indicators.	2
(c)	Explain the auditor's main considerations in respect of social and environmental matters and how they impact on entities and their financial statements (eg impairment of assets, provisions and contingent liabilities).	2
(d)	Describe substantive procedures to detect potential misstatements in respect of socioenvironmental matters.	2
(e)	Discuss the form and content of an independent verification statement (eg on an environmental management system (EMS) and a report to society).	2
5	**Other current issues**	
(a)	Discuss how the potential problems associated with the audit of small enterprises may be overcome.	2
(b)	Explain how International Standards on Auditing (UK and Ireland) affect smaller firms.	2
(c)	Discuss the dominance of the global firms and their influence and impact on the accounting profession.	2
(d)	Discuss the impact of developments in public company oversight on external auditors.	2
(e)	Explain current developments in auditing standards including the need for new and revised standards and evaluate their impact on the conduct of audits.	3
(f)	Discuss other current legal, ethical, other professional and practical matters that affect accountants, auditors, their employers and the profession.	3

Exam guide

You may be asked to discuss current developments and must be prepared to argue for or against any new proposals from the point of view of either a preparer or user of assurance reports.

1 Summary of current issues

This text has covered the wide range of current issues within the relevant topic chapters. The following summary should remind you of the issues you have studied up to this point.

	Chapter(s)
Professional, ethical and corporate governance topics	1, 2 and 3
Information technology	6
Transnational audits	11
Social and environmental auditing	15
Other	various

2 Update

2.1 The IAASB's clarity project

2.1.1 Overview

As you know, the IAASB is responsible for setting ISAs. However, in 2005 the IAASB reviewed the drafting conventions used in its ISAs, with a view to improving the clarity, and therefore the consistent application, of its ISAs.

This involves:

- Setting an overall objective for each ISA

- Clarifying the obligations imposed on auditors by the requirements of ISAs by using the word "shall" instead of the word "should" to emphasise that auditors are expected to comply with the requirements in virtually all engagements

- Incorporating guidance on considerations specific to the audit of smaller entities into the ISAs

- Improving the overall readability and understandability of the ISAs.

2.1.2 Progress to date

With this in mind, the IAASB reissued its *Preface to International Standards on Quality Control, Auditing, Review, Other Assurance and Related Services* in January 2007 in order to establish the conventions to be used by the board in drafting future ISAs. The IAASB has also implemented a plan to complete the revision of certain ISAs and the redrafting of all ISAs by the end of 2008.

Of the IAASB's 32 standards in issue currently, 11 are under full revision and will be issued in the clarity form, nine have been revised in the last few years but will be redrafted in the clarity form, and the remaining 12 will be redrafted in the clarity form without revision.

To date, four final ISAs have been issued which are drafted in accordance with the new conventions and several exposure drafts of ISAs redrafted in the new clarity form have been approved for public comment. These include ISA 200 (revised and redrafted) *Overall objective of the independent auditor, and the conduct of an audit in accordance with International Standards on Auditing*, ISA 250 (redrafted) *The auditor's responsibilities relating to laws and regulations in an audit of financial statements* and ISA 500 (redrafted) *Considering the relevance and reliability of audit evidence*.

2.1.3 Implications for auditors in the UK

The APB will not issue any new standards for the time being. Instead the APB will focus on responding to the IAASB exposure drafts resulting from the clarity project. There is some concern that the revised standards will have an increased level of prescription. The APB favour a more principles based approach and believe that too many rules can detract from auditors' judgement and lead to a "tick box" approach to auditing.

The EU has passed a directive on the audit of company accounts. This will apply in all member states from mid 2008 and will include the adoption of international auditing standards. The APB will be actively involved in the standards adoption process in the UK when, assuming that the European commission approves the "clarity" standards, it is these revised standards that will come into force for all UK statutory audits.

2.2 Guidance on smaller audits

The APB issued two consultation papers in January 2007 regarding guidance for auditors of smaller entities. These involve questions as to whether additional guidance is needed, if so who should issue it and how this relates to training responsibilities. In general terms the APB, along with the IAASB, take the view that "an audit is an audit" and that all audits should be conducted in accordance with the same auditing standards.

2.2.1 Documentation

The ISAs (UK and Ireland) were issued in December 2004. Most of the requirements were very similar to those in the previous standards but some, particularly ISA (UK and Ireland) 315 *Understanding the entity and its environment*, increased the requirements for documentation, in part to support external monitoring of audit quality. Some auditors have argued that these requirements are not cost effective in the context of audits of smaller entities.

This argument has been raised mainly in relation to audits that are conducted on a substantive basis. ISA 315 requires that even in those circumstances an understanding of internal control is necessary in order to identify the risks of misstatement and that this understanding should be documented.

One of the consultation papers, *Draft Guidance on Smaller Entity Audit Documentation* aims to show that such documentation does not need to be extensive and costly to prepare. Beyond this, the APB believes that this issue should be addressed through audit firms' internal training.

2.2.3 The need for specific guidance

The old UK standards were supplemented by Practice Note 13 *The Audit of Small Businesses*. This is now out of date as it is not based on the ISAs. The APB has considered whether a replacement should be issued but their view is that it should be withdrawn and not replaced. This decision has been influenced by the following:

- The EC is moving towards adoption of the "Clarity Project" ISAs. These will include guidance on specific points relating to small entity audits within the ISAs themselves.

- IFAC is developing an explanatory guide to the use of ISAs on small and medium-sized entity audits.

- There has been a significant reduction in the number of small company audits as a result of the increases in the audit exemption threshold.

Exam question bank

1 Fundamental principles

27 mins

Fundamental Principles require that a member of a professional accountancy body should behave with integrity in all professional, business and financial relationships and should strive for objectivity in all professional and business judgements. Objectivity can only be assured if the member is and is seen to be independent. Conflicts of interest have an important bearing on independence and hence also on the public's perception of the integrity, objectivity and independence of the accounting profession.

The following scenario is an example of press reports in recent years which deal with issues of objectivity and independence within a multinational firm of accountants:

'A partner in the firm was told by the regulatory body that he must resign because he was in breach of the regulatory body's independence rules, as his brother-in-law was financial controller of an audit client. He was told that the alternative was that he could move his home and place of work at least 400 miles from the offices of the client, even though he was not the reporting partner. This made his job untenable. The regulatory body was seen as 'taking its rules to absurd lengths' by the accounting firm. Shortly after this comment, the multinational firm announced proposals to split the firm into three areas between audit, tax and business advisory services; management consultancy; and investment advisory services.'

Required

Discuss the impact that the above events may have on the public perception of the integrity, objectivity and independence of the multinational firm of accountants **(Total = 15 marks)**

2 Aventura International (12/01)

27 mins

Aventura International, a listed company, manufactures and wholesales a wide variety of products including fashion clothes and audio-video equipment. The company is audited by Voest, a firm of Chartered Certified Accountants, and the audit manager is Darius Harken. The following matters have arisen during the audit of the group's financial statements for the year to 31 December 2006 which is nearing completion:

(1) During the annual stocktake of fashion clothes at the company's principal warehouse, the audit staff attending the count were invited to purchase any items of clothing or equipment at 30% of their recommended retail prices.

(2) The chief executive of Aventura International, Armando Thyolo, owns a private jet. Armando invoices the company, on a monthly basis, for that proportion of the operating costs which reflects business use. One of these invoices shows that Darius Harken was flown to Florida in March 2006 and flown back two weeks later. Neither Aventura nor Voest have any offices or associates in Florida.

(3) Last week Armando announced his engagement to be married to his personal assistant, Kirsten Fennimore. Before joining Aventura in September 2006, Kirsten had been Voest's accountant in charge of the audit of Aventura.

Required

Discuss the ethical issues raised and the actions which might be taken by the auditor in relation to these matters.

Note. Assume it is 6 June 2007. **(Total = 15 marks)**

3 PLD Associates

36 mins

PLD Associates plc, a large quoted company, was founded and controlled by Mr J Scott. The principal business of the company was to develop derelict land in city centres into office accommodation. In 1993, the Inland Revenue became suspicious of the nature of the operations being carried out by the company and an investigation into its affairs commenced.

The resultant report stated that the organisation's internal controls were weak and non-existent in many cases. The investigators found payments to unknown persons, and fictitious consultancy firms. In addition, J Scott had maintained a secret expense account that was used to disburse funds to himself. The board of directors of PLD Associates plc did not know of the existence of this account. The expense account was maintained by the partner of the firm of accountants responsible for the audit of the company. The auditors were heavily criticised in the report of the investigators.

The firm of auditors, Allcost & Co, had an aggressive marketing strategy and had increased its audit fees by 100% in two years. The audit firm had accepted the appointment in 1991 after the previous auditors had been dismissed. The audit report for the year ended 1990 had been heavily qualified by the previous auditors on the grounds of poor internal control and lack of audit evidence. J Scott had approached several firms of auditors in order to ascertain whether they would qualify the audit report given the present systems of control in PLD Associates plc. Allcost & Co had stated that it was unlikely that they would qualify their report. They realised that J Scott was 'opinion shopping' but were prepared to give an opinion in order to attract the client to their firm.

PLD Associates plc subsequently filed for insolvency and Allcost & Co were sued for negligence by the largest loan creditor, its bankers.

Required

(a)   Describe the procedures which an audit firm should carry out before accepting a client with potentially high audit risk such as PLD Associates plc.   **(6 marks)**

(b)   Discuss the ethical problems raised by the maintenance of the secret expense account for Mr J Scott by the audit partner.   **(5 marks)**

(c)   Suggest measures that audit firms might introduce to try and minimise the practice of 'opinion shopping' by prospective audit clients.   **(5 marks)**

(d)   Explain how audit firms can reduce the risk of litigation and its effects upon the audit practice.

(4 marks)

(Total = 20 marks)

4 Professional responsibilities

27 mins

You are required to write an essay, in which you consider the extent to which an auditor should be responsible for detecting fraud and other irregularities when auditing the accounts of limited companies. Your essay should:

(a)   Briefly outline on the extent to which an auditor is responsible for detecting irregularities and fraud (as expressed in the auditing guidelines)

(b)   Consider the extent to which it would be reasonable to extend the auditor's responsibilities beyond that and the practical problems of extending auditor's responsibilities

(c)   Reach a conclusion on and provide a definition of the extent to which you consider it reasonable for an auditor to be responsible for detecting irregularities and fraud.   **(Total = 15 marks)**

5 CD Sales

36 mins

CD Sales, a limited liability company, was a growth orientated company that was dominated by its managing director, Mr A Long. The company sold quality music systems direct to the public. A large number of sales persons were employed on a commission only basis. The music systems were sent to the sales agents who then sold them direct to the public using telephone sales techniques. The music systems were supplied to the sales agents on a sale or return basis and CD Sales recognised the sale of the equipment when it was received by the sales agents. Any returns of the music systems were treated as re-purchases in the period concerned.

The company enjoyed a tremendous growth record. The main reasons for this apparent expansion were as follows.

(a)   Mr A Long falsified the sales records. He created several fictitious sales agents who were responsible for 25% of the company's turnover.

(b)   At the year end, Mr Long despatched nearly all of his inventories of music systems to the sales agents and re-purchased those that they wished to return after the year end.

(c)   Twenty per cent of the cost of sales were capitalised. This was achieved by the falsification of purchase invoices with the co-operation of the supplier company. Suppliers furnished the company with invoices for non-current assets but supplied music systems.

(d)   The directors of the company enjoyed a bonus plan linked to reported profits. Executives could earn bonuses ranging from 50% to 75% of their basic salaries. The directors did not query the unusually rapid growth of the company, and were unaware of the fraud perpetrated by Mr A Long.

Mr A Long spent large sums of money in creating false records and bribing accomplices in order to conceal the fraud from the auditor. He insisted that the auditor should sign a 'confidentiality' agreement which effectively precluded the auditor from corroborating sales with independent third parties, and from examining the service contracts of the directors. This agreement had the effect of preventing the auditor from discussing the affairs of the company with the sales agents.

The fraud was discovered when a disgruntled director wrote an anonymous letter to the Stock Exchange concerning the reasons for CD Sales's growth. The auditor was subsequently sued by a major bank that had granted a loan to CD Sales on the basis of interim accounts. These accounts had been reviewed by the auditor and a review report issued.

Required

(a)   Explain the key audit tests which would normally ensure that such a fraud as that perpetrated by Mr A Long would be detected.
(7 marks)

(b)   Discuss the implications of the signing of the 'confidentiality' agreement by the auditor.

(4 marks)

(c)   Explain how the 'review report' issued by the auditor on the interim financial statements differs in terms of its level of assurance from the auditor's report on the year end financial statements.

(4 marks)

(d)   Discuss where you feel that the auditor is guilty of professional negligence in not detecting the fraud.

(5 marks)

(Total = 20 marks)

6 Marsden Manufacturing Ltd

45 mins

Marsden Manufacturing (MM) is an established audit client of your firm. You were involved with the audit last year as audit senior. This year, you are to act as audit supervisor. The engagement partner has asked you to plan the audit for the year ended 30 June 20X4. It is an old-fashioned audit, and the partner does not anticipate that you will require the use of the new laptops that the firm has just invested in.

MM has a sales ledger of approximately 100 customers, but in terms of value, 80% of the ledger is represented by just six. The company has just secured a new customer, Wallworths, which has only impacted on the sales ledger for 1 month in the current year, but is projected to represent 20% of sales in the year ending 30 June 20X5.

MM has a large bank loan with ABC Bank. There is a covenant attached to the loan. One of the conditions of the loan is that the company maintains certain financial ratios at the balance sheet date. The bank requires an interest cover of 2.5 and a current ratio of 1.5.

The major development in the year is that MM decided to factor their debts. In the past they had suffered a substantial bad debt expense when a major customer went bankrupt and they are concerned that the reoccurrence of such an event would affect their interest cover ratio. They sacked their sales ledger clerk at the end of the year, so have outsourced their sales ledger function to the factor.

The audit assistant attended the stock take 2 days ago. She observed that there appeared to be a high level of old stocks. They were nevertheless added into the count.

The following draft figures have been provided:

Balance sheet

	20X4		20X3	
	£'000s	£'000s	£'000s	£'000s
Fixed assets		210		243
Current assets				
Stock	460		370	
Debtors	324		250	
Cash	15		69	
	799		689	
Creditors: amounts falling due within one year				
Trade creditors	381		367	
Bank loan	10		10	
	391		377	
Net current assets		408		312
Creditors: amounts falling due in more than one year				
Bank loan		(250)		(260)
		368		295

Profit and loss account

	20X4	20X3
	£'000s	£'000s
Sales	2,534	2,967
Cost of sales	1,583	1,823
Gross profit (% 37.5/38.5)	951	1,144
Administrative expenses	476	488
Other expenses	400	432
Profit before interest and tax	75	224
Interest	14	14

Sally Forsyth, the sales ledger clerk has threatened to sue MM for unfair dismissal and sexual discrimination.

Wallworths is an audit client of the firm. You are aware that they were often in dispute with their previous supplier over their poor payment record and have changed supplier because the supplier broke off relations with them.

Required:

(a)   Comment on the level at which you would set materiality.   **(4 marks)**

(b)   Identify and explain the audit risks in the above scenario for the audit for the year ended 30 June 20X4.

(14 marks)

(c)   Outline the key administrative planning matters that remain outstanding.   **(3 marks)**

(d)   Discuss whether an audit conflict of interest arises in this situation and what steps the auditor might take in this situation.   **(4 marks)**

(Total = 25 marks)

7 Gasoleum   36 mins

Your firm is the auditor of Gasoleum, a limited liability company which operates 15 petrol stations in and around London. You are the senior in charge of the audit for the year ending 31 January 20X1, and are engaged on the audit planning.

Most of the company's sites are long established and, as well as supplying fuel, oil, air and water, have a car wash and a shop.

Over the last few years, due to the intense price competition in petrol retailing, the shops have been expanded into mini-markets with a wide range of motor accessories, food, drinks and household products. They also sell State Lottery tickets.

Point-of-sale microcomputers are installed in all the petrol stations, linked on-line via a network to the computer at head office. Sales and inventory data are input direct from the microcomputers.

The company has an internal auditor, whose principal function is to monitor continuously and test the operation of internal controls throughout the organisation. The internal auditor will also be responsible for co-ordinating the year-end inventory count.

Required

Prepare notes for a planning meeting with the audit partner which:

(a)   identify areas of potential risk which will have to be addressed by the audit;   **(10 marks)**

(b)   describe the extent to which the work performed by the internal auditor may affect your planning, and the factors that could limit the use you may wish to make of his work; and

(5 marks)

(c)   detail the analytical review procedures that you would adopt to obtain audit evidence on income and gross profit as part of your substantive testing.   **(5 marks)**

(20 marks)

8 Audit

20 mins

For the last few years your firm has helped Colin, a sole trader, prepare his accounts for the Inland Revenue. Colin is about to incorporate his business and has asked your advice on a number of issues.

Required

Advise Colin on the following.

(a)   The advantages to the company of having its accounts audited (you may assume that the company would be able to claim exemption from audit).

(b)   Whether the audit undertaken on his small company would be the same as an audit undertaken on a large one.

(c)   Whether he has any alternatives to audit that would still provide him with a degree of assurance.

9 Lambley Properties

36 mins

You are the manager in charge of the audit of Lambley Properties plc and you have been asked to prepare the letter of representation which will be signed by the company's directors.

You are aware that there are two material items in the accounts for the year ended 31 March 20X2 on which you want the company's directors to confirm that the treatment in the accounts is correct.

(a)   One of the company's subsidiaries, Keyworth Builders Ltd, is experiencing going concern problems, and you want the directors' confirmation that they intend to support the company for the foreseeable future.

(b)   Eastwood Manufacturing plc is in dispute with Lambley Properties over repairs required to a building they purchased from Lambley. Lambley Properties constructed the building for Eastwood, and three years after it was sold to Eastwood, the customer is claiming that repairs are required which will cost £3 million, and that Lambley is liable to pay for these repairs, as they are as a result of negligent construction of the building. In addition, Eastwood is claiming £2 million for the cost of disruption of the business due to the faults in the building and in the period when the repairs take place. Lambley Properties have obtained the advice of a lawyer and a surveyor, and the directors believe there are no grounds for the claim and any court action will find in their favour. However, Lambley Properties has included a note in its accounts concerning this contingency.

Required

(a)   Prepare a letter of representation which the directors will sign and send to you, as auditors. In the letter, you should include the two items above and any other matters which you believe should be included. **(8 marks)**

(b)   Discuss the reliability of a letter of representation as audit evidence and the extent to which the auditors can rely on this evidence. **(4 marks)**

(c)   Describe the work you will perform to check whether a provision should be included in the accounts for the legal claim from Eastwood Manufacturing plc. **(5 marks)**

(d)   Describe the matters you will consider and the further action you will take if the directors refuse to sign the letter of representation because of the legal claim from Eastwood Manufacturing plc.
(3 marks)

(Total = 20 marks)

10 Bestwood Electronics   36 mins

Your firm is the auditor of Bestwood Electronics plc which assembles microcomputers and wholesales them and associated equipment to retailers. Many of the parts for the computers and the associated equipment are bought from the Far East. These computers are used by businesses for accounting, word processing and other computing tasks.

You have been asked by the partner in charge of the audit to consider your firm's audit responsibilities in relation to subsequent sheet events, and the audit work you will carry out on these matters.

Required

(a)   Describe the responsibilities of the auditors for detecting errors in the accounts during the following periods:

   (i)   From the period end to the date of the auditors' report
   (ii)   From the date of the auditors' report to the issue of the financial statements
   (iii)   From the date the financial statements are issued to the date they are laid before the members   **(5 marks)**

(b)   Describe the audit work you will carry out in period (a)(i) above which involves consideration of subsequent events (or post balance sheet events).   **(11 marks)**

(c)   Describe the work you will carry out in period (a)(ii) above to ensure no adjustments are required to the accounts.   **(4 marks)**

(Total = 20 marks)

11 Bingham Engineering   45 mins

You are auditing the accounts of Bingham Engineering Ltd for the year ended 31 March 20X7, which is experiencing going concern problems.

The company prepares monthly, as well as annual accounts and its accountant has supplied you with the following forecasts to enable you to assess whether the company will be a going concern. The forecasts have been prepared on a monthly basis for the year to 31 March 20X8, and are:

(a)   Capital expenditure/disposal forecast
(b)   Profit forecast
(c)   Cash flow forecast

The capital expenditure/disposal forecast and profit forecast have been used to prepare the cash flow forecast.

Required

(a)   Briefly describe what you understand by the term 'going concern' and state the minimum period you would expect the company to continue in business for it to be considered a going concern.
                                                                                        (3 marks)

(b)   List the factors which may indicate that a company is not a going concern.   **(9 marks)**

(c)   Describe the work you would perform to verify that the value of items in the following forecasts, prepared by the company's accountant, are reasonable:

   (i)   Capital expenditure/disposal forecast
   (ii)   Profit forecast
   (iii)   Cash flow forecast   **(10 marks)**

(d)   Briefly describe the further work, in addition to that described in (b) and (c) above, you would perform to enable you to determine whether the company is a going concern.   **(3 marks)**

(Total = 25 marks)

12 Locksley

45 mins

The following is the draft balance sheet of Locksley Ltd for the year ended 31 January 20X3.

LOCKSLEY LIMITED
BALANCE SHEET AS AT 31 JANUARY 20X3

	20X3 £	20X2 £
Fixed assets		
Development expenditure	59,810	-
Tangible assets	99,400	73,000
Investments	85,100	101,400
	244,310	174,400
Current assets		
Stock	58,190	63,010
Debtors	184,630	156,720
Cash at bank and in hand	9,970	62,620
	252,790	282,350
Creditors: amounts falling due within one year	276,510	215,900
Net current (liabilities)/assets	(23,720)	66,450
Total assets less current liabilities	220,590	240,850
Creditors: amounts falling due after more than one year		
Provisions for liabilities and charges	53,100	46,320
Deferred taxation	3,080	2,520
	164,410	192,010
Capital and reserves		
Share capital	89,700	89,700
Share premium account	11,300	11,300
Revaluation reserve	19,750	9,750
Profit and loss account	43,660	81,260
	164,410	192,010

Locksley Ltd produces garden furniture and has incurred expenditure during the year ended 31 January 20X3 on the development of mouldings for a new range of plastic garden furniture. The directors wish to carry forward the development expenditure indefinitely as they feel that the company will benefit from the new moulding for many years. The product range is being developed because profits have been declining over the last few years owing to the uncompetitiveness of the products made by the company. The company has sold many of its fixed assets during the year and purchased new machinery which will enable the company's productivity to increase. The directors decided not to fund the above expenditure using outside finance but to generate the necessary resources internally by taking extended credit from its suppliers and utilising its liquid funds held at the bank. The company also sold part of its investments, which are made up of stocks and shares of public limited companies.

One of the reasons for this method of financing the expenditure was that the company already has a loan of £45,000 outstanding which has been included in the figure for 'creditors: amounts falling due after more than one year'. This loan is secured on the fixed assets of the company and is repayable over ten years. The sale of fixed assets and investments did not yield as much as was expected and a small loss on sale of £1,200 has been included in the profit and loss account as part of the amounts shown for 'other expenses'.

The company had the fixed assets revalued by a professional valuer, at the year end. The gain on revaluation of fixed assets has been credited by the company to the revaluation reserve.

The directors felt that the shareholders should share in the gain on the revaluation of the fixed assets and increased the proposed dividend accordingly. Over 90% of the shares of the company are held by the directors.

BPP
LEARNING MEDIA

Required

(a)   Describe the audit work to be performed to verify the value attributed to the development
        expenditure in the balance sheet of Locksley Ltd.   **(6 marks)**

(b)   Describe the audit procedures which should be carried out to verify the gain arising on the
        revaluation of fixed assets.   **(6 marks)**

(c)   Explain to the directors why development expenditure should not be carried forward indefinitely in
        the financial statements, and describe the circumstances in which the costs maybe deferred to the
        future.   **(8 marks)**

(d)   Describe the implications for the company and the auditors of the directors' decision to generate
        internally the funds required for the development of the business.   **(5 marks)**

                                                                             (Total = 25 marks)

13 Bainbridge   36 mins

You are the auditor of Bainbridge Ltd, a regional-based company which manufactures top of the range
kitchen units and accessories. The company is owned and run by the Bainbridge family who first set up
the business in the 1950s. In recent years the company has experienced increasing success fuelled by the
housing boom and the trend for home improvements. The draft accounts for the year ended 30 June 20X5
show revenue of £20.2 million, profit for the period of £1.6 million and total assets of £30 million. The
following matters remain outstanding from the audit fieldwork and have been brought to your attention:

Stocks

Stocks of finished goods are included in the draft accounts at a cost of £4.5 million. The majority of items
are produced for stock with the cost being calculated using a standard costing system. Standard costs are
calculated for:

*   Materials
*   Labour
*   Production overheads
*   Other overheads

The standards used have been kept the same as those applied last year and variance calculations have not
been performed. Management have justified this by saying that costs have remained constant over the last
two years and that historically variances have been negligible.

A small number of items in stock have been made to customer specification. In respect of these
management have included overheads relating to design.   **(7 marks)**

Warehouse

On 1 July 20X4 Bainbridge entered into a 10 year lease for a warehouse. Under the terms of the lease the
company have been given a one-year rent-free period after which the annual rental is £50,000 per year. At
the end of the initial term Bainbridge has the option to extend the lease for a further 2 years at a notional
rental.

Currently no charge has been included in the accounts in respect of the lease on the basis that the rent-
free period means that no charge has been incurred for the year. In future management intend to account
for the lease as an operating lease.   **(7 marks)**

Convertible debenture

On 1 July 20X4 Bainbridge issued a £5m debenture at par. The debenture carries interest at 4% and is
redeemable on 1 July 20X9 at which date the holder has the option to convert the debenture to 3 million
£1 ordinary shares in Bainbridge.

Currently the only entries that have been made in relation to the debenture were to credit the net proceeds to a long-term liability account and to record the first payment of interest on 31 June 20X5. **(6 marks)**

Required

For each of the above issues:

(i)   Comment on the matters you should consider, and

(ii)   The evidence you should expect to find,

in undertaking your review of the audit working papers and financial statements of Bainbridge.

(Total = 20 marks)

14 Griffin plc

36 mins

Griffin plc manufactures football kits. It has contracts with a number of Nationwide league football teams. It also produces 'unbranded' football wear, which it sells to a number of wholesalers.

The profit before tax for the year is £1.2m (2003 £3.5m). You are the manager responsible for the audit for the year end 30 June 2004. Today you have visited the client's premises to review the audit team's work to date. The audit senior has drafted the following 'points for the attention of the manager':

1   Griffin is seeking to enter the market in women's leisure clothes. In light of that fact, during the year it purchased 30% of the share capital of Bees Ltd, a company that manufactures sporty leisurewear at a cost of £750,000. **(7 marks)**

2   During the year a major competitor emerged in the branded football kit market. Two of the contracts with nationwide clubs which came up during the year have not been renewed. A number of key personnel have been headhunted by the competitor. **(6 marks)**

3   A legal requirement to adjust the seats at which machinists sit was passed in December 2005. The legislation required the seats to be adjusted by April 2006. Griffin has not yet carried out any adjustment. Also in April 2006, the government increased the national minimum wage. 5% of Griffin's employees receive less than the minimum wage. **(7 marks)**

Required

(a)   Comment on the matters you would consider, and

(b)   State the evidence you would expect to find during your review of the working papers and financial statements of Griffin Plc.

(Total = 20 marks)

15 Recognition

27 mins

Discuss the impact on the audit report of the proposed treatment of the following items in the financial statements.

(a)   Beak plc sells land to a property investment company, Wings plc. The sale price is £20 million and the current market value is £30 million. Beak plc can buy the land back at any time in the next five years for the original selling price plus an annual commission of 1% above the current bank base rate. Wings plc cannot require Beak plc to buy the land back at any time.

The accountant of Beak plc proposes to treat this transaction as a sale in the financial statements. You may assume that the amounts involved are material. **(6 marks)**

(b)   A car manufacturer, Gocar plc, supplies cars to a car dealer, Sparks Ltd, on the following terms.

Sparks Ltd has to pay a monthly fee of £100 per car for the privilege of displaying it in its showroom and is also responsible for insuring the cars. When a car is sold to a customer, Sparks Ltd has to pay Gocar plc the factory price of the car when it was first supplied. Sparks Ltd can only return cars to Gocar plc on the payment of a fixed penalty charge of 10% of the cost of the car. Sparks Ltd has to pay the factory price for the cars if they remain unsold within a four month period. Gocar plc cannot demand the return of the cars from Sparks Ltd.

The accountant of Sparks Ltd proposes to treat the cars unsold for less than four months as the property of Gocar plc and not show them as stock in the financial statements. At the year end the value of car stocks shown in the balance sheet was £150,720. The total assets on balance sheet are £1.3 m. The cars unsold for less than four months have a factory cost of £22,500.   **(9 marks)**

(Total = 15 marks)

16 Henshelwood plc

You are employed as an audit manager by Viewstream, a firm of Certified Accountants. You are currently involved in planning the final audit of the financial statements of Henshelwood plc, an IT consultancy, for the year ended 31 March 20X7.

The draft financial statements show a profit before tax of £192m (20X6 £167m) and total assets of £553m (20X6 £510m).

The following disclosures have been extracted from the draft financial statements:

(1)   **Share-based payments**

The fair value of all share-based remuneration is determined at the date of grant and recognised as an expense in the profit and loss account on a straight-line basis over the vesting period, taking account of the estimated number of shares that will vest. The fair value is determined by use of the relevant valuation model. All share-based remuneration is equity settled.

(Notes made by the audit senior during some preliminary analytical review refer to a share-based payment expense of £4.8m and an equity reserve, relating to the share-based payment scheme, of £8.7m.)

(5 marks)

(2)   **Pension costs**

UK Defined benefit scheme

(i)   The scheme, the Henshelwood Pension Scheme, is a defined benefit scheme where the benefits are based on employees' length of service and final pensionable pay. It is a funded approved defined benefit scheme and closed to new members on 1 July 2001. It is funded through a legally separate trustee administered fund.

The actuarial valuation was performed at 31 March 20X7 by the Scheme actuary, an employee of Milton Human Resource Consulting.

The amounts recognised in the consolidated income statement for the defined benefit schemes are as follows:

	20X7 £m
Current service cost	(8.1)
Past service costs	(0.1)
Total operating charge	(8.2)
Expected return on pension scheme assets	21.2
Interest on pension liabilities	(20.1)
Net financial income/(charge)	1.1
Total amount charged to the consolidated profit and loss account	(7.1)

The actuarial gains and losses have been recognised in the consolidated statement of total recognised gains and loses as follows:

	20X7 £m
Actuarial gain on scheme assets	19.1
Actuarial (losses)/gain on scheme liabilities	(4.7)
Impact of changes in assumptions relating to the present value of scheme liabilities	1.4
Net income recognised directly in consolidated statement of recognised income and expense	15.8

	20X7 £m
Deficit in the scheme brought forward	(69.7)
Current service cost	(8.1)
Past service costs	(0.1)
Contributions	5.1
Net financial return	1.1
Actuarial gain	15.8
Deficit in the scheme carried forward	(55.9)

The amount included in the balance sheet arising from the Group's obligations in respect of its defined benefit retirement scheme is as follows:

	20X7 £m
Present value of defined benefit obligations	(431.7)
Fair value of scheme assets	375.8
Defined benefit scheme deficit	(55.9)
Liability recognised in the balance sheet	(55.9)

(9 marks)

(3) **Provisions**

	Property £m	Other £m	Total £m
Balance at 1 July 2005	25.2	47.8	73.0
Exchange adjustments	-	0.1	0.1
Charged to income statement	-	0.2	0.2
Utilised	(8.2)	(14.3)	(22.5)
Balance at 30 June 2006	17.0	33.8	50.8

Property provisions are for rents and other related amounts payable on certain leased properties for periods in which they are not anticipated to be in use by the Group. The leases expire in periods up to 2013.

Other provisions comprise liabilities arising as a result of business disposals and the Group transformation including the following items:

- Provisions of £7.1 million (2005 – £8.9 million) relating to restructuring costs arising from the Group transformation and closure of former shared service facilities and the closure of the former head office. These provisions are expected to be utilised over the next 12 – 36 months.

- Provisions of £6.2 million (2005 - £160 million) for potential liabilities relating to the disposal of the European business including certain site restitution costs.

- Provisions of £19.1 million (2005 - £19.4 million) relating to possible warranty and environmental claims in relation to businesses disposed. It is not possible to estimate the timing of payments against these provisions.

(6 marks)

Required

For each of the three issues identified above

(a) Explain the matters you should consider to determine whether the amounts have been appropriately valued: and

(b) Describe the tests you should plan to perform to quantify the amount of any misstatement.

Note: The mark allocation is shown against each of the three issues

(Total = 20 marks)

17 Merger of audit firms 27 mins

The increase in the size of audit firms has been a source of concern to regulators and clients alike. Some audit firms feel that mergers between the largest firms of auditors are necessary in order to meet the global demand for their services. However their clients are concerned that such mergers will create a monopolistic market for audit services which will not be in their best interests.

Required

(a) Explain the reasons why the largest audit firms might wish to merge their practices. **(7 marks)**
(b) Discuss the potential problems created by mergers of the largest firms of auditors. **(8 marks)**

(Total = 15 marks)

18 Annabella Ltd 45 mins

Annabella Ltd has been an audit client of your firm for 13 years. It is a business which manufactures soft furnishings. It also has a shop, from which it sells its own soft furnishings, and other manufacturers' soft furnishings and small items of furniture.

On the first day of the year ending 30 June 2006, Annabella Ltd undertook a major reconstruction of its operations. It set up two subsidiary companies. Anna Ltd and Bella Ltd. It then transferred its trade to those companies. Anna Ltd took the manufacturing trade and Bella Ltd took the retail trade. On the same day, Annabella Ltd entered into a joint venture with its former chief designer. The joint venture, Annabella Designs Ltd, will provide designs for the soft furnishings manufactured by Anna Ltd and will also operate an interior design service, which will be advertised strongly by Bella Ltd.

Annabella Ltd is 100% owned by James Dancer, Annabella Ltd will charge Anna Ltd, Bella Ltd and Annabella Designs Ltd management charges.

The former chief designer, now a 50% shareholder in Annabella Designs Ltd is Annabel Dancer, James' only daughter. They make decisions about Annabella Designs jointly, and have agreed that the audit of Annabella Designs Ltd shall be carried out by David Turner and Co. David Turner is a friend of Annabel.

Required

(a) Identify and explain the audit planning issues in the above scenario. **(17 marks)**

(b) Describe the principal audit procedures on a consolidation. **(8 marks)**

(Total = 25 marks)

19 Anderson Group 27 mins

You are auditing the accounts of Anderson Group for the year ended 31 August 20X1. The group comprises Anderson, a public company and its wholly owned subsidiary Green, a limited liability company. The main activities of both companies are the manufacture and sale of household textiles. During the year under review Green made a substantial trading loss and the board of directors of Anderson has decided to sell the subsidiary. A suitable buyer was found and the sale which was approved and announced by the Board on 31 July 20X1, was legally completed on 31 August 20X1.

A summary draft profit and loss account for the year ended 31 August 20X1 (which is shown below) has been prepared, which divides the group profit between continuing operations (those of Anderson) and discontinued operations (those of Green).

	Continuing operations £'000	Discontinued operations £'000	Total £'000
Revenue	25,700	10,000	37,500
Profit/(loss) before tax	1,300	(1,000)	300
Tax expense	(700)	450	(250)
Profit/(loss) before exceptional item	600	(550)	50
Loss on sale of subsidiary (note 1)	-	(450)	(450)
Loss for the period	600	(1,000)	(400)

Notes to the accounts (extract)

1 Loss on sale of subsidiary.

	£'000
Net assets of Green at 31 August 20X1	1,800
Cash proceeds	(1,350)
Loss arising on disposal of subsidiary	450

The results of Green, included above, have been obtained from the company's management accounts. No audited accounts of Green are available as Green's new owners have a different year end from Anderson and Anderson no longer has control over Green.

In view of the substantial loss of Green, the directors of Anderson do not want to include the trading results of Green in the group accounts. They have suggested that the loss on disposal of the subsidiary should be shown as an exceptional item.

You have approached Green, and in view of the change in ownership, they have said that they are not prepared to allow you to carry out an audit of their accounts or to answer questions on the management accounts to 31 August 20X1. However, the directors of Anderson are prepared to give you as much information about the preparation of Green's accounts as they are able.

Required

Assuming that the results of Green for the year ended 31 August 20X1 are consolidated into the accounts of Anderson, describe the audit work you would perform and the matters you would consider in relation to the *profit and loss account* of Green which is included in the group accounts of Anderson as shown in the schedule above. Your answer should include consideration of:

(a)   the factors you would take into account in deciding whether the results of Green are sufficiently reliable to be included in the group accounts and receive an unqualified auditor's report; **(5 marks)**

(b)   the level of materiality (or acceptable error) you would accept in the results of Green which are included in the group profit and loss account; and   **(5 marks)**

(c)   how you would audit the item in note 1 to the accounts: 'Loss on sale of subsidiary'.   **(5 marks)**

(Total = 15 marks)

Note: You should assume that the disposal of Green meets the criteria to be classed as a discontinued operation under FRS 3 *Reporting financial performance.*

20 Business assurance   36 mins

Audit practitioners have recently initiated substantive changes in the audit approach. It appears to be the strategy that audit firms are moving away from the audit of financial statements and more to the provision of assurances on financial data, systems and controls in those systems. Auditors are focusing on providing 'business assurance' and 'business risk' which gives clients wider assurance than the traditional audit has offered. Auditors are reviewing the business from a process standpoint utilising benchmarking, performance measurements and best control practices as the key criteria. It seems that the audit is moving more to the analysis of business risk and the alignment of the audit much more to the management perspective.

A wide range of risk assessment services is now part of the audit service. The provision of internal audit services is becoming an increasingly larger part of the 'business assurance' service offered by auditors. It seems that the audit is becoming a management consultancy exercise with internal audit, external audit and consultancy assignments being seen as complementary services.

Required

(a)   Discuss the implications of the external auditor providing an internal audit service to a client, explaining the current ethical guidance on the provision of other services to clients.   **(10 marks)**

(b)   Explain the principal effects of the external auditor providing wider assurance to the client.

(6 marks)

(c)   Critically evaluate the move by large auditing firms to providing 'business risk and assurance' services rather than the traditional audit assurance for investors and creditors.   **(4 marks)**

(Total = 20 marks)

21 Trendy Group

Trendy Group Inc is an international group which manufactures costume jewellery and sells it through its own retail stores. It is a new client for your firm which was awarded the world-wide audit after submitting a competitive tender. You have just learnt that you are the senior assigned to the audit of Trendy Group Inc. As group audit senior, you will be responsible for the co-ordination of the world-wide audit for the year ending 30 September 20X2 and for the audits of the consolidation, the US parent entity, (Trendy Group Inc), and the US trading subsidiary, (Trendy (US) Inc). Your firm has offices in every country in which the Trendy Group has operations and you will instruct the relevant local offices to perform any overseas work required.

The audit manager has presented you with a copy of a background memorandum prepared in connection with the tender process **(Exhibit 1)**.

Required

Identify the key area of business risk associated with Trendy Group Inc. For each business risk area identified, include (perhaps in tabular format) the specific audit risks, if any, associated with that business risk, both at a group level and at an individual company level.

EXHIBIT 1

To:	The Files
From:	Kim Welsby (Audit manager)
Date:	30 May 20X2
Subject:	Trendy Group Inc Invitation to tender for world-wide audit Background information

This memorandum summarises background information obtained at a meeting with Mary Pegg (Group Finance Director) on 27 May 20X2.

Group structure

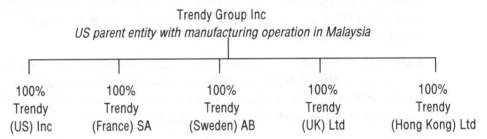

Trendy Group Inc
US parent entity with manufacturing operation in Malaysia

100% Trendy (US) Inc	100% Trendy (France) SA	100% Trendy (Sweden) AB	100% Trendy (UK) Ltd	100% Trendy (Hong Kong) Ltd

Local audit requirements

Full statutory audits are required for both US companies and for the subsidiaries in Sweden and Hong Kong. At all other locations, Mary wants the auditors to perform the minimum level of work necessary to give an overall opinion on the group financial statements.

Parent entity operations

The parent, Trendy Group Inc, has a factory in Malaysia. This factory manufactures costume jewellery using a local workforce and materials. All of the factory output is sold to Trendy Group Inc's trading subsidiaries at prices set in dollars at the beginning of each quarter. The prices charged by the factory include freight and are set to ensure that the factory makes a modest profit margin.

The parent is also responsible for design, international marketing and promotions, treasury management and certain other administrative activities. It charges the trading subsidiaries a royalty of 5% of retail sales to cover design costs and also levies management charges sufficient to recover its other overhead expenses.

Trading subsidiaries

The 5 trading subsidiaries each sell costume jewellery purchased from the Malaysian factory through retail stores in their own geographical area. All sales are made through the companies' own stores. Each trading subsidiary has a central warehouse at which deliveries from the Malaysian factory are received and distributed to individual retail stores. The subsidiaries are responsible for local marketing activities.

The US trading subsidiary, Trendy (US) Inc, also runs a factory outlet shop at which old inventories are sold at marked clown prices. Any inventories held in the retail outlets at the end of a fashion season are first reduced in a shop sale. If it has not been sold by the end of the sale, the trading subsidiaries sell the obsolete lines to Trendy (US) Inc for 50% of their original cost. These inventories are then sold through the factory outlet or, if this proves unsuccessful, destroyed. In order to protect its reputation, the group will not sell obsolete inventories to market traders.

Kim Welsby

22 Verity

36 mins

Verity, a limited liability company, has a credit facility with Cranley Bank of £6 million. The facility is due to expire on 31 December 20X1. The overdraft in the recently audited balance sheet at 30 September 20X1 is £5.5 million. The directors of Verity have started negotiations with their bankers for a renewal of the facility and to increase the amount to £9 million. To support this request the bank has asked Verity to provide a business plan for the coming 12 months consisting of a cash flow forecast supported by a forecast profit and loss account and balance sheet. The management of Verity has produced a cash flow forecast for the period 1 October 20X1 to 30 September 20X2 and, at the request of the bank, have asked their auditor to examine and report on it.

The audit manager, who has recently completed Verity's audit, has been asked to make a preliminary examination of the cash flow forecast and supporting material and she has noted the following observations.

(a) The cash flows from sales are based on the assumption of an overall increase in sales of 24% compared to the previous financial year. Analysis shows that this is based on an increase in selling price of 5% and an increase in the volume of sales of 18%. Just over a quarter of all Verity's sales are made to foreign customers.

(b) The cost of sales in the recently audited profit and loss account to 30 September 20X1 was 80% of sales revenue, giving a gross profit of 20%. In the forecast profit and loss account for the year to 30 September 20X2 the cost of sales has fallen to 72%, giving a gross profit of 28%. Manufacturing costs are made up of approximately one third each of materials, labour and production overheads.

(c) The trade receivables collection period used in the cash flow forecast to 30 September 20X2 is 61 days. In the year to 30 September 20X1 this period averaged 93 days. Management has stated that it is its intention to inform all customers of a new standard 60 day credit period. In addition an early settlement discount of 1% will apply to customers who settle their account within 30 days of the statement.

Conversely the credit period for trade payables has been extended from an average of 45 days in the current year to 90 days in the forecast.

(d) The cash flow forecast showed that the maximum credit required during the period would rise to nearly £9 million in August 20X2.

Required

(a) Describe the general matters an auditor should consider before accepting an engagement as a reporting accountant on forecast financial information. **(5 marks)**

(b) Detail the procedures that the reporting accountant should undertake in relation to the cash flow forecast of Verity for the year to 30 September 20X2. **(8 marks)**

(c) The negotiations with Cranley Bank resulted in a renewal of Verity's existing credit facility of £6 million, but the bank would not agree to increase it to £9 million. As a result of this Verity issued a circular to its existing shareholders inviting them to subscribe for a new £3 million issue of debentures. The purpose of the circular was to show the intended use and the future benefits from the debenture issue. It was supported by the same forecast financial information, including the accountant's report, that had been provided to Cranley Bank. However the directors of Verity had removed all references to its original purpose and restricted distribution.

The trading results of the first half of the year to 30 September 20X2 showed that the forecast information was proving to be over optimistic and that Verity was beginning to experience cash flow difficulties.

Discuss the basis on which a reporting accountant should form an opinion on forecast information, and consider whether the reporting accountants of Verity may be liable to:

(i) Cranley Bank; and

(ii) the investors who subscribe for the new debentures. **(7 marks)**

(Total = 20 marks)

Note. You are to assume that the accountant's report had expressed an unqualified opinion on the cash flow statement.

23 Scenarios

27 mins

You are a partner in a medium sized firm of chartered certified accountants. The following opportunities have arisen.

(a) A major audit client, Lilac Co, is seeking loan finance from its bank to fund an expansion into a new factory. The expansion should result in an increase in capacity of 30%. Lilac has conducted market research and is confident that they will be able to sell the added output. The financial director has recently telephoned you and mentioned that the bank are keen to obtain a reference from the audit firm, relating to Lilac's ability to repay the loan and whether the business plan is reasonable. He said 'they just need their forms filled, for their files. They know we can repay. We're one of their best clients.' Your audit team is about to commence the audit for the year ended 31 March 2006.

Required

Comment on the matters you would consider in relation to giving such a reference to the bank.

(7 marks)

(b) The finance director of Laurel Co, another audit client, telephoned you yesterday. He recently attended a half-day course on the importance of corporate governance run by your firm. Laurel's long term plans include the possibility of flotation on a stock exchange. The finance director has told the other directors the issues discussed at the course and they feel that it might be a good idea to engage the firm to undertake an assurance engagement to assess risk management and the internal control system at Laurel Co.

Required

Comment on the matters you would consider in relation to accepting and planning such an engagement. **(8 marks)**

(Total = 15 marks)

24 Harness Ltd

27 mins

(a) Briefly outline the reasons why social and environmental issues are of interest to an external auditor.

(5 marks)

(b) Harness Ltd is a wind-farm situated on an island in the North Sea. Harness was set up a number of years ago by an energy fanatic who was also a millionaire. It is predominately owned by the millionaire. Brewster Billings, who continues to loan it money, despite a history of loss-making.

Harness owns and operates 15 windmills which are situated on the island. The windmills are connected to a generator, which converts the wind power to electricity. The electricity is mainly supplied to Brewster's mansion on the East Coast of Scotland, but some is sold to various power supply companies. One of these companies, Scot Power, has a small stake in Harness Ltd.

The company has suffered some problems this year. Firstly, the erosion which as badly affected the island during the course of the company's occupation has finally struck some of the windmills. One fell into the sea at the end of the year, and the foundations of another three appear to have been affected. The generator lies within 10 metres of the cliff.

During the year, Harness invested in a stake in an oil pipeline which runs near the island. The co-owners of the pipeline have just advised Brewster, as a director of Harness, that they have discovered a substantial crack in the pipeline.

Required

Comment on the implications of the above on the audit of Harness Ltd for the year end June 2006.

(10 marks)

(Total = 15 marks)

25 Eastfield Distributors

Your firm is the external auditor of Eastfield Distributors, a limited liability company which has revenue of £25 million and a profit before tax of £1.7 million. The company operates from a head office at Eastfield and has sales and inventory holding centres in different parts of the country. The directors have decided the company has reached a size when it needs an internal audit department. As is becoming increasingly common, the directors have asked your firm to provide this service to the company as well as being the external auditor of the company's annual financial statements.

In answering the question, you should consider:

(a) the effects of the ACCA's Rules of Professional Conduct in relation to providing an internal audit service to Eastfield Distributors;

(b) the extent to which your audit firm can rely on the internal audit work when carrying out the external audit of Eastfield Distributors;

(c) the arrangements over control of the work and reporting of the internal audit staff:

   (i) the extent to which the internal audit staff should be responsible to Eastfield Distributors, and who should control their work;

   (ii) the extent to which the internal audit staff should be responsible to a manager or partner of the external audit firm, and whether the same manager and partner should be responsible for both the internal audit staff of Eastfield Distributors and the external audit.

Required

In relation to your audit firm becoming internal auditors of Eastfield Distributors:

(a)   describe the matters you should consider and the action you will take to ensure your firm remains independent as external auditor of the annual financial statements;   **(8 marks)**

(b)   describe the advantages and disadvantages to Eastfield Distributors of your firm providing an internal audit service;   **(7 marks)**

(c)   describe the advantages and disadvantages to your *audit firm* of providing an internal audit service to Eastfield Distributors.   **(5 marks)**

(Total = 20 marks)

26 Maple   27 mins

(a)   Explain the auditor's responsibility in respect of fraud and error.   **(5 marks)**

(b)   Maple, a limited liability company, designs and manufactures high quality wooden furniture. The audit is nearing completion and you are in the process of reviewing the audit file in your capacity as audit manager.

Draft accounts for the year ended 30 September 20X5 show a profit before tax of £100,000 and total assets of £4,562,500.

The following matters are brought to your attention.

(i)   The inventories figure of £675,000 includes £80,000 which has been valued based on the directors' estimate. This is due to the loss of the stock counting sheets for the Sherwood depot. The audit team were unable to find any other means of validating these stocks.

(ii)   During the year Maple made a loan to a director, Colin Wood, for £5,000. This is not disclosed in the accounts as the directors believe that the transaction is a personal issue.

(iii)   Trade debtors that total £525,000 include £47,000 due from Beech. This customer went into liquidation on 3 November 20X5. The audit senior has concluded that Maple is unlikely to recover the debt based on information provided by the liquidator.

The directors have refused to adjust the accounts.

The audit senior has drafted the auditor's report, extracts of which are as follows:

'*Modified opinion*

The stock balance includes an amount of £80,000 based on the directors' estimate. This is because the stock counting sheets for the Sherwood depot were lost and we were unable to find any other suitable means of confirming the stock value. Also, included in debtors is an amount of £47,000 due from a company which is in liquidation. We believe that this amount should have been fully provided against as it is unlikely that they will receive any payment in respect of this amount.

Except for the financial effects of the matters referred to in the preceding paragraph, in our opinion, the financial statements give a true and fair view, in accordance with United Kingdom Generally Accepted Accounting Practice, of the state of the company's affairs as at 30 September 20X5 and of its profit for the year then ended.'

The audit senior has also attached a note for you explaining that he has made no reference to the director's loan on the basis that the amount involved is not material.   **(10 marks)**

Required

Comment on the suitability of this report. Your answer should include an assessment of the materiality of each of the three outstanding issues.   **(Total = 15 marks)**

27 Reporting issues

27 mins

(a)   You are the engagement partner on the audit of Techie Ltd. The directors are developing the company's website and have intimated that they would like to provide access to the full financial statements, including the auditors' report through the site.

Required

Comment briefly on the issues this raises for the auditor.   **(5 marks)**

(b)   Later in the year, you undertake the audit of Techie Ltd.

The website is now operational, and Techie is trading through it. The website was developed by an external information technology expert. It will be maintained in the future by the company's IT staff. There is no continuing maintenance arrangement. The cost of developing the website, which was substantial, has been written off in the profit and loss account as part of administrative expenses. Techie has a reciprocal arrangement with another company. Trekkie Ltd, whereby the companies have free advertising banners on each other's websites. No provision has been made for the above arrangement in the financial statements.

Required

(i)   Comment on any evidence you would seek in relation to the above items
(ii)   Comment on the potential implications of the above items on the auditors' report

(10 marks)

(Total = 15 marks)

Exam answer bank

1 Fundamental principles

Independence

It is important that auditors are, and are seen to be, independent. **Independence** is at the heart of the auditing profession as auditors claim to give an **impartial, objective** opinion on the truth and fairness of the financial statements.

Objectivity

A **family relationship** between an auditor and the client **can substantially affect the objectivity** of the audit, so auditors are advised not to build close personal relationships with audit clients and should not audit a company where family are employed in a capacity which is sensitive to the accounts, for example, in the finance department, although this is **not prohibited by law** unless the auditor's 'partner' is an employee of the company.

In this instance, the **partner was not the reporting partner** for the audit client in which his brother-in-law was a financial controller. According to generally accepted ethical practice then, the firm appeared to be independent of the audit client if the related partner did not have anything to do with the audit.

Resolution?

The regulatory body required the audit partner to move 400 miles. This presumably implies that the partner was requested to change offices within the firm by which he was employed. Given current levels of computer networking and other **communications** common in business, this would appear to be an **arbitrary distinction**, as a partner in an office in Glasgow could have similar access and influence over a single audit carried out by the firm as a partner in London.

Independence in appearance

However, in this situation, the regulatory body appear to be concerned about the appearance of independence. They appear to be concerned that the public will not perceive the distinction between a partner and a partner who reports on a specific engagement. This may or may not be fair. Arguably, it is only in publicising the problem that the public are likely to have a perception at all.

Also, given the comments made about modern communications above, the public are unlikely to be convinced that moving a member of staff to a different office will solve this independence problem, if they perceive that there is one.

Split of audit firm

The decision of the firm to split into three divisions could **enhance the public perception of the independence of the audit department**. While there might be **underlying scepticism** relating to the reasons behind the split (which could merely be for marketing purposes or to enable non-audit divisions to raise capital more easily), the **underlying benefit for objectivity still exists**.

However, some audit clients will be unhappy with the move of the firm as it will entail their engaging will several different service providers to gain the services they previously got from the one audit firm.

2 Aventura International

Marking scheme

Marks

Ethical issues and actions to be taken
Generally 1 mark a point
Action ideas
- Enquire (ask)/discuss/review/inspect/accept/decline
- Safeguards
Reason ideas
- Ethical rules
- Risk – actual/perceived
For each matter
Max 4 marks for issues
Max 4 marks for actions
Max 6 marks for any one matter × 3

<u>Max 15</u>

Ethical situations arising in connection with the audit of Aventura International

(1) **Offer of goods**

At the stocktake, the auditors attending were invited to purchase stock at 30% of RRP, that is, at a 70% discount.

ACCA's guidance on accepting goods states that such benefits should only be accepted on 'normal commercial terms' or at a 'modest benefit'. What constitutes modest benefit will be a matter of judgement for the auditor. However, the APB's ES4 states that goods should not be accepted unless they are clearly insignificant.

Benefit

It is possible that this offer does approximate to offers made to staff at Aventura, as clothes commonly retail at prices with a substantial mark up on cost. It would not be unreasonable for a clothes retailer to give staff a 'cost' benefit. The auditor should determine whether such a benefit is made available to staff. If it is not made to staff it should not be accepted by the auditor.

The term 'modest benefit' should be considered both in terms of materiality to the auditor and the company. The offer is not material to Aventura, for whom clothes retail is only one division. However, the offer of unlimited fashion at a 70% discount is extremely likely to be material to junior audit staff (who are the grade most likely to be allocated to the stocktake). In this context, the benefit is **not** clearly insignificant.

Timing

It would be inappropriate to take up the offer at the stocktake, not least because this would constitute movement of stock during the count, which would be wrong.

Also, the junior staff members should not accept such goods without having discussed the matter with the audit partner (it is assumed in this answer that this is the first time such an offer has been made).

Lastly, if mistakes were to be made on the stock count, the audit might be open to charges of negligence if it appeared its staff members indulged in a shopping trip when they should have been auditing.

Action to be taken

The staff members should not have taken up the offer at the stocktake.

The audit partner should discuss the matter with management, ascertain whether a similar benefit is offered to staff and decide whether he feels it is appropriate for his staff to take up the offer. It may be inappropriate as Aventura might become perceived to be a 'reward' job by audit staff. Alternatively, it might be appropriate if the audit firm imposed a financial limit to the benefits their staff could accept.

(2) **Hospitality**

An invoice to the company for business use of the Chief Executive's jet shows that the audit manager was flown to Florida and back for a stay of two weeks.

Issues arising

(a) If the invoice was ostensibly for 'business use', what was the business? (Neither the client nor the auditor have offices in Florida.)

(b) If the invoice was not for business, the Chief Executive is wrong to invoice it to the company. Is this common practice?

(c) If it was for business, the cost of the auditor's flight should not have been charged directly to the company, but the audit firm, who could then have re-charged it. Was Darius Harken working for the weeks in question, or is it recorded as holiday in the audit firm's records?

(d) Does the invoice actually represent a significant example of hospitality being accepted by the audit manager?

(e) Did the audit manager travel alone, with family, or even with the Chief Executive? Does this indicate that the audit manager has a close personal relationship with the Chief Executive?

Hospitality/close personal relationship

It is possible that points (d) and (e) above may be indicated by the invoice.

In terms of accepting hospitality, ACCA's guidance is the same as was discussed above in relation to accepting goods. It is unlikely that paying for an auditor's flight would be considered normal commercial terms, because it would be traditional for the audit firm simply to recharge the cost of a business trip. Taking steps such as these would help to reduce the suggestion that something inappropriate has occurred, if the trip was genuinely business related. The APB's guidance states that hospitality should not be accepted unless it is reasonable in terms of its frequency, nature and cost.

If the trip was a pleasure trip (a) it should not have been charged to the company, which raises several auditing issues in its own right and (b) it does not come within the definition of 'modest commercial benefit'.

In terms of close business or personal relationships, ACCA's guidance states that these might adversely affect, or appear to affect, the objectivity of the auditor. It seems likely that in this instance, if the Chief Executive and the audit manager have been on holiday together, or at least a business 'jolly', then as a minimum, objectivity will **appear** to be threatened.

Action to be taken

(a) The audit firm should check their personnel records and see whether Darius Harken was working or holidaying at the relevant time.

(b) If the trip was business-related, the audit partner should check why the cost has been invoiced to the company by the Chief Executive and not by the audit firm.

(c) If the trip was personal, then the audit manager appears to have threatened the objectivity of the audit, and indeed, given that the trip appears to have been taken around the time the prior year audit was taking place, that audit is also adversely affected.

(d) The prior year audit files should be subjected to a cold review and the audit manager should be replaced on this year's audit, which should also be subject to a quality control review.

(e) All invoices rendered to the company in respect of the jet should be scrutinised by the audit team, for further evidence of personal expenses being charged to the company.

(3) **The impending marriage of the Chief Executive**

The Chief Executive's assistant is the former accountant in charge of the audit of Aventura, who is likely to have been involved with the audit of the previous year-end. She has just announced her engagement to the Chief Executive.

Issues arising

(a) Current year audit – there is a risk of loss of independence as the Chief Executive's assistant is aware of audit method.

(b) Prior year audit – there is a suggestion that the accountant in charge of the audit may have been in a personal relationship with the Chief Executive which may have adversely affected her objectivity.

Movement of audit staff

ACCA does not cover the issue of audit staff moving between the employments of the audit firm and audit clients. However, it is clear that this might adversely affect objectivity, so members involved in such activity should bear in mind the general guidance on objectivity.

The APB's ES2 states that in this situation the following factors should be considered:

• The position the individual had in the engagement team or firm,

• The position the individual has taken at the audit client

• The amount of involvement the individual will have with the engagement team (especially where it includes former colleagues)

• The length of time since the individual was a member of the engagement team or employed by the audit firm

Following the assessment of such threats, appropriate safeguards should be applied where necessary.

IFAC suggests a number of safeguards, such as:

• Considering the appropriateness of modifying the plan for the engagement

• Assigning the audit team to someone of sufficient experience in relation to the person who has left

• Involving an additional accountant not previously associated with the audit to review

Action to be taken

Although the accountant in charge was not the most senior staff member on the audit, it would have been prudent to modify the audit plan before this year's audit. However, this does not appear to have been done, and the audit is nearing completion.

Therefore, it is important that Voest implement the third bullet point above, and conduct a quality control review of this audit.

In relation to the suspicion that Ms Fennimore's objectivity may have been affected last year, it might also be a good idea to conduct a similar review of last year's audit work, evidence obtained and conclusions drawn. However, as the work should have been reviewed by an audit manager and partner after Ms Fennimore's involvement, the risk of a problem on last year's audit appears to be slight.

3 PLD Associates

> **Tutorial note**. The assessment of audit risk is a fundamental part of each audit and in considering whether to accept audit clients – it will *always* be necessary to carry out some kind of work to assess the overall risk at a client. Do not be tempted just to give a list of common risks, you must relate your answer to the situation given in the question. In this situation, you should have identified key words in the scenario, such as 'develop derelict land', 'Inland Revenue became suspicious', 'internal controls were weak'. This explains why the company was high risk and point you particularly to parts (iv) and (v) in the answer to (a). However, the requirement is (a) is not for you to identify the risk – so make sure you answer the question set and look past the risk to the procedures an audit firm would carry out to identify if the risk was too great to accept the audit. Remember also the importance of CDD procedures to avoid problems associated with clients who launder money.
>
> Part (b) requires assessment of information given in the question, but parts (c) and (d) can be answered without reference to the scenario. Do not fall into a trap of trying to relate your answer to these parts simply to this scenario. Use the scenario to prompt you if you wish, but you should use your general knowledge to answer much of this section.

(a)   PLD Associates plc is a high-risk client on two counts:

   (i)   The **nature of its business is property development**, a high-risk activity, and

   (ii)   The **weaknesses of the company's internal control system** and the lack of integrity of the founder Mr J Scott.

With such a potential client, the auditors must ensure that there are no independence or other ethical problems likely to cause conflict with the ethical code before accepting the appointment. They must also carry out customer due diligence to guard against accepting a client who launders money (remember, retaining the proceeds of any crime, eg tax evasion, is money laundering).

The procedures which an audit firm should carry out before accepting a potentially high audit risk client are as follows.

   (i)   **Request** the prospective clients' **permission to communicate** with the **previous auditors**. If such permission is refused the appointment should be declined.

   (ii)   On receipt of permission the prospective auditors should **request** in writing of the previous auditors all **information** which ought to be made available to them to enable them to decide whether they are prepared to accept nomination.

The information requested from the old auditors could go as far as asking about the integrity of the management of PLD Associates plc.

   (iii)   Ensure that the firm's **existing resources are adequate** to service the needs of the new client. This will raise questions of staff and time availability and the firm's technical expertise. This will be important in the case of PLD Associates plc as property development is a specialist area.

   (iv)   **Seek references** in respect of the new client company; it may be, as is often the case, that the directors of the company are already personally known to the firm; if not, independent enquiries should be made concerning the status of the company and its directors. Agencies such as Dun & Bradstreet might be of assistance together with a formal search at Companies House. The search at Companies House will uncover the qualified audit report if a copy of this has not already been obtained. It will be necessary to find out whether any regulatory authority has disciplined the company.

(v)   A **preliminary assessment of audit risk** should be made. This will involve discussions with the management of the client and assessing the internal control structure (which in the case of the PLD Associates plc is obviously poor).

(vi)   The **costs and benefits** of accepting the client should be estimated; this appointment may be considered too costly in terms of potential liability (or raised insurance premiums) and bad publicity.

(b)   Ethical guidelines issued by the accountancy institutes require that the auditors are **independent and objective**. It is the integrity of the auditors which gives weight to the audit opinion. In this case the partner has shown a singular lack of integrity by maintaining this secret fund; his objectivity as an auditor has been impaired by his lack of independence. He has also contravened ethical guidelines by carrying out the **preparation** of **accounting records** for a **quoted company**.

The partner has, however, gone farther than this omission of fundamental ethical principles; he has in fact **colluded** with the **managing director** to conceal questionable transactions from fellow directors and shareholders. In the worst case this could be with a view to defrauding the company of which he is auditor. He has also concealed transactions which should have been disclosed to the Inland Revenue and the DTI. His position as auditor is untenable and his audit opinion, once knowledge of his involvement is known, is valueless. He may also face criminal prosecution for money laundering.

(c)   The measures that audit firms might introduce to try and minimise the practice of 'opinion shopping' by prospective audit clients are as follows.

(i)   To **establish why the question is being asked**. Is the prospective client looking for auditors who will confirm his views on the treatment of a particular transaction? He may be trying to use this against his current auditors with whom he is in dispute.

(ii)   No **opinion** should be **given** until the **present auditors** have been **informed**. This is not only a matter of courtesy but may reveal other aspects to the problem which had not been forthcoming from the prospective client.

(iii)   If an audit firm decides to give an opinion it should do so **in writing** giving the facts of the problem as it has been presented to them. This will protect the audit firm against the situation where an incorrect opinion is given because the facts have been misrepresented by the prospective client to order to get the opinion which concurred with their own.

Current legislation exists to protect auditors, allowing them to present their case against removal to the members. Similarly, when the auditors resign they also have the right to make a **statement** regarding the resignation which must be sent to the **Registrar** and everyone who is entitled to receive the financial statements. Auditors often do not do so because of bad publicity etc.

In future the Review Panel might take a more active role in finding sets of accounts where an 'opinion shopper' has succeeded in obtaining an unqualified opinion which is unjustified.

(d)   Audit firms can reduce the risk of litigation and its effects upon the audit practice by ensuring:

(i)   **Auditing standards are applied** on all assignments

(ii)   **Adequate quality control procedures** are in force

(iii)   **Adequate review procedures** are in operation before a new client is accepted

(iv)   **Adequate PI insurance** is obtained (this does not reduce the risk of litigation but limits the damage it causes)

4 Professional responsibilities

> **Tutorial note.** You should expect at least one discussion question on your paper, which will probably be optional. This question requirement was not typical of a discussion question you could expect but is good practice for your essay skills.
>
> You should discuss who else has responsibilities in relation to fraud itself, given that actually auditors have no direct responsibility.
>
> Remember, when attempting an essay question, you should always set out all the sides to an argument, not just the ones you agree with, although you should always draw a conclusion at the end. Make sure your answer is justifiable given the arguments you have made. You should not introduce new arguments in your conclusions.

Responsibility of auditors

Before considering whether it is practical or desirable for auditors to accept a general responsibility to detect fraud and other irregularities it should be recognised that they already have a responsibility to plan the audit so that they have a reasonable expectation of detecting material misstatements in the financial statements resulting from irregularities or fraud.

It must also be acknowledged that the **primary responsibility** for preventing and detecting fraud must always **rest with the management of the enterprise.** It is they who have been given the responsibility to safeguard the assets of the enterprise while the auditor's primary responsibility is to express an opinion on the financial statements.

Extend responsibility?

However, it can be seen that the shareholders', the government's and the public's expectations of the auditor are changing and they are **increasingly calling on the auditor** to **widen his responsibility.**

One of the problems that may arise is the **difficulty of defining fraud.** Associated with this is the need for the auditor to determine an **appropriate level of materiality.**

Currently the auditor assesses materiality in relation to the true and fair view shown by the financial statements. This may no longer be the correct basis if all or most frauds have to be detected.

Fraud itself can cover several types of activities at various levels within the company. Should the auditor be expected to detect a petty theft committed by a junior employee? If not, how is a line drawn between insignificant and important frauds? The guidelines defines fraud as involving the use of deception to obtain an unjust of illegal financial advantage.

The desirability of changing the auditor's responsibility has to be considered in the light of different types of organisations and different interested parties. It would seem to be reasonable for the auditor of a financial institution, where depositors' savings are at risk, to have a greater responsibility for the detection of fraud than the auditor of a small private company run by proprietors. Similarly the auditors of public companies should have a greater responsibility than those of private companies. This would reflect the public's expectations of the role of the modern auditor and legislation should react to these expectations.

Since fraud invariably has an impact on either the accounting records of the financial statements, it is generally accepted that auditors need to plan their audits so that they have a reasonable expectation of detecting material misstatements caused by fraud.

While few people would disagree that the auditor should have some responsibility for the detection of fraud, it may be that widening the auditor's role would mean that additional audit costs would be incurred by all organisations to detect fraud in a mere handful of cases.

Perhaps auditors should advise management how to prevent and detect fraud and penalties for it should be increased so that there is a greater deterrent. If organisations could prevent fraud more effectively there would not be such a need for auditors to try to detect it.

As to the practicalities of detection, fraud can be very difficult to detect where internal control systems are very weak. Some types of fraud may require special expertise to be detected. All auditors should already be detecting frauds and irregularities which give rise to material errors in financial statements. Procedures used to detect immaterial frauds would principally be an extension of the usual audit procedures but the time taken to **extend the level of testing** would be considerable.

The auditor judges the amount of work necessary on the need to obtain sufficient, reliable evidence on which to form an opinion on the view shown by the financial statements. If the auditor's objective was changed, whilst the **method would principally be the same**, the amount of **work necessary** would **increase significantly.** The auditor would not accept a greater responsibility for detecting fraud without a **substantial fee increase.** It is questionable whether this would be considered worthwhile for most organisations.

There is also the **practical difficulty** of **to whom the auditors reports a fraud.** If senior management are involved and the auditor has no real proof and there is no material effect on the financial statements, then the auditor will have to seek legal advice on what action should be taken. The auditor is bound by his **duty of confidentiality** from disclosing it to the appropriate authorities without the client's permission. However, the duty of confidence is not absolute, and the auditors may disclose matters to a proper authority either in the public interest or for other specific reasons.

An associated problem which might arise is a **deterioration in the relationship** between the auditor and the client. If he had to report directly to the authorities, the client may be reluctant to provide information which might cast suspicion over everyone.

Conclusion

Auditors have the skills necessary to detect most types of fraud but the **cost** of so doing **may exceed the likely benefits.** The approach I recommend is for the auditor to make recommendations to management about how they could reduce the likelihood of fraud or irregularities and increase the possibility of detection.

5 CD Sales

(a) There are various key audit procedures which would have uncovered the fraud perpetrated by Mr A Long. Note that the first two tests would bring to the attention of the auditor the substantial inherent and control risk surrounding the accounts of CD Sales, thus increasing their perceived audit risk, and putting them on their guard.

Analytical review

The auditor should perform analytical procedures in order to compare the company's results with those of other companies in the same business sector. In particular, the auditor should look at sales growth rates and gross profit margins, but also inventory holding levels, non-current assets and return on capital. This should indicate that the company's results are unusual for the sector, to a great extent.

Review of service contracts

The auditor should examine the directors' service contracts. It is unusual for *all* directors to be paid such substantial bonuses, although the payment of bonuses of some sort to directors is common business practice. It is the size of the bonuses in proportion to the directors' base salaries which is the problem here. It increases both the inherent and control risk for the auditor because it reduces the directors' objectivity about the performance of the company. Audit risk is thus increased.

Testing of sales, purchases and inventories

(i) The main audit test to obtain audit evidence for sales would be to require direct confirmations from the sales agents. These confirmations would also provide evidence for the balance owed to CD Sales at the year end and the inventories held by the agent at the year end. Replies to such confirmations should be sent direct to the auditor who would agree the details therein to the company's records or reconcile any differences. Where replies are not received alternative procedures would be carried out which might include visits to the agents themselves to examine their records.

(ii) A selection of agents should, in any case, be visited at the year end to confirm the inventories held on sale or return by physical verification. The auditor should count such inventories and consider obsolescence, damage etc.

(iii) Fictitious agents might be discovered by either of tests (iii) and (iv), but a further specific procedure would be to check authorisation of and contracts with all the sales agents. Correspondence could also be reviewed from throughout the year.

(iv) The practice of 'selling' all the inventories to the agents and them repurchasing it after the year end should be detected by sales and purchases cut-off tests around the year end. All transactions involving inventory items returned after the year end should be examined.

Testing of non-current assets

Non-current asset testing should help to identify inventory purchases which have been invoiced as non-current assets.

(i) Samples of additions to non-current assets can be checked to the non-current asset register and to the asset itself.

(ii) Physical verification will ensure that an asset is being used for the purpose specified, and this should be relatively straightforward to check as the computers will each have individual identification codes.

(iii) Where the assets cannot be found, then it may be possible to trace the asset to inventories, perhaps via the selling agents' confirmations, or to sales already made.

Related parties review

The level of collusion with suppliers makes detection of fraud difficult, but the auditor may be put on guard if he discovers that the suppliers are related parties to CD Sales. A related party review would normally take place as part of an audit.

(b) The type of 'confidentiality agreement' signed by the auditor of CD Sales has reduced the scope of the audit to such an extent that it has become almost meaningless.

While it is understandable that companies would wish to protect sensitive commercial information, the auditor has the right to any information he feels is necessary in the performance of his duties. This agreement clearly circumvents that right. Moreover, such information would still be protected if released to the auditor, because the auditor is under a duty of confidentiality to the client.

In reducing the scope of the audit to this extent, the agreement prevents the auditor obtaining sufficient appropriate evidence to support an audit opinion. The auditor's report should therefore be modified on the grounds of limitation on scope, possibly to the extent of a full disclaimer.

In failing to issue such a modification, the auditor may well have acted negligently and even unlawfully in signing such an agreement.

(c) A review of interim accounts is very different from an audit of year end financial statements. In an auditor's report a positive assurance is given on the truth and fairness of the financial statements. The level of audit work will be commensurate with the level of the assurance given, that is it will be stringent, testing the systems producing the accounts and the year end figures themselves using a variety of appropriate procedures.

In the case of a review of interim financial statements, the auditor gives only negative assurance, that he has not found any indication that the interim accounts are materially misstated. The level of audit work will be much less penetrating, varied and detailed than in a full audit. The main audit tools used to obtain evidence will be analytical procedures and direct enquiries of the company's directors.

(d) It is not the duty of the auditor to prevent or detect fraud. The auditor should, however, conduct the audit in such a way as to expect to detect any material misstatements in the financial statements, whether caused by fraud or error. At the planning stage, the auditor should assess the risk that fraud is occurring both at the financial statement and the assertion level and plan his procedures accordingly. Where fraud is suspected or likely, the auditor should carry out additional procedures in order to confirm or deny this suspicion.

Even if a fraud is uncovered after an audit, the auditor will have a defence against a negligence claim if it can be shown that auditing standards were followed and that no indication that a fraud was taking place was received at any time.

Application of principles to this case

In this particular case, Mr A Long has taken a great deal of trouble to cover up his fraudulent activities, using accomplices, bribing people, cooking up fictitious documents etc. When such a high level fraud is carried out, the auditor might find it extremely difficult to uncover the true situation or even to realise anything was amiss. The auditor is also entitled to accept the truth of representations made to him and documents shown to him which purport to come from third parties.

On the other hand, the auditor should have a degree of professional scepticism. The auditor should be aware of the risks pertaining to the company and should recognise that controls can be overridden by collusion or by management actions. The suspicions of the auditor should have been aroused by the rapid growth rate of the company and fairly standard audit procedures on cut-off and non-current assets should have raised matters which required explanation.

Where the auditor has been most culpable, however, is in signing the confidentiality agreement. This restricted the scope of the audit to such an extent that the auditor should have known that there was insufficient evidence to support their opinion. The auditor will therefore find it difficult to defend a negligence claim.

6 Marsden Manufacturing Ltd

Tutorial note. In part (a), it is vitally important that you do not just bang out the percentage indicators, but that you show the examiner that you are considering qualitative factors as well. You will probably get one mark for the calculations – the rest are available for considered comment.

In part (b), remember the approach we set out in the EQB. Work through the scenario, looking out for items you think will be relevant of that raise question (or exclamation) marks in your head. The examiner doesn't just include things in exam questions to take up paper. Think to yourself 'what does that mean for the company/the audit?'. However, you don't have to get 100% on this question to pass the paper, so don't waste time trying to think of points for every word in the question – if you really can't see anything relevant in the information, move on to the next thing you are told.

Part (c) should represent easy marks, as there are three or four key administrative matters which require attending to on every audit, none of which have been mentioned in the scenario. Remember lists such as 'administrative planning matters' so that you can always get easy marks like these. But don't mention things on your list that the question has discounted – that is obviously a waste of your time. For example, in this question, don't talk about deciding whether to use computers on this audit, because the question states that the partner has decided not to.

Part (d) is another source of useful marks on this question. You should be able to discuss the basic issues relating to conflicts of interest, draw a conclusion in this case and then discuss steps to take such as discussing it with both parties. It is unlikely in this case that the firm should divest either audit – don't fall into the trap of making over the top suggestions.

(a)   **Materiality considerations**

Value indicators

The traditional indicators of materiality levels which would apply in this situation are as follows:

	Band A £	Band B £
Turnover (1/2% / 1%)	12,670	25,340
Profit before tax (5%)	3,050	-
Total assets (1% / 2%)	10,090	20,180
Net assets (2% / 5%)	7,360	18,400

A simple average of these indicators would give materiality of £13,870. This is a useful numerical indicator, but there are also some qualitative features that should be considered.

Qualitative features

As interest is an important figure to the company due to their agreements with the bank, it might be wise to include profit before interest and tax rather than profit before tax in the calculations. This would raise the average figure given above to £13,970.

Net assets are also important to the company, due to the bank agreement. The agreement requires current assets to be 1.5 times current liabilities. On the balance sheet given, that would be £586,000. The current assets are well above that at the moment. However, when considering materiality, the auditor should look at matters cumulatively. The ratio is material to the balance sheet, so any issues relevant to that ratio may be material, regardless of value.

Conclusion

I would therefore set planning materiality at £14,000. However, I would treat issues arising in relation to net current assets as potentially material, and consider the cumulative impact that any issues had.

(b) **Audit risks at Marsden Manufacturing**

Inherent risks

Using the components of audit risk might help you identify the risks, or a greater breadth of risks, in the scenario in the first place.

The key issue relating to the balance sheet in the year is the **factoring of debts**. This raises a number of issues for the audit.

Breaking up your answer into the components of audit risk helps to structure your answer

The first issue is questions behind the factoring of debt: **why have they been factored**? This is answered by the fact that the company is seeking a form of insurance against bad debts so that their interest cover will be maintained. However, it is important to check that this is the only reason, ie that the debt is not being factored because there are **cash flow** problems (which might also be indicated by the fall in cash in the year) which could in turn lead to suspicions of **going concern** issues.

You do not need to go into long detail about the requirements of FRS 5 here, but should be aware of the issues that make this risky for the audit.

Specifically in relation to **debtors**, it raises issues of whether they have yet been accounted for in the balance sheet and **properly disclosed** under **FRS 5**. Factoring of debts is given as an illustration in the FRS. It states that there are three ways of accounting for debt which has been factored. One of the ways is **derecognition**. This is when there is a high transfer of all significant risks and rewards to the factor and as the entire sales ledger function has been outsourced to the factor, this needs investigation. Derecognising debt would clearly be **material** to the balance sheet, and could have an impact on the covenant with the bank although there would also be a significant influx of cash, so the net effect on net assets might not affect the net assets ratio too badly. If the factoring has already been accounted for, then cash appears to be dangerously low (given that an injection of cash should have just occurred). This would have serious implications for the going concern assumption. However, as there is a large debit balance in debtors, it appears more likely that the factoring has not yet been accounted for.

The **relationship with the bank** is clearly important to the business, and has been mentioned already. However, the whole issue of relationship with the bank must be considered for audit purposes, particularly as there appears to be a **worsening cash position** and there is a question mark over the factoring of debts. **Going concern** is a risk on this audit, particularly if **accounting issues** such as the one mentioned above radically change the balance sheet and have an **impact on the debt covenants**.

Facts such as the compensation limits for dismissal claims are not within your syllabus. However, they are cumulative general knowledge from your ACCA studies and here are relevant materiality considerations. An auditor would know or find out such details. For your purposes, being aware that they would be material is sufficient.

Connected to the issue of the debt factoring is the position of the former sales ledger clerk, Sally Forsyth. As part of the re-structuring, she has been dismissed. She appears to be bringing a claim against the company for unfair dismissal and sexual discrimination. It is unclear whether she has grounds for such action.

The upper limit for compensation in unfair dismissal cases is £51,700 and there is no upper limit for discrimination cases. Hence, there is a **potential material contingent liability**. During the course of the audit it will be vital to investigate this affair and consider whether the potential liability falls within the **timing requirements of FRS 12** (when were the key dates?). If Ms Forsyth has been dismissed before the year end it is likely that there is a legal obligation arising, if she has a case. To consider whether she has a case or not, it may be necessary to **seek an expert legal opinion**.

Following up from the issues noted at the stock take, there appears to a be problem with **possible stock obsolescence**. In the absence of any further explanation for the stock increase, this is borne out by the fact that stock has risen on the balance sheet from last year. It is unclear whether this may be material or not, however, given that current assets are material by their nature given the agreement with the bank and the possible effects of FRS 5 on debtors, **this matter may be material by its nature**.

BPP
LEARNING MEDIA

Control risk

As part of control risk evaluation, the auditor must consider the **effect of debt factoring** on the systems of the business and the fact that the sales ledger function is now outsourced, and has been for a portion of the year under review. The **related controls must be assessed**. There is also a risk that the **controls over the transfer** from in house sales ledger to outsourced sales ledger may not have been strong, and that errors could have been made.

Detection risk

There are some key detection issues to consider. The first, as mentioned above, is that an **expert** may be required on this audit to obtain evidence about the contingent liability. The second is that the requirements of ISA 402 must be considered in relation to the outsourced sales ledger function. The auditor must ensure that he has all the **information he requires from the service provider**.

(c) **Administrative planning matters**

The engagement partner must organise a **planning meeting** to discuss the audit with the team.

The supervisor needs to obtain **key dates** relating to the audit, such as the dates of the manager and partner reviews, and client related dates such as when final accounts will be ready and when the accounts need to be signed by.

The supervisor needs to obtain **client permission to contact** the company's **solicitor** and the **debt factor** and he needs to **organise when the audit team will be able to liase with them**.

(d) **Conflict of interest**

Does a conflict exist?

The audit firm is in possession of information about Marsden's new client which Marsden would be interested in, which is sensitive information. However, it is also information they could have obtained by conducting a credit rating or search on the new customer, which they should have (and therefore may have) done for a customer of such magnitude.

It is obviously in Wallworth's best interests that their auditors do not share information about their poor payment history with their new supplier.

> It is important to set out that you are not in possession of enough details to come to a conclusion on this matter, stating what the relevant factors are.

Whether a conflict exists depends on the size of the audit firm and the procedures put in place in the audit department to maintain the independence of the two audits. In a small department it is likely that it will be difficult in practice to keep matters completely confidential. (In other words, one audit team is likely to be aware of facts relating to the other audit client.)

What steps should the auditor take?

In this situation, it is probably best that the auditor makes both parties aware that they are the auditors for both companies and restate their duty of confidentiality to both. It may be wise to revisit the engagement letter for both clients to ensure that the duties and procedures in relation to this potential conflict are set out.

> Remember, draw a reasonable conclusion, based on the facts.

7 Gasoleum

(a)   Areas of potential risk to be addressed by the audit

Income

A substantial proportion of sales made at the stations will be cash based therefore making completeness of income difficult to establish.

Sales records are updated via an on-line computer ie records are updated automatically and instantly. Any weakness in the operation of the computer be it manual input or systematic error will directly impact income. The key risk is however weak control over manual input.

Income could be missed via weak controls over the sale of car wash and air tokens.

Misclassification of income would render management accounts meaningless for analytical review purposes.

Inventories

The nature of inventories ie petrol requires an unusual method to quantify – dipping of tanks. This increases the risk that the value is inaccurate.

All goods stocked within the mini markets are potentially desirable by both staff and customers. They are also easily moveable and thus inventory losses could occur. If this remains undetected, year-end inventories and thus profit will be overstated.

Goods are also perishable. There is therefore a risk of inventory valuation being overstated where no provision/write off is made.

State lottery outlet

There is a potential risk that income from sales of tickets is inappropriately included within the company's income.

Outlets receive commission per ticket sold. There is a risk of inappropriate classification and also overstatement if weak controls exist over the handling and storage of lottery tickets.

Inherent risk due to price competition

Intense price competition could significantly reduce margins which could in turn lead to management manipulation of financial information ie potential overstatement of income and understatement of expenses.

Multi-locations

With there being 15 garages to audit, there is increased risk of not detecting error as it is more complicated to control and co-ordinate the audit.

(b)   The work performed by the internal auditor would impact planning to the extent that:

(1)   The results of his work on the company's internal controls during the year could reduce the risk attached to particular parts of the audit and thus reduce the extent of our detailed testing on it.

For instance, evidence that the microcomputer has operated satisfactorily during the year would provide us with increased assurance as to the completeness and accuracy of both income and inventory records and thus allow a modification in the nature and timing and reduce the extent of our work. This is obviously only the case if the audit work was done thoroughly and competently.

(2) Once we have determined that his work can be relied upon, the knowledge that he was responsible for co-ordinating the year-end inventory count would again increase our confidence in inventory quantity figures, provided we are satisfied that he is suitably independent of the warehouse and of the normal inventory control procedures.

Before deciding to make use of his work we would first need to establish its relevance and the reliability.

Relevance – has he been engaged in projects whose results are of interest to us. Given what we have been told about his duties it would appear that we have some common objectives.

Reliability – his work is ultimately only reliable provided he is competent at what he does, carries out his work with due professional care and is suitably independent.

Once these have been determined, other factors would also need to be considered:

(1) Do management within the company act upon the results of his work?

(2) The materiality of the area would need to be ascertained. For instance any work on the controls surrounding the sale of car wash and air tokens could reduce our testing to just a review of his working papers, whereas work on the operation of the on-line micro computers would give us confidence but not negate the need for some systems work to be done by our computer audit department.

(c) Analytical procedures on income and GP margin:

Income

(1) Obtain an analysis of income per petrol station and perform inter-branch comparisons to identify any branch with unusually high/low total income.

(2) Obtain an analysis of income per source for each station and again carry out inter-branch comparisons to identify any branch with an unusual mix/split of income.

(3) Compare income per source and per branch to last year. Are changes in line with our expectations and industry norms?

(4) Obtain management accounts and do a month by month review of sales comparing with both previous years and other branches.

(5) For all the above we need to discuss fluctuations with management, follow up any discrepancies and confirm any statements made by the directors.

Gross profit

(1) Perform a comparison of gross profit percentage per branch.

(2) Compare gross profit percentage this year to last year and against budget.

(3) Review aged inventories analysis between this year and last for slow moving products, to identify any overstatement of closing inventories and thus gross profit.

(4) Compare percentage of inventories written off after inventory counts branch by branch and investigate branches with low gross profit percentages.

(5) Compare margins on petrol to industry norms.

(6) Consider the impact that fluctuations in oil prices would have on profits made.

(7) Again, for all of the above we would need to discuss fluctuations, follow up any discrepancies and confirm any statements made.

8 Audit

> **Tutorial note.** This is not an exam standard question, but is a helpful exercise to remind yourself of the advantages of audit for a small company and also the alternative opinions available.

(a)   The advantages of having an audit include the following.

    (i)   **Shareholders** who are **not involved in management** gain **reassurance** from audited accounts about management's **stewardship** of the business.

    (ii)   Audited accounts are a reliable source for a **fair valuation of shares** in an unquoted company either for taxation or other purposes.

    (iii)   Some **banks** rely on accounts for the purposes of **making loans** and reviewing the value of security.

    (iv)   **Creditors and potential creditors** can use audited accounts to assess the potential strength of the company.

    (v)   The audit provides **management** with an **useful independent check** on the accuracy of the accounting systems; the auditors can recommend improvements in those systems.

(b)   **Audit of a small company**

The audit of a small company is still an exercise designed to express an opinion on the truth and fairness of the accounts.

However, the audit of a small company is often affected by certain factors:

- The concentration of ownership and management in one person
- The wider professional relationship between the auditor and the business
- The fact that small teams of auditors are involved with the audit

There is a Practice Note in existence giving guidance on the audit of small businesses and it outlines how specific auditing standards impact upon the audit of small businesses. For example, in relation to SAS 110, the practice note suggests that indicators of fraud in an owner managed business might be that the owner makes no distinction between business expenses and personal expenses.

So the methods of undertaking the audit will be the same, and the same auditing standards will be applied. However, the auditor must be aware of the different inherent risk in the audit of a small company and in applying auditing standards, consider all the relevant risks.

(c)   **Alternatives to audit**

A small company who does not require an audit under statute could engage a firm of accountants to carry out a review instead.

A review is an engagement similar to audit, which is designed to give a lower level of assurance that would be given by an audit. Often this is expressed in terms of negative assurance. The procedures undertaken to express an opinion in a review engagement are therefore less detailed and often comprise of enquiry and analytical procedures.

Colin needs to decide upon the level of assurance that is best for his business. This will involve him analysing the advantages of audit (giving a high level of assurance) discussed above in part (a) and deciding whether his business requires the higher level of assurance or not. Some of the advantages of the audit will also be given by a review.

9 Lambley Properties

Tutorial note. You should not just assume that if the directors refuse to sign the letter of representation a qualification of the audit report is automatically required. There are other procedures to undertake first. Remember the circumstances (given in (b)) in which it is permissible to rely on a letter of representation.

(a)

Lambley Properties plc
Farmer Estate
Brickley

ABC & Co
7 The High Street
Brickley   30 April 20X2

Dear Sirs

We confirm to the best of our knowledge and belief, and having made appropriate enquiries of other directors and officials of the company, the following representations given to you in connection with your audit of the company's financial statements for the year ended 31 March 20X2.

General

We acknowledge as directors our responsibility under the Companies Act 1985 for preparing financial statements which give a true and fair view and for making accurate representations to you. All the accounting records have been made available to you for the purpose of your audit and all the transactions undertaken by the company have been properly reflected and recorded in the accounting records. All other records and related information, including minutes of all management and shareholders' meetings, have been made available to you.

Financial support

Keyworth Builders Ltd a subsidiary of the company, is experiencing going concern problems. We confirm that the company will continue to make financial support available to the subsidiary for the foreseeable future.

Claim

Eastwood Manufacturing plc has made a claim against the company for £5m arising from alleged negligent construction of a printing machine. The claim comprises £3m for repairs and £2m for the cost of disruption to Eastwood's business. Following discussions with the company's professional advisers we consider that Eastwood has no claim on the company and hence no provision for these costs is required in the accounts for the year ended 31 March 20X2. However the contingency is fully explained in a note.

Transactions with directors

The company has had at no time during the year any arrangement, transaction or agreement to provide credit facilities (including loans, quasi-loans or credit transactions) for directors nor to guarantee or provide security for such matters, except as disclosed in note X to the financial statements.

Post balance sheet events

There have been no events since the balance sheet date which necessitate revision of the figures included in the financial statements or inclusion of a note thereto. Should further material events occur, which may necessitate revision of the figures included in the financial statements or inclusion of a note thereto, we will advise you accordingly.

Yours faithfully

Signed on behalf of the Board of Directors

.... Director

(b) **Reliability of letter of representation**

The letter of representation is a written record of statements made by management to auditors during the audit. As it is a written record, it is stronger evidence than oral representations by themselves would be.

However representations do not come from an independent source. They should not therefore be relied on when other evidence is available or expected to be available.

Nevertheless representations may be the only available evidence when **knowledge of facts is confined to management**, or the matter is **one of judgement** or opinion. Independent confirmation will not be available in these circumstances.

In this context s 389A Companies Act 1985 provides that an officer of the company commits an offence if he knowingly or recklessly makes a statement (written or oral) to the company's auditors which is misleading, false or deceptive concerning a material matter. (An officer in this context would include directors, company secretary and senior management.)

Reliance on letter

On receipt of a letter of representation the auditors will need to **ensure** that there is **no other evidence** that they have discovered during the course of their audit which conflicts with the written representation. They will then have to **review the representations** made and decide, given the results of the audit testing and their assessment of risk, whether they are able to rely on them to give an unqualified opinion on the accounts.

(c) Work to be performed to check whether a provision should be included in the accounts for the legal claim from Eastwood Manufacturing plc is as follows.

- **Obtain and review all correspondence** relating to the claim.

- **Review written advice** obtained from the company's lawyer and surveyor.

- **Review the original contract** between Eastwood and Lambley to assess the extent of Lambley's responsibility for repairs and any time period limitations.

- **Ascertain whether Lambley is covered by insurance** should the claim be payable.

- **Examine minutes** of meetings of the Board and management which deal with this matter.

These procedures will allow the probability of the company having to meet the claim to be assessed. Disclosure and/or provision to comply with FRS 12 *Provisions, Contingent Liabilities and Contingent Assets* will be required.

(d) In the circumstances where the directors refuse to sign the letter of representation because of the legal claim from Eastwood Manufacturing plc the following procedures could be considered.

(i) A **meeting** between the auditors and directors to discuss a revision of the wording of the letter, so allowing the directors to sign.

(ii) Failing this, a **letter of representation excluding the Eastwood claim** should be obtained.

(iii) The old APC auditing guideline recommended that where management refused to sign a letter of representation, the **auditors should prepare a statement** setting out their understanding of the principal representation and ask the management to confirm in writing that their understanding is correct. In this case this procedure could be carried out just for the Eastwood claim if a letter of representation excluding this matter had already been obtained.

Assuming that satisfactory representations are not obtained, either because the original letter is amended in such a way that the situation concerning the claim is not properly explained or that the directors refuse to confirm the auditors' statement, then the auditors will need to **consider the implications** of this scope limitation **for their report**.

Given that refusal by the management to give satisfactory representations concerning the claim indicates that they may be uncertain as to the eventual outcome, the auditors would probably decide to qualify their opinion on the grounds of uncertainty.

10 Bestwood Electronics

Tutorial note. A knowledge of FRS 21 is required here, as well as the practical knowledge of the audit procedures which must be carried out after the year end. This requirement to be aware of accounting matters will be reflected in your paper. You must be prepared to discuss accounting issues from the auditors' perspective.

(a) (i) Auditors should perform procedures designed to obtain sufficient appropriate audit evidence that all **material subsequent events** up to the date of their report which require adjustment of, or disclosure in, the financial statements have been **identified and properly reflected** therein.

These procedures should be applied to any **matters** examined during the audit which may be **susceptible to change** after the year end. They are in addition to tests on specific transactions after the period end, eg cut-off tests.

Non-adjusting subsequent events should be disclosed in the notes to the accounts of the company, whereas all adjusting events should be incorporated in the accounts.

(ii) The financial statements are the **directors' responsibility** and they would therefore be expected to inform the auditors of any material subsequent events between the date of the auditors' report and the date the financial statements are issued. The auditors do *not* have any obligation to perform procedures, or make enquires regarding the financial statements *after* the date of their report.

When, **after** the date of their **report** but **before** the **financial statements** are **issued**, the **auditors** become **aware** of **subsequent events** which may materially affect the financial statements, they should:

- Establish whether the financial statements need amendment
- Discuss the matter with the directors
- Consider the implications for their report, taking additional action as appropriate

When the financial statements are amended, the auditors should extend the procedures discussed above to the date of their new report, carry out any other appropriate procedures and issue a new audit report dated the day it is signed.

The situation where the statements are not amended but the auditors feel that they should be is discussed below.

(iii) Auditors have no obligations to perform procedures or make enquiries regarding the financial statements **after** they have been issued.

When, after the financial statements have been issued, but before they have been laid before the members or equivalent, auditors become aware of subsequent events which, had they occurred and been known of at the date of their report, might have caused them to issue a different report, they should

- **Consider** whether the financial statements need **amendment**
- **Discuss** the matter with the directors
- **Consider the implications** for their **report**, taking additional action as appropriate

There are two cases:

(1)   An event which **occurred before** the **date** of the **auditors' report**, but which the auditors became aware of thereafter, and

(2)   An **event** which **occurred after** the **date** of the **auditors' report**.

Under (1), the auditors and directors should consider whether the financial statements should be revised (eg under ss 245 to 245(c) CA 1985). In situation (2) there is no statutory provision for revising financial statements; the auditors might take legal advice on withdrawing their report. In **both** cases, a statement by the directors or auditors at the AGM may be feasible, but in any event legal advice may be helpful.

Where the directors do **not** revise the financial statements but the auditors feel they should be revised, and where the statements have been issued but not yet laid before the members; or if the directors do not intend to make an appropriate statement at the AGM, then the auditors should consider steps to take, on a timely basis, to prevent reliance on their report eg a statement at the AGM. Remember that the auditors have no right to communicate to the members directly in writing.

(b)   The audit work for post balance sheet events will normally be concerned with balance sheet values at and after the year end. The following procedures will be carried out.

(i)   **Fixed assets**

(1)   **Check for any sales** or proposed sales after the year end which may trigger a write down to net realisable value at the year end.

(2)   **Consider obsolescence** of fixed assets, for example plant used to make a discontinue line, which might only become apparent after the year end.

(ii)   **Stock**

(1)   **Check post year-end selling price** of major items of stock and compare to value in year end accounts. Consider write downs to net realisable value.

(2)   **Consider the possible existence of obsolete, damaged or slow moving stock** and the consequent value of any write down.

(3)   **Perform a (limited) stock take** after the year end **if the existence of all stock is not known** for certain.

(iii)   **Debtors**

(1)   Review post year end receipts to determine recoverability.

(2)   Take doubtful debts paid out of the provision and consider writing parts of the provision off for which no money has been received.

(3)   Review trade press and correspondence and consult the sales manager about any major customers who have become insolvent recently.

(4)   Check the issue of credit notes and return of goods after the year end to determine the provision for credit notes required in the accounts.

(iv) **Cash at bank**

(1) **Check that outstanding items** on the bank reconciliation have **cleared promptly after the year end** (to spot teeming and lading and late payment to creditors).

(2) **Write back any stale cheques** not cleared (over 6 months old).

(3) **Check all material payments and receipts around the year end** to check the completeness of both accruals and prepayments (including NI and PAYE sundry creditors).

(v) **Trade creditors**

(1) **Check reconciling items** on suppliers' statements have **cleared promptly** after the year end.

(2) If the creditors circularisation has been carried out then **examining post year end payments** will help to verify balances where there was no supplier's statement and no reply.

(vi) **Going concern problems and other matters**

The post balance sheet event review is important in terms of going concern investigations. The following procedures should be carried out as a matter of routine.

(1) **Check profit and cash flow forecasts.**

(2) **Review management accounts** and reports after the year end.

(3) **Review board minutes** after the year end.

(4) **Request any information** on post balance sheet events and going concern matters from the directors and check their information.

(5) The **directors should also state** they have given all such information in the letter of representation.

(vii) **Non-adjusting events**

Look for any matters which are non-adjusting but which should be disclosed in the accounts, for example, major sales of fixed assets, accidental losses and issues of shares and debentures.

(c) I will check whether there have been any material post balance sheet events in this period, particularly if there is a significant delay between the date of the auditors' report and the issue of their financial statements. I will not undertake such detailed enquiries as in (b) above, but I will perform the following procedures.

(i) **Ask the management or directors if any further material events have occurred** which might affect my opinion on the accounts.

(ii) **Review the latest board minutes, reports and management accounts** issued since the end of the audit.

(iii) Any **matters which were uncertain** at the end of the audit should be **reviewed** again to establish an outcome and any effect on the accounts. Examples would include doubtful debts, contingencies and stock obsolescence (perhaps due to new developments).

(iv) **Consider any matters** which have **arisen in the industry** or the economy which might affect the company.

11 Bingham Engineering

Tutorial note. This question combines the issue of the auditors' review of the going concern assumption in financial statements with the review of forecast information. Although you are given a brief scenario in the question, this question is largely based on your learning in these areas and you do not need to apply your knowledge to a scenario. As such, it is not exam standard, but it is a useful exercise to run through your knowledge on these important areas.

(a)   The 'going concern' concept assumes that the accounts are drawn up on the basis that the business will continue to exist as a viable commercial entity, without any need for any significant curtailment in its present level of activity for the 'foreseeable future'.

When forming his opinion at the conclusion of the post balance sheet period the auditor should have regard to the term 'foreseeable future' identified in SSAP 2 in the context of going concern. While the foreseeable future must be judged in relation to specific circumstances, the auditors should normally expect the directors to have considered information which relates to a minimum of 12 months following the date of approval of the financial statements.

(b)   The most common factors indicating that a company may not be regarded as a going concern are as follows.

- Adverse financial figures or ratios:
    - Recurring operating losses
    - Financing to a considerable extent out of overdue suppliers and other creditors
    - Heavy dependence on short-term finance for long-term needs
    - Working capital deficiencies
    - Low liquidity rates
    - Over-gearing, in the form of high or increasing debt to equity ratios
    - Under capitalisation, particularly if there is a deficiency of share capital and reserves

- Borrowing in excess of limits imposed by debenture trust deeds

- Defaults on loans or similar agreements

- Dividends in arrears

- Restrictions placed on usual trade terms

- Excessive or obsolete stock

- Long overdue debtors

- Non-compliance with statutory capital requirements

- Deterioration of relationship with bankers

- Necessity of seeking new sources or methods of obtaining finance

- The continuing use of old fixed assets because there are not funds to replace them

- The size and content of the order book

- Potential losses on long-term contracts

Other factors, not necessarily suggesting inability to meet debts, may be internal or external matters.

(i)   **Internal matters**

- Loss of key management or staff
- Significantly increasing stock levels
- Work stoppages or other labour difficulties

- Substantial dependence upon the success of a particular project or particular asset
- Excessive reliance on the success of a new product
- Uneconomic long-term commitments

(ii) **External matters**

- Legal proceedings or similar matters that may jeopardise a company's ability to continue in business

- Loss of a key franchise or patent

- Loss of a principal supplier or customer

- The undue influence of a market dominant competitor

- Political risks

- Technical developments which render a key product obsolete

- Frequent financial failures of enterprises in the same industry

The indications above vary in importance and some may only have significance as audit evidence when viewed in conjunction with others.

The significance of the indications above may diminish because they are matched by audit evidence indicating that there are mitigating factors. Indications that the business may be having to sell fixed assets to meet present cash demands may be mitigated by the possibility of obtaining new sources of finance or of renewing and expanding loan finance. Indications of problems that raise questions about the continuation of the business without suggesting inability to meet debts may be mitigated by factors relating to the enterprise's capacity to adopt alternative courses of action, for example, the likelihood of finding alternative sales markets where a principal customer is lost.

(c) (i) Under the present circumstances of the company, it is unlikely that the capital expenditure/disposal forecast will contain many items of capital expenditure because of the adverse effect that this would have on the company's cash flow. For such items as there are, the auditor should check that the quoted costs are reasonable, with any large value items being checked against price lists etc. Enquiries should be made of management as to whether there are any proposed items of capital expenditure not included in the forecast.

In relation to any intended disposals of fixed assets, the auditors should:

(1) Check whether the proceeds of sale appear to be reasonable with particular care being taken to see that any estimates are arrived at on a prudent basis.

(2) Consider whether the estimates of the timing of the receipt of sale proceeds appear to be reasonable and, once again, arrived at on a prudent basis.

(ii) The audit work required in relation to the profit forecast would be as follows.

(1) Check that the level of projected sales is reasonable, being similar to the previous year and consistent with current market conditions and the confirmed orders received from the company's customers.

(2) Consider whether the gross profit margin appears reasonable in the light of the company's recent experiences and there has been consistency in the recognition of those items affecting the calculation of this key ratio.

(3) Compare the level of profit and loss account items to the previous year, investigating carefully any areas of significant change. Any projected savings in expenditure must be justified and the auditor should take particular car to see that proper provision has been made for all bank charges and interest.

(4) All castings and extensions in the profit forecast should be checked and comparison made with common items dealt with in the other two forecasts.

     (iii)   The cash flow forecast which is based on the above two forecasts should be checked in the following way.

         (1)   The opening balance should be checked to the draft financial statements and the company's cash book. For the expired period of the forecast, the month end balance should also be checked to the cash book.

         (2)   All receipts and payments for the elapsed period of the forecast should be checked against supporting documentation.

         (3)   The reasonableness of the timing of future receipts and payments should be considered in the light of the normal period of credit taken by customers and extended by suppliers, due date for payment of PAYE, VAT etc.

         (4)   The consistency of items in the cash flow forecast with the other two forecasts should be considered, as well as consistency and accuracy of forecasts in previous years.

         (5)   All castings and extensions in the forecast should be checked.

(d)   The reasonableness of the three forecasts referred to above and the willingness of the company's bankers and other creditors to supply the required funds will be the main factors to consider in assessing whether the company is a going concern.

    If the work already carried out suggests that the forecasts are reasonable, then with the permission of the client, some direct confirmation of the future 'co-operation' of the bank and major suppliers should be sought. Such co-operation is more likely to be forthcoming if the company is forecast to make profits rather than losses and consideration should also be given to any security held by the various creditors and the chances of any single creditor precipitating a crisis by seeking to invoke his own security.

12 Locksley

> **Tutorial note**. The audit of these assets is relatively straightforward, but it relies on your knowledge of the relevant accounting standards. You should cover every aspect of the audit of these items, perhaps by considering the balance sheet and then the P & L account effects.

(a)   The relevant audit tests are as follows.

     (i)   The auditors should **obtain** from the client a **breakdown** of the figure for development expenditure which makes it possible to trace the amounts spent to the nominal ledger and the final accounts.

     (ii)   **Tests of controls** should be performed to ensure that a system exists for controlling the authorising and recording of development expenditure, and that the system is operating adequately. (This work may be covered where practicable by the audit tests performed on the company's purchases and payroll systems.)

     (iii)   Individual amounts should be **vouched** by reference to **supporting documentation**. The relevant documentation will vary according to the type of expenditure, but tests might include the following.

         (1)   Agree purchases to requisitions, orders, goods received notes, invoices, cash book and bank statement.

         (2)   Agree labour costs to the payroll and to supporting evidence, such as time sheets or job cards.

         (3)   If overheads have been included in the development figure, ensure that they have been calculated on a basis consistent with that used generally by the company.

The auditors will wish to set a materiality level for testing individual items; this will have to be established when the breakdown of the total figure is known. For instance, it may be possible to restrict testing considerably if one or two large invoices represent the bulk of the relevant expenditure.

(iv)   The **arithmetical accuracy** of the schedule of expenditure should be **checked**.

(v)   The auditors should **ensure** that there has been **no double-counting**, that is, that development items capitalised have not also been charged as an expense in the profit and loss account.

(vi)   Finally, the auditors should carry out a **review of the development figure** in order to be satisfied that it is reasonable and consistent with what else is known about the company and its business.

(b)   The following audit procedures may be performed to verify the revaluation gain arising on fixed assets.

(i)   Ensure that the **valuer** appears to be **appropriately qualified** and **independent** of the company. If these conditions are not fulfilled, the auditors will need to consider their possible impact on the results of the valuation.

(ii)   By reference to the instructions given to the valuer and the valuer's report, ensure that the **valuation** has been **performed on a basis reasonable and consistent** with previous valuations.

(iii)   Check that **profits or losses on individual fixed assets** have been **correctly calculated** by reference to the fixed asset register and the detailed analysis of the revaluation.

(iv)   **Check the arithmetical accuracy** of the compilation of the **revaluation schedule** and of the **calculation of asset profits and losses**.

(c)   SSAP 13 lays down the basis on which development costs may be carried forward. They may be carried forward only if, and to the extent that, they represent an **asset** which is likely to generate income for the company in the future. It would contravene the prudence concept to carry forward expenditure which is not reasonably expected to generate future income.

According to SSAP 13, development expenditure should be written off in the year it is incurred, unless there is a **clearly defined project**, and the **related expenditure is separately identifiable**.

The outcome of a project must then be examined for:

(i)   Its technical feasibility, and
(ii)   Its ultimate commercial viability considered in the light of such factors as:

(1)   Likely market conditions (including competing products or services)
(2)   Public opinion
(3)   Consumer and environmental legislation

A project will be of value:

(i)   Only if **further development costs** to be incurred on the same project, together with related production, selling and administration costs, will be more than **covered by related revenues**, and

(ii)   **Adequate resources exist**, or are reasonably expected to be available, to **enable the project to be completed** and to provide any consequential increases in working capital.

If, taking a prudent view of the available evidence, these conditions are met, development costs may be deferred and amortised over the period expected to benefit.

(d)   The decision to finance development internally has resulted in a large increase in creditors and a decrease in cash and bank balances. This may lead to liquidity problems, especially since the company will still need funds to finance the new product. These funds will have to be generated either by the sale of further investments, the raising of a loan from the directors or an outside investor, or by the issue of shares. If **funding** is **not available**, the **development expenditure** should be **written off** on the basis that it will not be possible to complete the project. This would eliminate the profit and loss reserve and would create doubts about the company's status as a going concern.

The auditors should discuss with the directors their plans for obtaining **additional finance**, and request that they produce cash flow forecasts in support of these. If the auditors do not obtain satisfactory evidence of the company's ability to obtain finance, it may be necessary to qualify the audit report on the grounds of going concern problems which have not been fully disclosed.

13 Bainbridge

Stocks

Matters to consider

- Risk that items produced for stocks are misstated due to out of date standards being applied.

  Stocks are also potentially misstated if no comparison with NRV has been made.

- Risk that bespoke items are overstated due to the inclusion in cost of design fees.

- Stock value as a whole is likely to be a material area of the accounts so this is an area where audit effort should be directed. The materiality of any adjustments required needs to be considered. The lowest level of materiality would be £16,000 (1% of profit).

- Whether management have considered the NRV of the stock on a line by line basis as required by SSAP 9 *Stocks and long-term contracts*.

- Whether the standard costing approach provides the fairest practical approximation to actual cost as required by SSAP 9.

- Whether the management are justified in maintaining the same standards as last year on the basis that they do reflect current prices. (SSAP 9 states that standard costs should be reviewed regularly and revised where necessary).

- Whether overheads have been allocated to stock based on the normal level of activity.

- Whether other overheads have been split between functions (ie production, administration) on a sensible basis.

- Whether the capitalisation of design fees relating to the bespoke items is in compliance with SSAP 9. Such 'other costs' can be capitalised only to the extent that they are incurred in bringing the stocks to their present location and condition.

Evidence to seek

- Confirm with management that they have considered the need to write down certain stock lines to their NRV. Review any schedules produced by the client to support their conclusions and check that any issues identified by the auditor at the inventory count or in the follow up work have been reflected in the final stock valuation.

- Obtain a schedule of the standards applied and compare to last year to determine whether they have remained the same.

- Agree major components to supporting documentation eg materials can be agreed to purchase invoices, labour can be agreed to payroll records

- Obtain an analysis of the production and other overheads allocated to stocks. Check that these costs are related to the production centre.

- For other overheads determine the way that management have allocated these costs between the different business centres. Determine whether the allocation is reasonable and consistent with previous years.

- Check the calculation of the 'normal' activity levels used to allocate the overheads to units of production. Establish that this does not include the effects of any abnormal events and that it is consistent with previous years.

- Obtain a schedule of design fees capitalised. Agree the details to sales contracts and establish the date on which they were incurred checking that this was before the commencement of production.

Lease

Matters to consider

- Risk that the lease is incorrectly classified. If it is a finance lease the lower of present value of the minimum lease payments and fair value should be capitalised and depreciated. If an operating lease the rentals should be expensed.

- Extent to which the risks and rewards of ownership have been transferred to the lessee. (eg who is responsible for maintenance, insurance). According to SSAP 21 *Accounting for leases and hire purchase contracts* if the risks and rewards of ownership remain with the lessor the lease would be of an operating nature.

- Basis on which management have decided that the lease is an operating lease. SSAP 21 states that the land element of a lease of land and buildings is not normally a finance lease unless title is expected to pass at the end of the lease, because, due to its indefinite economic life, the lessee does not receive substantially all the risks and rewards incidental to ownership. The building element, however, could be. This would suggest that the management have come to the right conclusion, at least for the land element.

- Treatment of the rent-free period. SSAP 21 states that operating lease rentals should be charged on a straight line basis over the lease term, even if the payments are not made on such a basis unless another systematic basis is representative of the time pattern of the user's benefit. On this basis the benefit of the rent free period should be spread over the lease term rather than being taken upfront. (Tutorial note: UITF 28 also requires that operating lease incentives should be spread).

- The likelihood of management taking up the option to extend the lease. SSAP 21 states that the lease term should include any further terms for which the lessee has the option to continue to lease the asset with or without payment if it is reasonably certain at the inception of the lease that the option will be exercised. This would affect the period over which the rentals would be spread.

- Materiality. Assuming that the option is to be exercised the total lease payments of £450,000 should be spread over the 12 year lease term. This would give a charge of £37,500. This represents 2.3% of profit so is likely to be material.

- Completeness and adequacy of disclosures. SSAP 21 requires a lessee to disclose the amounts to which he is committed broken down into payments due not later than one year, later than one year and not later than five years and over five years.

- Impact on the auditor's report. If it was concluded a material adjustment was required which management refused to make, the auditor's report would be modified (qualified – 'except for') on the grounds of disagreement.

Evidence to seek

- The lease agreement. The terms should be reviewed to confirm that the risks and rewards of ownership remain with the lessor. Details of the rent-free period, the rentals and the option to extend should be confirmed.

- Discussions with management should be held to determine the likelihood of the option to extend the lease being exercised. Conclusions should be confirmed in writing.

- Experience of treatment of any existing leases ie whether the company normally takes up the extension period.

- A recalculation of the allocation of total rentals over the lease term should be performed.

- Disclosures should be checked to confirm that they are in accordance with SSAP 21.

Matters to consider:

- The par value of the debenture is material to the balance sheet as it represents 16.7% of total assets. The coupon interest is material to the profit and loss account as it amounts to 12.5 % of profit after tax.

- The treatment does not appear to comply with FRS 26 *Financial Instruments: Recognition and Measurement.* Under FRS 26 it should be treated as a hybrid instrument, split into its equity and liability components. Normally the liability component should be calculated as the discounted present value of the cash flows of the debenture, discounted at the market rate of interest for a comparable borrowing with no conversion rights. The remainder of the proceeds represents the fair value of the right to convert and this element should be reclassified as equity.

- The treatment currently adopted by Bainbridge therefore appears to be incorrect.

- It is not possible from the information given to assess whether the reclassification would materially affect the view given by the balance sheet, but if it is, and the directors are not willing to change the classification then the audit opinion may have to be qualified on the grounds of disagreement.

Evidence to seek:

- A copy of the debenture deed showing the interest rate, and conversion terms.

- A schedule calculating the fair value of the liability at the date of issue, using interest rates quoted for similar borrowings without conversion rights.

- A copy of any disclosures relating to the debenture that have been prepared by the directors.

- A schedule showing the initial proceeds and interest payment agreed to the cash book and bank statement.

14 Griffin plc

Tutorial note. This question requires a good accounting knowledge as well as good auditing knowledge. You must anticipate that there will be at least one question on the paper that has such a requirement. It is essential for auditors to understand accounting problems and the audit issues that such matters raise.

It is also important that you show the examiner that you have used the details given to you to consider matters such as materiality. Whether an issue is material or not is critical to an audit manager, who will not want to waste audit time considering matters which are not material. Use the details given to you as much as you can. For example, in (1), the details about profits and cost of investment help you to make a sensible comment about the chances that the 'group' created by the investment in the associate will be large enough to require some sort of group accounts, or in this case, additional disclosures for the associate. Note that **consolidated** financial statements are **not** required -as there is no subsidiary involved.

Lastly, it is perfectly legitimate for you to include current issues in your answer if they seem relevant, and you will receive credit for them if they are relevant and you use them well. For example it is reasonable in the answer to (2) where it touches on going concern to mention that if a lot of Griffin's revenue comes from Nationwide league clubs, the company may be facing financial difficulties as an on-going results of problems with television revenues. You are training to be an accountant, you should be aware of current financial issues.

1   **Investment in Bees Ltd**

(a)   *Matters to consider*

Inclusion in Griffin's accounts

Bees Ltd may meet the criteria to be accounted for as an associate under FRS 9. This states that an associate is an entity (other than a subsidiary) in which another entity (the investor) has a participating interest and over whose operating and financial policies the investor exercises a significant influence.

Companies legislation states that a holding of >20% is presumed to be a participating interest. The auditors must consider whether this presumption is rebutted. It further provides that a company holding 20% or more of the voting rights in a company is presumed to exercise a significant influence. The auditors must check whether the shares held are voting shares.

Assuming that the entity is an associate, it should be included in Griffin's accounts as a fixed asset investment at cost, assuming that cost does not overstate the value of the asset. It is unclear whether the investment is material to Griffin's balance sheet.

Requirement for group accounts?

'Group accounts' here does **not** mean consolidation is required.

Griffin and Bees may represent a 'group' for which group financial statements are required, even though as there is no subsidiary involved, consolidated financial statements are not required.

If group accounts are required, a further set of accounts with the associated equity accounted is required. Alternatively, Griffin's accounts could contain additional disclosure of what the accounts would look like if Bees had been equity accounted.

The 'Griffin Group' would be exempt from group accounts if the group was small or medium sized. Pre-tax profit of £1.2million and the cost of the investment to Griffin of £750,000 both indicate that the group is not small (the limits for being a small group are: turnover, £2.8m, gross assets £1.4m, and employees, 50.) The auditor needs to consider whether group accounts are required.

Other auditors

If group accounts are required, our firm would be the principal auditors and would need to liase with the auditors of Bees Ltd (the other auditors.)

Related party transactions

There may be related party transactions requiring disclosure under FRS 8.

Dividends

Griffin may have received, or be due, dividend income from Bees Ltd which will require disclosure in the financial statements.

(b) *Audit evidence required*

The investment in Bees Ltd should be verified to a **share certificate**. In order to determine whether the shares are voting or not, the auditors should obtain and review the **register of members** at Bees Ltd, which is open to the public for a fee.

The cost of the investment should be verified to purchase documentation, and the payment should be agreed to bank statements.

The auditors must **review the financial statements** or the most up to date financial information available **of Bees Ltd** to ensure that the cost figure used for the investment is still reasonable and that all dividends have been accounted for correctly in Griffin's financial statements. This information may be passed on by the other auditors.

The **sales and purchase ledgers** and the **bank statements** should be **scrutinised** to assess whether there are any related party transactions in the normal course of business. This should also be **discussed with the directors**.

2 **Competitor**

(a) *Matters to consider*

Going concern

The entrance into the market of a major competitor, the failure of the clubs to renew their contracts and the loss of personnel to the competitor may raise issues relating to going concern. The auditors must assess whether the non-renewal of contracts was anticipated, and whether historic practice shows that such contracts are often swapped. They must also discover whether the directors have assessed the impact of the competitor on their business and consider whether these assessments have covered all the issues, and what the implications for the future of Griffin plc are.

Further indicators of going concern issues could be the large drop in profit, the plan to diversify (does this indicate the old market is shrinking?) and the Nationwide football league clubs facing current financial problems, some of whom may be customers of Griffin. However, there appears to have been sufficient cash available to make a substantial investment in Bees Ltd, which may indicate that going concern is not an issue. The auditor needs to check these matters.

Debtors

If the income from contracts with the League clubs has not been replaced, both turnover and debtors should have fallen on last year. We should check that this is the case.

Fixed asset impairment?

The entrance of a major competitor to the market is given by FRS 11 as a potential indicator of fixed asset impairment. The auditors need to consider whether fixed assets have been impaired, and whether the directors have considered if fixed assets have been impaired.

(b)   *Audit evidence required*

The auditors need to gain evidence about going concern issues. They should review the cash flow statement and the financial statements generally and **assess the cash position** of the company. They should consider how the investment in Bees Ltd has been financed. They should review **arrangements with the bank** and ensure that Griffin has sufficient cash to operate.

The auditors must **discuss** (and document) the loss of the contracts and the new competitor with the directors, particularly the sales director. They should **review budgets and sales projections** and ensure that these factors have been taken into account in them. They should review the current order book for signs that the budgets are unrealistic.

The reasons for the plans to diversify into women's leisure wear must be discussed (and documented) with the directors. There must be evidence on file that the auditors have investigated the issue of going concern and satisfied themselves either that the entity will continue in the foreseeable future, or that the directors have made sufficient disclosures in the financial statements that the situation is explained to the users of the financial statements.

The auditors should **review any correspondence** relating to the non-renewal of contracts to ensure that the contract has not been renewed. If no such information is available, the former customers should be included as part of the **debtors' circularisation** to ensure that no money is owed by them at the end of the year. There must be evidence on file that the level of debtors has been analysed in the light of known facts about customers and loss thereof. The auditors should also have reviewed discussions in the press about the financial viability of any clubs that are customers to assess the **recoverability of current debt**.

The auditors should identify whether the directors have carried out an **impairment review** and should review it to see if it is reasonable if they have done so. If no impairment review has been carried out, the auditors should consider whether one is required and discuss this with the directors. They may want to obtain **written representation** from the directors that no impairment review is required.

3   Legal requirements

(a)   *Matters to consider*

FRS 12

The provisions of FRS 12 must be considered in relation to the requirement to amend machinist's working conditions and the increase in the national minimum wage.

FRS 12 states that a provision is required if

- An entity has a present obligation as a result of a past event

- It is probable that a transfer of economic benefits will be required to settle the obligation, and

- A reliable estimate can be made of the amount of the obligation

Three situations arise for Griffin:

(i)   **Cost of adjustments**. As the adjustments have not yet been made, there is no present obligation to pay for them. The obligation to make the adjustments does not create a financial obligation to pay for them until a contract has been formed for the adjustments. No provision is therefore required for the cost of adjustment.

(ii) **Possibility of penalty**. As Griffin has not made the adjustments before the required date, it is possible that they are now subject to a penalty under the legislation. If this were to be in the form of a fine, this would result in the transfer of economic benefit. However, as it is only possible that such a penalty would occur (ie, no order has yet been made) no provision for fines would be required. However, the matter should be disclosed as a contingent liability, were it material.

(iii) **Liability to employees**. Some employees are not being paid the national minimum wage. If this is material, the auditor must consider whether there is a present obligation to pay those wages. However, as the shortfall is for 5% of employees and for 2 months of the year, it is extremely unlikely that this matter is material to the financial statements. Secondly, the auditor must consider whether any employees are taking action over the health and safety issue which has arisen over the seat adjustment.

ISA 250

Both issues arising here indicate that the entity is not complying with the laws and regulations concerning health and safety and to the national minimum wage.

Two considerations for the auditor result:

(i) Material effect on the financial statements? The auditors must consider whether examples of non-compliance will affect the financial statements in a material way. Given the considerations linked to FRS 12 above, it appears that this is not the case in this situation.

You are unlikely to be au fait with NMW law. Remember the requirement to report is in extreme cases, such as terrorism and drug-trafficking. Express a measured opinion

(ii) Reporting on non-compliance. When the auditors become aware of non-compliance with laws and regulations, they must discuss them with management. There may also be a requirement to report non-compliance to a third party, such as a regulator. In this instance, it is extremely unlikely that there is such a requirement.

(b) *Audit evidence required*

The auditor must identify whether a contract has been entered into to make the adjustments to the seats. This might become obvious from a review of board minutes, or discussions with directors.

The auditor should also review the minutes to establish whether any fines have been levied. There should also be correspondence on the legislation requirements to review, or correspondence from the company solicitor.

In terms of the national minimum wage, the auditors should review the payroll to assess the extent of the problem.

It may be necessary to contact the solicitors to establish whether any legal action has been threatened by employees over either the health and safety issues or the wage issues outlined. If so, the auditors might have to rely on the solicitor's expert opinion as to whether the claims were actionable and the possible outcomes.

15 Recognition

> **Tutorial note.** This question focuses on some accounting treatments and materiality consideration. In the exam, questions on the topics in Chapter 11 could also cover the following issues:
>
> - Whether disclosure a presentation is fair
>
> - Whether accounting treatments are reasonable or aggressive (in part (a), the treatment of revenue is aggressive)
>
> - Whether the issues raised are material or fundamental and therefore, pervasive to the financial statements

(a) **Accounting treatment**

Beak plc has sold the land to Wings plc at a price well under current market value for no discernible reason. It is able to repurchase that land at cost at any time in the next five years but cannot be forced to do so. Therefore unless the land value falls significantly it can be assumed that Beak plc will repurchase the land. Wings plc will not use the building or the land for redevelopment in that period otherwise on repurchase they would lose any investment they had made.

The **commercial effect** of this transaction, assuming land values do not fall significantly, is that of **a loan** to Beak plc secured on the land. The commission is in effect interest on the loan, payment being deferred until the repurchase takes place.

Hence Beak plc should not treat this transaction as a sale. The land should continue to be shown as an asset in the balance sheet and a loan of £20m should be recorded. The profit and loss account should be charged annually with the commission charge and the accrual shown as a deferral liability in the balance sheet.

As this is a material transaction, the auditors should qualify their report on the grounds of disagreement.

(b) **Accounting treatment**

The **substance** of this transaction appears to be that the **cars are part** of the **stock of Sparks Ltd** from the time they take delivery of them from Gocar plc. This is because Sparks Ltd bears the risks and rewards of ownership, ie it has to insure the cars, but only pays the wholesale price in force on the date the cars were first supplied, so avoiding subsequent price rises. The monthly rental is a form of interest charged by Gocar plc, varying with the length of time Sparks Ltd holds the stock.

This interpretation of the transaction is also supported by the fact that Gocar plc cannot demand the return of the cars from Sparks Ltd.

The cars unsold for less than four months should be treated as stock in the financial statements and the liability to Gocar plc for them recognised.

Materiality considerations

The auditors should make a judgement as to whether they feel the amounts are material. The value of the additional stock represents 15% of their stock already recognised on the balance sheet. It is 1.7% of the balance sheet total. Bearing in mind a general guideline for materiality of 1-2% of total assets, this is likely to be material.

Impact on audit report

If the matter is material to the profit and loss account (these details are not given in the question), or there are other errors in stock which would result in stock being increased in the balance sheet, they should qualify their report.

This would be on the grounds of disagreement, as before.

16 Henshelwood plc

(1) **Share-based payments**

    (a) *Matters to consider:*

- The share-based payment expense for the year is not individually material being only 2.5% of the profit before tax; the related equity reserve is material to the balance sheet being 1.6% of total assets.

- The nature of the share-based payment must be determined; the valuation of shares in a public company is likely to be easier to determine than the value of options.

- If the fair value of the equity has been based on an option pricing model, is the model one that complies with FRS 20 *Share-based payment.*

- The terms of the share-based payment and the assumptions as to the number of equity instruments that will vest.

    (b) *Tests:*

- Obtain a copy of the terms of the scheme and verify the details used in the calculation of the expense, including the number of instruments granted, grant date, vesting date and any conditions attached to the scheme.

- If the fair value calculation has been performed by an expert, obtain a copy of the valuation report and

    – Review the assumptions for reasonableness
    – Consider professional qualification and reputation of the expert

- Discuss with management their assumptions about the number of instruments that will ultimately vest and consider their reasonableness in the light of

    – Latest budgets and forecasts

    – Board minutes, and

    – Any events after the balance sheet date that might affect employee numbers or the likelihood of achieving any performance targets.

- Reperform the calculation of the expense for the year.

(2) **Pension costs**

    (a) *Matters to consider:*

- The net amount charged to the profit and loss account is not individually material being only 3.7 % of the profit before tax; the net deficit carried in the balance sheet is material, amounting to 10.1% of total assets.

- Whether the pension scheme accounts have been audited as at Henshelwood's year-end or a date close to that.

- Whether all the pension schemes operated within the group have been included in the figures in the draft financial statements.

- Whether the valuation of assets and liabilities have been performed on bases that are acceptable under FRS 17 *Retirement benefits.*

- The expected return on assets and the finance charge relating to the unwinding of the discount on the scheme liabilities carry a high risk of misstatement as they are based on the directors' judgement and hence may be manipulated.

(b) *Tests:*

- Obtain a copy of the latest audited accounts of the pension scheme and verify the asset valuation used in Henshelwood's draft financial statements.

- Obtain a copy of the actuarial valuation of the pension scheme liabilities and:

  - Check that the actuary is a member of a relevant professional body such as the Institute of Actuaries

  - Review the source data used relating to scheme members

  - Consider whether the actuarial assumptions appear reasonable and consistent with assumptions made elsewhere in the financial statements.

  - Compare the assumptions used with those used in previous years

- Obtain copies of all written communications from the actuary to the company directors concerning the findings of their work.

- Obtain explanations from the directors and actuary in respect of the expected rate of return for all main asset categories and consider whether these are consistent with, for example, changes in investment strategy.

- Compare the expected rate of return with market indices for fixed interest and index-linked securities.

- Discuss with directors the choice of discount rate and obtain explanations for any change in the rate.

- Compare the discount rate to the appropriate high-quality corporate bond rate at the start of the year.

- Perform a proof in total of the interest cost by applying the discount rate to an average of the liabilities at the beginning and end of the year and compare it to the actual charge.

- Discuss with directors and actuaries the factors affecting the current service cost.

- Discuss with directors and actuaries the underlying reasons for actuarial gains and losses.

- Obtain written representations from the directors confirming that all retirement benefits have been identified and properly accounted for and that the assumptions used in valuing the scheme liabilities are consistent with the directors' knowledge of the business.

(3) **Provisions**

(a) *Matters to consider:*

- The net effect of provision on the profit and loss account, a credit of £22.2m, represents 11.6% of profit before tax so is clearly material. The total liability, being 9.2% of total assets is also highly material.

- The risk of misstatement is always high in respect of provisions because estimate and judgement are involved. In the case of Henshelwood where there has been a significant write back to the profit and loss account there is a risk that the provisions could have been utilised incorrectly. FRS 12 *Provisions, Contingent Assets and Contingent Liabilities* requires that provisions are only used to offset those expenses for which they were originally established.

- There is also a risk that the company may have additional obligations that have not been provided for.

- Whether the leases of unused properties meet the criteria to be treated as 'onerous contracts' under FRS 12.

(b) **Tests:**

- Agree the opening balance on all provisions to the prior year's audit file.

- Review the estimates used in the provisions with reference to:

    - The latest rental agreement in respect of the unused leasehold properties

    - Recent budgets and projections relating to the restructuring costs.

    - Copies of any licences or other legal documentation relating to the site restitution in the European business.

    - The terms of the sales agreements relating to the warranty and environmental claims, and also to any correspondence between the purchasers of those businesses and the directors of Henshelwood.

- Obtain a breakdown of the expenses against which the provisions have been utilised to verify that they have only been utilised against the appropriate expenses.

- Review board minutes, budgets and projections, and discuss with directors whether there are any plans to resume using the leasehold properties or to sublet them in which case the provision would no longer meet the criteria of FRS12.

- Obtain written representations from the directors that no additional obligations exist that would require provisions and that there have been no events after the balance sheet date that would affect the carrying value of the provisions.

17 Merger of audit firms

Tutorial note. This is a topical question as these 'mega-mergers' have taken place relatively recently.

(a) The reasons behind a merger could include the following.

- The desire to operate on a **global scale** and increase market shares

- The wish to service **multinational clients** demanding an international presence

- Increased **expertise** and professional experience

- **Business expansion:** the competitive nature of auditing and consultancy services demands a larger firm to service clients globally

- **Increasing funds** available for investment. (Increasing investment in IT systems makes this necessary.)

- The need to **compete with banks** who are increasing management consultancy services

- To **resist liability claims**

- To reduce the ability of major clients to exert fee pressures and thus improve **financial independence**

- To increase the **range of opportunities** available to skilled staff

- To take advantage of **cost savings** achievable

(b)   Possible problems could include the following.

- A reduction in **choice of clients**
- Possible **conflicts of interest** arising from mergers of firms providing services to competing clients
- A reduction in **auditors' independence**, particularly as a result of increasing provision of consultancy services
- The emergence of '**audit giants**' which weakens the arguments for limiting auditors' liability
- **Domination** of the profession by 'giant firms'
- Increase in the **influence of large firms** on the standard setting process
- **Redundancies** caused by elimination of overlapping departments
- **Scrutiny of the mergers** by outside agencies
- **Disputes** emerging between partners as to management styles leading to resignation of disaffected partners and loss of experience
- A **loss of the 'personal touch'** which is a feature of smaller firms

18 Annabella Ltd

Tutorial note. Part (a) is a very general requirement for a large number of marks. This can be daunting, but as this would be a compulsory question in the exam, don't let that put you off. Start thinking through standard lists of planning matters and see if any of them apply in this situation. (Don't include them in your answer if they don't apply, you won't get any marks for them.) Then read through the scenario again slowly (it is only short), looking for points that raise question marks or that indicate issues the auditor will need to consider.

You should be able to identify key issues in the scenario from key words. For example, '*set up two subsidiary companies*' = group audit, '*transferred its trade*' = FRS 3, all the intercompany dealings should point you towards FRS 8. Remember also that as soon as Annabella Ltd sets up a group, you have several audits to consider: all the individual company accounts, and the consolidated ones. Don't talk about consolidation to the exclusion of the individual audits. Lastly, talk of group audits should always make you ask 'are there any other auditors?' and in this situation, there is the friend of the director.

Remember, it is not enough to identify that FRS 3 (say) may be an issue. You must explain what the specific impacts are going to be. This is true of all the points you raise.

Part (b) should be much more straightforward than part (a). It requires you to repeat things you have learnt, rather than apply anything. You might have wanted to tackle this part first. However, as always, remember not to spend too long on the easier part that provides fewer marks. You need to get a good number of marks in part (a) to pass the question.

(a)   **Planning issues**

Engagement letters

The audit firm needs to ensure that **every entity** that it audits is **covered in an engagement letter** so that there is no confusion over the audit that is undertaken. Annabella Ltd requires a **new engagement letter** itself because of the **radical overhaul** of its business and the impact that that will have on its own audit.

Impact on Annabella Ltd's individual accounts

(i) **Accounting for the investment in subsidiaries**. The auditors need to establish what the credit accounting entries were in Annabella Ltd's financial statements. If the trade and assets have been transferred, Annabella's **balance sheet is likely to be substantially different** from the previous year. As the firm were probably involved in the reconstruction and may have advised the journals, this information should be available at the firm.

(ii) **Profit on sale**. The auditors need to establish whether a profit on sale was made on the transfer of assets to the subsidiaries, as this would be an **exceptional item** and would require special disclosure under FRS 3.

(iii) **Other exceptional items**. The auditors should consider whether any **costs of reconstruction** (for example, **legal fees or accountancy fees**) represent exceptional costs under the requirements of FRS 3. If this is the case, these would also require special disclosure.

(iv) **Discontinued operations**. Disclosures should have been made in the previous year's accounts for discontinued operations under FRS 3. This should be checked in the **comparatives** for this year.

(v) **Accounting for the investment in a joint venture**. In the individual financial statements of Annabella Ltd, this should be **accounted at cost**. The auditors will need to check that the joint venture does **qualify** as a joint venture for accounting purposes under the requirements of **FRS 9**.

New subsidiaries

The audit firm will have to ensure that **financial statements** are being drafted for the new subsidiaries and that these are **to be audited**. They will have to determine an **audit approach** for these new audits. It is likely that they will be able to make use of **analytical evidence** from the previous business of Annabella Ltd, so while these will be first year audits, in many ways they will **not be a risky as first year audits can be**.

Related party transactions

In the individual company accounts there are going to be a number of related party transactions which **require disclosure** under FRS 8:

	Anna Ltd	Bella Ltd	Annabella Designs Ltd
Annabella Ltd	Transfer of assets and trade. Management charges.	Transfer of assets and trade. Management charges.	Management charges. Any transfer of assets and trade?
Anna Ltd		Trading on commercial terms?	Trading on normal commercial terms?
Bella Ltd			Advertising? Trading at all?

The relationships between the companies and directors and the ultimate controlling party will all require disclosure in the accounts. When the accounts are consolidated, intercompany trading will drop out, but the controlling party will still require disclosure.

Consolidation

(i) **Required?** The audit firm must determine whether the group will be required to publish group accounts. This will depend upon its **size**. If it qualifies as a small group, it may be exempt.

(ii) **Audited**. If the company is required to produce group accounts, then the consolidated accounts must be audited.

(iii) **Other auditors**. See below.

(iv) **Accounting**. The subsidiaries will require consolidating into the results of the group. The joint investment should be included in the group accounts under the gross equity method. Intercompany transactions will have to be stripped out.

(v) **Drafting**. The audit firm should determine who is to draft any required group accounts, in case the client would like them to. This would have to be included in the engagement letter and would also impact upon new fee quotes for the group.

Arrangements with the other auditors

(i) **Evaluation**. The firm is the principal auditor for the group, so it will need to evaluate the second audit firm (David Turner and Co) to assess **to what degree it is happy to rely on the audit of Annabella Designs Ltd**. It will need to satisfy itself particularly that the audit is going to be **objective** and independent, due to the personal relationship between the audit partner and the director of the firm. The firm may feel that the relationship is too close, the audit will not be objective, in which case they would have to discuss this matter with the directors of Annabella Ltd.

(ii) **Procedures**. If the auditors are happy that the audit will be objective and they are satisfied with the qualifications, resources and reputation of the other auditors, they will then have to **discuss the procedures and audit approach** with the other auditors.

(iii) **Timing**. The principal auditors will also need to outline the **deadlines** that they are working to, so the **time requirement** for the audit of Annabella Designs Ltd to be completed.

Costs and time budgets

As the group is new, it is **difficult to determine the time** that will be taken to complete the audit of the group, and this may **impact upon the fee**. The engagement partner should **discuss the fee level with the directors** and **possibly arrange** a margin by which it might rise, as it becomes apparent how long the audit will take.

The auditors will also require **good time budgets** upon which **to base future audits and billings**. The audit plan should require that **very detailed time records** are maintained, in particular, outlining time spent in the main because the audit of the group was **new** and on the **restructuring**.

(b) **Audit of a consolidation**

Step 1 Compare the audited accounts of each subsidiary/associate to the consolidation schedules to ensure figures have been transposed correctly.

Step 2 Review the adjustments made on consolidation to ensure they are appropriate and comparable with the previous year. This will involve:

- **Recording** the **dates** and **costs** of **acquisitions** of subsidiaries and the assets acquired

- **Calculating goodwill** and **pre-acquisition reserves** arising on consolidation

- **Preparing** an overall **reconciliation** of movements on reserves and minority interests

Step 3 For business combinations, determine:

- Whether acquisition or merger accounting has been appropriately used

- The appropriateness of the date used as the date for acquisition

- The treatment of the results of investments acquired during the year

- If acquisition accounting has been used, that the fair value of acquired assets and liabilities is reasonable (to ascertainable market value by use of an expert)
- Goodwill has been calculated correctly and if amortised, period of amortisation is reasonable

Step 4 For disposals:

- Agree the **date** used as the date for disposal to sales documentation
- Review management accounts to ascertain whether the **results** of the **investment** have been **included** up to the date of disposal, and whether figures used are reasonable

Step 5 Consider whether previous treatment of existing subsidiaries or associates is still correct (consider level of influence, degree of control)

Step 6 Verify the arithmetical accuracy of the consolidation workings by recalculating them

Step 7 Review the consolidated accounts for compliance with the law and standards and other relevant regulations. Care will need to be taken where:

- Group companies do not have coterminous accounting periods.
- Subsidiaries are not consolidated.
- Accounting policies of group members differ because foreign subsidiaries operate under different rules.

Other important areas include:

- Treatment of participating interests and associates
- Treatment of goodwill and intangible assets
- Foreign currency translation
- Treatment of loss-making subsidiaries
- Treatment of restrictions on distribution of profits of a subsidiary

Step 8 **Review** the **consolidated accounts** to confirm that they give a true and fair view in the circumstances.

19 Anderson Group

(a) *Availability and reliability of information*

Since no direct communication with subsidiary management is possible, and audit results are not available, the auditor should consider the results of Green in the light of:

(i) the reliability of management accounts in previous years;

(ii) any evidence that this year's management accounts have been prepared on a basis consistent with that applied in earlier years;

(iii) the amount of information and explanations which the management of Anderson are able to provide from their knowledge acquired whilst still in control of Green;

(iv) any audit work carried out on an interim visit and the extent to which useful audit evidence may be obtained by reviewing the work of Anderson's internal auditors on the accounts of Green in respect of the year ended 31 August 20X1;

(v) any year end audit work, such as attendance at inventory count and receivable circularisation, carried out before control of Green was lost.

(b)   *Materiality level (or acceptable error) in relation to Green's results*

There is no reason to suppose that the reported revenue of Green is incorrect: the main question mark would be against the extent of the pre-tax loss. The reliability of the figure for the reported loss would be very dependent on the matters considered above.

Under the circumstances prevailing, over or understatement of the pre-tax loss would be offset by a corresponding decrease or increase in the exceptional item, loss on sale of subsidiary. In the light of this compensating effect, the auditor of Anderson would be able to accept a higher level of error than would have been the case if the group structure had continued as before.

(c)   *Audit of loss on disposal of subsidiary*

The auditor of Anderson should check the loss arising on the disposal of its subsidiary Green as follows.

(i)   Confirm that the net assets of Green at 31 August 20X1 are equivalent to the reported net assets at 31 August 20X0 less the reported trading loss for the year ended 31 August 20X1.

(ii)   The cash proceeds should be confirmed to any agreement in relation to the sale of Green and agreed to post balance sheet receipts.

(iii)   The sale of the subsidiary should be confirmed to board minutes and a sales agreement.

(iv)   The journal posting the loss should be traced through to the nominal ledger.

(v)   The notes to the financial statements should be checked to ensure that adequate disclosure of the disposal is given.

20 Business assurance

Tutorial note. This question could have been answered with basic auditing knowledge and did not need an in-depth knowledge of the services currently performed by auditors. However, you need to feel confident and familiar with the subject.

(a)   Current ACCA guidance on the provision of other services to clients is very similar to IFAC guidance which applies in an international basis.

The view taken internationally by IFAC is that many companies would be restricted if they were unable to obtain the other services available from their auditors, provided these services do not interfere with the exercise of managerial functions and auditors' independence. It would seem that **IFAC guidance allows external auditors to act as internal auditors** of clients.

The view taken by the ACCA guidelines is as follows.

- The ACCA guidance states that **objectivity may be threatened** by the provision of non-audit services. Care must be taken not to give executive advice or to become part of the client's active management.

- Firms **should not provide accountancy services to plc clients.**

- If accounting records are prepared for a client, then the **client** must accept **responsibility for the records.**

- There is **no specific prohibition** from an external auditor undertaking the internal audit function.

Specific **problems** which could occur include the following.

- The **difficulty of reporting weaknesses** in internal controls in systems designed by employees of the auditor acting as internal auditors of the client.

- The **perceived difficulties in testing work** carried out by internal auditors who are colleagues of the external auditors.

- Internal audit programmes designed to **reduce the work** of external auditors.

- The danger of **breaching ACCA rules** of conduct if the internal audit department is deemed to be **part of the management** of the client.

- **Fee pressures** arising from the increase in fees for providing an internal audit service leading to breaching the fee guidelines.

- **Audit risk** assessed by the external auditor. The presumption is that control risk would reduce because of the involvement of the external auditor in the provision of internal audit services

(b)   The **effects** would be as follows.

- Increased **risk of liability claims**

- **Additional costs** to the auditor incurred in employing suitable staff to provide wider assurance

- An impact upon **fees** charged to clients

- Possible **increased expectations** of audit clients

- The difficulty in formulating and wording an appropriate **audit report** which could require legislative changes

(c)   The new approach could be seen as a **'repackaging'** of existing services where auditors concentrate upon providing services which add value to the audit fee in the eyes of the client. Basic audit work may be foregone as it is perceived as adding very little.

The difficulty with this approach is that auditors are increasingly faced with **litigation claims** and should therefore provide more basic assurance based lower materiality thresholds. It may be that external auditors came to view the roles of audit committees and internal audit departments as crucial in reducing control risk.

It is dangerous to assume that external audit is a consultancy exercise aimed at adding value because traditional audit assurance will be lost and overall levels of audit risk will rise.

21 Trendy Group

Business risks	Audit risks
(a) **Fraud and Loss**	
This obviously impacts on both the business and potentially affects the risk of an incorrect audit opinion if they result in material misstatements which go unadjusted.	As for business risk.
(b) **Foreign currency transactions**	
The parent entity is responsible for treasury management but no details are given as to how group FX risk is being controlled. In fact the current procedures may for intragroup transactions be creating further currency exchange problems.	The audit of purchases may appear easier if costs are fixed at the beginning of the year but this may well increase audit work required in stock provisioning and year end adjustments to reflect the stocks at their real cost to the group.
(c) **Single sourcing manufacture**	
Currently adverse price movements in the Malay employment or raw material market, or indeed inflation or interest rate movements, may result in the group having significantly reduced profits.	Quality may reduce as only one supplier has a monopoly on sales. This has an audit impact due to the risk of overvaluation of poor quality stocks.
As prices are set each quarter guaranteeing a modest Malaysian operation profit margin, this does not lead to future cost control strategies being effective. There is the ability of local management to live rather lavishly without effectively controlling costs.	
There is also a enhanced risk of fraud.	
Political unrest may also cut off supply and lead to significant going concern issues for the group.	
Over reliance on a single supplier would be a key non going concern indicator to be followed up by the auditors of the individual companies.	Non going concern risk
(d) **Design risks**	
Potentially US designed goods produced in Malaysia may not sell abroad.	This may lead to further inventory provisioning to be required again increasing audit risk associated with inventory over valuation.
	Design costs may have been capitalised in the parent entity's books. There is an audit risk of overstated intangible assets.

Business risks

Audit risks

(e) Inventory obsolescence and valuation

The ability to achieve good sales in the countries of the individual trading operations depends upon

– the design capability of the parent entity team
– the local advertising spend.

As the US trading company ultimately buys the obsolete lines at 50% of original transfer price this company could end up with substantial losses and stock provisions as a result of someone else's bad design and advertising decisions.

Stocks purchased at the set transfer price may be over-valued if not saleable at the year end.

In the individual companies stock provisions should bring stocks held down to the lower of cost and net realisable value.

There is a further audit risk that from a group perspective that the stock valuation is not appropriate.

The transfer of stocks around the group means that the individual companies are not reflecting the stocks at original cost to the group.

In addition any provision to reduce stocks to NRV should be based upon the NRV expected to be achieved according to where it is likely the stocks are going to be sold. If it is expected to be the US at marked down prices then the group accounts should reflect the full loss on original cost to the group.

(f) Cash rich environments

The retail stores are carrying significant levels of cash, credit card receipts and cheques. There is exposure to loss, theft and human error in giving out change and entering sales details.

Risk from lack of reliable audit evidence. Material misstatement of cash balances.

(g) Property

With retail stores and the Malaysian factory the group has many responsibilities and commitments:

– insurance
– security offered on loans
– repairs and maintenance
– payments on mortgages
– maintaining an acceptable level of return on the floor space
– refurbishments to maintain market presence

There is an audit risk the financial statements include:

– inflated revaluations to support loans and guarantees
– inappropriate depreciation charges/ policies
– wrongly capitalised repairs expenditure
– lack of necessary disclosures.

(h) Tax

The use of fixed transfer prices may expose the group to making profits in countries where the tax regime is not favourable.

22 Verity

(a) The factors that will affect the accountants' decision on whether to accept appointment are as follows.

    (i) **Previous experience of client**

        The accountants should draw on their knowledge of the client as gained during the audit. In particular they will be interested in the willingness of the client to provide information, the integrity and knowledge of the directors, and the reliability of the forecasts prepared for financial accounting purposes, for example for assessment of going concern or deferred tax.

    (ii) **How prepared**

        The accountants will need to consider how the forecast is being prepared, in particular:

        (1) how the forecast was compiled, and the staff who compiled it;

        (2) the extent to which the forecast is based on assumptions consistent with past events. The details given suggest that a more optimistic view is being taken than is warranted by the company's record in recent years;

        (3) whether the forecast represents management's best estimate of achievable results, or whether it represents hopeful targets or is based on certain hypothetical events taking place;

        (4) how the forecast takes account of factors which may invalidate the assumptions made;

        (5) the level of detail available supporting the forecast.

    (iii) **Terms of report**

        The accountants will need to consider the exact terms within which they are reporting, as this could have a bearing on their liability. This is discussed further in (c) below.

    (iv) **Users**

        The accountants should consider carefully the use to which the report will be put, and its audience.

(b) A major concern of the reporting accountant will be the assumptions on which the report is based. The level of evidence required will depend on the terms of the accountants' report, but some evidence will be required on the major assumptions made in the forecast.

    (i) **Sales**. It might be expected that the price increase would result in some lost sales, so extra sales will be needed from other customers to make up for the sales lost as well as achieving the planned increase. The auditor will need to focus on the plans to achieve that increase. Increases might be a result of a change in the sales mix or new products or customers; if these changes have already occurred, the accountants should consider what effect they have already had. Increased marketing and promotional activity may also be necessary, and this would need to occur rapidly in order to achieve the desired effect. This activity will probably be reflected in increased costs, and the accountants will need to check that these have been included in the forecast.

    (ii) **Cost of sales**. The accountants will need to consider whether economies have been planned to improve margins, whether these economies are likely to be achieved, and whether there will be consequential other costs that need to be reflected in the plan. For example reduction in the labour force is likely to mean redundancy costs, investment in more up-to-date plant and equipment to mean capital investment costs.

(iii) **Trade receivables**. The accountants should consider whether the decrease in settlement period is likely to be achieved. They should consider whether emphasising new credit limits and prompt settlement discounts will help achieve the required target, and also the effectiveness of any other measures the company takes, for example tighter checks on new customers and more rigorous pursuit of slow payers. In particular the accountants will need to review the position of foreign customers, as they may be less flexible in reducing settlement periods. The accountants should also check that the consequences of the prompt settlement discount, a reduction in amounts received, have been reflected in the forecast. For foreign customers, the accountants should also check any exchange rate effects have been reflected in the forecast.

(iv) **Trade payables**. The accountants should check that the increase in payable days will not breach terms of business with suppliers, leading to possible supply problems or withdrawal of credit terms and demands for immediate cash payments. They should also check that the forecast reflects other possible consequences of the increase, for example a loss of early settlement discounts.

(v) **Maximum finance**. The accountants should check whether the estimated increase in finance is reasonable or whether other sources will be required, either because the £9 million is an under-estimate or because other existing sources of finance will need to be repaid. The accountants should check that the consequences of the increase, particularly an increased interest burden, have been reflected. They should consider also whether the forecast shows that the company will be able to make the repayments comfortably, or whether the forecast margins are tight.

The accountants should also check that the forecast is internally consistent, for example that increased sales correspond with increased purchases, and reflects all non-trading cash flows. Consistency with forecasts made for other purposes, for example management accounting budgets, should also be checked.

(c) Liability will depend partly on the following general factors.

Extent of assurance

In this assignment accountants are focusing on uncertain future events, as opposed to an audit, where the report is based on a verification of data relating to past events. Therefore the level of assurance that can be given on this type of report is lower.

The exact level of assurance will depend on the form of the opinion given. Reporting under ISAE 3400 *The Examination of Prospective Financial Information* would require the accountants to report whether the forecast has been properly compiled on the basis of the stated assumptions and is presented in accordance with the relevant financial reporting framework. The report would state that nothing has come to the accountants' attention to suggest that the assumptions do not provide a reasonable basis for the prospective financial information. The accountants may go further, and make a positive report on the assumptions or less probably give a report on the achievability of the forecasts. If the report gives more positive assurance, this may increase the expectations of the report's readers as to the assurance given.

Other report issues

Whatever the exact terms of their opinion, the accountants should mention other matters in their report that will clarify for users what the accountants have done and hence what they are offering:

(i) the accountants should state why and for whom the report is being prepared;

(ii) reference should be made to the work done, and whether the work has been done in accordance with ISAE 3400;

(iii)   the report should state that the directors are responsible for the assumptions made;

(iv)   the accountants may be able to include specific disclaimers on the assumptions made and achievability of the forecasts. Even if they do not, they should make a statement about the uncertainty of the forecast, and the possibility that the actual outcomes will differ from what is predicted.

Cranley Bank

The accountants were on notice that the forecast was being prepared for the purposes of the bank, and thus the degree of the proximity that the law relating to professional liability requires has been established. If a claim arises, the courts will consider whether the forecast was properly prepared and based on reasonable assumptions that took account of the information that should have been known at the time of the forecast. If it was not, the court would then consider whether the accountants should have drawn the conclusion that they did or allowed themselves to provide some degree of implicit assurance on the forecast because of their association with it.

Certainly some of the assumptions made would appear to be doubtful and the bank may have a case against the accountants. However if the company fails to meet the forecast, it may well be difficult to assess how much this was due to factors that could have been predicted, and how much it was due to factors that could not have been forecast when the forecast was made.

The debenture holders

The accountants will probably not be liable to the debenture holders, The accountants stated in their report that it was prepared solely for the bank. The fact that the directors omitted this statement makes no difference to the accountants' liability, although it may render the directors liable. In addition had the report been prepared for the purposes of obtaining debenture finance it would have been prepared on different assumptions.

23 Scenarios

Tutorial note. Both scenarios given in this question should help you explore the issues that would be considered in practice, if an audit firm was going to offer assurance services.

Notice that you must think about a variety of issues: ethics, acceptance, planning, liability, reporting. You must be prepared to bring in all strands of your syllabus in questions set in scenarios.

Part (a) considers the position of an audit firm asked to report on a client to a third party but with no engagement. The auditor must consider whether it is possible to provide assurance in this situation. Is there an official assurance service that can be offered in this situation? Above all, the auditor must ensure that he is not accepting liability on this reference. The bank is seeking to reduce its risk – but the auditor must not allow that risk to be transferred to him. That might have dangerous implications for his audit independence, apart from the issue of personal risk.

Part (b) looks at the idea of providing assurance on the whole process of business systems. It is important that the terms of an engagement are settled. An assurance service cannot be undertaken if there is no clear requirements as to the nature of the service.

(a) **Lilac**

An audit engagement partner would have to consider the following things before issuing a reference on behalf of a client:

(i) Is any **additional work** required to give such a reference?

(ii) If so, the need to contact the bank and discuss whether a **separate engagement** might be appropriate.

(iii) The **inherent uncertainty** of future income and expenditure and therefore the **high risk** which is associated with giving such an opinion.

(iv) The **difficulty of issuing an opinion on current solvency**. The auditors are about to commence the audit for the past year, meaning they will be investigating information up to 15 months old.

(v) The fact that a **duty of care** to the bank is likely to arise if such a reference is given.

(vi) The need for **disclaimers of liability**, therefore, which will need to be reasonable in order to have legal force, perhaps the **need for legal advice** before such disclaimer is made.

(vii) Any need to negotiate a **liability cap**, although a disclaimer of liability should be sufficient/more appropriate.

(viii) Need for **written clarification** of the status of the reference, that is, explanation that there has been no engagement between the parties, that no fee has been paid, that it is given to the best of knowledge at the time.

(ix) The **form of the reference**. It is likely to be inappropriate to sign a bank's pre-printed document. The audit firm may have a standard reference document of its own, or may choose to compose each one according to the facts of the situation.

(b) **Laurel**

The directors of Laurel have expressed an interest in engaging the audit firm to undertake an assurance engagement in relation to their risk management and controls.

The following matters will be relevant:

Acceptance

Independence

The audit firm has to consider the issue of **independence**. It is vital that the provision of other services to the audit client does not **impair their objectivity towards the audit**. ACCA states that provision of other services may impair objectivity.

The IFAC guidance relates to assurance services relating solely to IT systems, which may be relevant or makes indications for how this would affect objectivity. It states that it would be vital that the assurance firm obtained the client's acknowledgement of responsibility for work done by the firm.

The amount that audit independence would be affected will depend on the exact nature of the service provided (see below). However, an assignment testing the operation of controls could be complimentary to the audit.

Nature of the service

The firm would not be able to accept the engagement as it has been currently set out. An assurance engagement should exhibit certain elements, key of which are subject matter, suitable criteria and an engagement process. It is very difficult to give assurance on the effectiveness of risk management, as there are no recognised criteria by which to judge it. However, the firm could provide an assurance service checking that controls are designed according to management criteria and they operate according to management policy, for example. This would need discussing and agreeing in writing before the engagement could be accepted.

Planning

In terms of planning such an engagement, once the details of the engagement had been agreed, the following matters would be relevant:

(i)   Is the firm **sufficiently independent** of the client to conduct the assurance service objectively? It may be that the fact that the company is an audit client would impair their objectivity towards this engagement.

(ii)   Are all the **elements** of an assurance engagement **present**? This has been discussed above.

(iii)   Have **the firm and the parties agreed terms**? In this case, the assurance service is likely to be carried out to benefit shareholders, so it may be necessary for a vote to be passed in general meeting to approve the service.

(iv)   Are the **criteria** for assessing the subject matter **suitable**? In this case, management policy would be a suitable criterion for evaluating the operation of systems.

(v)   The auditor must assess the **materiality and risk** of the engagement. These should be incorporated into a **fee** and into the **detailed procedures** planned for the engagement.

(vi)   What **form of report** is required by the parties? There is no such thing as a standard report, so it is important for the parties to agree upon the format of the report that will be produced at the end of the engagement.

24 Harness Ltd

Tutorial note. When it comes to the impact of social and environmental issues on the work of the external audit, two things are important. These two things are:

- Why the issues are relevant
- How the issues are relevant

In this question, these issues are addressed, but the 'how' aspect is addressed through an auditing scenario. Notice that the question in part (b) does not ask you to comment on the implications of the environmental issues on the audit, but more generally asks you to comment on the above. You should not restrict your answer to environmental matters then.

This question is overtly aimed at environmental matters. However, in the exam, issues like these will not necessarily have a neon sign over them. You may find that they are thrown into a more general risks and planning question. In such a case, it is for you to identify that such matters are important.

Notice that this question also requires a solid accounting knowledge to discuss issues such as fixed asset impairment, contingent liabilities and joint ventures. You must ensure that your accounting knowledge is up to scratch before attempting to sit P7. Auditors must have a good accounting knowledge to be able to identify risk matters in financial statements.

(a)   **Importance of social and environmental issues**

Social and environmental issues are important to the external auditor today for a variety of reasons.

(i)   *Importance to companies*

The first reason is that these matters are **important to the companies on whom the auditor is reporting**. Social and environmental matters which are important to the company form a necessary part of knowledge of the business.

Companies are increasingly reporting to their shareholders on matters of corporate responsibility. The external auditors report to the shareholders and have responsibilities to review other information presented with the financial statements which they have audited. Social and environmental issues are a natural part of corporate reporting in the 3rd millennium.

(ii)   *Impact on the financial statements*

Social and environmental issues may well have financial implications which impact on the financial statements. Several examples can be given:

- Fixed asset impairment (FRS 11)
- Provisions (FRS 12)
- Revenue recognition (FRS 5)
- Development costs (SSAP 13)
- Going concern issues (FRS 18)

(iii)   *ISA 250*

It will sometimes be the case that social and environmental issues will be regulated, in which case the auditing guidance contained in ISA 250 will become relevant to the auditor.

(b)   **Audit of Harness Ltd**

ISA 250

As part of the knowledge of the business exercise, when planning the audit, the auditors must ensure that they are **aware** of any **relevant regulations** relating to energy provision and/or piping oil which may impact on the financial statements.

Fixed assets

Harness Ltd appears to have accidentally **disposed** of a windmill in the year and three others show signs of being impaired. The auditors must ensure that the disposal has been **correctly accounted** for and whether any loss on disposal is an **exceptional item under FRS 3**. They must also discover whether Brewster has conducted an **impairment review** and, if so, whether the review is appropriate and reasonable.

Going concern

The loss of three or four windmills is likely to **severely affect operations** in terms of quantity of power generated. However, as the vast majority of the power goes to Brewster himself, it is likely that other customers will still be able to be accommodated.

However, the **generator also lies close to the eroding cliff**. The auditors must assess whether the generator is in danger of being affected by the erosion as this is more likely to impact severely on the going concern assumption. It appears that Brewster is happy to finance the loss-making business, but without a generator, it would not be able to operate anyway.

Cracked pipe line

Harness Ltd has invested in a pipeline which has a large crack in it. The auditors need to assess whether this gives rise to any **obligation to transfer economic benefits**.

If repair work has been commissioned, this might give rise to an obligation which might necessitate a **provision for repair costs**.

It is unclear whether the crack is going to result in **oil spill and resulting environmental contamination**. The auditors may need to obtain the opinion of an **expert engineer** as to the **likelihood** of that happening. If contamination is possible or probable, there may be a **contingent liability** arising in respect of fines or compensation.

Investment

Harness is the 'co-owner' of the pipeline. The auditors need to investigate the details of this **investment** to determine whether the pipe line is a fixed or current asset or whether it would constitute a joint venture or arrangement under FRS 9.

Going concern

The auditors need to investigate the potential impact the cracked pipeline could have on the business of Harness Ltd, because this could also impact upon the going concern basis, if fines or legal action was extensive.

25 Eastfield Distributors

(a)   The auditor should consider the following factors when assessing their independence.

(i)   The level of fee income from Eastfield should not exceed 15% of the practice's total income. If Eastfield is listed, the fees should not exceed 10%.

(ii)   As external auditor, the firm will be reviewing the work of internal audit; if the same staff were acting as external and internal auditors, they would be judging their own work. This obvious threat to objectivity can be lessened by different staff carrying out the detailed work, and different partners and managers being in charge of providing both services.

(iii)   There is a specific threat to independence if preparing Eastfield's accounts is part of the desired internal audit service. If Eastfield is a listed company, the audit firm's staff should not be involved in preparing the accounting records unless their work is of a mechanical nature. If Eastfield is not listed, it must accept responsibility for its accounts and accounting records, and the practice must carry out sufficient audit work on the accounting records.

(iv)   Similarly there is a threat to independence if the internal auditors become involved in the management of the company, because as external auditor the audit firm is reporting on the stewardship of management. However part of the internal audit service could be making recommendations about the design of systems and controls. The audit firm should thus ensure that the directors take responsibility for implementation of any recommendations, and their decisions are clearly recorded in board minutes.

(v)   Internal audit staff may be particularly likely to breach other independence guidelines that are applicable to them as employees of the firm carrying out the external audit. They should be reminded that they should not own shares in the client, accept a loan from the client, or obtain goods or services on more favourable terms than are offered to Eastfield's own staff.

(vi)   If Eastfield does fail to pay fees, there may be a greater danger of the amounts owing being akin to a loan because of their size and because they are amounts owed for a continuing service rather than an annual audit.

(vii)   The engagement letter should set out clearly the respective responsibilities of the audit firm and Eastfield. It should separately identify the work that the audit firm should carry out as external and internal auditors, and how fees will be calculated for each service. It should make clear to whom the audit firm's internal audit team will report.

(viii)   The firm should consider as part of its annual review of independence whether it is still sufficiently independent to be able to continue to act as external auditor.

(b)   The advantages for Eastfield of having the external auditor provide internal audit services are as follows.

(i)   The audit staff will be qualified or partly qualified accountants who are subject to professional standards and guidelines.

(ii)   Training costs will be saved, as the audit firm, not Eastfield will be responsible for staff training.

(iii)   The audit firm may be able to provide a range of expertise which would not be available to Eastfield without incurring considerable extra costs.

(iv) The efficiency of external audit would be enhanced, and hence its costs lowered, because internal auditors are using the same procedures to record and assess systems. Therefore the external auditor would not have to spend time checking whether appropriate work has been performed.

The disadvantages for Eastfield of using the internal auditors are as follows.

(i) Eastfield may want to use internal audit for a variety of tasks on the non-financial areas of its business, and the audit firm may not have staff with the expertise necessary in these areas.

(ii) As discussed in (a), the ACCA's independence requirements place limitations on the work that the internal auditors can carry out as a result of their firm also acting as external auditor.

(iii) The audit firm may not be able to guarantee continuity of internal audit staff. There may be regular staff changes as staff leave or are involved in other work, and the learning curve for new staff may add to the costs of internal audit.

(iv) The audit firm may not be able to provide the staff that Eastfield wants at the time Eastfield needs them because of commitments to other clients.

(v) The costs of the audit firm's staff will be higher than if Eastfield employed its own internal audit staff, because the audit firm will be charging Eastfield a mark-up on the staff's time as well as their salaries.

(vi) There may be conflicts over the reporting arrangements for internal audit staff. Eastfield would want to maintain control over their activities, but there has to be a mechanism for reporting to the audit firm as well, because the external firm is responsible for the staff's professional development and hence will need to assess how staff have performed.

(c) The advantages for the audit firm of carrying out both the internal and external audit are as follows.

(i) The audit firm will be able to gain greater assurance from their own staff's work as internal auditors than they are likely to be able to gain if the internal audit staff were employed by Eastfield. The firm will know that its staff have the necessary levels of competence and independence. It will also not have to spend time assessing the methods used to record and evaluate controls.

(ii) The extent of the work done by internal audit is likely to go beyond that necessary to support an external audit opinion, so the firm will have more evidence available than it would aim to have if it was just carrying out an external audit.

(iii) Working on a variety of internal audit tasks will enhance the professional development of the audit staff concerned.

(iv) The internal audit work might be able to be carried out at times of the year when the amount of other work is low, and thus staff will be used more efficiently.

The disadvantages for the firm of carrying out both services are as follows.

(i) The firm may have problems exercising control over the internal audit staff, because of their responsibility to report to the client.

(ii) Problems over the internal audit work may jeopardise the firm's role as external auditor.

(iii) The potential problems discussed in (a) in guaranteeing independence may prove insurmountable.

26 Maple

(a) **Auditor's responsibility in respect of fraud and error**

ISA 240 *The Auditor's Responsibility to Consider Fraud in an Audit of Financial Statements* states that the primary responsibility for the prevention and detection of fraud rests with both those charged with governance and the management of an entity. It is not the auditor's function to prevent fraud or error although the fact that an audit is carried out may act as a deterrent.

In respect of detection, ISA 240 states that the auditor should assess the risk of material misstatement due to fraud at both the financial statement and assertion level and determine overall responses to address the assessed risks. This might include changing the nature, timing and extent of audit procedures, e.g. more inspection, more work conducted during the year rather than at the year end and larger sample sizes.

The approach to error under ISA 315 *Understanding the Entity and Its Environment and Assessing the Risks of Material Misstatement* and ISA 330 *The Auditor's Procedures in Response to Assessed Risks* is broadly similar to the approach outlined for fraud above.

In practical terms the likelihood of detecting errors will be much higher than that of detecting fraud as deliberate attempts are normally made to conceal fraud including collusion and falsification of records.

In either case an audit is subject to an unavoidable risk that some material misstatements will not be detected.

If the auditor identifies an instance of fraud or error, he should document his findings and report them to the appropriate level of management and possibly to those charged with governance of the entity depending on their significance.

The auditor also needs to consider the potential impact on the audit opinion. If the fraud or error has a material effect on the financial statements the auditor's report may need to be modified. The nature of the modification would depend on the specific circumstances.

The auditor may need to consider whether there is a legal duty to report the occurrence of fraud or material error to regulatory or enforcement authorities.

(b) **Auditor's report**

Stock in Sherwood

An exact calculation of the required adjustment to stock cannot be performed as it is not possible to tell the extent to which the directors' valuation is incorrect. However the inventories figure of £80,000 overall is material to both the profit and total assets figure.

The issue here is a limitation on scope which is material (assuming that the audit manager agrees that no other procedures can be performed). In the draft auditor's report this has not been dealt with correctly. It appears that it has been dealt with as a disagreement.

The explanation of the problem has been correctly dealt with in the explanatory paragraph itself. The opinion paragraph should have acknowledged the limitation as follows:

'Except for the financial effects of such adjustments, if any, as might have been determined to be necessary had we been able to satisfy ourselves as to the validity of the stock figure, in our opinion the financial statements......'

Director's loan

The audit senior has made no reference to the loan on the basis that £5,000 is not material to the financial statements. Whilst this is true from a quantitative perspective, in this case the director's loan is material due to the sensitive nature of the balance. Both the Companies Act and FRS 8 *Related party disclosures* require disclosure of transactions with key management personnel.

If the directors of Maple still refuse to provide the necessary information the details of the loan should be included in the auditor's report. In addition the opinion would be modified (qualified – 'except for') on the grounds of a material disagreement for non compliance with legislation/FRS.

Bad debt

If the debt in respect of Beech were written off this would result in a reduction in profits of 47% and assets of 8.4%. On this basis it would have a material effect on the financial statements. Whilst material, the matter is isolated to the receivables balance and does not affect the truth and fairness of the financial statements overall. The audit senior has modified the audit opinion on the grounds of material disagreement with the decision not to provide against the debt. This is the correct treatment and the report has been correctly drafted in respect of this issue.

27 Reporting issues

> **Tutorial note**. Part (a) involves a fairly straightforward run through of the issues covered in Chapter 17 on this issue.
>
> Part (b) involves some more complex accounting and auditing issues. The answer mentions UITF Abstract 29. This is advanced financial reporting knowledge and you might not have known about it. Don't worry too much about the exact financial reporting requirements for an issue such as a website, just show the examiner that you are aware of the relevant issues. You don't need to know about Abstract 29 to raise the issue that the website is likely to qualify as a fixed asset of some description and to discuss the issues raised by that. You should be able to discuss issues of auditing evidence, what ever the accounting issues are. Don't spend too long on the first issue raised in the scenario to the detriment of the others.

(a)   **Electronic publication of auditors' report**

Publishing the auditors' report electronically will in practice make the report **available to a greater number of people** than is likely to have been the case previously. There are **three key risks** to which publication of the auditors' report on the website exposes the auditor:

- The risk that users will **misunderstand** which financial statements the auditors' report refers to, or that the report will be disconnected from the correct statements

- The risk that people will **assume** that the auditors' report **gives assurance on any financial information available on the website**

- The risk that the report could be **amended by unauthorised persons**

These risks could result in two things:

(i)   **Increase in expectations gap**. Such lack of understanding about a widely available audit report (as discussed above) will only serve to expand the expectations gap between what auditors do and what people think they do, which is to the detriment of the auditing profession.

(ii) **Impact on auditors' liability**. More pressingly for the auditor making public the information, it is possible that extending the audience of the audit report could impact on the liability of the auditor by having an effect on the auditors' duty of care. This would only be discovered in the courts (that is, if a case was brought).

(b) **Issues arising at Techie Ltd**

(i) *Audit evidence*

The website: The auditor should seek evidence about the assertions made by the directors in relation to the website. The key assertions are in relation to existence and valuation.

The auditors should **visit the website** to ensure that it exists and should perhaps check with an IT literate staff member whether the **complexity** of the website **bears out the cost** of developing it.

With regard to valuation, the auditors should **verify the cost to the invoices** tendered by the IT specialist who developed the website.

With regard to the **advertising**, the auditors should visit the other party's website to **vouch the existence** of the advertising. They should also review the **terms of the agreement** between the parties to verify that there is no liability or income on the arrangement.

(ii) *Implications for the audit report*

Website costs. The Statement of Principles states that **assets** are 'rights or other access to future economic benefits controlled by an entity as a result of past transactions or events'.

As the website is an arena for trading, controlled by the entity, it would **appear to fall within this description**. UITF Abstract 29 sets out the circumstances in which website costs should be capitalised. If this website meets the criteria for capitalisation, which it seems to under the definition of an asset, it should be included in the balance sheet, not the profit and loss account.

As the matter is considered **material** (it has been disclosed as an exceptional item) this matter would cause a **qualification due to disagreement** (except for qualification) if the directors do not amend the financial statements. However, it is **not pervasive** to the accounts, so the qualification **would not need to be an adverse opinion**.

Advertising banner. It is **possible** that the advertising banner **also falls within the definition of an asset given above**. As it is maintained on someone else's website, it could be argued that it is not under the entity's control. However, there is likely to be an agreement with the other entity under which Techie controls the nature and form of the advert.

FRS 10 states that **non-purchased assets** should not be capitalised unless they have a 'readily ascertainable market value'. This will be the case if it is a member of a group of homogenous assets with an active market. An advertising banner is **not comparable to a brand** which has no such market. **There is a market in advertising slots**.

The **engagement partner would have to take a view** on whether this advertising banner should be capitalised or not, **if the amounts involved were material** to the financial statements. **It is unlikely that they would be so**. However, if they were, and the directors disagreed with the auditors, another disagreement qualification might be required.

Index

BPP
LEARNING MEDIA

Note: **Key Terms** and their page references are given in **bold**

Review Form & Free Prize Draw – P7: Advanced Audit And Assurance (UK) (4/07)

All original review forms from the entire BPP range, completed with genuine comments, will be entered into one of two draws on 31 January 2008 and 31 July 2008. The names on the first four forms picked out on each occasion will be sent a cheque for £50.

Name: _____   Address: _____

_____

_____

How have you used this Text?
(Tick one box only)

☐ Home study (book only)

☐ On a course: college _____

☐ With 'correspondence' package

☐ Other _____

Why did you decide to purchase this Text? *(Tick one box only)*

☐ Have used BPP Texts in the past

☐ Recommendation by friend/colleague

☐ Recommendation by a lecturer at college

☐ Saw advertising

☐ Saw information on BPP website

☐ Other _____

During the past six months do you recall seeing/receiving any of the following?
(Tick as many boxes as are relevant)

☐ Our advertisement in *ACCA Student Accountant*

☐ Our advertisement in *Pass*

☐ Our advertisement in *PQ*

☐ Our brochure with a letter through the post

☐ Our website www.bpp.com

Which (if any) aspects of our advertising do you find useful?
(Tick as many boxes as are relevant)

☐ Prices and publication dates of new editions

☐ Information on Text content

☐ Facility to order books off-the-page

☐ None of the above

Which BPP products have you used?

Text	☑	Success CD	☐	Learn Online	☐
Kit	☐	i-Learn	☐	Home Study Package	☐
Passcard	☐	i-Pass	☐	Home Study PLUS	☐

Your ratings, comments and suggestions would be appreciated on the following areas.

	Very useful	Useful	Not useful
Introductory section (Key study steps, personal study)	☐	☐	☐
Chapter introductions	☐	☐	☐
Key terms	☐	☐	☐
Quality of explanations	☐	☐	☐
Case studies and other examples	☐	☐	☐
Exam focus points	☐	☐	☐
Questions and answers in each chapter	☐	☐	☐
Fast forwards and chapter roundups	☐	☐	☐
Quick quizzes	☐	☐	☐
Question Bank	☐	☐	☐
Answer Bank	☐	☐	☐
Index	☐	☐	☐

Overall opinion of this Study Text	Excellent ☐	Good ☐	Adequate ☐	Poor ☐

Do you intend to continue using BPP products?   Yes ☐   No ☐

On the reverse of this page are noted particular areas of the text about which we would welcome your feedback. The BPP author of this edition can be e-mailed at: jenniebruce@bpp.com

Please return this form to: Nick Weller, ACCA Publishing Manager, BPP Learning Media Ltd, FREEPOST, London, W12 8BR

Review Form & Free Prize Draw (continued)

Please note any further comments and suggestions/errors below

Free Prize Draw Rules

1   Closing date for 31 January 2008 draw is 31 December 2007. Closing date for 31 July 2008 draw is 30 June 2008.

2   Restricted to entries with UK and Eire addresses only. BPP employees, their families and business associates are excluded.

3   No purchase necessary. Entry forms are available upon request from BPP Learning Media Ltd. No more than one entry per title, per person. Draw restricted to persons aged 16 and over.

4   Winners will be notified by post and receive their cheques not later than 6 weeks after the relevant draw date.

5   The decision of the promoter in all matters is final and binding. No correspondence will be entered into.